EXAMPLES&EXPLANATIONS

International Law

International Law

Valerie Epps

Professor of Law
Co-Director of the International Law Concentration
Suffolk University Law School, Boston, MA

Lorie Graham

Professor of Law
Suffolk University Law School, Boston, MA

Wolters Kluwer
Law & Business

AUSTIN   BOSTON   CHICAGO   NEW YORK   THE NETHERLANDS

To contact Customer Care, e-mail customer.service@aspenpublishers.com,
call 1-800-234-1660, fax 1-800-901-9075, or mail correspondence to:

Aspen Publishers
Attn: Order Department
PO Box 990
Frederick, MD 21705

Printed in the United States of America.

1 2 3 4 5 6 7 8 9 0

ISBN 978-0-7355-9856-0

Library of Congress Cataloging-in-Publication Data

Epps, Valerie, 1943-
    International law : examples and explanations / Valerie Epps, Lorie Graham.
        p. cm.
    Includes index.
    ISBN 978-0-7355-9856-0
    I. Graham, Lorie (Lorie M.), 1962 II. Title.

    KZ1242.E675 2011
    341 — dc22

                                            2010052148

About Wolters Kluwer Law & Business

Wolters Kluwer Law & Business is a leading provider of research information and workflow solutions in key specialty areas. The strengths of the individual brands of Aspen Publishers, CCH, Kluwer Law International and Loislaw are aligned within Wolters Kluwer Law & Business to provide comprehensive, in-depth solutions and expert-authored content for the legal, professional and education markets.

CCH was founded in 1913 and has served more than four generations of business professionals and their clients. The CCH products in the Wolters Kluwer Law & Business group are highly regarded electronic and print resources for legal, securities, antitrust and trade regulation, government contracting, banking, pension, payroll, employment and labor, and health-care reimbursement and compliance professionals.

Aspen Publishers is a leading information provider for attorneys, business professionals and law students. Written by preeminent authorities, Aspen products offer analytical and practical information in a range of specialty practice areas from securities law and intellectual property to mergers and acquisitions and pension/benefits. Aspen's trusted legal education resources provide professors and students with high-quality, up-to-date and effective resources for successful instruction and study in all areas of the law.

Kluwer Law International supplies the global business community with comprehensive English-language international legal information. Legal practitioners, corporate counsel and business executives around the world rely on the Kluwer Law International journals, loose-leafs, books and electronic products for authoritative information in many areas of international legal practice.

Loislaw is a premier provider of digitized legal content to small law firm practitioners of various specializations. Loislaw provides attorneys with the ability to quickly and efficiently find the necessary legal information they need, when and where they need it, by facilitating access to primary law as well as state-specific law, records, forms and treatises.

Wolters Kluwer Law & Business, a unit of Wolters Kluwer, is headquartered in New York and Riverwoods, Illinois. Wolters Kluwer is a leading multinational publisher and information services company.

Summary of Contents

Contents		*xi*
Preface		*xxiii*
Acknowledgments		*xxv*

Chapter 1	Introduction to International Law	1
Chapter 2	Sources of International Law	5
Chapter 3	The Law of Treaties	29
Chapter 4	The Legal Status of Actors in the International Arena: States, International Organizations, Non-State Groups, Individuals, and Multinational Corporations	61
Chapter 5	International Dispute Settlement Including International Civil Courts and Civil Tribunals	103
Chapter 6	Jurisdiction	127
Chapter 7	Title to Territory	157
Chapter 8	International Human Rights	175
Chapter 9	Additional Topics in Human Rights	237
Chapter 10	The Use of Force Including War	265
Chapter 11	International Criminal Law	309
Chapter 12	The Law of the Sea	335
Chapter 13	International Environmental Law	375

Table of Cases	*405*
Treaties and Other International Documents Index	*409*
General Index	*415*

Contents

Preface   *xxiii*

Acknowledgments   *xxv*

Chapter 1   Introduction to International Law   1

§1.1   What Is International Law?   1
§1.2   Traditional Definition Challenged   2

Chapter 2   Sources of International Law   5

§2.1   The Doctrine of Sources (or Who Makes Up
         International Law?)   5
§2.2   Customary International Law   6
         §2.2.1   Regional Customary Law   10
         §2.2.2   Special or Local Customary Law   11
         §2.2.3   *Jus Cogens*   12
§2.3   Treaties   16
§2.4   The Relationship of International Law to Domestic
         (National) Law   18
§2.5   General Principles of Law   20
§2.6   Judicial Decisions   23
§2.7   Writers and Scholars   24
§2.8   United Nations' Resolutions   24
         §2.8.1   General Assembly Resolutions   24
         §2.8.2   Security Council Resolutions   25
         §2.8.3   Proliferation of International Regulatory
                    Systems   26
§2.9   The "Soft Law" or Non-Binding Rules Process   26

Chapter 3   The Law of Treaties   29

§3.1   Definition of a Treaty   30
§3.2   Capacity to Conclude a Treaty   30
§3.3   Ratification   31
         §3.3.1   Internal Ratification   31
         §3.3.2   International Ratification   32
§3.4   Reservations   32

§3.5   Entry into Force   36
§3.6   Observance and Application of Treaties   36
§3.7   Interpretation of Treaties   37
§3.8   Individual Rights Arising Under Treaties   38
§3.9   Invalidity   41
         §3.9.1   Error   41
         §3.9.2   Fraud and Corruption   41
         §3.9.3   Coercion   42
         §3.9.4   Conflict with a Peremptory Norm
                   (*Jus Cogens*)   43
§3.10   Termination and Suspension   44
         §3.10.1   Material Breach   45
         §3.10.2   Supervening Impossibility of
                   Performance   47
         §3.10.3   Fundamental Change of Circumstances:
                   (*Rebus Sic Stantibus*)   48
§3.11   The Effect of War on Treaties   51
         §3.11.1   The Effect of War on Human Rights
                   Treaties   52
§3.12   Procedure for Termination   54
§3.13   Remedies for Violation of a Treaty   54
         §3.13.1   Enforcement of Treaties in National
                   Courts   58
§3.14   State Succession in Respect of Treaties   59

Chapter 4   **The Legal Status of Actors in the
             International Arena: States, International
             Organizations, Non-State Groups,
             Individuals, and Multinational
             Corporations**   **61**

§4.1   Introduction   62
§4.2   The Definition of a State   62
         §4.2.1   A Defined Territory   63
         §4.2.2   A Permanent Population   64
         §4.2.3   A Government   64
         §4.2.4   Capacity to Enter into Relations with
                   Other States   65
         §4.2.5   Recognition of States   69
§4.3   Secession and Self-Determination   70
         §4.3.1   Introduction   70
         §4.3.2   Secession as a Legal Concept   71

Contents

	§4.3.3	The Evolution of the Meaning of Self-Determination	71
	§4.3.4	Court Cases Discussing Self-Determination or Secession	74
§4.4	State Responsibility		80
	§4.4.1	Attributing Conduct to a State	80
	§4.4.2	State Breaches of International Obligations Where Wrongfulness Is Precluded	83
	§4.4.3	The State's Obligation to Make Reparations for Breaches of International Obligations	85
		Satisfaction	86
		Restitution	87
		Compensation	88
	§4.4.4	A State's Capacity to Bring International Claims on Behalf of Individuals	89
§4.5	International Organizations		92
	§4.5.1	Inter-Governmental Organizations	93
		(a) The United Nations' International Legal Status	93
		(b) The Structure of the United Nations	94
		(c) The United Nations' Principal Organs	94
		The General Assembly	95
		The Security Council	95
		The Economic and Social Council (ECOSOC)	96
		The Trusteeship Council	97
		The International Court of Justice	97
		The Secretariat	97
	§4.5.2	Regional International Organizations	98
	§4.5.3	Non-Governmental International Organizations	98
§4.6	Non-State Groups		99
	§4.6.1	Protected Groups	99
	§4.6.2	Non-State Actors	100
§4.7	International Status of the Individual		100
§4.8	Multinational Corporations		101
§4.9	Conclusion		102

Chapter 5 International Dispute Settlement Including International Civil Courts and Civil Tribunals   103

§5.1	The Obligation to Settle Disputes	104
§5.2	Arbitration	104
	§5.2.1 The Permanent Court of Arbitration	105
§5.3	International Civil Courts	106
	§5.3.1 The Permanent Court of International Justice	106
	§5.3.2 The International Court of Justice	106
	(a) The Composition of the Court	107
	(b) The Jurisdiction of the International Court of Justice in Contentious Cases	108
	(i) "[A]ll cases which the parties refer to it (i.e., the Court) . . ."	109
	(ii) "[A]ll matters specially provided for in the Charter of the United Nations . . ."	110
	(iii) "[A]ll matters . . . in treaties and conventions in force"	110
	(iv) Compulsory Jurisdiction: Also Known as "The Optional Clause"	112
	(v) Jurisdiction *Forum Prorogatum*	120
	(c) The Jurisdiction of the International Court of Justice in Advisory Cases	120
	(d) The Power of the International Court of Justice to Issue Interim Measures of Protection	121
	§5.3.3 Examples of Other Major International Civil Courts and Tribunals	121
	(a) The International Tribunal for the Law of the Sea	121
	(b) Iran-United States Claims Tribunal	122
	(c) World Trade Organization: Dispute Settlement Body	122
	§5.3.4 Regional Courts	123
	(a) Europe	123
	(b) The Americas	123
	(c) Africa	124

		(d) Arab States	124
		(e) Asia	125
	§5.4	Conclusion	125

Chapter 6   Jurisdiction   127

§6.1	Introduction	127
§6.2	The Territorial Principle	128
§6.3	The Nationality Principle	130
§6.4	The Passive Personality Principle	132
§6.5	The Protective Principle	135
§6.6	The Universality Principle	136
§6.7	Extradition	138
§6.8	Immunity from Jurisdiction	139
	§6.8.1 Diplomatic Immunity	140
	§6.8.2 Consular Immunity	144
	§6.8.3 Head of State and Other Ministers' Immunity	146
	§6.8.4 Immunity for International Organizations	149
	§6.8.5 Sovereign Immunity	149
	Absolute Theory	149
	The Restrictive Theory	151

Chapter 7   Title to Territory   157

§7.1	*Terra Nullius*	158
§7.2	Discovery	159
§7.3	Occupation	160
§7.4	Conquest	162
§7.5	Cession	163
§7.6	Prescription	163
§7.7	*Uti Possidetis Juris*	164
§7.8	Accretion and Avulsion	167
§7.9	Special Territorial Regimes	168
	§7.9.1 The Arctic	169
	§7.9.2 The Antarctic	169
	§7.9.3 Celestial Bodies and Space	170

Chapter 8   International Human Rights   175

§8.1	Introduction	176
	§8.1.1 The Origins of International Human Rights Law	176
	§8.1.2 Theories of Human Rights	178

§8.2   The Law of Treaties in the Human Rights Context   181

      §8.2.1   Interpretation   182

      §8.2.2   Reservations   185

      §8.2.3   Non-Self-Executing   188

      §8.2.4   Termination   190

§8.3   Human Rights Law in the United Nations System   190

      §8.3.1   U.N. Charter and Universal Declaration of Human Rights   191

      §8.3.2   The International Covenant on Civil and Political Rights   193

          Rights and Freedoms Under the ICCPR   194

          States' Duties to Implement ICCPR Rights and Freedoms   195

          States' Powers to Derogate from or Limit ICCPR Rights   198

          Monitoring and Enforcement of Rights   202

          Optional Protocols   206

      §8.3.3   The International Covenant on Economic, Social, and Cultural Rights   209

          Rights and Freedoms Under the ICESCR   209

          States' Duties to Implement ICESCR Rights   211

          Monitoring and Enforcement Under the ICESCR   212

      §8.3.4   Customary International Human Rights Law   217

§8.4   Charter-based Bodies   221

      §8.4.1   U.N. High Commissioner for Human Rights   222

      §8.4.2   Human Rights Council   223

      §8.4.3   International Court of Justice   226

      §8.4.4   U.N. Security Council   229

Chapter 9   Additional Topics in Human Rights   237

§9.1   Introduction   237

§9.2   U.N. Conventions on Specific Human Rights Topics   238

§9.3   The Role of Non-Governmental Organizations   240

§9.4   Regional Human Rights Systems   242

      §9.4.1   The European Human Rights System   243

      §9.4.2   The Inter-American System   245

      §9.4.3   The African System   248

§9.4.4   The Emergence of Other Regional
            Human Rights Systems   251
§9.5   Group Rights   251
§9.6   Corporate Responsibility for Human Rights   258

Chapter 10   The Use of Force Including War   265

§10.1   Introduction   266
§10.2   Coercive Measures Not Amounting to Armed
         Force   267
         §10.2.1   Retorsions   268
         §10.2.2   Reprisals Not Involving Armed Force   268
§10.3   Pre-1945 Law on the Use of Armed Force   268
         §10.3.1   The Customary Law of Self-Defence   269
§10.4   Post-1945 Law   271
         §10.4.1   The Jus Ad Bellum   271
         §10.4.2   The United Nations Charter   271
                    (a) The Meaning of Force   272
                    (b) What Is a Threat of Force?   273
                    (c) Must Force Be Used for a Particular
                         Objective to Violate Article 2(4)?   274
                    (d) Exceptions to Article 2(4)   276
                         (i)   Self-Defence   276
                               a. What Level of Armed Force
                                  Gives Rise to the Right to
                                  Self-Defence?   276
                               b. Must an Armed Attack Be
                                  Carried Out by a State to
                                  Trigger the Right of Self
                                  Defence?   280
                         (ii) Preemption   280
                         (iii) Forceful Countermeasures   281
                    (e) Reprisals Using Force   281
         §10.4.3   The Rule of Non-Intervention   282
                    (a) Civil Wars and the Rule of Non-
                         Intervention   286
                    (b) Intervention in Particular
                         Circumstances   286
                         (i)   Intervening to Protect
                               Nationals Abroad   287
                         (ii) Humanitarian Intervention 287
                         (iii) The Responsibility to Protect   289

Contents

(c) The Security Council's Power to
    Intervene   289
    (i) Article 41 Measures   290
    (ii) Article 42 Measures   291
(d) United Nations Peacekeeping
    Forces   292
§10.5 The Jus In Bello   293
§10.5.1 Regulation of the Conduct of Hostilities 293
    (a) Modern-Era History: The Hague
        and Geneva Conventions   293
§10.5.2 Specific Rules of International
        Humanitarian Law (IHL)   297
    (a) Introduction   297
    (b) The Principle of Distinction and the
        Definition of Combatants/Military
        Objects and Civilians/Civilian
        Objects   297
    (c) Treatment of Those Captured in
        Armed Conflict   300
§10.5.3 Weapons Control   303
    (a) Historical Progression   303
    (b) Nuclear Weapons   304
        (i) Conventions and Declarations
             that Limit the Spread or Use of
             Nuclear Weapons   304
        (ii) Conventions that Call for the
             Reduction of Nuclear
             Weapons   305
        (iii) Conventions that Declare
             Certain Areas of the World
             Nuclear Weapons Free   305
        (iv) Conventions that Prohibit the
             Testing of Nuclear Weapons   305
        (v) The I.C.J.'s Advisory Opinion
             on Nuclear Weapons   305
§10.6 Conclusion   308

Chapter 11 International Criminal Law   309

§11.1 Introduction   310
§11.2 Definition of Crimes   310
§11.2.1 Genocide   311
§11.2.2 War Crimes   312

§11.2.3   Crimes Against Humanity   315
§11.2.4   The Crime of Aggression   316
§11.3   Individual Responsibility   321
§11.4   Defenses   323
§11.4.1   Specific Defenses   323
§11.5   State Responsibility   325
§11.6   International and Hybrid (National/International)
Criminal Tribunals   327
§11.6.1   International Criminal Tribunals:
Introduction   327
§11.6.2   The Nuremberg Trials   327
§11.6.3   The Tokyo Trials   327
§11.6.4   The International Criminal Tribunal for
the Former Yugoslavia   328
§11.6.5   The International Criminal Tribunal for
Rwanda   330
§11.6.6   The International Criminal Court   330
§11.6.7   Hybrid (National/International)
Criminal Tribunals: Introduction   331
§11.6.8   The Special Court for Sierra Leone   331
§11.6.9   The East Timor Tribunal   332
§11.6.10 The Extraordinary Chambers in the
Courts of Cambodia   332
§11.6.11 The Special Tribunal for Lebanon   333

Chapter 12   The Law of the Sea   335

§12.1   Introduction   336
§12.2   Internal Waters   337
§12.2.1   Bays   338
§12.2.2   Historic Bays   340
§12.3   The Territorial Sea   341
§12.3.1   Measuring the Territorial Sea   342
§12.3.2   Powers of the Coastal State in the
Territorial Sea and Foreign Ships' Right
of Innocent Passage   342
(a) The Meaning of Innocent Passage   343
(b) Coastal States' Right of Action
Against Non-Innocent Passage   344
§12.4   Archipelagos   346
§12.5   International Straits   347
§12.5.1   Definition of an International Strait   348
(a) Customary Law   348
(b) Treaty Law   348

§12.5.2 Transit Passage Through Some
International Straits 348
(a) Transit Passage Contrasted with
Innocent Passage 350
§12.6 The Contiguous Zone 351
§12.7 The Exclusive Economic Zone 353
§12.7.1 Coastal States' Rights in the Exclusive
Economic Zone 353
§12.7.2 Foreign States' Rights in the Exclusive
Economic Zone 354
§12.8 The Continental Shelf 356
§12.8.1 Delimitation of the Continental Shelf
with Opposite or Adjacent Coasts 357
§12.9 The High Seas 358
§12.10 The Deep Sea Bed 359
§12.10.1 The Deep Sea Bed Regime Under the
1982 Convention 359
§12.10.2 The Deep Sea Bed Regime Under the
1994 Agreement 360
§12.11 Settlement of Maritime Disputes 361
§12.12 Marine Pollution 361
§12.13 Jurisdiction Over Vessels 362
§12.13.1 The Genuine Link Requirement 364
§12.13.2 Remedy Where There Is No Genuine
Link 364
§12.14 Prohibited Activities on the High Seas 367
§12.15 Jurisdiction Over Foreign Vessels 370
§12.15.1 Jurisdiction in Internal Waters and Ports 370
§12.15.2 Jurisdiction in the Territorial Seas 370
§12.15.3 The Right of Hot Pursuit 371
§12.16 Fishing on the High Seas 374

Chapter 13   International Environmental Law   375

§13.1 Introduction 376
§13.2 State Responsibility for Environmental Harm 377
§13.3 Establishing the Standard for State Responsibility
for Environmental Harm 377
§13.3.1 Customary Law Standards 377
§13.3.2 Declarations and Treaty Law Standards 380
§13.4 Hazardous Waste 382
§13.5 Atmosphere, Ozone, and Climate 386
§13.6 Nature, Flora, Fauna, and Other Resources 387
§13.7 Nuclear Fallout 390

Contents

§13.8   Other Regimes   397
§13.9   Guiding Environmental Principles   398
         §13.9.1   The Precautionary Principle   398
         §13.9.2   The Principle of Intergenerational
                    Equity   400
         §13.9.3   The Principle of Sustainable
                    Development   401
         §13.9.4   The Polluter Pays Principle   401
         §13.9.5   The Environmental Impact Assessment
                    Principle   402
         §13.9.6   The Recognition of Differentiated
                    Responsibilities for Developed and
                    Developing States   403
§13.10   Conclusion   404

Table of Cases   405
Treaties and Other International Documents Index   409
General Index   415

Preface

In recent years, admissions directors in law schools and colleges have indicated that one of the most frequently asked questions by prospective students is what the particular institution has to offer in the area of international law. Law schools and colleges have expanded their course offerings in international law to cover a whole variety of specialized areas, such as international environmental law, international human rights, international business transactions, the law of the sea, and the laws of war, among many others. All of these specialized courses build on the introductory foundational course generally called, simply, "International Law." This book is designed to assist students taking the introductory international law course to understand the framework and subject matter of international law and to work through the EXAMPLES, which consist of real-world problems based on the materials provided. After each EXAMPLE, there follows an EXPLANATION that represents the authors' best attempts at answering the problems posed. The EXAMPLES give students a chance to apply the substantive material they have read and to test their ability to articulate a comprehensive answer. Students are advised to try to answer the problems themselves before reading the EXPLANATION. After answering the problem, students should check their answers with the EXPLANATION.

The book is best used as an aid throughout an entire international law course and will also be particularly useful in preparation for examinations. We have found that students grasp the different subjects of international law at a much better level when they have the opportunity to apply their knowledge to problems posed over the full semester in which the course is taught, not just at the end of the course in an examination. By providing substantive information as well as EXAMPLES and EXPLANATIONS related to international law, the authors hope that students will deepen their understanding of the subject and will be encouraged to develop their knowledge further in specialized courses.

December 2010
Valerie Epps and Lorie Graham
Suffolk University Law School
120 Tremont Street
Boston, MA 02108

Acknowledgments

We would like to thank all of the students who have taken our courses in International Law and International Human Rights at Suffolk University Law School. They have been a source of much inspiration and a spur to developing better materials for teaching these vital and fast-changing subjects. Special thanks goes to Mishell Fortes, who has typed, retyped, and corrected the whole of the text and all of the indexes with a calm assurance and much grace. We also want to thank Katrina McCusker and Heidi Lamirande for their research assistance, the reviewers for their helpful comments on drafts, and our families for all their support during the writing process. Finally, we would like to thank the team at our publisher, Wolters Kluwer; Carol McGeehan; Peter Skagestad; and Jay Harward for helping us bring this project full circle.

International Law

Introduction to International Law

§1.1 What Is International Law?
§1.2 Traditional Definition Challenged

§1.1 WHAT IS INTERNATIONAL LAW?

When students are considering whether to read a book about "International Law," quite naturally they wish to know, in general terms, what the subject covers. The dilemma faced by anyone seeking to answer this question is how to convey a broad sense of the subject matter to someone who does not yet grasp the specifics of the subject. Perhaps the best answer would be "wait and see," but that would probably infuriate a good number of potential readers. This introduction will, however, be very brief. The book will then plunge into some of the specific issues addressed by international law with "Examples" and "Explanations." By the end of the book many questions about the nature and application of international law will have been tackled, by which time the reader should have the necessary background to begin to appreciate the underlying concepts of international law and to understand how this area of law operates.

§1.2 TRADITIONAL DEFINITION CHALLENGED

A traditional definition of international law is that it concerns the legal relationships between sovereign states and covers a wide variety of topics, such as the law of the sea and the laws of war. More modern definitions would wish to include the legal relationships that exist between states and between and among international organizations, individuals, groups, multinational corporations, and other entities that are considered capable of possessing certain characteristics of international personality. For centuries the field of international law was only open to states, not because there was anything in the real world that prevented other entities from being players in this arena, but simply because the theory of international law, in those centuries, had defined the field with a neat precision: Only states possess international legal rights and duties; therefore, no other entities are capable of possessing international legal rights and obligations. As the role of the nation-state evolved and states took on an ever-widening array of activities, and as the corporation, international organizations, and the individual came to occupy a radically different place in the legal spectrum, it was clear that many subjects, originally considered as being outside the scope of international law, would have to be included in it. More recently, the rise of the paramilitary international non-state actor has again challenged the framework of international law.

Traditionally, the way in which a state treated its own citizens was considered to be a subject of that state's law alone. If state A passed laws allowing it to chop off a petty thief's hands, there was no body of law outside the municipal law of state A that exerted authority over the state. Most writers on international law would now maintain that every state is subject to a body of law, broadly called human rights, that would prohibit such treatment because it would violate the individual's right to be free from cruel or excessive punishments — and bodily dismemberment would be considered cruel and excessive for a petty thief. The individual is now seen as possessing international rights and also some international obligations.

As new entities and new concepts have gained acceptance in the international arena, the scope of international law has changed and broadened. The process will doubtless continue. The lesson it teaches us is that we must constantly ask ourselves why we define legal concepts in a particular way and what are the consequences of our insistence on a particular definition.

It is a truism that we exist in a "globalized" world but this truism has much to teach us about the continuing evolution of international law. The traditional definition regarded states as lonely entities that decided whether they did, or did not, wish to enter into relations with other states.

Only to the extent that the state chose to enter into relations with other states would it be governed by international law. The concept of this isolated state without the necessity of contacts with other states is now hardly possible. Even for states that remain to some extent cut off from outside contact, there are a variety of international agreements and structures that require their participation. Some examples will illustrate this point: postal agreements (unless a country does not want to be able to send and receive letters and goods across its borders), telecommunications agreements (unless it wishes to do without telephones, televisions, the Internet, etc.), environmental agreements (unless it is prepared to allow other countries to swamp it with pollution in all its forms), migration agreements (unless it is prepared to allow all comers to enter and remain), and trade agreements (unless it does not intend to engage in any international trade). As you can see from the above examples, a modern state has to engage in relations with other states, and it will necessarily find itself participating in an international regulatory structure. This great web of international agreements and practices, with their regulatory, administrative, and enforcements structures, make up a large part of international law, and this interwoven system also shapes what we mean by international law.

CHAPTER 2

Sources of International Law

§2.1 The Doctrine of Sources (or Who Makes Up International Law?)
§2.2 Customary International Law
 §2.2.1 Regional Customary Law
 §2.2.2 Special or Local Customary Law
 §2.2.3 *Jus Cogens*
§2.3 Treaties
§2.4 The Relationship of International Law to Domestic (National) Law
§2.5 General Principles of Law
§2.6 Judicial Decisions
§2.7 Writers and Scholars
§2.8 United Nations' Resolutions
 §2.8.1 General Assembly Resolutions
 §2.8.2 Security Council Resolutions
 §2.8.3 Proliferation of International Regulatory Systems
§2.9 The "Soft Law" or Non-Binding Rules Process

§2.1 THE DOCTRINE OF SOURCES (OR WHO MAKES UP INTERNATIONAL LAW?)

Most students have a fairly good notion of how law gets made in their own country. They know that the legislature enacts laws and that often legislative power is divided between federal, state, and local authorities. They also know that a variety of entities, broadly known as the executive branch of

5

government, has the authority to carry out or enforce the laws and that judges, who may be elected or appointed, interpret and apply the law in cases before them. But who makes international law? The answer is that states and other international entities largely make international law for themselves through a variety of mechanisms that will be studied below.

International law comes about in a number of ways. The most prominent sources are custom, treaties, general principles of law, judicial decisions, and the work of scholars and writers. Major multilateral treaties often establish regulatory and enforcement structures to implement the treaty, and these mechanisms will also contribute to the creation of international law. With respect to the work of writers and scholars, their work is regarded as evidence of what the law is, rather than strictly a source of law itself, but such work is often quite influential in shaping the development of international law. Each one of these sources will be studied separately though often a number of sources combine to create international law.

§2.2 CUSTOMARY INTERNATIONAL LAW

What is customary international law? It is a practice of states (or other international legal entities) engaged in by them out of a sense of legal obligation rather than out of a sense of kindness, courtesy, or convenience. This latter element, namely that the practice be regarded as law, is spoken of as *opinion juris* in many cases and texts. Below are some examples taken from cases where courts have faced the task of determining whether a particular state practice amounts to binding customary international law.

Example 2-1

In an early U.S. Supreme Court case, *The Paquete Habana*, 175 U.S. 677 (1900), the Court had to answer the question of whether small fishing vessels engaged in normal fishing activities were subject to capture as prize of war. In 1898 war broke out between the U.S. and Spain, which then ruled Cuba as a colony. The U.S. imposed a blockade around Cuba. Two small Cuban fishing vessels, who did not know of the blockade, were catching fish on the high seas off the coast of Cuba. They were captured as prize of war by American warships and condemned by the U.S. district court in Florida. Later the boats were auctioned with the proceeds going to the U.S. government. The Cuban owners of the boats argued that, as fishing vessels, they were exempt from capture by virtue of customary international law. There was no specific law in the U.S. answering the question, and so the Court examined the practice of a number of other states on the issue stretching over five centuries. The Court looked at orders issued by the

English King Henry IV to his admirals in the early fifteenth century during war with France; a treaty made between the Holy Roman Empire and France in the sixteenth century; various examples from French history; a treaty between the U.S. and Prussia and between the U.S. and Mexico; a British case concerning a Dutch fishing vessel; Austrian and German practice; and Japanese practice in relation to Chinese vessels. A number of well-known U.S. and foreign scholars of international law were also quoted on the subject. In the end, the Court concluded that the examples cited above led to the conclusion that the practice of exempting fishing vessels from capture as prize of war had become established as a binding international custom. The Court quoted with approval one of its earlier decisions:

> Undoubtedly no single nation can change the law of the sea. The law is of universal obligation and no statute of one or two nations can create obligations for the world. Like all the laws of nations, it rests upon the common consent of civilized communities. It is of force, not because it was prescribed by any superior power, but because it has been generally accepted as a rule of conduct. . . . This is not giving to the statutes of any nation extraterritorial effect. It is not treating them as general maritime laws; but it is recognition of the historical fact that by common consent of mankind these rules have been acquiesced in as of general obligation. . . . *The Scotia*, 81 U.S. 170, 188 (1871), as quoted in *The Paquete Habana supra*, at 711.

The paragraph dealing with way in which international law is incorporated into U.S. national law has become famous:

> International law is part of our law, and must be ascertained and administered by the courts of justice of appropriate jurisdiction as often as questions of right depending upon it are duly presented for their determination. For this purpose, where there is no treaty and no controlling executive or legislative act or judicial decision, resort must be had to the customs and usages of civilized nations, and as evidence of these, to the works of jurists and commentators who by years of labor, research and experience have made themselves peculiarly well acquainted with the subject of which they treat. Such works are resorted to by judicial tribunals, not for the speculations of their authors concerning what the law ought to be, but for trustworthy evidence of what the law really is. *Id.* at 700.

Three of the Justices dissented largely on the ground that: "the exemption of fishing craft is essentially an act of grace, and not a matter of right. . . ." *Id.* at 719.

    1) What was the custom that the Court found applicable in the *Paquete Habana* case?

    2) What persuaded the Court that the practice was indeed a binding international custom?

3) Why are the United States courts obliged to follow international custom?

4) Would the Court have followed the custom if Congress had passed a law indicating that no vessels were exempt from capture as prize of war?

5) If indeed there is an international custom, are states completely free to pass contrary legislation?

6) If states are free to pass legislation contrary to an international custom, won't that mean that custom will only exist if nation legislatures either approve (overtly or tacitly) of the custom or if they fail to enact contrary legislation?

Explanations

1) Fishing vessels are exempt from capture as prize of war.

2) The Court examined the practice of several states, in treaties and cases over five centuries, as well as scholarly writings, and determined that state practice always exempted fishing vessels from capture as prize of war. (A couple of possible contrary examples were distinguished.) The Court found a consistent practice of states engaged in out of a sense of legal obligation, i.e., binding international custom.

3) The U.S. treats international custom as part of its own law which can only be set aside where there is positive U.S. law to the contrary.

4) No. U.S. courts must follow positive U.S. law if it is contrary to international custom but the courts always try to reconcile U.S. law and custom. Only where it is impossible to reconcile the two will the courts follow the U.S. law. Virtually all other states follow this practice.

5) Generally, states are free to enact legislation contrary to customary law unless the custom is *jus cogens*, that is a fundamental norm. See §2.2.3 *infra*.

6) Yes. If enough states pass contrary legislation, then there will not be a consistent practice of states sufficient to establish custom. (But see §2.2.3 *infra* on fundamental norms.)

A much more recent example of a U.S. federal court finding custom occurred in the second circuit in 2009. *Abdullahi v. Pfizer, Inc.*, 562 F.3d 163 (2d Cir. 2009), cert. denied, 130 S. Ct. 3541 (2010). In that case several Nigerian children and their guardians sued the large pharmaceutical company, Pfizer, alleging that a joint U.S.-Nigerian team of doctors used an unapproved drug called "Trovan" to treat children suffering from meningitis in Nigeria. As a result, eleven children died and several others were left blind, deaf, paralyzed, or brain-damaged. The children claimed that such experimentation on them, without the knowledge or consent of either the children or their parents or guardians, violated a customary international norm prohibiting such nonconsensual experimentation. The trial court had dismissed the suit for failing to meet the threshold for claims brought under the Alien Tort Statute (ATS), 28 U.S.C. §1350, which permits aliens (non-U.S. citizens) to sue in U.S. courts "for a tort only, committed in violation of the law of nations or a treaty of the United States." Although the district court found that there was a customary norm prohibiting nonconsensual medical experimentation, the court determined that the norm did not create a private right of action under the ATS. The second circuit was therefore simply determining whether the plaintiffs had alleged sufficient facts to go forward with the claim (not whether the plaintiffs should win on the merits).

An earlier case had determined that "the law of nations" refers to the body of law known as "customary international law" which can be "discerned from myriad decisions made in numerous and varied international and domestic arenas. . . ." *Flores v. Southern Peru Copper Corp.*, 414 F.3d 233, 247-248 (2d Cir. 2003). In that case, the court stated that the Alien Tort Statute was limited to alleged violations of "those clear and unambiguous rules by which States universally abide, or to which they accede, out of a sense of legal obligation and mutual concern." *Id.* at 252.

In order to determine whether the prohibition on nonconsensual medical experimentation had become an established customary international norm the court examined, among other things: (1) the Nuremberg Code requiring the voluntary consent of patients to medical treatment; (2) the World Medical Association's Declaration of Helsinki which requires patient's informed consent in medical research; (3) guidelines prepared by the Council for International Organizations of Medical Services which require voluntary, informed consent of patients; and (4) article 7 of the International Covenant on Civil and Political Rights (ICCPR), 999 U.N.T.S. 171, which states that "no one shall be subjected without his free consent to medical or scientific experimentation."

The court examined the trials of Nazi doctors after World War II by U.S. military tribunals operating "under the aegis of the IMT [International Military Tribunal]." *Id.* at 177-178. There the doctors were found "guilty of war crimes and crimes against humanity for conducting medical experiments without the subjects' consent. . . ." *Id.* at 178. The *Abdullahi* court concluded that: "[S]ince Nuremberg, states throughout the world have shown through international accords and domestic law-making that they consider the prohibition on nonconsensual medical experimentation . . . as a norm of customary international law." *Id.* at 179. The court also considered article 7 of the ICCPR, quoted above, as authoritative as it had been ratified by more than 160 states, including the U.S. The Helsinki Declaration's Code of Ethics adopted by the World Medical Association was noted as prohibiting nonconsensual medical experimentation. At least eighty-four countries, including the U.S., were found to have statutory or regulatory requirements for informed consent by medical patients. The European Union was found to have promulgated a Directive which prohibits nonconsensual medical experimentation throughout the EU. The Convention on Human Rights and Biomedicine, 1997 E.T.S. No. 164, had also been adopted by the Council of Europe, which includes a similar prohibition. After weighing all of the above sources, the *Abdullahi* court concluded that: "the norm prohibiting nonconsensual medical experimentation on human subjects has become firmly embedded and has secured universal acceptance in the community of nations." *Id.* at 183-184.

The dissent strongly criticized the weight of the sources relied on by the majority in establishing customary law. Judge Wesley concluded that the ICCPR was of little utility and did not apply to private actors; the Convention on Biomedicine was only a regional treaty and had not been ratified by several key European nations, and anyway was only promulgated a year after the conduct alleged in this case; the European Directive also occurred after the conduct in question; the Declaration of Helsinki was issued by a non-governmental entity, as were the Ethical Guidelines; states' domestic laws do not establish international custom; and the Nuremberg Code and criminal convictions are at best a subsidiary means for determining custom. He ultimately concluded "that non-consensual medical experimentation by private actors, though deplorable, is not actionable under international law. . . ." *Id.* at 193.

Another very influential case in the United States was *Filartiga v. Pena-Irala*, 630 F.2d 876 (2d Cir. 1980), where a Paraguayan father and his daughter sued the Paraguayan Inspector of Police for the area of Asuncion, Paraguay, claiming that he was responsible for the kidnapping, torture, and death of Joelito Filartiga, the plaintiffs' son and brother, respectively. The court examined a variety of sources of law and concluded "that official torture is now prohibited by the law of nations." *Id.* at 884. It was significant that this case was decided several years before 1984 when the U.N. General Assembly adopted the Convention Against Torture and Other Cruel, Inhuman, or Degrading Treatment or Punishment, 1465 U.N.T.S. 85, which entered into force in 1987.

§2.2.1 Regional Customary Law

The Court has also accepted the idea of regional custom, that is the idea that a practice among states within a particular area of the world can be sufficiently well established and accepted as law that it is binding among the states of that region but not elsewhere. In the *Asylum* case (Colombia v. Peru), 1950 I.C.J. 266, the International Court of Justice stated:

> The Colombian government has finally invoked "American international law in general." In addition to the rules arising from agreements which have already been considered, it has relied on an alleged regional or local custom peculiar to Latin-American States. The Party which relies on a custom of this kind must prove that this custom is established in such a manner that it has become binding on the other party. *Id.* at 276.

Ultimately, the Court determined that Colombia had failed to establish a regional custom because there was "so much uncertainty and contradiction, so much fluctuation and discrepancy . . . that it is not possible to discern in all this any constant and uniform usage, accepted as law. . . ." Id. at 277.

§2.2.2 Special or Local Customary Law

Where two states have engaged in a practice with respect to each other over a long period of time, the Court may also be willing to find that this practice meets the requirements of customary law and has become binding on the states concerned as a special custom. In the *Right of Passage* case (Portugal v. India), 1960 I.C.J. 6, the Court stated:

> With regard to Portugal's claim . . . on the basis of local custom, it is objected on behalf of India that no local custom could be established between only two States. . . . The Court sees no reason why long continued practice between two States accepted by them as regulating their relations should not form the basis of mutual rights and obligations. Id. at 39.

Example 2-2

The St. Joseph river demarcates the border between State N to the north and State S to the south. By a treaty concluded between the two states in 1858, State N was given sovereign rights over the St. Joseph river but State S was given perpetual navigational rights on the river. Various disputes have arisen over navigational rights but recently State N has forbidden all fishing from the banks of the river from the territory of State S. State S protests that, at least since 1540, riparian dwellers have consistently engaged in subsistence fishing from the banks of the river from the State S side. State N never objected to this practice until six months ago. State N replies that the treaty of 1858 does not mention fishing rights and that the treaty should be read as a complete statement of the rights of both states with respect to the river. State S and State N agree to have the dispute settled by the I.C.J.

How should the Court rule?

Explanation

If State S can indeed document a continuous practice of riparian subsistence fishing in the St. Joseph river by inhabitants on the State S banks of the river both before and after the 1858 treaty, without objection by State N, the Court would likely find that the fishing constituted a local custom and would rule in favor of State S. On the other hand, if the language of the treaty indicated that it was to be the sole source of rights on the river, and if there were good reasons why State N may not have known of the fishing (such as a very sparsely populated, extremely remote area), the decision might hold that the practice of fishing was contrary to the treaty. Cf. *Dispute Regarding Navigational and Related Rights* (Costa Rica v. Nicaragua), 2009 I.C.J. _____.

§2.2.3 *Jus Cogens*

Although customary international law comes about by a consistent practice of states accepted as law, states are generally free to reject these rules by passing contrary laws. Such states are described as "persistent objectors," and they will not be bound by the custom. Are there, however, some customary rules which are so fundamental that states are not free to reject them? For some time, international law has accepted the notion of peremptory norms, or *jus cogens*, which bind all states, although there has been disagreement about which norms fall into this category. The Vienna Convention on the Law of Treaties, 1155 U.N.T.S. 331, article 53 provides: "a peremptory norm ... is a norm accepted and recognized by the international community of States as a whole as a norm from which no derogation is permitted...." Some candidates for *jus cogens* are: the prohibition on the use of force by one state against another; the prohibition against torture; the prohibition against racial discrimination; genocide; war crimes; crimes against humanity; slavery; and piracy.

The International Tribunal for the former Yugoslavia explained the concept of *jus cogens* in the context of the prohibition on torture in *Prosecutor v. Furundzija*, Case No. 17-95-17/IT, Judgment of the Trial Chamber, 10 Dec. 1998 at para. 153:

> Because of the importance of the values it projects, [the prohibition of torture] ... has evolved into a peremptory norm or jus cogens, that is, a norm that enjoys a higher rank in the international hierarchy than treaty law and even "ordinary" customary rules. The most conspicuous consequence of this higher rank is that the principle at issue cannot be derogated from by States through international treaties or local or special customs or even general customary rules not endowed with the same normative force. (Footnotes omitted).

It is not clear whether national courts would follow a *jus cogens* norm where there was contrary national law. For example, if a state had a presidential order permitting torture of detainees thought to possess useful enemy intelligence during wartime, the courts of that state might well follow the President's order, despite the fact that the prohibition of torture is considered a peremptory norm and despite the fact that the Convention Against Torture makes it clear that the prohibition applies in wartime. Similarly, some norms, such as high governmental ministers' immunity from the jurisdiction of foreign courts, might be held to prevail over the right or even obligation to prosecute those committing war crimes. See *Arrest Warrant of 11 April 2000* (D.R. Congo v. Belgium), 2002 I.C.J. 3.

Example 2-3

Below are some statistics on the prohibition of the death penalty imposed after conviction for crimes. In the U.S., fifteen states and the District of Columbia have banned the death penalty; thirty-five states permit it, as does federal law. The statutes for the International Criminal Tribunals for the former Yugoslavia and Rwanda and the International Criminal Court do not permit the death penalty. On December 18, 2008, the U.N. General Assembly passed a resolution calling on all states that maintain the death penalty to establish a moratorium on execution, with a view to abolishing the death penalty. G.A. Res. 63/168 (2008). The vote was 106 in favor, 46 against, with 34 abstentions. One hundred and thirty-nine countries have abolished the death penalty in law or in practice (i.e., no executions in the last ten years).

In Europe only one country, Latvia, retains the death penalty but only for certain crimes occurring during war time. The last execution occurred in 1996. In South America some states retain the death penalty but only for extraordinary circumstances.

In December 2008, Amnesty International reported that ninety-two countries had abolished the death penalty for all crimes; ten had abolished it for ordinary crimes; thirty-six had not executed anyone for at least ten years; and fifty-nine states retained the death penalty. Ninety-three percent of all executions carried out in 2008 took place in five countries: China, Iran, Saudi Arabia, Pakistan, and the U.S. Fifty-two states sentenced people to death in 2008, although only twenty-five of the fifty-nine countries that retain the death penalty carried out executions during that year. Some countries that had suspended the death penalty subsequently reintroduced it, such as India and Sri Lanka.

1) On the basis of the information given above, would you conclude that there is a international custom prohibiting the death penalty?

2) Would you conclude that in some areas of the world there is a regional custom prohibiting the death penalty?

Explanations

1) A binding international custom requires two factors: (a) a consistent practice of states, where (b) that practice is engaged in out of a sense of legal obligation. This latter requirement is known by its Latin name, *opinio juris*, "regarded as law." With fifty-nine states still retaining the death penalty in their criminal laws, it is not possible to maintain that there is currently an international custom prohibiting the death penalty.

2) It is clear, however, that some areas of the world, such as Europe, no longer impose the death penalty either as a matter of law, or, in the case of Latvia, within the last fourteen years. From that fact it may be possible to argue that in such areas there is a binding regional custom. Certainly there is a consistent practice of states prohibiting the death penalty in those areas but the requirement of demonstrating that the practice is engaged in out of a sense of legal obligation is more difficult. States do not often announce to the world the reasons why they have adopted a particular law, and when they do, there are often a myriad of motivational factors involved. Some eminent jurists have suggested that a consistent practice of states should give rise to the presumption that such a practice was engaged in out of a sense of legal obligation and if that presumption is challenged, the burden would fall on the challenger to prove otherwise. See, for example, Sir Hersch Lauterpacht, *The Development of International Law* 380 (1958). There has, however, never been agreement on the International Court of Justice with respect to how the second requirement for custom, *opinio juris*, is to be demonstrated.

Example 2-4

Below are some statistics on the practice of executing people who commit crimes when they are under the age of eighteen years (juveniles). In 1990, there were nine countries that permitted the execution of juveniles. Currently, there are only five states that permit juvenile executions: Democratic Republic of the Congo, Iran, Nigeria, Saudi Arabia, and Sudan. The Convention of the Rights of the Child, 1577 U.N.T.S. 3, forbids capital punishment for juveniles (art. 37(a)). The treaty entered into force in 1990 and has been signed by all countries and ratified by all except Somalia and the U.S. Some countries have deposited reservations to the Convention, such as a number of Islamic countries who frequently add a generic reservation stating that they do not agree to anything that violates the principles of Islam although they do not specifically mention article 37(a). In the U.S. the death penalty for juveniles was declared unconstitutional by the Supreme Court in *Roper v. Simmons*, 543 U.S. 551 (2005). Currently, throughout the world there are about 140 people sentenced to death for crimes committed when they were under the age of eighteen years. Iran executes about two-thirds of the juvenile offenders executed each year.

Does customary international law prohibit the execution of people who commit crimes when they are under the age of eighteen years?

Explanation

There is obviously a very widespread practice throughout the world prohibiting the execution of those who commit crimes while they are juveniles. The I.C.J. has not always insisted on total uniformity of practice in order to constitute custom. In *Anglo-Norwegian Fisheries* (U.K. v. Norway), 1951 I.C.J. 116, the Court stated that "too much importance need not be attached to the few uncertainties or contradictions, real or apparent" that occur in state practice. *Id.* at 138-139. In other cases the Court stated it was looking for "constant and uniform" practice, *Asylum* case (Colombia v. Peru), 1950 I.C.J. 266, at 276, although that was in the context of regional custom. A "constant" or "consistent" state practice also indicates that the practice usually needs to be established for some time. In the *North Sea Continental Shelf* cases (F.R. Germany v. Denmark; F.R. Germany v. Netherlands), 1969 I.C.J. 3, the Court stated:

> Although the passage of only a short period of time is not necessarily, or of itself, a bar to the formation of a new rule of customary international law on the basis of what was originally a purely conventional rule, an indispensable requirement would be that within the period in question, short though it might be, State practice, . . . should have been both extensive and virtually uniform. . . ." *Id.* at para. 74.

The prohibition on juvenile death penalty has been in place in many countries for decades but it has only been in the last ten years or so that the practice has been almost universal. That period of time, though fairly short, should not alone be a bar to finding the practice to be a binding custom. There are still five countries that permit the death penalty for juvenile offenders. If it were determined that the prohibition on execution of juvenile offenders is now an international custom, would those five countries be bound by any such custom? If the prohibition on juvenile death penalty was ordinary customary international law, then the five states permitting such a penalty would be regarded as "persistent objectors" to the rule, as their opposition to the custom is well known and presumably published in their criminal codes. If the prohibition against juvenile death penalty is regarded as a jus cogens customary rule, then no derogation is permitted from such a rule. Many scholars argue that the rule has reached the jus cogens level. The Inter-American Commission on Human Rights determined that the rule was jus cogens in *Domingues v. U.S.*, Report No. 62/02, Case No. 12.285 at paras. 84-85 (2002).

Although the death penalty will no doubt continue to be carried out on juveniles in the five listed countries, if jurisdiction could be obtained over those states in an international court (and that court regarded the rule as *jus cogens*) then those states would be found in violation of the rule. The states could not raise their contrary national law as an excuse for not abiding by the *jus cogens* customary rule. Cf. VCLT, art. 27.

§2.3 TREATIES

There has been a great deal of arcane debate over whether treaties simply create binding obligations between states which are parties to the particular treaty in question or whether a treaty itself can create obligations not just for the treaty partners but also for the international community as a whole and thus serve as a source of international law. Treaties most certainly do create obligations for states that choose to become parties to treaties. (See Chapter 3, The Law of Treaties.) Can treaties serve as a source of law for non-parties? The answer to this question is "yes," but most writers are then insistent that if a particular precept in a treaty is binding on non-parties it will be so because the precept itself has become part of customary law, so it will be the customary law (also expressed in the treaty), not the treaty as such, that will bind the non-parties. The process whereby treaties are expressive of pre-existing custom or where, over time, treaty concepts become binding customary norms has been expressly recognized by the International Court of Justice in the *North Sea Continental Shelf* cases (F.R. Germany v. Denmark; F.R. Germany v. Netherlands), 1969 I.C.J. 3. In the current era, a great number of areas of international concern have been codified in multilateral treaties, and often these treaties exert a powerful influence on the development of customary law and on national law. (See, for example, the U.N. Law of the Sea Convention, discussed in greater detail in Chapter 12.) Before World War II, treaties that were open to ratification by all states were a rarity. Treaties were more often signed by a limited number of states with similar interests. It was unlikely, therefore, and these treaties would give rise to the creation of a customary norm or were themselves expressive of existing universal norms. Since World War II, the number of treaties open for universal signature has proliferated. These treaties often combine large sections that are simply a codification of pre-existing customary law and sections that are new law for the treaty partners but which may rapidly come to express customary norms. This rapid progression toward a binding customary norm occurs because, where many states sign on to the treaty, other non-parties quickly recognize that the treaty provisions have become the way that the international community organizes itself on that particular matter.

Sometimes the drafters of a treaty will write an accompanying commentary indicating whether they consider each article to be already established law (*lex lata*) or rather new law (*lex ferenda*). See, for example, the commentary to the Vienna Convention on the Law of Treaties drafted by the International Law Commission (ILC). Draft Articles on the Law of Treaties, II Y.B. Int'l L. Comm'n (1966). U.N. Charter article 13(1)(a) calls upon the General Assembly to encourage "the progressive development of international law and its codification . . ."; the ILC was established in 1948 to help accomplish this goal. The Commission consists of thirty-four international law experts; much of their work consists of drafting treaties. The work of the ILC has been enormously influential, and a number of its draft treaties have been adopted by the international community of states, such as the Vienna Convention on the Law of Treaties, 1155 U.N.T.S. 331, and the Vienna Convention on Diplomatic Relation, 500 U.N.T.S. 95.

In the *North Sea Continental Shelf* cases *supra*, Denmark and the Netherlands were trying to persuade the I.C.J. that article 6 of the Convention on the Continental Shelf, 499 U.N.T.S. 31, which set out a methodology for delimiting continental shelves between adjacent states where they could not reach a settlement, should be applicable to Germany, as established custom, even though Germany was not a party to that treaty. Although the Court accepted the principle that treaties could: (1) express established custom or (2) become custom after the adoption or entry into force of the treaty by means of the subsequent practice of states, the Court refused to find that article 6 had become binding on Germany as custom. It found the examples of state practice cited by Denmark and the Netherlands "inconclusive, and insufficient . . . as evidence of . . . a settled practice. . . ." *Id.* at para. 79.

Example 2-5

In 1982 a multilateral conference adopted the text of the U.N. Convention on the Law of the Sea. Over 100 states immediately signed the treaty, but many states refused to sign mainly because they objected to the regime created for harvesting the resources of the deep sea bed. (See Chapter 12, The Law of the Sea.) For the first time in history, the Convention declared that coastal states could claim up to 200 nautical miles from their coastlines as an exclusive economic zone (EEZ). Although ships of all states would have rights of passage over these waters, all of the zone's resources could be claimed by the coastal state.

By 1994, sixty states had ratified the treaty, and it went into force for those states that had ratified the treaty. All of these states rapidly claimed an EEZ. Some states that had signed but not yet ratified the treaty also claimed an EEZ. Several states that had not signed or ratified the treaty also claimed such a zone. State A has not signed the Convention and has not claimed an EEZ. State B has not signed the Convention but claimed an EEZ in 1996. State A's fishermen have traditionally fished in the waters off State B, except for a three nautical mile wide strip known as the territorial sea.

After State B claimed an EEZ, will State A be violating international law if it instructs its fishermen that they may fish within 200 nautical miles of State B and State A's fishermen continue to fish in those waters?

Explanation

There is no binding treaty on this issue between State A and State B. The answer to this question will, therefore, depend upon whether the EEZ is well enough established to be regarded as custom. In fact, many of the new regimes, or expanded regimes that were created by the Law of the Sea Convention were very rapidly accepted by the community of states so that the International Court of Justice twice stated that the EEZ had been accepted as law even before the treaty had entered into force.

In *Delimitation of the Maritime Boundary in the Gulf of Maine Area* (Canada v. United States of America), 1984 I.C.J. 246 at para. 94, a Chamber of the Court concluded that the regime of the exclusive economic zone, created by the Law of the Sea Convention, 1833 U.N.T.S. 3, arts. 55-75, which at the time was not yet in force, could already "be regarded as consonant . . . with general international law on the issue." Again, in a dispute over the delimitation of a continental shelf, the Court stated in *Continental Shelf* (Libya v. Malta), 1985 I.C.J. 13: "It is the Court's view that, apart from [articles in the Law of the Sea Convention] . . . , the institution of the exclusive economic zone, with its rule on entitlement by reason of distance, is shown by the practice of States to have become part of customary law. . . ." Both Libya and Malta had signed the Law of the Sea Convention but, as the Court noted, "that Convention has not yet entered into force, and is therefore not operative as treaty-law. . . ." *Id.* at para. 26.

In the modern era, treaties have become the dominant source of international law. The specific terms of a treaty will, of course, govern the legal relationship between the parties with respect to issues covered by the treaty. What is also apparent is that widely ratified multilateral treaties can themselves rapidly regulate the practice of non-parties to the treaty by creating binding custom.

§2.4 THE RELATIONSHIP OF INTERNATIONAL LAW TO DOMESTIC (NATIONAL) LAW

A number of issues are presented by the question of the relationship of international law to domestic law. The academic debate on this issue has labeled two different approaches as: (1) "Monism," basically that international law and national law are part of one unified system; and (2) "Dualism," basically that international and national law are distinct forms of law, and international law can only operate nationally if it has been specifically incorporated into national law. The debate, though interesting, is best understood by examining how international law is incorporated into national law in various countries. As a matter of international law, international obligations are considered to persist at the international level whether or not incorporated into national law. The *Paquete Habana* case, *supra*, states the U.S. approach which incorporates international customary law into U.S. domestic law, provided it does not conflict with pre-existing domestic law. Most other common law and civil law countries take this approach.[1] For example, a number of the judges in the *Ex Parte Pinochet* litigation in the U.K. expressed the view that international law was part of British common law.[2] Similar expressions can be found in the Supreme Court of Canada's discussion in *Reference re Secession of Quebec*.[3] Germany's Basic Law 25 specifically incorporates "general rules of public international law. . . ." Further, such rules are stated to "take precedence over the laws. . . ." Professor Shaw sums up his survey on this issue: "Most countries accept the operation of customary rules within their own jurisdictions, provid[ed] there is no conflict with existing laws, and some will allow international law to prevail over municipal provisions."[4]

With respect to the role that treaties play in national law, the answer is complicated by the variety of ways that treaties are made, as well as the possibility of constitutional provisions addressing the role of treaties. Some states, such as the U.K., always require an act of parliament before a treaty can be operative as municipal law. Other states, such as the U.S., often require a certain percentage of legislators to vote in favor of a treaty before the treaty can be ratified by the President. For example, under article II, section 2, of the U.S. Constitution, the President is given the "power, by and with the advice and consent of the Senate, to make treaties, provided two-thirds of the senators present concur; . . ." This power is again complicated by the Executive's centuries-old practice of entering into Executive Agreements (another term for international agreements) without the advice and consent of the Senate. Article VI of the U.S. Constitution makes "all treaties . . . the supreme law of the land . . ." and has generally been interpreted as making treaties self-executing, that is, not requiring further legislation to become operative at the national level, unless encroaching on an

---

1. For an excellent survey of a number of countries' approaches to this issue, see Malcolm N. Shaw, *International Law* 138-179 (6th ed. 2008) [hereinafter Shaw].

2. See, e.g., [2000] 1 AC 61, 98; [2000] 1 AC 147, 276; see also IV *Blackstone's Commentaries*, ch. 5; but cf., *Regina v. Jones*, [2006] UKHL 16.

3. 161 DLR (4th) 385, 399, 2 S.C.R. 217 (1998).

4. Shaw, *supra* note 1, at 177.

area delegated by the Constitution to Congress, such as raising revenue, but this view has recently been challenged in the case of *Medellin v. Texas*.[5]

A further question is whether subsequent legislation can override treaties. (We have noted that states are generally free to disregard customary law by passing contrary legislation, except where the customary rule is *jus cogens*. See note on *Jus Cogens*, §2.2.3 *supra*). There is no general approach to this issue, and different states exhibit different stances. The U.S. follows a "latter in time" rule so that the last item to become operative, whether a treaty or a regular piece of legislation, will prevail. Other states hold that treaties prevail over regular legislation regardless of the date of the treaty or the contrary legislation.[6]

Despite all of these different ways of melding international law into domestic law while preserving the right to pass contrary legislation, it should be remembered that at the international level a state may not rely on its internal law to excuse the non-performance of an international obligation.[7]

§2.5 GENERAL PRINCIPLES OF LAW

The International Court of Justice, which is the judicial arm of the United Nations, operates under provisions in the U.N. Charter and its own statute that is annexed to the Charter. Article 38 of the Court's statute lists the sources of law upon which the Court may rely when it is deciding cases that come before it. Article 38 states that the Court is to apply:

a) international conventions, whether general or particular, establishing rules expressly recognized by the contesting states;

b) international custom, as evidence of a general practice accepted as law;

c) the general principles of law recognized by civilized nations;

d) subject to the provisions of Article 59,[8] judicial decisions and the teachings of the most highly qualified publicists of the various nations, as subsidiary means for the determination of rules of law.

---

5. 552 U.S. 491 (2008).
6. Shaw, *supra* note 1, at 178.
7. See Vienna Convention on the Law of Treaties, arts. 27 & 46, 1155 U.N.T.S. 331, signed May 23, 1969, entered into force January 27, 1980; *Cameroon v. Nigeria*, 2002 I.C.J. 303, 430-431; Request for Interpretation of the Judgment of 31 March 2004 (*Mexico v. U.S.*), 2009 I.C.J. ___, at para. 47.
8. Article 59 of the Statute of the International Court of Justice states: "The decision of the Court has no binding force except between the parties and in respect of the particular case." In practice the Court either follows the rules laid down in similar cases or seeks to distinguish the case before it from previous cases.

2. Sources of International Law

Although this article governs a particular international court, it has been widely regarded as an authoritative statement on the sources of international law. The article does not purport to indicate which of the listed sources should be resorted to first but most writers assume that the order in the article was meant to indicate a hierarchy of sources. If that is the case, then "general principles" will only come into play in the absence of a treaty or custom on a particular point. The term "recognized by civilized nations" has a paternalistic air to it and was obviously a product of the colonial era during which the Charter and statute were drafted. Nowadays, we tend to refer to general principles recognized by developed legal systems. What are these "general principles"? Nothing too startling. Occasionally an international court will find that it needs to resort to a legal precept found in national legal systems but never before used in an international court. Allowing international judges to rely on concepts common to the major national legal systems means that where there is a gap in international law the judges have some ability to fill it rather than simply announcing that the case cannot be decided because no international law currently exists on the topic. Examples of reliance on "general principles" have generally come from procedural or administrative areas of the law or notions of general legal liability. In the *Factory at Chorzów* case,[9] the Permanent Court of International Justice[10] stated that "a party cannot take advantage of his own wrong" and that "every violation of an engagement involves an obligation to make reparation." Some international tribunals have applied the concept of limitation (i.e., a claim is barred because too much time has passed between the alleged wrongdoing and the presentation of the claim).[11] The International Court of Justice has also used the principle of estoppel to bar a claim.[12] Some of the general principles are derived from the nature of the international legal system such as the legal equality of states or the prohibition against states operating on another state's territory. None of the above principles comes as a surprise to anyone versed in even a smattering of law, but allowing international courts to resort to these general principles has proved useful in a system that operates without a legislative system that might otherwise be relied on to fill in legal gaps. Sometimes an international court will also refer to equity or fairness as guiding its decision either to find an international obligation or to refuse to do so.[13] Some writers

---

9. 1927 P.C.I.J., Ser. A, No. 9, at 31.

10. The Permanent Court was the judicial arm of the League of Nations. When the League was disbanded, the Permanent Court ceased to exist but the Statute of the International Court of Justice is based upon the Statute of the Permanent Court.

11. Italy (Gentini) v. *Venezuela*, Mixed Claims Commission, 1903 (Ralston, *Venezuelan Arbitrations of 1903*, at 720 (1904)).

12. *Temple Case* (Cambodia v. Thailand), 1962 I.C.J. 6, at 33.

13. *North Sea Continental Shelf Cases*, 1969 I.C.J. 3 at paras. 88ff.

maintain that equity is not as such a source of law but rather simply influences the way the court applies the law.

Example 2-6

State B brings a claim against State C asserting that State C engaged in genocide against certain groups of citizens in State B.

Which party would you expect to bear the burden of proof in establishing the alleged fact of genocide drawing on what you understand to be general principles of proof before a court?

Explanation

Virtually all states have a general principle that it is the party asserting the fact that bears the burden of proving it. This rule is occasionally set aside in special circumstances in which another party has sole access to information about the events in question and that party refuses to divulge the information. In such a case, a court may order the reluctant party to produce the information, or it may be prepared to infer the facts from the limited evidence presented by the party alleging the fact.

The I.C.J. has often referred to the general rule on the burden of proof. For example, in *Military and Paramilitary Activities in and Against Nicaragua* (Nicaragua v. United States of America), 1984 I.C.J. 392, at 437 (Jurisdiction and Admissibility), the Court stated "[I]t is the litigant seeking to establish a fact who bears the burden of proving it. . . ." Again, in *Application of the Convention on the Prevention and Punishment of the Crime of Genocide* (Bosnia & Herzegovina v. Serbia & Montenegro), 2007 I.C.J. 1 at para. 204, the Court states: "On the burden or onus of proof, it is well established in general that the applicant must establish its case and that a party asserting a fact must establish it. . . ." The Court noted that Serbia and Montenegro had redacted certain portions of crucial documents, and Bosnia and Herzegovina had suggested that this refusal to supply full documents should reverse the burden. The Court noted that it had access to a great deal of material on the issue. Although it did not rule directly on Bosnia and Herzegovina's request, it stated that it had "not failed to note the Applicant's suggestion that the Court may be free to draw its own conclusions." *Id.* at para. 206. In the *Corfu Channel* case (U.K. v. Albania), 1949 I.C.J. 4, at 18, the Court was prepared to allow inferences from indirect evidence where one party was in control of a certain area. In *U.S. Diplomatic and Consular Staff in Tehran* (U.S. v. Iran), 1980 I.C.J. 3, at 10, where Iran was holding U.S. diplomats hostage in Tehran, thus blocking access to much information and where Iran refused to appear before the Court, the Court relied on a great deal of publically available information, as well as the U.S. submissions, to reach its determination of the facts.

§2.6 JUDICIAL DECISIONS

By virtue of article 59 of the I.C.J.'s Statute, the Court's decisions are only binding on the parties before it in respect of the particular case. One might expect therefore that the Court would approach each case on a clean slate regardless of whether the issues raised were similar to ones presented in an earlier case. Nothing could be further from the truth. In fact, if a case raises issues discussed in a previous case, the Court is often at pains to explain either why the issue will be resolved in the same way or why it should be distinguished. This approach makes sense as the Court obviously does not invent new law for each case before it. Why then was article 59 drafted as it was? The answer has at least two facets. First, the drafters of article 59 were convinced that cases that arise between states are, to some extent, unique. It is true they are not like the everyday automobile accident that bears the characteristics of thousands of other similar accidents, but, taking an historical perspective, inter-state disputes often, in fact, share common characteristics. Second, it was well known that in the common-law legal systems precedent is relied upon rather more heavily than in civil law systems. The civil law countries did not want the International Court taking off down the common-law precedent road. As a result the Court does not apply the rule of *stare decisis*. Nonetheless, international judicial decisions often influence future decisions, and the International Court often cites earlier cases.

For example, in *Avena and Other Mexican Nationals* (Mexico v. U.S), 2004 I.C.J. 12 at para. 119, the Court cited with approval a decision by the Permanent Court of International Justice (P.C.I.J.) which had stated:

> The essential principle contained in the actual notion of an illegal act — a principle which seems to be established by international practice and particularly by the decisions of arbitral tribunals — is that reparation must, as far as possible, wipe out all the consequences of an illegal act and reestablish the situation which would, in all probability, have existed if that act had not been committed. Quoting, *Factory at Chorzów*, 1928 P.C.I.J., Ser. A, No. 17, at 47.

Here the I.C.J. was citing an earlier decision of its predecessor Court for a principle of law established by arbitral tribunals.

In *Territorial and Maritime Dispute Between Nicaragua and Honduras in the Caribbean Sea* (Nicaragua v. Honduras), 2007 I.C.J. 659, the Court cites a decision of the Swiss Federal Council of 1922 and a 1933 decision of a Special Boundary Tribunal constituted by a treaty of arbitration between the two parties. *Id.* at paras. 133-134. Now that the I.C.J.'s web site (http://www.icj-cij.org) has an excellent search engine, it is very simple to find numerous references by the Court to its earlier decisions and to decisions of other international tribunals the Court has referenced.

§2.7 WRITERS AND SCHOLARS

National judicial decisions are often replete with long strings of citations to the works of eminent legal writers. This has been particularly so in recent decades in the developed world, in part because of the advent of the law clerk or judge's assistant and in part because of the availability of sophisticated electronic data retrieval systems. International decisions refer to authors' works much less frequently. This may be due in part to the comparative dearth of law clerks in the international arena but is much more probably due to the judges' fears of being perceived as relying too heavily on authors from one particular country or one particular legal system. If the American judge on the International Court of Justice started authoring opinions peppered with citations only to American scholars, fellow judges might not be willing to join those opinions, and the judge would rapidly get the reputation of deciding cases according to American notions rather than international norms. International judges have therefore often been more sparing in their citations to scholars' works, but this does not mean that international judges do not read scholars and other writers' works nor does it mean they are not influenced by this body of work. In the Court's advisory opinions (see Chapter 5, §5.3.2) the judges tend to cite scholars more frequently. See *Legality of the Threat or Use of Nuclear Weapons*, Advisory Opinion, 1996 I.C.J. 226 (July 8), which is full of references to such works. The International Law Commission (ILC) is a group of thirty-four scholars and jurists approved by U.N. General Assembly to encourage "the progressive development of international law and its codification. . . ." U.N. Charter, art. 13(1)(a). The ILC has drafted several very important treaties and its work has been most influential. National courts often rely on international scholars to support their determination of international law. See, e.g., *The Paquete Habana*, 175 U.S. 677 (1900); *Abdullahi v. Pfizer, Inc.*, 562 F.3d 163 (2d Cir. 2009) cert. denied, 130 S. Ct. 3541 (2010).

§2.8 UNITED NATIONS' RESOLUTIONS

§2.8.1 General Assembly Resolutions

Although the General Assembly of the U.N. has the authority to adopt binding resolutions with respect to the U.N. budget (U.N. Charter, art. 17) most of its resolutions are not considered binding as such (U.N. Charter, art. 14). Nonetheless, resolutions that receive overwhelming support are certainly treated as evidence of the practice of states and, as such, may themselves reflect custom. Some of the resolutions purport to confirm a norm of international law, such as a 1946 resolution which affirms that "genocide is a crime under international law" G.A. Res. 96 (I) (Dec. 11, 1946) or a 1960 resolution on granting independence to colonial peoples which declared: "1. The subjection of peoples to alien subjugation, domination and exploitation constitutes a denial of human rights, is contrary to the Charter of the United Nations and is an impediment to world peace and co-operation." G.A. Res. 1514 (XV) (Dec. 14, 1960). While these resolutions are not binding themselves, they reflect the opinions of states on binding legal norms and are often hugely influential in moving aspirations along a continuum toward universal acceptance as a binding norm. The I.C.J. has also recognized that consent by states to General Assembly resolutions "may be understood as acceptance of the validity of the rule or set of rules declared by the resolution. . . ." *Military and Paramilitary Activities in and Against Nicaragua* (Nicaragua v. U.S.), 1986 I.C.J. 14, 108.

(For a description of the General Assembly and its powers, see Chapter 4, §4.5.1.)

§2.8.2 Security Council Resolutions

The U.N. Charter grants the Security Council authority to:

> determine the existence of any threat to the peace, breach of the peace, or act of aggression and . . . make recommendations, or decide what measures shall be taken in accordance with Articles 41 and 42, to maintain or restore international peace and security. Art. 39.

Article 41 grants the Council the power to decide on non-forceful measures to carry out its decisions and article 42 gives the Council the power to order forceful measures. These orders can be binding on all member states (art. 25) if that is what the Council intends. Whether the Council intends a particular resolution to be binding will depend upon the interpretation of the language of the resolution. The Council can order such things as economic sanctions against a particular nation, as it has on numerous occasions, for example, against Iraq (e.g., S.C. Res. 661 (1990)), Libya (e.g., S.C. Res. 748 (1992)), and the former Yugoslavia (e.g., S.C. Res. 757 (1992)), and make the sanctions mandatory or voluntary as the Council determines. Economic sanctions are an example of non-forceful measures (art. 41). Alternatively, the Council may authorize member states to use force to achieve a particular objective such as driving Iraq out of Kuwait after Saddam Hussein invaded Kuwait in 1990 (art. 42). The Council requested (but did not require) member states to cooperate with Kuwait and use all necessary means (including armed force) to secure the withdrawal of Iraq from Kuwait (S.C. Res. 678 (1990)). More than twenty nations responded under a coalition force led by the U.S. and the U.K.

When the Security Council's resolutions are binding on U.N. members those resolutions create required actions for member states. In a way, this is a form of international legislation. Looking at the whole corpus of Security Council resolutions, both those that are recommendatory and those that are mandatory, the action taken by states in response to these resolutions creates patterns of state practice, often engaged in because the resolutions are considered binding, that is, regarded as law.

§2.8.3 Proliferation of International Regulatory Systems

In this chapter, most of the international law making process examined has been generated by states but, of course, with the very rapid expansion of the movement of goods, services, and people since the middle of the twentieth century, a whole host of international entities has grown up, or expanded, to deal with everything from postal services, air and sea travel, health standards, environmental standards, transfer of currencies, and many other topics. All of the international structures established to regulate these and many more fields also contribute to the creation of international law. The United Nations remains the pre-eminent international governmental organization, and its many organs and subsidiary organs have created a great web of international law. The U.N. Security Council can issue resolutions binding on all member states and, in recent years, it has begun to use these powers almost like a super-legislature on an ever-increasing variety of topics.

(For a description of the Security Council and its powers, see Chapter 4, §4.5.1.)

All of the methods of creating international law outlined in this chapter are at work within the rapidly expanding number of international regulatory systems to produce a highly dynamic system of international law creation.

§2.9 THE "SOFT LAW" OR NON-BINDING RULES PROCESS

One of the ways that all law develops, including international law, is the process by which a proposed rule is first adopted as a guiding principle but then, over time, gathers traction and ultimately becomes, or shapes, a binding law. To give some examples: If you read through the 1948 Universal Declaration of Human Rights (UDHR) (see also Chapter 8), you will find what looks like the guarantee of numerous human rights: "the right to life, liberty and security of person" (art. 3); not to be "subjected to torture or to cruel, inhuman or degrading treatment or punishment" (art. 5); to be "equal before the law" (art. 7); "the right to freedom of thought, conscience and religion" (art. 18); "the right to work . . . and to protection against unemployment" (art. 23(1)); "the right to rest and leisure" (art. 24); "the right to a standard of living adequate for the health and well-being of himself and of his family, including food, clothing, housing and medical care and necessary social services" (art. 25). The UDHR, however, starts with a preamble, which, among other things, states:

> Now, Therefore the General Assembly proclaims this Universal Declaration of Human Rights as a common standard of achievement for all peoples and all nations, to the end that every individual and every organ of society, keeping this Declaration constantly in mind, shall strive by teaching and education to promote respect for these rights and freedoms and by progressive measures, national and international, to secure their universal and effective recognition and observance, both among the peoples of Member States themselves and among the peoples of territories under their jurisdiction. UDHR, preamble at para. 8.

From this language, it is clear that the UDHR was aspirational and sought to set standards toward which members of the United Nations pledged to work. The UDHR was, at the time of its adoption by the U.N. General Assembly in 1948, soft law. It was, however, and continues to be, hugely influential and has led to the adoption of a number of treaties guaranteeing similar rights which are binding upon states parties to those treaties and which may also become binding custom. See, for example, the International Covenant on Civil and Political Rights, 999 U.N.T.S. 171; the International Covenant on Economic, Social and Cultural Rights, 993 U.N.T.S. 3; and the Convention Against Torture and Other Cruel, Inhuman or Degrading Treatment or Punishment, 1465 U.N.T.S. 85.

International environmental law, see Chapter 13, is another area where governmental or non-governmental conferences may well adopt working principles or aspirational normative rules which slowly, or rapidly, may develop into binding law. For example, in 1972, the United Nations Conference on the Human Environment issued the Stockholm Declaration which stated:

> The national resources of the earth . . . must be safeguarded for the benefit of present and future generations. . . . Stockholm Declaration, Principle 2, reprinted at 11 I.L.M. 1416 (1972).

2. Sources of International Law

At the time the Declaration was written, no one regarded it as creating binding obligations. This Declaration has, however, been very influential and has led to treaties such as the Convention on Biological Diversity, 1760 U.N.T.S. 79, and the United Nations Framework Convention on Climate Change, 1771 U.N.T.S. 107, which create binding legal obligations.

This process of law creation can now be observed in many areas of international law. Because of the revolution in communication, facilitated by the Internet, the movement from soft law to hard law can often be quite rapid.

The Law of Treaties

3

§3.1   Definition of a Treaty
§3.2   Capacity to Conclude a Treaty
§3.3   Ratification
    §3.3.1   Internal Ratification
    §3.3.2   International Ratification
§3.4   Reservations
§3.5   Entry into Force
§3.6   Observance and Application of Treaties
§3.7   Interpretation of Treaties
§3.8   Individual Rights Arising Under Treaties
§3.9   Invalidity
    §3.9.1   Error
    §3.9.2   Fraud and Corruption
    §3.9.3   Coercion
    §3.9.4   Conflict with a Peremptory Norm (*Jus Cogens*)
§3.10 Termination and Suspension
    §3.10.1 Material Breach
    §3.10.2 Supervening Impossibility of Performance
    §3.10.3 Fundamental Change of Circumstances: (*Rebus Sic Stantibus*)
§3.11 The Effect of War on Treaties
    §3.11.1 The Effect of War on Human Rights Treaties

§3.12 Procedure for Termination
§3.13 Remedies for Violation of a Treaty
    §3.13.1 Enforcement of Treaties in National Courts
§3.14 State Succession in Respect of Treaties

§3.1 DEFINITION OF A TREATY

The Vienna Convention on the Law of Treaties (VCLT), 1155 U.N.T.S. 331, which has been ratified by 111 states and which most states regard as highly authoritative (even if they have not consented to ratification), defines a treaty as: "an international agreement concluded between states in written form and governed by international law. . . ." Art. 2(1)(a). (Further articles of this treaty will be referenced as VCLT with the appropriate article number.) Such a document does not have to be called a treaty to be binding. Indeed there are many names for such documents, such as convention, covenant, pact, protocol, charter, exchange of notes and several others. Technically, the VCLT does not govern oral agreements between states although such agreements can be binding. Article 3 of the VCLT states that the fact that non-written agreements fall outside the scope of the VCLT "shall not affect . . . the legal force of such agreements." Many of the rules found in the VCLT are, in any event, customary rules and thus may be binding on oral agreements. See VCLT, art. 3(c). Oral agreements between state representatives have been found to be binding. *Legal Status of Eastern Greenland* (Denmark v. Norway), 1933 P.C.I.J., Ser. A/B, No. 53, at 194 (Apr. 5). Sometimes even unilateral statements made by governmental officials may be internationally binding, *Nuclear Tests* (Australia v. France), 1974 I.C.J. 253 at para. 51, and an agreement between a state and an international organization may also be binding at the international level.

§3.2 CAPACITY TO CONCLUDE A TREATY

States are free to designate anyone to represent the state for the purpose of concluding a treaty provided he or she has been duly authorized with "full powers." The term "full powers" means that the person concerned will have been issued an appropriate document indicating such powers have been conferred upon him/her. Certain representatives of a state are automatically considered to have "full powers" by virtue of their office: a head of state, a leader of the government, or a foreign affairs minister. VCLT, art. 7(2)(a).

Even if such persons do not in fact possess such powers under their own municipal law, if they hold themselves out as having the power to bind their country, international law will hold that other states have every right to rely on such representation and will find any agreement concluded by such a person binding. *Legal Status of Eastern Greenland* (Denmark v. Norway), 1933 P.C.I.J., Ser. A/B, No. 53, at 194.

§3.3 RATIFICATION

§3.3.1 Internal Ratification

Every state has its own internal law for determining which organs of government are empowered to make a treaty binding on the state. In the United Kingdom, for example, the Executive has the authority to enter into treaties but treaties need an enabling act of Parliament before they become part of British law. The same is true in the Netherlands. In the United States the executive branch negotiates and signs the treaty. From that point on, although the U.S. is not yet bound by the specific language of the treaty, as it has not yet ratified the treaty, it is nonetheless "obliged to refrain from acts which would defeat the object and purpose of [the] treaty . . . until it shall have made its intention clear not to become a party to the treaty. . . ." VCLT, art. 18. Although the U.S. is not a party to the VCLT, it appears to consider this principle as operative. In 2000, President Clinton signed the Rome Statute establishing the International Criminal Court. However, President Bush decided that the U.S. did not wish to be bound by VCLT article 18's requirement not to do anything to defeat the object and purpose of the treaty, and so, in 2002, the U.S. Department of State notified the Secretary-General that the U.S. did not intend to become a party to the Rome Statute. (The U.S. had persuaded a number of states who were parties to the Rome Statute to sign bilateral treaties with the U.S. promising never to surrender U.S. citizens to the ICC even if the U.S. citizen was in the territory of the treaty partner and the ICC had issued an indictment of that person. Many people argued that since the Rome Statute required the surrender of such a person, the bilateral treaties were designed to defeat the objects and purposes of the Rome Statute.) Generally, when the text has been signed by a duly appointed representative of the U.S., the treaty is sent by the executive branch to the Senate for its advice and consent by a two-thirds vote. After the Senate has given its consent, the treaty is returned to the President for his/her ratification, which he or she may complete or refuse to complete as he or she sees fit.

Note

In U.S. practice, the Senate gives its advice and consent to the ratification of treaties. **The Senate does not ratify treaties.** There is no constitutional obligation for the President to ratify a treaty even if the Senate has given its advice and consent.

The President is also empowered to conclude Executive Agreements to which Senate consent is not necessary. These agreements are equally binding upon the United States. The distinction between "treaties" which require Senate consent and "executive agreements" which do not is entirely unclear in U.S. constitutional law, although a fair amount of historic practice often dictates the route to be employed. Congress, by legislation, can also authorize the President to enter into Executive Agreements that then become binding law for the U.S. at both the domestic and international level. These agreements are called "Congressional-Executive Agreements" and have long been upheld by the U.S. Supreme Court. *J.W. Hampton, Jr. & Co. v. U.S.*, 276 U.S. 394, 410-411 (1928). Once the President has ratified a treaty under U.S. law, the ratification will be sent to the international depositary. If the treaty has entered into force for treaty parties, then the U.S. will be bound internationally to comply with the provisions of the treaty.

§3.3.2 International Ratification

After internal ratification has occurred, the state will send a formal indication of consent to be bound by the treaty either to the other states parties to the treaty or by depositing its consent with the depository organization designated by the treaty. If the state is also a member of the United Nations, the U.N. Charter requires the state to register the treaty with the U.N. Secretariat. (U.N. Charter, art. 102, para. 1.)

§3.4 RESERVATIONS

VCLT article 2(1)(d) defines a reservation as:

> a unilateral statement, however phrased or named, made by a state, when signing, ratifying, accepting, approving or acceding to a treaty, whereby it purports to exclude or modify the legal effect of certain provisions of the treaty in their application to that state.

In other words, a reservation allows a treaty party who does not like all of the terms of a treaty unilaterally to announce that certain parts of the treaty will not apply to it. At first blush, you might well think that such a system spells potential chaos. States being allowed to opt out of onerous parts of obligations at will hardly comports with the overarching principle of treaty law, *pacta sunt servanda*: Treaties are binding and to be performed in good faith. A good number of treaties, however, either prohibit or limit reservations. For example, article 309 of the United Nations Convention on the Law of the Sea, 1833 U.N.T.S. 3, states: "No reservations or exceptions may be made to this Convention unless expressly permitted by other articles of this Convention."

Example 3-1

The State of Alpha and the State of Beta enter into a treaty containing eight numbered articles. Both states complete their internal ratification procedures and mutually exchange ratification notifications. Alpha adds the following reservation: "The State of Alpha does not agree to article number eight and hereby notifies the State of Beta of its reservation to article eight." Beta's ratification did not include any reservations to the treaty.

What effect will Alpha's reservation have on the treaty?

Explanation

First, there can be no reservations to bilateral (two-party) treaties for the simple reason that if the two parties do not agree on any particular provisions then there is no agreement on that provision, that is, there is no binding obligation on that point. When Beta receives the notification of ratification from Alpha it has three choices: (1) It can agree to the modification, in which case the treaty will only have seven articles; (2) It can tell Alpha that if she is not prepared to accept article 8, Beta will not agree to the treaty; (3) Beta can ask Alpha to enter into further negotiations about article 8 (or any other articles).

Before the second half of the twentieth century, the rule on reservations had been that states were not permitted to make reservations to treaties unless all of the other parties to the treaty accepted the reservation. In many ways, this older system was orderly and predictable but the nature of treaty relationships was beginning to change, particularly in the human rights area, and it was thought that a more flexible system might be preferable.

In 1951, the International Court of Justice, the international court established by the U.N. Charter, articles 92-96, handed down an advisory opinion, *Reservations to the Convention on the Prevention and Punishment of the Crime of Genocide*, Advisory Opinion, 1951 I.C.J. 15 (May 28), which altered the unanimity rule, at least for human rights treaties that sought to attract as many treaty parties as possible. Considering the effect of reservations to the Genocide Convention, 78 U.N.T.S. 277, the Court ruled that where a state appended a reservation to the Genocide Convention and that reservation was accepted by some, but not all, of the parties to the Convention, then the reserving state could be considered a party to the treaty provided the reservation was not incompatible with the objects and purposes of the treaty. Although the Court seemed to indicate that there were objective criteria for assessing such compatibility, the Court also indicated that it was for each state party to the Convention to decide this issue for itself. If all of the states parties to the treaty rejected the reservation then the reserving state could not become a party to the treaty, but if, for example, the reservation was accepted by some states but rejected by other states, then the reserving state would be considered a party to the treaty and would have a treaty relationship with the states that had accepted the reservation but only with respect to the articles to which no reservation had been made. If the states that had rejected the reservation had done so because they regarded the reservation as incompatible with the objects and purposes of the treaty, then there would be no treaty relationship between those states and the reserving state.

Example 3-2

States A, B, C, D, and E wish to enter into a treaty. The treaty has ten different articles. States A, B, C, and D accept all ten articles without reservations. State E, however, does not agree with article 10, so it indicates that it wishes to make a reservation to article 10.

Under what circumstances can State E become a party to the treaty? If State E can become a party to the treaty, what is the treaty relationship between State E and States A, B, C, and D?

Explanation

Under the pre-1950s rule the answer to both questions was straightforward. State E could only become a party to the treaty if States A, B, C, and D all accepted State E's reservation. If any state rejected the reservation, State E could not become a party to the treaty. If all of the states (A-D) accepted E's reservation, then State E was regarded as a party to the treaty. There would be a treaty relationship between States A, B, C, and D binding them to all ten articles of the treaty. There would also be a treaty relationship between State E and all the other states but only with respect to articles 1-9. After the *Genocide Reservations* case *supra*, the answer changes.

It still remains true that if all states parties to the treaty reject the reservation as incompatible with the objects and purposes of the treaty, State E cannot become a party to the treaty. Similarly if States A-D accept the reservation, then E will be a treaty party and the treaty will be in effect between E and A-D but only with respect to articles 1-9. If A and B accept the reservation but C and D reject it, then E can be regarded as a treaty party and will have to abide by articles 1-9. A and B will be in a treaty relationship with E but only with respect to articles 1-9. C and D will not be in a treaty relationship with E.

If there were a court where the issue of the reservation's compatibility with the object and purpose of the treaty could be litigated, then such a court could make a determination about the permissibility of the reservation. If the reservation were ruled to be incompatible, then the reserving state would have to drop the reservation in order to become a party to the treaty. Even if such a court ruled that the reservation was not incompatible with the treaty, other states, parties to the treaty, are not required to accept the reservation or to enter into a treaty relationship with State E. If a state party to the treaty objects to the reservation but not because it views it as incompatible with the treaty, then that state can choose to enter into a treaty relationship with State E with the exception of the article to which State E made a reservation, although it is not required to enter into any such treaty relationship.

The drafters of the VCLT largely adopted the new rule on reservations announced by the Court in the *Genocide Reservations* case, see articles 19-23. Many modern treaties spell out whether parties are permitted to make reservations or not and, if so, usually indicate to which articles reservations may be made and which articles do not permit reservations. Where a treaty has such a provision, it will govern the question of the permissibility of reservations.

Example 3-3

The Convention Against Torture and Other Cruel, Inhuman or Degrading Treatment or Punishment, 1465 U.N.T.S. 85, states in article 2(2): "No exceptional circumstances whatsoever, whether a state of war or a threat of war, internal political instability or any other public emergency, may be invoked as justification of torture." State Y has recently been subject to a series of suicide bomb attacks in some of its major cities by dissidents who disagree with the country's foreign policy. State Y sends in its ratification of the Torture Convention with the following reservation: "State Y reserves the right to use any means necessary to protect its citizens from the threat of terrorist attacks where it is convinced that such means will protect human life."

You represent your country, State X, and your president has asked for your advice on whether State X should accept such a reservation. State X and Y are long time allies, and State X has been very supportive of State Y's attempt to curb terrorism. What will you advise your president? Remember that if you do nothing for a year after notification of Y's reservation, your country will be deemed to have accepted the reservation. VCLT, art. 20(5).

Explanation

First ask yourself exactly what State Y's reservation means. Presumably, if State Y was not contemplating activity that could be labeled as torture, there would have been no need for a reservation. As a result, one has to assume that State Y is reserving the right to torture in certain circumstances. Next ask yourself what is the underlying purpose of the Torture Convention. Next ask yourself whether article 2(2) of the Convention leaves any room for states to refuse to comply with the prohibition on torture in exceptional circumstances. If you view the Torture Convention as having the purpose of outlawing all torture, in all circumstances, then State Y's reservation will clearly undermine the object and purpose of the treaty and thus will not be acceptable. If you think there is some room for exceptions to a total ban on torture (though it is difficult to make such an argument), you may not find the reservation incompatible with the treaty. Again, if you come to the conclusion that article 2(2) of the Convention permits no reservations, no matter what the circumstances, then State Y's reservation is contrary to the Convention's own requirements and thus not acceptable. Many human rights lawyers would also argue that the total prohibition on torture is also a *jus cogens* norm of customary law from which no derogation is permitted. (See Chapter 2 on Sources of International Law and Chapters 8 and 9 on Human Rights.)

§3.5 ENTRY INTO FORCE

States are free to choose the manner in which, and date on which, a treaty enters into force. Most modern treaties have a provision specifying how and when the treaty enters into force, usually upon the ratification of a specified number of states. For example, the U.N. Convention on the Law of the Sea, 1833 U.N.T.S. 3, states that the treaty will enter into force one year after the deposit of the sixtieth ratification (art. 308). The sixtieth ratification was, in fact, deposited on November 16, 1993 and so the Convention entered into force on November 16, 1994. If a treaty does not specify when entry into force occurs then it will occur "as soon as consent to be bound by the treaty has been established for all the negotiating states," VCLT art. 24(2).

§3.6 OBSERVANCE AND APPLICATION OF TREATIES

The great overriding principle of treaty law is often expressed in Latin: *pacta sunt servanda*, which article 26 of the VCLT translates as "Every treaty in force is binding upon the parties to it and must be performed by them in good faith." VCLT article 27 makes it clear that internal law cannot be raised as a justification for the failure to keep a treaty. Article 46 makes that limitation specifically applicable with respect to competence to conclude a treaty unless it is objectively manifest that the party purporting to bind the state had no such authority. Treaties are deemed to be prospective and are applicable to the state's entire territory unless they indicate otherwise.

§3.7 INTERPRETATION OF TREATIES

When the VCLT was being drafted by the International Law Commission, two schools of treaty interpretation emerged. One group wished to concentrate on *the meaning of the text*. It was assumed that most treaties are negotiated by educated and sophisticated people, so that by the time a text is arrived at, the ambiguities will have been largely eliminated, and the text will in fact reflect the intention of the parties. Such a view leads naturally to rules of interpretation that restrict quite severely the types, and occasions on which, extrinsic evidence (evidence arising outside the four corners of the document) may be introduced to prove the meaning of the treaty. The other group focused on *the intention of the parties* and were much more willing to establish rules that would allow the introduction of a broad array of evidence that might throw light upon the intention of the parties. It is fair to say that the first group largely won the day. Both groups were sometimes willing to take into account the overall object and purpose of the treaty. VCLT, arts. 31-33. The International Court of Justice has stated that "interpretation must be based above all upon the text of the treaty." *Territorial Dispute* (Libya v. Chad), 1994 I.C.J. 6 at para. 41. However, in the same paragraph of that case, the I.C.J. also mentions other aids to treaty interpretation: the "ordinary meaning," "context," "object and purpose," and, as "a supplementary measure recourse may be had to means of interpretation such as the preparatory work of the treaty and the circumstances of its conclusion." Id.

Article 31 of the VCLT establishes the rule of interpreting a treaty in accordance with its ordinary meaning but adds that this rule operates in light of the treaty's context and its overall objective. The meaning given to context and objective is fairly limited. The only occasions when supplementary means of interpretation may be resorted to, such as "*travaux préparatoires*" (preparatory works) are when the ordinary meaning method "leaves the meaning ambiguous or obscure" or when that method of interpretation leads to an "absurd or unreasonable" result. VCLT art. 32(a) & (b). See *Kasikili/Sedudu Island* (Botswana v. Namibia), 1999 I.C.J. 1045.

In the *Territorial Dispute supra*, between Libya and Chad, the I.C.J. settled the boundary between the parties on the basis of a 1955 treaty. Under article 3 of that treaty the parties " 'recognize . . . that the frontiers . . . are those that result' from certain international instruments." *Id.* at para. 42. Libya contended that the 1955 treaty only meant to recognize a frontier where such a frontier had been agreed on prior to 1955, but if a frontier had not been fixed before that date, the 1955 treaty should not be interpreted as creating a frontier. The Court disagreed with such an interpretation.

> In the view of the Court, the terms of the Treaty signified that the parties thereby recognized complete frontiers between their respective territories . . . no relevant frontier was to be left undefined. . . . [To agree with the Libyan interpretation] would be to deprive Article 3 of the Treaty . . . of [its] ordinary meaning. *Id.* at para. 43.

The United States is not a party to the VCLT but has often stated that it regards much of the treaty as reflecting customary law. One area, however, where U.S. courts differ from the VCLT is on the methodology of treaty interpretation. Although different views on the topic have been expressed by various members of the U.S. Supreme Court, it is fair to say that U.S. courts are quite liberal in allowing the presentation of outside evidence when interpreting treaties. See the sharply differing views expressed in *U.S. v. Stuart*, 489 U.S. 353 (1989).

§3.8 INDIVIDUAL RIGHTS ARISING UNDER TREATIES

Treaties are entered into by states or international organizations. The rights and responsibilities, therefore, usually only apply to the parties to the treaty and do not normally apply to individuals. Parties to treaties are, however, free to confer rights upon individuals if they intend to do so. Currently, it is recognized that "treaties . . . sometimes confer rights that would support a cause of action by private parties" (Restatement of the Law Third, Foreign Relations Law of the United States §111, reporter's note 4) and that a defendant may be "able to invoke a treaty in his defense." Restatement Third §111, reporter's note 4, citing *Asakura v. Seattle*, 265 U.S. 332 (1924). Whether states parties to a particular treaty have in fact conferred rights upon individuals is a matter of treaty interpretation.

Example 3-4

The Vienna Convention on Consular Relations, 596 U.N.T.S. 261, spells out the rights and duties of consuls when they are serving their own country abroad. Article 36, para. 1 of the Consular Convention also states:

> With a view toward facilitating the exercise of consular functions relating to the nationals of the sending State:

(a) consular officers shall be free to communicate with nationals of the sending State and to have access to them. Nationals of the sending State shall have the same freedom with respect to communications with and access to consular officers of the sending State;

(b) if he so requests, the competent authorities of the receiving State shall, without delay, inform the consular post of the sending State if, within its consular district, a national of that State is arrested or committed to prison or to custody pending trial or is detained in any other manner. Any communication addressed to the consular post by the person arrested, in prison, custody or detention shall be forwarded by the said authorities without delay. The said authorities shall inform the person concerned without delay of his rights under this subparagraph;

(c) consular officers shall have the right to visit a national of the sending State who is in prison, custody or detention, to converse and correspond with him and to arrange for his legal representation. They shall also have the right to visit any national of the sending State who is in prison, custody or detention in their district in pursuance of a judgment. Nevertheless, consular officers shall refrain from taking action on behalf of a national who is in prison, custody or detention if he expressly opposes such action.

Your client, a Mexican national living in the U.S., has been accused of murder in Texas. He was arrested and read his *Miranda* rights (*Miranda v. Arizona*, 384 U.S. 436 (1966)), under which he was advised that he did not have to say anything and that he had a right to a lawyer. Your client, nonetheless, confessed to the murder. Both Mexico and the U.S. are parties to the Consular Convention. The defendant was never told that he could get in touch with the Mexican Consul in the district where he was arrested, nor was the Mexican Consul informed that the defendant had been arrested. You would like to raise the lack of Consular Convention notification as a defense in your client's trial.

Does your client have rights as an individual arising under the Consular Convention? (This question does not address the issue of the appropriate remedy for violations of rights in a treaty. For discussion of remedies, see §3.13.)

Explanation

First, read the language of the Consular Convention, as quoted above, carefully. Ask yourself whether you think the state parties to the treaty intended to grant individual citizens rights under the treaty. The International Court of Justice has twice addressed this issue in the *LaGrand* case and the *Avena* case, both described below. In *LaGrand* (Germany v. U.S.), 2001 I.C.J. 466, Germany had sought relief for two German brothers convicted of murder in the United States. Neither had been informed of his right to get in touch with the German Consul. The Court stated that:

The United States contends that rights of consular notification and access in the Vienna Convention are rights of States, and not of individuals, even though these rights may benefit individuals by permitting States to offer them consular assistance. It maintains that the treatment due to individuals under the Convention is inextricably linked to and derived from the right of the State, acting through its consular officer, to communicate with its nationals, and does not constitute a fundamental right or a human right. The United States argues that the fact that Article 36 by its terms recognizes the rights of individuals does not determine the nature of those rights or the remedies required under the Vienna Convention for breaches of that article. It points out that Article 36 begins with the words "[w]ith a view to facilitating the exercise of consular functions relating to nationals of the sending State," and that this wording gives no support to the notion that the rights and obligations enumerated in paragraph 1 of that article are intended to ensure that nationals of the sending State have any particular rights or treatment in the context of a criminal prosecution. The *travaux préparatoires* of the Vienna Convention according to the United States, do not reflect a consensus that Article 36 was addressing immutable individual rights, as opposed to individual rights derivative of the rights of States. *LaGrand* at para. 76.

Despite the U.S. argument, the Court ruled that:

Article 36, para. 1(b), spells out the obligations the receiving State has towards the detained person and the sending State. It provides that, at the request of the detained person, the receiving State must inform the consular post of the sending State of the individual's detention "without delay". It provides further that any communication by the detained person addressed to the consular post of the sending State must be forwarded to it by authorities of the receiving State "without delay." Significantly, this subparagraph ends with the following language: "The said authorities shall inform the person concerned without delay of his rights under the subparagraph" (emphasis added). Moreover, under Article 36, paragraph 1 (c), the sending State's right to provide consular assistance to the detained person may not be exercised "if he expressly opposes such action." The clarity of these provisions, viewed in their context, admits of no doubt. . . . Based on the text of these provisions, the Court concludes that Article 36, paragraph 1, creates individual rights, which, by virtue of Article I of the Optional Protocol, may be invoked in this Court by the national State of the detained person. These rights were violated in the present case. (*LaGrand* at para. 77.)

Again, in *Avena and Other Mexican Nationals* (Mexico v. U.S.), 2004 I.C.J. 12, where Mexico complained that over fifty Mexicans on death row in the U.S. had not received Consular Convention rights the Court stated: "in cases where the breach of the individual rights of Mexican nationals under article 36, paragraph 1(b), of the Convention has resulted, in the sequence of judicial proceedings that has followed, in the individuals concerned being subjected to prolonged detention or convicted and sentenced to severe penalties, the legal consequences of this breach have to be examined and taken into account in the course of review and reconsideration." (*Avena* at para. 140.)

Article 36, para. 1(b) of the Consular Convention also requires that the foreign detainee be informed of his rights "without delay." In *Avena*, the Court also interpreted this phrase of the Convention, see paras. 83-88.

---

§3.9 INVALIDITY

There are several grounds upon which a treaty may be found invalid.

§3.9.1 Error

This ground of invalidity has seldom been invoked. One can reasonably expect that state negotiators of a treaty will be properly informed about the subject under discussion. This article does not include errors in the wording of a treaty which is covered by article 79. To be invoked as a ground of invalidity the error must relate "to a fact or situation which was assumed by that State to exist at the time when the treaty was concluded and formed an essential basis of its consent to be bound by the treaty." VCLT, art. 48(1). If the state claiming error "contributed by its own conduct to the error" or had notice of the error, then the state is not permitted to claim invalidity. Occasionally this ground has been raised with respect to the alleged inaccuracy of maps that were relied upon in settling a border dispute. *Temple of Preah Vihear* (Cambodia v. Thailand), 1962 I.C.J. 6. Despite the Court's judgment settling the border dispute between Thailand and Cambodia, fighting broke out again in 2008 over a plot of land near the temple.

§3.9.2 Fraud and Corruption

Article 49 provides that a state may claim invalidity of a treaty if it "has been induced to conclude a treaty by the fraudulent conduct of another . . . State. . . ." The Vienna Convention does not define fraud and the International Law Commission decided that it would not attempt to define the term but rather "leave its precise scope to be worked out in practice. . . ." 1966, II Y.B. Int'l L. Comm'n 244.

If a treaty has been procured by the corruption of its representative by another negotiating state that may be grounds for invalidity. Again there are few cases. Not too many states will admit to, or leave evidence of, attempts at corruption, and those who may have succumbed to such attempts are unlikely to reveal it willingly. The International Law Commission was aware of the practice of some states to give and receive gifts when treaties are signed, sometimes on quite a lavish scale. Although it did not address this practice directly, it did note that the article "did not mean to imply that . . . a small courtesy or favour shown to a representative in connection with the conclusion of a treaty may be invoked as a pretext for invalidating the treaty." *Id.* at 245.

§3.9.3 Coercion

VCLT article 51 declares that if a treaty has been "procured by the coercion of its representative through acts or threats directed against him [it] shall be without any legal effect." There are only a few examples of such coercion which have come to light. The threats referred to in article 51 have to be directed against the representative personally rather than against his/her state.

Example 3-5

In 1939 the representatives of Czechoslovakia were subject to extreme pressure to sign a treaty establishing German control over their state.

> "The German ministers [Goering and Ribbentrop] were pitiless. . . . They literally hunted Dr. Hácha [the President of Czechoslovakia] and M. Chavlkovsky [the Foreign Minister] round the table on which the documents were lying, thrusting them continually before them, pushing pens into their hands. . . ." Quoted in William L. Shirer, *The Rise and Fall of the Third Reich* 446 (1960).

During these proceedings Dr. Hácha fainted and was revived by an injection from Dr. Morell, Hitler's physician.
Was the treaty signed by the Czech representatives valid?

Explanation

Clearly not. It is hard to think of a more graphic example of illegal coercion of state representatives. They were subject to excessive personal coercion to try to force them to sign the document. Any such document is void.

Article 52 declares a treaty void if it is the result of "the threat or use of force in violation of the principles of international law embodied in the Charter of the United Nations." This article refers directly to the prohibition contained in article 2(4) of the U.N. Charter where the threat or use of force is directed against the state itself. Historically, international law had not prohibited the use of force and indeed throughout the centuries force had been a principal method of settling interstate disputes with the victor imposing its wishes on the vanquished. During the twentieth century a movement was begun to bring the use of force within the umbrella of international law. This movement culminated in the adoption of the U.N. Charter in 1945. Article 2(4) of the Charter states: "All members shall refrain in their international relations from the threat or use of force against the territorial integrity or political independence of any state, or in any other manner inconsistent with the Purposes of the United Nations." (See Chapter 10.) The limits on the use of force contained in the Charter are now established as customary law. The proposal to include other forms of coercion, such as economic coercion, was rejected by the drafters of the Convention.

Example 3-6

State X launches an unprovoked attack on State Y and completely defeats State Y within a month. State X then insists that State Y sign a peace treaty ceding half of its territory to State X.

Is the peace treaty valid?

Explanation

If State X violated U.N. Charter article 2(4), then VCLT article 52, which declares that treaties made as a result of coercion against the state are void *ab initio*, clearly nullifies the treaty. (In real life, of course, State X would put forward some reason explaining why its attack did not violate article 2(4) and, if State Y was considerably weaker than State X or lacked powerful friends, there may not be any immediate remedy available. The problem of remedy, however, pervades all law and is by no means unique to international law.)

§3.9.4 Conflict with a Peremptory Norm (*Jus Cogens*)

VCLT article 53 declares a treaty void "if, at the time of its conclusion, it conflicts with a peremptory norm of general international law." Article 64 states that if an existing treaty conflicts with newly emerging peremptory norms the treaty "becomes void and terminates." Article 53 defines a peremptory norm as "a norm accepted and recognized by the international community of States as a whole as a norm from which no derogation is permitted. . . ." While there is often disagreement about whether a particular rule has reached the level of a peremptory norm, a number of international rules have clearly reached that status, such as the prohibition of the use of force found in article 2(4) of the U.N. Charter and the prohibition of genocide reflected in the Genocide Convention, 78 U.N.T.S. 277.

Example 3-7

State F is concerned about terrorism. It is a party to the Torture Convention (1465 U.N.T.S. 85) which prohibits torture under all circumstances. Article 2, para. 2, states: "No exceptional circumstances whatsoever, whether a state of war or a threat of war, internal political instability or any other public emergency, may be invoked as a justification of torture." State F is a democratic state with a vigorous free press. It knows that if it tortured suspected terrorists on its own territory, the press would find out and expose the acts. State F therefore enters into an agreement with autocratic State G, well known for its shocking human rights record and not a party to the Torture Convention. State F promises to pay State G $250,000 annually for every suspected terrorist shipped to State G. State G agrees to hold the suspects in prison and to reveal to State F any relevant information concerning terrorist plots against State F that State G may extract from such prisoners "by any methods of State G's choosing."

Is such an agreement valid?

Explanation

The clear impact of the agreement between State F and State G appears to be to allow State G to torture the suspects to get information on possible terrorist threats against State F and that State G will then pass on any such information to State F. There are now 147 states parties to the Torture Convention, and most scholars would agree that the prohibition against torture, in all circumstances, is a peremptory norm of international law. If the treaty is interpreted to permit torture, it is therefore void. State F is also violating its obligations under article 3 of the Torture Convention which states: "No State Party shall expel, return (refouler) or extradite a person to another State where there are substantial grounds for believing that he would be in danger of being subjected to torture." (Of course, there may be divergent views as to whether particular coercive treatment actually amounts to torture as defined by the treaty in article 1, para. 1.)

§3.10 TERMINATION AND SUSPENSION

Modern treaties almost always have a termination article, unless they deal with certain fundamental rights, such as human rights. A termination clause would typically provide that upon the giving of a specified term of notice any party to the treaty may terminate its consent to be bound and withdraw from the treaty. VCLT article 54 makes it clear that termination is perfectly permissible provided it is done in conformity with the terms of the treaty or with the consent of all the other treaty partners. If a treaty does not contain a termination provision, article 56 states that "it is not subject to denunciation or withdrawal unless" the parties intended to allow such or such a right can be implied from the treaty, in which case the parties must give at least a year's notice of their intent to withdraw from the treaty. If all the parties to an existing treaty conclude a later treaty on the same subject matter, the earlier treaty is terminated if that was the intent of the parties or if the provisions of the later treaty are incompatible with the earlier treaty. Art. 59.

§3.10.1 Material Breach

It is important to note that not all breaches of treaties give rise to a right to terminate. Many treaties are full of technical provisions and to allow termination for minor breaches would undermine the principle of *pacta sunt servanda*. The Vienna Convention defines a material breach as either "a repudiation of the treaty not sanctioned by the present Convention" or "the violation of a provision essential to the accomplishment of the object or purpose of the treaty." Art. 60(3)(a) & (b). The International Court of Justice discussed an example of a permissible termination of a treaty after a material breach in its advisory opinion in the *Namibia (South West Africa)* case, Advisory Opinion, 1971 I.C.J. 16 (June 21) where the General Assembly of the United Nations had determined that by imposing apartheid on Namibia, South Africa had repudiated the terms of a League of Nations Mandate (subsequently taken over by the U.N. Trusteeship system). This Mandate, which required South Africa "to ensure the moral and material well-being and security of the indigenous inhabitants of . . . [Namibia]," was determined to be incompatible with the imposition of apartheid. Because South Africa had repudiated the Mandate by imposing the system of apartheid, such action was deemed to violate a provision essential to the accomplishment of the object and purpose of the treaty, and thus the General Assembly could terminate South Africa's Mandatory powers over Namibia.

The termination provisions for a material breach are specifically stated not to apply "to provisions relating to the protections of the human person contained in treaties of a humanitarian character. . . ." Art. 60(5). The notion here is that if, for example, a state party to the Torture Convention, 1465 U.N.T.S. 85, suddenly starts practicing torture on its citizens, that does not permit other parties to the Convention to terminate their obligations under the Treaty and start torturing their own citizens.

Example 3-8

The Vienna Convention on Diplomatic Relations, 500 U.N.T.S. 95, outlines the obligations of diplomats serving in foreign countries and states that: "The person of the diplomatic agent shall be inviolable. He shall not be liable to any form of arrest or detention." Art. 29. It also states that: "The premises of the mission [embassy] shall be inviolable. The agents of the receiving State may not enter them, except with the consent of the head of the mission." Art. 22(1). All diplomats are also required to "respect the laws and regulations of the receiving state" (art. 41(1)) but they "enjoy immunity from the criminal jurisdiction of the receiving State." Art. 31(1). The Convention gives the receiving state the right "at anytime and without having to explain its decision" to notify "the sending State that the head of the mission or any member of the diplomatic staff of the mission is *persona non grata* [an unwelcome person]. . . ." In such a case, "the sending state shall, as appropriate, either recall the person concerned or terminate his functions with the mission." Art. 9(1). The "privileges and immunities" granted to a diplomat "shall normally cease at the moment when he leaves the country, or on the expiry of a reasonable period in which to do so, but shall subsist until that time, even in case of armed conflict." Art. 39(2). State H and State I have entered into diplomatic relations and each has sent a diplomatic mission to the other country. State I has recently become convinced that the ambassador from State H is using the State H embassy, located in the capital of State I, for prostitution. State I is a strictly religious state and prostitution is forbidden. State I enters State H's embassy, arrests the ambassador and deports the rest of the embassy staff. State H's ambassador is held in jail while he awaits trial.

Did State I's arrest of State H's ambassador violate the Diplomatic Relations Convention? Does State H now have the right to arrest State I's ambassador? Is State I and/or State H entitled to terminate its obligations under the Convention? If State H announced its termination of the Convention at 10 A.M., could it then arrest State I's ambassador at 10:15 A.M.?

Explanation

Even though there may be more than probable cause to believe that the ambassador from State H is using the embassy for prostitution, and although that might violate the laws of State H so that the ambassador would have violated article 41(1) of the Diplomatic Relations Convention, the Convention makes it clear that the only remedy permitted in such circumstances is to declare the diplomat "*persona non grata*," to require him to leave the country (see article 9) and, if thought necessary, break off diplomatic relations with the sending state. Under no circumstances is the receiving state permitted to enter the embassy or arrest the diplomats. (The host state is free to ask State H to waive the ambassador's diplomatic immunity so that he can be prosecuted but State H is not obliged to waive immunity. Art. 32. Although states occasionally waive immunity in serious cases, such as vehicular homicide or drug trafficking, usually the diplomat is sent home and dropped from the diplomatic service.) In *United States Diplomatic and Consular Staff in Tehran* (U.S. v. Iran), 1980 I.C.J. 3, where Iranian students had entered the U.S. embassy in Tehran and taken more than fifty diplomats hostage, the International Court of Justice ruled: "even if the alleged criminal activities of the United States in Iran could be considered as having been established" [Iran had accused the U.S. of, *inter alia*, engineering the overthrow of the Iranian government in 1953 and restoring the Shah to the throne, see para. 80] the invasion of the embassy and taking the diplomats hostage could not be regarded as justified. *Id.* at para. 83. The Convention provides the only remedy in article 9 (requiring that the diplomat be recalled by his state) or more generally a state may use "the power which every receiving State has, at its own discretion, to break off diplomatic relations with a sending State and to call for the immediate closure of the offending mission." *Id.* at para. 85. Just because State I may have violated the Convention by arresting State H's ambassador, that does not allow State H to arrest State I's ambassador. Certainly, the arrest of State H's ambassador is a material violation of the treaty and does permit State H to terminate its obligations under the Convention toward State I, break off diplomatic relations and declare all of the diplomats *persona non grata*, but diplomats must be given a reasonable period of time in which to leave the country (art. 39(2)) before they can be treated as regular foreign visitors.

§3.10.2 Supervening Impossibility of Performance

Occasionally it will be impossible to carry out a treaty because "an object indispensable for the execution of the treaty" (art. 61) has permanently disappeared or been destroyed. Article 61 recognizes these conditions as permitting termination or withdrawal from a treaty. The International Law Commission's Commentary supplies some examples: "the submergence of an island, the drying up of a river or the destruction of a dam or hydroelectric installation indispensable for the execution of the treaty." If the condition creating the impossibility is only temporary, then the treaty will be suspended until conditions have returned to the *status quo ante*. Impossibility of performance may not be invoked by a party to the treaty where the impossibility results from a breach of that party's obligations under the treaty. If a state party to the treaty ceases to exist, the rules of state succession to treaties apply. (See §3.14.)

§3.10.3 Fundamental Change of Circumstances: (*Rebus Sic Stantibus*)

It was with some reluctance that the International Law Commission included a provision for invalidity of treaties on the basis of a fundamental change of circumstances. It was well understood that if this provision were drafted too broadly it would provide an easy escape route for those wishing to break treaties. At the same time, most modern scholars accept the principle of *rebus sic stantibus* which posits a tacit implied clause in all treaties which rests the treaty's validity on "things remaining as they are." This idea essentially means that if the conditions under which the treaty was negotiated change radically, then the whole basis of the treaty is vitiated. The problem for the drafters of the Vienna Convention was to keep this principle within reasonable bounds. Article 62 states that a fundamental change of circumstances can only be invoked as a ground for terminating or withdrawing from a treaty when: "(a) the existence of those circumstances constituted an essential basis of the consent of the parties . . . and (b) the effect of the change is radically to transform the extent of the obligations still to be performed. . . ." Specifically excluded from this doctrine are boundary treaties or where "the fundamental change is a result of a breach by the party invoking it. . . ." (Art. 62(2)(a) & (b).)

Example 3-9

Two states, A and B, concluded a treaty for the building of a dam, the production of electric power and the construction of flood control mechanisms on a river that marked the border between the two countries. Each state owned the waters and bed of the river to the midpoint in the river. The project was time consuming and complex. Work progressed slowly. After ten years, State A declared it was terminating the treaty because it had become clear that the dam would not improve conditions in State A but rather would cause irreparable environmental damage. State A argued further that, in fact, international environmental law would now prohibit the treaty from being completed because the project would markedly increase pollution.

Run through all of the arguments made by State A for terminating the treaty and pinpoint the grounds for termination under the VCLT paying attention to the precise language of each article. Are the reasons given by State A sufficient to permit termination of the treaty?

Explanation

The arguments advanced by State A for terminating the treaty are very similar to some of those argued by Hungary when it wished to terminate its treaty with Slovakia under which both parties had agreed to build a dam and various other structures on the Danube River. *Gabčíkovo-Nagymaros Project* (Hungary v. Slovakia), 1997 I.C.J. 7.

Grounds for Termination of the Treaty
(i) changed standards required by international environmental law and
(ii) changed understanding of the environmental consequences of the project.

In theory, these grounds for termination could possibly serve as an argument both for Fundamental Change of Circumstance and for Supervening Impossibility of Performance.

(a) Change in the Law

(i) *Fundamental Change of Circumstances*

The argument here rests on two grounds: (a) change in the law and (b) change in the expected results of the treaty project.

The International Court of Justice has recognized that in theory: "changes in the law may under certain conditions constitute valid grounds for invoking a change of circumstances affecting the duration of a treaty. . . ." *Fisheries Jurisdiction* (U.K. v. Iceland), 1973 I.C.J. 3 at para. 32. The Court has, however, never upheld such an argument as applied to the circumstances in cases before it. To invoke a fundamental change of circumstances, sufficient to terminate a treaty, the state must show that the change was not foreseen by the parties, that the original circumstances (now changed) "constituted an essential basis of the consent of the parties . . ." (VCLT, art. 62(a)) and that "the effect of the change is radically to transform the extent of obligations still to be performed under the treaty." VCLT, art. 62(b). Unless all of these requirements are met, including that State A's obligations under the treaty are now radically altered because of a change in the law, a court is not likely to look favorably on this argument. In practice, if a court agreed that the law had changed, it might well require the parties to demonstrate exactly what extra work would need to be undertaken to bring the project into conformity with new environmental standards. If the work required, and its costs, were not large in comparison to the overall cost of the project, the court might well refuse to permit termination.

(b) Change in the Expected Results of the Treaty Project

The I.C.J. has also recognized that a change in events in the world can also count as a reason for invoking the fundamental change in circumstances ground. In the *Fisheries* case *supra*, Iceland had argued that the increased exploitation of fishery resources taken from the sea around Iceland was a fundamental change. The U.K. argued that the catch level of fish in those waters had not altered appreciably and thus there was no fundamental change of circumstances. This was obviously a factual dispute and any state wishing to rely upon factual fundamental changes will have to convince the court of its version of the facts. Even if the state is successful on the factual issue, it will then have to demonstrate that the facts as they were before the changes were an essential basis of the treaty, that the change was unforeseen, and that the change has radically transformed the remaining obligations of the complaining state.

(i) *Supervening the Impossibility of Performance*

The arguments relating to the environment might also try to invoke Supervening Impossibility of Performance. This ground for termination is also hedged about with conditions. The impossibility of performance must result "from the permanent disappearance or destruction of an object indispensable for the execution of the treaty." VCLT, art. 61(1). State A might argue that the prospect of a joint treaty that was consistent with international environmental law and that would bring environmental benefits had permanently disappeared and thus that there was a supervening impossibility of performance. Some commentators argue that article 61 of the VCLT is only meant to apply to the physical disappearance or destruction of the physical objects that are the subject of a treaty or upon which the treaty relies and does not relate to the destruction of the likely benefits of a treaty. The I.C.J. skirted this issue in *Gabčíkovo-Nagymaros Project* (Hungary v. Slovakia), 1997 I.C.J. 7 at para. 103, but did suggest that inability to continue a project because of financial difficulties would not justify termination for impossibility of performance although it might preclude "the wrongfulness of non-performance by a party of its treaty obligations. . . ." *Id.* at para. 102.

Again, State A might try to argue that the prospect of an environmentally beneficial project had permanently disappeared. The I.C.J. has shown considerable reluctance in accepting such an argument where there is any possibility of re-negotiating an agreement to improve the outcome. *Id.* at para. 103.

Caveat

Courts will also refuse relief to a party where that party's own conduct may have contributed to the current problems with carrying out the treaty.

For example, if State A was supposed to have completed its part of the project eight years ago and the environmental norms have only changed recently or the delay has contributed to the adverse environmental consequences, the court will likely reject State A's argument. Excessive delay might also qualify as a material breach of the treaty.

§3.11 THE EFFECT OF WAR ON TREATIES

The VCLT does not address the question of the effect of war on treaties. The International Law Commission, when drafting the VCLT, considered that:

> the study of this topic would inevitably involve a consideration of the effect of the provisions of the Charter concerning the threat or use of force upon the legality of the recourse to the particular hostilities in question; and it did not feel that this question could conveniently be dealt with in the context of its present work upon the law of treaties. 1966, II Y.B. Int'l L. Comm'n 176 at para. 29.

Older authorities had tended to use a general rule: "That provisions [in the treaty] compatible with a state of hostilities, unless expressly terminated, will be enforced, and those incompatible rejected." *Techt v. Hughes*, 229 N.Y. 222, 241, 128 N.E. 185, 191, cert. denied, 254 U.S. 643 (1920) (opinion by Cardozo, J). (Incidentally, this case is a joy to read. Cardozo's wonderful language is inspirational.)

The U.N. Charter seeks, among other things, to outlaw the use of force. In earlier centuries war was often a limited engagement largely carried on between the armed forces of the warring states. World War II changed that pattern dramatically with both sides engaging in widespread bombing of civilian areas. The concept of "total" war was born, so the notion of continuing treaty relationships between belligerents became less acceptable. VCLT article 63 makes it clear that the mere severance of diplomatic or consular relations between treaty partners does not terminate or suspend treaties between them "except in so far as the existence of diplomatic or consular relations is indispensable for the application of the treaty." On the effect of hostilities between treaty partners, the Restatement Third §336, cmt. e states:

> Under traditional international law, the outbreak of war between states terminated or suspended agreements between them. [This view differs from the opinion in *Techt v. Hughes supra*.] However, not all agreements were necessarily affected. In particular, agreements governing the conduct of hostilities

survived, since they were designed for application during war. However, the United Nations Charter prohibits the use of armed force between states except in limited circumstances, and was intended to outlaw war. . . . The consequences of these principles for the law as to the effect of hostilities on treaties remains uncertain.

Reporters' Note 4 to §336 elaborates further:

Since 1945, when the United Nations Charter came into effect, there has been uncertainty about the impact of hostilities upon international agreements. The Vienna Convention, Article 73, disclaims any judgment on the question. The full import of the provisions of the Charter prohibiting the use of force is debated, but the Charter clearly intended to outlaw war. See §905, Comment g. It has been suggested that it effectively abolished war as a legal regime (although, for humanitarian reasons, it has been accepted that the Geneva Conventions on the Law of War continue to be applicable). However, since the traditional effect of war on treaties derived from the fact that continuing treaty relations generally were deemed inconsistent with the state of war, perhaps as a special application of the doctrine of *rebus sic stantibus*, it is arguable that major hostilities are "changed circumstances" providing a basis for suspending or terminating a treaty, regardless of whether there is a lawful state of war. In any event, the victim of aggression in violation of Article 2(4) of the Charter can surely be justified in treating treaty obligations as suspended. On the other hand, the aggressor may not invoke his own unlawful act as a basis for exemption from the obligation of treaties and would be liable for consequent violation of treaty obligations (as well as for violation of the Charter), but not for violation of an agreement of the type not applicable during hostilities.

§3.11.1 The Effect of War on Human Rights Treaties

Recently, considerable attention has been given to the question of the effect of war on human rights treaties. One view is that once international armed conflict occurs, then the conflict is entirely governed by the laws of armed conflict, including the four Geneva Conventions of 1949. This area of law is known as international humanitarian law, which is applicable during armed conflict and distinct from human rights law. Another view is that human rights treaties continue throughout war unless they conflict with the specific provisions of a law regulating war. Some treaties already provide that they are to operate both in peacetime and in wartime as we have seen in the Torture Convention *supra*, art. 2, para. 2. The International Court of Justice has addressed this issue in several of its opinions.

3. The Law of Treaties

In the *Legal Consequences of the Construction of a Wall in the Occupied Palestinian Territory*, Advisory Opinion, 2004 I.C.J. 136 (July 9), the Court was examining the legal consequences arising from Israel's construction of a wall parts of which were on territory occupied by Israel after the 1967 war. The Court stated:

103. On 3 October 1991 Israel ratified both the International Covenant on Economic, Social and Cultural Rights of 19 December 1966 and the International Covenant on Civil and Political Rights of the same date, as well as the United Nations Convention on the Rights of the Child of 20 November 1989. It is a party to these three instruments.

104. In order to determine whether these texts are applicable in the Occupied Palestinian Territory, the Court will first address the issue of the relationship between international humanitarian law and human rights law and then that of the applicability of human rights instruments outside national territory.

105. In its Advisory Opinion of 8 July 1996 on the *Legality of the Threat or Use of Nuclear Weapons*, the Court had occasion to address the first of these issues in relation to the International Covenant on Civil and Political Rights. In those proceedings certain States had argued that "the Covenant was directed to the protection of human rights in peacetime, but that questions relating to unlawful loss of life in hostilities were governed by the law applicable in armed conflict." (*I.C.J. Reports 1996* (I), p. 239, para. 24).

The Court rejected this argument, stating that:

"the protection of the International Covenant of Civil and Political Rights does not cease in times of war, except by operation of Article 4 of the Covenant whereby certain provisions may be derogated from in a time of national emergency. Respect for the right to life is not, however, such a provision. In principle, the right not arbitrarily to be deprived of one's life applies also in hostilities. The test of what is an arbitrary deprivation for life, however, then falls to be determined by the applicable *lex specialis*, namely, the law applicable in armed conflict which is designed to regulate the conduct of hostilities." (*Ibid.*, p. 240, para. 25).

106. More generally, the Court considers that the protection offered by human rights conventions does not cease in case of armed conflict, save through the effect of provisions for derogation of the kind to be found in Article 4 of the International Covenant on Civil and Political Rights. As regards the relationship between international humanitarian law and human rights law, there are thus three possible situations: some rights may be exclusively matters of international humanitarian law; others may be exclusively matters of human rights law; yet others may be matters of both these branches of international law. In order to answer the question put to it, the Court will have to take into consideration both these branches

of international law, namely human rights law and, as *lex specialis*, international humanitarian law.

In general then, the Court concluded that human rights treaties continue to operate during armed conflict unless their provisions are ousted by a particular rule of the law of armed conflict. Although the right not to be arbitrarily deprived of life will continue throughout warfare, the lawful combatant's privilege to target military personnel and kill them (see Chapter 10) will be the *lex specialis* applied during armed conflict and will supersede the right to life for military personnel.

§3.12 PROCEDURE FOR TERMINATION

The International Law Commission was concerned that the rules on invalidity might provoke a plethora of unilateral claims of termination of treaties so it laid down stringent rules to be followed by parties invoking grounds for termination. VCLT arts. 65-68. First, the party invoking termination, withdrawal, or suspension must notify in writing the other parties and indicate what measures it intends to take. Three months after notification, if no objection has been registered, the party making the notification may go ahead with its measures. If objection has been raised then the parties are required to use the means indicated under article 33 of the U.N. Charter ("negotiation, inquiry, mediation, conciliation, arbitration, judicial settlement . . ."). If no solution is reached within twelve months from the raising of an objection then any party to a dispute arising under article 53 (treaties conflicting with a peremptory norm) or article 54 (termination under a treaty's provisions or consent of the parties) may submit it to the International Court of Justice for resolution. Any party to a dispute arising under any other part of Part V of the VCLT (invalidity, termination and suspension) may "set in motion the procedure specified in the Annex to the Convention. . . ." (The procedure outlined in the Annex provides for the creation of a conciliation commission.)

§3.13 REMEDIES FOR VIOLATION OF A TREATY

The previous sections on termination and withdrawal from treaties in specified circumstances are examples of remedies for treaty violations but a state that accuses another state of violating a treaty may want further remedies.

3. The Law of Treaties

In *Avena and Other Mexican Nationals* (Mexico v. U.S.), 2004 I.C.J. 12 at para. 119, the I.C.J. stated that:

> The general principle on the legal consequences of the commission of an internationally wrongful act was stated by the Permanent Court of International Justice in the *Factory at Chorzów* case as follows: "It is a principle of international law that the breach of an engagement involves an obligation to make reparation in an adequate form." (*Factory at Chorzów, Jurisdiction*, 1927, P.C.I.J., *Series A, No. 9*, p. 21.) What constitutes "reparation in an adequate form" clearly varies depending on the concrete circumstances surrounding each case and the precise nature and scope of the injury, since the question has to be examined from the viewpoint of what is the "reparation in an adequate form" that corresponds to the injury.

In a subsequent phase of the same case, the Permanent Court went on to elaborate on this point again:

> The essential principle contained in the actual notion of an illegal act — a principle which seems to be established by international practice and in particular by the decisions of arbitral tribunals — is that reparation must, as far as possible, wipe out all the consequences of the illegal act and reestablish the situation which would, in all probability, have existed if that act had not been committed. (*Factory at Chorzów, Merits*, 1928, P.C.I.J., *Series A, No. 17*, p. 47.)

Sometimes a state will offer a formal apology for the violation of a treaty but in certain instances the I.C.J. has held that an apology is insufficient. *LaGrand supra*, at para. 125. International courts and tribunals have ordered a wide variety of remedies for breaches of international law. The Restatement Third §901, cmt. d describes the range of remedies available:

> d. *Forms of reparation*. All forms of reparation are designed to provide redress for the breach of the international obligation that gave rise to the claim. Ordinarily, emphasis is on forms of redress that will undo the effect of the violation, such as restoration of the *status quo ante*, restitution, or specific performance of an undertaking. For instance, if a foreign embassy has been occupied by a mob, there is an obligation to remove the mob and to return the embassy to its diplomatic staff; there may also be an obligation to pay compensation for the damage to the building and to its contents, and for the injuries and indignities suffered by the embassy's staff. Compensation is a common remedy for monetary damage, Comment *e*, and in some instances compensation may be required even though no monetary damage had occurred. Acknowledgment of a violation and an apology are common forms of redress, sometimes supplemented by compensation. There is variety also in the remedies that may be ordered by a third party to which a claim has been presented for resolution. Principles of international law concerning remedies are not rigid or formalistic

and give an international tribunal wide latitude to develop and shape remedies, but the tribunal is usually restricted to measures proposed by the parties.

Other examples cited by the Restatement are: "compensation in case of an oil spill [which] may include the cost of clean-up, replacement of the property destroyed, and damage for lost tourist business; compensation for a wrongful seizure of a ship may included cost of repair, seamen's wages paid during the seizure, and lost revenue. . . ." Restatement Third *supra*, §901, cmt. e.

Example 3-10

Return to Example 3-4 beginning on page 38 and reread the fact pattern. Suppose that you did raise the lack of Consular Convention rights at your client's murder trial. The U.S. admits that your client was not told that he could get in touch with the Mexican Consul and that the Mexican Consul was not informed that your client had been arrested. The trial court has ruled that the defendant has individual rights under the treaty. The U.S. has apologized to the Mexican Foreign Minister and admitted that it failed to inform either the Mexican Consul or your client of their rights under the Consular Convention.

What remedies will you seek on behalf of your client for violations of his treaty rights?

Explanation

As the text above makes clear, the scope of remedies available for the breach of an international obligation is not bound by any rigid rules but must be designed to put the parties back in the position they were in before the breach occurred. What all lawyers want who represent clients on death row (or where any severe penalty is possible) is either to get the charges dismissed or to radically reduce the evidence that the prosecutor is permitted to introduce in court, with a view either to getting a dismissal of the charges by the court, or to getting an acquittal by the jury or, failing that, getting a considerably reduced sentence. There are a range of possible remedies you might request. You will probably have to make an argument about when the treaty rights attached to the defendant. Obviously, the earlier the better. If you argue that the treaty rights attached as soon as the defendant was arrested, then you might ask that any evidence gained from the defendant following arrest should be excluded from court. There may, of course, be extensive physical evidence linking the defendant with the crime, but if most of the case was based on the defendant's confession, then excluding such evidence would be very helpful. If such evidence was a major part of the prosecutor's case, and you are successful in having it excluded, you might ask for the case to be dismissed or the conviction to be overturned.

If the case will stand even without the evidence you have asked to be excluded, you might ask for the sentence to be reviewed by the court and request a considerably lighter sentence. You might also ask for monetary reparations on behalf of your client. You could also request that the U.S. undertake a solemn pledge not to violate the Convention in the future, or that the court should require the government to undertake extensive training programs for law enforcement personnel to instruct them on the requirements of the treaty.

What remedies are you likely to get for violation of the defendant's Consular Convention rights? In the *Avena* case *supra*, almost all of the above remedies were sought by Mexico on behalf of the Mexicans sitting on death-row in the U.S., except monetary reparations. The Court ruled that "partial or total annulment of the conviction or sentence" (as requested by Mexico) did not provide "the necessary and sole remedy." *Avena* at para. 123. Nonetheless, the Court did not rule out the possibility of such a remedy. What the Court required was that the United States must "permit review and reconsideration of . . . [the] cases by United States courts . . . with a view to ascertaining whether in each case the violation of Article 36 committed by the competent authorities caused actual prejudice to the defendant in the process of administration of criminal justice." *Avena* at para. 121. The Court stated that the U.S. courts should focus on the "question of whether the violations of Article 36, paragraph 1 [of the Consular Convention] are to be regarded as having, in the causal sequence of events, ultimately led to convictions and severe penalties . . . in the process of review and reconsideration." *Avena* at para. 122.

One of the complicating factors in the U.S. cases that have raised Consular Convention violations has been that almost all of the defendants were found to have been read their *Miranda* rights, told they could remain silent and have an attorney, but, nevertheless, often decided to waive those rights and either confessed to the crime or gave other inculpatory evidence. Practically all of the U.S. courts that have addressed the remedy question, after a knowing and intelligent waiver of *Miranda* rights, have conflated the rights protected by *Miranda* and the rights protected by the Consular Convention and have then ruled that a waiver of the one (*Miranda* rights) obviated the need for the other (Consular Convention rights) and that therefore no remedy was due. It was thought that many of these issues would be resolved by the U.S. Supreme Court in the case of *Medellin v. Dretke*, cert. granted, 543 U.S. 1032 (2004) but the petition for certiorari was subsequently dismissed as improvidently granted, 544 U.S. 660 (2005), in light of the fact that President George W. Bush had written a memorandum to the Attorney General of the U.S., which noted that the U.S. was a party to the Consular Convention and stated that: "I have determined, pursuant to the authority vested in me as President by the Constitution and the laws of the United States of America, that the United States will discharge its international obligations under the decision of the International Court of Justice in the . . . *Avena* [case] . . . by having State courts give effect to the decision in accordance with general principles of comity in cases filed by the 51 Mexican nationals addressed in that decision." The case was remanded to the Texas courts where the state court had to decide how to implement the *Avena* decision in light of the President's memorandum. The Texas courts took the position that the President had no power to interfere with the state's administration of criminal justice. The case made its way back to the Supreme Court, *Medellin v. Texas*, 552 U.S. 491 (2008), where the Supreme Court refused to enforce the I.C.J's decision either as a treaty obligation or in compliance with the President's memorandum, although it indicated that Texas was free to comply with the *Avena* decision if it wished to do so. Since then, Mexico has again sought enforcement in the I.C.J., *Request for Interpretation of Judgment of 31 March 2004* (Mexico v. U.S.), 2009 I.C.J. _____, where the I.C.J. found that by executing José Medellin the United States had violated the Court's order and again reaffirmed the continuing binding obligations of the U.S. under the *Avena* judgment. Courts throughout the U.S. are now struggling with the issue of whether and/or how to comply with the *Avena* decision.

§3.13.1 Enforcement of Treaties in National Courts

A great number of states have ratified many important treaties. All of those states have national court systems, so you may be wondering why individuals don't simply seek to enforce their treaty rights through their own national courts. The answer to this question is somewhat complex and turns upon the status of a treaty in a particular country's legal system as well as the interpretive issue of whether the treaty intended to create an enforceable right or remedy for individuals. It may also be complicated by the scope of sovereign immunity accorded to the government or to government officials in the particular country as well as the integrity of the judicial system.

Some countries follow a doctrine that provides that once treaties are ratified they become part of the national laws, just like enacted statutes. The United States Constitution, for example, provides that: "This Constitution, and the laws of the United States which shall be made in pursuance thereof; and all treaties made, or which shall be made, under the authority of the United States, shall be the supreme law of the land. . . ." (U.S. Constitution, art. VI, para. 2.) Some scholars hold that this language indicates that U.S. treaties were to be regarded as part of U.S. law, that is, they were automatically self-executing and did not need implementing legislation to become effective. Other writers insist that whether a U.S. treaty is self-executing or not depends upon the intention of the United States in ratifying the treaty. Certain U.S. courts have tended to follow this latter approach when resolving the issue, although there are many U.S. cases where the courts have assumed that the treaty is self-executing without even discussing the issue. The recent U.S. Supreme Court case, *Medellín v. Texas*, 552 U.S. 491 (2008), exposed a wide division on the Court concerning the methodology to be used to determine whether treaties are self-executing with the majority looking for explicit treaty language indicating self-execution. This approach has been very controversial.

Under the United States Constitution, there are some areas that are within the exclusive law-making authority of Congress, such as the appropriation of money or the determination that certain acts constitute a federal crime. When a treaty undertakes to provide monies or declare certain international crimes to be federal offenses, it is generally held that such treaties will need implementing legislation to become effective as U.S. law. In recent years, when giving its consent to the ratification of a treaty, the U.S. Senate has sometimes stipulated that the President shall not ratify the treaty until Congress has passed implementing legislation. After the *Medellín* case, the Senate has sometimes indicated whether it considers a treaty to be self-executing.

When an individual seeks to rely upon the provisions of a treaty in national courts, the first question to be answered is whether the treaty is self-executing. If it is not, then the individual cannot rely upon the treaty as such, although s/he may be able to argue that the treaty is evidence of a customary norm which is binding in the national courts. If the treaty is self-executing or has been implemented by legislation, the next question to be answered is whether the treaty or the implementing legislation intended to create a right or remedy in favor of the individual bringing the claim. This is often a difficult question to resolve even after a careful reading of the treaty or the legislation. United States courts will seek to discover the meaning of the treaty or legislation in this regard and have fairly liberal views about the type of evidence that may be introduced to throw light upon the drafters' intent.

§3.14 STATE SUCCESSION IN RESPECT OF TREATIES

The question of what happens to a state's obligations under treaties when the state ceases to exist, becomes a new entity, separates from a part of its territory, acquires more territory, declares its independence from a former ruler or somehow evolves into a different entity is a hotly disputed question in international law. This issue has become particularly important with the reunification of the two Germanies, the disintegration of the former Yugoslavia and the breakup of the Soviet Union.

3. The Law of Treaties

The Vienna Convention on Succession of States in Respect of Treaties, 1946 U.N.T.S. 3, was signed in 1978 and entered into force in 1996 but has received only a very modest number of ratifications. The two competing views on this issue are generally termed "the clean slate theory" and "the continuity theory." The clean slate view basically allows a new entity to start on a clean slate, that is to adopt only those treaties it wishes to be bound by and to reject the others. The continuity view holds the new entity to the obligations that attached to the same territory under the old entity. The Vienna Convention largely adopts the clean slate approach but with some notable exceptions. The clean slate theory does not apply to boundary treaties, treaties relating to the use of, or restrictions upon territory for the benefit of another state or for the establishment of foreign military bases on the territory. There are also special rules for uniting or separating states.

The I.C.J. has had occasion to discuss this issue in the *Application of the Convention on the Prevention and Punishment of the Crime of Genocide* (Bosnia and Herzegovina v. Yugoslavia [later Serbia-Montenegro]), 1996 I.C.J. 595 (Preliminary Objections), but succession was not determinative of the issues before the Court.

The Legal Status of Actors in the International Arena

States, International Organizations, Non-State Groups, Individuals, and Multinational Corporations

§4.1 Introduction
§4.2 The Definition of a State
    §4.2.1 A Defined Territory
    §4.2.2 A Permanent Population
    §4.2.3 A Government
    §4.2.4 Capacity to Enter into Relations with Other States
    §4.2.5 Recognition of States
§4.3 Secession and Self-Determination
    §4.3.1 Introduction
    §4.3.2 Secession as a Legal Concept
    §4.3.3 The Evolution of the Meaning of Self-Determination
    §4.3.4 Court Cases Discussing Self-Determination or
        Secession
§4.4 State Responsibility
    §4.4.1 Attributing Conduct to a State
    §4.4.2 State Breaches of International Obligations Where
        Wrongfulness Is Precluded
    §4.4.3 The State's Obligation to Make Reparations for Breaches
        of International Obligations
        Satisfaction
        Restitution
        Compensation
    §4.4.4 A State's Capacity to Bring International Claims on
        Behalf of Individuals

§4.5 International Organizations
§4.5.1 Inter-Governmental Organizations
(a) The United Nations' International Legal Status
(b) The Structure of the United Nations
(c) The United Nations' Principal Organs
The General Assembly
The Security Council
The Economic and Social Council (ECOSOC)
The Trusteeship Council
The International Court of Justice
The Secretariat
§4.5.2 Regional International Organizations
§4.5.3 Non-Governmental International Organizations
§4.6 Non-State Groups
§4.6.1 Protected Groups
§4.6.2 Non-State Actors
§4.7 International Status of the Individual
§4.8 Multinational Corporations
§4.9 Conclusion

§4.1 INTRODUCTION

In Chapter 1 it was stated that the classic definition of international law was that it encompassed the legal relationships between sovereign states. Unless an entity could claim statehood it could not claim any international rights or responsibilities. The classic definition has altered considerably in the last half century. Now various international forms of organizations as well as individuals have gained international legal status for certain purposes. This chapter will take a brief look at the following list of subjects as they relate to international legal status: the definition of a state; secession and self-determination; state responsibility; a state's capacity to bring international claims on behalf of an individual; the international status of international organizations (including a description of the structure of the United Nations); non-state groups; and the international status of individuals and multinational corporations.

§4.2 THE DEFINITION OF A STATE

Since states are still the principal actors in international law it is well to discuss the definition of the state. Most definitions of a state set out four requirements: a defined territory; a permanent population; a government;

and the capacity to enter into relations with other states. See Montevideo Convention on Rights and Duties of States, 165 L.N.T.S. 19, art. 1; Restatement of the Law Third, Foreign Relations Law of the United States §201 (1987). Although the International Court of Justice's advisory opinion on Kosovo does not address the characteristics of a state: *Accordance with International Law of the Unilateral Declaration of Independence in Respect of Kosovo*, Advisory Opinion, 2010 I.C.J. _____ (July 22), the Separate Opinion of Judge Cançado Trindade has some instructive discussion. Judge Cançado Trindade surveys the changing nature of international law which he views as shifting from a state-sovereignty centered model toward a human-development centered model. Separate Opinion at paras. 169-211. He also reviews the idea of statehood in light of this shifting emphasis. *Id.* at paras. 169-172. While acknowledging the historic importance of the four requirements, population, territory, government and capacity to enter into relations with other states, *id.* at para. 173, he views the past as obsessed with territorial considerations, *id.* at para. 169, but now moving toward "a normative . . . people-centered outlook. . . ." *Id.* at para. 170.

§4.2.1 A Defined Territory

Most states have well defined boundaries accepted by other states. Within their boundaries, states have the exclusive right to display sovereignty and the corollary duty to protect the international rights of individuals, whether nationals or aliens, within the state and to protect the rights of other states and entities as they interact with the state.

A number of states either have been, or are currently, embroiled in territorial disputes. These disputes may emanate from within the state or from other states. Within the state, various groups may be claiming that they have been unjustly deprived of their lands. Such issues will ultimately be settled by the internal dispute settlement machinery. Those claims do not usually impinge upon the question of statehood. If a particular group not only claims territory but also asserts a right to secession, then the state's boundaries are indeed questionable just as they would be if another state laid claim to part of the state's territory. Provided a state has some area of land that it definitely controls, international law is usually willing to treat the entity as a state. Israel was admitted to the United Nations in 1948 when its borders were far from clear. Negotiations concerning the ultimate status of the Palestinian-occupied territories mean that Israel's borders and the extent of the territory it occupies are likely to alter; but, despite this uncertainty, Israel is regarded as a state. What indicia of statehood the Palestinians will have to demonstrate before the world decides to recognize Palestine as a state is yet to be determined. The International Court of Justice has been called on to settle a number of inter-state land disputes but the existence of the disputing states, as states, was not questioned. See, e.g., *Sovereignty Over Pedra Branca/Pulau Batu Puteh, Middle Rocks and South Ledge* (Malaysia v. Singapore), 2008 I.C.J. 12; *The Frontier Dispute* (Benin v. Niger), 2005 I.C.J. 90; *Sovereignty Over Pulau Ligitan and Pulau Sipadan* (Indonesia v. Malaysia), 2002 I.C.J. 625.

§4.2.2 A Permanent Population

All populations are always in flux in terms of numbers but in order to be considered a state, the entity must have some people. Earlier in the twentieth century there were suggestions that an entity must have a certain minimum number of inhabitants to qualify for statehood but that view has now been rejected. A number of micro-states have been admitted to the United Nations such as Liechtenstein with a population of roughly 31,000 and Nauru with roughly 12,000 inhabitants. A number of states also have nomadic populations who spend part of the year in one state and part in another. Again, this is not considered to negate statehood provided the state always has a core of inhabitants.

Some areas of the globe are very inhospitable to human habitation such as the Arctic and Antarctic regions. The Antarctic is subject to a number of overlapping territorial claims on the part of several states. There is no permanent population in the Antarctic. Its status is now governed by the Antarctic Treaty, 402 U.N.T.S. 71, but it is not considered a state.

§4.2.3 A Government

A state must have an organized governmental structure which is largely independent from outside authority. States are, of course, free to enter into alliances with other states and to make agreements with other states promising to perform or refrain from performing certain acts. Most states have always entered into a whole variety of different networks of international agreements on a host of topics. No one suggests that these agreements jeopardize an entity's statehood. If, however, aspects of a state's foreign, defense, monetary, or domestic policy are governed by another state, the international community may be unwilling to treat the entity as a state. After Finland declared its independence from the Soviet Union following the revolution of 1917, chaos erupted, which the new Finnish government was only able to subdue with difficulty. The League of Nations Commission of Jurists discussed the question of when Finland became a state in the course of its decision in the *Aaland Islands* case. The Commission stated:

> In the midst of revolution and anarchy, certain elements essential to the exist-
> ence of a State, even some elements of fact, were lacking for a considerable

period. Political and social life was disorganized; the authorities were not strong enough to assert themselves . . . the Government had been chased from the capital and forcibly prevented from carrying out its duties. . . . It is, therefore, difficult to say at what exact date the Finnish Republic, in the legal sense of the term, actually became a definitely constituted sovereign State. This certainly did not take place until a state political organization had been created, and until the public authorities had become strong enough to assert themselves throughout the territories of the State without the assistance of foreign troops. League of Nations O.J., Spec. Supp. 3, 4 at 8-9 (1920).

Many governments undergo rebel attacks or civil wars. The British government was attacked by the Irish Republican Army for several decades but the turmoil was insufficient to persuade the international community that the United Kingdom no longer existed as a state. At various times, Lebanon has undergone severe internal strife as well as outside control of certain areas by both Syria and Israel, and yet Lebanon continued to be recognized as a state. A civil war may simply result in a new government's coming to power but sometimes it results in the creation of a new entity. The civil war in Ethiopia eventually resulted in the new state of Eritrea being created out of the northern part of the country in 1993. In Nigeria, however, the breakaway state of Biafra was ultimately unsuccessful in achieving statehood and returned to the Nigerian Federation in 1970.

§4.2.4 Capacity to Enter into Relations with Other States

An entity that wishes to enter into relationships with other states obviously needs a fairly high degree of governmental organization. Those persons conducting the external relationships on behalf of the entity have to be perceived by other states as having a credible claim to represent the entity. Ultimately, an entity's ability actually to enter into relationships with other states depends only in part on its capacity to conduct such relationships. Other states must be willing to treat the entity as a state and to conduct relationships with the entity on a state-to-state basis.

There have been a number of entities throughout history that have possessed all four indicia of statehood but the international community has nevertheless refused to recognize them as states or to have any dealings with them. In 1965, Ian Smith, the Prime Minister of the British self-governing colony of Rhodesia declared independence from Great Britain. The Smith government wanted to retain a system of government that kept almost all governing powers in the hands of the minority white population. The British government insisted on universal suffrage and no white racial preferences, although it is fair to say that such a position was of recent origin and that prior to the 1960s the British government had not objected to white domination in Rhodesia. Britain refused to recognize Smith's declaration of independence and the rest of the world followed suit. The U.N. imposed broad-based economic sanctions on the Smith government and called upon all states "not to recognize this illegal racist minority regime. . . ."[1] By 1979, the guerilla independence movement had toppled the Smith government, and the independent state of Zimbabwe was declared and rapidly recognized by the international community.

There was no doubt that the Smith regime possessed all of the requirements of statehood in an objective sense but the world community had condemned the regime for its racist politics and refused to recognize it as a state. Some authors have used the example of the Smith regime to argue that there is a fifth requirement for statehood, namely that the entity should meet with the approval (either on moral and/or legal grounds) of the world community before it fully possesses the requirements for statehood. When the apartheid government of South Africa created the so-called independent states of Transkei, Bophutgatswana, Venda, and Ciskei in the 1970s and 1980s, these states were perceived by the world as manifesting the racial separation policies of the South African government. As a result no other state was willing to recognize them as international entities.

Example 4-1

Below is the name of an area of the world together with some basic information relating to the area.

Bermuda

Bermuda is a collection of 138 islands lying in the Atlantic Ocean about 640 miles west-northwest of North Carolina. The islands were discovered by the Spanish in 1503 but in 1609 were claimed by the British and are now designated as a British Overseas Territory. Bermuda adopted a constitution in 1967 granting universal suffrage to all adults. The population numbers about 65,000. The islands have a two-party political system led by a premier who nominates cabinet members. There is a British governor of the islands appointed by the British Crown who officially appoints cabinet members. There is a bicameral parliamentary system consisting of an upper house, known as the Senate, and a lower house, known as the House of Assembly. The Senate has eleven members nominated jointly by the premier and the leader of the opposition party, and officially appointed by the governor.

---

1. Question Concerning the Situation in Southern Rhodesia, Nov. 12, 1965, S.C. Res. 216, U.N. SCOR, 20th Sess., Resolutions and Declarations, at 8 (1965).

The House of Assembly consists of thirty-six members elected by the adult population. There are a few diplomats from other nations, including the U.S., posted to Bermuda.

Britain remains largely responsible for Bermuda's defense and foreign affairs; the Bermudan government is responsible for internal affairs. Currently the only military post in Bermuda consists of the Bermuda Regiment, formed mainly by conscription of young Bermudan men who serve part time for three years. There is an independent judiciary that includes a Supreme Court, although final appeals in certain cases can be heard in the U.K. courts.

In 2009, the government of Bermuda agreed with the U.S. to accept four Chinese Uighurs who had been detained by the U.S. at Guantanamo Bay in Cuba. They had been suspected of assisting the Taliban but were later cleared for release. They did not wish to return to China because of fears that they might be tortured. The British were not consulted and were considerably annoyed by the Bermudan government's failure to consult them. The British Foreign Office stated: "We've underlined to the Bermuda Government that they should have consulted with the United Kingdom as to whether this falls within their competence or is a security issue, for which the Bermudan Government does not have delegated responsibility."

Bermuda enjoys a very high standard of living and in 2005 had the highest gross domestic income per capita in the world. A referendum on complete independence from Britain was soundly defeated in 1995. Britain maintains that she is ready to grant Bermuda independence should the population ever express a wish for it.

Is Bermuda a state? Explain your reasoning.

Explanation

In trying to determine whether a particular entity is a "state" what we look for are various indicia of sovereignty. What we discover is that, like many abstract concepts, "sovereignty" tends to consist of a spectrum of other features. The four agreed features of a defined territory, a permanent population, a government, and capacity to enter into relations with other states appear to be met by Bermuda.

Bermuda passes laws for the islands, prosecutes and jails transgressors, and carries on day-to-day governance without interference. Nonetheless, Bermuda's general lack of control over foreign affairs and defense (despite the Uighur incident) tends to indicate that it does not enjoy full sovereignty. It has rejected independence and agrees that it is a British Overseas Territory. The permanent residence in Bermuda of the British-appointed governor with certain powers under the Bermuda Constitution again indicates that Bermuda is not a fully independent state. What we have in Bermuda is an internally self-governing entity that, at least in recent years, appears to have acquiesced in its partially dependent status, thus preventing full statehood. Would we regard Bermuda as a state if, for example, the islands had been fully independent for several decades but then decided to ask a more powerful state to take on aspects of government, such as defense or foreign affairs, on behalf of Bermuda? In other words, if the powers exercised by the British were delegated to them by Bermuda, would that alter our analysis, even though the reality would be similar? Because Bermuda is not fully independent and has not yet claimed full independence, the international community is not willing to treat it as a state, despite the fact that it exhibits many of the characteristics of sovereignty.

Example 4-2

Below is some information relating to an entity headquartered in Rome, Italy.

The Sovereign Military Order of Malta

This Roman Catholic Order, also known as the Knights of Malta, was founded in 1050 as a hospital to care for pilgrims to the Holy Land. At various times it has ruled certain areas: the Island of Rhodes (1310-1523) and Malta (1530-1798). The Order was driven out of Malta by Napoleon. It currently has 12,500 members, 80,000 permanent volunteers, and 20,000 medical workers providing humanitarian aid on five continents. It claims sovereign status, has diplomat relations with roughly 100 states, and has observer status at the United Nations.

Is the Sovereign Military Order of Malta a state? Explain your reasoning.

Explanation

This Order clearly has operated as a state at various times in its history. To some extent it has certain characteristics of a sovereign. For example, it sets its own rules, and the pieces of property that it owns in Italy are not subject to Italian jurisdiction (rather like foreign embassies). However, The Order currently does not rule over any territory, and it cannot claim a permanent population. Although it sets its own internal rules, they are limited to its restricted purposes of humanitarian aid and do not govern such things as monetary policy, criminal laws, or environmental concerns, all of which we would expect to find on a state's agenda. Laudable though the Order's work is, somehow the scope of its activities seem too narrow for it to qualify as a state. It is one of a few remaining historical, semi-sovereign anomalies that some states choose to treat as a fellow state, at least for purposes of diplomatic relations.

Example 4-3

Nagorno-Karabakh

In the 1990s armed conflict took place between Armenia and Azerbaijan. Armenian forces occupied an area of Azerbaijan known as Nagorno-Karabakh together with certain surrounding areas where ninety-five percent of the population is ethnically Armenian. In 1991 Nagorno-Karabakh declared its independence from Azerbaijan. The U.N. Security Council has adopted resolutions reaffirming the original territorial integrity of Azerbaijan. Nonetheless, the self-proclaimed Nagorno-Karabakh Republic rules a land-locked area of 1,699 square miles within Azerbaijan. There is a Prime Minister, a Vice-Premier, and various ministries. The Organization for Security and Cooperation in Europe (OSCE) has created a negotiating group with a view to bringing about a permanent resolution of the conflict between Armenia and Azerbaijan over Nagorno-Karabakh. Neither Armenia nor Azerbaijan exercises any power within Nagorno-Karabakh. No country has diplomatic relations with Nagorno-Karabakh.

Is Nagorno-Karabakh a state? Explain your reasoning.

Explanation

The area of Nagorno-Karabakh is representative of the many claims to secession and independence that have always been apparent throughout history. It does have a defined territory, a permanent population, and a functioning government. No other state is, as yet, however, willing to give it recognition as a state. It has the capacity to enter into foreign relations with other states, but other states are not willing to treat it as a state. If the OSCE can work out a settlement granting the area independence, then do doubt the international community will rapidly recognize it as a state. If, however, all that is agreed is some form of greater autonomy for the area, recognition will not be forthcoming even if Nagorno-Karabakh continues to insist that it is an independent republic.

§4.2.5 Recognition of States

During the second half of the twentieth century and continuing into the twenty-first century, many new states have emerged often in fractious circumstances. The former Yugoslavia broke into five states in the 1990s. One of those new states, Serbia and Montenegro, formed in 1992, then broke into two separate states in 2006. More recently a portion of Serbia, known as Kosovo, declared independence in 2008 and is seeking recognition as a state by the international community of states. So far over seventy states have recognized Kosovo as a state but many states have not done so.

Two philosophical approaches have emerged with respect to the recognition of states. One approach is called the "declaratory theory" which holds that once an entity meets the objective criteria for statehood (see the four requirements above), then the entity is a state. The other approach is called "the constitutive theory," which states that only when other states decide that an entity has met the objective criteria and in fact treat the entity as a state does that entity actually become a state. In practice, these two theories often merge because general recognition as a state based on fulfilling the criteria will be necessary before the entity can operate as a state in the international arena.

The European Community (now called the European Union) issued *Guidelines on the Recognition of New States in Eastern Europe and the Soviet Union*.[2] The *Guidelines* set out standards to be met by applicants before recognition would be accorded to them by European states. Most of the standards set out relate to democracy, rule of law, human rights, and peaceful settlement of disputes. A Commission, known of the Badinter Commission, was established to create a mechanism under which entities could seek to establish that they had met the requirements to be recognized as a state. Ultimately, the Commission issued fifteen opinions addressing a variety of issues including recognition.[3] The *Guidelines* and the Commission's Opinions moved the European Union toward a process of collective recognition and created a quasi-judicial mechanism for resolving issues of territorial status even though the recognition practice of EU member states did not always follow the Commission's decisions.

§4.3 SECESSION AND SELF-DETERMINATION

§4.3.1 Introduction

New states can come about in a variety of ways. Sometimes a larger territorial unit will decide to split up, as was the case when Czechoslovakia separated peacefully into the two states of the Czech Republic and Slovakia in 1993 or when Norway and Sweden separated in 1905. Sometimes a state will disintegrate into several states such as when the former Yugoslavia started to crumble in the early 1990s. It has so far evolved into six new states: Bosnia-Herzegovina, Croatia, Macedonia, Montenegro, Serbia, and Slovenia. The status of a region within Serbia, known as Kosovo, which declared its independence in 2008, is not yet fully determined although over seventy states have recognized it as an independent state. The breakup of the Soviet Union encountered little opposition, and by May 1992 the three Baltic states and the other twelve constituent republics were all admitted to the United Nations as independent states.

---

2. *EC Guidelines*, 31 I.L.M. 1486 (1992).
3. See discussion in Thomas D. Grant, *The Recognition of States* 159ff (1999).

The more difficult cases of the creation of new states arise in the context of separatists' claims to secession from a larger territorial state. Separatist uprisings, not always involving armed conflict, span the globe from South Ossetia and Abkhazia in Georgia/Russia, to Indian-administered Kashmir, from the Basque region of Spain, to Scotland in the United Kingdom, from Quebec in Canada, to Chechnya in Russia, from the Uighur region of Xinjiang Province in China, to Somaliland in Africa. Most of these claim fester for a long period of time and usually, although not always, arise out of a sense of injustice perpetrated, in the separatists' view, by the larger state upon the people of the area claiming secession.

War sometimes brings success for the separatists' claims to independence, although at great human and material costs, as it did in Eritrea, which gained independence from Ethiopia in 1993 and in East Timor, which became independent from Indonesia in 2002.

§4.3.2 Secession as a Legal Concept

The late Professor Hersch Lauterpacht took the view that: "International law does not condemn rebellion or secession aiming at the acquisition of independence."[4] This view is largely reiterated by Professor James Crawford who states: "secession is neither legal nor illegal in international law, but a legally neutral act the consequences of which are regulated internationally."[5] You might well think that such authoritative statements would end the discussion but, in fact, the concept of secession has burrowed its way into another legal term, "self-determination," which, over time, has gained much legal legitimacy even though the outer edges of this concept are by no means well defined.

§4.3.3 The Evolution of the Meaning of Self-Determination

The term "self-determination" has undergone considerable historical transmutation since it was tossed into the international arena by U.S. President Woodrow Wilson after World War I when the victorious powers were busy carving up the rubble of the Austro-Hungarian and Ottoman Empires.[6]

---

4. Hersch Lauterpacht, *Recognition in International Law* 8 (1947).
5. James Crawford, *The Creation of States in International Law* 390 (2d ed. 2006), discussing various Security Council resolutions on the issue.
6. President Wilson stated: "National aspirations must be respected; peoples may now be dominated and governed only by their own consent. Self-determination is not a mere phrase. It is an imperative principle of action, which statesmen will henceforth ignore at their peril." *War Aims of Germany and Austria*, in 3 *The Public Papers of Woodrow Wilson: War and Peace* 177 (Ray Stannard Baker & William E. Dodds eds. 1927).

The Covenant of the League of Nations did not mention self-determination although the Mandate System was charged with ensuring the "well-being and development" of peoples within the areas governed by the Mandatory Powers.[7] The United Nations Charter states that "The Organization is based on the principle of the sovereign equality of all its Members." Art. 2, para. 2. The "Members" must be states meeting certain obligations. Arts. 3-6. The Charter, however, mentions "self-determination" twice. Article 1, para. 2 states that a purpose of the U.N. is "to develop friendly relations among nations based on respect for the principle of equal rights and self-determination of peoples. . . ." Article 55 notes that "peaceful and friendly relations among nations" should be "based on respect for the principle of equal rights and self-determination of peoples. . . ." These articles were referring to the peoples who were transferred from the League's Mandate System to the U.N.'s Trusteeship System plus territories that were detached from enemy states after World War II. The Charter accepted a colonial system for the administration of dependent states but, at least within the Trusteeship System, it contemplated a form of self-government or even independence at some future, undetermined, date.

By the 1960s, the movement toward decolonization was underway. Decolonization began to link self-determination to the right to political participation in governance. In 1960, the General Assembly declared that: "All peoples have the right to self-determination; by virtue of that right they freely determine their political status and freely pursue their economic, social and cultural development."[8] This resolution concludes, however, as do many similar declarations, with a prohibition against reading the right of self-determination as a right of secession: "Any attempt aimed at the partial or total disruption of the national unity and the territorial integrity of a country is incompatible with the purposes and principles of the Charter of the United Nations."[9] On the one hand, the U.N. wanted to operate on an inter-state level accepting the state-centered framework of the international community. On the other hand, it wanted to confer certain rights on peoples within the existing state framework. The question left open was: What happens when peoples cannot "freely determine their political status and freely pursue their economic, social and cultural development"? Do they get some sort of right to disassociate themselves from the governmental structure currently ruling them? There is yet another question lurking here: Who are these "peoples"? The whole of the inhabitants in an existing state or certain groups of them? If the term applies to certain groups,

---

7. Covenant of the League of Nations, art. 22 (1919-1924).
8. *Declaration on Granting Independence to Colonial Countries and Peoples*, G.A. Res. 1514, GAOR, 15th Sess., Supp. No. 16, at 67, U.N. Doc. A/L 323 and Add. 1-6 (1960).
9. *Id.* at para. 4.

which groups? The answers to these questions have caused, and continue to cause, much controversy.

Once the process of decolonization began to gain momentum, different groups within the boundaries of existing colonies began to question whether the boundaries, as drawn up by the administering empire, could be challenged. Colonial powers had often drawn colonial boundaries with little regard for ethnic, racial, religious, or even geographic divisions. See §7.7. The principle of *uti possidetis juris* (as you did possess so you shall possess) under which colonial territories claiming independence must accept the territorial boundaries as they were drawn and administered by the colonial power was rapidly accepted both by Latin American states and by African states. The International Court of Justice has reaffirmed this principle in a number of cases in part "to prevent the independence and stability of new States being endangered by fratricidal struggles provoked by the challenging of frontiers following the withdrawal of the administering power."[10] Dismantling the colonial system did not dismantle the idea of the state and the need for territorial integrity, rather it enunciated a norm of self-government within pre-existing colonial boundaries. Self-government began to be seen in terms of a right attaching to persons to participate in their own governance as well as a right not to be ruled by foreigners.

The idea of rights attaching to persons, or groups of persons, has seen exponential growth since the middle of the twentieth century when the modern human rights movement began its remarkable progress. Once the human rights movement began to establish rights in treaties, self-determination began to make an appearance in treaty language. Self-determination is mentioned in both the International Covenant on Civil and Political Rights[11] and the International Covenant on Economic, Social and Cultural Rights.[12] Both covenants declare: "All peoples have the right of self-determination. By virtue of that right they freely determine their political status and freely pursue their economic, social and cultural development." These treaties were intended to apply to all people, not only to people in U.N. Trust territories or colonies. In our discussion of secession, we are then left with two overarching questions: (1) Who are the *peoples* to whom the right of self-determination attaches? and (2) does the right of self-determination ever include the right of secession?

As for the *peoples* who can claim self-determination, there seems little doubt that it refers to colonial peoples. They have a right to throw off colonial rule and to organize their own governance system. But can the term *peoples* also refer to a subgroup of the whole body of an existing state's citizenry. Some scholars maintain that the concept does not go beyond the

---

10. *Frontier Dispute* (Burkina Faso v. Mali), 1986 I.C.J. 554, at 565.
11. 999 U.N.T.S. 171, at art. 1.
12. 993 U.N.T.S. 3, at art. 1.

colonial context. Others maintain that subgroups defined by such things as race, ethnicity, culture, religion, language, history, and tradition may qualify as *peoples*.

From the early 1990s, international documents began to appear stating that governments must "represent . . . the whole people belonging to a territory. . . ."[13] These documents also begin to expand the groups to whom self-determination attaches. Colonial peoples are certainly included but people under "other forms of alien domination or foreign occupation . . ." are also given the right to self-determination.[14] All of these groups are stated to have the right "to take any legitimate action . . . to realize their inalienable right to self-determination."[15] What these declarations do not describe is what rights or remedies accrue to unrepresented *peoples* if a state does not have a government representing the whole people, nor do they describe what might constitute "legitimate action." This is where the so-called right to secession comes in. The argument is that if people have a right to self-determination, and if, as part of that right, a state has an obligation to ensure the establishment of a government that represents the whole people, then, if the state has failed in its obligation, the prohibition on secession disappears and any subset of the people that can credibly claim nonrepresentation, can then secede in order to ensure their own self-determination. This jump, from the failure to fulfill an obligation to the creation of the remedy for such a failure, remains highly controversial but, in many ways, it is what drives every established state's recognition of independence when claimed by a part of a larger pre-existing state, whether some European states' recognition of Kosovo or Russian recognition of Abkhazia and South Ossetia. It should be noted, however, that many scholars, jurists, and international practitioners maintain that there is no right to secession outside the colonial context. Some might add that the right to secession can be exercised where the government engages in gross violations of human rights against a distinct subset of the people it rules.

§4.3.4 Court Cases Discussing Self-Determination or Secession

Perhaps the leading case, to date, discussing self-determination and secession comes from the Supreme Court of Canada. The Canadian Court was asked for an advisory opinion on whether the province of Quebec had a right to secede from Canada either under Canadian law or under international law. In the circumstances of the case, the Court answered "No" to both questions but in doing so it assessed the state of international

---

13. *Vienna Declaration and Programme of Action*, U.N. Doc. A/CONF. 157/24 (pt. I), para. 2 (1993).
14. *Id.* at para. 2.
15. *Id.*

law on self-determination and secession.[16] The Court came to the conclusion that generally the right to self-determination must be exercised within the framework of the state structure. This notion the Court called "internal self-determination." Nonetheless, the Court noted that "a people" may be interpreted to include "only a portion of the population of an existing state."[17] It also recognized that in "exceptional circumstances a right of secession may arise."[18] Such a right "arises in only the most extreme of cases and, even then, under carefully defined circumstances."[19] The Court listed three examples of extreme cases. First, the right of colonial peoples to declare independence was considered undisputed.[20] Second, where, outside the colonial context, a people "is subject to alien subjugation, domination or exploitation" there was a right to secede.[21] This situation the Court also believed to be settled law. Third, "when a people is blocked from the meaningful exercise of its right to self-determination internally, it is entitled, as a last resort, to exercise it by secession. . . ."[22] The Court conceded that this last circumstance was not yet "an established international law standard."[23] Although the Court was clear that none of these extreme circumstances applied to Quebec, it went on to discuss what it called "The Effectively Principle."[24] This principle, operative in all law, describes the way that law, usually, adapts to political reality. The Court recognized that if Quebec did declare independence and if, over time, the international community broadly recognized it as an independent state, then, at some point, the law would rearrange itself to recognize the new state even though the secession originally came about illegally.[25]

The International Court of Justice has also discussed self-determination in a number of cases. Most of those cases either relate to colonies or to non-self-governing territories within the Mandate System. In those contexts, the Court has made it clear that self-determination, in the sense of self-government, applies to all peoples in non-self-governing territories.[26] In its 2004 Advisory Opinion on the *Legal Consequences of the Construction of a Wall in the Occupied Palestinian Territories*[27] the Court notes that the principle of

---

16. Reference re Secession of Quebec, 2 S.C.R. 217 (1998).
17. Id. at 124.
18. Id. at 122.
19. Id. at 126.
20. Id. at 132.
21. Id. at 133.
22. Id. at 134.
23. Id. at 135.
24. Id. at 140.
25. Id. at 141.
26. *East Timor* (Portugal v. Australia), 1995 I.C.J. 102; *Western Sahara*, Advisory Opinion, 1975 I.C.J. 12 (Oct. 16); *Legal Consequences for States of the Continued Presence of South Africa in Namibia (South West Africa) Notwithstanding Security Council Resolution 276 (1970)*, Advisory Opinion, 1971 I.C.J. 16 (June 21).
27. Advisory Opinion, 2004 I.C.J. 136 (July 9).

"self-determination of peoples has been enshrined in the United Nations Charter and reaffirmed by the General Assembly in resolution 2625 (XXV). . . ."[28] It also noted that: "the existence of a 'Palestinian people' is no longer in issue"[29] and that the right of self-determination was a legitimate right of the Palestinians.[30] In this case then, the Court recognizes a right of self-determination as attaching to a people who do not yet constitute a state when they are under alien occupation.

The Court has now issued an advisory opinion on Kosovo's declaration of independence from Serbia.[31] The General Assembly asked the Court: "Is the unilateral declaration of independence by the Provisional Institutions of Self-Government of Kosovo in accordance with international law?"[32] Unfortunately, the Court missed an opportunity to give substantive guidance on the law of self-determination and secession. It restricted itself to answering whether the declaration of independence itself was, or was not, in accordance with international law and determined that "the act of promulgating the declaration" was not "regarded as contrary to international law." Id. at para. 79. In other words the Court sliced off "the declaration" from the legal significance of its consequences and refused to rule on anything except the act of making a declaration of independence.

The Separate Opinion of Judge Cançado Trindade does contain a definitive statement on the right to secession for oppressed peoples:

> The entitlement to self-determination of the victimized population emerged, as the claim to territorial integrity could no longer be relied upon by the willing victimizers. Id. at para. 181.

> Grave breaches of fundamental human rights (such as mass killings, the practice of torture, forced disappearance of persons, ethnic cleansing, systematic discrimination) are in breach of the *corpus juris gentium*, as set forth in the U.N. Charter and the Universal Declaration . . . and are condemned by the universal juridical conscience. Any State which systematically perpetrates those grave breaches acts criminally, and loses its legitimacy, ceases to be a State for the victimized population. . . . Id. at para. 205.

However, it is important to note that this is the separate opinion of one judge on the Court.

---

28. Id. at 171.
29. Id. at 182-183.
30. Id. at 183.
31. *Accordance with International Law of the Unilateral Declaration of Independence in Respect of Kosovo*, Advisory Opinion, 2010 I.C.J. _____ (July 22).
32. G.A. Res. 10764; U.N. GAOR, 63d Sess.; U.N. Doc. A/RES/63/3 (Oct. 8, 2008).

Example 4-4

Below are some very brief excerpts (with footnotes omitted) from two written statements filed in the I.C.J. addressing the question of whether Kosovo (an area of Serbia) meets the requirements of statehood and whether its declaration of independence accords with international law. The first statement was filed by Serbia and runs to 372 pages in full. The second statement was filed by the United Kingdom and runs to 130 pages in full. Both statements also have numerous appendixes. No less than thirty-six countries, plus Kosovo, filed written statements in this advisory case. There were also further comments filed by fourteen states, plus Kosovo. All of these statements and comments can be read on the I.C.J.'s web site: http://www.icj-cij.org/. Obviously, these brief excerpts only cover one of many issues addressed in the statements.

1) *Excerpt from Serbia's 2009 Written Statement to the I.C.J. in the Kosovo Advisory Case*

Part III
General International Law Provides No Ground for the Independence of Kosovo

* * *

The Unilateral Declaration of Independence is in Contradiction with the Principle of Respect for the Territorial Integrity of States

412. The principle of respect for the territorial integrity of States constitutes a foundational principle of international law. It is one of the key constituent principles of the overarching concept of the sovereignty of States and from it flows a series of consequential norms. For the international community to accept a rule of international law positing a non-consensual right of secession from sovereign States would be tantamount to breaking the previously entrenched international consensus concerning the territorial integrity of States in a way that would have quite dramatic consequences. Such would be the inevitable result of accepting the UDI by the provisional institutions of self-government of Kosovo.

* * *

476. It is, therefore, beyond dispute that international practice has been remarkably consistent in affirming the territorial integrity of States, both generally and particularly with regard to States faced with internal conflicts or disputes. Such practice, which confirms and reinforces the foundational norm of territorial

integrity, demonstrates that there exists an international rule to that effect which applies not only to neighbouring and other States, but also to those groups within the State in question that seek non-consensual secession.

2) *Excerpt from the United Kingdom's 2009 Written Statement to the I.C.J. in the Kosovo Advisory Opinion*

*   *   *

The Creation of States: General Issues

5.9   The protection of the territorial integrity of States is a protection in "international relations." It is not a guarantee of the permanence of a State as it exists at any given time. Nor does it apply to secessionist movements within the territory of a State. Generally speaking, international law does not prohibit the separation of part of the territory of a State arising from internal processes.

5.10   To put the same proposition in other terms, although a State's territorial integrity is protected under international law, as a general matter this protection has been extended only insofar as the use of force and intervention by third States are concerned. It has not been extended to the point of providing a guarantee of the integrity of a State's territory against internal developments which may lead over time to the dissolution or reconfiguration of the State.

5.11   This is not to say that international law *favours* the dismemberment of a State's territory, nor, in particular, that it favours secessionist claims. Rather, international law favours the territorial integrity of States in the interests of stability and the peaceful settlement of disputes, including disputes arising within a State. Under international law, secessionist movements — or the populations they claim to represent — have no legal right to independence, outside the special context of colonial self-determination. International law seeks to avoid the dissolution or dismemberment of its subjects, but not to the point of guaranteeing that these situations can never occur.

*   *   *

5.17   But it is one thing to say that there is no right to secede in international law and another to say that secession is *contrary* to international law or that it is legally impossible. Seceding entities did not rely on international law as giving them a right to independence. International law, however, was flexible enough to acknowledge these situations, once they had achieved the necessary stability and effectiveness, so that a successful reassertion of sovereignty by the former State was practically excluded.

* * *

5.33 To summarise, international law favours the territorial integrity of States. Outside the context of self-determination, normally limited to situations of colonial type or those involving foreign occupation, it does not confer any "right to secede." But neither, in general, does it prohibit secession or separation, or guarantee the unity of predecessor States against internal movements leading to separation or independence with the support of the peoples concerned.

Would you agree that the principle of the territorial integrity of states should always trump claims to secession? If not, when should claims to secession be permitted (or acknowledged) by international law?

Explanation

Law evolves over time. Before the anti-colonial movement which, in the modern era, started when India gained independence from Britain in 1947, one could say (with a fair amount of certainty) that international law prohibited secession. Secession did take place, the U.S. independence from the U.K. in 1776 being a prominent example, and, over time, law adapted to treat the U.S. as a fully legal independent state. It did not, however, condone the act of secession. More recently, international law has bestowed a wide variety of human rights on individuals and on certain groups, including the right to equal treatment and fair representation by government. Where a government does not treat its population equally and/or is not representative of all of its people, it has failed to meet its international obligations. The argument being made by those who favor secession, in certain circumstances, is that the remedy for the government's failure to meet its obligation toward a portion of its population is that those people get a right to secede. (The U.K. position above is that internal dismemberment of a state is not addressed by international law.) Turning to the case of Kosovo and its claim to independence from Serbia, someone supporting its right to secession would need to present a detailed catalog of the relationship between the Kosovars and the Serbian government before any decision could be made about whether Kosovo meets the criteria for secession. Because there are also many U.N. Security Council resolutions relating to the situation those too would need to be examined. In law, as in life, sometimes there are no easy answers.

§4.4 STATE RESPONSIBILITY

States have responsibility for a variety of obligations imposed on them by international law, for example, complying with its treaty obligations (see Chapter 3) or not causing injury to other states by the emission of noxious fumes (see Chapter 13). Every time you read a decision from the International Court of Justice where one state has filed a claim against another state, the claimant state is asserting that the respondent state failed to meet its internationally required responsibilities and that some sort of remedy is due to the claimant. The International Law Commission (ILC), which consists of thirty-four members elected by the General Assembly, is required to work toward "encouraging the progressive development of international law and its codification. . . ." U.N. Charter, art. 13, para. 1(a). ILC web site: http://www.un.org/law/ilc/. The Commission has work for many years on a series of draft articles on state responsibility. In 2001, the ILC adopted the Draft Articles on Responsibility of States for Internationally Wrongful Acts. Although these articles are considered authoritative by many scholars, certain provisions are controversial. As yet, there is no comprehensive treaty in this area. The central principle is that any state's internationally wrongful act requires reparation. This much might well be expected in any legal system. The Draft Articles *do not* spell out what is an internationally wrongful act but rather leave that to the other areas of international law, such as treaty law or international environmental law. The Draft Articles do, however, address a number of other useful areas of this subject matter.

§4.4.1 Attributing Conduct to a State

A "State" is a legal concept. There is not any particular entity that we can name or point to that characterizes the "State" in all circumstances. Rather, people, agencies, different parts of governments, organizations and various other entities may purport to act as the "State" or on behalf of the "State." The Draft Articles relating to attribution of conduct to the State lay down rules on how closely an entity must be connected to the State before the State will be held responsible for the act or omission. You can find these provisions at articles 4-11 of the Draft Articles. A very brief summary of the actors which are considered part of the state for purposes of attributing their conduct to the state, in certain circumstances, appears below:

> State organs exercising legislative, judicial, executive or any other functions (art. 4) while acting in a governmental capacity even if the organ exceeds its authority or contravenes instructions (art. 7);

A person or entity empowered by the law of the State to exercise elements of governmental authority while acting in a governmental capacity (art. 5) even if the person or entity exceeds its authority or contravenes instructions (art. 7);

An organ placed at the disposal of a State by another state if the organ is exercising governmental authority of the State at whose disposal it was placed (art. 6).

Persons or groups of persons acting on the instructions of, or under the direction or control of, a State (art. 8) even where the person or group is exercising elements of governmental authority in the absence or default of official authorities where the circumstances call for the exercise of such authority (art. 9);

An insurrectional movement when it becomes the new government of the State (art. 10, para. 1);

The entity which succeeds in establishing a new State in part of a pre-existing State (art 10, para. 2);

Any person or entity where the State acknowledges and adopts the person's or entity's conduct as its own (art. 11).

Of course, the above rules of attribution are very general and any particular application will no doubt generate debate.

Example 4-5

Two members of the armed forces, Tom and Harriet, of the State of Acla were posted abroad to take part in a long-running war between Acla and the State of Zeda. All members of Acla's armed forces are instructed that if any of Zeda's armed forces are taken prisoner, they are to be treated humanely in accordance with the Geneva Conventions to which both Acla and Zeda are parties. Tom and Harriet captured seven members of Zeda's armed forces in a remote region of the conflict. They disarmed the Zedans and took them to a nearby cave where they proceeded to torture them over the course of several days. One Zedan died.
Will the actions of Tom and Harriet be attributable to the State of Acla?

Explanation

Yes. Any member of a state's armed forces are part of that state's government. The State of Acla is responsible for all the actions of any member of its armed forces even where the action is contrary to specific instructions or training. (Article 91 of Additional Protocol I to the Geneva Conventions of 1949, 1125 U.N.T.S. 3, has the same rule. Tom and Harriet will probably also face prosecution under Acla's code of military justice. If they are not prosecuted by Acla, or if Acla's prosecution is a sham and Tom and Harriet are exonerated, they may face prosecution in an international criminal court for war crimes. See Chapter 11.)

Example 4-6

The Beta State Oil Company is owned and run by the State of Beta and directly controlled by Beta's Ministry of Oil. Recently, the company was drilling an oil well in Beta's territorial waters which were part of the Aqua Sea. Three states border this sea: Beta, Ceta, and Deta.

Suddenly, the drilling equipment failed, and a huge, continuous fountain of oil started to gush into the Aqua Sea. The Beta State Oil Company tried in vain for two weeks to contain the oil. The State of Beta then contracted with a private oil company, named Etoil, registered in the State of Eta, another state in the region. The Betan Oil Ministry instructed Etoil "to do whatever it takes to contain the oil flow in the Aqua Sea." Etoil decided the only way to contain the oil would be to use a high grade explosion to blast the oil well out of existence. Beta's Oil Ministry had not asked to be consulted about the method to be used to contain the oil well. Etoil laid massive explosives near the well. Warnings were given to all the population thought to be in range of the explosion, and they were evacuated. The explosion turned out to be much more devastating than estimated. As a result, more oil poured into the Aqua Sea. Thousands of people were killed in all three states bordering the Sea. It took Etoil another two months to contain the oil by more conventional methods. The Aqua Sea is completely filled with oil. No flora or fauna survived the combined effects of the blast and the oil pollution.

Will the State of Beta be responsible for the activities of Etoil?

Explanation

Etoil is not part of the government of Beta but article 8 of the Draft Articles on State Responsibility for Internationally Wrongful Acts provides:

> The conduct of a person or group of persons shall be considered an act of a State under international law if the person or group of persons is in fact acting on the instructions of, or under the direction or control of, that State in carrying out the conduct.

In this case Etoil was acting on the *instructions* (vague though they were) of the Betan Oil Ministry which is part of the Betan government thus Beta would be responsible for Etoil's activities. Note that article 8 also attributes conduct to a state if the person or group of persons act *under the direction or control* of the state. The latter part of this rule has led to some disagreement in different international courts. On the one hand, the I.C.J. refused to attribute all of the activities of the *Contra* forces to the U.S. government. The *Contras* were a private rebel group fighting the government of Nicaragua. It was, in large part, financed, organized, trained, and equipped by the U.S. government. The U.S. was held to have violated various international laws by this support of the *Contras*. The *Contras* were also alleged to have committed violations of human rights and humanitarian law but the Court ruled that to hold the U.S. responsible for such violations "it would . . . have to be proved that . . . [the U.S.] had effective control of the military or paramilitary operations in the course of which the alleged violations were committed." *Military and Paramilitary Activities in and Against Nicaragua* (Nicaragua v. U.S.), 1986 I.C.J. 14 (Merits), para. 115, see also paras. 109 & 110. Clearly, the I.C.J. was looking for evidence of day-to-day control where there was actual participation or direction given by the U.S. to the *Contras* before the U.S. would be held responsible for every illegal activity undertaken by the *Contras*. On the other hand, the Appeals Chamber of the International Tribunal for the former Yugoslavia thought that the I.C.J. standard was too stringent. It stated that:

> The requirement of international law for the attribution to States of acts performed by private individuals is that the State exercise control over the individuals. The degree of control may, however, vary according to the factual circumstances of each case. The Appeals Chamber fails to see why in each and every circumstance international law should require a high threshold for the test of control. *Prosecutor v. Duško Tadić*, I.C.T.Y., Case IT-94-1-A, 1518, para. 117, at 1541 (1999).

The I.C.T.Y. was obviously willing to attribute individual's actions to the state when the state exercised overall control even if it did not exercise day-to-day, minute-by-minute, control.

In the case of Etoil, Beta hardly exercised any control of Etoil's activities. (Indeed, one might argue that Beta's lack of careful control amounted to wrongful conduct by omission.) Nonetheless, in this case Etoil was operating under the instructions of Beta and thus Beta is responsible for Etoil's activities.

§4.4.2 State Breaches of International Obligations Where Wrongfulness Is Precluded

The Draft Articles also outline situations where even though the activity in question will constitute the breach of an international obligation attributable to the state, it will, nevertheless not be considered wrongful. Below is a brief summary of the articles (20-27) indicating the circumstances when failure to meet international obligations is not regarded as wrongful:

When a state engages in illegal activity against another state but the injured state has consented to the illegal activity (art. 20);

When a state exercises self-defence where the self-defence is in conformity with the U.N. Charter (art. 21);

When a state engages in legitimate countermeasures taken against another state's illegal acts (art. 22);

When a state's actions are compelled by *force majeur*, an irresistible force, or unforeseen events that make it impossible to fulfill international obligations (art. 23),

When a state's actions are required to save the actor's life, in a situation of distress, and there is no other reasonable way, to save that life or other lives entrusted to the actor's care (art. 24);

When the state acts out of necessity but only when it is the sole way to safeguard an essential interest against a grave and imminent peril and does not impair an essential interest of the states to whom the international obligation exists (art. 25);

Article 26 notes, however, that the wrongfulness of failure to comply with a peremptory norm of international law is never precluded.

Example 4-7

Take the facts as discussed in Example 4-6 but alter them a little, as follows. Suppose that the Beta Oil Company had successfully drilled for oil in the Aqua Sea and had been pumping out several hundred barrels of oil a day for two years without incident. Now suppose that a massive earthquake erupted directly under the oil well, causing oil to gush into the Aqua Sea. Suppose also that earthquakes have never been experienced anywhere in the area before. The Beta Oil Company manages to cap the well within ten days but not before the whole of Aqua Sea has suffered devastating pollution.

Has the State of Beta committed an internationally wrongful act because of the pollution from the oil well?

Explanation

Article 23 of the Draft Articles on State Responsibility for Internationally Wrongful Acts provides:

> The wrongfulness of an act of a State not in conformity with an international obligation of that State is precluded if the act is due to *force majeure* [superior force], that is the occurrence of an irresistible force or of an unforeseen event, beyond the control of the State, making it materially impossible in the circumstances to perform the obligation.

The Commentary to this Article states:

> Material impossibility of performance giving rise to *force majeure* may be due to a natural or physical event (e.g., stress of weather . . . earthquakes, floods or drought). . . .

In this case, there is no issue of attributing the conduct to the State of Beta. The Beta Oil Company is a state-owned and -controlled entity, part of the governmental machinery. Clearly, Beta has an international obligation not to pollute the Aqua Sea (see Chapters 12 and 13), but the earthquake that caused the damage to the oil well and the resulting pollution was due to *force majeure*. The damage was caused by an irresistible force, which was an unforeseen event. It was beyond the control of Beta, and the earthquake made it materially impossible to perform the obligation not to pollute. As a result, the pollution, which would otherwise have been wrongful, is considered not wrongful in these circumstances. (As a political matter, one suspects that Beta would offer to pay for the cleanup.) Of course, if earthquakes were a frequent occurrence in the Aqua Sea, the event would not be unforeseen and thus Beta's wrongful acts would not be "precluded."

§4.4.3 The State's Obligation to Make Reparations for Breaches of International Obligations

The ILC's Draft Articles make it clear that when a state breaches an international obligation, it remains bound by that obligation (art. 25). The breaching state is also required to make reparation for the breach to the state or states to whom the obligation was owed. An early case from the Permanent Court of International Justice (P.C.I.J.) stated the general principle of reparation:

> It is a principle of international law that the breach of an engagement involves an obligation to make reparation in an adequate form.[33]

---

33. *Factory at Chorzów* (Germany v. Poland), 1927 P.C.I.J., Ser. A, No. 9, at 21 (July 26) (Jurisdiction).

More recently, the I.C.J. has stated:

> What constitutes "reparation in an adequate form" clearly varies depending upon the concrete circumstances surrounding each case and the precise nature and scope of the injury, since the question has to be examined from the viewpoint of what is the "reparation in an adequate form" that corresponds to the injury. *Avena and Other Mexicans Nationals* (Mexico v. U.S.), 2004 I.C.J. 12, at 59.

In a later phase of the *Factory at Chorzów* case, the Permanent Court stated:

> Reparation must, as far as possible, wipe out all consequences of the illegal act and reestablish the situation which would, in all probability, have existed if that act had not been committed.[34]

In trying to put the parties back in the position they would have been in if the illegal act had not occurred, courts have awarded a variety of types of reparations. The Draft Articles characterize the main forms of reparation as: restitution, compensation, and satisfaction (art. 34).

Satisfaction

Satisfaction may take the form of a court's decision that a wrong was committed; an acknowledgment by a party that it had breached its obligations; an apology to the injured party; and/or a promise of non-repetition. In *Pulp Mills on the River Uruguay*, Argentina requested the Court to find that Uruguay violated its obligations under a treaty. It also asked the Court to issue an order to Uruguay to immediately cease from the wrongful acts. Below is the Court's ruling on this request:

> The Court considers that its finding of wrongful conduct by Uruguay in respect of its procedural obligations per se constitutes a measure of satisfaction for Argentina. As Uruguay's breaches of the procedural obligations occurred in the past and have come to an end, there is no cause to order their cessation.[35]

In the *LaGrand* case,[36] the Court determined that the U.S. had failed to comply with its treaty obligations of consular notification to German detainees held in the U.S. criminal system. The U.S. apologized to Germany but Germany was not satisfied with a simple apology and demanded an assurance of non-repetition of the failure and changes in U.S. law and practice. The U.S. outlined to the Court the leaflets and training programs it was preparing to comply with its notification obligations. With respect to the

---

34. 1928 P.C.I. J., Ser. A, No. 17, at 47 (Sept. 13) (Merits).
35. (Argentina v. Uruguay), 2010 I.C.J. _____, para. 269.
36. (Germany v. U.S.), 2001 I.C.J. 466.

apology, the Court held that "an apology is not sufficient in this case . . ."[37] but that

> the commitment expressed by the United States to ensure implementation of the specific measures adopted in performance of its obligations . . . must be regarded as meeting Germany's request for a general assurance of non-repetition.[38]

Ultimately the Court also ruled that in the case of the conviction of a defendant who had not received consular notification where the sentence was the death penalty or prolonged detention:

> it would be incumbent upon the United States to allow review and reconsideration of the conviction and the sentence by taking account of the violation of the rights set forth in the Convention.[39]

Restitution

The I.C.J. has defined restitution as: "the reestablishment of the situation which existed before the occurrence of the wrongful act."[40] It added that: "where restitution is materially impossible or involves a burden out of all proportion to the benefit deriving from it, reparation takes the form of compensation or satisfaction, or even both. . . ."[41] The P.C.I.J. spoke of: "Restitution in kind, or if this is not possible, payment of a sum corresponding to the value which a restitution in kind would bear. . . ."[42] In its advisory opinion, *Construction of a Wall*, the I.C.J. stated that the construction of a wall in the Occupied Palestinian Territories was "contrary to various of Israel's international obligations. . . ."[43] The Court, therefore, concluded that Israel was "under an obligation to return land, orchards, olive groves and other immovable property seized from any natural or legal person for purposes of construction of the wall in the Occupied Palestinian Territory."[44] In *U.S. Diplomatic and Consular Staff in Tehran*, where the Court had found that Iran was responsible for the wrongful takeover of the U.S. Embassy and Consulates in Iran and the illegal detention of U.S. diplomats and U.S. nationals, the Court decided that Iran

---

37. *Id.* at 512.
38. *Id.* at 513.
39. *Id.* at 514.
40. *Pulp Mills on the River Uruguay* (Argentina v. Uruguay), 2010 I.C.J. _____, para. 273.
41. *Id.*
42. *Factory at Chorzów* (Germany v. Poland), 1928 P.C.I.J., Ser. A, No. 17, at 47 (Sept. 13) (Merits).
43. *Legal Consequences of the Construction of a Wall in the Occupied Palestinian Territory*, Advisory Opinion, 2004 I.C.J. 136, 197 (9 July).
44. *Id.* at 198.

must immediately terminate the unlawful detention of the United States Chargé d'affaires and other diplomatic and consular staff and other United States nationals now held hostage in Iran . . . [and] must immediately . . . [turn over to an appointed Protecting Power] the premises, property, archives and documents of the United States Embassy in Tehran and of its Consulates in Iran. . . .[45]

Compensation

Compensation as a form of reparation is designed to make the injured party whole. There is a large amount of case law which addresses the standards for the appropriate level of compensation including methods of valuation and how any interest might be calculated. The I.C.J. prefers the parties to settle issues of compensation once the Court has determined that reparations are due for damages.[46] In the *Nicaragua* case the Court decided that the U.S. was under an obligation to make reparation to Nicaragua for a wide variety of obligations having to do with breaches of a treaty of friendship, as well as violations of the customary rules on the use of force, nonintervention, humanitarian law, and respect for state sovereignty.[47] Nonetheless, the Court indicated that the parties should arrive at a "negotiated settlement."[48] In the *Gabčíkovo-Nagymaros Project* case the Court determined that both parties had engaged in wrongful conduct and were entitled to claim compensation but were also required to pay compensation.[49] Here the Court concluded:

> It is a well established rule of international law that an injured State is entitled to obtain compensation from the State which has committed an internationally wrongful act for the damage caused by it. In the present Judgment, the Court has concluded that both parties committed internationally wrongful acts, and it has noted that those acts gave rise to damage sustained by the Parties; consequently Hungary and Slovakia are both under an obligation to pay compensation and both are entitled to obtain compensation.
>
> *   *   *
>
> Given the fact, however, that there have been intersecting wrongs by both Parties, the Court wishes to observe that the issue of compensation could satisfactorily be resolved in the framework of an overall settlement if each of the Parties were to renounce or cancel all financial claims and counterclaims.[50]

---

45. *U.S. Diplomatic and Consular Staff in Tehran* (U.S. v. Iran), 1980 I.C.J. 3, at 44-45.
46. *Military and Paramilitary Activities in and Against Nicaragua* (Nicaragua v. U.S.), 1986 I.C.J. 14, at 143.
47. Id. at 146-150.
48. Id. at 143.
49. (Hungary v. Slovakia), 1997 I.C.J. 7, at 81.
50. Id.

§4.4.4 A State's Capacity to Bring International Claims on Behalf of Individuals

If an individual is injured by a foreign state (a state other than the individual's state of citizenship), the individual's own state is permitted to pursue the claim at the international level against the state causing the injury but only under certain conditions. First, the individual must seek a remedy in the offending state. All administrative and judicial avenues must be exhausted. Second, the individual must have the citizenship of the state espousing the claim at the time when the injury occurred and continuously through to settlement of the claim. Throughout the world there are a variety of ways that states confer citizenship: through birth in the territory, through consanguinity or marriage, through naturalization upon the fulfillment of certain conditions, after successful claims for political asylum, or even because a state would like an athlete on its national team. International law does not set down any requirements for the conferring of citizenship (other than prohibiting forceful impositions of citizenship), but international law does require a certain level of relationship between the individual and the state before the state is permitted to bring an international claim on behalf of an individual.

In the *Nottebohm* case, the I.C.J. ruled that even though Friedreich Nottebohm had acquired citizenship in Liechtenstein in compliance with Liechtenstein law, Liechtenstein could not represent his claim at the international level before the I.C.J.[51] Nottebohm was German by birth. At the age of twenty-four he went to Guatemala where he lived and pursued various commercial interests. Shortly after the outbreak of World War II, he applied for Liechtenstein nationality which was granted three weeks later. He then returned to Guatemala. Although the court stated that: "international law leaves it to each State to lay down the rules governing the grant of its own nationality,"[52] in order for a state to represent a citizen at the international level "the legal bond of nationality [must] accord with the individual's genuine connection with the State which assumes the defence of its citizens by means of protection as against other States."[53] The citizenship must represent "a legal bond having as its basis a social fact of attachment, a genuine connection of existence, interests and sentiments, together with the existence of reciprocal rights and duties."[54] The person to be represented at the international level must be "more closely attached by his tradition, his establishment, his interests, his activities, his family ties, his intentions for the near future to [the state seeking to represent him] . . . than to any other

---

51. (Liechtenstein v. Guatemala), 1955 I.C.J. 4.
52. Id. at 23.
53. Id.
54. Id.

State."[55] Nottebohm had hardly any connection with Liechtenstein. He had considerably more both with Germany and with Guatemala. The Court ruled that Liechtenstein was not qualified to represent Nottebohm's claims at the international level against Guatemala.

When an individual has more than one nationality, which given the great mobility of the current world's population occurs quite frequently, international law will generally look to the dominant nationality by examining the individual's ties to the various states in which s/he holds citizenship. The state deemed to possess the closest ties to the individual will be the only state able to represent the individual at the international level. The state with the less dominant ties will not be permitted to reject a claim simply on the ground that the individual is also a citizen of the state against which the claim is made. The Iran-U.S. Claims Tribunal has had to resolve a number of dual-nationality issues.[56]

Whether a state chooses to take up an individual's claim at the international level is left to the discretion of the state. Obviously, a whole variety of factors will be taken into account such as the size of the claim, whether there are other similar claims against the same state, the seriousness of the injury and the nature of the state's relationship with the injuring state.

Example 4-8

In 1980, a woman called Jasmine Alba was born in a country named Azza which, under its Constitution, automatically confers citizenship on persons born in its territory. Jasmine's parents were citizens of the country of Balna. At the time of Jasmine's birth, they were visiting Azza as distinguished scholars at a leading university there. As the child of two citizens of Balna, Jasmine also acquired citizenship in Balna at birth. Her parents acquired both an Azzan and a Balnan passport for Jasmine when she was six months old. The Alba family remained in Azza until Jasmine was eight years old when the family returned to Balna. From the age of eight to eighteen, Jasmine lived and went to school in Balna. At eighteen, she returned to Azza to attend college, returning home to Balna for all vacations. She graduated with a physics degree in 2002 and continued her studies in Azza at the graduate level.

Jasmine has traveled about the world both with her parents and by herself after she reached the age of eighteen. She sometimes uses her Azzan passport, and she sometimes uses her Balnan passport to enter or leave foreign countries. Her choice of passport is usually dictated by the

---

55. *Id.* at 24.
56. The Iran-United States Claims Tribunal was established to resolve disputes arising out of the 1979 detention of fifty-two U.S. nationals in the U.S. Embassy in Tehran. The Tribunal sits in The Hague, the Netherlands: http://www.iusct.org/. See Charles N. Browler & Jason D. Brueschke, *The Iran-United States Claim Tribunal* 289-296 (1998); Case No. A/18 Decision No. DEC 32-A18-FT (6 April 1984); 5 Iran-U.S. Cl. Trib. Rep. 251, 254 (1984).

length of the line waiting to get through customs and immigration inspection. The shorter the line, the more likely she is to use that passport. In 2005, Jasmine married a fellow graduate student. Her husband is a citizen of Azza. The wedding was celebrated at the bride's home in Balna but after a two-week honeymoon, the couple returned to their studies in Azza, where they recently jointly purchased a small condominium. Jasmine also has a teaching assistantship in Azza. In 2007, Jasmine's parents made a gift of their summer home in Balna to Jasmine. Jasmine and her husband take their annual month-long vacation in Balna using Jasmine's summer home, which they have now redecorated and refurbished at considerable expense. Jasmine has two brothers who live in Balna, and she always visits her parents and her brothers in the summer.

In January of 2009, war broke out between Azza and Balna over a border dispute. Immediately after the outbreak of war, Balna confiscated "all property owned by enemy aliens." Jasmine's summer house was confiscated, and the Ministry of War informed her that: "as a citizen of Azza, you are considered an enemy alien." Jasmine had been visiting her parents in Balna when the war broke out but two months later she returned to Azza. Finally, in July of 2010, the war ended with a peace treaty. The treaty established a Claims Tribunal under which "the States of Azza and Balna are permitted to pursue claims on behalf of their citizens against the other State." The treaty also stipulates that: "in the case of dual nationals, the dominant or effective nationality shall be determinate."

Can the State of Azza represent Jasmine against the State of Balna in a claim seeking the return of, or compensation for, the expropriated summer house in Balna? Note: only address the issue of representation. Do not address the merits of the claim. Assume that all remedies available to Jasmine in the administrative and court systems of Balna have been exhausted.

Explanation

This is a case in which the facts are fairly evenly balanced between Jasmine's ties to Azza and her ties to Balna. Jasmine was born in Azza and resided there from birth to age eight. She carries an Azzan passport. She again took up residence in Azza during the academic year from the age of eighteen until the present, a further twelve years. She currently works and studies in Azza and jointly owns a condominium there.

On the other hand, Jasmine's parents live in Balna, she has always carried a Balnan passport, she lived there from age eight to eighteen, and she returned there frequently while she was in college. She currently owns a home in Balna and often visits her relatives there.

If we look at the time when the claim arose through to the present, 2009-2010, Jasmine's main ties seem focused in Azza. She mainly lives there, works there, is married to an Azzan citizen and jointly owns property in Azza. During the war, she spent two months in Balna and the rest of the time in Azza. Her Balnan property was expropriated because Balna considered her an Azzan citizen, an enemy alien. In these circumstances, a tribunal would probably determine that Jasmine's main ties were with Azza, and thus Azza could represent her claim before the tribunal against Balna.

Note how very fact specific these determinations are. They often consist of long catalogs of facts tying the claimant to one state, followed by another list of facts tying the clamant to the other state. For a post–World War II case concerning payment for a grand piano and other personal property, see *U.S. ex rel. Mergé v. Italian Republic*, 14 U.N.R.I.A.A 236 (1955).

§4.5 INTERNATIONAL ORGANIZATIONS

Groups of states have entered into alliances ever since states took over governance from tribes, clans, and other governing entities. In the modern era, the creation of international organizations to facilitate inter-state communication and policy making began early in the nineteenth century. Such organizations have proliferated particularly since the end of WWII. These organizations may be governmental or non-governmental. They may address multiple issues or focus on single issues. They may represent millions of people or only a handful. It is fair to say that international organizations have become very influential in the field of international law. Many fields of human endeavor literally could not operate without the international cooperative and standard-setting work of many of these international organizations. For example, international mail services are facilitated by the Universal Postal Union; international air flight is coordinated by the International Air Transport Association; hurricanes are predicted and tracked by the World Meteorological Organization; and standards for oil tankers are governed by the International Maritime Organization. These are just a few of the thousands of international organizations that are essential to our daily lives. As Professor Malcolm Shaw says: "International organizations (or institutions) have now become indispensable."[57] Whether any particular international organization possesses international legal personality depends upon the powers granted to it by its members in its constitutional documents as well as its actual functioning in a particular case. In an early advisory opinion, the I.C.J. made it clear that the United Nations (an international, inter-governmental organization) had the capacity to bring international claims against states on behalf of injury to itself and its agents.[58]

---

57. Malcolm N. Shaw, *International Law* 1284 (6th ed. 2008).
58. *Reparation for Injuries Suffered in the Service of the U.N.*, Advisory Opinion, 1949 I.C.J. 174 (April 11).

§4.5.1 Inter-Governmental Organizations

An international, inter-governmental organization is an entity created by an agreement between states and having states as its constituent members. The United Nations is a prime example of such an entity. Its principal constitutional agreement is the U.N. Charter, and membership was opened to all the states that participated in the San Francisco Conference of 1945 and to "all other peace loving states which accept the obligations contained in the present Charter and, in the judgment of the Organization, are able and willing to carry out these obligations." U.N. Charter, art. 4, para. 1. As mentioned above, the extent to which an international organization possesses international capacity (often called *personality*) will depend, in part, upon the degree of capacity conferred upon it by its constitutional documents. Its capacity may also evolve through practice and may be deduced from its overall purposes. To some degree the extent to which an international organization is able to exercise the international capacity conferred upon it by its charter will be determined by the will of its members. Below is a brief description of the status and structure of the United Nations which has almost universal state membership.

(a) The United Nations' International Legal Status

When seeking to determine the international capacity of an organization the first place to look is its constitutional documents. The U.N. Charter is largely silent on this matter although article 104 provides: "The Organization shall enjoy in the territory of each of its Members such legal capacity as may be necessary for the exercise of its functions and the fulfillment of its purposes." Similarly, article 105 states:

> 1. The Organization shall enjoy in the territory of each of its Members such privileges and immunities as are necessary for the fulfillment of its purposes.
> 2. Representatives of the Members of the United Nations and officials of the Organization shall similarly enjoy such privileges and immunities as are necessary for the independent exercise of their functions in connection with the Organization.
> 3. The General Assembly may make recommendations with a view to determining the details of the application of paragraphs 1 and 2 of this Article or may propose conventions to the Members of the United Nations for this purpose.

These two articles only confer capacity on the U.N. and its representatives within the territories of its members. Nothing is said about the general international capacity of the organization or about its capacity in its relations with nonmembers.

The next place to search for legal capacity of an organization is any agreements it may have entered into with its members. In 1946 the General Assembly adopted the Convention on the Privileges and Immunities of the United Nations. 1 U.N.T.S. 15. This convention is an agreement between the United Nations and each of its members and provides for the U.N.'s juridical capacity (art. I); specifically, the capacity "(a) to contract; (b) to acquire and dispose of immovable and movable property; (c) to institute legal proceedings" (art. I, §I). It also provides for a broad range of privileges and immunities for the U.N. in order to facilitate its work. Wherever the U.N. has offices, it enters into an agreement with the host state, under which the host state agrees to grant the U.N., its representatives, and officials various privileges and immunities. See, for example, 11 U.N.T.S. 11.

Constitutional documents and agreements between an international organization and its members cannot hope to cover the myriad of issues relating to capacity that may arise in the course of the organization's development. Such issues can only be resolved through practice and legal inference.

(b) The Structure of the United Nations

The League of Nations, which was founded in 1919 to limit resort to war and to provide a mechanism for settlement of international disputes, collapsed during World War II. After the war, the determination to provide an international organization that could "maintain international peace and security" (U.N. Charter, art. 1(1)) bore fruit at the San Francisco Conference of 1945, where fifty nations met and the U.N. Charter was drafted. The principal purpose of the U.N. was directed to the maintenance of peace and collective security but the Charter outlined far broader purposes such as developing "friendly relations among nations" (art. 1(2)), "equal rights and self-determination of peoples" (art. 1(2)), "international cooperation in solving . . . economic, social, cultural [and] humanitarian" problems (art. 1(3)), and "promoting and encouraging respect for human rights and for fundamental freedoms for all without distinction as to race, sex, language or religion" (art. 1(3)). Many of these concepts have become almost common place today (though few are fully realized), but in 1945 they were nothing short of radical. Below is a brief description of the structure of the United Nations.

(c) The United Nations' Principal Organs

Article 7 of the Charter establishes six principal organs of the U.N.; the General Assembly, the Security Council, the Economic and Social Council, the Trusteeship Council, the International Court of Justice, and the Secretariat.

The General Assembly

The General Assembly is made up of all the member states of the United Nations, now numbering over 190. Each member may have up to five representatives in the Assembly (art. 9(2)) but each state has only one vote. Voting is generally by simple majority but "important questions" (art. 18(2)) require a two-thirds vote of the members present and voting. "Important questions" are defined in article 18(2) and include such matters as the election of non-permanent members of the Security Council, the expulsion of members and budgetary questions. Clearly, a one-state-one-vote system is far from democratic. The most heavily populated states such as China or India, with over one billion people, have one vote as does Nauru which has about 12,000 people. Numerous suggestions have been made to alter the General Assembly's voting system but no reform has been agreed upon.

The General Assembly "may discuss any questions or any matters within the scope of the present Charter or relating to the powers and functions of any organs provided for in the present Charter and . . . may make recommendations to the Members . . . or to the Security Council . . ." (art. 10). If the Security Council has a matter under consideration then the General Assembly "shall not make any recommendations with regard to that dispute . . ." (art. 12(1)).

The main work of the General Assembly consists of "initiating studies and making recommendations" (art. 13(1)) to promote international political cooperation; to encourage the development of international law; to promote cooperation in the "economic, social, cultural, educational and health fields" (art. 13(1)(b)); and to assist in realizing "human rights and fundamental freedoms for all without distinction as to race, sex, language or religion" (art. 12(1)(b)). The General Assembly also considers and approves "the budget of the Organization" (art. 17(1)). This latter task has been fraught with difficulties over the years as various nations have refused to pay their assessed portions of the budget.

The Security Council

The Security Council has the "primary responsibility for the maintenance of international peace and security . . ." (art. 24(1)). All members of the U.N. "agree to accept and carry out the decisions of the Security Council . . ." (art. 25). The Charter intended that member states would enter into agreements with the Security Council undertaking "to make available to the Security Council . . . armed forces, assistance, and facilities . . . necessary for the purposes of maintaining international peace and security" (art. 43(1)). In fact, no such agreements have been negotiated. Although the United Nations has sent peacekeeping troops to a variety of locations round the globe and has authorized certain states to use all necessary means to quell certain threats to the peace, the troops used on such occasions have been supplied by individual states on an *ad hoc* basis. There are no permanent U.N. armed forces as envisioned by the Charter.

States may refer disputes to the Security Council for recommendations on settlement. The Council has the power to "determine the existence of any threat to the peace, breach of the peace, or act of aggression" (art. 39) and makes decisions on the measures to be taken. The measures taken can be non-forceful actions, such as economic sanctions or severance of diplomatic relationships (art. 41), or the Security Council may take action "by air, sea, or land forces as may be necessary to maintain or restore international peace and security" (art. 42). The Council provides a forum where states can raise issues implicating threats to the peace. The Security Council has frequently called upon parties to settle their disputes. It has dispatched peacekeeping forces, increasingly so in recent years (e.g., to the former Yugoslavia and to Somalia), and it has authorized state-led military actions against states determined to have breached the peace (e.g., resolutions relating to the Gulf War (1990-1991), where the U.S. and U.K. led a coalition of other states against Iraq after its invasion of Kuwait).

There are fifteen members of the Security Council: five permanent members (China, France, Russia, the United Kingdom, and the United States) and nine non-permanent members elected for two-year terms. Members of the Security Council each have one vote. Nine votes are needed to pass a resolution in the Security Council, and that vote must include all five permanent members, except when voting on procedural matters (art. 27). In practice, the abstention of a permanent member is not counted as a vote against a resolution. The preeminence accorded to the five permanent members may have given recognition to the major powers in 1945 but certainly does not reflect the distribution of political power today and is not in any way democratic. Again, there have been numerous suggestions on reforming the membership and voting in the Security Council but none has been adopted.

The Economic and Social Council (ECOSOC)

The Economic and Social Council consists of twenty-seven members with nine members elected each year for three year terms. The Council's principal function is to study and report to the General Assembly, the members, and the specialized agencies on economic, social, cultural, educational, health, and human rights matters.

ECOSOC has established many commissions and committees to report on subjects within its competence. It coordinates the work of the long list of specialized agencies such as the United Nations International Children's Emergency Fund (UNICEF) and the World Health Organization (WHO). It also has the power to give non-governmental organizations consultative status when their expertise would be useful to the work of ECOSOC. The number of organizations granted consultative status now runs to several thousand. Each member of the Council has one vote and a majority of the members present, and voting is required to pass a resolution.

The Trusteeship Council

The Trusteeship Council operates under the authority of the General Assembly. The main task of the Council was to move dependent territories toward self-government. It played a major role in the decolonization era which rapidly gathered steam during in 1960s. There are relatively few territories left under its jurisdiction now so that its role is much less significant.

The International Court of Justice

The International Court of Justice is the "principal judicial organ of the United Nations." Article 92. It is established by the U.N. Charter (arts. 92-96) and functions in accordance with a Statute annexed to the Charter which "forms an integral part of the Charter." Art. 92. For materials on the structure, competence, and jurisdiction of the International Court of Justice, see Chapter 5, §5.3.2.

The Secretariat

Currently there are over 50,000 members of the U.N. staff located at the U.N. headquarters in New York City and throughout the world at other headquarters. The "chief administrative officer" is the Secretary-General who "shall be appointed by the General Assembly upon the recommendation of the Security Council." Article 97. In effect this means that no Secretary-General can be appointed without the positive endorsement of the five permanent members of the Security Council. The Secretary-General is the chief officer of a very large bureaucracy. A number of nations have called for a reduction in the size of the staff, and the Secretary-General's office has effected across-the-board cuts in staffing levels in recent years.

The Secretary-General performs any functions entrusted to him or her by the General Assembly, the Security Council, the Economic and Social Council, and the Trusteeship Council and "makes an annual report to the General Assembly on the work of the Organization." Article 98. The Secretary-General also has the power to "bring to the attention of the Security Council any matter which in his opinion may threaten the maintenance of international peace and security." Article 99. This latter power permits the Secretary-General to play a prominent role in bringing to world attention international crises. A number of Secretaries-General have undertaken active peace negotiation roles in attempts to resolve international disputes and can be very influential in shaping the worldwide agenda for the United Nations.

Members of the Secretariat do not represent their particular countries. The U.N. Charter, article 100, makes it clear that "the staff shall not seek or receive instructions from any government or any other authority external to the Organization." The member states of the U.N. undertake to respect the notion of international responsibility of the staff and agree "not to seek to influence them in the discharge of their responsibilities." Art. 100, para. 2.

§4.5.2 Regional International Organizations

Regional international organizations consist of organizations that represent governments in particular regions of the world and may focus on a particular set of problems or address a very broad scope of issues. For a detailed description of the regional structures focusing on human rights, see Chapter 9, §9.4. Various parts of the world now have structures in place to facilitate their ever expanding operations. If you go to the web sites of the regional organizations listed below you will get a sense of their activities: the European Union (EU): http://europa.eu/; the Organization of American States (OAS): http://www.oas.org/; the African Union (AU): http://www.africa-union.org/; the League of Arab States: http://www.arableagueonline.org/; the Shanghai Cooperation Organization: http://www.sectsco.org/; the Eurasian Economic Community: http://www.photius.com/eaec/. There are, of course, many others.

§4.5.3 Non-Governmental International Organizations

A non-governmental international organization (NGO) is a private organization made up of individuals or groups with chapters of the organization in more than one country. There has been an enormous proliferation of such organizations, particularly since the 1960s. These organizations address a myriad of topics relating to international issues, and they have had a profound impact on the development of international law in such areas as civilian and combatants' rights in armed conflict; human rights; environmental concerns; animal rights; workers and employers rights; marine matters and fishing; health, food, and hunger; religious rights; and scientific progress.

Article 71 of the U.N. Charter states that the Economic and Social Council (ECOSOC) "may make suitable arrangements for consultation with non-governmental organizations which are concerned with matters within its competence." Several thousand NGOs now have consultative status with ECOSOC.

A few examples of NGOs that have performed critical roles in the international arena are Amnesty International (political repression, death penalty, and human rights); the International Committee of the Red Cross/Red Crescent (development of the laws of war and the supply of humanitarian assistance during hostilities or natural disasters); the World Wildlife Fund (species conservation and environmental matters); Greenpeace (environmental matters); and Oxfam (world hunger). These organizations are often the first to bring issues to international attention and frequently provide the structure and the energy necessary to formulate and to implement solutions. They have helped draft international treaties and have worked vigorously for their worldwide ratification and enforcement. The NGOs provide the framework for the ordinary person to be intimately involved in international problems and their solutions.

§4.6 NON-STATE GROUPS

§4.6.1 Protected Groups

Some international human rights treaties recognize the rights of certain sub-state groups based on factors such as race, ethnicity, religion, culture, gender, age, or language. There has also been a concerted effort to establish rights for Indigenous Peoples in many parts of the world. The right of self-determination is said to attach to "peoples," which has been recognized as being a smaller group than the entire state. Some groups, such as those based on race, possess what might be called "immutable characteristics." Other groups, such as those based on religion, are changeable. All such group characteristics, however, depend upon perceived differences ascribed either by the group itself, or by non-group members, or by both members and nonmembers of the group. To some extent, the rights (or duties) allocated to the group will also depend upon the perceived need for special treatment. We don't find any particular rights being given to "Caucasian, upper income, college-educated males," for example, because such a group has not been seen as needing special protection. Although group rights have now found increasing areas of recognition, particularly in the field of human rights, the recognition of groups being permitted to enforce their rights as a group is only just beginning to emerge. For detailed treatment of group rights in the human rights field, see Chapter 9, §9.5.

§4.6.2 Non-State Actors

Recently, loosely structured international non-governmental paramilitary organizations have successfully launched attacks on a number of targets throughout the world. The bombing of the World Trade Center in New York City and the Pentagon in Washington, D.C., in September 2001, by hijacking airplanes and crashing them into the targeted buildings, was apparently masterminded by Osama Bin Laden, who is said to head a worldwide organization called Al-Qaeda, aimed at eliminating Western influence in certain Islamic states. Almost 3,000 people were killed in those attacks. In response, the United States launched an attack on Afghanistan against the Taliban government who, at that time, controlled roughly ninety percent of the country. The United States argued that such an attack was justified as self-defense, because the Taliban had permitted Osama Bin Laden to run training camps for Al-Qaeda in Afghanistan. The task here has not been to confer rights on such groups or to enable them to enforce rights, but rather to find an entity that can be held liable for the group's actions. States that facilitate or acquiesce in these groups' criminal activities may well be held liable under principles of state responsibility. See §4.4. Individuals within the group may be held criminally responsible under national law, or international law provided there is an international tribunal with jurisdiction over them. International law has not yet found a satisfactory place for these non-state actors in the existing framework of international law.

§4.7 INTERNATIONAL STATUS OF THE INDIVIDUAL

Before the recognition of individual human rights in international law, states had recognized that they owed certain duties to aliens traveling within their borders. Generally, a state has no obligation to admit aliens to its territory but, if it does so, then it owes the alien a duty of care. If that duty of care is breached, the alien can seek a remedy in the foreign state. If no remedy is forthcoming, then the alien's own state can seek a remedy against the foreign state at the international level. See §4.4.4. In theory, the state pursing a claim at the international level arising out of a citizen's injury abroad was pursuing a remedy for injury to itself, not directly on behalf of the citizen. If a citizen was injured, the theory was that a component of the state had been injured so that the state had suffered an injury.

As the law of human rights developed (see Chapters 8 and 9), it became clear that people had personal rights that attached to the individual regardless of his/her status as an alien. Increasingly human rights agreements began to give the individual the right to bring a complaint against the state. In other words, the individual was given the capacity to sue the state for an internationally based claim.

At the same time that the individual was gaining international rights, it began to be recognized that individuals may also have responsibilities for breaches of certain obligations attaching to the individual's conduct. The Nuremburg International Criminal Tribunal, which was set up by the Allies to try war criminals after World War II, was clear that responsibility for war crimes could be attributed to individuals. Sentences punishing wartime commanders and civilian officials were handed down by the Tribunal thus establishing individual responsibility for the commission of international crimes. The International Criminal Court for the former Yugoslavia and for Rwanda and the newly established permanent International Criminal Court (see Chapter 11) are also proceeding on the concept of individual responsibility for international offenses. A number of hybrid national/international courts, such as those in East Timor, Sierra Leone, and Cambodia are proceeding on the same assumption.

Individuals are increasingly being accorded international rights and responsibilities. The availability of a forum in which the individual can claim such rights or be prosecuted for the violation of international responsibilities has not moved ahead with the same speed as the acceptance of the notion of individual rights and responsibilities at the international level. As a result, the availability of a forum to pursue claims or adjudicate responsibilities depends upon (1) the willingness of states to agree to subject themselves to such suits or to allow such prosecutions to go forward in their national courts and (2) the willingness of the international community to establish and support international or quasi-international tribunals for the adjudication of violations of state or individual responsibilities. Such fora are increasing.

§4.8 MULTINATIONAL CORPORATIONS

Corporations are, of course, creatures of national law. Their structure and powers are dictated by domestic legislation. When a corporation operates across state borders, however, it finds itself subject to a variety of international regimes, including everything from taxation to labor standards. A number of transnational corporate activities have now created specialized areas of international law such as the international sale of goods or intellectual property licensing.

When corporations decide to invest in another state, they will often enter into an agreement with the state where the investment is located through an internationalized contract which spells out the terms and conditions of the investment and mandates that disputes arising under the contract will be settled by international arbitration rather than by the domestic courts. These contracts will often seek to protect the corporation's investment from expropriation by the local government. Most states seeking foreign investment now recognize that offering contractual protections to multinational corporations works to their benefit. Without certain international assurances, corporations may simply not be willing to risk investing in less developed countries.

Codes of conduct for multinational corporations have also developed around areas such as working conditions for corporate employees or environmental standards for conducting business. Although these Codes are not technically binding, many multinational corporations adopt them in an attempt to meet acceptable standards for conducting transnational business. Corporations that operate in more than one country have become major players in the international arena, employing thousands of workers and creating wealth both for investors and for the countries where they operate.

§4.9 CONCLUSION

Just as the subject matter covered by international law has rapidly expanded, so has the number of recognized entities within the international legal framework. International law, like law more generally, changes as the world changes. As the number of international transactions relentlessly increases, functional necessity has put pressure on international law to expand the types of entities it recognizes as having international legal capacity. No doubt this trend will continue.

International Dispute Settlement Including International Civil Courts and Civil Tribunals

§5.1 The Obligation to Settle Disputes
§5.2 Arbitration
 §5.2.1 The Permanent Court of Arbitration
§5.3 International Civil Courts
 §5.3.1 The Permanent Court of International Justice
 §5.3.2 The International Court of Justice
  (a) The Composition of the Court
  (b) The Jurisdiction of the International Court of Justice
   in Contentious Cases
   (i) "[A]ll cases which the parties refer to it (i.e.,
    the Court) . . ."
   (ii) "[A]ll matters specially provided for in the
    Charter of the United Nations . . ."
   (iii) "[A]ll matters . . . in treaties and conventions
    in force"
   (iv) Compulsory Jurisdiction: Also Known as
    "The Optional Clause"
   (v) Jurisdiction *Forum Prorogatum*
  (c) The Jurisdiction of the International Court of
   Justice in Advisory Cases
  (d) The Power of the International Court of Justice
   to Issue Interim Measures of Protection
 §5.3.3 Examples of Other Major International Civil Courts and
  Tribunals
  (a) The International Tribunal for the Law of the Sea

        (b) Iran–United States Claims Tribunal
        (c) World Trade Organization: Dispute Settlement Body
    §5.3.4 Regional Courts
        (a) Europe
        (b) The Americas
        (c) Africa
        (d) Arab States
        (e) Asia
§5.4 Conclusion

§5.1 THE OBLIGATION TO SETTLE DISPUTES

The United Nations Charter requires states to settle their disputes peacefully. Article 33 provides:

> 1. The parties to any dispute, the continuance of which is likely to endanger the maintenance of international peace and security, shall, first of all, seek a solution by negotiation, enquiry, mediation, conciliation, arbitration, judicial settlement, resort to regional agencies or arrangements, or other peaceful means of their own choice.
>
> 2. The Security Council shall, when it deems necessary, call upon the parties to settle their dispute by such means.

On the whole, states prefer to settle disputes themselves by direct negotiations without the interference of third parties. Negotiations may be undertaken by ministers or their deputies from the states involved, or they may be undertaken by the country's respective ambassadors or special envoys.

Other informal methods of dispute settlement, usually involving a third party, are called: *good offices*, where a third party facilitates the negotiations between the parties; *mediation*, where an intermediary operates between the parties to settle the dispute; *conciliation*, where an outside party will study the dispute and may propose a settlement; *commissions of inquiry*, where a commission seeks to establish the factual basis of the dispute and may suggest a framework for settlement.

§5.2 ARBITRATION

Arbitration is a more formal, quasi-judicial method of settling disputes and one that has found increasing favor in the international community in recent years. The International Law Commission has defined international arbitration as: "a procedure for the settlement of disputes between States by a binding award on the basis of law and as a result of an undertaking voluntarily accepted." 1953, II Y.B. Int'l L. Comm'n 202. In the typical international arbitration, the parties will work out an agreement on the structure of the arbitral panel or tribunal; the appointment of the members of the panel; the substantive and procedural law to be applied; and the particular dispute, or group of disputes, to be settled by the arbitral tribunal. In many ways the parties create their own "court" for the settlement of the dispute. You may well ask why the parties do not use an existing court rather than go to the trouble of creating one themselves. The answer lies partly in the lack of any international courts until the twentieth century and their limited jurisdiction and partly in the amount of control that the parties can exercise over the structure and proceedings of an arbitral tribunal. One or more of the parties may not like the substantive or procedural law of existing courts, or they may think that the judges would be prejudiced against them, or they may think that the court procedure takes too long or is too expensive. Arbitration generally affords the parties a great deal more flexibility than existing courts. The parties are not obliged to accept any particular procedure or judge, and they can work out the framework for the tribunal to their mutual satisfaction.

Arbitration has a long history but in the modern era the practice has been for states to enter into agreements setting out the specific conditions for the establishment of the arbitral tribunal. Often each state involved in a dispute will be given the right to appoint an arbitrator, and a neutral person or entity, such as the Secretary-General of the United Nations, will also appoint an arbitrator. In the arbitral agreement the parties to the dispute will agree to abide by the arbitrators' decision. Arbitration agreements may relate to a particular dispute such as a territorial dispute. For example, the territorial dispute over Clipperton Island between France and Mexico was resolved by an arbitral tribunal, *Clipperton Island Arbitration* (France v. Mexico), reprinted at 26 Am. J. Int'l L. 390 (1932). On the other hand, the agreement may relate to a variety of claims arising out of an international dispute. For example, the Iran-U.S. Claims Tribunal was established by the Declaration of Algeria, reprinted at 20 I.L.M. 233ff (1981). The Tribunal was given authority to hear claims from citizens and corporations from both states arising out of the Iran hostage crisis.

§5.2.1 The Permanent Court of Arbitration

The Permanent Court of Arbitration was established in 1900 pursuant to the 1899 Hague Convention for the Pacific Settlement of International Disputes which was modified by the 1907 Convention. This agreement essentially allows parties to the Convention to nominate up to four arbitrators from which a list of arbitrators is created. The disputants can select judges from the list. The machinery of the "Court" only goes into operation if an arbitral panel is requested. Although the "Court" was relatively active in its early years, it then became relatively quiescent probably because there were many more avenues for the settlement of disputes available, such as the International Court of Arbitration of the International Chamber of Commerce in Paris, France. In recent years, the Court has experienced a resurgence in its use. Its work can be viewed on its web site: http://www.pca-cpa.org/. There are currently seven pending cases. Five cases were resolved in 2009 and three cases in 2008. The United Nations Commission on International Trade has developed the UNCITRAL Arbitration Rules, which are widely used in international commercial arbitration by corporations and other business entities. The rapid growth of international trade and finance has necessitated the creation of dispute settlement mechanisms. The 1965 Convention on the Settlement of Investment Disputes between States and Nationals of Other States, 575 U.N.T.S. 159, established the International Center for the Settlement of Investment Disputes (ICSID) in Washington, D.C. The American Arbitration Association (AAA) facilitates arbitrations and has also developed its own set of rules.

§5.3 INTERNATIONAL CIVIL COURTS

The twentieth century began the modern practice of establishing an ever growing number of international civil courts. (The development of international criminal courts is outlined in Chapter 11.)

§5.3.1 The Permanent Court of International Justice

The Permanent Court was set up under the League of Nations Covenant in 1920 and functioned from 1922 until the League was dissolved in 1946. It operated under a Statute annexed to the Covenant and decided a number of important cases. Its cases and documents can now be viewed on the web site of the International Court of Justice: http://www.icj-cij.org/. When the United Nations was established in 1945, the International Court of Justice was established under the United Nations Charter.

§5.3.2 The International Court of Justice

The framework of the Court is set out in the United Nations Charter, articles 92-96. The Court is "the principal judicial organ of the United Nations."

(Art. 92). It functions in accordance with a Statute which is annexed to the U.N. Charter which is said to form "an integral part of the . . . Charter." (Art. 92). All member states of the United Nations are parties to the Court's statute (art. 93(1)) but this *does not* mean that the Court has jurisdiction over all members of the U.N. What it means is that all member states of the U.N. are free to submit to the jurisdiction of the Court for the settlement of their international disputes. Under article 94 of the Charter every member of the U.N. "undertakes to comply with the decision of the International Court of Justice in any case to which it is a party." (Art. 94(1)). If a state fails to comply with the Court's judgment against it, the other party before the Court "may have recourse to the Security Council, which may, if it deems necessary, make recommendations or decide upon measures to be taken to give effect to the judgment." (Art. 94(2)). Although there have been several cases where the losing party has failed to comply with the Court's judgment, the enforcement procedure outlined in article 94 has only been invoked once. Nicaragua went to the Security Council and sought enforcement of the judgment rendered in its favor against the United States in *Military and Paramilitary Activities in and Against Nicaragua* (Nicaragua v. U.S.), 1986 I.C.J. 14 (Merits). The United States vetoed the proposed resolution which called for "immediate compliance" with the Court's judgment.

Article 95 of the Charter makes it clear that states are free to submit their disputes to any tribunal for settlement and that the International Court of Justice is simply one mechanism available for international legal dispute settlement. Article 96 vests the Court with advisory jurisdiction under which the Court is empowered to issue an advisory opinion when so requested by the General Assembly or Security Council or other duly authorized United Nations organ or agency. The Courts comprehensive web site can be found at: http://www.icj-cij.org/.

(a) The Composition of the Court

The rules governing the Court are set out in the Statute of the International Court of Justice which is an integral part of the United Nations Charter. There are fifteen judges on the International Court of Justice. Five judges are elected every three years; each judge holds office for nine years and may be re-elected. Judges are nominated by national groups and must receive an absolute majority vote in both the Security Council and the General Assembly. No country is ever permitted to have more than one judge of its nationality on the Court. Generally all the permanent members of the Security Council (China, France, Russia, United Kingdom, and United States) have a judge on the Court, and the rest of the judges are distributed throughout the various regions of the world.

The Court began sitting in 1946 and has since decided over eighty contentious cases and has issued more than twenty advisory opinions.

The disputes resolved have covered a large range of topics, such as territorial and border disputes, maritime and continental shelf delimitation, fishing rights, the use of force and intervention, diplomatic relations, hostage taking, rights of asylum, and questions of nationality.

The Court has two official languages (French and English) and is located at the Peace Palace at The Hague in the Netherlands. It generally sits as a full Court but under the Rules of the Court it may also establish a special chamber. The chamber procedure was first used in the Delimitation of the Maritime Boundary in the *Gulf of Maine Area* case (Canada v. U.S.), 1984 I.C.J. 246, and has been used in several subsequent cases. Article 38 of the Court's statute requires it to apply treaties and conventions recognized by the states appearing before the Court, international custom, the general principles of law, and, as subsidiary means, judicial decisions and the teachings of the most highly qualified publicist of the various nations. (For further information on the sources of international law, consult Chapter 2.)

(b) The Jurisdiction of the International Court of Justice in Contentious Cases

First, bear in mind that under the Court's contentious jurisdiction only states can be parties. The Court does not hear cases brought by or against individuals although a state may litigate where it claims injury as a result of violations of the international rights of its citizens. When one state brings a case against another state in the Court those cases are said to be within the Court's contentious jurisdiction. In other words the Court is asked to resolve a specific dispute between the states involved. Before a state can become a party before the International Court of Justice it must first submit to the Court's jurisdiction. This makes the Court a very different institution from most other courts. In national courts defendants or respondents cannot choose whether they wish to be subject to the Court's jurisdiction. Statutes will spell out the scope of the particular court's jurisdiction, and if a party falls under the court's jurisdiction in a case before it, it will do no good for that party to announce that it does not consent to the court's jurisdiction.

How does a state give its consent to the Court's jurisdiction? There are a number of different ways by which a state can express its consent to the Court's jurisdiction, which are explained in the Court's Statute; we shall study them in the order laid out in the Court's Statute. Article 36(1) of the Court's Statute provides:

> The jurisdiction of the Court comprises all cases which the parties refer to it and all matters specially provided for in the Charter of the United Nations or in treaties and conventions in force.

(i) "[A]ll cases which the parties refer to it (i.e., the Court) . . ."

Disputing states may decide that they would like the Court to settle the issues giving rise to the dispute. They will then draw up an agreement between them that spells out the precise nature of the dispute, stating that the states involved agree to litigate the issues before the Court for its determination. The special agreement (sometimes called by its French name of "*compromis*") gives the Court jurisdiction over the parties to the dispute and also defines the scope of the issues to be settled. The Court is not free to explore other areas touching upon the dispute. It may only decide the particular questions presented to it in the special agreement. An example of this type of agreement can be found in the special agreement entered into between the United States and Canada when both states asked the Court to settle the boundaries of the continental shelves and exclusive fishing zones between them in the Gulf of Maine; Delimitation of the Maritime Boundary in the *Gulf of Maine Area* (Canada v. U.S.), 1984 I.C.J. 246.

Example 5-1

Two neighboring states, A and B, had long had a border dispute. Every decade or so this dispute erupted into warfare, ending with death and injuries on both sides. Finally, States A and B decide they would like the I.C.J. to settle the border dispute if that is possible. Both states are members of the United Nations. You are the chief legal advisor to State A.

The President of State A asks you how State A and State B can proceed in order to place the border issues before the I.C.J. for a decision. What will you advise?

Explanation

First, you should remind the President that as members of the United Nations State A and State B are parties to the Statute of the I.C.J., U.N. Charter, art. 93(1). As such, States A and B have a right to appear before the Court provided they accept the Court's jurisdiction. Next, explain that the jurisdiction of the Court "comprises all cases which the parties refer to it. . . ." Statute of the I.C.J., art. 36(1). Explain that this means that State A and State B can draw up an agreement stating that they submit to the Court's jurisdiction for the purposes of determining the correct line of the border running between State A and State B. That agreement should then be submitted to the Court. The Court will then schedule the dispute for argument and will set a time schedule for the filing of briefs. You will probably also suggest some well-known international lawyers, who may or may not be nationals of your state, that the President may wish to ask to argue the case on behalf of State A. (No doubt you will also suggest your own name.) If you would like to see the language of an agreement between two states asking the Court to resolve their border dispute go to the Court's web site at: http://www.icj-cij.org/; click on the language you wish to read (English); click on "Cases" in the left-hand column; click on "Contentious Cases"; click on "See by State party to a case" (the States are listed alphabetically); scroll down to "Burkina Faso"; there you will find one case, *Frontier Dispute* (Burkina Faso v. Mali), 1986 I.C.J. 554; click on "More"; click on "Judgments"; click on the PDF sign below "Judgment of 22 December 1986." The case will come up with French and English pages appearing alternately. You will find the agreement at paragraph 2 of the Court's opinion. Note: the State now called Burkina Faso was named Upper Volta until 1984. As the agreement was drawn up in 1983, the State is called Upper Volta in the agreement, see paragraph 4 of the opinion.

(ii) "[A]ll matters specially provided for in the Charter of the United Nations . . ."

In fact there are no matters specially referred to in the Charter which confer jurisdiction on the Court. Why then does article 36 of the Statute refer to such "matters"? The late Professor Michael Akehurst unraveled the confusion for us:

> The explanation of this paradox is that Article 36(1) of the Statute of the Court was drafted at a time when it looked as if the Charter would provide for compulsory jurisdiction [i.e., states would be required to submit their international disputes to the Court for settlement]; the San Francisco Conference [where the U.N. Charter was drafted] subsequently rejected proposals to provide for compulsory jurisdiction in the Charter, but forgot to delete the cross-reference in the Statute.[1]

(iii) "[A]ll matters . . . in treaties and conventions in force"

A good number of treaties currently in force include a provision which states that parties to the treaty agree that, with respect to disputes arising under the treaty, any party to the treaty may bring the dispute to the Court against any other party to the treaty. For example, article IX of the Convention on the Prevention and Punishment of the Crime of Genocide, 78 U.N.T.S. 277, states:

> Disputes between the Contracting Parties relating to the interpretation, application or fulfillment of the present Convention, including those relating to the responsibility of a State for genocide or any of the other acts enumerated in

---

1. Peter Malanczuk, *Akehurst's Modern Introduction to International Law* 283 (7th rev. ed. 1997).

Article III, shall be submitted to the International Court of Justice at the request of any of the parties to the dispute.

When the Court acquires jurisdiction through the operation of a clause in a treaty it is only empowered to decide issues arising under that treaty. It is not free to decide other issues even though they may be closely related to the treaty issue.

Example 5-2

The Vienna Convention on Diplomatic Relations, 500 U.N.T.S. 95, sets out what is expected of diplomats posted abroad and what obligations the host state undertakes when it agrees to receive foreign diplomats. Among other things, the Convention provides:

> The person of a diplomatic agent shall be inviolable. He shall not be liable to any form of arrest or detention. . . . Art. 29.

There is also a separate treaty appended to the Vienna Convention to which states are free to become parties, if they wish to do so. This treaty is called the Optional Protocol Concerning the Compulsory Settlement of Disputes to the Vienna Convention on Diplomatic Relations, 500 U.N.T.S. 241. The Optional Protocol provides:

> Disputes arising out of the interpretation or application of the Convention [Vienna Convention on Diplomatic Relations] shall lie within the . . . jurisdiction of the International Court of Justice and may accordingly be brought before the Court by an application made by any party to the dispute being a Party to the present Protocol. Art. 1.

State X and State Y are both parties to the Vienna Convention on Diplomatic Relations and to the Optional Protocol. State X and State Y have sent diplomatic representatives to each other's countries for many decades. Recently, State X's ambassador to State Y was arrested for drunk driving and vehicular homicide when he slammed his car into a sidewalk and killed a pedestrian in the capital city of State Y. The ambassador was arrested but he pulled out his diplomatic passport and demanded to be released. The local police contacted State Y's Minister for Foreign Affairs for instructions. The Minister requested State X to waive the ambassador's immunity but State X refused. The local police were told to book the ambassador and keep him in jail for trial.

You are the chief legal advisor to the President of State X. The President is furious with State Y for arresting the ambassador. The President tells you he wants this handled at the international level, and he says he wants the

International Court of Justice to resolve the issue. Please advise the President about whether there is a basis for invoking the Court's jurisdiction over this dispute.

Explanation

You should explain to the President that because both State X and State Y are parties to the Vienna Convention on Diplomatic Relations, which provides for immunity for the ambassador from arrest or detention in State Y, and that the dispute is about his arrest and detention, the dispute does in fact arise under the Diplomatic Relations Convention. Next, explain that because both State X and State Y are also parties to the Optional Protocol, they have both agreed that when a dispute arises under the Diplomatic Relations Convention, any state party, which is also a state party to the Optional Protocol, can take any other state party to the Convention and the Protocol before the I.C.J. to resolve the dispute. If you would like to cite an example where the Court found that it had jurisdiction in similar circumstances, you should refer to *United States Diplomatic and Consular Staff in Tehran* (U.S. v. Iran), 1980 I.C.J. 3, paras. 45-49. (You might also point out that although the case did not involve drunk driving or vehicular homicide, the Court upheld the inviolability of the diplomatic agents. In addition, you might note that all remedies in State Y's courts must first be exhausted.)

(iv) *Compulsory Jurisdiction: Also Known as "The Optional Clause"*

Article 36, paras. 2-4, of the Court's Statute explain yet another method by which states can submit to the jurisdiction of the Court:

> 2. The parties to the present Statute may at any time declare that they recognize as compulsory *ipso facto* and without special agreement in relation to any other state accepting the same obligation, the jurisdiction of the Court in all legal disputes . . .
>
> 3. The declaration referred to above may be made unconditionally or on condition of reciprocity on the part of several or certain states, or for a certain time.
>
> 4. Such declarations shall be deposited with the Secretary-General of the United Nations, who shall transmit copies thereof to the parties to the Statute and to the Register of the Court.

This means that states can deposit a declaration with the U.N. Secretary-General that they accept the Court's jurisdiction for the settlement of international legal disputes they may have with other states that have also accepted the Court's jurisdiction. This type of jurisdiction is often called "compulsory" jurisdiction but you should note that the states are completely free to decide whether they will accept such jurisdiction; in other words, accepting such jurisdiction is *optional*.

Example 5-3

Below are two actual examples of the acceptance of compulsory jurisdiction of the Court deposited with the U.N. Secretary-General.

A.

Sweden

[Translation from the French]   6 IV 57.

On behalf of the Royal Swedish Government, I declare that it accepts as compulsory *ipso facto* and without special agreement, in relation to any other State accepting the same obligation, the jurisdiction of the International Court of Justice, in accordance with Article 36, paragraph 2, of the Statute of the said Court, for a period of five years as from 6 April 1957. This obligation shall be renewed by tacit agreement for further periods of the same duration unless notice of abrogation is made at least six months before the expiration of any such period. The above-mentioned obligation is accepted only in respect of disputes which may arise with regard to situations or facts subsequent to 6 April 1947. New York, 6 April 1957.

(Signed) Claes Carbonnier, Permanent Representative of Sweden to the United Nations.

(Sweden had previously made a declaration on April 5, 1947, which had been made for a period of ten years.)

Note that this acceptance of compulsory jurisdiction has very few limitations (also called "reservations"). Jurisdiction is accepted in relation to any other state that also accepts the Court's compulsory jurisdiction over legal disputes outlined in article 36, para. 2 of the Court's Statute, namely:

a. the interpretation of a treaty;
b. any question of international law;
c. the existence of any fact which, if established, would constitute a breach of an international obligation;
d. the nature or extent of the reparation to be made for the breach of an international obligation.

There are also two temporal conditions: (1) the dispute must arise after April 6, 1947; and (2) a five-year limitation on the acceptance but tacit renewal for similar periods unless six months notice before expiration is given indicating that Sweden will terminate its acceptance.

B.

United States of America

26 VIII 46.

I, Harry S. Truman, President of the United States of America, declare on behalf of the United States of America, under Article 36, paragraph 2, of the Statute of the International Court of Justice, and in accordance with the Resolution of 2 August 1946 of the Senate of the United States of America (two-thirds of the Senators present concurring therein), that the United States of America recognizes as compulsory *ipso facto* and without special agreement, in relation to any other State accepting the same obligation, the jurisdiction of the International Court of Justice in all legal disputes hereafter arising concerning —

(a) the interpretation of a treaty;
(b) any question of international law;
(c) the existence of any fact which, if established, would constitute a breach of an international obligation;
(d) the nature or extent of the reparation to be made for the breach of an international obligation;

Provided, that this declaration shall not apply to —

(a) disputes the solution of which the parties shall entrust to other tribunals by virtue of agreements already in existence or which may be concluded in the future; or
(b) disputes with regard to matters which are essentially within the domestic jurisdiction of the United States of America as determined by the United States of America; or
(c) disputes arising under a multilateral treaty, unless (1) all parties to the treaty affected by the decision are also parties to the case before the Court, or (2) the United States of America specifically agrees to jurisdiction; and

Provided further, that this declaration shall remain in force for a period of five years and thereafter until the expiration of six months after notice may be given to terminate this declaration.

(*Signed*) Harry S. Truman

Done at Washington this fourteenth day of August 1946.

Note

On April 6, 1984, the United States attempted a partial withdrawal from the Court's compulsory jurisdiction. On October 7, 1985, in the wake of the International Court of Justice's decision in the *Military and Paramilitary Activities* in and Against Nicaragua (Nicaragua v. U.S.), 1986 I.C.J. 14 (Merits), President Ronald Regan terminated the United States acceptance of compulsory jurisdiction to be effective six months later.

Note also that the first part of the U.S. acceptance as well as the temporal limitation is very like Sweden's acceptance, but that the clauses prefaced by "Provided that this declaration shall not apply to _____" raise different issues. Paragraph (a) is not problematic as U.N. Charter, article 95, allows U.N. members to entrust their disputes to other tribunals. Paragraph (c) seems straightforward, but the Court found a way around this limitation in the Nicaragua case supra, which will be discussed later.

Article 36, para. 6, of the Court's Statute states:

> In the event of a dispute as to whether the Court has jurisdiction, the matter shall be settled by the decision of the Court.

The U.N. Charter's article 2, para. 7, also states:

> Nothing contained in the present Charter shall authorize the United Nations to intervene in matters that are essentially within the domestic jurisdiction of any State or shall require the Members to submit such matters to settlement under the present Charter; . . .

You are Sweden's chief legal advisor. Assume that the U.S. has just reaccepted the Court's compulsory jurisdiction in the same terms as President Truman's acceptance. You have just read this new acceptance. Does paragraph (b) of the U.S. limitations on its acceptance of the Court's compulsory jurisdiction raise any legal problems?

Explanation

On a first reading of the U.S. paragraph (b), you might think that it simply mirrored the U.N. Charter, article 2, para. 7. On a closer reading, however, you would notice that the last phrase of paragraph (b) states: "as determined by the United States of America; . . ." In other words, it will be for the U.S. to determine whether an issue falls within the domestic jurisdiction of the U.S. or whether it fits within the Court's jurisdiction as an international legal dispute. Such a limitation would appear to run counter to the Court's Statute which indicates that it is the Court that will determine whether it has jurisdiction in the event that jurisdiction is disputed. The question then becomes whether a state that purports to accept the Court's compulsory jurisdiction can do so in a manner that contravenes one of the Court's own rules. If you think of other rules that govern the Court such as the number of judges (15), or that decisions do not have to be unanimous, and you ask yourself whether a state could stipulate that only nine judges could sit in judgment or that the decision must be unanimous, you will immediately see that such limitations would be impossible, indeed illegal. There is yet another more systemic problem: in a way the U.S. is purporting to accept the Court's compulsory jurisdiction but always giving itself a way to wiggle out of jurisdiction. It is as if the U.S. is saying: "We accept the Court's compulsory jurisdiction unless we let the Court know, in any particular case, that we do not accept the Court's jurisdiction (because we think it lies within the domestic jurisdiction of the U.S.)." When you think of the U.S. acceptance in this way, you will see that, in many ways, it is not really an acceptance of the Court's jurisdiction at all. Ask yourself, exactly when is the U.S. bound to accept the Court's decision that it has jurisdiction over the U.S.? Although the Court has never ruled on the merits of such an acceptance (and a number of other states have similar limiting clauses) Judge Lauterpacht wrote a separate opinion in the case of *Certain Norwegian Loans* (France v. Norway), 1957 I.C.J. 9, in which France had a similar limitation on its acceptance of the Court's jurisdiction. He noted that such a limitation was: "contrary to the Statute of the Court;" *id.* at 44, and he stated that: "An instrument in which a party is entitled to determine the existence of its obligation is not a valid and enforceable legal instrument of which a court of law can take cognizance. It is not a legal instrument." *Id.* at 48.

The limitation that we have examined in the U.S. acceptance of jurisdiction also appears in similar form in the French acceptance. The French limitation, or reservation stated: "This declaration does not apply to differences relating to matters which are essentially within the national jurisdiction as understood by the Government of the French Republic." These types of clauses are often called "self-judging, domestic affairs reservations." Another problem has arisen with such clauses. The next Example will test whether you can figure out what this problem might be.

Example 5-4

France had accepted the Court's jurisdiction in the terms indicated above, namely with a self-judging, domestic affairs reservation. France wished to sue Norway on behalf of French holders of Norwegian bonds. Norway had accepted the Court's compulsory jurisdiction without a self-judging, domestic affairs reservation. States only accept the Court's jurisdiction under such declarations "in relation to any other state accepting the same obligation." That clause ensures that states that *have not accepted* the Court's compulsory jurisdiction cannot use such a declaration to sue states that *have accepted* the compulsory jurisdiction. A state that has not accepted the Court's compulsory jurisdiction is not a "state accepting the same obligation" in relation to a state that has accepted the Court's compulsory jurisdiction.

Think about how this notion of reciprocity should work when one state accepts the Court's jurisdiction with certain limitations or reservations, but the other state accepts the Court's jurisdiction without limitations.

France files suit against Norway. You represent Norway in the International Court of Justice. How will you argue that the Court does not have jurisdiction even though both states have accepted the Court's compulsory jurisdiction?

Explanation

You might argue that Norway has only accepted the Court's jurisdiction "in relation to any other State accepting the same obligation" (Statute of the I.C.J., art. 36, para. 2) and that because France has a self-judging, domestic affairs reservation, and Norway does not, then France is not a "State accepting the same obligation" and thus the Court has no jurisdiction over Norway. This may well seem a plausible argument but the Court has not taken that route. In general, it has allowed states to deposit acceptances of compulsory jurisdiction with all sorts of reservations. If you read the I.C.J. Statute, article 36, para. 3, it states: "The declarations referred to above [declarations accepting the Court's compulsory jurisdiction] may be made unconditionally or on condition of reciprocity on the part of several or certain states, or for a certain time." You might well think that was intended to put severe limitations on the types of reservations that would be acceptable. Indeed, this may well be what was intended by the Statute but the Court has allowed many types of reservations to operate as a limit on the Court's compulsory jurisdiction, perhaps because only about one-third of the U.N. members have accepted the Court's compulsory jurisdiction, and many of those states have fairly broad reservations. When a case is filed in the Court using compulsory jurisdiction and the parties have differing types of reservations, the Court has decided that it has jurisdiction "only to the extent to which the Declarations coincide in conferring it." *Certain Norwegian Loans supra*, at 23. Norway went before the Court and argued that the legality of the treatment of the French holders of Norwegian bonds was a matter which was "essentially within the national jurisdiction [of Norway] as understood by" the Norwegian government, despite the fact that Norway had no self-judging domestic affairs reservation in its acceptance of the Court's compulsory jurisdiction. The Court ruled that it lacked jurisdiction because:

> France has limited her acceptance of the compulsory jurisdiction of the Court by excluding beforehand disputes "relating to matters which are essentially within the national jurisdiction as understood by the Government of the French Republic." In accordance with the condition of reciprocity to which

acceptance of the compulsory jurisdiction is made subject in both Declarations and which is provided for in Article 36, paragraph 3, of the Statute, Norway, equally with France, is entitled to except from the compulsory jurisdiction of the Court disputes understood by Norway to be essentially within its national jurisdiction. . . . *Id.* at 24.

The Court did not address the question of whether such self-judging reservations were compatible with the Court's statute because the "validity of the reservation ha[d] not been questioned by the Parties." *Id.* at 27.

The practical lesson to be learned from the outcome of this case is that any of the reservations put into a state's acceptance of the Court's compulsory jurisdiction can also be used by an opposing party. Self-judging clauses in an applicant's acceptance can, therefore, always be used by an opposing party. Self-judging clauses in an applicant's acceptance of the Court's jurisdiction can, therefore, always be used by respondents to defeat the Court's jurisdiction.

Judge Lauterpacht, in his separate opinion, considered self-judging clauses to be invalid, as noted above. He then considered whether the invalid reservation could be severed from the rest of the French acceptance of jurisdiction so that the acceptance of compulsory jurisdiction would remain without the domestic self-judging clause. He came to the conclusion that the clause could not be severed from the rest of the acceptance because the self-judging clause was "an essential and deliberate condition of the Acceptance." *Id.* at 55. The Vienna Convention on the Law of Treaties, 1155 U.N.T.S. 331, art. 44, also addresses the issue of severing clauses from treaties. In treaty law the term used is "separability."

Example 5-5

State N had accepted the Court's compulsory jurisdiction without any temporal limitation. State A had accepted the Court's compulsory jurisdiction but had indicated that it reserved the right to terminate its acceptance of jurisdiction upon the giving of six months notice. It was rumored that State N was about to file suit in the Court against State A arguing, among other things, that State A had violated the U.N. Charter by laying mines and damaging ships, ports, oil facilities, and a naval base in State N. State A decided that it did not wish to be sued by State N in the International Court of Justice on such charges. State A therefore sent in a notice to the Court indicating that it was terminating its acceptance of the Court's compulsory jurisdiction immediately. Three days later State N filed suit against State A for various violations of international law.

Will State A's termination be effective immediately so that it will not have to answer State N's complaint?

Explanation

No, State A's attempt at immediate termination of its acceptance of the Court's compulsory jurisdiction will not be effective. Why not? At first glance, you will remember that State A has a six month notice of termination provision in its acceptance of the Court's jurisdiction. Can you think how State A could construct an argument that it was not bound by such a reservation? Think about reciprocity. Could State A argue that because State N had no notice of termination provision in its acceptance of the Court's jurisdiction, that must mean that State N could terminate its acceptance at any time, even immediately? If State N could terminate its acceptance immediately, then, on the basis of reciprocity and the notion that the Court only has jurisdiction to the extent that the acceptances of jurisdiction coincide (case of *Norwegian Loans supra*), then State A should also be able to terminate its acceptance immediately. Well, it's an interesting argument, but it will fail for a number of reasons: (1) The premise is incorrect: A state that has no termination provision in its acceptance of the Court's jurisdiction *cannot* terminate its acceptance immediately. Without a reservation to be able to terminate immediately, the normal rules of treaty renunciation come into play. Except for human rights treaties, treaties without a termination provision can usually be terminated by a state party if the right to terminate can be implied from the treaty but only upon the giving of reasonable notice. (The Vienna Convention on the Law of Treaties, 1155 U.N.T.S. 331, art. 56, now requires twelve months' notice.) Here State N filed suit three days after State A's attempted withdrawal from the Court's jurisdiction. However long "reasonable notice" is, it is longer than three days. (2) Before State N filed its suit, there was nothing against which State A could claim reciprocity. Thus when State A attempted its immediate withdrawal, there was no other state against which it could claim reciprocity. (3) Does reciprocity work for what might be thought of as the "procedural" niceties of filing an acceptance of jurisdiction, including termination language? The Court has ruled that reciprocity does not work for such conditions, although it has not explained why not, or where the line is between substantive and procedural conditions of the acceptance of jurisdiction. To see the full force of this Example, read *Military and Paramilitary Activities in and Against Nicaragua* (Nicaragua v. U.S.), 1984 I.C.J. 392 (Jurisdiction and Admissibility).

Currently sixty-six of the member states of the United Nations have accepted the compulsory jurisdiction of the Court, and many of those states have appended reservations (or exceptions) to their acceptances. Many hundreds of states are parties to specific treaties with clauses granting the Court jurisdiction to resolve disputes between parties that arise under the particular treaty. Nonetheless, many states are reluctant to accept the Court's jurisdiction. Why is this so? A variety of reasons are given by various states.

Some states are reluctant to submit to the authority of any outside body. Somehow they regard compliance with judicial decisions rendered by non-national bodies as diminishing their own sovereignty or their own control over the dispute. Some states contend that the decisions of the Court are unpredictable. It may indeed be difficult to predict the outcome in cases where the facts are in dispute or where the issues raised are on the cutting edge of the law but that is always true in all law cases. Developing states may fear that the law applied has largely been made by the developed states, and they may not agree with some of the customary rules. All of these fears have elements of validity in them but the main argument in favor of using the Court to settle disputes (or indeed any other method designed to settle disputes peacefully) is that the alternatives often involve the use of force with its inevitable trail of calamities. In an address at Delhi University in 1959, U.S. President Dwight Eisenhower made the point succinctly. He said: "It is better to lose a point now and then in an international tribunal and gain a world in which everyone lives at peace under the rule of law."

(v) *Jurisdiction* Forum Prorogatum

The Court also has jurisdiction over states if they consent to the Court's jurisdiction by specifically indicating their consent or engaging in conduct from which their consent may be deduced. The principle that a court has jurisdiction if the parties consent to its jurisdiction is known as the doctrine of *forum prorogatum* (having asked the court). For example, a state's consent may be expressed in a letter to the Court or implied from the fact that a state has argued the case on the merits without objecting to the Court's jurisdiction. See *Questions of Mutual Assistance in Criminal Matters* (Djibouti v. France), 2008 I.C.J. 177, paras. 60-94.

(c) The Jurisdiction of the International Court of Justice in Advisory Cases

The Court can also issue opinions when requested to do so by the General Assembly, the Security Council, or specialized agencies of the United Nations when authorized to request an opinion by the General Assembly. These opinions fall within the court's *advisory* jurisdiction (U.N. Charter, article 96).

Since 1946 the Court has issued over twenty advisory opinions on topics ranging from the legality of the threat or use of nuclear weapons to the territorial status of South West Africa (Namibia). Although advisory opinions are not binding in the same way that contentious cases are binding on the parties before the Court, there is no doubt that the body of advisory opinions have been influential not only within the United Nations but also in the development of international law generally.

(d) The Power of the International Court of Justice to Issue Interim Measures of Protection

Under article 41 of the Court's Statute it is given the power "to indicate, if it considers that circumstances so require, any provisional measures which ought to be taken to preserve the respective rights of either party." (Art. 41, para. 1). This mechanism allows the parties to request a fairly rapid decision aimed at preventing irreparable harm to a party that might occur if that party had to wait until the Court had deliberated and decided first, whether it had jurisdiction over the case, and then, if so, how it would rule on the merits. In interim measures proceedings, the Court first makes what it calls a "*prima facie*" (first look) decision that there appears to be a basis for the Court's jurisdiction. The Court has stated that it will only issue interim measures of protection if there is an urgency and that failure to issue the orders would result in irreparable prejudice to the rights of one of the parties to the dispute. For example, in *LaGrand* (Germany v. U.S.), 2001 I.C.J. 466, Walter LaGrand was about to be executed in the United States, so Germany requested, and was granted, interim measures of protection. Before the hearings on jurisdiction or the merits began the Court ordered that: "The United States should take all measures at its disposal to ensure that Walter LaGrand is not executed pending the final decision in these proceedings . . ." In *LaGrand*, the Court also ruled that interim measures of protection were legally binding. 2001 I.C.J. 466 at paras. 98ff.

§5.3.3 Examples of Other Major International Civil Courts and Tribunals

(For international criminal courts and country-specific hybrid — national/international — courts, see Chapter 11.)

(a) The International Tribunal for the Law of the Sea

The International Tribunal for the Law of the Sea was created by the United Nations Convention on the Law of the Sea, 1833 U.N.T.S. 3, Annex VI. It is located in Hamburg, Germany and began sitting in 1996. The Convention requires state parties to settle their maritime disputes peacefully by means of their own choosing. If the parties cannot settle a dispute themselves, then the Convention requires them to resort to compulsory dispute settlement by opting to use one of four means of dispute settlement, namely, the International Court of Justice; the International Tribunal for the Law of the Sea; an arbitral tribunal constituted under Annex VII to the Convention; or a special arbitral tribunal constituted under Annex VIII to the Convention. The Law of the Sea Tribunal has twenty-one judges elected by the member states with a system in place to ensure an equitable geographic balance. No state may have more than one judge on the Tribunal. Judges are elected for nine years and may be re-elected. The jurisdiction of the Tribunal consists of:

> all disputes and all applications submitted to it [the Tribunal] in accordance with this Convention and all matters specifically provided for in any other agreement which confers jurisdiction on the Tribunal. Convention, Annex VI, art. 21.

The Tribunal applies the Law of the Sea "Convention and other rules of international law not incompatible with this Convention." Convention, art. 293. It has created specialized chambers in accordance with its Statute. You can read its judgments and other proceedings on the Tribunal's web site: http://www.itlos.org/. (For further information on the Law of the Sea, see Chapter 12.)

(b) The Iran-United States Claims Tribunal

This Tribunal was created as part of the settlement agreement between Iran and the United States after the detention of fifty-two U.S. diplomats and citizens in the U.S. Embassy in Tehran in 1979, which was followed by the freezing of Iranian assets by the U.S. In return for Iran's agreement to release the detainees, both parties agreed that legal proceedings in U.S. courts against Iran and Iranian claims against the U.S. arising from the dispute should be exclusively settled by the Claims Tribunal. Algiers Accords of 1981, 20 I.L.M. 223ff (1981). The Tribunal is located at The Hague in the Netherlands and began sitting in 1981. There are nine Arbitral Members of the Tribunal. Almost 4,000 claims have been filed with the Tribunal, which sits either as a three-member chamber or with the full complement of arbitrators. The extensive database can be searched on the Tribunal's web site: http://www.iusct.com/.

(c) World Trade Organization: Dispute Settlement Body

The World Trade Organization (WTO), which supervises and seeks to liberalize international trade, was established in 1995 developing out of, and expanding, the earlier General Agreement on Tariffs and Trade (GATT). The WTO regulates trade between member countries, presently numbering over 150. There is a mandatory dispute settlement mechanism. Where one state concludes that another state is violating WTO trade agreements, that state must use the dispute settlement mechanism rather than taking unilateral action. Although member states are encouraged to settle their own trade disputes, if such disputes cannot be settled, then they can be brought before a panel of the Dispute Settlement Body (DSB). The decisions of the DSB are binding on the parties to the dispute. Having a binding dispute settlement mechanism within the WTO is regarded by many as a unique contribution to world trade stability. Most disputes between member states are settled before they reach a DSB panel; nonetheless, the panels and the appellate body have seen an ever-growing number of case. You can search these cases at http://www.wto.org/english/tratop_e/dispu_e/dispu_e.htm.

§5.3.4 Regional Courts

(a) Europe

The European Union (EU), which was created by a series of treaties, is a political and economic partnership currently consisting of twenty-seven member states. Europe has two main regional courts: the Court of Justice, located in Luxembourg City, Luxembourg, which was created by the EU and the European Court of Human Rights, located in Strasbourg, France. The Human Rights Court was created by the European Council, which actually has a broader membership than the European Union. For example, Russia and Turkey are members of the European Council but are not members of the EU. (For more information on the European Court of Human Rights, see Chapter 9.) The Court of Justice of the European Communities was established in 1952. Its tasks have expanded as the European Community, now called the European Union, has enlarged the scope of its authority and the number of member states. Each member state has a judge on the Court which usually sits in smaller chambers. The Court ensures that European legislation is interpreted and enforced uniformly throughout the Union, and it has the power to settle disputes between member states, institutions, corporations, and individuals. The Court's extensive work can be viewed on its web site: http://curia.europa.eu/jcms/.

(b) The Americas

The Organization of American States was created by a Charter signed in 1948 and entered into force in 1951. The Charter has since been amended several times. The Organization was created to establish "peace and justice . . . to strengthen collaboration, and to defend [member states'] sovereignty, . . . territorial integrity, and . . . independence." OAS Charter, art. 1. It currently consists of thirty-five member states. It has a number of political units such as the General Assembly but no court with general jurisdiction. It has two entities that protect human rights: the Inter-American Commission on Human Rights, which sits in Washington, D.C., and the Inter-American Court of Human Rights, which sits in San José, Costa Rica. The work of these two entities is discussed in Chapter 9.

(c) Africa

The Charter of the Organization of African Unity (OAU) was established in 1963 and created the framework for a regional governmental organization within the African continent. The OAU was disbanded in 2002 and replaced by the African Union (AU), which is based in Addis Ababa, Ethiopia. The AU was established by the Constitutive Act, which was adopted in 2000 and came into force for member states in 2001. The African Charter on Human and Peoples' Rights (also known as the Banjul Charter) was adopted by the OAU in 1981 and entered into force in 1986. The African Charter protects a broad range of civil, political, economic, social, and cultural rights. Certain rights are fundamentally different from those found in the European or American Conventions.

The African Union's Constitutive Act establishes a number of operational organs of the AU, including the Peace and Security Council, which dispatched its first group of cease-fire monitors and military personnel to Sudan in 2004 following widespread attacks by the Janjaweed Militia against the civilian population.

Perhaps the most important organ of the AU concerning human rights, to date, is the African Commission on Human and Peoples' Rights. The Commission has the power to undertake educational activities, appoint Special Rapporteurs, adopt recommendations for governmental action, and can hear state versus state complaints.

In 1998 the Assembly of the OAU adopted a Protocol to the African Charter for the establishment of an African Court on Human and Peoples' Rights. The Protocol came into force on January 15, 2004, upon the deposit of the fifteenth ratification. Under the Protocol, the Commission, State parties, African Regional Organizations, certain NGOs with observer status at the AU, and (provided their country has agreed) individuals can bring suit in the Court. The Court will hear disputes concerning "the interpretation and application of the Charter, this Protocol and any other relevant Human Rights instruments ratified by the States concerned." Some judges were elected by the Executive Council in 2006 and 2008, but no cases have yet been heard. (See also Chapter 9, §9.4.3.)

(d) Arab States

The League of Arab States, informally known as the Arab League (AL), was founded in Cairo in 1945. It is a voluntary association of mainly Arabic speaking states based in Cairo, Egypt. Its purpose is to strengthen ties among members by coordinating policies and promoting common interests. The members have established a Joint Defense Council, an Economic Council, and Permanent Military Command, as well as a number of Specialized Organizations and Committees with specific areas of concern. In February of

2004, the Yemeni president proposed replacing the AL with a European Union–style Arab Union. At present there is no inter-state Arab court system. The League adopted an Arab Charter on Human Rights in 1994, which was revised in 2004 and entered into force in 2008. It reiterates many of the principles in the foundational human rights treaties, but all rights are stated to be subject to Islamic Shari'ah law (arts. 24 & 25). The Charter is to be enforced by an Arab Human Rights Committee (arts. 45-48), but there is no Arab League human rights court.

(e) Asia

Asia does not have an official regional structure and thus has no regional courts or regional human rights system, but the Shanghai Cooperation Organization (SCO) and the Eurasian Economic Community are rapidly developing the scope of their activities and the number of participating countries and might, one day, create a court system. The SCO started in 1996 as an inter-governmental organization focused on military relations between China, Kazakhstan, Kyrgyzstan, Russia, and Tajikistan. Uzbekistan was admitted in 2001. India, Iran, Mongolia, and Pakistan have observer status. Afghanistan is part of a contact group. The U.S. applied for observer status but was turned down in 2005. Originally focused on military and security issues, the SCO has rapidly evolved to tackle social development, drug crimes, terrorism, economic cooperation, transportation, movement of goods, currency and fiscal policies, food production, energy supplies, and cultural exchanges.

There is also a Eurasian Economic Community (EAEC), established by treaty in 2000 and signed by Belarus, Kazakhstan, Kyrgyzstan, Russia, and Tajikistan, which set out to deepen "Integration in the Economic and Humanitarian Spheres . . ." and promote a customs union. Uzbekistan was admitted as a member in 2005, with Armenia, Moldova, and Ukraine as observer states.

The European Union started out as a purely trade-related group. It is possible that the above organizations will eventually encompass a regional court system.

§5.4 CONCLUSION

The current era has seen a rapid expansion of the fora available for the settlement of international disputes and a growing willingness on the part of some states to use existing courts, tribunals, and other settlement mechanisms to resolve otherwise intractable areas of conflict. At the same time, the rate of the outbreak of internal and international hostilities does not appear to have diminished. The trend toward the creation of the settlement mechanisms for international disputes is likely to continue, in part because of the exponential explosion in international transactions. International settlement mechanisms have become a functional necessity for the international community. Whether these mechanisms will ultimately contribute to permanent reductions in hostilities remains to be seen.

CHAPTER 6

Jurisdiction

§6.1 Introduction
§6.2 The Territorial Principle
§6.3 The Nationality Principle
§6.4 The Passive Personality Principle
§6.5 The Protective Principle
§6.6 The Universality Principle
§6.7 Extradition
§6.8 Immunity from Jurisdiction
  §6.8.1 Diplomatic Immunity
  §6.8.2 Consular Immunity
  §6.8.3 Head of State and Other Ministers' Immunity
  §6.8.4 Immunity for International Organizations
  §6.8.5 Sovereign Immunity
     Absolute Theory
     The Restrictive Theory

§6.1 INTRODUCTION

American law students usually spend part of their first year at law school learning about civil procedure. One of the topics studied is the question of when a state (such as California or Massachusetts) within the United States may exercise jurisdiction (broadly speaking, power, either legislative or executive or judicial) over a person or entity. It is accepted that if the person or entity has no connection with a state, that state may not exercise jurisdiction over the person or entity. For example, if one resident of California killed another resident of California in Los Angeles, the State of Massachusetts could not exercise its criminal jurisdiction over the alleged murderer. But what would be the case if the victim normally lived in Massachusetts and was simply on a short vacation in Los Angeles? There is a long line of U.S. Supreme Court cases that seek to identify the *minimum level of contacts* that the persons, entities, or transactions involved must have with the forum state in order for the state to exercise jurisdiction. This body of law has grown up out of the Supreme Court's interpretation of the Due Process Clause of the Fourteenth Amendment to the United States Constitution. International law has a similar counterpart. Broadly, it addresses the question of when a nation-state has sufficient connection to or interest in a person, entity, or activity so that it may exercise its jurisdiction. Jurisdiction is divided into three categories: (a) jurisdiction to prescribe ("the authority of a state to make its law applicable to persons or activities")[1]; (b) jurisdiction to adjudicate ("to subject particular persons or things to it judicial process"); and (c) jurisdiction to enforce or execute ("to use the resources of government to induce or compel compliance with its law").

The international law relating to jurisdiction is by no means complete and has usually arisen in the criminal as opposed to the civil context. No state is obliged to exercise its jurisdiction even if international law would raise no objection to its doing so. Each state passes its own internal laws indicating in what circumstances it will exercise jurisdiction. There are five bases of jurisdiction recognized in international law. Some of the categories are more broadly accepted than others.

§6.2 THE TERRITORIAL PRINCIPLE

International law permits a state to exercise its *jurisdiction to legislate* (prescribe) with respect to:

(a) conduct that, wholly or in substantial part, takes place within its territory;
(b) the state of persons, or interests in things, present within its territory;
(c) conduct outside its territory that has or is intended to have substantial effect within its territory.[2]

---

1. The three categories of jurisdiction are those outlined in the Restatement of the Law Third, Foreign Relations Law of the United States, Introductory Note to Part IV, at 231 (1987) [hereinafter Restatement Third].
2. Restatement Third §402(1).

6. Jurisdiction

The state will also have *jurisdiction to adjudicate* under the territorial principle if the exercise of jurisdiction is "reasonable." What constitutes reasonableness is fairly vague, but again, basically takes into account how closely the person, entity, or activity is connected with the territory of the state. Again, *jurisdiction to enforce*, under the territorial principle, is limited by reasonableness measured by connection to the territory.

If you ask yourself the question: "Could the French legislature pass laws making it a crime for one Englishman to kill another Englishman in London?" You will immediately sense that the answer to this question is "No." If you ask "Why not?" the answer is that the murder has no connection with France. On the other hand, if you ask "Could the French legislature make it a crime for a Frenchman (or a citizen of any other country) to kill another Frenchman (or citizen of any other country) in Paris?" you would immediately answer "Yes." Again, if asked "Why?" you would reply that the activity took place on French soil and may have involved French citizens. Suppose the murder took place in Paris but the culprit and the victim were Spanish citizens? Then France would have legislative jurisdiction on the basis of the territorial principle and Spain would have legislative jurisdiction on the basis of the nationality principle (see *infra*). When more than one state has a basis on which to claim jurisdiction, the conflicting claims will usually be settled between the two states. In the example above doubtless the French authorities would try the culprit and if convicted, he would probably (though not definitely) be protected from subsequent prosecution by Spanish authorities, if he ever returned to Spain.

Most of the instances where a state asserts jurisdiction on the basis of the territorial principle are not particularly controversial. There is no disagreement that the state has the right to assert jurisdiction where the conduct being regulated takes place within a state (e.g., murder) or when the state regulates persons or entities within the state (e.g., people's status, such as the definition of a minor) or interests in things (e.g., a shareholder's rights in a corporation). More controversial are some of the instances where the state attempts to regulate "conduct outside its territory that has or is intended to have substantial effect within its territory."[3] No one disputes that if a person stands on the Canadian side of the U.S.-Canadian border and fires a gun at a person standing on the American side of the border, injuring or killing that person, both Canada and the United States may assert jurisdiction on the basis of the territorial principle; Canada may do so because the conduct took place substantially within the Canadian territory and the United States may do so because the conduct outside its territory was intended to have, and did have, a substantial effect within its territory. The more difficult cases involve a state's attempt to regulate the conduct of persons or entities outside its

---

3. Restatement Third §402(1).

territory where the conduct has an economic effect within the state's territory.

For example, if the U.S. passed a law stating "every contract, combination . . . or conspiracy, in restraint of trade or commerce among the several States, or with foreign nations, is declared to be illegal" (as it has done under section one of the Sherman Antitrust Act, 15 U.S.C. §1 (1890)), would that law be interpreted by U.S. courts as encompassing activities carried out by foreign companies in a foreign country? Your first reaction might well be: "Surely not," and your instinct would generally be correct as U.S. courts start with the assumption that U.S. laws do not apply outside the territory of the U.S. unless congressional intent to apply the law extraterritorially is clear. Compare *Smith v. U.S.*, 507 U.S. 197, 204-205 (1993) with *Foley Bros. v. Filardo*, 336 U.S. 281, 285 (1949). However, in *U.S. v. Aluminum Co. of America*, 148 F.2d 416 (2d Cir. 1945), in a famous decision by Judge Learned Hand, the court held that fixing prices and setting quotas for the production and sale of aluminum was prohibited by the Sherman Act, even though the agreements to limit production were made in Switzerland by a Swiss corporation (made up of one French, two German, one Swiss, one British, and one Canadian corporation) where the agreements "were intended to affect imports [into the U.S.] and did effect them." *Id.* at 444. The court acknowledged that:

> we are not to read general words . . . without regard to the limitations customarily observed by nations upon the exercise of their powers. . . . On the other hand, it is settled law . . . that any state may impose liabilities, even on persons not within its allegiance, for conduct outside its borders that has consequences within its borders which the state reprehends. . . . *Id.* at 443.

The worldwide scope of the U.S. antitrust laws has been controversial and many countries maintain that certain applications of the law go beyond what is permissible under international law. Several countries have passed laws designed to undo what they regard as the impermissible reach of the U.S. antitrust laws. E.g., U.K. Protection of Trading Interests Act of 1980, 21 I.L.M. 384 (1982); Canadian Uranium Information Security Regulations, Can. Stat. O. & R. 76-644 (P.C. 1976-2368, Sept. 21, 1976). It is significant that these laws have generally been passed by political and economic allies of the U.S.

§6.3 THE NATIONALITY PRINCIPLE

This principle permits a state to exercise jurisdiction over a person or entity on the basis of the nationality of the person or entity. For example, in the United States all male U.S. citizens are required to register under the military service laws when they reach the age of eighteen years regardless of where in the world they might be living at the time. 50 U.S.C.A. App. §453. The Foreign Corrupt Practices Act, 15 U.S.C. §78dd-1 et seq., makes various actions by U.S. corporations and citizens illegal even when the activities occur outside the U.S. Similarly the U.S. tax code makes all income of U.S. citizens taxable regardless of the location of the source of the income or the location of the citizen. Internal Revenue Code, 26 U.S.C. §1 (1986). For example, a U.S. citizen living and earning wages in the United Kingdom has an obligation to pay taxes both to the U.S. (nationality principle) and to the U.K. (territorial principle). Such double taxation obligations would obviously be burdensome, so many countries (including U.S. and the U.K.) have entered into double taxation treaties, which would be better named "anti-double taxation treaties." See, e.g., U.S.-U.K. Treaty, 31 U.S.T. 5668, T.I.A.S. No. 9682. These treaties essentially allow the treaty parties to collect taxes on the basis of the place from where the income is generated and the parties agree to forgo collecting taxes on the basis of citizenship.

Common law countries exercise jurisdiction on the basis of nationality very sparingly with few of their laws applying to a citizen while the citizen is outside the country. Civil law countries tend to use this basis of jurisdiction more frequently and a few countries make their criminal law entirely applicable to all of their citizens no matter where they were when they committed the offense. For example, if a citizen of India murdered someone in New York City, that person would certainly have violated the laws of New York; but the Indian citizen would also have violated the laws of India because India's criminal law applies to all Indian citizens wherever they may be in the world. Indian Penal Code §4 (3d ed. Raju 1965). Here again, we have an example of two nations with concurrent jurisdiction. No doubt the New York authorities would arrest and try the culprit and India would probably respect the decision and not retry the offender should s/he ever return to India. If, however, New York did not assert jurisdiction over the offense, India could certainly do so under the nationality principle. In order for India to have jurisdiction over the person alleged to have committed murder, the Indian suspect will either have to return to India or India could seek extradition from the U.S. under the U.S.-Indian extradition treaty, S. Treaty Doc. No. 105-30; 1997 WL 602447, signed June 25, 1997; entered into force July 21, 1999. Just because India has an adequate basis for legislative jurisdiction (here declaring murder outside India by an Indian citizen to be a violation of India's criminal law) that does not mean that India can assert personal jurisdiction over the suspect while he remains outside India. No state has the right to exercise its executive powers in another state except where a state permits a foreign state to operate within its borders.

Example 6-1

State A passes the following criminal law:

Any citizen of State A who travels abroad and engages in sexual relations with a person under the age of sixteen years shall be guilty of a felony and may be sentenced to up to fifteen years in jail and/or a fine of up to $100,000. It shall be no defense to this crime that the person under the age of sixteen consented to the sexual relationship or that such relationships are not illegal in the territory where the acts were committed.

Mr. X, a citizen of State A, travels to State T and engages in sexual intercourse with a fifteen year old girl in a brothel licensed by State T. Mr. X paid $100 to visit the brothel and his acts were not illegal in State T. When Mr. X returns to State A, he is arrested and tried under the law quoted above. He is convicted and sentenced to five years in jail.

Does Mr. X's criminal conviction in State A violate international law?

Explanation

No. Mr. X's criminal conviction is permissible under international law based on the Nationality Principle. States are free to criminalize their citizens' (or residents') activities even when those activities are carried on outside the State's own territory. For example, under the Prosecutorial Remedies and Other Tools to end the Exploitation of Children Today (PROTECT) Act of 2003, 117 Stat. 650, §105, 18 U.S.C. §2423, the U.S. criminalizes commercial sex with anyone under the age of eighteen and certain non-commercial sex when the person is under the age of sixteen years, even if the activity occurs outside the U.S. The Foreign Corrupt Practices Act, 15 U.S.C. §§78a, 78dd-1 et seq., criminalizes the activities of U.S. citizens and U.S. corporations if they seek to bribe foreign officials in order to gain improper business advantages even if the activities occur outside the U.S.

§6.4 THE PASSIVE PERSONALITY PRINCIPLE

This principle affirms that a state may assert jurisdiction on the basis of the nationality of the victim over certain offenses regardless of where the offense occurs or the nationality of the perpetrator. The principle has not been widely accepted but recently a number of international treaties, designed to curb various types of terrorism, have incorporated the principle.[4]

---

4. E.g., Convention on Offenses and Certain Other Acts Committed on Board Aircraft, art. 4(b), 704 U.N.T.S. 219, 20 U.S.T. 2941, T.I.A.S. No. 6768, signed September 14, 1963; entered into force December 4, 1969. See also Omnibus Diplomatic Security and Anti-terrorism Act of 1986, 18 U.S.C. §2231 (1986).

The Restatement Third §402, cmt. g states that the principle "is increasingly accepted as applied to terrorist and other organized attacks on a state's nationals by reason of their nationality, or to assassination of a state's diplomatic representative or other officials."

The principle does not apply to ordinary crimes or torts. If a German tourist in Italy is robbed or murdered in Milan, the German courts will not have jurisdiction over the crime on the basis of the passive personality principle.

Example 6-2

A Lebanese citizen called Fawaz Yunis, together with four associates, hijacked a Jordanian-registered civilian plane at the airport in Beirut, Lebanon. The pilot was forced to take off as Yunis threatened him with a gun. All of the crew and passengers were tied up. The hijackers wanted publicity for a political cause they believed in. Yunis explained to the passengers that he wanted the plane to fly to Tunis, capital of Tunisia, where he would address a meeting of the Arab League and inform the delegates about the need to remove all Palestinians from Lebanon. The plane tried to land at a number of airports, including Tunis, but could not get clearance. Eventually, the plane returned to Beirut where the passengers disembarked, severely shaken by their thirty-hour ordeal, but physically unharmed. On the plane there were 145 passengers from twenty-one different countries, including two U.S. citizens.

The U.S. had enacted the following statute as part of its criminal code: 18 U.S.C. §1203, the Hostage Taking Act:

(a) [W]hoever, whether inside or outside the United States, seizes or detains and threatens to kill, to injure, or to continue to detain another person in order to compel a third person or a governmental organization to do or to abstain from any act . . . shall be punished by imprisonment by any term of years or for life.

(b) (1) It is not an offense under this section if the conduct required for the offense occurred outside the United States unless —

(A) The offender or the person seized or detained is a national of the United States;

(B) The offender is found in the United States; or

(C) The governmental organization sought to be compelled is the Government of the United States.

Assume that Yunis turned up in France. The U.S. requested his extradition, and he was duly extradited to the U.S. Does the U.S. have an acceptable basis for the assertion of criminal jurisdiction over Yunis? If so, on what basis?

Explanation

So far you have learned about three bases of jurisdiction: (1) territorial, (2) nationality, and (3) passive personality. Run through these bases of jurisdiction to see if the requirements are met here. First, the events did not take place in the U.S. or on a U.S.-registered plane. Was the conduct outside the U.S. intended to have, or did it have, a substantial effect in the U.S.? The answer seems to be "No." You might say that the activity had a substantial effect on the two U.S. passengers and presumably on their families and friends in the U.S., but, if such effects were sufficient, it would mean that all crimes committed abroad against U.S. citizens could fall within U.S. jurisdiction on the basis of the territorial principle. This stretches the territorial principle too far.

Next, the alleged perpetrator, Yunis, is not a U.S. citizen and thus there is no basis for nationality jurisdiction.

Finally, two of the victims of the hijacking were U.S. citizens. Is the type of activity in this example sufficient to satisfy the passive personality rule? Note: When any court examines its jurisdiction, it will be looking for a statute granting it jurisdiction and the activity must fit within the statute. Does the activity fit with the Hostage Taking Act? Read the statute carefully. Section (a) seems to be satisfied: Yunis seized and detained other people and threatened to injure them in order to compel the pilot to fly the plane to Tunis. What about section (b)? The activity is outside the U.S. so normally would not be an offense under the Act unless "(A) . . . the person seized or detained is a national of the United States." Two of the passengers on the plane were U.S. citizens. Does the statute require that (B) also be satisfied, i.e., "the offender is found in the United States"? In other words, did Congress mean that there was an "and" between (A) and (B), or only an "or," as there is between (B) and (C). In any event would that section be satisfied through extradition even if Yunis was not originally found in the U.S.? Clearly section (C) is not relevant as the governmental organization sought to be compelled was not the "Government of the United States." In U.S. v. Fawaz Yunis, a/k/a Nazeeh, 924 F.2d 1086 (D.C. Cir. 1991) the court found that the statute should be read disjunctively; i.e., with an "or" not an "and" between (A) and (B) and that the requirements of the statute were met in similar, although not identical, circumstances to the Example. Defense counsel had tried to argue that the statute went beyond what was permitted under international law but the court stated that as a U.S. court it was only interested in meeting the requirements of the U.S. statute but that anyway international law would permit the assertion of jurisdiction in this case under the passive personality principle. Note: Although it is true that national courts are governed by their own statutes and Constitutions, the U.S. and many other courts also subscribe to a doctrine of statutory interpretation that was also expressed by the Yunis court: "[A]n act of congress ought never to be construed to violate the law of nations, if any other possible construction remains. . . ." *Id.* at 1091, quoting *Murray v. The Schooner Charming Betsy*, 6 U.S. (2 Cranch) 64, 118 (1804).

§6.5 THE PROTECTIVE PRINCIPLE

This principle permits a state to exercise jurisdiction over "certain conduct outside its territory by persons not its nationals that is directed against the security of the State or against a limited class of other state interests."[5] A state may well pass laws prohibiting espionage, counterfeiting, or falsifying official documents and make the legislation applicable not only to activity within the state but also to activities abroad carried out by non-nationals.[6] Nations may be tempted to define their security interests too broadly and may provoke the wrath of other nations if this principle is used excessively. Where the activities in question are clearly directed against the security of the state, its property, or citizens, the principle is less controversial.

Example 6-3

Adam, a citizen of State A and Cain, a citizen of State C, worked together to bomb the foreign embassy of State G located in State H. The bombing was successful in the sense that the entire State G embassy complex was blown up; twenty-three embassy employees were killed (all citizens of State G) and thirty-four civilian citizens of State H, who were in the vicinity of the embassy, were injured. Eventually, agents of State H captured Adam and Cain in State H. State H agreed to extradite Adam and Cain to State G under a duly ratified extradition treaty. State G put Adam and Cain on trial for conspiracy to murder State G's embassy staff and for destroying State G's embassy buildings and property. They were convicted and sentenced to life in prison.

Do the trials and convictions of Adam and Cain violate international law?

Explanation

No. The trials and convictions of Adam and Cain fall within the permissible scope of protective jurisdiction where the statutes are applied to protect the vital interests of the State such as the carrying out of foreign relations through the establishment of foreign embassies staffed by members of the State's foreign affairs ministry. See, e.g., *U.S. v. Bin Laden*, 92 F. Supp. 2d 189 (S.D.N.Y. 2000) aff'd sub nom. *U.S. v. Odeh*, 548 F.3d 276 (2d Cir.

---

5. Restatement Third §402(3).
6. See, e.g., *U.S. v. Birch*, 470 F.2d 808 (4th Cir. 1972).

2008). (Convictions of non-nationals upheld for bombing U.S. embassies in Kenya and Tanzania, including 223 counts of murder.)

§6.6 THE UNIVERSALITY PRINCIPLE

Certain activities have been considered so reprehensible by the international community that the usual rules of jurisdiction are waived and any state apprehending the alleged perpetrator is deemed competent to exercise its jurisdiction. The obligations not to engage in such activities is said to be an obligation *erga omnes*; that is, the obligation is owed to the entire international community, not just the victim or the state representing the victim and consequently, all states have the right to complain of a breach of such an obligation. There is a certain amount of agreement over core activities that trigger universal jurisdiction. Piracy, slave trade, operating a "stateless vessel," genocide, torture, crimes against humanity, and war crimes have all reached the level of being defined as "universal crimes." Other activities such as hijacking of aircraft and various forms of terrorism are not so widely accepted as conferring universal jurisdiction though such jurisdiction has often been conferred by states entering into an international treaty on the subject.[7]

You might well wonder why such a principle of jurisdiction is thought necessary or desirable. One answer to that question is that powerful rulers who commit these very serious crimes are unlikely to be tried in their own country, even if they ultimately fall from power. Other states, such as the state of the victims may be too weak or lacking in resources to go forward with requests for extradition or prosecution. Thus it may be that all of the states with more traditional bases of jurisdiction do not pursue the criminal. Universal jurisdiction expands the number of states who might assert jurisdiction to the entire community of nations but that very fact also brings with it a variety of other problems.

Although the principle of universal jurisdiction has been widely accepted in theory, very few states have enacted statutes that permit the assertion of such jurisdiction in its pure form, that is, when there is no connection at all to the forum state. Even when an activity might well permit universal jurisdiction, such as genocide, most often national statutes require some form of connection to the prosecuting state. The U.S. statute on genocide, for example, limits prosecution to when the offense occurs in the U.S. or when the genocidal action is committed by a U.S. citizen. 18 U.S.C.

---

7. E.g., The Hague Convention on the Suppression of Unlawful Seizure of Aircraft, 860 U.N.T.S. 105, 22 U.S.T. 1641, T.I.A.S. No. 7192, reprinted at 10 I.L.M. 133 (1971), entered into force October 14, 1971; International Convention Against the Taking of Hostages, 1316 U.N.T.S. 205, T.I.A.S. No. 11081, reprinted at 18 I.L.M. 1456 (1979), entered into force June 3, 1983.

§1091(d) (2000). Note also the statutes cited in *Arrest Warrant of 11 April 2000* (D.R. Congo v. Belgium), 2002 I.C.J. 3 at paras. 20-21 (Joint Separate Opinion of Judges Higgins, Kooijmans, and Buergenthal).

Belgium enacted a statute in 1993 prohibiting various war crimes that are violations of the four Geneva Conventions of 1949 and their two Additional Protocols even if the violations were committed outside Belgium and were carried out by non-Belgians against non-Belgians.[8] Criminal complaints under this statute could be filed by non-Belgians as well as Belgian citizens. A number of complaints were filed against internationally known people such as Augusto Pinochet, President of Chile; Fidel Castro, President of Cuba; Ariel Sharon, Prime Minister of Israel; George H.W. Bush and George W. Bush, both U.S. Presidents, and Tony Blair, U.K. Prime Minister. As you can imagine, these indictments caused a furor. Eventually Belgium scaled back on the scope of its jurisdiction, so that now complaints can only be filed by Belgian citizens or residents or where the victim is a Belgian citizen or resident. All of the indictments lacking connection with Belgium were ultimately dismissed.

Example 6-4

Two neighboring states Rutland and Shropland fought a bloody war in 2008. Rutland's military, under command of President Rugo, invaded Shropland without provocation. Cities were burned wholesale, thousands of women were raped, children were slaughtered. All of these actions are serious war crimes. Rutland took over Shropland including its valuable natural resources. After three years, Shropland's government-in-exile persuaded the United Nations Security Council to authorize a coalition force to drive Rutland out of Shropland. The coalition force was formed in January of 2009 and within three months Rutland's military and civilian occupiers had been driven out of Shropland. In the summer of 2009, elections were held in Rutland and President Rugo was voted out of office. The new administration decided it would be too disruptive to prosecute former President Rugo and the newly installed government in Shropland decided that rebuilding the country's institutions, restoring infrastructure, and strengthening international relations were far more important than seeking Rugo's extradition from Rutland.

Rutland has seventy-five bilateral extradition treaties with other countries, including the State of Teeland. Teeland is situated 5,000 miles from Rutland. Several other countries and an ocean lie between Teeland and Rutland. Teeland had enacted a statute permitting prosecution in Teeland for war crimes "when committed by a national of Teeland or of any other State regardless of where the crimes occur." No citizens of Teeland were victims of the Rutland/Shropland war. Teeland asks Rutland for Rugo's extradition.

---

8. Law of June 16, 1993, Moniteur Belge 17751 (Aug. 5, 1993), reprinted 28 Rev. Belge de Droit Int'l 668, 680 (1995).

Assume that the requirements for extradition from Rutland to Teeland under the extradition treaty are satisfied and that former President Rugo is not entitled to immunity. Does Teeland have an adequate basis for the assertion of jurisdiction over war crimes committed by a non-national, outside its territory, against non-nationals?

Explanation

Teeland can assert jurisdiction over war crimes on the basis of universal jurisdiction. If Rugo is extradited to Teeland, then prosecution can proceed. It is generally agreed that grave crimes, as defined by the Geneva Conventions, including the crimes alleged here, are sufficient to satisfy universal jurisdiction. Israel asserted jurisdiction over Adolf Eichmann, one of the main architects of the attempt to exterminate Jews and other minorities during World War II, despite the fact that the crimes had not been committed within the boundaries of what later became Israel, Eichmann was a German citizen, not an Israeli, and despite the fact that none of the victims was an Israeli. (In fact, the State of Israel was not established until 1948, which raised other issues related to retroactive application of the law.) The Israeli courts upheld Eichmann's conviction asserting various possible bases of jurisdiction, including universal jurisdiction. *Attorney General of the Government of Israel v. Eichmann*, S. Ct. Isr. (May 29, 1962); 16 Piske Din 2033 (1962).

In the joint separate opinion of Judges Higgins, Kooijmans, and Buergenthal in *Arrest Warrant of 11 April 2000 supra*, the judges surveyed universal jurisdiction based on national statutes, national case law, treaties, and scholarly writings. *Id.* at paras. 19-52. They concluded that:

> There are . . . certain indications that a universal jurisdiction for certain international crimes is clearly not regarded as unlawful. The duty to prosecute under those treaties which contain the *aut dedere aut prosequi* provisions [the obligation either to hand over the alleged perpetrator for prosecution or to proceed to prosecute] opens the door to a jurisdiction based on the heinous nature of the crime rather than on links of territoriality or nationality (whether as perpetrator or victim). The 1949 Geneva Conventions lend support to this possibility and are widely regarded as today reflecting customary international law. *Id.* at para. 46.

§6.7 EXTRADITION

If someone commits a crime in State A and flees to State B, State A may request extradition of the offender. Extradition is the process by which one state hands over an alleged offender to another state. Some states engage in this practice on an informal, reciprocal basis but most states spell out their respective duties in bilateral or multilateral extradition treaties. These treaties either list the offenses for which extradition is required (usually more serious offenses) or state that if both states criminalize similar conduct, extradition is required, provided the minimum sentence imposed is at least a specified minimum number of years. Most treaties allow each state to refuse to extradite their own nationals. Common law countries are usually prepared to extradite their own nationals but civil law countries often have specific statutes forbidding the extradition of nationals. If a state refuses extradition of a national, the extradition treaty usually imposes an obligation on that state to try the offender. You may wonder how a state can try someone who committed an offense in another state but you should bear in mind that civil law countries exercise jurisdiction on the basis of nationality much more frequently than common law countries.

There have been a number of cases where a serious offender has fled from the place of the crime and extradition has been requested but refused. If the case is considered serious enough the state may seek other means to bring the offender back for trial. The *Eichmann* case *supra*, is a famous example of the forcible abduction of an offender. Israeli agents captured Eichmann in Argentina and flew him to Israel. Argentina originally filed a complaint with the United Nations Security Council claiming a violation of her sovereignty but the claim was dropped when Israel and Argentina mutually agreed to declare the incident closed.

When there has been a forcible abduction of a fugitive, the defendant will usually argue that his/her illegal abduction defeats the court's jurisdiction. Courts are often hostile to such arguments. They hold that the defendant cannot raise such a defense either because the defendant does not have rights arising under the treaty generally, or that although the abduction may have violated the sovereignty rights of the fugitive's country of residence, those rights do not run to the fugitive. (*Eichmann supra* at para. 13.) The U.S. Supreme Court has ruled that such abduction does not violate the provisions of the extradition treaty where the treaty did not specifically state that abduction would violate the treaty (*U.S. v. Alvarez-Machain*, 504 U.S. 655 (1992)). That case provoked a vigorous dissent that argues that abduction violates the whole idea of extradition and should result in the court's not having jurisdiction over the defendant. Some countries have now concluded that where there is an extradition treaty, failure to follow the requirements of the treaty defeats the court's jurisdiction, *Regina v. Horseferry Road Magistrate's Court, ex parte Bennett*, 95 I.L.R. 380 (1993) (U.K.); *Regina v. Hartely*, 77 I.L.R. 330 (1978) (New Zealand).

§6.8 IMMUNITY FROM JURISDICTION

Over the course of centuries, states have decided to accord certain representatives of foreign states differing levels of immunity from jurisdiction when those foreign state representatives visit other states. These practices have sometimes resulted in treaties that detail which persons or entities are entitled to immunity and how broad that immunity is.

§6.8.1 Diplomatic Immunity

There is a long history of one state granting immunity to accredited diplomats from another state. There is no obligation on the part of any state to engage in relations of any sort with other nations but, if a state does enter into diplomatic relations with another state and receives an accredited diplomat, international law clearly requires almost total immunity from civil and criminal jurisdiction for the diplomat. If the host state disapproves of the diplomat's activities or otherwise wishes to break relations with the diplomat's state, the host state's only remedy is to ask the diplomat to leave and to give him/her a reasonable amount of time to get out of the country. The Vienna Convention on Diplomatic Relations (VCDR)[9] has been ratified by a great number of countries and many of its provisions are declaratory of customary law. The Convention provides differing levels of immunity for the diplomat, his or her family, the administrative and technical staff, the service staff, and private servants. The main idea behind the Convention was that diplomats needed immunity in order to carry out their functions freely and without fear of reprisal.

From time to time relations between states may become strained and, without immunity, it would be far too easy for the host state to seize the diplomats on some trumped up charges and use them as bargaining chips in any ensuing negotiations. You may well wonder what happens if in fact a diplomat does break the criminal law of the host country. Suppose the diplomat is suspected of murdering someone. First, the Vienna Convention puts a positive obligation on diplomats to observe the laws of the host state (art. 41(1)) but it is clear that immunity from arrest and criminal prosecution attaches to the diplomat even for the most heinous of crimes (arts. 29 & 31). The host state may at any time declare any diplomat a *persona non grata*, in which case the sending state must either recall the person or terminate his/her functions within the mission (art. 9). Even if the person is no longer regarded as a diplomat by either the sending or receiving state, immunity still attaches to those official activities carried out while the person was a diplomat (art. 39(2)).

The persons accredited as diplomatic agents are declared "inviolable" and the host state is obligated to treat the diplomat with "due respect and . . . take all appropriate steps to prevent any attack on his person, freedom, or dignity" (art. 29). The premises of the diplomatic mission are declared inviolable

---

9. 500 U.N.T.S. 95, 23 U.S.T. 3227, T.I.A.S. No. 7502, signed April 19, 1961; entered into force April 24, 1964.

under the Convention (art. 22(1)) and the host state has an obligation to protect the premises "against any intrusion or damage and to prevent any disturbance of the peace of the mission or impairment of its dignity" (art. 22(2)). The mission's official correspondence is also declared inviolable (art. 27(2), and the diplomatic bag "shall not be opened or detained" (art. 27(3)).

You may wonder why a state would grant diplomats total immunity from criminal jurisdiction and almost total immunity from its civil jurisdiction. The answer lies in examining how the host state would like its own diplomats treated when they are abroad and by bearing in mind that although there have been some celebrated accusations of criminal activity on the part of diplomats, these are few and far between. For example, a member of the Libyan diplomatic mission in London, U.K., shot and killed a British policewoman in 1984. The entire Libyan diplomatic contingent was given two weeks to leave the country and Britain broke off all diplomatic relations with Libya until 1999 when Libya accepted responsibility for the policewoman's death and offered her family compensation. Occasionally there have been suggestions that the scope of immunity should be narrowed but so far these suggestions have not met with success.

Another case involved a member of the diplomatic mission from the Republic of Georgia who was initially arrested in 1997 for drunk driving when he crashed his car in Washington, D.C., killing one woman and injuring several other people. When the police realized that he was a diplomat he was released but the U.S. government asked the Republic of Georgia to waive the diplomat's immunity (VCDR, art. 32(1)). (Note: It is only the diplomat's state that has the power to insist on immunity or waive immunity, not the diplomat.) Initially, Georgia refused to waive the diplomat's immunity, but after negotiations, agreed to the waiver. The diplomat was prosecuted for involuntary manslaughter and aggravated assault. He was convicted and sentenced to jail. See report of the case in a related civil proceeding, *Knab v. Republic of Georgia*, No. 97-CV-03118 (TFH), 1998 U.S. Dist. Lexis 8820 (D.D.C. May 29, 1998) (mem).

There are also some notorious examples of a host state failing to live up to its obligations under the VCDR. During 1979 the Shah of Iran was deposed. The Shah's family had to flee the country and the United States agreed to admit the Shah, ostensibly for medical treatment. This action provoked protests in Iran specifically at the U.S. embassy in Tehran and at some U.S. consulates in other Iranian cities. On November 4, 1979, a crowd of students and protesters took over the U.S. embassy in Tehran. The Iranian security forces offered no assistance in curbing the demonstration or in restoring the embassy to the Americans once it had been taken by force. The embassy staff and two private American citizens who were visiting the embassy were seized by the protesters. After some negotiations the women and black hostages were released, leaving fifty remaining diplomatic and consular staff and two private citizens still in custody.

The embassy premises, archives and documents were ransacked. The United States applied to the International Court of Justice for interim measures of protection asking for the return of the embassy, the release of the hostages and safe passage out of the country for all personnel being held. The Court promptly granted all of the U.S. requests. (Order of Provisional Measures, 15 December, 1979 I.C.J. 7.) Iran refused to comply with the order. (While the Court was considering the case on the merits, U.S. military forces entered Iran and attempted to rescue the hostages. The attempt was unsuccessful and eight U.S. military personnel were killed in a collision between two U.S. aircraft.) The U.S. claim for relief was based on a number of treaties to which both the U.S. and Iran were parties, including the VCDR and the Vienna Convention on Consular Relations (VCCR).[10]

The Court ruled in favor of the U.S. holding that the State of Iran had violated its obligations under the treaties by failing to subdue the students, release the hostages, and restore the embassy and consulates to the U.S. when it clearly could have done so. Iran was also held responsible for the students' actions because it engaged in various forms of activities that endorsed those actions. *U.S. Diplomatic and Consular Staff in Tehran* (U.S. v. Iran), 1980 I.C.J. 3. The Court made it clear that although Iran might accuse the U.S. of a variety of violations of international law against Iran, the VCDR and the VCCR make it clear that the only permissible remedy against diplomats and consuls is to ask them to leave the country and, if desired, break off all diplomatic relations with the offending country. Although Iran did not comply with the Court's judgment, that judgment laid the groundwork for the eventual settlement of the case and release of the hostages in a U.S.-Iran treaty known as the Declaration of Algeria, reprinted in 20 I.L.M. 223 (1981).

In *Armed Activities on the Territory of the Congo* (D.R. Congo v. Uganda), 2005 I.C.J. 168, the Court also ruled that an attack by the D.R. Congolese armed forces on the Ugandan embassy in Kinshasa, their maltreatment of Ugandan diplomats both at the embassy and at an airport, and D.R. Congo's failure to protect the Ugandan embassy and diplomats violated Congo's obligations to Uganda under the VCDR. The Court also stated that the VCDR "continues to apply notwithstanding the state of armed conflict that existed between" D.R. Congo and Uganda. *Id.* at para. 323.

Example 6-5

The wealthy country of Wadcash has diplomatic missions all over the world and it pays its diplomatic staff very well. Even in the small, sparsely populated, and very poor country of Norevenue, Wadcash has a luxurious embassy and a diplomatic staff of sixty people in the capital city of

---

10. 596 U.N.T.S. 261, 21 U.S.T. 77, T.I.A.S. No. 6820, signed April 24, 1963, entered into force March 19, 1967.

Rundown. Wadcash's ambassador to Norevenue is a well-connected former legislator called Augustus Moneypound. Mr. Moneypound always drives around in a large embassy car whenever he travels in Norevenue. He parks wherever he chooses. This means that the embassy car is frequently parked on pedestrian crossings, in "disabled only" parking spots, in "no parking any time" zones and even in the "ambulance parking only" bays at hospitals. The local police are infuriated by this and usually attach parking tickets to the car although it is widely known that Mr. Moneypound ignores the tickets.

1) Can the State of Norevenue insist that Mr. Moneypound pay the parking tickets or, if not, be subject to fines?

2) Could the city of Rundown refuse to issue a registration certificate to Mr. Moneypound's car unless he pays the tickets? (Such a certificate is necessary to drive on the Norevenue roads and Rundown, as the capital city, is authorized to set the regulations for registration.)

3) Could the State of Norevenue insist that the Wadcash embassy deposit a lump sum (say $40,000.00) from which any amount owed for the parking tickets by Wadcash to Norevenue would be deducted? Norevenue agreed to remit interest of two percent per annum to the State of Wadcash at the end of each year and to return the remaining sum if Wadcash ever decided to withdraw its diplomatic staff from Norevenue.

Explanations

1) Mr. Moneypound cannot be arrested or detained or required to appear in court. The ambassador enjoys immunity from criminal jurisdiction and from civil jurisdiction (with a few minor exceptions with respect to civil jurisdiction). VCDR, arts. 29 & 31. Although most states take the view that the tickets can be issued and forwarded to the mission for payment, most states take the view that the fines cannot be collected unless paid voluntarily. The general practice is to cancel the tickets at some point after seeking payment. But see Restatement Third §464, RN 9. If Norevenue gave foreign aid to Wadcash, it could cut off such aid unless the tickets were paid. This has been a technique used by the U.S. Foreign Operations, Export Financing, and Related Programs Appropriations Act, Public Law No. 107-115, §545, 115 Stat. 2118, 2155 (2002) but in this case the shoe is on the other foot; Wadcash is the rich country and Norevenue is the poor country.

2) Probably not. The City of New York, which has many diplomats working at the U.N. headquarters who enjoy similar immunities, threatened to tow diplomat's cars and impound them unless all tickets were paid but, after negotiation with the U.S. Department of State, the matter was dropped. No doubt the State Department either argued that New York had no power to interfere in U.S. foreign relations, or that the issue was preempted by federal policy, or that such activity was implicitly illegal under the VCDR as

essentially impeding the free functioning of the diplomats. See *A Ticket for Corruption*, The Economist, Aug. 10, 2006; *U.S.-UN Dispute over Parking Fines*, 97 Am. J. Int'l L. 190-192 (2003).

3) If such an agreement were entered into as a condition of engaging in diplomatic relations, it would probably be legal. The U.S. requires all diplomatic cars to carry very heavy liability insurance. If a person is injured by a diplomatic car, the individual can sue the insurance company. Technically the insurer is representing the insured, so presumably the insurer could argue that the diplomat had no liability, but that does not happen. Since the insurance company is receiving payments, presumably these payments are for liability coverage. A lump sum agreement would serve a purpose similar to liability insurance but relating to parking tickets rather than car accidents.

§6.8.2 Consular Immunity

The traditional role of the consul was to represent his/her state abroad, usually not in the capital city, and to deal with administrative and trade matters as opposed to political and foreign relations issues that were handled by the embassy. Today there is a great deal of overlap in the functions carried out in consulates and embassies. Consular staff enjoy a more limited immunity from the host state's jurisdiction than diplomatic staff.

The Vienna Convention on Consular Relations (VCCR) was signed in 1963 and entered into force in 1967.[11] It provides for immunity from civil and criminal jurisdiction for consular officers "in respect of acts performed in the exercise of consular functions." Art. 43(1) with minor exceptions, arts. 43(2)(a) & 43(2)(b). When the criminal act did not arise from official actions, the consular officer may not be arrested or detained pending trial "except in the case of a grave crime and pursuant to a decision by the competent judicial authority." Art. 41(1). Note that this provision only relates to arrest and detention before trial. It does not prohibit a trial. For grave crimes, not arising out of official duties, consular officers can be detained pending trial after a judicial order for such detention.

The consular officers' accompanying family members have very limited immunity extending only to taxes, customs duties on articles for personal use, immigration controls and military obligations. The sending state has the authority to waive all immunities under the Convention should it wish to do so. Art. 45.

The Convention also provides for the inviolability of consular premises, the inviolability of consular archives and documents, freedom of movement

---

11. 596 U.N.T.S. 261, 21 U.S.T. 77, T.I.A.S. No. 6820, signed April 24, 1963, entered into force March 19, 1967.

for members of the consular post and freedom of communication by means of official correspondence, including the consular bag. For other aspects of a consul's rights and duties with respect to citizens of the consul's state detained in the foreign country where the consul is serving see *LaGrand* (Germany v. U.S.), 2001 I.C.J. 446, and *Avena and Other Mexican Nationals* (Mexico v. United States of America), 2004 I.C.J. 12 *supra*, Chapter 3, §3.8.

There are very few cases where consular officials are prosecuted largely because, if they are suspected of illegal activity, the host state will request their removal and the case will never find its way to court. Occasionally, however, a host state will prosecute a more egregious crime. See, for example, *U.S. v. Sihadej Chindawongse/U.S. v. Boripat Siripan*, 771 F.2d 840 (4th Cir. 1985) (no immunity for consular officers for conspiring to distribute heroin).

Example 6-6

Inge Tomalu is the consul for the State of Grasp posted to Birmingham, U.K. Ms. Tomalu has expensive tastes in handbags. A luxury store in Birmingham discovered that several of its very costly handbags were missing. The store's videotapes showed that Ms. Tomalu loaded the bags into a large plastic shopping container. The local police have also come to the conclusion that three years after taking up her post, Ms. Tomalu started using illegal immigrants to paint the interior and maintain the grounds of the consulate. The U.K. is a party to the VCCR.

Can the U.K. prosecute Ms. Tomalu for (1) shoplifting and (2) employing illegal immigrants at the consulate? You should assume that both activities are normally considered to be crimes under U.K. law.

Explanations

1) The U.K. can certainly prosecute Ms. Tomalu for shoplifting luxury handbags. Although Ms. Tomalu may well need to maintain a smart appearance for her official duties, shoplifting cannot be described as falling within "the exercise of consular functions." VCCR, art. 43(1).

2) Prosecution for employing illegal immigrants on consular premises is more problematic. No doubt the illegal immigrants could be prosecuted and/or deported. The immunity from immigration controls only applies to the consul and his/her accompanying family members (art. 46). Although article 46 states that consular employees are exempt from immigration controls, the term "consular employee" is defined as "any person employed in the administrative or technical service of a consular post." The host state would need to approve the list of consular employees before they start work, which presumably was not the case with the painters and grounds keepers. The painters and grounds keepers could not be arrested on the consular

premises without Ms. Tomalu's consent as the premises are largely inviolable. Art. 31.

Whether Ms. Tomalu can be prosecuted for employing the illegal aliens to work on the consulate building and grounds presents a difficult question. On the one hand, the upkeep of the fabric of the consulate is clearly necessary for the carrying out of official functions. On the other hand, the act of employing illegal immigrants is not itself "the exercise of consular functions." Art. 43. Consular functions are described in more detail in article 5, which does not include employing persons to work on the upkeep of the consulate, but which is not considered an exhaustive list of consular functions.

As a practical matter, the host state would probably explain to Ms. Tomalu that employing illegal immigrants to work on the consulate is illegal under U.K. law and all such workers will be arrested once they leave the consular premises.

§6.8.3 Head of State and Other Ministers' Immunity

Until very recently, there were almost no attempts to subject leaders of foreign states to the jurisdiction of national courts. Those leaders were viewed as representatives of the foreign state and thus entitled to Foreign Sovereign Immunity (infra §6.8.5) or to an immunity analogous to diplomatic immunity, supra. Once the concept of universal jurisdiction began to gain ground, together with the idea of individual responsibility for violation of international obligations, states began to consider whether incumbent foreign leaders, or former leaders, could be subjected to national court jurisdiction.

A famous early case arose in the U.K. courts, *Regina v. Bartle and the Commissioner of Police for the Metropolis and Others Ex Parte Pinochet*, House of Lords, U.K. (24 March 1999), 119 I.L.R. 135 (1999). The former President of Chile, Augusto Pinochet, traveled to Britain in 1998 to undergo medical treatment. While there, Spain sought his extradition to stand trial for a litany of crimes that allegedly took place during Pinochet's presidency and occurred almost exclusively in Chile, committed against Chilean citizens. Spain's claimed jurisdiction largely on the basis of universality. (There were a few criminal counts linked to Spain but they are not relevant here.) The issue arose as to whether Pinochet was entitled to immunity. In the end, the case turned on the double criminality provision of the extradition treaty between Spain and the U.K. That provision required that the crime for which extradition was sought should also be a crime in Britain. Under the double criminality provision, Britain asked itself not only whether the substantive crime for which extradition was requested was an offense in the U.K. but also whether, in similar circumstances, Britain would have jurisdiction over the offense. The U.K. High Court determined that Pinochet, as a former head of state, could claim immunity (similar to a former diplomat) for all of the official acts occurring during his time in office, including crimes — with one exception. Spain had requested extradition for torture. Prior to 1988, Britain had not asserted jurisdiction over torture occurring outside Britain but after that date, when the U.K. enacted implementing legislation for the Torture Convention, 1465 U.N.T.S. 85, torture occurring anywhere, committed by a citizen of any state against a citizen of any state, became a crime under U.K. criminal law. Thus the court determined that Pinochet could be tried for torture in the U.K. courts after 1988 and thus the double criminality provision of the extradition treaty was met. In turning to the question of whether Pinochet was entitled to immunity for torture, the court concluded that normally Pinochet could claim immunity but, because the Torture Convention describes torture as various acts "inflicted by or at the instigation of or with the consent or acquiescence of a public official or other person acting in an official capacity" (art. 1(1)), the Convention, and thus the U.K. legislation, could not have intended to give state officials (such as Pinochet) immunity. The U.K. court thus ruled that Pinochet was able to be extradited on charges of torture arising after 1988. (In the end, U.K. officials determined that Pinochet was unfit to stand trial and he returned to Chile in 2000. Various criminal charges were pending against him in Chile at the time of his death in 2006.) In other words, the U.K. court had upheld the notion of Spain's power to assert criminal jurisdiction over a former foreign head of state on the basis of universality and had rejected the claim to immunity from prosecution for the former head of state but only when the definition of the crime appeared to make such a claim impossible. Note, however, that the U.K. court upheld immunity for all regular crimes occurring while Pinochet was in office.

In *Arrest Warrant of 11 April 2000* (D.R. Congo v. Belgium), 2002 I.C.J. 3, the I.C.J. appears to have severely restricted the possibility of prosecuting incumbent presidents or ministers in foreign national courts. In that case, Belgium issued an international arrest warrant against the incumbent Minister for Foreign Affairs for D.R. Congo for war crimes and crimes against humanity occurring outside Belgium and committed against non-Belgians. As discussed *supra*, war crimes are widely perceived as permitting the asserting of universal jurisdiction and many maintain that crimes against humanity also permit universal jurisdiction. Instead of examining the permissible scope of Belgium's jurisdiction, the Court simply addressed the question of whether an incumbent minister from a foreign country was entitled to immunity in national courts (much as a foreign diplomat would be) and concluded that:

> In international law it is firmly established that, as also diplomatic and consular agents, certain holders of high-ranking office in a State, such as the Head of State, Head of Government and Ministers for Foreign Affairs, enjoy immunities from jurisdiction in other States, both civil and criminal. *Id.* at para. 51.

Belgium was therefore ordered to cancel the arrest warrant. The Court did point out that heads of state and other ministers can be prosecuted in their own nation's courts, or in foreign courts provided their own state waives immunity, or for acts occurring before or after their period of office, or for private acts engaged in while in office. Similarly, such persons may be prosecuted in international criminal tribunals where the tribunal's statute bars such claims of immunity. *Id.* at para. 61.

Example 6-7

State B arrests the President of State C when the President is visiting State B on vacation. The President is put on trial for torture of State C citizens occurring in State C last year. He is convicted and sentenced to life in prison. The President was elected to office in State C in 2002 and has been the President of State C ever since. State B has a statute that allows it to assert universal jurisdiction over persons from any country suspected of torture occurring anywhere in the world and perpetrated against the citizens of any state.

Does the arrest, trial, and conviction of the President of State C by State B for torture occurring in State C against State C citizens violate international law?

Explanation

At first blush, it appears that such an arrest and trial would violate the I.C.J.'s judgment in the *Arrest Warrant* case *supra*, where the Court held that Belgium could not issue an arrest warrant against the Foreign Minister of D.R. Congo because incumbent ministers have immunity from such an assertion of a foreign state's jurisdiction. That case involved accusations of war crimes and crimes against humanity. Those crimes usually involve some level of governmental authority, whether it be the commanding general of an army or the civilian guard at a prison camp. In the case of torture, the definition of the crime states that it must be "inflicted by or at the instigation of or with the consent or acquiescence of a public official or other person acting in an official capacity." Torture Convention *supra*, art. 1(1). As the U.K. High Court in the *Pinochet* case observed:

> Under the Convention the international crime of torture can only be committed by an official or someone in an official capacity. They would [under normal immunity doctrines] all be entitled to immunity. It would follow that there can be no case . . . in which a successful prosecution for torture can be brought unless . . . [the official's State] is prepared to waive its right to its official's immunity. Therefore the whole elaborate structure of universal jurisdiction over torture committed by officials is rendered abortive. . . .

If the *Arrest Warrant* case *supra*, requires the dismissal of the case against the President of State C, then torturers will never be able to be prosecuted at the national level except in their own courts or if their own state waives immunity and permits prosecution in a foreign state. Either the definition of the crime of torture operates as an implicit waiver of official immunity or we can expect almost no trials for torture in national courts.

§6.8.4 Immunity for International Organizations

If a state decides to allow an international organization to operate from a base within its territory, that state will negotiate an agreement with the organization spelling out the scope of the immunities to be enjoyed. For example the United States entered into an agreement with the United Nations when it was decided that the United Nations was to be headquartered in New York City.[12] These immunities are those associated with facilitating the purposes of the international organization and will usually include immunity from legal process and criminal jurisdiction. There is also a General Convention on the Privileges and Immunities of the United Nations[13] which grants a broad based immunity to the assets and other property of the United Nations. Representatives of members of the United Nations are granted immunity "from personal arrest or detention and from seizure of their personal baggage, and, in respect of words spoken or written and all acts done by them in their capacity as representatives, immunity from legal process of every kind." Art. IV, §11(a). This latter type of immunity attaches while the representatives are "exercising their functions and during their journey to and from the place of meeting. . . ." Art. IV, §11.

§6.8.5 Sovereign Immunity

Absolute Theory

In the past, most monarchs were held to represent the sovereignty of the state and to be above the law. They were not subject to any legal procedures within their own state and when they traveled abroad they enjoyed immunity from jurisdiction, largely based on a theory of the equality of sovereigns. If indeed sovereigns were equal, the theory stated, one sovereign could not subject another sovereign to its legal process. During this period, the courts adhered to the theory of absolute sovereign immunity under which

---

12. Agreement between the United Nations and the United States Regarding the Headquarters of the United Nations, 11 U.N.T.S. 11, 61 Stat. 3416, T.I.A.S. No. 1676.
13. Adopted by the General Assembly, Feb. 13, 1946, 1 U.N.T.S. 13, 21 U.S.T. 1418, T.I.A.S. No. 6900.

foreign sovereigns or foreign governments were generally not subject to any legal proceedings. *The Schooner Exchange v. McFadden*, 11 U.S. (7 Cranch) 116 (1812).

The modern state gradually evolved from absolute monarchy to constitutional monarchy (with severe limitations on the power of the crown) to a variety of republics with different representative forms of government. The role of the state expanded from mustering armies and carrying on foreign relations to engaging in a whole variety of enterprises from regulating trade, to running steel mills and trains, to providing pensions and health care. The modern state is often the largest single employer within a nation and generally engages in a host of activities both commercial and governmental.

As the state expanded its activities so it was more likely to find itself in legal disputes with the general population. On the domestic front people began to press for a waiver of their own state's immunity in their own local court system. Somehow it did not seem fair that, for example, a paper manufacturer who supplied paper to the Department of Agriculture should be unable to sue for the price of goods delivered when the Department failed to pay just because the defendant in the case happened to be the government. The people's representatives soon got busy passing legislation that waived sovereign immunity for their own government on a fairly broad basis. See e.g., the Tucker Act, 28 U.S.C. §1346(a)(2)(1982); the Federal Tort Claims Act, 28 U.S.C. §1346(b)(1982).

There was a reluctance to tackle the issue of a foreign sovereign's immunity, however, because:

(a) that might subject your own state to reciprocal treatment elsewhere under a legal system that might be very different from your own, and;

(b) such legislation, subjecting foreign sovereigns to jurisdiction, would certainly have a major impact on foreign relations.

In an era where most people did not have dealings with foreigners, sovereign or otherwise, the existence of immunity for foreign sovereigns did not weigh too heavily on the public consciousness. Gradually, however, as the role and activities of the state expanded and as international travel became commonplace, many more people and organizations began to have international contacts. Today, the overwhelming majority of businesses in developed countries have some aspect of their enterprise that stretches beyond national borders. The result has been that more people and corporations have dealings with foreign governments. If a dispute arose with a foreign government, the government could always claim absolute sovereign immunity and avoid any type of settlement as long as the doctrine of absolute sovereign immunity prevailed. Sometimes the person could sue the foreign government in its own state courts but that would depend on the extent to which immunity had been repealed in the foreign state and anyway litigating claims abroad would inevitably be expensive. The cry went up to limit the scope of immunity afforded to foreign sovereigns in national courts.

The Restrictive Theory

The doctrine of restrictive sovereign immunity states that foreign sovereigns will not be subject to suit in disputes involving *governmental* matters but will be subject to the courts' jurisdiction in *commercial* matters. Application of this doctrine began as early as 1886 in a case from the Court of Cassation in Naples, Italy. A number of other courts began to follow suit and by the middle of the twentieth century a sizable number of states had abandoned absolute sovereign immunity and embraced the restrictive theory.[14] The courts often referred to governmental activities as sovereign or public acts (*jure imperii*) and spoke of commercial activities as private acts (*jure gestionis*). The great task for the courts, once they had accepted the restrictive theory of sovereign immunity, was in sorting out the dividing line between governmental activities and commercial activities. Not an easy task.

At the beginning of the 1950s about the only major states still adhering to absolute sovereign immunity were the United States, the United Kingdom and the Soviet Union. These states were beginning to recognize the inequality of the situation. For example, a U.S. citizen who had a dispute with the Italian government concerning commercial activity could not sue the Italian government in the courts of the United States, whereas an Italian citizen who had a dispute with the U.S. government concerning commercial activity could sue the U.S. government in Italian courts. In 1952, Jack B. Tate, Acting Legal Adviser to the U.S. Department of State, wrote a now famous letter to Acting Attorney General Philip B. Perlman of the Department of Justice. In the letter Mr. Tate reviews state practice of granting immunity to foreign sovereigns and concludes that his Department will henceforth follow the restrictive theory of sovereign immunity when advising U.S. courts on pleas of immunity from foreign sovereigns. Mr. Tate was well aware that the U.S. courts were not bound to follow the State Department's suggestions but, in light of the fact that the U.S. courts generally defer to the executive department in matters touching on international relations, he thought it likely that the courts might be willing to follow the State Department's advice. 26 Dep't St. Bull. 984 (1952).

After the Tate letter, both the Department of State and the courts struggled with drawing the line between those activities which merited immunity and those which did not. It is fair to say that there was little agreement on the

---

14. *Dralle v. Republic of Czechoslovakia*, Supreme Court of Austria, (1950) Int'l L. Rep. 155 (H. Lauterpacht ed.).

matter. One line of argument was that the *purpose of the government's acts* should be examined. The problem with this approach was that all acts of government are presumably carried out for a public purpose with the result that all governmental activity ends up being immune from jurisdiction. Another line of argument was that *nature of the government's acts* should be examined. The problem with this approach is that it gives no guidance as to which acts are to be treated as private (and therefore subject to jurisdiction) and which acts are to be treated as public (and therefore not subject to jurisdiction). The courts in the U.S. and other countries struggled on with tenuous line drawing. See *Victory Transport, Inc. v. Comisaria General de Abastecimiento y Transportes*, 336 F.2d 354 (2d Cir. 1964) cert. denied, 381 U.S. 934 (1965).

Eventually the legislatures of various countries decided to enact statutes that were meant to resolve the difficulties the courts had been facing. In the United States, for example, Congress passed the *Foreign Sovereign Immunities Act of 1976*.[15] In Britain, the government passed the *State Immunity Act of 1978*[16] and in Canada the legislature enacted the *State Immunity Act of 1982*.[17]

All of the above acts adopt the restrictive immunity principle and spell out which types of foreign governmental acts will be immune from jurisdiction and which types of acts will be subject to jurisdiction. The courts now struggle with the definitions provided by the statutes. There is still room for much disagreement but it is fair to say that foreign governments now have a much smaller scope for claiming immunity than previously.

Example 6-8

Henry Wall is a citizen of the State of Atra by virtue of being born there. He spent the first three months of his life in Atra before his parents, both citizens of the State of Bula, moved back to Bula. Henry lived in Bula until he was twenty when he joined an international art auction house located in Calla, the capital of the State of Callaria. Since then Henry has led a fast-paced life moving in the world of buying and selling high-priced art, sculpture, and antique furniture. Over the course of his career, three priceless Rembrandt portraits, all originally owned by the State of Callaria's National Gallery of Art, disappeared shortly after they were consigned to Henry's portfolio at the auction house. Though the police never ruled him out as a suspect, no evidence ever came to light linking Henry with the disappearance of the portraits.

At the age of forty-five in 2001, Jacob suddenly retired from his job and went to live in the State of Duma. He is apparently living in great luxury. Six months after he arrived in Duma, the Duma legislature passed a special bill

---

15. 28 U.S.C.A. §§1330, 1332, 1391, 1441, 1602-1611 (1976).
16. Reprinted at 17 I.L.M. 1123 (1978).
17. 29, 30, 31 Eliz. 2, ch. 95; reprinted at 21 I.L.M. 798 (1982).

conferring citizenship upon Henry. He now has two passports, one from Atra and one from Duma.

Six months ago the Callaria police unearthed some evidence that directly linked Henry to the disappearance of the Rembrandts. The evidence seems to suggest that Henry took the portraits from Callaria to Bula and that he was paid large amounts of money to deliver the Rembrandts to a well-known Bulan criminal who promptly disappeared with the portraits. The Callarian authorities have indicted Jacob for the art thefts and have asked the Duma authorities to extradite Jacob to Callaria. Callaria and Duma are parties to a bilateral extradition treaty which obligates both parties to surrender criminally indicted fugitives to the other state. The treaty also provides that neither party is obligated to surrender its own citizens under the treaty. Duma refuses to extradite Henry on the grounds that he is a citizen of Duma, and also refuses to prosecute him because Duma's statutes do not make theft outside Duma an offense under Duman law. Callaria sends undercover agents to Duma. They capture Henry and bring him back to Callaria where he is put on trial for the theft of the portraits.

1) Does the State of Atra have legislative jurisdiction to prosecute Henry for theft of the portraits? In other words, if Atra had made theft occurring in the circumstances outlined in the example a crime, would that be permissible under international law?

2) Does the State of Bula have jurisdiction to prosecute Henry for the theft of the portrait?

3) Does the State of Callaria have jurisdiction to prosecute Henry for theft of the portraits?

4) On what grounds might Henry object to being tried by the Callarian courts?

5) If you were representing the State of Duma in negotiations with the State of Callaria, what violations of international law would you complain had been violated and what remedy would you seek and on whose behalf?

Explanations

1) Henry is a citizen of Atra and owns an Atran passport. Even though he also has a Duman passport, there is no evidence that Henry has renounced his Atran citizenship or that Atran law does not permit dual citizenship. (Some states would revoke Henry's citizenship on learning that he had acquired another citizenship, but many states permit dual citizenship.) As such, Atra can assert legislative jurisdiction on the basis of Henry's nationality. Atra is free to make theft by Atran citizens occurring anywhere in the world an offense under Atran law.

2) Although Henry had been a resident of Bula, he has never been a citizen. The thefts did not take place from Bula but the evidence seems to suggest that the stolen portraits were brought to Bula and that they were sold

to a Bulan criminal. Bula would not have jurisdiction on the basis of nationality but would have jurisdiction on the basis of territoriality. Here the stolen goods were brought into Bula and sold in Bula to a Bulan criminal.

3) The portraits were originally located in Callaria's National Gallery of Art and were consigned to Henry at an auction house in Callaria. Henry then allegedly stole the portraits in Callaria and took them out of the country. A good deal of the criminal activity allegedly occurred in Callaria. Callaria can make such activities occurring within its territory a criminal offense on the basis of territoriality.

4) Duma refused to extradite Henry on the basis that he was a Duman citizen. At the international level, there might be objections to this very rapid conferral of citizenship. (See the *Nottebohm* case, Chapter 4, §4.4.4.) However, such objections do not give Callaria the right to enter Duma, capture Henry, and remove him to Callaria. Henry might well object to the Callarian court's jurisdiction over his person. He might argue that his abduction violates the Callarian-Duman extradition treaty. Even if there is no specific clause stating that such an abduction violates the treaty, Henry might argue that the reason why states enter into such treaties is because they know they cannot chase fugitives across international borders. There is no "hot pursuit" doctrine similar to that in the Law of the Sea (see UNCLOS, art. 111; Chapter 12, §12.15.3). One state is not permitted to enter another state without that state's permission. Callaria has therefore violated Duma's rights. As we saw in the *Alvarez-Machain* case *supra*, some courts would refuse to find the abduction to be a violation of the treaty but some courts might find the dissent in that case more persuasive and thus find the treaty violated. If the court finds that the abduction violates the treaty, the next questions are: (a) What is the appropriate remedy, and (b) to whom does the remedy run? Some courts, such as the Israeli court in the *Eichmann* case *supra*, would say that any remedy for the violation of the state's territorial integrity (in that case there was no extradition treaty) only runs to the injured state. It does not run to the individual who was abducted. Other courts might hold that the treaty protects both the state and individuals from violations of sovereignty and thus any remedy should run both to the injured state and the injured individual. The general rule for remedying violations of treaties is to put the parties back in the position they were in before the violation of the treaty occurred. Chapter 3, §3.13. In this case, Henry would argue that he should be repatriated to Duma which was where he was before being illegally abducted. Note: Most courts are very reluctant to allow a person in Henry's situation to escape prosecution. Judges tend to say: "We are not interested in how you arrived here. You are here now and there is a statute permitting your prosecution, thus the prosecution will proceed."

5) Duma would want an acknowledgment that Callaria had wrongfully entered its territory and wrongfully abducted Henry. Duma would also want an apology from Callaria and an undertaking never to repeat such activity.

6. Jurisdiction

Duma might also ask for monetary damages and/or perhaps some favorable treatment in ongoing negotiations on other issues, such as trade. Duma might well press for the return of Henry if Henry is still being held by Callaria and might ask for reparations on his behalf. Duma might threaten to prosecute the Callarian agents who carried out the abduction. Presumably Duma would request their extradition but Callaria would probably refuse extradition on the ground that Callaria is not required to extradite her own citizens and the agents are Callarian citizens. Note: Duma probably has many extradition treaties with other countries so that if the agents traveled to any of those countries, they might be subject to extradition.

Title to Territory

§7.1 Terra Nullius
§7.2 Discovery
§7.3 Occupation
§7.4 Conquest
§7.5 Cession
§7.6 Prescription
§7.7 Uti Possidetis Juris
§7.8 Accretion and Avulsion
§7.9 Special Territorial Regimes
    §7.9.1 The Arctic
    §7.9.2 The Antarctic
    §7.9.3 Celestial Bodies and Space

Modern national systems of law have a method for recording title to territory in some official register. Buyers of property receive a title that furnishes proof of ownership. Unfortunately, there is no such system operative in the international arena, and disputes over title to territory are frequent and often give rise to devastating wars. Some of the international rules concerning title to territory may seem antiquated and to hark back to the time when intrepid discoverers roamed the globe in search of lands that they could claim for their sovereign. Some of the cases definitely have an ancient ring to them, and may well turn upon the interpretation of old treaties or settlement patterns dating back many centuries, but without a thorough understanding of the international rules used to determine title to territory, it is often impossible to determine whether one side or the other (or both) has violated international law when conflicts erupt over territorial disputes. In recent years, the International Court of Justice has increasingly been called upon to settle land disputes. See, e.g., *Sovereignty Over Pedra Branca/Pulau Batu Puteh, Middle Rocks and South Ledge* (Malaysia v. Singapore), 2008 I.C.J. 12; *The Frontier Dispute* (Benin v. Niger), 2005 I.C.J. 90; *Sovereignty Over Pulau Ligitan and Pulau Sipadan* (Indonesia v. Malaysia), 2002 I.C.J. 625; *The Land and Maritime Boundary Between Cameroon and Nigeria* (Cameroon v. Nigeria: Equatorial Guinea intervening), 2002 I.C.J. 303. All of these cases are very fact specific, and the Court pays great attention to the details of treaties, history, conduct of the parties, and sometimes how other states have treated the area. The Court also struggles with the weight to be attached to various types of evidence, particularly when the evidence presented is many centuries old.

§7.1 *TERRA NULLIUS*

If land is occupied by no one and not claimed by any state, no state owns the territory and it is said to be *terra nullius*. Such land is open to an ownership claim. In previous centuries powerful states sent out envoys to discover areas of the globe and claim them for the sending sovereign. Often the areas claimed would in fact be inhabited by tribes or groups of Indigenous Peoples. The inhabitants would be subjugated and frequently forced to sign treaties of cession or required to acknowledge the sovereignty of the foreign intruder. This process represented the age old example of more technologically advanced people subjecting less technologically advanced people to their rule. The general name for this process was colonialism.

The United Nations has spoken out against colonialism in recent decades and now international law prohibits "[t]he subjection of peoples to alien subjugation, domination and exploitation. . . ." Declaration on the Granting of Independence to Colonial Territories and Peoples, G.A. Res. 1514 (XV) Dec. 14, 1960, G.A.O.R., 15th Sess., Supp. 16, p. 66. That same declaration asserts that "[a]ll peoples have the right to self-determination; by virtue of that right they freely determine their political status. . . ." When the United Nations was established in 1945, it took over the League of Nations' Mandate System under which developed states took on the obligation of administering certain less developed states or territories. Covenant of the League of Nations, art. 22. The U.N. Charter created a Trusteeship System (U.N. Charter, arts. 75-91) by which developed states took on the task of running non-self-governing territories with a view to promoting "their progressive development toward self-government or independence . . ." (art. 76(B)). Since the 1960s virtually all of the former colonies of the few remaining empires have achieved independence though a few territories remain in dependent status.

§7.2 DISCOVERY

If an unoccupied territory was discovered, or in earlier centuries an occupied territory became subject to foreign domination, how did the discoverer or dominator acquire title to the territory? From the fifteenth century onward, many of the great empires sent envoys on long voyages to discover new lands and claim them for their sovereigns. Some popes allocated vast areas of the globe to Catholic rulers. See Papal Bull of 1493, *Inter Caetera*, awarding to Spain everything 100 miles west of the Azores and Cape Verde not already ruled by a Christian sovereign. The mere fact of finding an island or an unoccupied area of land was apparently never considered fully sufficient to establish sovereignty. It seems that some sort of ceremony claiming sovereignty over the territory in the name of a particular sovereign was necessary to establish a claim to title to the territory. Such a claim "was deemed good against all subsequent claims set up in opposition thereto unless, perhaps, transferred by conquest or treaty, relinquished, abandoned, or successfully opposed by continued occupation on the part of some other state." Arthur S. Keller, Oliver J. Lissitzyn, and Frederick J. Mann, Creation of Rights of Sovereignty through Symbolic Acts 1400-1800, 148-149 (1938) (reprinted 1974). International Arbitrator, Max Huber, discussing Spain's claim to title through discovery of the Island of Palmas, states: "The title of discovery . . . would, under the most favorable and most extensive interpretation, exist only as an inchoate title, as a claim to establish sovereignty by effective occupation. An inchoate title however cannot prevail over a definite title founded on continuous and peaceful display of sovereignty." *The Island of Palmas* case (or, *Miangas*) (Netherlands v. U.S.), 2 R.I.A.A. 829 (1928). Pre-U.N. Charter cases were unconcerned with the right of a people to govern themselves as this right only developed after WWII. Very few displays of sovereignty were required to establish title in remote or sparsely populated areas. *Legal Status of Eastern Greenland* (Denmark v. Norway), 1933 P.C.I.J., Ser. A/B, No. 53, at 46.

Example 7-1

In 1858 a French ship came across an island 670 miles southwest of Mexico. The captain proclaimed sovereignty over the island on behalf of Emperor Napoleon III. The captain had been authorized to make such a claim by a French Minister. Three days later some of the crew went ashore for a few hours; the ship then sailed for Hawaii. The captain informed the French Consulate in Honolulu of the claim, which was published in a Honolulu

English-language journal. The island had no population, and the French government never set up any form of administration.

In 1897, Mexico sent a gunboat to the island and landed a small group of officers and marines. The Mexican flag was raised. France immediately protested but Mexico stated that it owned the island. Assume that the claimants agreed to international arbitration in 1930.

Which state had good title to this uninhabited island?

Explanation

In the above example neither state had done very much in the way of administration or other displays of sovereignty. Since France appears to have arrived on the uninhabited island first and to have publicly declared its sovereignty, a court is likely to favor the French claim over the Mexican claim. France's immediate protest at Mexico's attempted claim indicates that France had not abandoned her title. See *Clipperton Island Arbitration* (France v. Mexico), 26 Am. J. Int'l L. 390 (1932).

§7.3 OCCUPATION

If unoccupied territory was claimed by a state and occupied by that state, then the occupation operated to confer title on the claimant. But what if the territory was inhabited by tribes of Indigenous Peoples? The International Court of Justice has stated that: "Territories inhabited by tribes or peoples having a social and political organization were not regarded as *terra nullius*." *Western Sahara* case, Advisory Opinion, 1975 I.C.J. 12, at 39 (Oct. 16). This would certainly be true today, but in earlier times, Indigenous Peoples were usually conquered or forced to agree to pay tribute to the invader.

Example 7-2

Blueland is a large island in the middle of a great ocean. It is 500 miles from west to east and 300 miles from north to south. Eight centuries ago explorers from the state of Norseland discovered the western part of the island. Settlers were sent out from Norseland to western Blueland. They constructed houses and schools, engaged in fishing, and cultivated crops during the short summer season. The climate was harsh and the Norselanders only occupied a narrow strip of land on the western coast of Blueland. They never ventured inland beyond about fifty miles. Over the centuries, more Norselanders arrived but many left, so that sometimes there were only a dozen or so inhabitants. By 1990, only six Norselanders remained in the western Blueland settlement.

In 1991, explorers from the State of Scanland discovered the eastern coast of Blueland. They built a camp and trekked inland for 200 miles. They saw no one and discovered no evidence of settlement. They returned to their camp, hoisted the Scanland flag, and returned to Scanland. The explorers reported their findings to the Scanland government, which authorized the explorers to return to Blueland, claim the land on behalf of Scanland, and build a permanent research station. They were instructed to map the land. All of this was accomplished within six months. They did see the settlement on the west coast but it appeared abandoned. No inhabitants were located anywhere. (In all probability the inhabitants were on an extended fishing trip.)

When the explorers returned to Scanland, the government claimed the whole of Blueland as Scanland territory. The government of Norseland heard about the claim and immediately sent a protest to Scanland's government. Norseland maintained that "since time immemorial Norseland has always claimed sovereignty over the whole of Blueland."

Scanland and Norseland agree to submit their dispute over title to Blueland to the International Court of Justice for settlement. Should the Court confirm Scanland's or Norseland's title to Blueland?

Explanation

It appears that Norseland first discovered and settled the western coast of Blueland many centuries ago and thus would claim title through discovery and occupation of terra nullius. Presumably, Norseland can document an early claim to Blueland. If not, Norseland's claim to the whole island will be weaker. The problem, however, lies in determining exactly what Norseland discovered and exactly what it reasonably could lay claim to. Norseland settled a small part of the western coast and never ventured more than fifty miles inland. There is no evidence that Norseland knew the extent of the island.

Scanland discovered the eastern part of the island first. The explorers traveled throughout the island and mapped it at a time when only six Norselanders remained in the western settlement. Those settlers were absent on fishing trips from time to time. No doubt Scanland would claim title to the whole of the island by discovery of terra nullius together with settlement and mapping.

The Court might determine that Norseland had good title to the western settlement and any part of the island for which Norseland could present evidence of earlier discovery at least where such discovery was communicated to the Norseland government. If Norseland can document her claim to the specific land that had been discovered then she has a good claim to that part of the island. Without some acts relating to the rest of the island, it is doubtful that the Court would award the whole of the island to Norseland.

Scanland had discovered all of the remaining area of the island first and had claimed title to the whole of the island. The explorers had also built a camp and a research station and had mapped the whole of the island. On these bases the Court would probably award title to the remaining area of the island to Scanland. Cf. *Legal Status of Eastern Greenland* (Denmark v. Norway), 1933 P.C.I.J., Ser. A/B, No. 53.

§7.4 CONQUEST

In the past, if one state invaded another state and defeated it in war, the most usual outcome was that the victor forced the vanquished to sign a treaty ceding the territory to the victorious party. Before the twentieth century, conquest was a frequent mode of acquiring territory. Now a number of international agreements and the Charter of the United Nations prohibit the use of force in international relations. U.N. Charter, art. 2(4), cf. art. 51. The result of this prohibition is that generally a state may not now acquire territory through the use of force.

It has been suggested that if force is used in self-defense, as permitted by article 51 of the U.N. Charter, and if the exercise of self-defense results in the acquisition of territory such acquisition is valid. This argument has been roundly criticized as contrary to the Declaration on Friendly Relations which states that: "No territorial acquisition resulting from the threat or use of force shall be recognized as legal." G.A. Res. 2625, U.N. GAOR, Supp. No. 28, 25th Sess. (1970). It has also been argued that under the laws of war the right of self-defense only continues until the armed attack (or possibly the threat of armed attack) has been repelled. Once the danger has been contained, the right to use force in self-defense evaporates and with it the right to retain any territory taken while exercising the right of self-defense. The Security Council has criticized Israel's retention of areas captured during the 1967 war, which are currently gradually being returned to Arab control.

In July 2004, the International Court of Justice issued an Advisory Opinion: *Legal Consequences of the Construction of a Wall in the Occupied Palestinian Territory*, Advisory Opinion, 2004 I.C.J. 136 (9 July). The General Assembly of the United Nations had asked the Court to answer the following question:

> What are the legal consequences arising from the construction of the wall being built by Israel, the occupying Power, in the Occupied Palestinian Territory, including in and around East Jerusalem, as described in the report of the Secretary-General, considering the rules and principles of international law, including the Fourth Geneva Convention of 1949, and relevant Security Council and General Assembly Resolutions?

In the course of its opinion, the Court stated:

> On 24 October 1970, the General Assembly adopted resolution 2625 (XXV), entitled "Declaration on Principles of International Law concerning Friendly Relations and Co-operation among States" (hereinafter "resolution 2625 (XXV)"), in which it emphasized that "No territorial acquisition resulting from the threat or use of force shall be recognized as legal." As the Court stated in its Judgment in the case concerning *Military and Paramilitary Activities in and Against Nicaragua (Nicaragua v. United States of America)*, the principles as to the use of force incorporated in the Charter reflect customary international law (see I.C.J. *Reports 1986*, pp. 98-101, paras. 187-190); the same is true of its corollary entailing the illegality of territorial acquisition resulting from the threat or use of force. (At para. 87).

Later, the Court added that "both the General Assembly and the Security Council have referred, with regard to Palestine, to the customary rule of 'the inadmissibility of the acquisition of territory by war' . . ." (at para. 117).

It should be noted, however, that there are several areas of the world which have been taken by force even after World War II but which remain in the hands of the conqueror. For example, India took over the Portuguese enclaves of Goa, Danao, and Diu in 1961 and still controls them. India claimed that she was "liberating" the territory from the illegal colonial power.

§7.5 CESSION

Cession is the process whereby one sovereign gives title to territory to another sovereign. The process is usually effected by a treaty of cession. Sometimes land is acquired under a treaty through purchase such as the United States' Louisiana purchase from France in 1803, 8 Stat. 200, T.S. 86, 7 Bevans 812, and its Alaskan purchase from Russia in 1867, 15 Stat. 539, T.S. 301, 11 Bevans 1216.

§7.6 PRESCRIPTION

In many municipal systems of law there is a provision for the acquisition of real property through the continuous and open use of it for a prescribed number of years despite the fact that the property is registered in another owner's name. In the common-law tradition this is known as "adverse possession" and normally takes at least twenty years. The question of whether one state can acquire title to territory despite an earlier recognized title by another state is much debated in international law. Of course, if the earlier title holder abandoned the territory there is nothing to stop a subsequent claim to title, but exactly what constitutes abandonment is again debatable. A classic example of these dilemmas is provided by the Falkland Islands/Islas Malvinas dispute between Argentina and the United Kingdom. Argentina claims that she held good title to Islas Malvinas when the British forcibly occupied the islands in 1833. Britain has remained in possession since that time except for several weeks in 1982 when Argentina invaded the islands and claimed them as the rightful owner. Britain responded with force and drove the Argentinians out. Argentina claims that she was wrongfully ousted in 1833 and has never abandoned her claim to title. Britain disputes Argentina's right to title in 1833 but maintains that more than a century and a half of occupation and administration of the islands confers good title.

In 2008, the I.C.J. decided a territorial dispute between Malaysia and Singapore[1] that certainly indicates that good title can be lost. The case concerned a sovereignty dispute over a small island, a cluster of small rocks, and another rock that was only visible at low tide. The case is replete with very detailed evidence of history, treaties, correspondence, and conduct of the parties. With respect to the island the Court ruled that prior to 1844 the island of Pedra Branca/Pulau Batu Puteh had belonged to the Sultanate of Johor (which ultimately became part of Malaysia), but that "by 1980 sovereignty over [the island] had passed to Singapore." Id. at para. 276. Singapore, which had been a British colony until it became independent in 1963, based its claim on a British treaty with the Dutch (the other empire operating in the area from the eighteenth century); various activities on, or related to, the island; and the fact that Johor/Malaysia "took no action at all on [the island] from June 1850 for the whole of the following century or more." Id. at para. 275. Moreover, the "Acting Secretary of State of Johor in 1953 [stated] that Johor did not claim ownership of Pedra Branca/Pulau Batu Puteh." Id. In this case, the Court makes it clear that even if a state has good title, it can lose that title if another state engages in a variety of activities on, or relating to, the territory over a long period of time, where the original title holder does nothing and actually declares that it does not own the territory.

§7.7 UTI POSSIDETIS JURIS

Although the rule of uti possidetis juris (as you did possess, so you shall possess) traces its root to Roman civil law, it has been adapted in international law to

---

1. *Sovereignty over Pedra Branca/Pulau Batu Puteh, Middle Rocks and South Ledge* (Malaysia v. Singapore), 2008 I.C.J. 12.

provide a rule for states emerging from colonial rule. Colonial powers often drew the borders of colonized countries to suit their own purposes with little regard for ethnic, racial, religious, or even natural geographic divisions. After World War II, almost all colonized states claimed independence. The rule of uti possidetis juris required the newly independent states to accept the boundaries as they had been drawn up by the colonial administrators. The International Court of Justice has often incorporated the uti possidetis juris rule into decisions on territorial disputes. In the frontier dispute between Burkina Faso and Mali, the Court stated that the purpose of uti possidetis juris "is to prevent the independence and stability of new States being endangered by fratricidal struggles provoked by the challenging of frontiers following the withdrawal of the administering power." Frontier Dispute (Burkina Faso v. Mali), 1986 I.C.J. 554 at para. 23. The rule was expressly accepted by African states in the Cairo Declaration of 1964, and has also been applied in the European context. See, e.g., Statement of the European Arbitration Commission relating to the breakup of the former Yugoslavia: "it is well established that, whatever the circumstances, the right to self-determination must not involve changes to existing frontiers at the time of independence (uti possidetis juris) except where the States concerned agree otherwise." 92 I.L.R. 168 (1992). The rule has also been applied in South America. See, e.g., Land, Island and Maritime Frontier Dispute (El Salvador v. Honduras: Nicaragua intervening), 1992 I.C.J. 351.

Questions sometimes arise concerning which rule, of various territorial rules, takes precedence. For example, can uti possidetis juris be nullified by subsequent occupation? This question was answered by the Court in Frontier Dispute (Burkina Faso v. Mali), 1986 I.C.J. 554 at para. 23, where it stated that one aspect of the rule of uti possidetis juris "is found in the pre-eminence accorded to legal title [arising from uti possidetis juris] over effective possession as a basis of sovereignty."

More recently, the Court has indicated that although the rule of uti possidetis juris might clearly have settled a mainland territorial dispute, as it did with respect to the Honduran/Nicaraguan land border, that rule would not necessarily resolve a dispute over the sovereignty of offshore islands. With respect to such islands the Court concluded: "that the principle of uti possidetis affords inadequate assistance in determining sovereignty over these islands because nothing clearly indicates whether the islands were attributed to the colonial provinces of Nicaragua or of Honduras prior to or upon independence." Territorial and Maritime Dispute Between Nicaragua and Honduras in the Caribbean Sea (Nicaragua v. Honduras), 2007 I.C.J. 659 at para. 167. In other words, where there had been no indication by the colonial power concerning which of the two colonies could claim the islands and no attempt at demarcation, then the islands could not be claimed using the uti possidetis rule.

The Court then went on to examine whether "title may be inferred from the effective exercise of powers appertaining to the authority of the State over a given territory." *Id.* at para. 172. The Court ultimately ruled that: "having examined all of the evidence related to the claims of the Parties as to sovereignty over the islands . . . , including the evidentiary value of maps and the question of recognition by third States, [it] concludes that Honduras has sovereignty over these islands." *Id.* at para. 227.

Example 7-3

Assume that Sportuan, a great European power, administered vast areas of Asia during the eighteenth and nineteenth centuries. Two adjacent territories were administered as separate colonies, Nord (to the North) and Sord (to the South), although large parts of both colonies had never been explored or inhabited. In 1961, Sportuan was forced to grant independence to Nord and Sord, who declared their sovereignty over the land as administered as the colony of Nord and Sord, respectively. Since 1962 Sord has sent annual expeditions into the uninhabited areas of Nord. It has erected permanent research stations in dense forest areas and has issued licenses to some of its own citizens to fish in the rivers of those areas. Nord has never protested these activities probably because it did not know about them.

In 2010, Sord filed a suit in the I.C.J. against Nord claiming the uninhabited areas of Nord "on the basis of more than forty years continuous occupation and displays of sovereignty in areas where no other sovereign exercises any authority."

Will the Court rule in favor of Sord's or Nord's title to the uninhabited areas?

Explanation

The Court has indicated that the principle of *uti possidetis juris* will trump subsequent occupation. It has declared that: "a key aspect of the principle [of *uti possidetis*] is the denial of the possibility of *terra nullius*." *Land, Island and Maritime Frontier Dispute* (El Salvador v. Honduras: Nicaragua intervening), 1992 I.C.J. 351 at para. 42. Similarly in an Arbitral Award of the Swiss Federal Council of 1922 concerning the boundary between Colombia and Venezuela (1 R.I.A.A. 228) quoted with the approval by the I.C.J. in the *Land, Island and Maritime Frontier Dispute supra* at para. 42, the tribunal stated:

> This general principle [of *uti possidetis juris*] offered the advantage of establishing an absolute rule that there was not in *law* . . . any *terra nullius*; while there might exist many regions which had never been occupied by the Spaniards and many unexplored or inhabited by non-civilized natives, these regions were reputed to belong in law to whichever of the Republics succeeded to the Spanish province to which these territories were attached by virtue of the old Royal ordinances of the Spanish mother country. These territories, although not

occupied in fact were by common consent deemed to be occupied in law . . . by the new Republic. . . ."

Some scholars point out that the rule of *uti possidetis juris* directly conflicts with another rule of international law, the right of peoples to self-determination. (For details of this principle, see Chapter 4, §4.3.) They argue that the rigidity of the rule has often given rise to ethnic conflicts and may in fact be one of the main exacerbators of civil wars. Joshua Castellino and Steve Allen, *Title to Territory in International Law: A Temporal Analysis*, ch. 1 (2003).

§7.8 ACCRETION AND AVULSION

Occasionally natural events occur to the geography of a region to alter the shape of the territory. There may be a gradual increase in the land through silt deposits or shifts in the sea shore or river beds. These processes are known as accretion. Violent subterranean eruptions also cause the emergence of territory or the alteration in the shape of existing land. This activity is known as avulsion. Usually states must just put up with the configuration of the land that nature ascribes to them (although the Dutch have rather successfully resisted this type of resignation through an ingenious system of dikes). If accretion occurs on an international boundary, as on a boundary river, the general view is that the international boundary will shift. If avulsion occurs on an international boundary the general view is that the boundary will not be altered. Such occurrences are rare. See *Kasikili/Sedudu Island* (Botswana v. Namibia), 1999 I.C.J. 1045. The U.S. Supreme Court is sometimes asked to rule on issues of accretion and avulsion in boundary disputes between different states within the U.S. In 1998, the Supreme Court stated: "We have long recognized that a sudden shoreline change known as avulsion (as distinct from accretion, or gradual change in configuration) 'has no effect on boundary' . . . and that this 'is the received rule of law of nations on this point, as laid down by all the writers of authority', . . . including Sir William Blackstone. . . ." *New Jersey v. New York*, 523 U.S. 767, 784 (1998) (citations omitted).

Example 7-4

The Elizabeth River marks the boundary between State N and State S. State N is located to the north of State S. A 1914 treaty between the two states mainly concerned exports and imports between the states but mentioned that "the middle of the Elizabeth River marks the boundary between State N and State S." Over the decades the Elizabeth River had shifted its course so that now the river loops several yards farther south than it did in 1914.

Will State S be successful when it claims that the boundary between State S and State N should be calculated by reference to the middle of the Elizabeth River as it was in 1914 rather than the middle of the river as it now is?

Explanation

No. State S will not be successful unless State S could point to language in the treaty that said something like: "and the boundary shall not be considered to be altered when or if the river alters its course." There is no such language here and so any international court would find that the gradual shifts in the river had occurred by the process of accretion and thus the boundary would have shifted as the middle of the river shifted.

Example 7-5

Suppose that State S had gradually filled in the land along the river's edge by adding several yards to the southern shore of the river and thus pushing the middle of the river several yards to the north.

Would State S be successful in arguing that because the middle of the river had now shifted north, the boundary had also shifted?

Explanation

No. State S would not be successful. Filled land would, in all probability, be treated as a form of avulsion and thus the boundary would not shift. Compare, *New Jersey v. New York*, 523 U.S. 767 (1998). (New York did not gain sovereignty over land added to Ellis Island [owned by New York], where the filled land was on the New Jersey side of the river.)

§7.9 SPECIAL TERRITORIAL REGIMES

Certain areas of the universe are very inhospitable to human habitation, such as the Arctic or Antarctic or the Moon. Many internationalists would like these areas not to be subject to the usual rules of territorial acquisition and to be declared: "the common heritage of mankind." This view has however, met with some resistance.

§7.9.1 The Arctic

Most of the Arctic is a solid mass of ice or ice floes, rather than "land" as such. This raises the question as to whether any states can claim sovereignty over the area. Many environmentalists would like to see the area declared incapable of acquisition but several states have laid claim to the Arctic, principally Canada, Denmark, Finland, Norway, Russia, Sweden, and the U.S. Some of these states claim areas of the Arctic based on the sector system. By this system a state pinpoints its most easterly and westerly claims to territory and draws a triangle from these points to the pole, claiming all the territory within the triangle. These claims have not been recognized by the world community, and there is some hope that interested nations will work cooperatively to achieve an internationally protected conservation area in the Arctic.

Recently, however, scientists seem to agree that the Arctic ice cap is melting. Mining for minerals and regular sea lanes may become possible. On May 28, 2008, five states that border the Arctic Ocean issued the *Ilulissat Declaration* in which they pledged to work cooperatively in the region. They also declared that they "see no need to develop a new comprehensive international legal regime to govern the Arctic Ocean." Some have viewed this latter statement as bid to keep other states from weighing in on the issue of sovereignty in the area.

§7.9.2 The Antarctic

Numerous states have claimed various portions of the Antarctic, and many of these claims are overlapping. Some states refuse to recognize any land claims to the Antarctic, while others have recognized some claims but not others. In an effort to stabilize the operative regime in the area, the Antarctic Treaty was signed in 1959 and entered into force in 1961, 402 U.N.T.S. 71. All of the states currently claiming territory in the Antarctic are parties to the treaty (Argentina, Australia, Chile, France, New Zealand, Norway, and the United Kingdom). In addition, a number of other states are also parties to the treaty. The treaty requires that "Antarctica shall be used for peaceful purposes only" and prohibits "any measures of a military nature . . ." (art. I). The treaty also guarantees "[f]reedom of scientific investigation" (art. II) and prohibits "nuclear explosions" and "disposal . . . of radioactive waste material . . ." (art. V). Territorial claims are frozen (!) "while the present Treaty is in force" (art. VI). The treaty has two amendment procedures. First, it may be amended by a unanimous vote of all the treaty partners named in the preamble to the treaty, and second, it provides that after thirty years from the treaty's entry into force (i.e., 1991), any such treaty partner may call for a conference to review the treaty (art. XII).

There have also been a large number of measures taken to protect the Antarctic environment including the Convention for the Conservation of Antarctic Marine Living Resources, signed in 1980 and entered into force in 1982, 1329 U.N.T.S. 47, and the Protocol on Environmental Protection to the Antarctic Treaty, signed in 1991 and entered into force in 1998, which imposes a moratorium on mining in Antarctica, reprinted at 30 I.L.M. 145 (1991). At the moment the world community seems unwilling to treat the territory of Antarctica as regular territory subject to claims of sovereignty and exploitation. The increased understanding both of the fragility of the environment and of global environmental interdependence may preserve for Antarctica a legal regime different from the traditional notion of state sovereignty.

§7.9.3 Celestial Bodies and Space

The major treaty operative in this arena, the Treaty on Principles Governing the Activities of States in the Exploration and Uses of Outer Space, Including the Moon and Other Celestial Bodies, 610 U.N.T.S. 205, creates a regime that is described as "the province of all mankind" (art. I). This treaty entered into force in 1967 and has been ratified by over ninety states. The Outer Space Treaty, as it is known, states that all exploration shall be carried out "for the benefit and in the interests of all countries . . ." (art. I) and that outer space "is not subject to national appropriation by claim of sovereignty, by means of use or occupation, or by any other means" (art. II). The area is to be used "exclusively for peaceful purposes" (art. IV), and nuclear weapons are prohibited (art. IV). A later treaty, the Agreement Governing the Activities of States on the Moon and Other Celestial Bodies, 1363 U.N.T.S. 3, entered into force in 1984 and emphasizes that the natural resources of the area are the common heritage of mankind.

Other recent agreements include the 1968 Agreement on the Rescue of Astronauts, the Return of Astronauts and the Return of Objects Launched into Outer Space, 672 U.N.T.S. 119, which governs cooperation in rescuing and returning astronauts and the 1972 Convention on International Liability for Damage Caused by Objects Launched into Outer Space, 961 U.N.T.S. 187, which imposes strict liability on the launching state for "damage caused by its space object on the surface of the earth or to aircraft in flight" (art. II) and fault liability for "damage being caused elsewhere than on the surface of the earth to a space object of one launching state or to persons or property on board such space object by a space object of another launching state . . ." (art. III). It is clear from the above treaties that the traditional notions of sovereignty and ownership are not operative in outer space or on the moon or other celestial bodies.

Note

International law, like domestic law, generally applies what is called *inter-temporal law*. This concept means that: "a judicial fact must be appreciated in the light of the law contemporary with it, and not of the law in force at the time which a dispute in regard to it rises or falls to be settled." *The Island of Palmas* case (or, *Miangas*) (Netherlands v. U.S.), 2 R.I.A.A. 829, at 845 (1928). Nonetheless, the arbitrator in the *Island of Palmas* case also stated that an effective title is not only required for the act of acquiring title but is also required "for the maintenance of the right [to title]. . . . The same principle which subjects the act creative of a right to the law in force at the time the right arises, demands that the existence of the right, in other words its continued manifestation, shall follow the conditions required by the evolution of law." *Id.* This latter concept, namely that if the rules on the maintenance of title changes, the title holder must meet the new requirements of the law in order to continue to hold good title, is controversial.

Example 7-6

The State of Astra claims to have discovered the island of Walm in the sixteenth century. Astra has various state documents describing the discovery that date back to 1560. At that time Walm was inhabited by a tribe known as the Walmans. The island is five miles in length and three miles in width and is blessed by a temperate climate and much nutritious vegetation. It lies 200 miles off the south coast of Astra, which is the nearest mainland. Recently large deposits of gold have been found on the eastern tip of the island.

During the sixteenth and seventeenth centuries Astra occasionally sent settlers to Walm. The Astran flag was planted near the main settlement, and an Astran official was sent to the island for two months every year to carry out geographic surveys and to write a report on the state of the indigenous population. Some time toward the end of the seventeenth century this official was conferred the title "Governor of Walm," although his activities remained the same as they had been previously.

In 1714 a naval vessel from the State of Balud came across the island by accident after a storm had blown the ship off course. The crew went ashore and finding only indigenous Walmans, the captain of the ship planted Balud's flag, and the crew built several log cabins. No evidence was found of Astran presence. Presumably the Astran flag had succumbed to a storm or otherwise been removed, and any Astran settlers who might have lived there had either returned home or died. The captain of the Balud ship left several crew members on the island and returned to Balud, a state 700 miles to the west. Later that year, seventy-five Balud settlers were sent to the island. They quickly established homes and farms and, apart from a few skirmishes with the Walm tribesmen, seemed to enjoy a pleasant existence. A Balud governor was installed a few months later.

Later in the year, when the Astran governor came for his annual two-month-long trip to the island, he was amazed to find the Balud settlement. He immediately protested to the Balud governor, who dismissed Astran claims to the territory as "fanciful."

Six months later the Astran navy launched an attack on the island in an attempt to retake it. The Astran navy was soundly defeated by the Balud settlers and some tribesmen who had been persuaded to join the Baluds in the fight.

Since then, Balud has ruled Walm as a colony. The settlers have multiplied and intermarried with the tribesmen, and the governor remains in residence. Astra has issued official protests from time to time in any forum willing to listen and, since 1945, when both Astra and Balud joined the United Nations, has frequently filed protests with the General Assembly. No action has ever been taken by the General Assembly on the matter.

Does either Astra or Balud have good title to Walm?

Explanation

The fact pattern of Example 7-6 above is characteristic of many disputed titles. The resolution of these claims is frequently very fact specific and may require the court or arbitral tribunal to evaluate evidence dating back many centuries. The "facts" presented by a particular state are often challenged by the other claimant, which may well present a quite different version of history.

Astra appears to be able to document its discovery of Walm in the mid-sixteenth century. Although there were Indigenous Peoples on the island, international law, at that time, did not prohibit claims of ownership by foreigners provided the foreign nation "displayed sovereignty." Astra planted its flag, sent settlers to the island, carried out surveys, and by the late 1600s had appointed a governor. All of the above acts were probably sufficient to confer good title under international law at that time. There is the issue of whether sending a governor for only two months a year, who only seems to have carried out geographic surveys and written reports on the inhabitants, constitutes a sufficient display of sovereignty to warrant good title but in all probability the answer is that such activities were sufficient at that time to confer title, at least on a small, remote island.

We can probably conclude, fairly easily, that Astra had good title to Walm by the end of the seventeenth century, at least up until the time when the Balud ship arrived. (At that time international law did not recognize the right of Indigenous Peoples to self-determination. Today, such peoples would have a right to determine their own form of government, and colonization is no longer accepted by international law. See Chapter 4.)

7. Title to Territory

When the Balud ship arrived in 1714, they found no evidence of the Astrans and planted Balud's flag, presumably representing a claim of sovereignty. Balud settlers then arrived, and a governor from Balud was installed. Although Astra protested to the Balud government upon finding the Balud settlers and governor in Walm later in 1714, which might be viewed as preserving Astra's earlier title, Astra has never been able to reestablish its presence on the island. Astra's attempt to retake the island by force was unsuccessful.

The problem above presents the as yet unresolved question of whether it is possible for state to loose its good title when another state moves into the territory either initially by force, or, in this case, initially largely peacefully but then by successfully forcefully resisting the attempt to retake the island by the original title holder. Today, the acquisition of title to territory by force is not permitted but in 1714 international law did not prohibit the use of force, so that its use by Balud to retain the island did not violate international law. Balud would, therefore, appear to have the stronger claim. The *Pedra Branca/Pulau Batu Puteh* case *supra*, is distinguishable in that Johor/Malaysia had declared it did not claim ownership at a time when Singapore (Britain) did claim title.

There have been examples of states that have successfully regained title to lands that they considered wrongfully taken from them. In the middle of the nineteenth century, the British defeated the Chinese in the Opium Wars and acquired title "in perpetuity" to Hong Kong Island under the 1842 Treaty of Nanking. Later, Kowloon, the part of Hong Kong attached to mainland China, was leased to Britain for ninety-nine years. At the end of the ninety-nine-year lease, China announced that it would not renew the lease and that she was also going to take back Hong Kong island (which she had ceded to Britain in perpetuity) because it had wrongfully been taken by an "unlawful war." By 1997, political realities dictated that Britain had to hand back to China Hong Kong island and the rest of the leased territories. 1984 Agreement between China and U.K. reprinted at 23 I.L.M. 1366 (1984). The people of Hong Kong played no role in determining their status.

International Human Rights

§8.1 Introduction
    §8.1.1 The Origins of International Human Rights Law
    §8.1.2 Some Theories of Human Rights
§8.2 The Law of Treaties in the Human Rights Context
    §8.2.1 Interpretation
    §8.2.2 Reservations
    §8.2.3 Non-Self-Executing
    §8.2.4 Termination
§8.3 Human Rights Law in the United Nations System
    §8.3.1 U.N. Charter and Universal Declaration of Human
           Rights
    §8.3.2 The International Covenant on Civil and Political Rights
           Rights and Freedoms Under the ICCPR
           States' Duties to Implement ICCPR Rights and Freedoms
           States' Powers to Derogate from or Limit ICCPR Rights
           Monitoring and Enforcement of Rights
           Optional Protocols
    §8.3.3 International Covenant on Economic, Social,
           and Cultural Rights
           Rights and Freedoms Under the ICESCR
           States' Duties to Implement ICESCR Rights
           Monitoring and Enforcement Under the ICESCR
    §8.3.4 Customary International Human Rights Law
§8.4 Charter-based Bodies
    §8.4.1 U.N. High Commissioner for Human Rights

§8.4.2 Human Rights Council
§8.4.3 International Court of Justice
§8.4.4 U.N. Security Council

§8.1 INTRODUCTION

Where, after all, do universal human rights begin? In small places, close to home — so close and so small that they cannot be seen on any maps of the world. Yet they are the world of the individual person; the neighborhood he lives in; the school or college he attends; the factory, farm, or office where he works. Such are the places where every man, woman, and child seeks equal justice, equal opportunity, equal dignity without discrimination. Unless these rights have meaning there, they have little meaning anywhere. Without concerted citizen action to uphold them close to home, we shall look in vain for progress in the larger world. — *Eleanor Roosevelt*

§8.1.1 The Origins of International Human Rights Law

Whereas international law generally governs the conduct and relations between States, human rights law transcends state boundaries by seeking to define and uphold those rights held universally by every person regardless of nationality. Thus, human rights law differs from the rest of international law in that it deals with the way a State acts toward individuals and groups, and in particular, its own citizens. The "law" of international human rights is fairly new in the sense that prior to World War II, how a State treated its own citizens was predominately a matter of domestic concern and thus beyond the reach of international law. With that said, the origins of human rights law stem at least as far back as the American Declaration of Independence (1776), the American Constitution and Bill of Rights (1789), and the French Declaration of the Rights of Man and the Citizen (1789), many of which speak to the "rights of man" to such things as "life," "liberty," and "property." Moreover, prior to World War II, there were a few international treaties addressing some human rights issues, such as the Slavery Convention, 60 L.N.T.S. 253 (1926), the International Convention for the Suppression of Traffic in Women and Children, 60 U.N.T.S. 416 (1921), and a few treaties that addressed the rights of minorities within various States. There were also international rules that governed a State's treatment of aliens (noncitizens) found within its borders. Yet, in those early years, there was no systematic approach to promoting and protecting human rights.

Following World War II, an "internationalization" of human rights took place. In other words, nation-states began to accept the notion that human rights were not merely matters of domestic concern, but rather the concerns of all states interested in promoting and maintaining world peace and security.[1] A multitude of declarations and treaties relating to human rights followed, including the Charter of the United Nations (U.N. Charter) and the Universal Declaration of Human Rights. However, the primary purpose of the modern human rights movement was not to supplant national laws relating to human rights, but rather to supplement and enhance those protections. This was done (1) by "internationalizing" human rights (that is, making them a matter of both domestic and international concern) and (2) by "universalizing" many of those rights (that is, articulating through treaties a core set of rights that attached to individuals by virtue of their personhood and, more recently, by virtue of their membership in a group).

Example 8-1

Citizens of State I are peaceably protesting the re-election of their president on the grounds of electoral fraud. To quiet protests, government forces have begun to arrest demonstrators, holding them without charge and without the right to contact family or lawyers for months at a time. The United Nations High Commissioner for Human Rights has urged State I to observe due process in its dealings with protesters, including the right not to be subject to prolonged arbitrary detention. The State maintains that the political protests involve the citizens of State I and thus are solely the concern of State I.

Is State I correct that these are matters of domestic concern only?

Explanation

Historically, State I was correct. How a State acted toward its own citizens was once beyond the purview of international law. Today, however, there are many international human rights laws that will apply to State I's actions, particularly as they relate to the question of disappearance and prolonged arbitrary detention. A complete answer to this question may well turn on whether State I is a party to various international human rights instruments, such as the International Covenant on Civil and Political Rights (see §8.3.2). Some "human rights," such as the right not to be arbitrarily detained for prolonged periods of time or rules against causing the disappearance of

---

1. An important turning point in this regard were the trials at Nuremberg and Tokyo, in which individuals were held accountable for domestic acts that amounted to gross violations of human rights. *The Nuremberg Judgment*, 6 F.R.D. 69, 110 (1946). For a more detailed discussion of these early tribunals, see Chapter 11, International Criminal Law.

individuals, have risen to the level of customary law and thus would be binding on State I regardless of whether it is a party to any human rights treaties (see §§2.2 and 8.3.4).

§8.1.2 Some Theories of Human Rights

We have already discussed some of the foundational instruments that articulated the notion of individual rights. However, how do we know what rights fall under the umbrella of international human rights? Do they merely encompass such things as life, liberty, property, and equality; or do they include various necessities such as food, water, shelter, or employment? This question in turn opens the door to a host of additional queries, such as: What is meant by this idea of "rights"? Where do these rights and freedoms come from? Are they really applicable to everyone at all times, or are they limited and relative to one's circumstance? There are different theories of human rights law, which may provide us with some preliminary responses to these questions, but they are not strictly "legal" questions that can be answered simply. By considering different philosophical theories and views of human rights law, we can discern more fully the roots of human rights norms, as well as some possible reasons for lack of compliance with those norms. The following materials are a brief sampling of some of those theories.

One such perspective is the idea of natural justice, espoused early on in the writings of Aristotle and in later centuries in the writings of Immanuel Kant and John Locke. Natural law theorists posit that people are born with certain inalienable rights that cannot be taken away by the State because they are tied to one's personhood. At the core of natural law theory is the idea that law and morality are intertwined and that, although humans make laws, a law that is immoral is also invalid because it goes against nature. William Blackstone described natural law as "binding over all the globe, in all countries, and at all times: no human laws are of any validity, if contrary to this." William Blackstone, *Commentaries on the Law of England* 27 (1979). This language used by Blackstone could perhaps be used to describe the theory behind peremptory norms (see §§2.2.4 and 8.3.4), showing the connection between modern human rights theory and the philosophy of natural law. Of course, in making this point, we cannot ignore some of the early origins of international law, when religious tenets defined a process of colonialism that espoused the natural rights of human beings, but was often brutal in terms of its selectivity and application. Other human rights theorists argue that human rights law is grounded in the foundational principles of liberty, equality, and human dignity, which are in turn linked to concepts of justice and democracy. Another source of human rights law is known as legal positivism. Legal positivism may be contrasted with natural law theory in that it is said to be made by humans as a reflection of social norms that are then codified and advanced by the State, rather than by any inherent concept of right and wrong. Positivism is essential to considering the foundations of human rights, since in modern times the study of human rights is primarily grounded in positive law, such as treaties and other such agreements. With that said, modern international human rights law also draws on natural law tradition in terms of its conception of rights as being inherent or universal.

While there are a host of other human rights theories to be explored,[2] this later point on the "universality" of rights brings us to the issues of universalism, communitarianism, and relativism — that is, whether human rights exist in some abstract universal form or must be tied in some way to community and culture. As earlier noted, this notion of universality of human rights is one of the foundational principles of international human rights law. As the Universal Declaration of Human Rights (see *infra* §8.3.1) declares, "[a]ll human beings are born free and equal in dignity and rights." G.A. Res. 217A, art.1, U.N. GAOR, 3d Sess., 1st plen. mtg., U.N. Doc. A/810 (Dec. 12, 1948). However some critics have argued against the concept of universality, on the grounds that such a view does not reflect all of the various cultures of the world, but rather is a product of the cultural values held by some groups of people to the exclusion of others. This idea is called cultural relativism, and it is the notion that human rights law is not universal in nature because morality and ethics differ between cultures, making it impossible for human rights to be globally uniform.[3] Cultural relativism is often brought up in discussions about cultural practices that facially seem to violate universal norms, such as the case of domestic property laws that preclude women from owning or inheriting property. Others speak more in terms of the ethics of community, rather than notions of "relativism," which allow for the development of a tentative list of "rights."[4] Also, it is not necessarily always a question of cultural relativism versus universality. There is the issue of respecting cultural difference and diversity, while at the same time promoting a universal concept of "human dignity." As one United Nations body has stated, "the defence of cultural diversity is an ethical imperative, inseparable from respect for human dignity." See Universal Declaration on Cultural Diversity, UNESCO Res. 25, UNESCO Doc. 31 C/25 (Nov. 2, 2001). Questions involving the right to culture are explored more fully in the section on group rights in Chapter 9 (see §9.5).

---

2. For a more general discussion of the theories of human rights law, see Jerome J. Shestack, *The Philosophic Foundations of Human Rights*, 20.2 Hum. Rts. Q. 201, 201-234 (1998).
3. For a critique of this theory, see generally Fernando Teson, *International Human Rights and Cultural Relativism*, 25 Va. J. Int'l L. 869 (1985); Jack Donnelly, *Cultural Relativism and Universal Human Rights*, 6 Hum. Rts. Q. 400 (1984).
4. See, e.g., Chris Brown, *Universal Human Rights: A Critique*, 1 Int'l J. Hum. Rts. 41 (1997).

Example 8-2

Mia, a woman from State Y, inherits a piece of property left to her by her father through a validly executed will. State Y is a party to the major international human rights treaties, which uniformly call for a prohibition on discrimination based on sex. However, inheritance in State Y is also determined by customary law. Community norms prohibit women such as Mia from inheriting or selling lands within the community, regardless of whether her father has bequeathed them to her by will. Mia sues in court to enforce her ownership rights to the property.

Under the various theories of human rights law discussed above, how might a court address Mia's claim to property?

Explanation

The scope of the rights of women to own and dispose of real property is an ongoing human rights issue in a number of countries. For instance, in the Tanzanian case of *Ephraim v. Pastory*, the High Court of Tanzania upheld the right of women to inherit and sell property, despite customary laws to the contrary. 87 Int. L. Rep. 106 (1992). The High Court stated that the Tanzanian Bill of Rights and its incorporation of the Universal Declaration of Human Rights, as well as Tanzania's ratification of the African Charter on Human and Peoples' Rights, all required Tanzania to prohibit discrimination based on sex. The High Court thus refused to apply a cultural practice that allowed only males to inherit and sell land, noting that the cultural law had outlived its usefulness. In doing so, the High Court of Tanzania adhered to a universal view of human rights as it related to issues of equality. In addition, the existence of various treaties prohibiting discrimination against women created positive law that the court felt compelled to follow, which in turn impacted the social norms and customs of the state.

A similar question was posed before the Supreme Court of Zimbabwe with a somewhat different result. In the case of *Magaya v. Magaya*, SC No. 210-98 (Zimbabwe, Feb. 16, 1999), a woman asserted her rights as the eldest child of her deceased father to inherit her father's estate intestate as against another later-born son. Unlike the Tanzanian High Court in the above case, the Supreme Court of Zimbabwe upheld a customary law that gave preference to males as heirs. According to the lower court, a daughter was excluded from inheriting her father's estate under the laws of her community regardless of birth order. This was so, according to the court, because she had certain obligations to her new marital family that would conflict with any obligation she might have had to her original family as the heir of that estate. There were a number of positive laws, including the Constitution of Zimbabwe, that prohibited discrimination based on sex. However, the court found that the Constitution also permitted the question of the devolution of property on death to be controlled by customary law. As such, one might argue that the court adopted a relativist view of human rights law as it relates to certain cultural practices and the question of "equality" or "nondiscrimination." Others might conclude that the court was upholding and promoting community mores and practices as they relate to familial rights and responsibilities. The differing conclusions reached by these two courts illustrate how various theories of rights may impact the application of human rights precepts.[5]

The following statement, adopted by consensus at the U.N.'s 1993 World Conference on Human Rights, is a useful guide to working through issues of relativism, universalism, and the application of law:

> All human rights are universal, indivisible and interdependent. . . . The international community must treat human rights globally in a fair and equal manner. . . . While the significance of national and regional particularities and various historical, cultural, and religious backgrounds must be borne in mind, it is the duty of States, regardless of their political, economic or cultural systems, to promote and protect all human rights and fundamental freedoms. World Conference on Human Rights, Final Declaration and Programme of Action, U.N. Doc. A/CONF.157/23 (July 12, 1993), sec. I. para. 5.

§8.2 THE LAW OF TREATIES IN THE HUMAN RIGHTS CONTEXT

Chapter 3 of this book provides a detailed discussion of the law of treaties and should be read in conjunction with this section. As noted in that chapter, the law of treaties has long been a part of international customary law and was eventually codified in the Vienna Convention on the Law of Treaties (VCLT), 1155 U.N.T.S. 331 (1969). While the United States is not a party to the VCLT, it does recognize the provisions of that convention as reflecting customary international law. Historically, treaties involved reciprocal benefits and burdens between and among various states. Human rights treaties have also been made between and among states and govern state behavior. Yet, the primary beneficiaries of those agreements are not the states, but rather individuals and, in some cases, groups. Given the unique status of human rights treaties, some scholars and human rights organizations maintain that there is a "special" body of law that applies in the context of

---

5. For a more nuanced analysis of this case, see Bigge & Briesen, *Conflict in the Zimbabwean Courts: Women's Rights and Indigenous Self-Determination in Magaya v. Magaya*, 13 Harv. Hum. Rights J. 289 (2000).

interpreting these types of treaties. This section articulates some of the issues and rules relating specifically to human rights treaties.

§8.2.1 Interpretation

The general rules on the interpretation of treaties are discussed in §3.7 of this book. Article 31 of the VCLT establishes the basic rules of interpretation: that a treaty is to be read in "good faith in accordance with [its] ordinary meaning," in "context," and in "light of its object and purpose." In ascertaining the meaning of any treaty, an international court or human rights body may consult both the text of the instrument, as well as any agreement relating to that treaty. This might include subsequent agreements and practices of the contracting parties that relate to the application or interpretation of that treaty, as well as any "relevant rules of international law" applicable to the parties. VCLT art. 31(1)-(3). Supplementary means of interpretation, and most notably preparatory work, though, is limited primarily to situations where the ordinary meaning suggests either ambiguity or absurd or unreasonable results. VCLT, art. 32.

These rules of interpretation are particularly relevant with respect to human rights treaties, the primary "object and purpose" of which is to provide basic protection of rights for individuals and groups. Thus, an objective interpretation of these treaties that is based on ascertaining the meaning of the text, rather than some subjective interpretation that is based on ascertaining the "intent of the parties," makes sense in the human rights context. Regional human rights bodies, which are covered in Chapter 9 (see §9.4), have taken a similar view of human rights treaty interpretation. For instance, the European Court of Human Rights and the Inter-American Court have noted the "special character" of human rights treaties, which requires them to be interpreted in light of "present-day conditions" and not past convictions.[6]

This does not mean, however, that treaty interpretation in the human rights context is at all static. As "living instruments whose interpretation must consider the changes over time and present-day conditions," the interpretation of these instruments is in fact a "dynamic" one.[7] As we will see in the European human rights system, this "objective" but "dynamic" interpretation is layered with a "margin of appreciation," which basically means that there might be some differences among States when it comes to interpreting a treaty provision. This "margin of appreciation" is primarily a rule of interpretation in the European human rights context, and its scope is

---

6. See *Soering v. United Kingdom*, 11 Eur. Hum. Rts. Rep. 439 (1989); see *Selmouni v. France*, 199-V Eur. Ct. H.R. (Grand Chamber) (July 28, 1999), para. 101.
7. See *Juan Humberto Sanchez* case, Inter-Am. Ct. H.R. (ser. A) No. 102 (Nov. 26, 2003), para. 56.

dependent on the type of right in question and how fundamental that right is in a democratic society (see §9.4.1).[8]

Example 8-3

State Z is considering whether to extradite an individual to State A for prosecution in a capital case. State Z does not utilize capital punishment and is a party to a human rights treaty that absolutely prohibits "torture and cruel, inhuman, degrading treatment." The individual has filed a claim with a human rights court claiming that his rights not to be subjected to "torture" or "cruel and inhuman treatment" will be violated should State Z proceed with the extradition. He claims that this is so because he would be subjected to what is known as the "death row" phenomenon. The human rights treaty does not specifically define what constitutes "torture" or "cruel, inhuman, or degrading treatment."

In ascertaining the meaning of this treaty provision, what rules of treaty interpretation might be relevant to the court's analysis?

Explanation

According to article 31 of the VCLT, the human rights court should consider the "ordinary meaning" of the terms "torture" or "cruel, inhuman, and degrading treatment." The court must also consider what interpretation would be consistent with the treaty's object and purpose to absolutely prohibit torture and other such behavior. In addition, the court might consider the "context" surrounding the treaty, including other provisions of the treaty that might shed some light on the meaning of these terms or other subsequent regional or international agreements or practices that might be relevant to this question.

This example is factually similar to the case of *Soering v. United Kingdom*, Eur. Ct. H.R. (ser. A) No. 161 (1989), which involved an interpretation of the meaning of torture under article 3 of the European Convention on Human Rights in cases of extradition to countries with capital punishment. In that case, the European Court of Human Rights looked to a host of factors in ascertaining the meaning of torture, including other provisions of the treaty that when read together with article 3 suggested an absolute prohibition against torture even in times of war or national emergency. It also considered what other international human rights instruments with similar prohibitions on torture had to say about the issue, such as the International Covenant on Civil and Political Rights (see §8.3.2), the U.N. Convention

---

8. See, e.g., *Handyside v. United Kingdom*, 24 Eur. Ct. H.R. (ser. A) No. 5493/72 (1979) (relating to freedom of expression under article 10 of the European Convention).

Against Torture and Other Cruel, Inhuman or Degrading Treatment or Punishment (see §9.2), and the American Convention on Human Rights (see §9.4.2).

Example 8-4

Assume in the above example that the preparatory work surrounding the drafting of the human rights treaty suggested a narrow definition of the term "torture" or "cruel and inhuman treatment" that would not necessarily preclude extradition to a country with capital punishment.

1) Would the preparatory work preclude the court from finding that State Z would violate its obligation under the treaty if it proceeded with the extradition?

2) What if State Z expresses concerns over becoming a "safe haven" for fugitives from justice, particularly those states that still utilize capital punishment? Is this a matter that the court could consider in interpreting the meaning of the term "torture" or "cruel and inhuman treatment?"

Explanation

On the question of preparatory work, it is not particularly relevant in the context of interpreting human rights treaties, except in limited circumstances. It is more important to consult the treaty itself and "present-day" conditions surrounding the meaning of such terms. For instance, in *Selmouni v. France*, 199-V Eur. Ct. H.R. (Grand Chamber) (July 28, 1999), the European Court noted that certain acts that were classified in the past as not being "torture" could be classified differently in the future. This was so because human rights treaties are "living instrument[s] which must be interpreted in the light of present-day conditions." *Id.*

With respect to the question of the relevance of State Z becoming a safe haven for fugitives, the European Court of Human Rights in *Soering* took the position that a "fair balance between the demands of the general interest of the community and the requirements of the protection of the individual's fundamental rights" must be "among the factors to be taken into account in the interpretation and application of the notions of inhuman and degrading treatment or punishment in extradition cases."[9] With that said, the court ultimately held that the U.K. would violate its obligations under the Convention should it proceed with the extradition, primarily because of the type of right at issue; that is, the right not to be subject to torture.

---

9. *Soering v. United Kingdom*, Eur. Ct. H.R. (ser. A) No. 161 (1989).

§8.2.2 Reservations

Articles 19-21 of the Vienna Convention on the Law of Treaties articulate the general rules on reservations, understandings, and declarations (RUDS). These rules are discussed in Chapter 3, The Law of Treaties (see §3.4). However, since RUDS are a common part of international human rights treaties, some discussion regarding their use in the human rights context is necessary. This section discusses some of the general issues that arise in the use of RUDS. More specific examples relating to individual treaties, such as the International Covenant on Civil and Political Rights (ICCPR) and the International Covenant on Economic, Social, and Cultural Rights (ICESCR), are discussed in §§8.3.2 and 8.3.3 of this chapter.

Generally speaking, a "reservation" is a unilateral statement by a treaty party that it will not comply with certain parts of a treaty, thereby limiting the state party's legal obligation under that treaty. "Understandings" are merely one state's interpretation of various provisions of a treaty, but they don't limit the state's legal obligation under that treaty. Simply because a state refers to something as an "understanding" as opposed to a "reservation," however, doesn't make it so. If the "understanding" actually limits or modifies the state's legal obligations under the treaty, then it is a "reservation." Some human rights treaties have provisions that address the use of reservations (see, e.g., Convention on the Elimination of Racial Discrimination, art. 20(2)), but most do not. A State may rely on RUDS because it may not agree with every provision contained in the document or may wish to provide its own interpretation of a provision. In the human rights context, where you want to encourage as many States as possible to sign on to the treaties, RUDS may be an important part of achieving that aim. At the same time, RUDS may provide an out for States wishing not to comply with the more onerous aspects of the treaty, including those aspects that would require a change in domestic law in order for the State to be in compliance. This tension between large-scale acceptance of a treaty and the acceptance of multiple reservations that may undermine any real responsibility on the part of a State is dealt with in part through rules of interpretation.

As Example 3-1 explains, the permissibility of a reservation in the human rights context is governed by the reservation's compatibility with the object and purpose of the treaty, unless of course the treaty expressly prohibits or limits the use of reservations (see VCLT, art. 19). What this "object and purpose" test basically means is that the reservation cannot undermine the essence of a human rights treaty, especially as it relates to the core aims of protecting and promoting fundamental rights and freedoms. This rule was originally laid down in the International Court of Justice (ICJ) case of *Reservations to the Convention on the Prevention and Punishment of the Crime of Genocide*, Advisory Opinion, 1951 I.C.J. 15 (May 28, 1951) and then later codified under article 19 of the Vienna Convention on the Law of Treaties.[10]

Another contentious aspect of reservations, particularly in the human rights context, is who gets to decide whether a reservation is in fact consistent with its object and purpose? While there is some dispute over this question, it is fair to say that international human rights bodies have the power to assess whether a state's reservation is permissible when that assessment is necessary for the exercise of their duties in terms of monitoring or enforcement. (See generally International Law Commission Annual Report, U.N. Doc. A/CN.4/SER.A/1997/Add.1 (Part 2), Ch. V., para. 82.)

A State may not assert a reservation to a treaty provision that has the character of a peremptory norm (*jus cogens*). Remember that this is a norm that binds all States regardless of any rule to the contrary, such as the prohibition against genocide (see §§2.2.4 and 8.3.4). Some international human rights bodies also maintain that no reservations may be made to human rights provisions that are non-derogable, i.e., rights that may not be suspended even in times of national emergency, or that have risen to the level of customary law. See, e.g., HRC, General Comment No. 24, U.N. Doc. CCPR/C/21/Rev.1/Add.6 (1994). The reason why such reservations are problematic is because they may well violate the object and purpose of the treaty.

Example 8-5

Assume State B is a party to the International Covenant on Civil and Political Rights (ICCPR) and makes the following "understanding" with respect to that human rights treaty: "To the extent that various provisions of this treaty conflict with the laws and constitution of State B, this treaty is to be read in a manner consistent with the laws and constitution of State B."

Is this a permissible "understanding" under the law of treaties?

Explanation

First, you must first consider whether State B's statement is, in fact, an understanding or a reservation in disguise. As one U.N. human rights body has noted, "if a statement, irrespective of its name or title purports to exclude or modify the legal effect of a treaty in its application to the State, it constitutes a reservation." HRC, General Comment No. 24. This is exactly what the statement of State B does; it limits the legal effect of the human rights treaty, proclaiming that even if the treaty calls for even greater individual or group rights than the laws and constitution of State B, State B

---

10. Another really confusing aspect of reservations relates to objections by one state party to reservations advanced by another state party. This issue is dealt with in Chapter 3 (see §3.4 and Example 3-2).

is merely bound by its domestic law and not the international treaty. Thus, it is a reservation and not an understanding.

Second, you must consider whether such a broad statement would be inconsistent with the "object and purpose" of the ICCPR. As noted in the introduction, one of the primary aims of international human rights law is to articulate fundamental rights and freedoms that we are all entitled to regardless of our nationality. If State B can avoid this obligation by merely proclaiming its domestic laws to be supreme in all situations where they conflict with its international obligations, it would undermine the very purpose of human rights treaties. Clearly reservations to certain provisions of the ICCPR are allowed (see §8.3.2). However, State B's reservation indicates an unwillingness to bring any of its laws into compliance with the international treaty. Such a reservation would render ineffective all those treaty provisions that would require a change in national law, which State B cannot do. See, e.g., HRC, General Comment No. 24, U.N. Doc. CCPR/C/21/Rev.1/Add.6 (1994), para. 12.

Example 8-6

State C submits the following reservation with respect to its obligations under an international human rights treaty known as the Convention on the Elimination of Discrimination Against Women (CEDAW): "In case of contradiction between any term of the Convention and the religious tenets of the State, State C is not under any obligation to observe the contradictory terms of the Convention." CEDAW states that "a reservation incompatible with the object and purpose of the present Convention shall not be permitted." State C seeks to preserve various religious and cultural tenets that are in conflict with the Convention, but many of these tenets incorporate rules that treat women differently than men with respect to property, marriage, and education.

Is this a permissible reservation?

Explanation

Once again the object and purpose of the treaty will control here. State C is obviously interested in preserving certain customs and religious beliefs and may not have ratified the treaty regime without the right to do so through the use of reservations. On the other hand, the underlying object and purpose of the CEDAW is to promote rights of nondiscrimination for women. This would include changes in domestic law and practices that perpetuate discrimination against women, no matter how entrenched those practices might be.

As discussed Chapter 9, this continues to be a difficult question with respect to the CEDAW, given the sheer number of reservations that have been made to that human rights treaty. See §9.2. Various human rights bodies have worked behind the scenes to encourage States to withdraw reservations that are legally questionable, with some degree of success.[11]

§8.2.3 Non-Self-Executing

The self-executing nature of treaties, that is whether they are directly enforceable in national courts, is dealt with in Chapter 3 of this book, which should be reviewed prior to reading this section. See §3.12.1. This issue is particularly important in the human rights context, since a proclamation that a treaty is non-self-executing may in fact impact the right of an individual or group to have an "effective remedy" for violation of an internationally protected human right.

What does it mean for a treaty to be self-executing? Generally speaking, it means that once a treaty is ratified, it becomes part of the national laws of that country and can be enforced without the need for implementing legislation. The question of whether a treaty is self-executing is in the first instance a matter of domestic law, and since it arises mainly in the United States context, the focus here will be on U.S. law.

Some U.S. human rights scholars argue that human rights treaties are part of the "supreme" law of the land pursuant to the Supremacy Clause of the U.S. Constitution and therefore are self-executing, except in limited circumstances. For instance, when a treaty requires the State party to make some act a crime, such as the Genocide Convention, it would obviously require legislative action. Others, including U.S. courts, maintain that the intention of the United States in ratifying a treaty controls the question of whether that treaty is self-executing and, since the U.S. government has declared all human rights treaties to be non-self-executing, the intent is clear.

It is also an issue of international human rights law. All the major human rights agreements require States to provide remedies to individuals for violations of their rights. Thus, the important question here is whether a declaration of "non-self-executing" in a treaty, without any further implementing legislation, would be consistent with the object and purpose of the treaty? We will explore this question more closely later in this chapter when we review the rules on implementation of treaty obligations by States (see, e.g., §8.3.2).

Even if it a State declares a human rights treaty to be non-self-executing, the treaty is nevertheless still legally binding on the State from an

---

11. See, e.g., Donna Sullivan, *Women's Human Rights and the 1993 World Conference on Human Rights*, 88 Am. J. Int'l L. 152 (1994); Reservations to CEDAW, available at http://www.un.org/womenwatch/daw/cedaw/reservations.htm.

international law standpoint. Moreover, the treaty may not be the only source of international law that an individual can look to in order to assert rights, particularly if the rights are also protected under customary law (see §8.3.4).

Example 8-7

Assume that State X has ratified the International Covenant on Civil and Political Rights and submits with its ratification, the following declaration: "State X declares that the provisions of articles 1-27 of the Covenant are not self-executing." Assume State X follows U.S. principles on the issue of non-self-executing treaties. The ICCPR also prohibits the application of the death penalty on persons under the age of eighteen. A defendant files a claim in a domestic court claiming that his treaty rights not to be subject to the death penalty for a crime he committed while he was a minor are being violated.

Can the domestic court of State X hear the claim based on a violation of the human rights treaty?

Explanation

We need to start with State X's domestic law regarding the issue of non-self-executing treaties, which is identical to the laws of the United States. Some critics would argue that State X cannot declare an entire human rights treaty to be non-self-executing without violating the Supremacy Clause; it is up to the courts to decide on a case-by-case basis what is or is not self-executing. Others, including U.S. domestic courts, maintain that the intent of the federal government controls and, since the intent is clear, the defendant has no right to bring a claim in federal court, regardless of whether there is a substantive violation of the treaty.

Still others would argue that such a blanket declaration undermines the domestic judicial remedies contemplated by international human rights treaties and therefore may be inconsistent with the object and purpose of those treaties. Remember that State X is still legally bound to abide by the provisions of the treaty, even if individuals cannot bring claims in domestic courts.

We can come back to this question of whether such a declaration would be consistent with the object and purpose of the treaty after we have looked at the implementation provisions of the ICCPR (see §8.3.2). In the case of the United States, this question was further complicated by the fact that in 1992, when the United States ratified the ICCPR, it also had an express reservation to the ICCPR's prohibition against the application of the death penalty to persons under 18. Since that time, the U.S. Supreme Court has held, relying in part on international human rights norms, that application of the death penalty to juveniles violates the U.S. Constitution.[12]

§8.2.4 Termination

The last issue to consider in the human rights context is whether such treaties can be terminated, an issue that is discussed more fully in §3.7. Some human rights treaties, such as the Convention against Torture, contain provisions that allow for termination or withdrawal. The two major human rights treaties — the International Covenant on Civil and Political Rights and the International Covenant on Economic, Social and Cultural Rights — contain no such provisions. Article 56 of the Vienna Convention on the Law of Treaties addresses termination generally. Yet some international human rights bodies maintain that no withdrawal or denunciation of these human rights treaties is allowed given the nature of these instruments. Since they represent universal rights that are not of a temporary character and that attach "to the people living in the territory of the State party," unilateral termination or denunciation by the State is difficult to justify in light of this purpose. See HRC, General Comment No. 26, U.N. Doc. A/53/40, annex VII (Dec. 8, 1997).

§8.3 HUMAN RIGHTS LAW IN THE UNITED NATIONS SYSTEM

This section discusses the various sources of international human rights law, focusing on the two primary treaties that are part of the International Bill of Human Rights — the International Covenant on Civil and Political Rights (ICCPR) and the International Covenant on Economic, Social and Cultural Rights (ICESCR). In addition, it will briefly cover the U.N. Charter and the Universal Declaration on Human Rights. Finally, it ends with a discussion of international customary law, which is tailored to the particular issues that arise in the context of human rights. You should consult Chapter 2 for other sources of international law, such as general principles of law, as well as for a broader discussion of international conventional and customary law.

---

12. See *Roper v. Simmons*, 543 U.S. 551 (2005).

§8.3.1 U.N. Charter and Universal Declaration of Human Rights

The preamble to the U.N. Charter declares that the people of the United Nations "reaffirm faith in fundamental human rights, in the dignity and worth of the human person, in the equal rights of men and women." Additionally, article 1(3) specifically notes that one of the purposes of the Charter is to promote and encourage "respect for human rights and fundamental freedoms for all without distinction as to race, sex, language, or religion." The other two major provisions of the Charter relating to human rights are articles 55 and 56.

Article 55 states:

> [T]he United Nations shall *promote* . . . higher standards of living, full employment, and conditions of economic and social progress and development; . . . solutions of international economic, social, health, and related problems, and international cultural and educational co-operation; and . . . universal respect for, and observance of, human rights and fundamental freedoms for all without distinction as to race, sex, language or religion. . . .

Article 56 declares:

> All Members *pledge* themselves to take joint and separate action in co-operation with the Organization for the achievement of the purposes set forth in Article 55. . . . (emphasis added).

Another major provision of the Charter that mentions human rights is article 13, which states that the "General Assembly shall initiate studies and make recommendations for the purpose of . . . promoting international co-operation in the economic, social, cultural, educational, and health fields, and assisting in the realization of human rights. . . ." Finally, articles 62 and 68 authorize the Economic and Social Council to make recommendations regarding the promotion of human rights, including setting up Commissions.

When the Charter was written in 1945, this idea of "human rights" was not well understood, either in terms of what it might entail or what duties and responsibilities it might impose upon States. Some human rights organizations and countries advocated for a stronger, clearer statement in support of human rights in the Charter; other countries resisted such efforts. In the end, the Charter speaks more in terms of aspirations ("to pledge" and "to promote" human rights), than legally binding obligations on Member States. However, despite this vagueness, the U.N. Charter accomplished two important goals: It made clear that human rights would no longer merely be a matter of domestic concern and it empowered various bodies within the U.N. to define and codify specific human rights norms.

One of the first U.N. instruments to articulate human rights standards was the 1948 Universal Declaration of Human Rights, which was adopted by the General Assembly by a vote of forty-eight in favor, none against, and eight abstentions. G.A. Res. 217A, U.N. GAOR, 3d Sess., pt. I (Dec. 10, 1948). The instrument is, in fact, a "Declaration" and not a treaty or covenant. United Nations declarations are not per se legally binding, as a treaty or customary international law norm would be. Standing alone, they are generally perceived as "recommendations" without legally binding character. However, the Universal Declaration is generally ascribed a higher degree of authority, primarily because of what many of the provisions of that Declaration have come to represent over time — an accepted part of customary international law. See *infra* §8.3.4. Moreover, any resolution designated and adopted as a "declaration" by the General Assembly represents a "formal and solemn instrument, resorted to only in very rare cases relating to matters of major and lasting importance where maximum compliance is expected."[13]

The Declaration contains both civil and political rights (articles 1-21) and economic, social, and cultural rights (articles 22-28). Some argue that the first category of rights represents "negative" rights (rights in which a State can meet its international duties by merely refraining from violating them, such as freedom of expression, equal protection and nondiscrimination, right to life, freedom from slavery, freedom from torture, freedom from arbitrary arrest or detention, freedom of movement, and right to a fair trial) and the second category representing mainly "positive" rights (rights in which a State must take positive action to meet its duties, such as the right to social security; the right to work; the right to join a trade union; the right to an adequate standard of living; right to food, clothing, housing, and medical care; and right to education). Yet these rights are not always that easy to categorize. As we will see in the next section on the ICCPR and ICESCR, these various categories of rights may contain both positive and negative rights (e.g., the right to form trade unions), and many are interrelated and interconnected (e.g., the right to life and the right to foodstuffs). While the Declaration contained no means by which to monitor or enforce "rights," it served as a foundation for later treaties and for the formation of customary human rights law (see §8.3.4).

---

13. Report of the Commission on Human Rights, U.N. Doc. E/3616/Rev.1, para. 105, 18th Sess., Economic and Social Council, March 19-April 14, 1962, United Nations, New York.

Example 8-8

State C is a Member of the United Nations. A man from State C has been arbitrarily detained by State C's secret police and has been held in custody for over three months without being brought before a court or having the right to seek counsel. The man's parents claim that their son's human rights have been violated by the actions of State C under the U.N. Charter, which states that all Members will "pledge" to protect and promote human rights. Additionally, they assert that the man's right under article 9 of the Universal Declaration of Human Rights that he not "be subjected to arbitrary arrest, detention or exile" has been violated as well.

Does the man have a claim against State C for violations of the U.N. Charter or Declaration?

Explanation

While State C may have violated the man's human right not to be arbitrarily detained (as well as a host of other human rights), the U.N. Charter and the Universal Declaration create no per se legally binding obligations on State C with respect to those rights. This means that the man would not be able to bring a legal claim for a breach of State C's duties under either of those documents, because the relevant provisions are merely aspirational, functioning more like a recommendation than hard law. With that said, many human rights bodies maintain that the core concepts of human rights found in both the Charter and the Declaration are part of customary international law binding on all nations. If the right not to be arbitrarily detained for prolonged periods has become part of customary law (which, as noted in the customary law section, many believe that it has reached that level, see §8.3.4), then State C has violated a legally enforceable right and the man or his parents may be able to seek a remedy in an appropriate forum. Moreover, as the next section demonstrates, State C may also have binding treaty obligations.

§8.3.2 The International Covenant on Civil and Political Rights

While the Universal Declaration of Human Rights was significant in establishing international recognition of human rights, it was not a legally binding document. In the years subsequent to its passage, human rights advocates and States began to work toward the creation of positive law, which would impose binding obligations on states to respect and promote human rights. The problem that arose was that most States agreed that some rights listed in the Universal Declaration were undoubtedly universal in nature, but there were others that States could not agree on. Thus, two treaties were created: the International Covenant on Civil and Political Rights (ICCPR), G.A. Res. 2200, 999 U.N.T.S. 171 (1966), and the International Covenant on Economic, Social, and Cultural Rights (ICESCR) (discussed *infra* §8.3.2), G.A. Res. 2200, 993 U.N.T.S. 3 (1966). While the Declaration was divided into two separate covenants (which is another name for a treaty), the General Assembly has proclaimed by resolution that the covenants are nevertheless "interconnected" and "interdependent" (G.A. Resolution 421(V), sec. E (Dec. 4, 1950)). One of the primary arguments in support of two covenants was that civil and political rights could be implemented immediately, whereas economic, social, and cultural rights might need to be implemented over time. To date, 165 States have become a party to the ICCPR and 160 States have ratified the ICESCR. The United States is a party to the ICCPR (with some reservations), but has not ratified the ICESCR.

Rights and Freedoms Under the ICCPR

The rights contained in the ICCPR are often referred to as "first generation" rights because they were the earliest human rights to receive recognition. Among the rights contained in this covenant are "the right of self-determination" (art. 2); "the equal right of men and women to the enjoyment of all civil and political rights" (art. 3); "the inherent right to life" (art. 6); the right not to be "subjected to torture" (art. 7); the right not to be "held in slavery" (art. 8); "the right to liberty and security of person" (art. 9); the right to be informed of any charges against an accused person and to "be brought promptly before a judge . . . [and to receive a hearing] before a court" (art. 9(2)-(4)); "the right to liberty of movement" (art. 12); the right to "be equal before the courts" (art. 14); the right to a variety of criminal due process protections (arts. 14 & 15); "freedom of thought, conscience and religion" (art. 18); the right to freedom of expression, including the right "to seek, receive, and impart information" (art. 19); the prohibition against any propaganda for war or "advocacy of national, racial or religious hatred that constitutes an incitement to discrimination, hostility or violence" (art. 20); "the right to peaceful assembly" (art. 21); "freedom of association" (art. 22); the right to "marry and to found a family" (art. 23(2)); the rights of children with respect to nondiscrimination and nationality (art. 24); the right "to vote" (art. 25(b)); the right to equal protection of the laws (art. 26); and the right to cultural integrity for all ethnic, religious, and linguistic minorities (art. 27). In considering the scope and meaning of the rights articulated in this covenant, it is important to keep in mind the law of treaty interpretation and reservations discussed in §8.2 of this chapter.

States' Duties to Implement ICCPR Rights and Freedoms

Once a State ratifies the ICCPR and becomes a party to that covenant, it must implement the provisions of the treaty into domestic law, including taking "the necessary steps . . . to adopt such legislative or other measures as may be necessary to give effect to the rights recognized in the present covenant." ICCPR art. 2(2). This means that any existing domestic law in conflict with the Covenant must be changed to adhere to the ICCPR, unless the State has a legally valid reservation that is consistent with the Covenant's object and purpose. In addition, a State party must "respect" and "ensure" the Covenant's rights in a manner that is nondiscriminatory. ICCPR art. 2(1). The word "respect" suggests that States and their officials must refrain from violating ICCPR rights. The word "ensure" indicates that State parties are also obligated to take positive steps to ensure those rights are not being violated by others who are located within the State's territory or jurisdiction, such as corporations or individuals. Thus, while the ICCPR does not address its human rights norms to private persons (either natural or juridical), States may nevertheless be held responsible for their conduct. Note that the ICCPR is not limited to the State party's citizens, but rather the provisions apply to all individuals and groups located within a State's territory or who may be subject to the State's jurisdiction outside its territory. ICCPR art. 2(1).

In order to meet its obligations under article 2 of the ICCPR, States must not only adopt domestic measures to bring their law in compliance with the treaty, they must also provide an "effective remedy" to any person whose rights or freedoms have been violated. ICCPR art. 2(3). This remedy can include relief by "competent judicial, administrative, or legislative authorities," or any other competent authority provided for by the State's legal system. *Id.* art. 2(3)(b). In addition, States are obligated under article 40 of the Covenant to report to the U.N. Human Rights Committee (HRC) on what measures they have taken to give effect to the rights recognized in the treaty. The HRC is the treaty body that monitors state compliance under the ICCPR and is discussed in more detail below.

Finally on the question of whether a State can declare this treaty to be "non-self-executing," the HRC has noted that while States may choose the way in which they want to incorporate their obligations contained in the ICCPR into domestic law, direct application of the Covenant into a state's judicial system provides for "enhanced protection" of rights. HRC, General Comment No. 31, para. 13, U.N. Doc. CCPR/C/21/Rev.1/Add.13 (2004). This is especially true where (1) a State has not ratified the Optional Protocol to the ICCPR, allowing for individual complaints to be submitted directly to the HRC, and (2) there is an absence of domestic provisions "to ensure that Covenant rights may be sued on in domestic courts." HRC, General Comment No. 24(52), para. 1, U.N. Doc. CCPR/C/21/Rev.1/Add.6 (1994)).

Example 8-9

State Z has signed and ratified the ICCPR. Alan and Elizabeth, citizens of State Z, wish to marry. However, Alan and Elizabeth are of different religions and State Z has a law banning such marriages. Alan claims that his right to marry (art. 23) and his ability to enjoy his right to be free from discrimination under the law (arts. 2 & 26) have been violated by State Z.

1) Under article 2 of the ICCPR, what must State Z do to address Alan's claim?

2) Would it matter if it were a territory or province within State Z that had such a law on its books, rather than a national law?

3) What if State Z had no procedure in place for individuals to challenge provincial laws such as this one?

Explanation

Because State Z has ratified the ICCPR, it must take immediate steps to bring its laws in compliance with the provisions of the ICCPR. As the HRC has stated, "Where there are inconsistencies between domestic law and the Covenant, article 2 requires that the domestic law or practice be changed to meet the standards imposed by the Covenant's substantive guarantees." HRC, General Comment No. 31, para. 13, U.N. Doc. CCPR/C/21/Rev.1/Add.13 (2004). This means that State Z's law forbidding marriages of persons of different religions must be changed to the extent that it violates both the nondiscriminatory provisions of the Covenant (arts. 2 & 26), as well as the right of "men and women of marriageable age to marry" (art. 23).

In addition, the State is obligated to "respect and ensure" all the rights in the Covenant to any individual within its territory or its jurisdiction. Thus, it should not matter whether it was a national or provincial law (although State Z's own domestic law may raise difficult questions for State Z on this point).

Finally, to the extent that State Z has no procedure in place for the couple to vindicate their rights, it is not meeting its obligation under article 2 of the ICCPR to ensure that they have accessible and effective "remedies." As the HRC has noted, "the enjoyment of the rights recognized under the Covenant can be effectively assured . . . in many different ways . . . including direct applicability of the Covenant, application of comparable constitutional or other provisions of law, or the interpretive effect of the Covenant in the application of national law." HRC, General Comment No. 31, para. 15. However, "cessation of an ongoing violation is an essential element of the right to an effective remedy." Id.

Example 8-10

State E has a military base located within the exterior borders of State Y. State E is a party to the ICCPR, but State Y is not. Individuals from various States from around the world are being detained at State E's military base.

Must State E "respect and ensure" the rights of all the individuals currently being detained on the military base, even though the base is not located within State E's own territory?

Explanation

The phrase "within its territory and subject to its jurisdiction" of article 2 has been construed to include all persons in a State's territory or under its control. Since these individuals are being held on a military base controlled by State E, they are entitled to the protections of the ICCPR. See, e.g., HRC, General Comment No. 31, paras. 10-12 (regarding "persons under control" of a State party).

Example 8-11

Let us assume now that a multinational oil company is operating within the borders of State E, and State E has ratified the ICCPR. The oil company is accused by local community members of forcing them to work on the building of a pipeline through their community, which has in turn caused massive environmental damage and pollution to their lands, thereby undermining their ability to grow crops or graze their animals. To the extent that the community members have protested against this behavior, they have been detained and in some cases severely beaten by individuals of State E's military, who have been hired by the oil company for security purposes.

Is State E responsible under the ICCPR for the actions of the corporation and its military?

Explanation

This example raises questions with respect to the negative and positive obligations imposed on State parties under the ICCPR. There is no doubt that State E must refrain from violating the civil and political rights of the community members as they relate to the ICCPR (e.g., arbitrary detention; right not to be held in slavery or servitude; the right not to be tortured or subject to cruel, inhuman, or degrading treatment). This would include all aspects of the State, including its military. Moreover, to the extent that the individuals are acting outside their official capacity, the State still has assumed certain obligations under the ICCPR with respect to their actions. This is also true with respect to the multinational oil company. As the HRC has noted in its general comments:

> [T]he positive obligations on State Parties to ensure covenant rights will only be fully discharged if individuals are protected by the State, not just against violations of Covenant rights by its agents, but also against acts committed by private persons or entities that would impair the enjoyment of Covenant rights. . . . (HRC, General Comment No. 31, para. 8.)

For more information on individual accountability under human rights norms, see Chapter 11. The issue of direct corporate responsibility under human rights norms is dealt with later in Chapter 9 (see §9.6).

States' Powers to Derogate from or Limit ICCPR Rights

Not all of the rights in the Covenant are absolute. Some of the articles contain express limitations, such as article 19 on freedom of expression, which states that the exercise of this right carries with it "special duties and responsibilities" and therefore "may be subject to certain [legal] restrictions" necessary for the "respect of the rights and reputations of others" or for "the protection of national security or of public order . . . , or of public health or morals." Other provisions that allow for legal limitations on rights include such articles as article 12 with respect to freedom of movement, article 14 with respect to exclusion of press and public from criminal trials, and article 18 on freedom of thought, conscience, and religion.

Additionally, the ICCPR has a general "derogation" provision. Unlike limitations, which are not restricted to emergencies, article 4 of the ICCPR allows States to temporarily derogate from their obligations under the Covenant, "in times of public emergency which threatens the life of a nation." When a State derogates from guaranteed rights it must inform the Secretary-General of the United Nations. The HRC has noted, "not every disturbance or catastrophe qualifies as a public emergency, which threatens the life of a nation." HRC, General Comment No. 29, U.N. Doc. CCPR/C/21/Rev.1/Add.11 (2001), para. 3. For instance, it may include situations of international or domestic armed conflict, but only if those conflicts threaten the life of the nation. To the extent that a State wishes to derogate in other situations not involving armed conflict, the HRC notes that States "should carefully consider the justification and why such a measure is necessary and legitimate." HRC, General Comment No. 29, para. 3. These other situations might include a major natural disaster or perhaps widespread internal disorder.

In order to derogate from the Covenant, the State has to meet certain criteria. First, it must "officially proclaim" a state of emergency. Second derogation is limited to "the extent strictly required by the exigencies of the situation." Third, it cannot be done in a manner that violates other international legal obligations, such as international humanitarian law. With respect to the issue of being "strictly required by the exigencies of the situation," the HRC has stated that State measures must be appropriately limited in duration, geographical coverage, and material scope. See HRC, General Comment No. 29, para. 4. In other words, the derogation measures cannot last any longer, cover any more territory, or be greater in scope than what is called for by the situation. This is referred to as the "principle of proportionality." Regional bodies, such as the European Court of Human Rights, have dealt with derogation in a similar manner.[14]

Certain specific rights are non-derogable under article 4, including the right to life; the right not to be tortured; the right not to be held in slavery or servitude or to be imprisoned because of inability to fulfill a contract; the right not to be held guilty of an offense that did not constitute a crime at the time it was committed; the right to be recognized as a person before the law; and the right to freedom of thought, conscience, and religion. These enumerated non-derogable provisions are "related to, but not identical with, the question of whether human rights obligations bear the nature of peremptory norms of international law." HRC, General Comment No. 29, para. 11. In other words, many involve fundamental rights from which no State can derogate at any time. See §§2.2.4 and 8.3.4. This includes such provisions as article 7's prohibition against torture. States cannot obviously derogate from any rights found in the ICCPR that have obtained the status of a peremptory norm, regardless of whether it is expressly listed in article 4. Nor can it avoid its obligations under humanitarian law (law that applies during time of armed conflict) merely because some right protected under that law is not expressly listed as non-derogable under article 4 of the ICCPR. The HRC has articulated other rights that may not be subject to derogation even though they are not expressly listed in article 4 as being non-derogable, such as the right of all persons deprived of their liberty to be treated with humanity and dignity under article 10, the prohibition against unacknowledged detention, and the right of nondiscrimination with respect to minorities prevalent throughout various articles of the Covenant. HRC, General Comment. 29, para. 13(a-e). The issue here is the appropriateness of expanding the list of non-derogable rights beyond what is expressly stated in the treaty itself. Such a reading of the ICCPR may be supported by article 5, which precludes States from using the language of the ICCPR (including article 4) as an excuse for engaging in activities that would violate fundamental human rights precepts protected elsewhere.

---

14. See, e.g., *Brannigan and McBride v. United Kingdom*, 258-B Eur. Ct. H.R. (ser. A) (1993); *Brogan and Others v. United Kingdom*, 145-B Eur. Ct. H.R. (ser. A), at 30-34 (1988).

Finally, we need to consider the question of whether a State can reserve its rights to provisions that are clearly non-derogable or whether such derogation would be inconsistent with the ICCPR's object and purpose. The HRC has stated that, "while there is no automatic correlation between reservations to non-derogable provisions, and reservation which offend against the object and purpose of the Covenant, a State has a heavy onus to justify such a reservation." HRC, General Comment No. 24, para. 11. If those provisions represent a "peremptory norm," a strong argument could be made that no reservation to that right is permissible under the treaty, since such rights are non-derogable under principles of international law.

Example 8-12

State V claims that as a result of a recent hurricane that has devastated communities along the southern portion of the State, it is suspending indefinitely all movement by its citizens within the borders of State V, as well as any attempts by its citizens to leave the country. Article 12 of the ICCPR protects the "right to liberty of movement" and the freedom of everyone "to leave any country, including his own."

What are the issues with respect to State V's state of emergency proclamation under article 4 of the ICCPR?

Explanation

The first issue is whether this is, in fact, a "public emergency that threatens the life of a nation." This of course will depend on the extent of the natural disaster and the impact it is having on the ability of the nation to function. The facts suggest that the hurricane, while clearly devastating to some, is not widespread, but rather limited to the southern portions of State V. This leads us to the question of "proportionality." Is State V's response to suspend all movement within and from the country proportional to the proclaimed emergency? It would seem to suffer from defects in terms of its (1) geographical coverage (restriction of movement in all of State V, rather than merely the southern portion); (2) duration (indefinite suspension of the right); and (3) material scope (applying to all citizens of State V rather than just those directly affected by the disaster, including limiting the rights of those who wish to leave the country, which seems to have little or nothing to do with the proclaimed emergency).

Article 12 is not one of those rights listed in article 4 of the ICCPR as "non-derogable," nor would it necessarily be an issue of a peremptory norm. In fact, article 12 allows for legal limitations on the right to movement even absent a public emergency when it is necessary to "protect national security, public order, public health or morals, or the rights and freedoms of others." Even if State V relied on this limitation as opposed to its power to derogate under article 4, such a limitation must still be done in a manner that is consistent with the ordinary meaning of the treaty and its object and purpose. Such a blanket order by State V restricting the movement of all of its citizens would seem to be contrary to these principles.

Example 8-13

State G was recently the victim of a major terrorist attack in the City of Y, in which hundreds of people were killed. In response to the attack, State G has officially proclaimed a "war on terror" and has chosen to indefinitely detain any individual who State G thinks may either be associated with terrorists groups or have useful information about future attacks. These individuals are being held at a military base located outside the borders of State G. Many have been there for three years or more without being brought before any type of court or charged with any crime. Article 9 of the ICCPR states that "no one should be subjected to arbitrary arrest or detention" and that "anyone who is deprived of his liberty by arrest or detention shall be entitled to take proceedings before a court."

Analyze State G's obligations under article 4 of the ICCPR. What will State G argue with respect to its rights to derogate from article 9? What are possible counterarguments?

Explanation

The example is more complicated than the previous one, although it raises some of the same issues. First, it is complicated by the fact that State G sees itself in a state of "war," which may well raise issues of humanitarian law. If State G were in fact at "war," the rules articulated in Chapter 10 regarding the laws of war would be relevant to your analysis. Let us assume for a moment that there are no ongoing hostilities, but rather State G is taking proactive steps to counter any threat in the form of future terrorist attacks. Merely because the individuals are being held outside the territory of State G does not preclude the application of the provisions of the ICCPR (see art. 2(1)). State G will proclaim that it does in fact have a "state of emergency" (war on terror) that threatens the life of the nation (immediate security concerns that impact its citizens and territory) and therefore has a right to derogate from certain provisions of the ICCPR under article 4(1). Since article 9 is not one of those non-derogable rights listed in article 4(4), it has the right to take such action for as long as is necessary to counter the imminent threat of attack against State G. State G may also argue that it has leeway in determining what constitutes a public emergency and what the response to that emergency will be, especially in this case where there are ongoing and immediate threats to State G in the form of future attacks.

In response, the individuals detained may argue that there is no public emergency here since the life of the nation is not immediately threatened by the possibility of future attacks. In other words, article 4 was not intended to cover events that may or may not threaten State G in the future, but are not currently underway. The detained individuals may further argue that even if the war on terror is a public emergency that threatens the life of the nation, State G's actions may violate the proportionality requirements of article 4. The individuals are being detained "indefinitely" and without any opportunity for judicial process, both of which are a violation of article 9 and may not be necessary to protect the life of the nation.

Additionally, they make argue that it is not just the language of the ICCPR that constrains State G here, but other principles of international law as well. No State can claim a right to derogate from any principle that is considered to be a peremptory norm, even if that norm is not expressly listed in article 4 as being non-derogable. Since the right not to be subject to *prolonged arbitrary detention as a matter of state policy* is by itself arguably a peremptory norm (in addition to being prohibited under article 9 of the ICCPR), State G cannot derogate from that norm and hold these individuals indefinitely without some due process. Finally they may argue that even if article 9 is not listed as a non-derogable right, it is nevertheless essential to the protection of other non-derogable rights, such as the right to life and the right not to be tortured. As the HRC has noted, "in order to protect non-derogable rights, the right to take proceedings before a court to enable a court to decide without delay on the lawfulness of detention" is an essential aspect of the ICCPR, which "must not be undermined by a State party's decision to derogate from the Covenant." HRC, General Comment No. 29, para. 16.

Some regional bodies, such as the European Court of Human Rights, have allowed States leeway in dealing with these kinds of ongoing threats. However, issues of proportionality are still relevant to a State's decision to derogate from certain rights and oversight is provided in the form of the right of individual petition to a human rights court.[15]

Monitoring and Enforcement of Rights

Even if a State ratifies the ICCPR, how does the United Nations know that States are adhering to their obligations mandated by the ICCPR and what "remedies" are available to individuals who believe their rights are being violated? Remember, article 2 requires States to amend their laws to give effect to the rights protected under the ICCPR, and it also requires them to

---

15. See, e.g., Ireland v. United Kingdom, 25 Eur. Ct. H.R. (ser. A), at 207 (1978); Lawless v. Ireland, 3 Eur. Ct. H.R. (ser. A) (1961), 1 EHRR 15; see also Brannigan and McBride v. United Kingdom, 258-B Eur. Ct. H.R. (ser. A), at 55 (1993); Brogan and Others v. United Kingdom, 145-B Eur. Ct. H.R. (ser. A), at 30-34, paras. 55-62 (1988).

ensure that persons whose rights have been violated have an effective domestic remedy before a "competent authority." Thus, the ICCPR contemplates both implementation and enforcement through domestic legal systems.

The HRC, which oversees the implementation and enforcement of these rights by States (ICCPR, arts. 28-39), consists of eighteen members, all of whom are considered "experts" in the area of civil and political rights. The Committee's principal function is to receive reports on measures that States have taken to implement the Covenant's rights and transmit its comments on those reports back to the States. Article 40(1) of the ICCPR requires "State Parties to . . . submit reports on the measures they have adopted which give effect to the rights recognized herein and on the progress made in the enjoyment of those rights." It also requires the HRC to "study the reports submitted by the States" and provide "general comments" to the States regarding those reports. ICCPR art. 40(4). The HRC has adopted a fairly robust interpretation of its duty "to study" the reports. It holds long sessions with State representatives, examining various aspects of a State's article 40 report and offering comments and suggestions on each provision of the ICCPR. The HRC does not just rely on the report itself in examining the State; it also relies on information that it obtains from other sources, such as non-governmental organizations (see §9.3). The HRC then submits written comments to each State regarding the article 40 report.

Under article 40 of the ICCPR, the obligation for states to submit reports is mandatory, and occurs within the first year of a State becoming a party and "whenever the Committee so requests" (art. 40(1)(b)), which is every five years thereafter, according to the HRC. In addition, a State can declare recognition of the competence of the HRC to hear claims received from other States against it pursuant to article 41 of the ICCPR. While some States have recognized the authority of the HRC to hear state-against-state complaints, those States have never invoked this process. As discussed later, there is a chronic problem with late reports that is often, although not always, tied to resource questions.

The HRC also publishes general comments regarding various provisions of the ICCPR explaining how such provisions should be interpreted in light of the whole treaty. These general comments are very important in attempting to understand how the various rights contained in the treaty relate to one another and offer a more in-depth examination of what each right encompasses. We have already encountered a number of these general comments in our previous examples.

What impact do the article 40 reports and general comments issued by the HRC have in terms of state compliance? Is this really an "enforcement" mechanism or merely a question of monitoring state behavior? Some argue that the reporting requirement is a relatively weak "enforcement" mechanism, since the HRC does not issue legally binding decisions. Others maintain that since one of the purposes behind the human rights treaty regime is to encourage compliance through an objective and constructive dialogue with States, the reporting system is in fact the best way to achieve this end. Because it is less threatening to States in terms of their sovereignty than a court system with authority to issue legally binding decisions, the reporting system also ensures maximum participation by States, as evidenced by the large number of ratifications. Moreover, while the HRC is not a judicial body with the power to bind States, it does have the power of interpretation, which States must as a matter of good faith abide by, absent legally valid reservations. The HRC has also been known to put pressure on States that fail to implement its recommendations, most notably through follow-up reporting and review. Finally, the work of the HRC and its observations with respect to article 40 reports are made public, and the court of public opinion can be a powerful tool. When citizens of a State are made aware of a State's human rights record, it may in turn put pressure on that State to improve its record. Clearly this is not always the case, particularly with those States that seek to maintain tight control over their society and citizens. Other tools, such as the ones explored below in §8.4, may well be needed to move those States toward compliance.

Example 8-14

State T recently ratified the ICCPR and has submitted its first report under article 40. State T offers the following statement in its article 40 report: "State T is not currently violating any of the rights of its citizens and therefore is in full compliance with the spirit and purposes of the ICCPR. It will continue to ensure that its citizens have all of the rights and freedoms articulated therein."

Is this report sufficient under articles 2 and 40 of the ICCPR? Who has the power to make that determination?

Explanation

There is little question that it is within the competence of the HRC to review State T's article 40 report and comment on State T's compliance with various provisions of the ICCPR. In order for the HRC to perform its monitoring role, it will need more detailed information from State T. While the HRC may be able to discern the extent of State T's compliance with the ICCPR through its established examination process, articles 2 and 40 of the ICCPR suggest that State T must do more to be in compliance with the Covenant. Under article 2, a state must adopt "legislative, judicial, administrative, educative, and other appropriate measures" in order to fulfill its legal obligations under the Covenant. See HRC, General Comment No. 29, para. 7. Thus, a mere proclamation by the State that it is not violating any rights of its citizens is not enough; it has to take positive steps to ensure that the ICCPR rights are being protected and advanced (such as passing relevant laws or providing individuals with a right of review before some competent authority). Additionally, article 40 specifically requires States to report on all the "measures" it has taken to meet its treaty obligations, as well as information on any difficulties it has had in meeting its treaty obligations. A statement that State T is in compliance with the "purposes and spirit" of the Covenant would, therefore, be insufficient under article 40.

Example 8-15

What if instead State T adopts a reservation to the ICCPR that "[w]hile it is willing to take steps to comply with the provisions of the ICCPR, it declines to submit any article 40 reports for review by the HRC due to limits on State T's resources to provide such information at this time, and reserves its right not to appear before the HRC for examination of its compliance with the treaty. It also reserves its rights not to abide by any comments offered by the HRC regarding its interpretation of the covenant."

Analyze whether you think this would be a permissible reservation under the rules of interpretation that we explored in §8.2 and under the principles discussed in this section with respect to the scope of HRC's powers under the ICCPR.

Explanation

The treaty clearly contemplates a "monitoring" role for the HRC with respect to state compliance and this reservation undermines that role. The treaty regime established by the ICCPR envisions compliance through open dialogue and communication, as opposed to the issuance of legally binding decisions. Through this process, the HRC is given the opportunity to assist States in determining what more needs to be done to bring them in compliance with their treaty obligations. Additionally, it creates a very "public" process by which human rights violations are brought to the attention of the world. Thus, State T's reservation is incompatible with the monitoring and compliance aspects of the ICCPR.

Additionally, State T seems reluctant to accept the legitimacy of the HRC in interpreting the provisions of the treaty. While there is no express language in article 40 requiring the HRC to issue general comments regarding the meaning of each provision of the treaty, it would seem to be an implicit part of HRC's duty to "study" article 40 reports and provide "general comments" to the States regarding their report. The HRC has noted specifically with respect to a State's reluctance to abide by HRC's interpretation that:

> The Committee's role under the Covenant, whether under article 40 or under the Optional Protocols, necessarily entails interpreting the provisions of the

Covenant and the development of a jurisprudence. Accordingly, a reservation that rejects the Committee's competence to interpret the requirements of any provisions of the Covenant would also be contrary to the object and purpose of that treaty. HRC, General Comment No. 24, para. 11.

The resource question is a difficult one. It is true that many States fail to meet the deadlines for submitting their article 40 reports and that some have difficulty doing so because of the lack of resources. Human rights experts have proposed a list of steps for dealing with a State's chronic failure to file its reports, such as replacing reporting with a list of detailed questions from the human rights body; having the treaty bodies proceed in the absence of the report relying on any information available to them regarding the State's human rights record; or offering advisory services to help states prepare their reports.[16]

Optional Protocols

In addition to the main text of the ICCPR, the treaty has two optional protocols that States may choose to ratify, but do not have to agree to in order to be parties to the ICCPR. The First Optional Protocol to the ICCPR was adopted at the same time as the main treaty. G.A. Res. 2200A (XXI), 999 U.N.T.S. 171 (1966). It permits individuals to submit human rights communications directly to HRC alleging that their rights under the ICCPR have been violated. The HRC receives the individual's "written communication," makes a determination as to whether the submission is admissible (e.g., whether domestic remedies have been exhausted), and then brings that communication to the attention of the accused State. The State then responds to the communication with "written explanations" in terms of allegations and remedies (art. 4(2)). In making its decision, the HRC relies solely on written submissions. It has no power under the Protocol to compel testimony or engage in fact finding, although some argue that it could perhaps collect additional information with a State's permission. Once the HRC has reviewed the written submissions, it then forwards its views to the State party and to the individual. Over 100 States are parties to this Protocol and several hundred complaints have been filed under the procedures provided. The United States is not a party to the First Protocol.

In exercising its powers under the First Optional Protocol, the HRC acts more like a court than it does with respect to its monitoring functions under article 40 of the ICCPR. The "views" that it forwards to the States actually look like a court decision: allegations of the party, response by the State, decision on admissibility, any interim measure taken, discussion of the

---

16. See Final Report on Enhancing the Long-term Effectiveness of the U.N. Human Rights System, U.N. Doc. E/CN.4/1997/74.

"law" that the HRC relied on to reach its decisions (including relevant treaty provisions and prior cases or general comments interpreting those provisions), and a final statement of the State's obligations in light of HRC's findings. Additionally, the HRC has established a default judgment mechanism in situations where a State fails to respond to a communication and the allegations are "plausible and substantiated." Following the issuance of its views, the HRC will require a State to respond to its findings, may appoint HRC members to follow up on a State's response to the views, publish a State's compliance, and identify publically any State that refuses to implement its views.

The HRC's "views" may not be legally binding in the same manner as judicial decisions of the ICJ or the European Court of Human Rights. However, since the HRC's views articulate what a State must do to be in compliance with the ICCPR and the provisions of that treaty are legally binding on the State absent any valid reservation, so should the HRC views be considered binding on a State.

The Second Optional Protocol, added in 1989, is focused on the abolition of the death penalty. G.A. Res. 44/128, 1642 U.N.T.S. 414 (1989). Many states believe that article 6 of the ICCPR, which provides for the right to life, means that the practice of putting people to death cannot be reconciled with this fundamental right to life. Currently, the Second Protocol has been ratified by seventy-two states.

Example 8-16

In Example 8-7, we looked at the following facts: In ratifying the ICCPR, State Z declares that the treaty provisions of the ICCPR are "non-self-executing" (not directly enforceable in State Z's domestic court). State Z has not acted to implement the rights articulated in the ICCPR through legislation or "other [such] measures" as called for in article 2(2). Let us assume further that State Z is not a party to the First Optional Protocol.

Is State Z in compliance with its obligations under article 2 to provide individuals with an "effective remedy"?

Explanation

Remember in the explanation of Example 8-7, we discussed how States have the option to determine how they want to incorporate the obligations contained in the ICCPR into domestic law, including whether they want to make the Covenant directly applicable in the courts. HRC, General Comment No. 31, para. 13. However, the ICCPR does require States to provide individuals with an "effective remedy" with respect to their rights. In other words, the ICCPR is about rights as well as providing effective guarantees of those rights. In State Z, the ICCPR rights are not directly applicable in the courts, no steps are being taken to implement those rights and remedies into domestic law, and individuals of State Z cannot bring complaints before the HRC under the First Optional Protocol. Thus, State Z's actions are contrary to the object and purpose of the ICCPR, because they undermine the guarantees of an "effective remedy" provided for in article 2.

Example 8-17

An individual named Jon alleges that he and his brother have been detained several times by State L's police for periods ranging from several days to two months, without ever being charged. Then one day, both he and his brother were arrested and put in prison. While in prison, the two were subject to physical violence that included regular beatings and were denied basic food and water. After a time, Jon was released. He has had no information about his brother for four years. The authorities will not give Jon or his family any information pertaining to his brother, nor will they confirm his death. In fact, State L denies having any information regarding the whereabouts of Jon's brother. Assume State L is a party to both the ICCPR and the First Optional Protocol.

What steps might Jon pursue in bringing an action against State L?

Explanation

Since State L is a party to the ICCPR and its First Optional Protocol, Jon can submit a communication directly to the HRC regarding the disappearance of his brother. For the communication not to be dismissed, Jon must show that all domestic remedies have been exhausted or at least that one was never available, which seems to be the case here because the State is denying any knowledge of the brother's whereabouts. Note that Jon must submit his communication with his name on it; anonymous complaints will not be considered. This can, of course, create a difficult situation for someone like Jon who might fear retaliation from the State.

The communication must set forth the facts from the complainant's point of view and note the availability of any witnesses or other evidence that can offer corroboration. Once the communication is received by the HRC, the Committee then gives the State party time to respond. Unfortunately, some States will ignore the HRC, in which case the HRC will make findings of fact based on "plausible and substantiated allegations" under its default judgment mechanism. When a State party does respond, the Committee will consider all of the communications before issuing its "views." Once the views have been issued, and if a violation of the ICCPR is found, the HRC gives the State party an opportunity to respond with the measures it has taken to rectify the violations. The facts above are based on a recent communication heard by the HRC. See *El Hassy v. Libyan Arab Jamahiriya*, Views,

Human Rights Comm., 91st Sess., No. 1422/2005, U.N. Doc. CCPR/C/91/D/1422/2005 (2007).

§8.3.3 International Covenant on Economic, Social, and Cultural Rights

The International Covenant on Economic, Social, and Cultural Rights (ICESCR) was adopted at the same time as the ICCPR, yet is sometimes referred to as "second-generation" rights. The reason that the ICCPR and ICESCR were not adopted as one document is because States could not reach a consensus over the rights contained in the ICESCR. Some States felt that the rights enumerated in the ICESCR were secondary to civil and political rights, while others considered the rights in the ICESCR not rights at all, but privileges. Still others claimed that as "positive" rights, they were difficult to implement or perhaps were contrary to a State's particular economic or constitutional structure.

Yet, despite the separation of rights into two groups, the General Assembly has proclaimed on a number of occasions that all human rights and fundamental freedoms, regardless of whether they are labeled "social, economic, and cultural" or "civil and political" are indivisible, interdependent, and interrelated. See, e.g., G.A. Res. 41/128, annex 41, U.N. Doc. A/41/53 (1986). Both the U.N. Charter and the Universal Declaration on Human Rights address economic, social, and cultural rights as well as civil and political rights, and many of their provisions are part of customary international law. See, e.g., U.N. Charter, art. 55; Universal Declaration, arts. 22-27. Moreover, many of the rights contained in the ICCPR are connected or related to the rights found in the ICESCR—for instance, the right to life found in article 6 of the ICCPR and the right to adequate foodstuffs found in article 11 of the ICESCR. As you read through the ICESCR, consider how much overlap or possible conflict exists between the two major human rights treaties. One positive aspect of separating the ICESCR from the ICCPR is that it allowed for civil and political rights to be immediately implemented, while leading to a bolder approach on economic, social, and cultural rights than might have been achieved if the two treaties had been combined. The down side is that economic, social, and cultural rights don't always get the attention they deserve in domestic spheres with respect to promoting and protecting basic human rights. To date, 160 States have become a party to the ICESCR, on par with 165 ratifications of the ICCPR.

Rights and Freedoms Under the ICESCR

Some of the rights and freedoms protected by this Covenant are: "the right of self-determination" (art. 1); "the right to work" (art. 6); the right to "just and favourable conditions of work," including "safe and healthy working conditions" and "equal opportunity" (art. 7); the right "to form trade unions" and "to strike" (art. 8); the right "to social security" (art. 9); the right of mothers to be accorded "special protection . . . during a reasonable period before and after child birth . . . [and] working mothers . . . [to be] accorded paid leave or leave with adequate social security benefits" (art. 10(2)); the right of children to be afforded "special measures of protection," including limits on "child labour" (art. 10(3)); the right "to an adequate standard of living . . . , including adequate food, clothing and housing" (art. 11(1)); the right "to be free from hunger" (art. 11(2)); the right "to the enjoyment of the highest attainable standard of physical and mental health" (art. 12(1)); the right "to education," including compulsory free primary education (art. 13(1) & (2)); "the liberty of parents . . . [or] legal guardians to choose for their children schools . . . to ensure the religious and moral education of their children" (art. 13(3)); and the right "to take part in cultural life," including enjoying "the benefits of scientific progress" (art. 15).

Many (but not all) of the rights contained in the ICESCR are what are known as "positive rights" because they require a State to take action that will allow its citizens to enjoy these rights, such as the right to social security. This is in contrast to "negative rights," in which a State need only refrain from violating that right, such as the prohibition against torture. Because positive action by a State often requires resources and money, many of the rights in the ICESCR can only be fully realized over time and by countries that are fairly stable from an economic standpoint. However, all State parties have an obligation to take steps to meet certain minimum core obligations, such as the right to essential foodstuffs and healthcare, as well as basic shelter and education. See Committee on Economic, Social and Cultural Rights (CESCR), General Comment 3, U.N. Doc. E/1991/23, para. 10 (1990). In addition, certain rights, such as the enjoyment of these rights without discrimination (arts. 2(2) & (3)), may in fact be capable of "immediate application by judicial and other organs." CESCR, General Comment 3, para. 5. Another important point to remember is that while this treaty is focused primarily on individual rights, the issue of collective rights is particularly relevant in the economic, social, and cultural rights context since many of these rights are essential to the survival of collectivities, most notably Indigenous Peoples. These issues are further explored in §9.5. In terms of persons protected by the treaty, it extends to all individuals and groups within a State. However States that are "developing countries" may, "with due regard to human rights and their national economy," determine to what extent they will "guarantee the economic rights" of the ICESCR to "non-nationals." ICESCR, art. 2(3).

States' Duties to Implement ICESCR Rights

Article 2 of the Covenant lays out the duties of State parties with respect to implementation. Unlike the ICCPR, which is immediately applicable in all cases, each State party to the ICESCR agrees to "take steps, individually and through international assistance . . . to the maximum of its available resources," to "progressively [achieve] the full realization of the rights recognized" in the Covenant. Let us take a closer look at these elements. First, the language clearly requires States to "take steps" upon ratification, which means that a State must take immediate steps to meet its legal obligations under the treaty, even if the full realization of the rights in the Covenant might take some time. Indeed, the Covenant recognizes that full realization of all economic, social, and cultural rights will be "achieved progressively," and not necessarily in a short period of time. Yet State parties have a duty to "move as expeditiously and effectively as possible" toward the goal of full realization. CESCR, General Comment 3, para. 7, 14/12/90; U.N. Doc. E/1991/23.

In terms of what kinds of steps need to be taken, the treaty specifically notes the "adoption of legislative measures." ICESCR, art. 2(1). Other measures may be appropriate as well, such as "administrative, financial, educational and social measures." CESCR, General Comment 3, para. 7. Judicial remedies may also be necessary, particularly with respect to those rights that are capable of immediate action by a court or other such body, such as the equal rights of women and men to economic, social, and cultural rights (art. 3) or the right of everyone to form or join a trade union (art. 8). CESCR, General Comment 3, para. 5; General Comment 9, paras. 9-15, E/C.12/1998/24. According to the Committee that oversees this Covenant, "there are some obligations, such as (but by no means limited to) those concerning non-discrimination, in which the provision of some form of judicial remedy would seem indispensable in satisfying the requirements of the Covenant. In other words, whenever a Covenant right cannot be made fully effective without some role for the judiciary, judicial remedies are necessary." CESCR, General Comment 9, para. 9. On the question of whether the ICESCR norms are self-executing (that is, capable of being directly applied by the courts), the same Committee has stated:

> [I]t is especially important to avoid any a priori assumption that the norms should be considered to be non-self-executing. In fact, many of them are stated in terms which are at least as clear and specific as those in other human rights treaties, the provisions of which are regularly deemed by courts to be self-executing. CESCR, General Comment 9, para. 11.

What if the State lacks the resources to take steps to meet its obligations? Article 2 specifically notes that State parties need to take steps, but only to "the maximum of its available resources." States claiming failure to achieve rights due to the lack of resources must show "that every effort has been made to use all resources that are at its disposition in an effort to satisfy, as a matter of priority, its minimum obligations." CESCR, General Comment 3, para. 10. These minimum core obligations include ensuring that significant numbers of individuals are not denied essential foodstuffs, essential primary health care, basic shelter and housing, and basic forms of education. The Committee has concluded that these obligations are at the heart of the ICESCR, and are therefore an essential part of its overall object and purpose.

In addition, States have a duty to seek "international assistance and cooperation" in order to achieve the rights articulated in the Covenant. CESCR, General Comment 3, para. 14. While the Covenant doesn't mandate that a State party assist other State parties in meeting their treaty obligations, both the U.N. Charter (arts. 55-56) and general principles of international law impose an obligation on all member States to provide "international cooperation for development," which would arguably include economic, social, and cultural rights. CESCR, General Comment 3, para. 14.

There is no derogation clause in the ICESCR, but article 4 does allow States to limit Covenant rights at any time (not just during public emergencies), so long as such limitations are "determined by law," done in a manner that is consistent with the object and purpose of the treaty, and for the purpose of "promoting the general welfare" of the people. This article has been read narrowly to allow for the prioritizing of resources when they are limited, but only to the extent that resources are actually needed for the State to meet its treaty obligations. The ICESCR doesn't always require the expenditure of resources for the rights to be advanced by States. For instance, little or no expenditures would be necessary when it is just a matter of a State *respecting* the rights of individuals and groups to meet their own needs, such as the land and resource rights of Indigenous Peoples, or when it is just a matter of *protecting* those rights against violation by others, such as through legislation that provides individuals and groups a remedy to sue violators in the domestic courts. Finally, on the issue of limitations, article 5 does not allow a State party to use the Covenant as a pretext for violating other human rights protected under either conventional or customary law.

Monitoring and Enforcement Under the ICESCR

Just as the ICCPR has a monitoring body, the ICESCR has its own monitoring body called the Committee on Economic, Cultural, and Social Rights (CESCR), established by the Economic and Social Council. The monitoring mechanisms of the ICESCR are similar to the reporting requirements found in the ICCPR, but do not provide for-state-against state or, at the moment, individual-against-state complaints. Thus, states must submit periodic reports to the CESCR showing their progress and compliance with the treaty, but like the HRC, the CESCR does not have the power to issue any binding decisions regarding those reports. It does, however, have the power to review the submissions and provide guidance to the States on their treaty obligations. Similar to the HRC, the CESCR does this through: (1) review of the reports in the presence of state representatives on an article-by-article basis; (2) consultation with specialized U.N. agencies, such as the World Health Organization or the United Nations Economic Social and Cultural Organization; (3) follow-up procedures in the form of written questions and, in some cases, fact finding and investigation (but only with the permission of the State); and (4) concluding observations that are adopted in public session and made available to the State as well as the general public.

Finally, although the ICESCR does not have a complaint mechanism, there is an Optional Protocol to the Covenant that was unanimously adopted by the General Assembly in 2008. G.A. Res. 63/117, U.N. Doc. A/RES/63/117 (2008). The Protocol is currently open for signature and ratification, and ten States must ratify it before it enters into force. Like the First Optional Protocol to the ICCPR, this new ICESCR Protocol allows for individuals and States to bring complaints directly to the Committee, which must in turn examine the communications and where appropriate issue its "views" on those communications. Additionally, this new Protocol has an "inquiry" mechanism that will allow the CESCR to make investigations into serious and ongoing human rights violations committed by States, so long as a State has recognized the competence of the Committee under article 11 of the Protocol. G.A. Res. 63/117, U.N. Doc. A/RES/63/117 (2008).

Example 8-18

Assume State R has proposed the following "understanding" with respect to the ICESCR: that "the articles are goals to be achieved progressively, but do not require immediate implementation or action upon ratification."

Would such an "understanding" be permissible under the rules on Reservations, Understandings and Declarations (see §8.2) or under article 2 of the ICESCR?

Explanation

The first issue we need to explore is whether this statement is in fact an "understanding" or a "reservation." To figure that out we need to know what State R's duties are under the ICESCR. It is true that the State has time to implement the Covenant rights fully and completely, which is what the language "to achiev[e] progressively" in article 2 means. The problem with State R's "understanding" is that it assumes it has no obligation to take any steps whatsoever toward that end, which is not the case. The Covenant clearly requires State parties to take immediate steps toward the full realization of rights, including, but not limited to, legislative measures. Thus, the State's understanding really appears to be a reservation to its obligation to begin to implement the Covenant rights as "expeditiously and effectively as possible." As such, it would appear to undermine and be incompatible with one of the basic objects and purposes of the Covenant.

Example 8-19

State E, a developing country, makes the following reservation to the ICESCR: "The Government of State E reserves the right to postpone the application of article 13(2)(a) of the Covenant, in so far as it relates to primary education; since, while the Government of State E fully accepts the principles embodied in the same article and agrees to take the necessary steps to apply them in their entirety, the problems of implementation, and particularly the financial implications, are such that full application of the principles in question cannot be guaranteed at this stage." Article 13(a)(2) of the ICESCR states: "Primary education shall be compulsory and available free to all."

What might State E argue with respect to the validity of this reservation?

Explanation

Free primary education is one of the minimum core obligations that the CESCR has held as essential to guaranteeing economic, social, and cultural rights on the whole, as well as perhaps many civil and political rights. CESCR, General Comment 3, para. 10. Thus, any reservation to meeting this right needs to be closely analyzed, particularly as it relates to the overall object and purpose of the treaty. State E is obviously relying on its duty to take steps, but only to "the maximum of its available resources" to delay full implementation of this core right. This may well be a valid reservation, since State E accepts its general obligation to provide free primary education and because it agrees to take some steps toward full application of this right. Before it can completely rely on the lack of resources to delay full implementation of this right, the Committee will want assurances from State E that it has made "every effort" to use "all resources that are at its disposition . . . to satisfy, as a matter of priority" this minimum core obligation. CESCR, General Comment 3, para. 10. This would include seeking international assistance and cooperation under article 2(1) of the Covenant. Note that the inability of State X to implement a free primary educational system does not prevent it from becoming a party to the ICESCR and being bound by the other provisions of the treaty.

Example 8-20

State F, a developed country, is facing a severe recession, huge budget deficits, and massive unemployment. It is at the same time contemplating whether to ratify the ICESCR. It is currently a party to the ICCPR. Critics to ratification claim that now is not the time to ratify a treaty that would impose additional legal obligations on the State with respect to economic and social programs. For instance it takes issue with the fact that the treaty would require it to adopt massive governmental programs to provide everyone who is currently unemployed with a job, in order to meet its obligation under article 6 ("State Parties to the Covenant recognize the right to work"). They would in many instances prefer to provide incentives to private businesses, which would in turn create new jobs. Additionally, critics argue that current deficits suggest the need for the government to limit certain programs, such as healthcare to the elderly and food stamps for those who are living below the poverty line (which could impact approximately 20 million people out of a population of 300 million).

What would State F's obligations be with respect to these issues (employment, healthcare, food stamps) if it did in fact move forward with ratification of this Covenant?

Explanation

First, it is important to acknowledge that the treaty does impose real obligations on State F with respect to taking steps toward achieving the full realization of the rights articulated in the treaty, including the right to work, the right to basic healthcare, and access to basic foodstuffs. It is also important to remember that State F does not have to be in complete compliance with all of these norms before becoming a party to the treaty; rather, it just has to be willing to move progressively in that direction.

With that said, the treaty is written in such a way as to allow for progressive implementation of the rights based on a State's available resources, so long as the State is taking some steps toward meeting these rights. In this case, because State F is faced with a huge budget deficit, the language of the Covenant would suggest that it has leeway in prioritizing its otherwise limited resources. Of course, State F could not use this as a reason for failing to meet its obligations under the Covenant that do not require an expenditure of resources, such as the passage of laws that ensure equal employment opportunities or that prevent fraudulent behavior in the marketplace that might drive up the costs of healthcare and foodstuffs. Additionally, State F would need to be sure that it is at the very least using all of its available resources to meet minimum core obligations, such as ensuring that significant numbers of individuals are not being denied essential foodstuffs or basic healthcare.

Another key aspect of State F's dilemma, however, is whether it has to adopt massive social programs to meet its obligations with respect to jobs, healthcare, and foodstuffs. Another way to think about this question is whether the ICESCR is best suited for one particular type of economic or political structure (e.g., socialist versus free market approach). The CESCR specifically notes that "in terms of political and economic systems the Covenant is neutral and its principles cannot accurately be described predicated exclusively upon the need for, or the desirability of a socialist or a capitalist system, or a mixed, centrally planned, or laisser-faire economy, or upon any other particular approach." CESCR, General Comment 3, para. 8. Moreover, the language of the Covenant is itself sufficiently flexible to take into consideration different State values on how to meet these rights, as well as different levels of development and approaches to implementation. Thus, in our current problem, nothing in the ICESCR precludes State F from creating conditions in the marketplace that are more conducive to job creation, as opposed to putting everyone to work through some governmental jobs program. Additionally, on the issue of healthcare and foodstuffs, there is nothing in the ICESCR that would preclude State F from developing measures that might help bring down their costs, thereby making them more affordable for all. Should these core rights continue to be denied to a significant portion of the population, additional measures may well be necessary, but the Covenant doesn't dictate what those measures need to be with respect to State F.

Finally, on the issue of whether this treaty is a priority for State F, that is something only the citizens of State F can answer through its political process. It is important to note that some of the rights in the treaty may already be binding on State F should they rise to the level of customary law or overlap with other core human rights, such as the right to life under the ICCPR, which would presume, among other things, adequate foodstuffs to prevent starvation.

Example 8-21

State N is party to the ICCPR but not the ICESCR. State N's water supply is in very poor condition. Many families do not have access to drinking water, and the water that is available is dangerous for young children and the elderly because of the potential of contracting waterborne illnesses. According to the World Health Organization (WHO), about 1.8 million people around the world die from diarrheal diseases each year, and about eighty-eight percent of those deaths are due to unsafe water and poor sanitation and hygiene. In State N, children account for the biggest share of deaths that have occurred in that country due to poor water quality. As the CESCR has noted with respect to clean water, "[t]he right should . . . be seen in conjunction with other rights enshrined in the International Bill of Human Rights, foremost amongst them the right to life and human dignity." CESCR, General Comment 15, The Right to Water, para. 3, U.N. Doc. E/C.12/2002/11 (2002). While not explicitly mentioned in the ICESCR, the right to water is part of both the right to an adequate standard of living (art. 11) and the right to the highest attainable standard of health (art. 12). CESCR, General Comment 15.

Even though State R is not a party to the ICESCR, what obligations might it have under the ICCPR and the Universal Declaration, both of which are part of the International Bill of Human Rights?

Explanation

This example is intended to demonstrate that many of the rights found in the human rights treaties are interconnected. Implicit in both the right to life under the ICCPR and the right to human dignity under the Universal Declaration is a right of access to clean drinking water. Thus, even though State R is not a party to the ICESCR, an individual from State R is still entitled to clean water as part of State R's obligation under the ICCPR (as a State party) and under the Universal Declaration (as part of customary law). Therefore State R needs to take immediate steps to address the water contamination and access problem in its country, relying both on domestic and international resources, as well as perhaps the assistance of NGOs that specialize in helping communities establish clean water sources.[17]

§8.3.4 Customary International Human Rights Law

Both of the major human rights treaties, the ICCPR and the ICESCR, create binding obligations on States that choose to sign and ratify them. Yet, sometimes a State that has not ratified a human rights treaty may still be in violation of the norms that are articulated in those treaties. This is because those norms have become part of international customary law. Remember that customary law is defined as general and consistent practices of States that are followed from a sense of legal obligation. The concept of customary law is explored in detail in §2.2 and should be reviewed before working through the examples in this section.

As mentioned earlier, the Universal Declaration was not binding when adopted by the United Nations. Yet today, many of its provisions are considered part of customary international law due to its far-reaching acceptance in the international community. Furthermore, some of the rights contained in the ICCPR and the ICESCR have also become part of customary

---

17. See, e.g., Global Water, Our Approach, available at http://www.globalwater.org/approach.htm (last visited Oct. 2, 2010).

law, due in part to the fact that the treaties have been ratified by a large number of States. It is important to remember that to be part of customary law, a practice does not have to be universally adopted, just widely accepted and consistently followed by States. Although no set amount of time is necessary in establishing whether something is customary law, the longer the custom has been around the more likely it is being followed out of a sense of legal obligation.

Why worry about customary law in the human rights context if most human rights norms are part of international conventional law (that is, they have been codified in some instrument, such as the ICCPR or the ICESCR)? Customary international law still plays an important role in the field of human rights, both because a State may not be a party to one of those treaties and because some of the treaty provisions have risen to the level of customary law, which may in turn limit a State's ability to place a reservation on those rights. Some of the law on whether a State can have a reservation to a treaty provision that is also part of customary law is a bit murky, but perhaps less so if you are dealing with a peremptory norm, which is a right that no State may derogate from as a matter of international law (see §2.2.4). It is important to remember that the permissibility of a reservation is controlled by both the language of the treaty (for instance, does it allow for reservations at all), as well as the question of whether it is consistent with the object and purpose of the treaty. According to the HRC:

> Reservations that offend peremptory norms would not be compatible with the object and purpose of the [ICCPR]. Although treaties that are mere exchanges of obligations between States allow them to reserve *inter se* application of rules of general international law, it is otherwise in human rights treaties, which are for the benefit of persons within their jurisdiction. Accordingly, provisions in the Covenant that represent customary international law (and *a fortiori* when they have the character of peremptory norms) may not be the subject of reservations. HRC, General Comment No. 24, para. 8.

Section 2.2 explores the issue of what constitutes customary law in the international law sense, including what is meant by the notion of "general and consistent practices of a State." These same principles are relevant in the human rights context. What constitutes a "state practice" is perhaps a bit more expansive in the human rights context. For instance, we have already discussed why treaties such as the ICCPR, which are widely accepted, would be part of state practice. What else might we look to in order to determine "general and consistent practices" in the human rights context? Well, it might include such things as widely accepted adherence to the U.N. Charter, Universal Declaration or other such instrument, adoption by consensus of U.N. human rights resolutions, human rights principles that have been formulated and advanced through regional bodies or organizations, and invocation of human rights principles in national laws or policies. Additionally, while there is no definitive list for what human rights norms might already raise to the level of customary law, the Restatement of the Law Third, Foreign Relations Law of the United States provides us with some guidance in this regard:

> A State violates international law, if, as a matter of state policy, it practices, encourages or condones: (a) genocide; (b) slavery or slave trade; (c) the murder or causing the disappearance of individuals; (d) torture or other cruel, inhuman, or degrading treatment or punishment; (e) prolonged arbitrary detention; (f) systematic racial discrimination, or (g) a consistent pattern of gross violations of internationally recognized human rights. Restatement Third §702 (1987).

As the Restatement notes, this list is not exhaustive. Restatement Third §702 cmt. a. The Restatement also notes that the list of human rights norms given in §702 (a)-(f) are not only part of ordinary customary law, they are also peremptory norms (jus cogens), which means that no State can derogate from them and that any international agreement that violates them is void. Restatement Third §702, cmt. n. While a State may consistently object to a customary practice to avoid being bound by it, this is not the case with peremptory norms.

Where else might we look for a list of existing customary norms? U.N. treaty bodies that were discussed earlier have provided some guidance on this. For instance, the HRC has stated with respect to civil and political norms that:

> [P]rovisions in the Covenant that represent customary international law . . . may not be subject to reservations. Accordingly, a State may not reserve the right to engage in slavery, to torture, to subject persons to cruel, inhuman or degrading treatment or punishment, to arbitrarily deprive persons of their lives, to arbitrarily arrest and detain persons, to deny freedom of thought, conscience and religion, to presume a person guilty unless he proves his innocence, to execute pregnant women or children, to permit the advocacy of national, racial or religious hatred, to deny to persons of marriageable age the right to marry, or to deny to minorities the right to enjoy their own culture, profess their own religion, or use their own language. And while reservations to particular clauses of article 14 may be acceptable, a general reservation to the right to a fair trial would not be. HRC, General Comment No. 24, U.N. Doc. CCPR/C/21/Rev.1/Add.6 (Nov. 4, 1994), para. 8.

Not all States would agree with this list or with the idea that it cannot reserve its rights to articles of a treaty that are also part of customary law. Some States might argue that what they are doing is merely reserving their rights with respect to one form of enforcement or monitoring of that norm, not to the norm itself. In other words, the State may well be bound by that norm generally, but is not willing to open itself up to review or criticism by some treaty body (such as the HRC) for violation of that norm. Again, this interpretation of a State's obligation under a treaty, and its relationship to customary law, is a bit murky. What is clear, however, is that State parties cannot use reservations to treaties as a means of avoiding their general duties under international law, including customary law, nor can they do anything that is inconsistent with the object and purpose of the treaty.

Example 8-22

A citizen of State T is kidnapped and severely beaten by a member of the secret police of State T during official interrogation. As a result of the beating, the citizen dies. Unfortunately this is a common practice in State T with respect to the interrogation of individuals who oppose the policies of State T's government. State T has not ratified either the ICCPR or any other relevant treaty relating to torture or cruel, inhumane, or degrading treatment or punishment, such as the Convention Against Torture (see §9.2). His family seeks to bring suit in a domestic court of State U where the member of the secret police who carried out the beatings is currently residing. State U's laws allow for suits in its domestic court for any tort committed by a State or its agents in violation of the "law of nations" (that is, international customary law).

Since the act was committed by an agent of a State that is not a party to any of the relevant human rights treaties, on what basis might the family argue that State T's agent nevertheless violated international law?

Explanation

The family will need to rely on customary law, which is in fact part of international law. According to Restatement §702(d), torture committed, encouraged, or condoned as a matter of state policy violates customary law. In this instance, a member of the police force of State T, an actor of the state, committed the acts of torture that led to the death of a citizen who opposed State T's policies, which means his family can argue that the official was acting in violation of customary law. But how do we know that this prohibition against torture or cruel and inhuman treatment has arisen to that level? Is it because there are longstanding and widely recognized human rights treaties that prohibit such conduct? Is it because so many States have domestic laws or policies against torture? This was a question faced by a United States federal court in *Filartiga v. Pena-Irala*, 360 F.2d 876 (1980). The facts of that case were similar to the facts of this problem. The court found that a prohibition of state-sanctioned torture existed in customary international law by looking to the U.N. Charter, the Universal Declaration, a U.N. Declaration on the Protection of All Persons from Being Subjected to Torture, and the American Convention on Human Rights, all of which had been widely accepted by States. It noted that "[t]he international consensus surrounding torture has found expression in numerous international treaties and accords" and thus "we have little difficulty discerning its universal renunciation in the modern usage and practice of nations." *Filartiga*, 360 F.2d at 883. In other words, such actions clearly violate universal customary norms.

Example 8-23

Now assume that State T is in fact a party to the ICCPR, but has a reservation to article 7's prohibition of torture or cruel, inhuman, or degrading treatment. State T is also a party to the First Optional Protocol to the ICCPR.

What international remedies might the family pursue and what might State T argue with respect to the allegation of torture or cruel and inhuman treatment?

Explanation

Assuming the family has exhausted all of their domestic remedies or shown that such remedies were not available to them, they can submit a communication with the HRC claiming a violation of article 7 of the ICCPR. Although State T is a party to the Optional Protocol, it may point to its reservation to article 7 as one reason for not moving forward with the communication. The HRC is likely to conclude that the reservation is invalid, since State T is trying to reserve its rights to a provision of the ICCPR that has the character of a peremptory norm. Thus, as a matter of customary and conventional law, State T should be bound by article 7 of the ICCPR.

The State may try to argue that while it is not exempt from customary law with respect to the issue of torture, it has reserved its rights with respect to one form of enforcement or monitoring of that norm. A strong argument could be made that the State's reservation is inconsistent with the object and purpose of the ICCPR, since article 7 is one of those rights that cannot be derogated from under article 4 and is also a peremptory norm.

§8.4 CHARTER-BASED BODIES

The U.N. human rights bodies created to oversee the various human rights treaties, such as the HRC and CESCR, do not have the power to exact decisions that legally bind State parties; instead, they function more as monitors of State progress of human rights implementation. Other major U.N.

"monitoring" bodies include the Human Rights Council (formerly the Human Rights Commission) and the High Commissioner for Human Rights, both of which are discussed in this section. There is also the U.N. General Assembly, which is made up of all member States to the United Nations. Pursuant to the U.N. Charter, the General Assembly offers recommendations and initiates studies relating to human rights matters, which include the power to adopt human rights treaties such as the ICCPR and the ICESCR. Finally, there is the Economic and Social Council that has similar powers relating to the studying and monitoring of "international economic, social, cultural, education, health and [other] related matters." U.N. Charter, art. 62.

There are other bodies, both within the United Nations and outside of it, that serve to enforce the principles of human rights law by creating binding judgments against states and individuals. Chapter 11 on international criminal law introduces several tribunals established by the United Nations that serve to hold individuals responsible for gross violations of human rights, including war crimes and crimes against humanity. Chapter 11 also introduces the newly formed International Criminal Court, which is a judicial body that operates much like the specific tribunals, but with broader jurisdiction. You should refer to Chapter 11 for more information about these entities, but do keep in mind that this individual accountability is where international criminal law and human rights law intersect. Additional enforcement bodies outside the United Nations include various regional bodies, such as the European Court of Human Rights, the Inter-American Court of Human Rights, and the newly formed African Court of Human and Peoples Rights (see §9.4). In terms of additional "enforcement" of human rights norms within the United Nations system, there is the International Court of Justice and the U.N. Security Council, both of which are discussed in this section.

§8.4.1 U.N. High Commissioner for Human Rights

The Office of the High Commissioner for Human Rights (OHCHR) oversees the United Nations human rights system. The High Commissioner is the top human rights official, a position created by the General Assembly "to promote the universal respect for and observance of all human rights, in the recognition that, in the framework of the purposes and principles of the Charter, the promotion and protection of all human rights is a legitimate concern of the international community." G.A. Res. 48/141, U.N. GAOR, 48th Sess., Agenda Item 1149(b), at 1, U.N. Doc. A/RES/48/141 (1993). The OHCHR works to support various human rights organs, such as the Human Rights Council, the Economic and Social Council, and the General Assembly, and must submit annual reports of its activities to the Human

Rights Council and ECOSOC. The OHCHR also works directly with state governments, legal systems, and other organizations to promote human rights and to aid countries in developing mechanisms to ensure these rights. In this way, the High Commissioner acts as a liaison between States and the various U.N. bodies, such as the Human Rights Council. The High Commissioner's mandate includes investigating and reporting upon human rights abuses. U.N. Doc. E/CN.4/1995/98. The Office also coordinates various informational and educational efforts relating to human rights.[18] Yet the High Commissioner must also "[f]unction within the framework of the Charter of the United Nations . . ." and is required to "respect the sovereignty, territorial integrity and domestic jurisdiction of States. . . ." U.N. Doc. A/RES/48/141 (1993), para. 3(a). Thus, the Office must struggle with the same dilemma that many U.N. human rights bodies face — finding the appropriate balance between the promotion of international human rights norms and the international commitment to respecting state sovereignty. Since its inception in 1993, the various High Commissioners have visited a large number of countries and have established regional and country offices throughout the world.

§8.4.2 Human Rights Council

The Human Rights Council, created by G.A. Res. 60/251, is the successor to the United Nations Commission on Human Rights. Whereas the Commission was under the mandate of the Economic and Social Council, the Human Rights Council has been elevated to the status of a subsidiary body of the Assembly. The forty-seven seats in the Council are distributed among the U.N.'s regional groups: thirteen for Africa, thirteen for Asia, six for Eastern Europe, eight for Latin America and the Caribbean, and seven for the Western European and Others Group. G.A. Res. 60/251, para. 7. Each State must be approved by a majority vote of the General Assembly in a secret ballot. Council membership is also limited to two consecutive terms. By a two-thirds vote of the Assembly, any Council member may be suspended by the General Assembly for committing human rights violations. G.A. Res. 60/251, para. 8. The Resolution adopting the new Human Rights Council acknowledged that the former Commission on Human Rights suffered from various "shortcomings," and therefore sought to develop a procedure that would promote "universal respect for the protection of all human rights and fundamental freedoms for all, without distinction of any kind and in a fair and equal manner." G.A. Res. 60/251, Preamble, para. 2.

---

18. For the text of High Commissioner's recent Strategic Management Plan, see http://www.ohchr.org/Documents/Press/SMP2008-2009.pdf.

Much like the periodic reporting process used for the individual treaties discussed earlier, the Council is empowered to undertake a universal periodic review (UPR) of the human rights records of all U.N. member States once every four years. G.A. Res. 60/251 at para. 5(e). Note that the UPR procedure applies to *any* State that is a member of the United Nations. The standard of evaluation of the Human Rights Council's periodic review process includes: the Charter, the Universal Declaration, and any human rights instruments to which a State is a party. See *Report of the Human Rights Council*, Annex to Resolution 5/1, *delivered to the General Assembly*, U.N. Doc. A/62/53 (June 18, 2007). The actual assessment includes a self-evaluation by the State under review, a report from the Office of the High Commissioner relating to applicable treaties and other information obtained from the U.N. system, and relevant information submitted by NGOs and other interested parties. The information is presented to the UPR Working Group, which in turn engages the State in an interactive dialogue regarding the human rights system in its country. After the review session, an "outcome document" is prepared and adopted by the Council.

In addition to the UPR, the Human Rights Council also oversees a "complaint procedure" modeled after the former Commission on Human Rights' 1503 procedure.[19] Much like the 1503 procedure, the new complaint procedure is designed to address "consistent patterns of gross and reliably attested violations of all human rights and all fundamental freedoms occurring in any part of the world and under any circumstances."[20] Moreover, similar to 1503, this procedure retains its "confidential nature" as a means of enhancing cooperation from the relevant State. While it is intended to be a "victim-oriented" procedure, there still must be evidence of a consistent pattern of human rights violations. Individuals or groups of individuals claiming to be victims of such violations of human rights, or relevant NGOs representing those victims, may submit a communication, which is then reviewed by the Working Group on Communications. In order for a communication to be admissible, it must be submitted by or on the behalf of a victim of a human rights violation, must not be politically motivated, must not already be under review by another U.N. body, and must demonstrate that domestic remedies have already been exhausted. If admissible, the complaint is transferred to the Working Group on Situations, which considers the complaint and makes recommendations to the Human Rights Council on what actions need to be taken.

---

19. For more information on this procedure, see Human Rights Council Complaint Procedure, available at http://www2.ohchr.org/english/bodies/chr/complaints.htm.
20. See Human Rights Council Complaint Procedure, available at http://www2.ohchr.org/english/bodies/chr/complaints.htm.

The Council also is responsible for overseeing "special procedures,"[21] a function carried over from the Commission on Human Rights. Special procedures are created under either a country mandate, where the Council feels that a particular State needs its human rights situation to be monitored in an ongoing fashion, or under a thematic mandate, where there is a certain human rights violation occurring in places around the world. Those who carry out these mandates have taken two forms, as special rapporteurs, who are individuals, or working groups that are normally composed of five people. These experts undertake various activities, such as responding to individual complaints, conducting studies, providing advice on technical cooperation at the country level, and engaging in educational activities. One of the main tasks these mandate holders do is receive information on specific human rights violations and send urgent appeals to State governments requesting clarification of the alleged violations. Thus, these procedures are an important tool for NGOs and other human rights workers who are working on behalf of individuals or groups that face specific human rights violations. Currently, there are thirty-one thematic mandates and eight country mandates. The thematic mandates cover many of the civil and political rights we have explored thus far in this chapter, such as prolonged arbitrary detention, enforced or involuntary disappearances, freedom of expression, and torture. The mandates also include a host of economic and social issues, such as housing, education, cultural rights, and health.

Example 8-24

State Y has been fighting a civil war for the past fifteen years. The major victims of that war have been children from rural indigenous communities, many of whom have been forced from the age of ten to fight on behalf of armed forces or armed opposition groups. The children are subjected to daily beatings in order to make them more compliant, and many have been subjected to sexual abuse as well. Those who chose not to fight are often killed or maimed. None of the children are allowed any schooling and most suffer from malnutrition and parasitic diseases that they acquire during their time as foot soldiers. "AI," an international NGO focused on the rights of children during armed conflict, has begun a campaign in support of the children of State Y.

Example 9-1 builds on the same set of facts and discusses the substantive treaty violations that exist, as well as principles of customary law. This example focuses on questions of procedure. State Y is a member of the United Nations and is also a party to the ICCPR, the First Optional Protocol to the ICCPR, and the ICESCR.

---

21. See Special Procedures of the Human Rights Council, available at http://www2.ohchr.org/english/bodies/chr/special/index.htm.

1) What communications or complaint procedures might the NGO "AI" utilize on behalf of these children?

2) What other steps might it consider taking beyond the communications or complaint procedures?

Explanation

Since State Y is a party to the ICCPR and its First Optional Protocol, "AI" could elect to submit a communication to the HRC on behalf of the victims or victims' families. The ICESCR does not currently have a complaint mechanism, but may have one in the future if the recently adopted Optional Protocol to the Covenant is ratified by enough States. Other possibilities for "AI" include the confidential complaint procedure of the Human Rights Council. The fact pattern suggests that this is exactly the kind of "consistent pattern of gross violations of human rights" that the Council's complaint procedure was intended to address. Many children from State Y, especially those from rural communities, have been forced to fight in the armed forces of State Y or its armed opposition groups. Since State Y seems to officially practice as well as condone this behavior, this suggests a pattern of gross violations, from forced disappearances to torture and slavery.

In addition to these procedures, "AI" should determine which of the many thematic procedures are relevant to the human rights violations being committed against the children and submit information directly to those working groups or special rapporteurs. This may well include multiple submissions to multiple experts covering a range of issues, including discrimination, torture, forced disappearances, slavery, education, health, and so on. Finally, "AI" should determine if State Y is already part of a country mandate, which means that there is a mandate-holder looking at human rights issues relating to that State. If no mandate has been established, it may well be an issue to bring to the attention of the Human Rights Council. The NGO should also determine when State Y will face universal periodic review by the Human Rights Council and be ready to provide information to that process. Finally, there may be relevant regional human rights bodies that "AI" will want to explore as well (see §9.4).

§8.4.3 International Court of Justice

The International Court of Justice (ICJ) does not play a huge role in the interpretation or application of human rights law because its primary function is to hear contentious cases involving disputes between States that have consented to its jurisdiction. The scope of the ICJ's jurisdiction is discussed in Chapter 5. Contentious jurisdiction may be found when a treaty provides for the ICJ to handle disputes among parties to the treaty.

For instance, several human rights treaties, such as CERD and the Genocide Convention, specifically recognize ICJ jurisdiction over disputes between State parties that arise under those treaties. When States ratify these treaties, they accept ICJ jurisdiction, unless they make a reservation to it. Many states have in fact made such reservations against the exercise of ICJ jurisdiction. For instance, the United States has the following reservation with respect to the Genocide Convention: "[B]efore any dispute to which the United States is a party may be submitted to the jurisdiction of the International Court of Justice under [article IX], the specific consent of the United States is required in each case." 132 Cong. Rec. 2350 (1986).

The ICJ also has what is called advisory jurisdiction, where it may issue a nonbinding opinion on any relevant legal question, which is offered up at the request of the U.N. Security Council, the General Assembly or other appropriate U.N. bodies. U.N. Charter, art. 96. The requesting body can then use the ICJ's interpretation of the law to decide how to proceed when dealing with issues of international concern, such as human rights matters. For instance, one of the earliest advisory opinions given to the General Assembly by the ICJ concerned the Genocide Convention. Reservations to Convention on Prevention and Punishment of Crime of Genocide, Advisory Opinion, 1951 I.C.J. 15 (May 28). One of the questions before the ICJ was whether a State could be a party to the Convention if another State party objected to that State's reservation. The court found that the reserving State could still be party to the treaty so long as the reservation was consistent with the treaty's object and purpose. The ICJ reasoned that one of the primary goals of the Genocide Convention was to have universal acceptance by all States, and therefore a minor reservation should not undermine this aim:

> The object and purpose of the Genocide Convention imply that it was the intention of the General Assembly and of the State which adopted it that as many States as possible should participate. The complete exclusion from the Convention of one or more States would not only restrict the scope of its application, but would detract from the authority of the moral and humanitarian principles which are its basis. . . . The object and purpose of the convention thus limit both the freedom of making reservations and of objecting to them. Reservations to Convention on Prevention and Punishment of Crime of Genocide, 1951 I.C.J. at 24.

In deciding various questions relating to human rights, the ICJ will consider all relevant law (see Chapter 2), including the provisions of the human rights treaties that were earlier discussed. Even though the ICJ is not the monitoring body for any of these human rights treaties, it has the power to consider them in resolving cases under its contentious or advisory powers, in part because those treaties are part of international law that it is bound to apply under article 38(1) of the Statute of the International Court of Justice.

Example 8-25

State I is a party to the two major human rights treaties, the ICCPR and the ICESCR. State I built a security wall in and around areas known as the "occupied territories," which are currently occupied by individuals who are not citizens of State I, but who maintain claims to the land in the occupied areas. While much of the barrier is on State I's own territory, some of it is built on the "occupied territories" either for logistical or security reasons. State I has been the subject of numerous terrorist attacks from the occupied territories. It considers the wall to be a necessary means of stopping such attacks, and addressing the ongoing conflict between State I and the members of the occupied territories. In some places the wall completely encircles the occupied territories, cutting off communities and individuals from access to work, social services, and religious and cultural amenities. The General Assembly has submitted the following question to the ICJ for an advisory opinion: "What are the legal consequences arising from the construction of the wall being built by State I in the occupied territories?"

In considering the General Assembly's request for an advisory opinion, what substantive international human rights norms may the ICJ consider? Does it matter that some of State I's actions are occurring outside its own territories? Does it matter that State I is in a state of conflict in terms of the general applicability of human rights norms (to fully answer this question you should consider the materials in Chapter 10 on humanitarian law)?

Explanation

Consistent with its powers under the Statute of the International Court of Justice, the ICJ would look to various sources of international law, including human rights treaties, to determine whether the construction of the wall was in violation of human rights norms. Among other things, the ICJ might find that State I's construction of the wall through the occupied territories impedes the liberty of movement of the inhabitants of the territory as guaranteed by the ICCPR. This situation in turn impacts the inhabitants' rights to work, health, education, and an adequate standard of living as proclaimed in the ICESCR. Also, since State I's actions are occurring within an area that is under the control and jurisdiction of State I, these treaty rights would be applicable to those areas (see, e.g., ICCPR, art. 2(1)). Finally, on the question of "the relationship between international humanitarian law and human rights law," the ICJ has found that:

> [T]he protection offered by human rights conventions does not cease in case of armed conflict, save through the effect of provisions for derogation of the kind to be found in Article 4 of the International Covenant on Civil and Political Rights. . . . [T]here are three possible situations: some rights may be exclusively

matters of international humanitarian law; other may be exclusively matters of human rights law; yet others may be matters of both these branches of international law. In order to answer the question put to it [by the General Assembly], the Court will have to take into consideration both these branches of international law, namely human rights law and, as *lex specialis*, international humanitarian law. *Legal Consequences of Construction of Wall in Occupied Palestinian Territory*, 2004 I.C.J. at para. 102-113.

Thus human rights law continues to apply during times of armed conflict, unless humanitarian law has some specific rule that would oust the human rights rule (see §§10.4 and 10.5). This example is similar to the facts found in the ICJ's advisory decision on the *Legal Consequences of the Construction of a Wall in the Occupied Palestinian Territory*, Advisory Opinion, 2004 I.C.J. 136 (July 9).

§8.4.4 U.N. Security Council

The other U.N. body that has "enforcement" powers relating to gross human rights violations is the Security Council. A general overview of the Security Council is provided in §4.5. Additionally, §10.5.2 discusses the Security Council's power to intervene in matters that would otherwise be within the domestic jurisdiction of a State. This latter section includes a discussion on "humanitarian intervention," which would include the use of military force to address massive violations of human rights. All these sections should be read in conjunction with this one in order to get a complete picture of the power of the Security Council to address such violations.

This section is intended to provide a brief overview on two important questions: (1) What role does the Security Council play in preserving and promoting human rights, especially in the context of massive violations of rights? (2) What, if anything, can member States do when the Security Council fails to authorize protective measures relating to human rights abuses? It is important to note at the outset that there are some grey areas here in terms of powers and duties, which will be highlighted in the text and in the examples.

Articles 55 and 56 of the U.N. Charter call on all member nations to promote and respect universal human rights and to take joint and separate action in order to fulfill these obligations. As §10.4 notes, the Charter also reinforces the general rule of non-intervention: that every State is prohibited from interfering with the internal affairs of another State, which includes the use of force except in limited circumstances. U.N. Charter, arts. 2(4), 2(7) & 51. This rule of non-intervention does not apply to enforcement measures taken by the Security Council under chapter VII of the U.N. Charter (see U.N. Charter, art. 2(7)), nor does it impact the ability of the Security

Council to act under chapter VI of the U.N. Charter relating to "pacific settlement of disputes." It is these Charter powers that are relevant to understanding what role the Security Council might play in preventing or addressing widespread human rights violations.

Chapter VI of the U.N. Charter (arts. 33-38) relates to noncoercive measures that can be taken by the Security Council in addressing disputes that are "likely to endanger the maintenance of international peace and security." Chapter VI basically encourages all parties to resolve disputes through peaceful means, such as arbitration, mediation, or judicial settlement, while empowering the Security Council to take appropriate steps to help bring about a peaceful settlement. On the other hand, chapter VII of the U.N. Charter (arts. 39-51) authorizes the Security Council to take coercive measures to address "any threat to the peace, breach of the peace, or act of aggression" as may be necessary to "maintain or restore international peace and security" (art. 39). Before taking such coercive measures, the Security Council may issue provisional measures to attempt to remedy the situation (art. 40). If this fails to work, the Security Council may then invoke its powers under article 41 to "decide what measures not involving the use of armed forces are to be employed to give effect to its decisions." Examples of such measures include sanctions, embargos, and severance of diplomatic relations. Should such measures prove to be inadequate, then article 42 of the Charter permits the Security Council to use force in order to maintain or restore international peace and security. Such measures include the use of "air, sea or land forces," for purposes of "demonstrations, blockade, and other operations" (art. 42). The Security Council itself doesn't perform these steps; rather, it is the member states of the United Nations that are obligated to do so (arts. 42 & 43).

When the Security Council "decides" to take action under one or more of these articles of the U.N. Charter, it will issue a resolution, which is binding on all member States (see art. 25). Remember that in order for the Security Council to issue such a resolution, it needs the consent of all five permanent members and at least four nonpermanent members.

It is also important to remember that the coercive powers of the Security Council are in fact limited by article 39, which requires it to determine in the first instance whether there is any "threat," "breach," or "act of aggression" as it relates to international peace and security. This raises the question of intervention in matters that are seemingly contained within the borders of one State, but involve gross violations of human rights. As many of the examples below demonstrate, most conflicts of this nature have consequences that extend well beyond the borders of an individual State and therefore constitute a "threat" to or even perhaps a "breach" of international peace and security. For instance, humanitarian crises may generate refugees who move into other States' territories. Also a failure to act on the part of the Security Council in the face of massive human rights violations may result in individual States taking action to halt the violations, thereby resulting in inter-state conflict. With that said, the substantive legal standards governing this type of humanitarian intervention are arguably still evolving. In addition, there are a host of political and logistical factors that impact the Security Council's decision to act.

So what happens if the Security Council is unwilling or unable to act? Do States have the power to act without Security Council approval in order to address widespread human rights violations? There is no easy answer to this question. U.N. officials, scholars, government officials, and others have all voiced their opinion on whether unilateral intervention by a State or group of States is permissible absent Security Council approval, even in the case of massive human rights violations. Some argue that it is not a permissible action under international law; others see it as an emerging principle that may be necessary to address the worst kinds of human rights violations.[22] Let us take a brief look at what the U.N. Charter has to say about this question.

First, if we are talking about the use of "force" then we need to turn to article 2(4) of the Charter, which prohibits members from using force or threatening to use force "against the territorial integrity or political independence of any state, or in any manner that is inconsistent with the Purposes of the United Nations" (see §10.4.2). Some scholars maintain that intervention for purposes of addressing widespread human rights violations is not barred under article 2(4) because such intervention is not aimed at changing the country's borders or impacting its political independence. They may also point to the fact that all members to the United Nations "pledge" under article 56 to take joint and *separate* action to promote human rights.

In response, some have argued that anytime one country uses force against another, even in the context of addressing gross violations of human rights, it impacts the territorial integrity and political independence of that country. Thus, such action would not be permissible under article 2(4) of the Charter, absent some other specific exception, such as the right to self-defence (see §10.4.2). They may also argue that such action is contrary to the primary "purpose" of the United Nations, which is to promote and maintain international peace and security. Two other arguments

---

22. For a broad array of scholarly opinions on this matter, see, e.g., Jonathan Charney, *Anticipatory Humanitarian Intervention in Kosovo*, 93 Am. J. Int'l L. 834 (1999) (concluding unilateral humanitarian intervention constitutes a violation of international law); Ruth Wedgwood, *NATO's Campaign in Yugoslavia*, 93 Am. J. Int'l L. 828 (1999) (stating intervention may be a "limited and conditional right" when taken by "a responsible multilateral organization and the Security Council does not oppose the action"); Louis Henkin, *Kosovo and the Law of Humanitarian Intervention*, 93 Am. J. Int'l L. 824 (1989) (explaining the "law is . . . that unilateral intervention by military force . . . is unlawful unless authorized by the Security Council").

against unilateral humanitarian intervention posit that it creates a "slippery slope" in terms of what abuses warrant such intervention and that it undermines the legitimacy of the Security Council, which has the power under the U.N. Charter to take such enforcement action.

Note that nothing in article 2(4) of the Charter seems to preclude States from taking nonforcible steps against a State who is committing or condoning human rights abuses, such as economic sanctions or severance of diplomatic relations. Finally, there is a great deal of discussion right now around a doctrine known as the "Responsibility to Protect," which basically stands for the idea that States have a duty to prevent or address certain types of atrocities, including massive human rights abuses. This "Responsibility to Protect" doctrine has been endorsed at various levels of the United Nations,[23] but is probably not considered part of customary international law in part because it raises a number of the same questions discussed above with respect to the use of unilateral force (see §10.4.3).

Example 8-26

State I invades State K without any claims to self-defense. Around the same time, State I begins a brutal campaign to wipe out a minority group that occupies the northern portion of State I. Many from that group are fleeing to neighboring States out of fear for their life.

1) What action if any can the Security Council take to address these two situations?

2) Do they warrant difference responses given their different factual circumstances, one being an attack on the sovereignty of another State and the other being an "internal" dispute?

Explanation

This example is based in part on Iraq's invasion of Kuwait in 1990 and its subsequent campaign against the Kurdish minority in the northern part of Iraq. The Security Council, pursuant to its chapter VII powers, authorized the collective use of force against Iraq on the grounds that Iraq's invasion of Kuwait violated article 2(4) of U.N. Charter, which prohibits the use of force against another country's territorial integrity or political independence. U.N. Doc. S/RES/678 (1990). Before approving the use of force against Iraq, the Security Council first demanded that Iraq

---

23. See, e.g., The Responsibility to Protect, Report of the International Commission on Intervention and State Sovereignty (2001); Report of the U.N. High-Level Panel on Threats, Challenges and Change, *A More Secure World: Our Shared Responsibility*, U.N. Doc. A/59/565 (Dec. 2, 2004). See generally Carsten Stahn, *Responsibility to Protect: Political Rhetoric or Emerging Legal Norm?* 101 Am. J. Int'l L. 99 (2007).

withdraw from Kuwait, and then imposed comprehensive sanctions on Iraq pursuant to article 41. U.N. Doc. S/RES/660 (1990); S/RES/661 (1990).

At the end of the Gulf War, Iraq forcibly suppressed an uprising by the Kurdish people of the north (and Shiites of the south), resulting in a massive exodus to Turkey and Iran, as well as to remote areas of Iraq. This action led to the adoption of Security Council Resolution 688, which was construed by the United States and other coalition forces to allow for the protection of the Kurds in northern Iraq through the use of armed forces. U.N. Doc. S/RES/688 (Apr. 5, 1991). Despite the fact that Iraq claimed this was an "internal" matter and that the resolution violated its sovereign rights, the Security Council found a threat to international peace and security, in part due to the "massive flow of refugees towards and across international frontiers and to cross-border incursions" U.N. Doc. S/RES/688. Thus, "intervention" was warranted under its chapter VII powers to address massive human rights violations that were threatening international peace and security in the region.

Example 8-27

A number of conflicts have broken out in and around the dissolution of State Y. Group B, one of the three ethnic groups living in parts of the former State Y, has declared its independence as State B. This territory is also populated by two other distinct ethnic groups — C and S. Civil war has broken out in the newly established State B, which was recently recognized by the Security Council as an independent State. The main aggressor is Group S, which has begun a campaign to destroy members of Group B. This includes the execution of thousands of men and boys from Group B, as well as the separating of women from Group B into camps where they are subjected to mass rape and other such violations. Members of Group B also are being forced to migrate to neighboring States.

Surrounding States with connections to Groups C and S are supplying these groups with military and logistical support. Additionally there are human rights abuses being committed on all sides, although Group S is committing the primary abuses in the form of executions and rapes. Finally various factions are interfering with the delivery of humanitarian aid to citizens of State B, who are currently without adequate food, water, or shelter.

Assume you are a legal advisor to the U.N. Secretary-General and have been asked to assess whether this is a matter for the Security Council. If so, what steps might the Security Council take in addressing this ongoing conflict?

Explanation

This example shows how complicated the issue of intervention in the name of human rights abuses can be, especially when you have multiple States and multiple offenders involved. As a legal advisor, you could recommend that the Security Council take the following steps:

1. Take action under chapter VI of the U.N. Charter in the form of a resolution that would encourage all parties to end the ongoing conflict and recognize the sovereign rights of State B.

2. Take action under chapter VII in the form of a resolution authorizing a mandatory arms embargo against the States that are providing logistical and military aid to Groups S and C in their attacks against State B and members of that ethnic group. This would be permissible under chapter VII given the involvement of multiple countries in the affairs of State B, resulting in a clear threat to, if not an actual breach of, international peace and security.

3. Take action under chapter VII in the form of a resolution authorizing member States to use military force to provide humanitarian relief to the people of State B. This is warranted given the massive humanitarian crisis that is unfolding in the region.

4. Additionally, the resolution could declare unlawful the "ethnic cleansing" and other such human rights violations being committed against civilians and provide for the necessary U.N. member "forces" to protect civilians that are being targeted by Group S. Again the basis for the Security Council's power to act would be chapter VII and the continued threat to international peace and security as the result of the ongoing conflict. While most of the atrocities are being committed within the borders of State B, various groups are being aided and abetted by neighboring countries, and there is a massive humanitarian crisis unfolding in the entire region.

5. Finally, the Security Council could authorize an international criminal tribunal to address the crimes against humanity and war crimes being committed in the course of this armed conflict (see Chapter 11).

The above example is similar to the situation that took place in Bosnia from 1992-1995. While the war involved multiple parties (e.g., Serbia, Croatia, Bosnia), the primary attacks were against Bosnian Muslims or Bosniaks by Bosnian Serbs. The Security Council took many of the actions outlined above, including declaring an arms embargo (U.N. Doc. S/RES/713 (1991)) and creating "safe areas" where humanitarian aid could be distributed to civilians (U.N. Doc. S/RES/819 (1993)). Bosnian Serbs nevertheless breached these "safe areas," leading to the execution of over 7,000 Bosniak men and boys just in the town of Srebrenica alone. This was due in part to the limited scope of the Security Council's mandate.[24] The war was finally brought to end through NATO intervention and negotiation, steps that had been authorized by the Security Council pursuant to its chapter VII powers. The Security Council also established the International Criminal Tribunal for the former Yugoslavia (ICTY) to prosecute individuals who committed atrocities against civilians (see Chapters 10 and 11).

Example 8-28

Internal armed conflict has erupted in State S. The conflict is between different factions vying for control of the government. Much of the population of State S lives in rural areas with limited resources and food due to severe drought. Thus, the citizens of State S depend on humanitarian aid from other countries in order to survive. Since the conflict began, humanitarian aid has been disrupted, as the militants in State S have begun intercepting the aid vehicles, thereby preventing the distribution of goods and food. Millions of people in State S are in danger of starvation and death from disease, which some fear may lead to a mass exodus to neighboring countries.

Can (or should) the Security Council use its power to "maintain international peace and security" to intervene in this internal conflict, or is this a merely a matter of "domestic concern" that does not warrant Security Council action?

Explanation

This is perhaps a somewhat more difficult situation than the two previous examples, where you had a clear breach or at least a threat to regional peace and security. In this case, intervention would be based predominately on humanitarian grounds, although the possibility of a mass exodus to other countries could certainly be seen as a destabilizing force in the region. This example is similar to the situation that arose in Somalia in 1991. The Security Council opted, among other things, to authorize the use of military force to address the growing humanitarian crisis in that country. S.C. Res. 794, U.N. Doc. S/RES/794 (Dec. 3, 1992). As robust as this mandate appeared to be in terms of addressing these kinds of massive human rights violations, the political climate for such interventions declined quickly following the death of 18 U.S. Army rangers in an armed clash with Somalia factions in Mogadishu. Many believe that this failed peace enforcement experience in Somalia set the stage for the Security Council's failure to authorize a military

---

24. See, e.g., Roy Gutman, *Bosnia: Negotiation and Retreat*, in *Soldiers for Peace: Fifty Years of United Nations Peacekeeping* (Barbara Benton ed. 1996).

intervention to halt the 1994 genocide in Rwanda.[25] Since then, Security Council involvement in addressing widespread human rights violations has been sporadic at best.

Example 8-29

State Y's armed forces have begun to attack the citizens of province K, who wish to declare their independence from State Y. The attacks have resulted in massive killings, as well as large-scale displacement from homes and communities into neighboring states, as well as a host of other human rights violations. A regional alliance of States has sought to negotiate a settlement with State Y in order to bring about peace in the region and to prevent what it perceives to be the makings of a massive humanitarian crisis. Although the U.N. Security Council has adopted several resolutions condemning the actions of State Y, it has not authorized U.N. member States to use force to implement these resolutions.

Can this regional organization take military action against State Y in the name of "human rights" absent such a resolution?

Explanation

This example raises the difficult question of whether a state or group of states can use force to avert a humanitarian crisis, absent an explicit resolution from the Security Council (see also §10.4). Many would argue that such action is clearly illegal under the U.N. Charter because it constitutes a use of force in violation of the territorial integrity and political independence of State Y. Only the Security Council has the power under the U.N. Charter to authorize forcible intervention in the domestic matters of State Y, in order to avert the impending humanitarian crisis. Others would argue that such action is warranted when it is necessary to avert an overwhelming and imminent humanitarian catastrophe in the region where these States are located, especially where, as here, all other means to resolve the situation have been exhausted.

This example is similar to the situation that unfolded in Kosovo in 1999, where NATO used force to intervene on behalf of Kosovo's ethnic Albanians. The actual Kosovo situation was complicated by the fact that the Security Council had previously adopted several resolutions relating to the Kosovo crisis pursuant to chapter VII, although none expressly provided for the use of force. Additionally, a draft resolution condemning the NATO attacks was defeated by the Security Council by a twelve-to-three vote shortly after the start of military operations in 1999, suggesting tacit approval on the part of the Security Council with respect to those operations.

---

25. See Philip Gourevitch, *We Wish to Inform You that Tomorrow We Will be Killed With Our Families: Stories from Rwanda* (1999). Over 800,000 Rwandan Tutsis and moderate Hutus were killed in that genocide.

Additional Topics in Human Rights

§9.1 Introduction
§9.2 U.N. Conventions on Specific Human Rights Topics
§9.3 The Role of Non-Governmental Organizations
§9.4 Regional Human Rights Systems
    §9.4.1 The European Human Rights System
    §9.4.2 The Inter-American System
    §9.4.3 The African System
    §9.4.4 The Emergence of Other Regional Human
            Rights Systems
§9.5 Group Rights
§9.6 Corporate Responsibility for Human Rights

§9.1 INTRODUCTION

This chapter discusses additional treaty regimes that relate to specific human rights topics, such as women and children, or that arise in the context of regional systems, such as the Council of Europe and the Organization of American States. Additionally, it touches upon some contemporary topics of human rights that are both timely and evolving in scope, such as group rights and corporate responsibility for human rights.

§9.2 U.N. CONVENTIONS ON SPECIFIC HUMAN RIGHTS TOPICS

There are a growing number of conventions that seek to protect a broad range of human rights, many of which are protected in the two main human rights treaties, but need additional monitoring and enforcement because of their special character (e.g., torture, genocide, discrimination) or because of the individuals they seek to protect (women and children). Some of these treaties are briefly discussed in this section.

They include such treaties as the Convention on Prevention and Punishment of the Crime of Genocide (78 U.N.T.S. 277 (1948)), which proclaims genocide to be a crime under international law. The Genocide Convention defines genocide as any act (such as killing members of a group, causing them seriously bodily or mental harm, taking actions to bring about their physical destruction, or forcibly transferring their children) that is "committed with intent to destroy, in whole or in part, a national, ethnical, racial or religious group." Genocide Convention, Art. 2. For additional information on the Genocide Convention, see §11.2.1.

Another specialized human rights treaty is the Convention against Torture and other Cruel, Inhuman or Degrading Treatment or Punishment, also known commonly as the Convention against Torture or CAT, G.A. Res. 39/46, 1465 U.N.T.S. 85 (1987). This treaty places an absolute ban on torture, which is defined as:

> [A]ny act by which severe pain or suffering, whether physical or mental, is intentionally inflicted on a person for such purposes as obtaining from him or a third person, information or a confession, punishing him for an act he or a third person has committed or is suspected of having committed, or intimidating or coercing him or a third person, or for any reason based on discrimination of any kind, when such pain or suffering is inflicted by or at the instigation of or with the consent or acquiescence of a public official or other person acting in an official capacity. Convention against Torture, art. 1.

The prohibitions against genocide and torture are peremptory norms (see §8.3.4).

Another important treaty is the International Convention on the Elimination of All Forms of Racial Discrimination, G.A. Res. 2106 (XX), 660 U.N.T.S. 195 (1965). This Convention (CERD) was adopted at the same time as the two major human rights treaties, the ICCPR and ICESCR, and all three contain important nondiscrimination provisions. CERD defines racial discrimination as:

> [A]ny distinction, exclusion, restriction or preference based on race, colour, descent, or national or ethnic origin which has the purpose or effect of

nullifying or impairing the recognition, enjoyment or exercise, on an equal footing, of human rights and fundamental freedoms in the political, economic, social, cultural or any other field of public life. CERD, art. 1.

The treaty requires States to take proactive measures to prevent discrimination and has been widely accepted by 173 States.

Two other human rights treaties are the Convention on the Elimination of All Forms of Discrimination against Women (CEDAW) (G.A. Res. 34/180, 1249 U.N.T.S. 14 (1979)) and the Convention on the Rights of the Child (CRC) (G.A. Res. 44/25, 1577 U.N.T.S. 3 (1989)). CEDAW recognizes that women often suffer human rights abuses disproportionately to men and are often the subject of extensive discrimination, particularly in the areas of civil, political, economic, and social rights. Despite being signed and ratified by a large number of States (185), many State parties have adopted reservations that impact the Convention's overall effectiveness. The United States is the only developed country that has not ratified the Convention. The CRC recognizes children as a class of individuals in need of special human rights protections, setting minimum standards for the protection of their rights. It guarantees civil and political, as well as economic, social, and cultural rights. One of the primary aims of the Convention is to address violence against children. The CRC has two optional protocols. The First Optional Protocol is for the prevention of child soldiering. The Second Optional Protocol is to protect children from being sold into slavery or sex work. The CRC is one of the most widely adopted human rights treaties, with 193 ratifications. The United States and Somalia are the only nations that have not ratified this treaty.

Much like the HRC and the CESCR, the implementation of these treaties are monitored by human rights bodies, including the Committee on the Elimination of Racial Discrimination, the Committee Against Torture, the Committee on the Rights of the Child, and the Committee on the Elimination of Discrimination Against Women.

Example 9-1

These are the same facts found in Example 8-24. State Y has been fighting a civil war for the past fifteen years. The major victims of that war have been children from rural indigenous communities, many of whom have been forced from the age of ten to fight on behalf of armed forces or armed opposition groups. The children are subjected to daily beatings in order to make them more compliant, and many have been subjected to sexual abuse as well. Those who chose not to fight are often killed or maimed. None of the children are allowed any schooling and most suffer from malnutrition and parasitic diseases that they acquire during their time as foot soldiers. "AI," an international non-governmental organization (see §§4.6 and §9.3) that is focused on the rights of children during armed conflict, has begun a campaign in support of the children of State Y.

    1) Which of the treaties might be relevant to AI's efforts on behalf of the child soldiers in State Y?

    2) Is there any customary law or peremptory norm that State Y may also be violating by allowing its armed forces to use child soldiers to fight rebel forces?

Explanation

This example is intended to demonstrate the interconnectedness of human rights law. Certainly the provisions of the ICCPR relating to the right to life, prohibition against torture or cruel and inhuman treatment, and the right to nondiscrimination would be applicable, as would the provisions of the ICESCR relating to foodstuffs, education, health, and special measures of protection as a result of their status as children. Yet equally relevant would be the more specific treaties that protect against systematic racial discrimination (CERD), torture or cruel and inhuman treatment (CAT), or that articulate a host of rights aimed at the well-being of children (CRC and its optional protocols). Each of these treaties has its own monitoring body that "AI" could reach out to in addressing its concerns about State Y's practices, assuming of course that State Y has in fact ratified all of these instruments. If State Y has not, then it may well be in violation of relevant customary norms and even perhaps peremptory norms (e.g., the prohibition against torture, slavery, arbitrary deprivation of life, prolonged arbitrary detention, and systematic racial discrimination to name a few). "AI" could not seek direct assistance from any of the treaty bodies should State Y not be a party to any of the relevant treaties, since the powers of the treaty bodies emanate from and are limited by those instruments. Section 8.4 discusses other U.N. processes that may be available and open to "AI" in its efforts to address the human rights violations against the children of State Y.

§9.3 THE ROLE OF NON-GOVERNMENTAL ORGANIZATIONS

There are non-governmental actors that play a very important role in human rights implementation and enforcement known as Non-Governmental Organizations or NGOs (see also §4.6). NGOs are invaluable information gatherers that may work in conjunction with U.N. or other government agencies, but also work independently to provide human rights relief without the stigma of government and politics attached. Human rights bodies, such as the U.N. Human Rights Committee (HRC), will look to NGOs to provide them with information pertaining to a specific State and its progress toward implementation of treaty obligations. This is because NGOs often have resources and expertise available to them that the U.N. or State party may not. For instance, when a State submits its article 40 report to the HRC, it may work with an NGO to assist in the reporting process. Other times, an NGO may file what is called a counter-report if the organization believes that the State's report was not accurate or detailed enough. The U.N. human rights bodies can use this information to create a more realistic picture of what is happening in a State. Additionally, NGOs may submit questions for a State to be used during public sessions, as well as assist individuals in bringing claims against their governments for human rights violations. Finally, NGOs may assist in the drafting of general comments, specifically when an organization specializes in the subject about which the comment will be written.

Example 9-2

State R is a party to the ICCPR and the First Optional Protocol to the ICCPR. Mikela, a woman from State R, has not seen or heard from her husband in two years. The last time she saw him, he had been taken by the local police force. Mikela's husband is a journalist and editor of a local newspaper that had been writing articles on corruption by local officials. On two previous occasions, Mikela's husband had been detained for several weeks after writing a series of articles on corruption relating to the building of a highway project. On other occasions, he and other local journalists have been subjected to phone threats and beatings by individuals that were never pursued or prosecuted by the local authorities. Mikela has attempted to contact police to find her husband but they have refused to help. She has also tried to hire a lawyer to bring a suit, but no lawyer will help her because of fear of retribution from the government. Intimidation, forced disappearances, and targeted killings of journalists and human rights activists have become a common occurrence in State R, and as a result, a number of NGOs have located human rights specialists in the country in order to better assess the human rights situation regarding journalists and the right to freedom of expression.

1) How might an NGO be able to help Mikela approach the HRC with her husband's situation?

2) How might an NGO be able to inform the HRC more generally about the pattern of disappearances in State R? You may also want to review the materials on the ICCPR (§8.3.2), including the procedures under the First Optional Protocol to the ICCPR, before answering this question.

Explanation

As noted in earlier examples in Chapter 8, forced disappearances violate a number of political and civil rights found in the ICCPR, such as the right to life, the right not to be arbitrarily detained, and the right to be free from torture. This example raises additional concerns as it relates to freedom of expression and freedom to seek, receive, and impart information. ICCPR, art. 19. Since State R is a party to both the ICCPR and the First Optional Protocol, Mikela can submit an individual complaint to the HRC on behalf of her husband. In order to submit an individual complaint before the HRC, however, it must be shown that all domestic remedies have been exhausted or were not available in the first place. Here, Mikela has attempted to invoke domestic remedies but has not been successful due to a lack of cooperation from the police of State R and the unwillingness of attorneys to get involved.

As far as choosing a way to have her complaint voiced, NGOs provide the means for people like Mikela, who may not have the ability on their own, to approach the HRC or other relevant international or regional human rights bodies. Given the large number of NGOs located in State R to document abuses against journalists, Mikela should be able to find an NGO that, in addition to data collecting, also works with victims and their families to submit individual communications to the HRC. When the NGO submits the complaint to the HRC, it must demonstrate why Mikela's husband was unable to submit the complaint himself, which will not be difficult as it is the disappearance of Mikela's husband that is one of the human rights violations being claimed. In addition to aiding Mikela with a complaint regarding the disappearance of her husband, an NGO may also compile information generally on the treatment and intimidation of journalists in State R. It can use this information in the form of a counter-report to State R's article 40 report. That way, if State R ignores the issue of disappearances and intimidation of journalists in its report, the HRC will be better informed as to the situation at hand. Additional remedies available to Mikela through the NGO are discussed in Chapter 8 with respect to the newly formed U.N. Human Rights Council (see §8.4.2).

§9.4 REGIONAL HUMAN RIGHTS SYSTEMS

So far, Chapter 8 and parts of Chapter 9 have examined the human rights framework put in place by the United Nations, which operates at a global level. However, the U.N. system relies more on monitoring and less on enforcement, in part because States are often reluctant to submit to any other type of oversight. At the same time, smaller human rights systems centered in different regions of the world have taken hold. Given their regional focus, these systems may be somewhat more effective in terms of enforcement or even monitoring when it comes to local or regional human rights problems. The European human rights system is perhaps one of the most robust systems in terms of the sheer number of human rights cases it addresses each year. Other well established systems include the Inter-American system and, more recently, the African system. The Arab system in the Middle East is just beginning to take hold, while Asia still lacks a human rights framework of its own. Since these systems are not often covered in depth in a course on international law, the following section is intended merely as an introduction.

§9.4.1 The European Human Rights System

The European Convention for the Protection of Human Rights and Fundamental Freedoms, 213 U.N.T.S. 221 (1950), was one of the first treaties to protect human rights at the regional level. The Convention is open to all members of the Council of Europe, which has as one of its primary functions the "the maintenance and further realization of human rights and fundamental freedoms." The European Convention gives protection to a long list of human rights in the area of civil and political rights, many of them similar to those found in the Universal Declaration and the ICCPR. A number of optional protocols have expanded the list of protected rights. Many of the listed rights are subject to restrictions prescribed by law to protect such interests as national security, public safety, and prevention of disorder or crime. In §8.2 we explored how some of those restrictions have played out in terms of treaty interpretation and the "margin of appreciation."

The European Convention on Human Rights and Fundamental Freedoms allows individuals, groups, or corporations to file complaints against States (art. 34). It also allows for state-against-state complaints (art. 33). The enforcement system for the Convention has evolved and has been altered considerably over time. Originally, the complaint procedures were optional, but today the complaint procedures have become mandatory. Domestic remedies in the State against which the complaint is brought must be exhausted (or otherwise not available) before seeking review. Member States have the primary responsibility for the enforcement of the Convention, with the Court only available where no further relief is available at the state level. The European Court now has the power to tell member States that their own laws violate their obligations under the Convention, which means that national laws might have to be repealed or altered to comply with the Convention. Additionally, member States must provide remedies for violations of certain Convention rights. The European Court of Human Rights is the body empowered to hear cases, and can sit as a Chamber, consisting of seven judges, or as a Grand Chamber of seventeen judges.

Europe has adopted two other primary human rights documents besides the Convention. The European Social Charter (529 U.N.T.S. 89 (1961)) protects a number of economic and social rights, such as the right to work and to just conditions of work; the right to organize; protections against child labor; protections for employed women; protection of health, social security, social and medical assistance; the right to training for the physically and mentally disabled; and protections for the family and migrant workers. States parties to the Charter are required to submit annual reports on implementation to the European Committee of Social Rights, which monitors compliance with the Charter's obligations. The other major human rights instrument is the European Convention for the Prevention of Torture and Inhuman or Degrading Treatment or Punishment (Nov. 26, 1987 Europ. T.S. 126, 27 I.L.M. 1152), which establishes a Committee whose job it is to visit places of detention and ensure that detainees are not subject to torture or other forms of severe mistreatment. After visiting places of detention, the Committee issues a confidential report to the State party. The Convention should be read in conjunction with article 3 of the European Convention on Human Rights, which prohibits torture.

Example 9-3

Article 9 of the European Convention on Human Rights reads:

> 1. Everyone has the right to freedom of thought, conscience and religion; this right includes freedom to change his religion or belief and freedom, either alone or in community with others and in public or private, to manifest his religion or belief, in worship, teaching, practice and observance.
> 2. Freedom to manifest one's religion or beliefs shall be subject only to such limitations as are prescribed by law and are necessary in a democratic society in the interests of public safety, for the protection of public order, health or morals, or for the protection of the rights and freedoms of others.

A woman in State T wants to attend a public university. She wears a scarf on her head as part of her religious practice. The university has a policy that does not permit the wearing of any religious clothing or items while on campus. She claims that the university's policy violates, among other things, her right to freedom of religion under article 9 of the European Convention. State T says that this rule was created to uphold the state's constitutional principles of secularism and equality. State T is a party to the European Convention.

How might State T use article 9 to justify the public university's rule? What tools of treaty interpretation might the Court use in order to decide whether State T is violating the woman's article 9 rights?

Explanation

This example is similar to the case of *Sahin v. Turkey*, App. No. 44774/98, 41 Eur. H.R. Rep. 8 (2004), where Turkey argued that its ban on headscarves at the State University was necessary for the continuance of a secular and equal society, which was consistent with the limitations allowed under article 9(2) of the Convention. That paragraph provides for limitations on the freedom of religion if they are "necessary in a democratic society." The Court found, among other things, that Turkey had shown secularism and equality to be essential parts of Turkey's constitutional structure and that the ban on headscarves was done to protect the rights and freedoms of others, making it a necessary action for Turkey to be a democratic society. Thus, the university's policy was found not to violate article 9 of the European Convention.

Turkey also argued that its ability to impose the ban on religious attire is within its margin of appreciation that every State has in its interpretation of the rights protected under the Convention. The Court agreed, noting that there was a "margin of appreciation" in interpreting article 9(2): "A margin of appreciation is particularly appropriate when it comes to the regulation by the Contracting States of the wearing of religious symbols in teaching institutions, since rules on the subject vary from one country to another depending on national traditions . . . and there is no uniform European conception of the requirements of the protection of the rights of others and of public order." *Sahin*, App. No. 44774/98 at paras. 101-102. Additional reasoning for the majority's finding that Turkey had not violated the European Convention, as well as the dissenting opinion with respect to an article 9 violation can be found at *Sahin v. Turkey*, App. No. 44774/98, 41 Eur. H.R. Rep. 8 (2004).

§9.4.2 The Inter-American System

The Inter-American system of human rights, existing under the Organization of American States (OAS), is based around two documents: the American Declaration on the Rights and Duties of Man (O.A.S. Res. XXX (1948)) and the American Convention on Human Rights (1144 U.N.T.S. 123 (1969)). See also Charter of the Organization of American States, 119 U.N.T.S. 3 (1948) [hereinafter OAS Charter]. The Declaration was adopted at the same time as the creation of the OAS, which was just before the Universal Declaration of Human Rights was adopted. This document differs from others discussed so far in that it places positive duties on individuals, not only states. For instance, the Declaration says that people have a general duty to society, a duty to vote, a duty to work, and a duty to obey the law, among others. O.A.S. Res. XXX, art. 29-38. In 1967, the OAS Charter was amended to make the contents of the American Declaration equivalent to "fundamental rights" mentioned in the Charter itself. It has been argued that through this amendment the human rights outlined in the American Declaration have become binding on all OAS members, regardless of whether they are parties to the American Convention on Human Rights.

The American Convention was adopted in 1979 and reaffirmed almost all of the rights protected by the Declaration, with a few differences. For instance, the American Declaration lists many social and culture rights, such as the right to social security (art. XVI) and a minimum standard of well-being (art. XI). The American Convention addresses these rights in a somewhat different manner, requiring State parties to "undertake to adopt measures . . . with a view to achieving progressively . . . the full realization of . . . the economic, social, educational, scientific and cultural standards set forth in the Charter . . ." (art. 26). The other rights protected under the Convention are similar to, but not identical to, those found in the ICCPR.[1]

Much like the ICCPR, State parties are permitted to derogate from the guarantee of certain rights but only "[i]n time of war, public danger, or other emergency that threatens the independence or security of a State party . . . provided that such [derogations] . . . do not involve discrimination on the ground of race, color, sex, language, religion or social origin." American Convention, art. 27. There are certain rights and freedoms from which American states may not derogate, but this list is much longer than that found in article 4 of the ICCPR, and includes: the right to juridical personality, the right to life, the right to humane treatment, freedom from slavery, freedom from ex post facto laws, freedom of conscience and religion, rights to a family, the right to name, rights of the child, the right to a nationality, the right to participate in government, and the right to judicial guarantees. American Convention, art. 27(2).

The Inter-American system has two human rights bodies: the Inter-American Commission on Human Rights (IACHR), which derives its powers from the Charter, the Declaration, and the American Convention; and the Inter-American Court of Human Rights, which derives its powers from the Convention. The IACHR is a permanent body that has the power to examine allegations of human rights violations. Under the Convention, the Commission can receive individual, group, or NGO petitions. American Convention, art. 44. The Commission has the power to investigate the allegations, request information from the relevant entities, conduct hearings, and if necessary, conduct on-site visits. American Convention, art. 48. The aim of the petition process is to promote a "friendly settlement of the

---

1. For instance, the right to "the use and enjoyment of . . . property" (art. 21(1)), and the right not to be "deprived of . . . property except upon payment of just compensation" (art. 21(2)) are protected under the Inter-American Convention, but not the ICCPR.

matter." Once the Committee has considered the merits of the petition, it will issue a report detailing its recommendations and conclusions. From there, the State party has a specified time to comply with the Commission's report. After this time period has expired, the Commission can publish the report or refer the case to the Inter-American Court.

The Commission also has the power under the OAS Charter to undertake investigations into situations where it has reason to believe that there are widespread violations of human rights. If the Commission wishes to undertake in-state investigation, it must receive that state's permission. OAS Charter, art. 87 The Commission is authorized to publish any report it makes after such an investigation. The Commission also has the power to hear communications from individuals or NGOs alleging violations by states under the American Declaration.[2] After investigating the allegations, it will issue a report stating the facts, conclusions, and recommendations. The Commission will then publish these reports.

The Inter-American Court of Human Rights was established in 1979 with the purpose of enforcing and interpreting the provisions of the American Convention on Human Rights. It has both contentious and advisory jurisdiction. It can hear contentious cases only after the Commission has submitted its report to the state concerned, and only on referral from the Commission or a state party. The state involved in the case must have agreed to the Court's jurisdiction for the case to proceed, either by accepting jurisdiction under article 62(1) of the Convention or by special agreement. The Court has the power to issue binding judgments; and the Commission does the monitoring of the execution of the judgment, unless the Court specifies another body. In the past, the Court has noted that governments have an affirmative legal obligation to investigate, prosecute, and punish human rights violators, including non-State actors, through their national judicial system. *Velasquez Rodriguez* case, Inter-Am. Ct. H.R. (ser. C) No. 4, at para. 174 (July 29, 1988). It has also said that it is the duty of the State to make reparations to victims of serious human rights violations and, when possible, to attempt to restore the right violated and provide compensation for damages resulting from the violations. *Id.* The Court can also issue advisory decisions under Article 64 of the Convention, relating to the interpretation and application of the Convention or some other human rights standard.

---

2. See O.A.S. Res. XXX (1948), O.A.S. Off. Rec. OEA/Ser. L/V/I.4 Rev. (1965), reprinted at 43 Am. J. Int'l L. Supp. 133 (1949). This area of the Commission's jurisdiction has been contested by some states. See, e.g., Donald T. Fox, *Inter-American Commission on Human Rights Finds United States in Violation*, 82 Am. J. Int'l L. 601 (1988).

Example 9-4

State C, a member of the OAS and a party to the American Convention, passes a law that imposes compulsory licensing of journalists, who must be admitted to a professional association in order to qualify for the practice of journalism. Journalists who are unable to obtain these legal credentials claim that, among other things, their freedoms of expression and information are being violated. These rights appear both in the American Declaration and the American Convention.

1) Can a citizen of State C bring a claim to the Inter-American Court alleging that his rights to expression and information are being violated?

2) What if State C has not consented to the Court's general jurisdiction over claims against it?

3) What if State C was not a party to the American Convention? Could the Commission or Court hear a claim against it?

Explanations

1) Unlike the European system, the citizen could not bring a claim directly to the Inter-American Court, even though State C is a party to the Convention. The citizen would have to first submit a complaint to the Commission, who could then decide to refer it to the Court.

2) If State C has not filed its consent to appear in front of the Inter-American Court, the court does not have jurisdiction over the state. However, State C may consent to jurisdiction in this instance if it so chooses, without being bound by the jurisdiction of the Court in the future.

3) If State C were not a party to the American Convention, it would be held to the standards of the American Declaration on the Rights and Duties of Man. The Commission has jurisdiction to interpret and hear claims arising from the Declaration, but cannot issue legally binding decisions. The Court derives its powers to hear contentious cases through the Convention, and thus would not be able to hear the claim if State C was not a party to the Convention.

The facts of this example are based on an advisory opinion requested by Costa Rica regarding its compulsory licensing requirements for journalists. See *Compulsory Membership in an Association Prescribed by Law for the Practice of Journalism* (Arts. 13 & 29, American Convention on Human Rights), Advisory Opinion OC-5/85, Inter-Am. Ct. H.R. (ser. A) No. 5 (Nov. 13, 1985).

§9.4.3 The African System

In 1981 the Organization of African States, now the African Union (AU), adopted the African Charter on Human and Peoples' Rights, 1520 U.N.T.S. 217 (1981). While the Charter protects political and civil, as well as economic, social, and cultural rights, it also protects additional rights that reflect the continent's own historical and colonial experiences. These rights include such things as the right of "colonized or oppressed peoples . . . to free themselves from the bonds of dominion" (art. 20(2)), the right to development (art. 22(2)), the right to a healthy environment (art. 24), and States' duty to prevent foreign economic exploitation (art. 21(5)). Like the American Declaration on the Rights and Duties of Man, the African Charter places affirmative duties on individuals, such as the duty to work and the duty to society. African Charter, arts. 27 & 29. It also places regionally specific duties on people, like the duty to "preserve and strengthen positive African cultural values" and the duty to "contribute . . . to the promotion and achievement of African unity." Id. art. 29. Similar to the duties imposed at the international level, when a State becomes a party to the African Charter, it assumes four levels of duties: to *respect* human rights by not interfering with peoples' enjoyment of them, to *protect* rights-holders by providing remedies for infringements of rights, to *promote* human rights by making sure the State tells the people that they have these rights, and to *fulfill* the rights in the Charter by taking positive steps so that every individual can enjoy them. See *Social and Economic Rights Action Center & the Center for Economic and Social Rights v. Nigeria*, African Comm'n on Human and Peoples' Rights, Comm. 155/96 (2001), paras. 44-47.

The African Commission on Human and Peoples' Rights is charged with interpreting the African Charter and monitoring states' progress toward giving effect to the rights contained in the Charter. The Commission functions are similar to the HRC. It serves as a monitoring body, reviewing states' periodic reports and considering communications of human rights violations. Like the HRC, the African Commission does not have the power to issue binding declarations. Rather, it issues reports and recommendations to State parties, detailing how they should proceed with respect to a human rights issue. Communications will be heard if they are substantiated by more than just media reports, and all domestic remedies have been exhausted. African Charter, art. 56. The Commission may submit a case before the African Court of Human Rights and, conversely, the Court may transfer cases to the Commission. See Protocol to the African Charter on Human and Peoples' Rights on the Establishment of the African Court on Human and Peoples' Rights, art. 6, OAU/LEG/MIN/AFCHPR/PROT.1 rev/2 (1997).

The enforcement body of the African Charter is the African Court on Human and Peoples' Rights. The court was established by a Protocol to the African Charter, which entered into force in 2004. The Court is not yet operational due to some additional steps that need to be taken, although some judges were recently elected to the body. The jurisdiction of this court will be much broader than the jurisdiction of the European or Inter-American courts, in that it will hear cases regarding the interpretation and application of the African Charter as well as any other human rights document that has been ratified by the state in question (although other regional bodies do consider such documents in the interpretation of their regional instruments). This means, for example, that the African Court would have jurisdiction to hear a claim involving a violation of the ICCPR or the ICESCR, so long as a State is a party to those instruments. What the protocol does, then, is incorporate these rights into the regional system of human rights law. The Court also has advisory jurisdiction over these matters at the request of an AU state or other body of the AU, so long as the Commission is not already dealing with the matter. Moreover, the Court has contentious jurisdiction to hear claims from individuals, NGOs that have observer status, and states belonging to the AU. The admissibility requirements of complaints are the same as those for communications to the Commission. The judgments of the Court are binding on States, and they may be ordered to pay compensation to their victims or take provisional measures if the situation needs immediate attention.

Example 9-5

The Endos peoples live in State K. For hundreds of years before State K even existed, the Endos have occupied lands beside a large lake that they rely on for subsistence and cultural purposes. Recently the government of State K notified the Endos that they could no longer remain on the land because it is going to be incorporated into a game preserve, which brings much needed tourism to State K. The Endos peoples were not consulted or given compensation before being forced off the land. The Endos claim that State K is violating numerous rights contained in the African Charter, such as their right to practice religion (art. 8), their right to property (art. 14), and their right to culture (art. 17). The Supreme Court of State K has dismissed the Endos case on the grounds that it is a matter of political concern only. State K is a member of the AU and a party to the African Charter.

1) Which bodies may hear the Endos complaint and what requirements will they have to meet to have their complaint considered?

2) What if State K is not a party to the African Charter, but is a party to the ICCPR and the ICESCR?

Explanations

1) Both the African Commission and the African Court, if it were operational, would be able to hear the Endos' complaint. Unlike the Inter-American system, individuals will have standing before the African Court, so long as the State has recognized its jurisdiction. For the Endos to approach either body, they must show that they have suffered a human rights violation, be able to offer evidence to substantiate the claim, and show that domestic remedies have been exhausted. Here, the Endos have well substantiated claims that numerous rights under the Charter are being violated and since State K's courts refuse to hear their claims, and they have clearly exhausted their domestic remedies. In terms of the Commission, it is

currently able to hear individual communications alleging violations and issue recommendations to States regarding those communications. Moreover, as we will see below in §9.5 on Group Rights, it doesn't matter that the claims are being asserted by a group of peoples, since the group claims are as viable, and in many ways interconnected to, individual claims.

2) Even if State K was not a party to the African Charter, the jurisdiction of the African Court extends to all human rights agreements that the state has ratified. This means that the Court would be able to hear claims against State K for violations of its duties under the ICCPR and ICESCR. The Commission has also looked to these international norms in interpreting the rights and responsibilities of States under the Charter, as it did in a communications brought by the Endorois peoples of Kenya against the Kenyan government. See *Centre for Minority Rights Development (Kenya) and Minority Rights Group International on behalf of Endorois Welfare Council v. Kenya*, African Comm. Decision of May 2009, Communication No. 276/2003. The substantive aspects of the case are discussed in the section on Group Rights (see §9.5).

§9.4.4 The Emergence of Other Regional Human Rights Systems

In 2004, the League of Arab States (LAS) adopted a second version of the Arab Charter on Human Rights, reprinted at 12 Int'l H.R. Rep. 893 (2005). The revision of the Charter calls for a modernization in line with other international human rights treaties, the greater protection of rights for women and children, and cooperation among Arab States for the protection of human rights. The Charter is very similar to the ICCPR and ICESCR in the rights protected, as well as times from which they may be derogated. Article 45 establishes an Arab Human Rights Committee to act as a monitoring body and is composed of seven representatives from seven members of the LAS. States are required to submit periodic reports every three years on their progress toward implementing the rights in the Charter to the Secretary-General of the LAS, who will pass the reports on to the Committee. The Committee will issue its findings and recommendations in a report that will be made public. At this time, there is no human rights court that serves to hear cases arising from the Arab Charter.

§9.5 GROUP RIGHTS

Most human rights discussions are centered on the rights that each person holds as an individual. Yet, some rights involve more than just the individual person; they include the society in which the person belongs. For example, article 27 of the ICCPR states that:

> In those States in which ethnic, religious or linguistic minorities exist, persons belonging to such minorities shall not be denied the right, in community with the other members of their group, to enjoy their own culture, to profess and practise their own religion, or to use their own language.

In its General Comment No. 23, the HRC noted that:

> Although the rights protected under Article 27 are individual rights, they depend in turn on the ability of the minority group to maintain its culture, language or religion. Accordingly, positive measures by States may also be necessary to protect the identity of a minority and the rights of its members to enjoy and develop their culture and language and to practise their religion, in community with the other members of the group. U.N. Doc. CCPR/C/21/Rev.1/Add.5 (1994).

Group human rights are not limited to cultural and linguistic rights. For example, Indigenous Peoples hold special rights to lands and resources, as well as rights to political autonomy and self-determination. Moreover, the current international human rights framework contemplates both collective and individual rights and, as the examples below suggest, the two sets of rights are interconnected and interrelated.

Perhaps one of the most important group rights to be recognized in the international human rights context is the right of self-determination, which is recognized in the first articles of both the ICCPR and the ICESCR. Chapter 4 of this book explores this right as it relates to the question of secession. Secession is only one facet of what self-determination means as a whole. As both of the two major human rights treaties note, self-determination includes the right of "peoples" to "freely determine their political status and freely pursue their economic, social and cultural development" (ICCPR and ICESCR, art. 1(1)). This includes the right to "freely dispose of their natural wealth and resources" and to not be deprived of one's "own means of subsistence" (art. 1(2)). As articulated, this right of self-determination is essential to a group's survival or way of life, particularly where Indigenous Peoples' are concerned. Given the extensive amount of international and regional law that has emerged in the last 25 years in the area of Indigenous Peoples' rights, the remaining part of this section will focus on those aspects of group rights.

Much has been written on the application of this principle of "self-determination" to Indigenous Peoples.[3] Following World War II,

---

3. See, e.g., S. James Anaya, *Indigenous Peoples In International Law* 98 (2004).

"self-determination of peoples" became a part of international conventional law, most notably in the U.N. Charter (art. 1(2)). In the 1960s, it served as a springboard for the process of decolonization and became an integral part of the international human rights movement, codified under art. 1 of the ICCPR and the ICESCR. Today, self-determination is an accepted principle of international law.

Contemporary debates on the principle of self-determination often focus on two questions: Who are the "peoples" entitled to this legal right, and how far does this right extend? While these are complicated issues with no clear-cut answers, there are some general guidelines to consider with respect to this right, at least where Indigenous Peoples are involved. First, domestic and international bodies have defined the term "peoples" to include subnational groups that are part of a larger territorial sovereign unit.[4] When one considers the common factors that make up these subnational groups — such as common racial, ethnic, linguistic, religious, or cultural history; some claim to territory or land; and a shared sense of political, economic, social, and cultural goals — Indigenous Peoples easily meet these criteria. Another major controversy is the meaning of "self-determination" itself. As noted earlier, it is often equated with secession and independent statehood, which may be an appropriate remedy for violation of this right under certain limited circumstances (see §4.2). Its meaning under contemporary international law extends well beyond this statist framework. For instance, the two major human rights covenants link self-determination to notions of cultural survival, economic development, political freedoms, and other basic human rights. This suggests that "self-determination is not separate from other human rights norms; rather [it] is a configurative principle or framework complemented by the more specific human rights norms that in their totality enjoin the governing institutional order."[5] Thus, self-determination for Indigenous Peoples embodies in its fullest sense the right to live and develop as culturally distinct groups, in control of their own destinies, and under conditions of equality.

The recognition of these core human rights for Indigenous Peoples culminated in the U.N. General Assembly voting overwhelmingly in support of the U.N. Declaration on the Rights of Indigenous Peoples. G.A. Res. 61/295 (2007). We know from our earlier discussion of "declarations" in Chapter 8 that they are not per se legally binding (compared to a treaty or customary international law norm). Standing alone, they are generally perceived as "recommendations." We also know that some have been ascribed a higher degree of authority, such as the 1948 Universal

---

4. See, e.g., Reference Re Secession of Quebec, 37 I.L.M. 1340, 1373 (1998); Report of the Human Rights Committee, U.N. GAOR, 47th Sess., Supp. No. 40, at 52, U.N. Doc. A/47/40 (1992).
5. Anaya, *supra* note 3, at 99.

Declaration of Human Rights, primarily because of what many of the provisions of Universal Declaration have come to represent over time — an accepted part of customary international law. We also know that any resolution designated and adopted as a "declaration" by the General Assembly represents a "formal and solemn instrument, resorted to only in very rare cases relating to matters of major and lasting importance where maximum compliance is expected";[6] and that any U.N. Declaration may "by custom become recognized as laying down Rules binding upon States."[7] Thus, the U.N. Declaration on Indigenous Peoples Rights represents a solemn and authoritative response of the international community of States to the claims of Indigenous Peoples. Additionally, some of the rights in the Declaration are already firmly established as a matter of international conventional or customary law, such as the right to maintain and develop their distinct cultural, linguistic, and spiritual identity (see, e.g., ICCPR, art. 27); the right to wide-ranging autonomy (see, e.g., ICCPR, art. 1 & ICESCR, art. 1); and the rights to certain traditional lands and resources.[8]

In addition to the adoption of the Declaration by the General Assembly, the U.N. Human Rights Council has re-established a thematic procedure on Indigenous Peoples. Consistent with the Council's own universal periodic review process, the special rapporteur to this thematic procedure undertakes a review of State conduct as it relates to Indigenous Peoples, relying in part on norms established in the Declaration.[9] U.N. human rights bodies, such as the Committee on the Elimination of Racial Discrimination, are also relying on these norms in their interpretation of a State's treaty obligation toward Indigenous Peoples.[10] Other relevant U.N. human rights mechanisms include a Working Group on Indigenous Populations, an Expert Mechanism on the Rights of Indigenous Peoples, and a Permanent Forum on Indigenous Issues.

The regional human rights organizations also play an important role in upholding the human rights of Indigenous Peoples. For instance, the Inter-American Commission on Human Rights has compiled an extensive study on the situation of Indigenous Peoples (OAS Doc. OEA/Ser.L/V/II.108, Doc. 62 (Oct. 20, 2000)), and both the Commission and the Inter-American

---

6. Report of the Commission on Human Rights, U.N. Doc. E/3616/Rev.1, para. 105, 18th Sess. ECOSOC Supp. No. 8 (1962), para. 105.

7. Report of the Commission on Human Rights, U.N. Doc. E/3616/Rev.1, para. 105, 18th Sess. ECOSOC Supp. No. 8 (1962), para. 105.

8. See, e.g., S. James Anaya & Siegfried Wiessner, *The UN Declaration on the Rights of Indigenous Peoples: Towards Re-empowerment*, Jurist Forum, Oct. 3, 2007, available at http://jurist.law.pitt.edu/forumy/2007/10/un-declaration-on-rights-of-indigenous.php.

9. See *Report of the Special Rapporteur on the Situation of Human Rights and Fundamental Freedoms of Indigenous People*, U.N. Doc. A/HRC/9/9, paras. 85 & 88 (Aug. 11, 2008), available at http://www2.ohchr.org/english/bodies/hrcouncil/docs/9session/A-HRC-9-9AEV.doc.

10. See, e.g., Concluding Observations of the Committee on the Elimination of Racial Discrimination: United States of America, 14/08/2001, U.N. Doc. A/56/18, para. 400 (Aug. 14, 2001) available at http://www.law.arizona.edu/depts/iplp/advocacy/shoshone/documents/36CERDConcObs.pdf.

Court have decided a number of important cases involving the land and resources rights of Indigenous Peoples.[11] Furthermore, the OAS has a Proposed American Declaration on the Rights of Indigenous Peoples that is currently in a final revision stage. OAS Doc. OEA/Ser.L/V/II.95 Doc. 6 (Feb. 26, 1997). The African Commission on Human and Peoples' Rights has created a Working Group on Indigenous Populations/Communities in Africa. The Working Group has compiled a general report detailing the human rights situation of Indigenous Peoples in Africa, as well as having conducted a number of individual country visits. The Working Group works in conjunction with numerous NGOs and U.N. bodies, and seeks to disseminate information about the U.N. Declaration on the Rights of Indigenous Peoples to African states. Additionally, the Commission has decided several important cases involving land and resources, as well as cultural rights of Indigenous Peoples.[12]

Example 9-6

State C has a federal law that states that any "Indian" woman who marries outside her "band," loses all rights and benefits to the lands and services held by that indigenous community, and ceases to be entitled to reside by right on the reserve set aside for that band. The law has been in existence for almost 100 years and has impacted thousands of indigenous women and their children, in terms of separating them from their communities and families. State C justifies the law on the grounds that, among other things, it protects the special privileges granted to "Indian" communities, by limiting through definition those who are actually entitled to these rights. Sandra, a Maliseet "Indian" woman who married a non-Maliseet man, wants to challenge State C's law. She and her children can no longer be members of the Maliseet community or reside within the community's borders. The highest court of State C has already ruled on the legality of State C's law, concluding that it was a political matter relating to state/tribal relations and therefore not an issue for the courts. State C has recently become a party to the ICCPR and the First Optional Protocol, but was not a party to these treaties at the time that Sandra lost her membership status.

1) Using the information contained in §8.3.2 on the ICCPR and §9.5 on Group Rights, where might Sandra now challenge State C's laws given the recent domestic ruling upholding this law?

2) What, if any, human rights violations have occurred?

---

11. See, e.g., *Case of Mary Dann and Carrie Dann v. United States*, Case No. 11.140, Inter-Am. C.H.R., Report No. 75/02 (Dec. 27, 2002); *Case of Mayagna (Sumo) Awas Tingni Community v. Nicaragua*, Inter-Am. C.H.R. (ser. C) No. 79 (Aug. 31, 2001).

12. See, e.g., *Centre for Minority Rights Development (Kenya) and Minority Rights Group International on behalf of Endorois Welfare Council v. Kenya*, African Comm. Decision of May 2009, Communication No. 276/2003, para. 241.

3) Do you think it matters that State C was not a party to these international treaties at the time Sandra was originally denied her membership rights?

Explanations

1) This example is similar to the facts found in *Sandra Lovelace v. Canada*, Communications No. R. 6/24, U.N. Doc. Supp. No. 40 (A/36/40) at 166, decided by the HRC in 1981. Given that Sandra has exhausted her domestic remedies, she can now file a communications with the HRC. Both the ICCPR and the First Optional Protocol allow individuals to file communications directly to the HRC, so long as the State has ratified these treaties, which State C has clearly done.

2) In terms of the human rights violations, multiple claims could be made, but for purposes of this communications, the violations must relate directly to the ICCPR because that is the treaty under which the HRC operates. In terms of the ICCPR, there are multiple provisions that the HRC could consider, such as the right to nondiscrimination under articles 3 and 26, or perhaps even the right to marry under article 23. In the *Lovelace* case, the Committee considered article 27 (right to culture, outlined above) as being most applicable to Sandra's case, because Canada's law denied Sandra and her children the right to be part of their community and culture. U.N. Doc. Supp. No. 40 (A/36/40), para. 15.

How about the right to self-determination protected under article 1 of the ICCPR? Can she assert a violation of that right using the Optional Protocol procedure of the ICCPR? The HRC has answered that question in the negative because self-determination is, in essence, a "group" right and the Optional Protocol relates to *individual* claims. With that said, the HRC has noted the clear substantive linkages between an individual's right to his or her culture and the group right to self-determination. This issue has been addressed in several HRC decisions involving Indigenous Peoples.[13]

3) In terms of the question of whether it matters that State C was not a party to the ICCPR or the Optional Protocol when Sandra was first denied her rights to her community and culture, the HRC noted in the *Lovelace* case that it was empowered to consider such communications "when the measures complained of, although they occurred before the entry into force of the Covenant, continued to have effects which themselves constitute a violation of the Covenant after that date." U.N. Doc. Supp. No. 40 (A/36/40), para. 7.3. In our example, Sandra and her children continue to be denied

---

13. See, e.g., *Lubicon Lake Band v. Canada*, Communication No. 167/1984, U.N. Doc. Supp. No. 40 (A/45/40), para. 13.3 (Mar. 26, 1990) ("the Covenant recognizes and protects in most resolute terms a people's right of self-determination and its right to dispose of its natural resources, as an essential condition for the effective guarantee and observance of individual human rights and for the promotion and strengthening of those rights").

their basic rights to culture and community because of State C's laws. Thus the complaint against State C can move forward, even though the first set of violations occurred prior to State C becoming a party to the ICCPR.

Example 9-7

Recall Example 9-5 regarding the Endos peoples from State K who were forcibly removed from their ancestral lands for a game reserve without prior consultation or compensation in the form of land and resources. Prior to the removal, the Endos had practiced a sustainable way of life that was linked directly to the lake and its surrounding fertile lands. The area was also essential to their religious and cultural practices. For instance, the Endos peoples believe that the spirits of their ancestors dwell on the lake and that certain festivals must be performed each year in that location. Since their removal, the Endos have been living in pockets of semiarid areas and have been divided as a community. They face extreme hardship in the form of food shortages, health problems, and familial dislocation.

What arguments might you make before the African Commission on behalf of the Endos peoples and its individual members with respect to State K?

Explanation

The Endos peoples as a group may claim a violation of their right to "self-determination," which includes the right not to be "deprived of their own means of subsistence" or to be denied their right to "economic, social, and cultural development." Additionally, the individual members of the Endos community have a host of potential claims relating not only to their right to practice their culture and religion, but their rights to a livelihood, food-stuffs, property, housing, and so on. Understanding how collective and individual rights are linked together from a human rights perspective was central to a recent African Commission decision involving the Endorois peoples of Kenya, on which this example is based. The Commission noted in particular that the African Charter weaves together a "tapestry" of rights, which includes "civil and political rights; economic, social and cultural rights; and group and peoples' rights." On the issue of culture, the Commission noted that the African Charter "protect[s] on the one hand, individuals' participation in the cultural life of their community and, on the other hand, oblig[es] the state to promote and protect traditional values recognised by a community."[14] Thus, in our example, we have multiple categories of rights that are being implicated and that impact one another,

---

14. *Centre for Minority Rights Development (Kenya) and Minority Rights Group International on behalf of Endorois Welfare Council v. Kenya*, African Comm. Decision of May 2009, Communication No. 276/2003, para. 241.

such as the denial of the right to land and resources or cultural practices leading to communal and familial dislocation. These violations can be viewed from an individual and communal perspective; that without the protection of group rights, an individual's ability to provide housing, food, and shelter for oneself and family becomes impaired as well.

§9.6 CORPORATE RESPONSIBILITY FOR HUMAN RIGHTS

Human rights law focuses on the duties of States to promote and protect the rights of individuals and groups. Increasingly, however, as businesses expand and operate in multinational settings with operating budgets that may well exceed the gross domestic product (GDP) of some countries, there has been a push to determine what, if any, responsibility corporations have with respect to promoting and protecting human rights. There is little question that in this age of globalized markets, corporate behavior can greatly affect the rights and environments of millions of people. States already have a duty under certain human rights instruments, such as the ICCPR, to regulate the policies and practices of multinational corporations that are headquartered or operating within their borders to the extent that those policies or practices impact the rights of others (see ICCPR, art. 2 in Chapter 8, §8.3.2). This type of regulation doesn't always occur, for a host of economic and political reasons. Thus, there has been a movement within and outside the United Nations to expand human rights law to cover corporations directly. This section offers a brief overview of some of the principles and initiatives taking hold in the area of corporate responsibility and human rights law.

Some corporations have voluntarily adopted within their own institutions "codes of conduct" with respect to human rights, in part due to pressure from shareholders and customers.[15] Additionally, some "soft law," which creates no legal binding obligations on corporations, has developed in the international arena. One such example is the U.N. Global Compact, which has been described as "a strategic policy initiative for businesses that are committed to aligning their operations and strategies with ten universally accepted principles in the areas of human rights, labour, environment and anti-corruption."[16] Since the ten principles are not backed up by any treaty or covenant, they don't impose any legally binding obligations on corporations; yet, they may over time create some important customary law in this area.

---

15. See, e.g., Sean D. Murphy, *Taking Multinational Corporate Codes of Conduct to the Next Level*, 43 Colum. J. Transnat'l L. 389 (2005).
16. United Nations Global Compact, available at http://www.unglobalcompact.org/.

As a complement to this initiative, the former United Nations Commission on Human Rights established a Special Representative of the Secretary-General (SRSG) on human rights and transnational corporations and other businesses. In his final report to the new Human Rights Council, the SRSG proposed a policy framework that would help guide relevant actors with respect to issues of business and human rights. The framework included three core principles: "the State's duty to protect against human rights abuses by third parties, including business; the corporate responsibility to respect human rights; and the need for more effective remedies." See Human Rights Council, *Protect, Respect and Remedy: A Framework for Business and Human Rights, Report of the Special Representative of the Secretary-General on the Issue of Human Rights and Transnational Corporations and Other Business Enterprises*, U.N. Doc. A/HRC/RES/8/5 (Apr. 7, 2008) (prepared by John Ruggie). Recently the Human Rights Council extended the SRSG's mandate for three more years to help "operationalize" the framework. The new mandate includes creating a set of recommendations for corporations to abide by, working with corporations to aid them in following those recommendations, and working with State governments to help protect against human rights abuses committed by corporations. *Id.* at para. 4. The Special Representative must report the progress of these tasks to the Human Rights Council on an annual basis.

The Human Rights Council also adopted a resolution regarding corporate accountability, which states "transnational corporations and other business enterprises have a responsibility to respect human rights." Human Rights Council, *Report of the Special Representative of the Secretary-General on the Issue of Human Rights and Transnational Corporations and Other Business Enterprises*, U.N. Doc. A/HRC/RES/8/7 (June 18, 2008). As the High Commissioner for Human Rights notes, the Council's position marks "an important milestone in the evolving understanding of human rights in our societies." See Navanethem Pillay, U.N. High Comm'n for Human Rights, Speech to the Human Rights Council: The Corporate Responsibility to Respect: A Human Rights Milestone (June 2, 2009).

There are also domestic movements afoot, such as using domestic statutes like the Alien Tort Claims Act, as a basis for asserting claims against corporations in U.S. courts. The Alien Tort Claims Act, also called the Alien Tort Statute (ATS), 28 U.S.C. §1350, has been part of U.S. law since 1789. It states: "The district courts shall have original jurisdiction of any civil action by an alien for a tort only, committed in violation of the law of nations or a treaty of the United States." *Id.* In order for a claim to be successfully brought in a U.S. federal court under this statute, a claimant must show that the court has jurisdiction over the claim, and that the claimant is alleging a violation of customary international law or a "well-established, universally recognized norm[] of international law." *Filartiga v. Pena-Irala*, 630 F.3d 876, 887-888 (2d Cir. 1980); see also *Khulumani v. Barclay Nat'l Bank Ltd.*, 504 F.3d 254, 267 (2d Cir. 2007). Recent case law from the U.S. Supreme Court suggests that the ATS will be applicable in limited circumstances, where there is a violation of an international norm that is specifically defined, universally accepted, and of obligatory or mutual concern.[17]

The ATS has been used against both individuals and corporations. See, e.g., *Kadic v. Karadzic*, 70 F.3d 232, 240 (2d Cir. 1995); *Doe I v. Unocal Corp.*, 395 F.3d 932 (9th Cir. 2002) (settlement obtained); *Wiwa v. Shell*, 392 F.3d 812 (5th Cir. 2004) (settlement obtained). In more recent circuit court cases involving corporate liability, some procedural and substantive limitations have been put in place, such as the requirement that any aiding and abetting liability must be accompanied by a finding "that the defendant provided substantial assistance with the purpose of facilitating the alleged offenses."[18] And one panel of the Second Circuit recently ruled in the case of *Kiobel v. Royal Dutch Petroleum Co.* that the jurisdiction granted by the ATS doesn't extend at all to civil actions against corporations.[19] In doing so, the court looked to international customary law (the "law of nations") to determine whether corporations could be subject to liability under the ATS. Since corporate liability is not well established under international law (according to the court, not a discernible, universally recognized norm of customary law), there can be no liability pursuant to the ATS. There are those who might disagree with this analysis and argue instead that U.S. domestic law determines the scope of corporate liability, whereas international law relates solely to the question of what conduct (e.g., torture, right to life) is prohibited under the law of nations. With that said, the court did not foreclose suits under the ATS against a corporation's employees or other such persons aiding and abetting international law violations, since individual liability is well established under international principles.[20] The plaintiff is likely to seek en banc review in the case and, depending on the outcome, appeal to the U.S. Supreme Court.

Example 9-8

Corporation U, whose parent company is located in the United States, is accused of working with State B to force local villagers to work on the construction of a gas pipeline through their village. The pipeline has resulted in the destruction of numerous homes, as well as lands that the villagers depend upon to grow their crops. The villagers have not been compensated

---

17. See *Abdullahi v. Pfizer, Inc.*, 562 F.3d 163, 187 (2d Cir. 2009) (citing *Sosa v. Alvarez-Machain*, 542 U.S. 692, 731-733, 738 (2004)).

18. See *Presbyterian Church of Sudan v. Talisman Energy, Inc.*, 582 F.3d 244, 247 (2d Cir. 2009). See generally *Sinaltrainal v. Coca-Cola Co.*, 578 F.3d 1252 (11th Cir. 2009); *Flores v. Southern Peru Copper Corp.*, 414 F.3d 233 (2d Cir. 2003).

19. See 2010 U.S. App. Lexis 19382 (plaintiffs sued under ATS, alleging defendant aided and abetted in host of actions violating the law of nations, such as torture, arbitrary arrest, violation of life, forced exile, and property destruction).

20. *Kiobel v. Royal Dutch Petroleum Co.*, 621 F.3d 111 (2d Cir. 2010).

for the loss of their homes or lands. State B is a party to the ICCPR and the ICESCR, but not any of the optional protocols.

Do the villagers have a claim against the oil company and if so, on what basis?

Explanation

Currently there is no conventional or customary law that directly binds Corporation U. Since State B is a party to both the ICCPR and ICESCR, it has a duty to protect the villagers against human rights abuses by third parties, including Corporation U. The problem is that State B is implicated in the alleged violations, and thus is not likely to take any action against Corporation U. The "soft" law that was discussed earlier with respect to the Global Compact establishes ethical standards for Corporation U to consider, but they impose no legal obligation on the corporation. Recent statements by the Human Rights Council and other international bodies suggest that this may well change in the future.

Another possibility is to bring an action in U.S. courts under the ATS, which is exactly what thirteen Burmese villagers did in 1997. They filed suit against Unocal and its parent company, alleging, among other things, that the Company was aiding and abetting State B in its human rights violations by using forced labor to construct the Yadana gas pipeline project.[21] Unocal eventually agreed to settle the case, compensating plaintiffs and providing additional funds for such things as improved living conditions, health care, and education.[22]

However, ATS claims may be more difficult to prove now than when the Unocal case was filed given the decisions in the Second Circuit, depending on what happens in those cases. For instance, as noted earlier, one federal circuit court recently held that under international law, "the mens rea standard for aiding and abetting liability in ATS actions is purpose rather than knowledge alone," which means that the "claimant must show that the defendant provided substantial assistance with the purpose of facilitating the alleged offenses."[23] Thus, in our example there would need to be a showing that Corporation U not only knew about the forced labor and other violations, but also provided substantial assistance to State B with the purpose of facilitating those violations. Finally, the human rights violations alleged must be of a specific and universal character in order to be actionable under the ATS. Since forced labor may itself constitute a modern form of slavery, it is probably universal and specific enough to be actionable under the ATS.

---

21. See Doe I v. Unocal Corp., 395 F.3d 932 (9th Cir. 2002).
22. See Earthrights, Final Settlement Reached in Doe v. Unocal, available at http://www.earthrights.org/legalfeature/final_settlement_reached_in_doe_v._unocal.html.
23. Presbyterian Church of Sudan v. Talisman Energy, Inc., 582 F.3d 244, 247 (2d Cir. 2009).

This point is further addressed in the next example. Finally, there may be restrictions on *who* can be sued under the ATS, namely corporations themselves (as opposed to individuals or those acting within their official capacity).[24]

Example 9-9

A pharmaceutical company is creating a new antibiotic for children to be sold in the United States. The company gains the permission of State N, a developing country, to test the drug on sick children in State N. The company sends doctors to State N to test the experimental drug on a number of sick children. The doctors fail to inform the children or their parents that the drug has not yet been approved for safe use, or to inform them that there are other well-tested drugs that may cure their child's illness. Hundreds of children in State N die or are severely injured by the experimental drug.

If a parent, on behalf of his child, wanted to sue the pharmaceutical company in U.S. courts for conducting medical experiments on humans without informed consent, what law might allow them to proceed, and what will the parents need to show regarding medical experimentation and informed consent?

Explanation

In this example, the State is responsible for its own conduct, as well as the conduct of the corporation that was operating with its permission inside the country. But what about the corporation itself? Can it be directly liable to the children and their guardians? The parents could try to bring a claim under the ATS. Although the ability to bring a claim under the ATS may be somewhat limited given the standards set out by the Supreme Court in *Alvarez-Machain*, there was no indication that the Court intended to limit those claims to individuals acting in their official governmental capacity. That case did not involve corporate liability and at least one recent Second Circuit decision suggests that claims against corporations (as opposed to individuals within that corporation) may not be viable under the ATS.[25]

Assuming that such cases can move forward in some circuits, or at least against individuals within the corporation, the plaintiffs will still need to follow the standards set out by the Supreme Court in *Alvarez-Machain* and other more recent cases. Thus, with respect to the prohibition on medical

24. Cf. *Samantar v. Yousuf*, 130 S. Ct. 2278 (2010) (holding the Foreign Sovereign Immunities Act does not shield individuals acting in their official capacity from being sued under ATS or Torture Victims Protection Act of 1991). The Court, however, did not rule on the question of common law immunity.
25. See *Kiobel v. Royal Dutch Petroleum Co.*, 2010 U.S. App. Lexis 19382.

experimentation without consent, the parents will need to demonstrate that it is a sufficiently well defined norm of international law in order for the claim to be actionable under the ATS. This can be done by providing examples of international treaties and agreements containing such a prohibition, by showing that states in general require informed consent when conducting medical experiments on humans, and by providing writings by scholars in the field that attest to the need for informed consent. In other words, the parent must show that informed consent for medical experimentation is part of customary international law.

The facts of this example are similar to a case from the Second Circuit involving the drug company Pfizer and the State of Nigeria, which was decided before its most recent case regarding corporate liability generally. Cf. *Abdullahi v. Pfizer Inc.*, 562 F.3d 163 (2d Cir. 2009) *with Kiobel v. Royal Dutch Petroleum Co.*, 2010 U.S. App. Lexis 19382. In the Pfizer case, the Second Circuit ruled that the plaintiffs, family members of the Nigerian children who had suffered as a result of Pfizer's drug testing, could bring a claim against Pfizer under the ATS. *Abdullahi*, 562 F.3d at 187. The court found, using the *Alvarez-Machain* standard, that the prohibition on uninformed medical experimentation was universal, specific, and of mutual concern to all states. *Id.* The court considered that the prohibition against such experimentation had existed since the Nuremberg Trials, where Nazi doctors had been charged with conducting medical experiments on those held in concentration camps and that the Nuremberg Tribunal had named unauthorized human experimentation as a crime against humanity. *Id.* at 178-179. The court also noted that the prohibition against medical experimentation without consent could be found in a host of international instruments, such as article 7 of the ICCPR, as well as being followed as a matter of practice for decades by many countries, including the United States. *Id.* at 179-183. The existence of the prohibition on nonconsensual medical experimentation in many international documents and state practices allowed the court to determine that it was indeed a *universal* practice. The fact that the human right was spelled out in those documents and elsewhere in almost identical language allowed the court to say that the norm had been defined with great enough *specificity*. *Id.* at 184. Finally, the existence of binding international agreements entered into by many States that declared the need for informed medical consent showed the *obligatory* or *mutual* concern of States to prevent this type of human rights violation. *Id.* at 185. An appeal of this case to the Supreme Court was recently denied (see 130 S. Ct. 3541 (2010)), and it looks as though Pfizer might be heading toward a settlement of the suit, working directly with the country involved.[26]

---

26. Business & Human Rights Resource Centre, Case Profile: Pfizer Lawsuit, http://www.business-humanrights.org/Categories/Lawlawsuits/Lawsuitsregulatoryaction/Lawsuits Selectedcases/PfizerlawsuitreNigeria (last visited Oct. 4, 2010).

The Use of Force Including War

§10.1 Introduction

§10.2 Coercive Measures Not Amounting to Armed Force

    §10.2.1 Retorsions

    §10.2.2 Reprisals Not Involving the Use of Armed Force

§10.3 Pre-1945 Law on the Use of Armed Force

    §10.3.1 The Customary Law of Self-Defence

§10.4 Post-1945 Law

    §10.4.1 The Jus *Ad Bellum*

    §10.4.2 The United Nations Charter

        (a) The Meaning of Force

        (b) What Is a Threat of Force?

        (c) Must Force Be Used for a Particular Objective to Violate Article 2(4)?

        (d) Exceptions to Article 2(4)

            (i) Self-Defence

                a. What Level of Armed Force Gives Rise to the Right to Self-Defence?

                b. Must an Armed Attack Be Carried Out by a *State* to Trigger the Right of Self-Defence?

            (ii) Preemption

            (iii) Forceful Countermeasures

        (e) Reprisals Using Force

    §10.4.3 The Rule of Non-Intervention

        (a) Civil Wars and the Rule of Non-Intervention

      (b) Intervention in Particular Circumstances
         (i)   Intervening to Protect Nationals Abroad
         (ii) Humanitarian Intervention
         (iii) The Responsibility to Protect
      (c) The Security Council's Power to Intervene
         (i)   Article 41 Measures
         (ii) Article 42 Measures
      (d) United Nations Peacekeeping Forces
§10.5 The Jus In Bello
   §10.5.1 The Regulation of the Conduct of Hostilities
      (a) Modern Era History: The Hague and Geneva
         Conventions
   §10.5.2 Specific Rules of International Humanitarian Law (IHL)
      (a) Introduction
      (b) The Principle of Distinction and the Definition of
         Combatants/Military Objects and Civilians/Civilian
         Objects
      (c) Treatment of Those Captured in Armed Conflict
   §10.5.3 Weapons Control
      (a) Historical Progression
      (b) Nuclear Weapons
         (i)   Conventions and Declarations that Limit the
            Spread or Use of Nuclear Weapons
         (ii) Conventions that Call for the Reduction
            of Nuclear Weapons
         (iii) Conventions that Declare Certain Areas
            of the World Nuclear Weapons Free
         (iv) Conventions that Prohibit the Testing
            of Nuclear Weapons
         (v) The I.C.J.'s Advisory Opinion on Nuclear
            Weapons
§10.6 Conclusion

§10.1 INTRODUCTION

For as long as history has been recorded individuals and groups have fought, maimed, and killed each other. This type of extreme activity is prohibited at the individual level by state criminal law. Carefully fashioned exceptions and defenses to the prohibited acts have arisen over the centuries. When a group organizes itself to attack another group we generally call the activity "war." The attacks may take place between clans, tribes, or gangs, and may occur within a nation-state or across state lines. When these attacks are launched there will usually be an articulated reason for the show of force, which may be based on fact or fancy. International law has generally divided the use of force into (1) inter-state armed conflict and (2) intra-state armed conflict, although the distinctions are now blurring. Inter-state conflict was generally thought of as one state (or a coalition) using force against another state (or a coalition). Intra-state conflict was regarded as conflict between different armed groups within a state that were usually vying for governmental power. Recently, with the rise of international, non-governmental, armed groups, that may operate in several countries, the above categories of conflict are being challenged.

The rules governing inter-state warfare have generally been divided into two categories: the rules that govern when it is permissible to initiate an attack, which has become known as "*jus ad bellum*," and the rules that govern behavior during war, known as "*jus in bello*." From time to time, most major religions have produced doctrines that define the occasions when fighting a war is justified. Medieval Europe developed elaborate rules governing behavior during war, and Shakespeare's Henry V has frequent references to permissible and impermissible activity during war. All of the above doctrines or codes have only been followed by particular groups at particular moments in history. It was not until the end of the nineteenth century and the beginning of the twentieth century that there was any movement to urge the adoption of universal rules governing inter-state warfare. By this time, in Europe at least, the power of the Church had been superseded by the power of the secular state. War was an instrument of state policy and was used when seen as promoting the state's interests. Despite early efforts of some international scholars to promote rules governing warfare, it is fair to say that, prior to the end of the nineteenth century, war was beyond the scope of anything recognizable as law.

§10.2 COERCIVE MEASURES NOT AMOUNTING TO ARMED FORCE

States, particularly powerful states, often try to influence the conduct of other states. Influence can take many forms but usually constitutes either the proverbial carrot or stick. The carrot may consist of economic aid or offering favorable trade conditions. The stick may mean engaging in a variety of nonforceful, unfriendly acts that may or may not be illegal.

§10.2.1 Retorsions

The term "retorsion" refers to unfriendly, nonforceful, but not illegal, retaliatory actions taken by one state against another in response to actions that are regarded as hostile, unfriendly, or not in keeping with the policy aims of the responding states. This type of retaliation can take a variety of forms. It may consist of breaking off trade or diplomatic relations or imposing embargoes on the export or import of goods from or to the offending state. Nationals of the offending state may be denied entry visas. Vessels may be denied entry to ports. Aircraft may be denied rights of overflight. It may even go as far as the massing of troops near the offending state's border but a large troop maneuver might constitute an illegal threat of force. One essential element of a retorsion is that the action undertaken is not illegal. For example, if State A had a treaty obligation to allow State B to fly over its territory, its suspension of overflight rights would amount to an illegal breach of the treaty and would not be classified as a retorsion.

§10.2.2 Reprisals Not Involving the Use of Armed Force

A reprisal is an illegal act taken as a measure of self-help in response to a prior illegal act. Provided the state undertaking the reprisal is correct in its assessment that the other state's prior actions were indeed illegal and provided the reprisal is proportionate to the initial wrongdoing, then the reprisal is not considered unlawful. Reprisals not involving armed force are often called "countermeasures" to distinguish them from armed reprisals. (Armed reprisals are now governed by the U.N. Charter and the laws of war.) One arbitral tribunal explained the law of reprisals in this way:

> If a situation arises which, in one State's view, results in the violation of an international obligation by another State, the first State is entitled, . . . to affirm its rights through 'counter-measures.' . . .
>
> It is generally agreed that all counter-measures must, in the first instance, have some degree of equivalence with the alleged breach. . . . It has been observed, generally, that judging the 'proportionality' of counter-measures is not an easy task and can best be accomplished by approximation. . . . *Air Services Agreement* case (France v. U.S.), 18 R.I.A.A. 416, paras. 81 & 83 (1978).

§10.3 PRE-1945 LAW ON THE USE OF ARMED FORCE

World War I caused death and suffering on an unprecedented scale. It has been estimated that between ten and thirteen million military personnel died and a further six million were seriously injured. About seven million civilians were killed and roughly twelve million civilians were injured. The League of Nations arose out of the Peace Conference of Paris at the close of World War I in an attempt to provide some international mechanism where nations could meet and discuss their differences and thereby resolve disputes without the necessity of going to war. The Covenant of the League of Nations, which was signed in 1919, attempted to govern the procedural steps necessary before going to war. Article 12(1) provides that the members of the League agree that "they will submit [disputes] . . . either to arbitration or judicial settlement or to enquiry by the Council, and [that] they agree in no case to resort to war until three months after the award by the arbitrators or the judicial decision, or the report by the Council." Members were also obligated not to go to war with another member as long as that member was complying with an arbitral award or judicial decision or with a unanimous report by the Council. The idea behind these requirements was that a cooling-off period would benefit all parties to disputes and that a decision by an outside (presumably impartial) body was infinitely preferable to the devastation of conflict. If a member resorted to war contrary to the Covenant, other members were obliged to "subject it to the severance of all trade or financial relations, the prohibition of all intercourse between their nationals and the nationals of the covenant-breaking State, and the prevention of all financial, commercial or personal intercourse. . . ." Art. 16.

Despite the Covenant's high aspirations, the League failed to take decisive action when Italy invaded Abyssinia (Ethiopia) in 1935. Abyssinia reported the invasion to the League's Council, and Italy was found in violation of the Covenant. Sanctions were drawn up but the powerful nations prevented embargoes on coal, steel, and oil. The limited sanctions imposed proved insufficient, and the League took no further action against Italy. With the outbreak of World War II the League ultimately collapsed.

There had also been other movements to outlaw war. In 1928, sixty-three nations had signed the General Treaty for the Renunciation of War, also known as the Kellogg-Briand Pact. 94 L.N.T.S. 57. The parties condemned "recourse to war for the solution of international controversies, and [they] renounce[d] it as an instrument of national policy in their relationships with one another." Art. I. They pledged that "the settlement of all disputes or conflicts of whatever nature . . . which may arise among them, shall never be sought except by pacific means." Art. II. These early efforts at renouncing and regulating war proved insufficient to prevent the outbreak of World War II.

§10.3.1 The Customary Law of Self-Defence

Note: Spelling of "defence" follows the English spelling that is found in all international documents and I.C.J. cases.

A most useful discussion of the law of self-defence prior to 1945 can be found in official correspondence between the U.S. and the U.K. (1841-1842). The correspondence grew out of a particular set of circumstances described below.

In 1837, a rebellion occurred in Canada against the British authorities, which at that time still ruled Canada. The leaders of the rebellion had persuaded a number of Americans to assist them. The American group occupied Navy Island in Canadian waters of the Niagara River and from there launched raids upon the Canadian shore and attacked British ships. An American ship called the *Caroline* supplied the insurgents. On December 29, 1837, the *Caroline* was moored at the American port of Schlosser. The British forces seized the *Caroline*, set fire to her, and sent her over the Niagara Falls, which resulted in the death of at least two Americans. Several other men were never accounted for. A British subject, Alexander McLeod, was arrested and put on trial in New York for his alleged participation in the destruction of the *Caroline* and the murder of the two Americans. Extensive correspondence on the matter took place between Daniel Webster, the U.S. Secretary of State, and both Mr. Henry Fox, the British Minister, and Lord Ashburton, the British Special Emissary.

Mr. Webster to Mr. Fox (April 24, 1841).

It will be for . . . [Her Majesty's] Government to show a necessity of self-defence, instant, overwhelming, leaving no choice of means, and no moment for deliberation. It will be for it to show, also, that the local authorities of Canada, even supposing the necessity of the moment authorized them to enter the territories of The United States at all, did nothing unreasonable or excessive; since the act, justified by the necessity of self-defence, must be limited by that necessity, and kept clearly within it. It must be shown that admonition or remonstrance to the persons on board the *Caroline* was impracticable, or would have been unavailing; it must be shown that day-light could not be waited for; that there could be no attempt at discrimination between the innocent and the guilty; that it would not have been enough to seize and detain the vessel; but that there was a necessity, present and inevitable, for attacking her in the darkness of the night, while moored to the shore, and while unarmed men were asleep on board, killing some and wounding others, and then drawing her into the current, above the cataract, setting her on fire, and, careless to know whether there might not be in her the innocent with the guilty, or the living with the dead, committing her to a fate which fills the imagination with horror. A necessity for all this, the Government of The United States cannot believe to have existed.

Lord Ashburton to Mr. Webster (July 28, 1842).

It is so far satisfactory to perceive that we are perfectly agreed as to the general principles of international law applicable to this unfortunate case.

Apart from being Secretary of State, Daniel Webster was also a dramatic orator and poet. Scholars have long poured over these papers. There seems to be some level of agreement on the precondition of necessity before a use of force can be initiated and for proportionality once force has been used, although there was no agreement on whether these conditions had in fact been met in the *Caroline* incident. It is also not clear whether both writers were referring simply to self-defence after an armed attack had already occurred, or whether the British also meant to include anticipatory self-defence. Certainly attacks had taken place on British (Canadian) soil carried out by, and facilitated by, American citizens, but the British reasonably expected further attacks, and so the correspondence might also be referring to self-defence carried out in anticipation of a future attack. Note also that the attacks were not carried out by a state but by armed groups of citizens (terrorists or revolutionary heroes, depending on one's point of view).

§10.4 POST-1945 LAW

The six years of World War II heaped further devastation upon Europe and the Far East. Here the estimates for death are staggering. Total deaths are listed as between fifty to seventy million, with civilian deaths accounting for more than forty-five million. The allied powers emerged determined to establish a worldwide framework for ensuring peace. The Charter of the United Nations was signed in 1945 and declares one of its main purposes to be "to unite our strength to maintain international peace and security, and to ensure . . . that armed force shall not be used, save in the common interest. . . ." U.N. Charter, Preamble.

§10.4.1 The *Jus Ad Bellum*

The law relating to when it is permissible for one state to use armed force against another state is mainly (some would argue entirely) found in the U.N. Charter.

§10.4.2 The United Nations Charter

Article 2(4) of the Charter provides:

> All Members shall refrain in their international relations from the threat or use of force against the territorial integrity or political independence of any state, or in any other manner inconsistent with the Purposes of the United Nations.

Although this article is addressed only to members of the United Nations, it is now considered to be a binding rule of customary international law applicable to all states.

(a) The Meaning of "Force"

Article 2(4) does not use the term "war" but rather refers to "the threat or use of force." Use of force short of war is clearly encompassed by the article, but does the article only refer to military force? What about economic, political, ideological, or psychological force? The Preamble to the Charter declares that "armed force shall not be used, save in the common interest. . . ." Article 51 preserves the "right of individual or collective self-defence if an *armed attack* occurs . . ." (emphasis added). In 1970 the General Assembly adopted the *Declaration on Principles of International Law Concerning Friendly Relations and Co-operation Among States in Accordance with the Charter of the United Nations.* G.A. Res. 2625 (1970). This resolution was adopted without vote by consensus but is considered an authoritative statement on the interpretation of certain provisions of the Charter. The Declaration reiterates article 2(4) and elaborates upon the occasions when the threat or use of force is prohibited but it does not address the question of whether force includes nonmilitary force within the scope of the Charter. The Declaration also states that "[n]othing in the foregoing paragraphs shall be construed as enlarging or diminishing in any way the scope of the provisions of the Charter concerning cases in which the use of force is lawful." Certain types of armed and nonarmed intervention are prohibited by the Declaration: "No State or group of States has the right to intervene, directly or indirectly, for any reason whatever, in the internal or external affairs of any other State. Consequently, armed intervention and all other forms of interference or attempted threats against the personality of the State or against its political, economic and cultural elements, are in violation of international law." The above sentence and various other sentences in the Declaration address the use of nonmilitary force but in the context of other international obligations, such as the obligation not to intervene in the affairs of another state.

A number of developing nations have maintained that "force" includes nonmilitary force but the developed states have resisted this view while conceding that nonmilitary force of various kinds may be outlawed by other principles of international law. More recently, it has been suggested that certain cyber attacks should come within the scope of article 2(4). The discussion here has focused on *who* is carrying out the cyber attack, *what entity* is attacked, and what is the *level of harm.* Some would maintain that where State A's military forces launch a cyber attack on the military computer system of State B, totally disabling State B from taking any defensive (or offensive) action, then if State A subsequently invades State B, the cyber attack should count as a prohibited use of force under article 2(4).

(b) What Is a Threat of Force?

The issue of what constitutes a "threat . . . of force" has received little attention. The late Professor Schachter admitted that it was difficult to define what minimum show of force was contemplated by the phrase, particularly in light of the interplay of power politics, but that at least: "A blatant and direct threat of force to compel another state to yield territory or make substantial political concessions (not required by law) would have to be seen as illegal under article 2(4), if the words 'threat of force' are to have any meaning."[1] The International Court of Justice refused to find military manoevres held by the U.S. near the Nicaraguan border constituted a threat of force. "The Court is however not satisfied that the manoevres complained of, in the circumstances in which they were held, constituted on the part of the United States a breach, as against Nicaragua, of the principle forbidding recourse to the threat or use of force. . . ."[2]

In one part of its Advisory Opinion, *Legality of the Threat or Use of Nuclear Weapons*, 1996 I.C.J. 226, the I.C.J. focused on the issue of whether the possession of nuclear weapons should be treated as a "threat" to use force under U.N. Charter, article 2(4). The Court stated:

> Whether this [possession of nuclear weapons] is a "threat" contrary to article 2, paragraph 4, depends upon whether the particular use of force envisaged would be directed against the territorial integrity or political independence of a State, or against the Purposes of the United Nations or whether, in the event that it was intended as a means of defence, it would necessarily violate the principles of necessity and proportionality. In any of these circumstances the use of force, and the threat to use it, would be unlawful under the law of the Charter. Id. at 246-247.

In other words, the Court determined that if the contemplated use of force would be legally permissible, then the threat to use force in those circumstances, including threatening use of nuclear weapons, would also be permissible. If, on the other hand, the contemplated use of force was legally prohibited, then any threat to use force in those circumstances would also be prohibited. Ultimately, the Court did not answer the question of whether the use of nuclear weapons could ever be legally permissible, although the Court did hold that their threat or use "would generally be contrary to the rules of international law applicable in armed conflict, and in particular the principles and rules of humanitarian law. . . ." Id. at 266.

---

1. Oscar Schachter, *International Law in Theory and Practice* 111 (1991).
2. *Military and Paramilitary Activities in and Against Nicaragua* (Nicaragua v. U.S.), 1986 I.C.J. 14 at para. 227.

The Court added:

> However, . . . the Court cannot conclude definitively whether the threat or use of nuclear weapons would be lawful or unlawful in an extreme circumstance of self-defence, in which the very survival of a State would be at stake. . . . Id. at 266.

By being unable to answer this question definitely, the Court has left open the possibility that the use of nuclear weapons might be permissible where the state used such weapons in self-defence in order to prevent the annihilation of the State. It has, therefore, also left open the question of whether a threat to use such weapons, in similar circumstances, might also be permissible.

Judge Schwebel appended a detailed dissenting opinion indicating that, in 1990, the U.S. Secretary of State, James Baker, had indicated to his Iraqi counterpart that if Saddam Hussein used chemical or biological weapons against coalition forces, the U.S. people would seek vengeance. Schwebel maintained that this language was perceived by Iraq as a threat to use nuclear weapons. No chemical or biological weapons were used by the Iraqi forces. Schwebel thus concluded that the U.S. threat was a legitimate threat to use nuclear weapons.

(c) Must Force Be Used for a Particular Objective to Violate Article 2(4)?

Article 2(4) prohibits the threat or use of force "against the territorial integrity or political independence of any State . . ." This raises the question of whether force used for ends other than attacking the territorial integrity or political independence of a state is permitted. For example, can a state use force to rescue a group of its own citizens under imminent threat in another state? Can force be used to promote or protect human rights or democracy or to preserve "peace and security"? To attempt to answer this question it should be remembered that force is also forbidden when it is used "in any manner inconsistent with the Purposes of the United Nations." Art. 2(4). The main purposes of the Charter are spelled out in the Preamble and article 1 and embrace a variety of aims encompassing human rights, equality, justice, social progress, tolerance, and friendly relations among nations. The principal purpose appears in article 1(1):

> To maintain international peace and security, and to that end: to take effective collective measures for the prevention and removal of threats to the peace, and for the suppression of acts of aggression or other breaches of the peace, and to bring about by peaceful means, and in conformity with the principles of justice and international law, adjustment or settlement of international disputes or situations which might lead to a breach of the peace.

Since the use of force for any purpose creates an immediate potential for a breach of the peace and since its use cannot be viewed as the peaceful settlement of an international dispute it would appear that the threat or use of force is contrary to article 2(4) unless it falls within specific Charter exceptions. (See §10.4.2(d)(i) and 10.4.3(c), *infra*.)

Example 10-1

In 1999, the North Atlantic Treaty Organization (NATO) forces bombed the Federal Republic of Yugoslavia (now Serbia). The bombing raids lasted for three months. This attack had not been authorized by the Security Council. NATO sought to justify its invasion on the basis of what it perceived as gross violations of the human rights of the population living in an area of Yugoslavia known as Kosovo. This population was largely made up of ethnic Albanians who were mostly Muslim. The rest of Yugoslavia was largely ethnically Slav and Orthodox Christian. In 2008, Kosovo declared independence from Serbia. Serbia maintains that Kosovo remains part of Serbia.

Did the NATO bombing violate U.N. Charter, article 2(4)?

1) Make an argument that the bombing did violate article 2(4).

2) Make an argument that the bombing did not violate article 2(4).

Explanations

1) If one views article 2(4) as prohibiting all uses of armed force by one state against another (unless justified as self-defence under article 51 (see below) or authorized by the Security Council under article 42 (see below)), then the NATO bombing clearly violates article 2(4). Even the argument that the bombing was not a "use of force against the territorial integrity or political independence of" another state is not convincing because a use of force to enter the air space of another state shatters the territorial integrity of that state. A portion of Serbia's territory, Kosovo, has now declared its independence and, to date, has been recognized as an independent country by roughly seventy states. Even if NATO argues it did not intend to break up the territorial integrity of Yugoslavia, the bombing raids were the acts that started the chain of events leading to Kosovo's declaration of independence.

2) Article 2(4) only prohibits the use of force against another state when it is used against the territorial integrity or political independence of that state or when it is against the purposes of the U.N. Charter. Here, the NATO bombing was entirely aimed at preventing the ethnic cleansing that was being carried out by the Yugoslav government against the Kosovars, an ethnic and religious minority group. The U.N. Charter was written not simply to "maintain international peace and security" but also to "promote human rights." In this case the protection of human rights could only be achieved by the use of force. The fact that Kosovo declared independence

nine years after the NATO bombing does not indicate that the bombing was against Yugoslavia's territorial integrity.

(d) Exceptions to Article 2(4)

(i) *Self-Defence*

Article 51 provides:

> Nothing in the present Charter shall impair the inherent right of individual or collective self-defence if an armed attack occurs against a Member of the United Nations, until the Security Council has taken measures necessary to maintain international peace and security. Measures taken by Members in the exercise of this right of self-defence shall be immediately reported to the Security Council and shall not in any way affect the authority and responsibility of the Security Council under the present Charter to take at any time such action as it deems necessary in order to maintain or restore international peace and security.

Some authors maintain that the Charter law subsumes all pre-existing law on the use of force and that the entire right of self-defence is spelled out in the Charter. They argue that article 51 precludes anticipatory self-defence and requires an armed attack to have taken place against a state before it has a right of self-defence. Other writers argue that the phrase "inherent right of self-defence" indicates that the Charter intended to incorporate the customary law of self-defence, including anticipatory self-defence, when facing imminent attack. Without addressing the issue of anticipatory self-defence, the International Court of Justice has recognized that the right to individual and collective self-defence were part of customary international law predating the Charter and that the Charter recognized this by its reference to "the inherent right (or *'droit naturel'*) which any State possesses in the event of an armed attack. . . ." *Nicaragua* case, *supra*, 1986 I.C.J. 14 at para. 193.

a. What Level of Armed Force Gives Rise to the Right of Self-Defence?

Note: Article 2(4) prohibits the *use of force*, whereas article 51 grants a right of self-defence if *an armed attack occurs*. Note the difference in this language. Do all prohibited uses of *armed force* automatically give rise to the right to self-defence? Are *armed attacks* a special subset of the *use of force*? These types of questions had long puzzled academics and jurists. The *Nicaragua* case, *supra*, addressed these questions. The Nicaraguan government accused the United States of laying mines in Nicaraguan waters and damaging ships, ports, oil facilities, and a naval base. They also accused the U.S. of arming, training, and financing the *Contra* forces — a rebel force seeking to overthrow the Nicaraguan government. The *Contras* were trained in Honduras, across Nicaragua's northern border. The U.S. sought to justify its activities on the basis of collective self-defence on behalf of El Salvador, one of Nicaragua's neighbors. The U.S. argued that Nicaragua had engaged in armed attacks against El Salvador; thus El Salvador had a right of self-defence, and the U.S. had a right to exercise collective self-defence on behalf of El Salvador. The Court therefore had to address the question of whether El Salvador had suffered an *armed attack*. The Court stated:

> As regards certain particular aspects . . . , it will be necessary to distinguish the most grave forms of the use of force (those constituting an armed attack) from other less grave forms. . . . Id. at para. 191.
>
> There appears now to be general agreement on the nature of the acts which can be treated as constituting armed attacks. In particular, it may be considered to be agreed that an armed attack must be understood as including not merely action by regular armed forces across an international border, but also "the sending by or on behalf of a State of armed bands, groups, irregulars or mercenaries, which carry out acts of armed force against another State of such gravity as to amount to" (*inter alia*) an actual armed attack conducted by regular forces, "or its substantial involvement therein." This description, contained in Article 3, paragraph (g), of the Definition of Aggression annexed to General Assembly resolution 3314 (XXIX), may be taken to reflect customary international law. The Court sees no reason to deny that, in customary law, the prohibition of armed attacks may apply to the sending by a State of armed bands to the territory of another State, if such an operation, because of its scale and effects would have been classified as an armed attack rather than as a mere frontier incident had it been carried out by regular armed forces. But the Court does not believe that the concept of "armed attack" includes not only acts by armed bands where such acts occur on a significant scale but also assistance to rebels in the form of the provision of weapons or logistical or other support. Such assistance may be regarded as a threat or use of force, or amount to intervention in the internal or external affairs of other States. *Nicaragua* case, *supra*, at para. 195.

Although the Court conceded that there had been:

> An intermittent flow of arms routed via the territory of Nicaragua to the armed opposition in [El Salvador]. . . . The Court was not however satisfied that assistance ha[d] reached the Salvadorian armed opposition, on a scale of any significance. . . . As stated above, the Court is unable to consider that, . . . the provision of arms to the opposition in another State constitutes an armed attack on that State. Id. at para. 230.

In other words, the Court distinguishes low-level uses of force or less grave uses of force that do not constitute an armed attack and, therefore, do not give rise to the right of self-defence under article 51, from more grave or higher level uses of force that do constitute an armed attack and do give rise to the right of self-defence. Lower level uses of armed force will violate article 2(4) and may also violate the principle of non-intervention (see below) but do not trigger the right to self-defence.

Imagine a long pole. At the bottom are low-level uses of inter-state force, at the top are the highest level uses of inter-state force. Somewhere on the pole is a line. Below the line, the uses of force do not amount to an armed attack (even though they violate article 2(4)). Above the line, the uses of force do amount to an armed attack, and violate article 2(4), but also gives rise to the right of self-defence for the attacked state. We do not yet know exactly where this line is drawn. Armed attacks also justify the exercise of collective self-defence on the part of third-party states seeking to defend the attacked state provided the attacked state has declared itself to be a victim of an armed attack and has asked for assistance. See *Nicaragua* case, *supra*, at para. 232. All exercises of self-defence must be reported to the Security Council. See the language of article 51. In the end, the U.S. argument seeking to justify its action against Nicaragua on the basis of the collective self-defence of El Salvador did not get off the ground because the Court determined that whatever the low-level uses of force there might have been emanating from Nicaraguan territory, they were not grave enough to amount to an armed attack. As a result, El Salvador had no right of self-defence, and thus no other state could invoke the right of collective self-defence on behalf of El Salvador.

Note that the Court stated that "assistance to rebels in the form of the provision of weapons or logistical or other support . . ." (*id.* at para. 195), does not constitute an armed attack. Judge Robert Jennings in his dissenting opinion disagreed with this rather sweeping statement. He stated:

> It may readily be agreed that the mere provision of arms cannot be said to amount to an armed attack. But the provision of arms may, nevertheless, be a very important element in what might be thought to amount to armed attack, where it is coupled with other kinds of involvement. Accordingly, it seems to me that to say that the provision of arms, coupled with 'logistical or other support' is not an armed attack is going much too far. *Id.* at 543.

Obviously, Judge Jennings would draw the line on our imaginary pole at a different place from the majority of the Court at least with respect to supplying rebels.

Example 10-2

State A is building a nuclear reactor. It claims the reactor is for peaceful purposes. The neighboring country, State B, is concerned that the reactor will be used to make nuclear weapons, probably within the next five years. State B has nuclear weapons. State A has no nuclear weapons. State A and State B have long had a tense relationship although they have never been at war. State B decides to bomb State A's nuclear reactor before the reactor can produce weapons grade materials that might be used against State B. State B bombs the reactor in State A. The reactor was completely demolished and twenty-four State A workers were killed. State B claims it was exercising self-defence.

Did State B have a right to self-defence?

Explanation

The text of article 51 only gives a right to self-defence after an armed attack has occurred. Fear that a neighboring state *might* use a nuclear reactor to make nuclear weapons at some future date (probably not being operational for at least five years) and then *might* use the weapons against State B, is far too speculative to count as even a threat of an armed attack. Even if one accepts the notion of anticipatory self-defence, the possibility of an attack five years away is, again, far too speculative to fall within the traditional notion of anticipatory self-defence that requires the threat of an imminent attack.

Compare: In 1981, Israel bombed an Iraqi nuclear reactor located at Osirak. The Security Council condemned the attack as a "clear violation of the Charter of the United Nations and the norms of international conduct." S.C. Res. 487 (1981). In 2007, Israel bombed a partly constructed Syrian nuclear reactor that was much further from completion than the Osirak reactor. Although a number of countries expressed concern, the Security Council did not condemn the attack.

Example 10-3

Assume the same facts as state in Example 10-2 above.

Had State A suffered an armed attack giving it the right of self-defence?

Explanation

Bombing a nuclear complex, completely destroying it, and killing twenty-four workers at the plant would, in all probability, count as a grave form of the use of force and would amount to an armed attack giving rise to the right of self-defence on the part of State A. Among the uses of force that do not amount to an armed attack the Court has identified: "a mere frontier incident"; "assistance to rebels in the form of provision of weapons or logistical or other support"; "an intermittent flow of arms" that was not on a significant scale; the mining of a warship "which was severely damaged but not sunk, and without loss of life"; and a missile attack on an oil tanker that caused damage to the ship and injury to six crew members.

The latter two examples can be found in the *Oil Platforms* case (Iran v. U.S.), 2003 I.C.J. 161.

b. Must an Armed Attack Be Carried Out by a State to Trigger the Right of Self-Defence?

We noted that article 2(4) is generally read as prohibiting the inter-state use of armed force. Internal uses of force are generally dealt with by domestic criminal law. Article 51 permits the right of self-defence "if an armed attack occurs against a member of the United Nations. . . ." We now know that the use of force necessary to trigger the right to self-defence must be at a fairly high level but must the high-level use of force be initiated by a *state* before the right to self-defence comes into existence?

In September 2001, members of an international paramilitary organization known as Al Qaeda, hijacked several civilian airplanes and crashed them into buildings in New York and Washington, D.C., in the United States, killing nearly 3,000 people. In the wake of the hijackings, the Security Council passed a resolution recognizing "the inherent right of individual or collective self-defence in accordance with the Charter." S.C. Res. 1368 (2001). NATO invoked article 5 of the NATO Treaty, 34 U.N.T.S. 243, which states that "[t]he Parties agree that an armed attack against one or more of them . . . shall be considered an attack against them all . . ." and goes on to state that, in such circumstances, all of the members will assist the attacked member as an exercise of individual or collective self-defence under article 51. Al Qaeda is not a state, although it is possible to argue that the State of Afghanistan was responsible for the actions of Al Qaeda because it allowed it to have bases and train on the territory of Afghanistan. Nonetheless, many have argued that since article 51 does not indicate that the "armed attack" has to be initiated by a state, only that the attack has to be directed against a state, any use of armed force at a high-enough level will trigger the right to self-defence regardless of the characteristics of the attacker. The attackers in the *Caroline* incident, above, were citizens of the U.S., not the U.S. government. Of course, this argument poses a variety of problems, such as whether it is possible to engage in self-defence against a non-state group without violating the territorial integrity of a state. Non-state actors must, presumably, be located on the territory of some state.

(ii) Preemption

In March 2003, the United States initiated armed force against Iraq. The United States sought to justify its attack on the basis of a new doctrine under which it maintained the right to use force preemptively because it stated that it had received "reliable intelligence" that Iraq had "weapons of mass destruction" (WMD), which Iraq was capable of using against the United States or its allies. Later, other justifications were added to the rationale for the attack, such as Iraq's violation of Security Council resolutions relating to the conditions imposed on Iraq after Iraq's invasion of Kuwait in 1990. The announcement of the preemption doctrine caused a torrent of debate especially when it became clear that there were no weapons of mass destruction in Iraq and that the "reliable intelligence" data had in fact never been considered "reliable," even by many within the U.S. intelligence agencies.

Previously, scholars who had accepted the argument for anticipatory self-defence had always insisted that the threatened attack must be "imminent." The preemption doctrine either stretches the term "imminent" beyond normal linguistic limits or simply dispenses with the need for any imminence. Any future attack, however remote or speculative, would then justify self-defence. Needless to say, this doctrine is highly controversial. For a reasoned explanation of many scholars' views of this issue in the Iraq war context, see *Agora: Future Implications of the Iraq Conflict*, 97 Am. J. Int'l L. 553-642 (2003). Of course, the doctrine of preemption is very far from a literal reading of article 51. It is worth asking, however, whether our view of preemption would be different if, in fact, WMD had been found in Iraq and they were capable of striking the U.S. or its close allies or both. Of course, in such a case, one might argue, that the fear of an imminent attack was justified thus placing the action more securely within the traditional doctrine of anticipatory self-defence.

(iii) *Forceful Countermeasures*

You may well be wondering what a state may do when it suffers a low-level use of force not amounting to an armed attack. It does not have a right of self-defence, but does it simply have to sit there and suffer the low-level force that violates article 2(4) and the principle of non-intervention (see below)? In the *Nicaragua* case, *supra*, the Court indicated that the less grave uses of force would justify "proportionate counter-measures on the part of the State which had been the victim of these acts. . . ." *Id.* at para. 249. On the other hand, the Court rejected the idea of any right to the collective use of forceful countermeasures.

> While an armed attack would give rise to an entitlement to collective self-defence, a use of force of a lesser degree of gravity cannot . . . produce any entitlement to take collective counter-measures involving the use of force. *Id.* at para. 249.

(e) Reprisals Using Force

Earlier in this chapter a reprisal was defined as "an illegal act taken as a measure of self-help in response to a prior illegal act." That earlier section discussed reprisals not involving force. What if a reprisal in fact involves force, such as a bombing raid into a neighboring territory or the dispatch of a commando unit to rescue hostages held by another state? The International Court of Justice has stated that "armed reprisals in time of peace . . . are considered to be unlawful." *Nuclear Weapons*, 1996 I.C.J. 226 at para. 46. The Court also added that with respect to "belligerent reprisals . . . any right of recourse to such reprisals would, like self-defence, be governed *inter alia* by the principle of proportionality." Reprisals that take place during war are also governed by the laws of war including the four Geneva Conventions of 1949. (See §10.5 *infra*.)

If a prior illegal action amounted to an armed attack, the prior actions would trigger the right to self-defence but, as the *Nicaragua* case makes clear, not all armed illegal activities by one state against another amount to an armed attack giving rise to the right of self-defence.

Although the Security Council has frequently condemned armed reprisals, it remains true that many states engage in armed reprisals. The international community has not created an effective mechanism to redress illegal armed inter-state acts, with the result that states are often ready to use self-help in the form of armed reprisals at an ever-escalating level.

§10.4.3 The Rule of Non-Intervention

Article 2(1) of the United Nations Charter declares that "[t]he Organization is based on the principle of the sovereign equality of all its Members." The principle of the equality of states carries with it the notion that every state is prohibited from interfering in the internal affairs of another state. Interference can take many forms. If it comes in the form of force it is governed by U.N. Charter articles 2(4) and 51 as well as customary law governing the use of force but it may also constitute illegal intervention. If interference does not amount to the use of force, then a state's conduct is governed by the rules relating to non-intervention.

In 1965, the General Assembly issued the *Declaration on the Inadmissibility of Intervention in the Domestic Affairs of States and the Protection of Their Independence and Sovereignty*. G.A. Res. 2131 (1965):

> 1. No State has the right to intervene, directly or indirectly, for any reason whatever, in the internal or external affairs of any other State. Consequently, armed intervention and all other forms of interference or attempted threats against the personality of the State or against its political, economic and cultural elements, are condemned;
>
> 2. No State may use or encourage the use of economic, political or any other type of measures to coerce another State in order to obtain from it the subordination of the exercise of its sovereign rights or to secure from it advantages of any kind. Also, no State shall organize, assist, foment, finance, incite or tolerate subversive, terrorist or armed activities directed towards the violent overthrow of the regime of another State, or interfere in civil strife in another State;

3. The use of force to deprive peoples of their national identity constitutes a violation of their inalienable rights and of the principle of non-intervention;

4. The strict observance of these obligations is an essential condition to ensure that nations live together in peace with one another, since the practice of any form of intervention not only violates the spirit and letter of the Charter but also leads to the creation of situations which threaten international peace and security;

5. Every State has an inalienable right to choose its political, economic, social and cultural systems, without interference in any form by another State;

6. All States shall respect the right of self-determination and independence of peoples and nations, to be freely exercised without any foreign pressure, and with absolute respect for human rights and fundamental freedoms. Consequently, all States shall contribute to the complete elimination of racial discrimination and colonialism in all its forms and manifestations;

7. For the purpose of this Declaration, the term "State" covers both individual States and groups of States;

8. Nothing in this Declaration shall be construed as affecting in any manner the relevant provisions of the Charter of the United Nations relating to the maintenance of international peace and security, in particular those contained in Chapters VI, VII, and VIII.

In the *Nicaragua* case the Court indicated that it considered this Declaration to be an expression of customary law. (See *Nicaragua* case at para. 203.) States do, of course, try to influence the behavior of other states in a variety of ways. The line between permissible diplomatic influence and illegal intervention is often hard to distinguish.

The International Court of Justice discussed one aspect of intervention in the *Corfu Channel* case (U.K. v. Albania), 1949 I.C.J. 3. After British warships had been damaged by mines while exercising their right of innocent passage in Albanian territorial waters that were also designated as an international strait, other British warships were sent back into the Corfu Channel to sweep for mines on a mission named "Operation Retail." The British were convinced that the Albanians had put the mines in the Channel, and they argued that they had a right to intervene to acquire and preserve evidence in order to submit it to an international tribunal.

The Court rejected this argument and stated:

The Court can only regard the alleged right of intervention as a manifestation of a policy of force, such as has, in the past, given rise to most serious abuses and such as cannot, whatever be the present defects in international organization, find a place in international law. . . .

The United Kingdom . . . has further classified "Operation Retail" among methods of self-protection or self-help. The Court cannot accept this defence either. Between independent states, respect for territorial sovereignty is an essential foundation of international relations. *Id.* at 35.

In the *Nicaragua* case, *supra*, the Court discussed the principle of non-intervention at length. In discussing the content of the principle, the Court noted:

> [T]he principle forbids all States or groups of States to intervene directly or indirectly in internal or external affairs of other States. A prohibited intervention must accordingly be one bearing on matters in which each State is permitted, by the principle of State sovereignty, to decide freely. One of these is the choice of a political, economic, social and cultural system, and the formulation of foreign policy. Intervention is wrongful when it uses methods of coercion in regard to such choices, which must remain free ones. The element of coercion, which defines, and indeed forms the very essence of, prohibited intervention, is particularly obvious in the case of an intervention which uses force, either in the direct form of military action, or in the indirect form of support for subversive or terrorist armed activities within another State. As noted above (paragraph 191), General Assembly resolution 2625 (XXV) equates assistance of this kind with the use of force by the assisting State when the acts committed in another State "involve a threat or use of force." These forms of action are therefore wrongful in the light of both the principle of non-use of force, and that on non-intervention. *Id.* at para. 205.

Although the Court condoned assistance to other governments (*Nicaragua* at para. 246), the Court declared that there was no right to support opposition in another State and that such support contravenes the rule of non-intervention. It stated:

> The Court considers that in international law, if one State, with a view to the coercion of another State, supports and assists armed bands in that State whose purpose is to overthrow the government of that State, that amounts to an intervention by the one State in the internal affairs of the other. . . . *Id.* at para. 241.

Humanitarian aid to factions fighting within a state is only permissible where it make no discrimination based on political opinion or other factors but simply seeks to relieve suffering. Such aid cannot be supplied to one faction and not to other factions without violating the principle of non-intervention.

Example 10-4

Assume State A has been facilitating the supply of guns and tanks across its border into State B to assist the rebel force in State B. This rebel force is trying to overthrow the government of State B by violence. State A also knows that segments of its population are sympathetic to the rebel cause in State B and that several hundred of its citizens have crossed the border into State B in order to assist the rebels. State A has not sought to curb this activity.

What may State B do in light of the above activities of State A?

Explanation

First, we have to decide whether the activities of State A are sufficient to amount to an armed attack. The sending of guns and tanks alone probably does not amount to an armed attack. The additional information about State A's citizens going across the border to assist the rebels, without being stopped by State A, brings the example closer to: "sending by or on behalf of a State of armed bands, groups, irregulars or mercenaries, which carry out acts of armed force against another State of such gravity to amount to . . . an actual armed attack. . . ." *Nicaragua* case, *supra*, at para. 135. Before we can be sure of the answer, we would need to know how deeply State A was involved in allowing or encouraging its citizens to take part in the rebellion. We would also need to be able to assess the level of armed activity engaged in by State A's citizens.

If the activity did amount to an armed attack, then State B would have a right of self-defence. Such activities would have to be both necessary (no other way to settle the dispute) and proportionate (only sufficient to repel the attack). If, on the other hand, the activity did not amount to an armed attack (but was a violation of article 2(4) and the rule against non-intervention), then State B could only engaged in similar low-level forceful countermeasures against State A.

Example 10-5

Assume the same facts as stated in Example 10-4 above and that State B has a close ally, State C.

What may State C do to assist State B after the activities by State A against State B?

Explanation

If the activity by State A against State B amounts to an armed attack, then State B can declare itself a victim of an armed attack and request assistance from State C. State C can then exercise collective self-defence against State A on behalf of State B. If State A's activities against State B do not amount to an armed attack, State C can certainly assist State B in whatever way requested but it cannot, itself, undertake direct forceful action against State A because there is no right to collective forceful countermeasures. It could, of course, engage in a number of nonforceful actions directed against State A, such as breaking off diplomatic relations with State A or refusing to allow citizens of State A to enter State C.

(a) Civil Wars and the Rule of Non-Intervention

The clear import of the Court's opinion in the *Nicaragua* case, *supra*, is that states have no right to support *rebel* groups in other states even if requested to do so and even if they are convinced that the rebels' cause is just. This prohibition of support for rebels even extends to humanitarian aid unless it is made equally available to government forces.

At the present time international law does not prohibit the initiation of civil wars. Article 2(4) of the U.N. Charter and the customary laws of war are directed toward the prohibition of international hostilities. The laws addressing the conduct of hostilities do apply to the conduct of civil wars in certain instances. (See §10.5 on *Jus in Bello*.) The internal law of all states prohibits rebellion. What constitutes rebellion varies dramatically from state to state but all states are likely to prosecute and punish convicted rebels severely. Of course, if the rebels are successful they will become the new government of the state.

May a state support a foreign *government* when that government is threatened by rebel forces? The International Court of Justice appeared to endorse such support in paragraph 246 of the *Nicaragua* case. A good number of powerful states have come to the aid of friendly governments threatened by rebels, and some states maintain that temporary assistance to restore internal order is not a violation of international law. Some authors disagree and maintain that "[s]ince international law recognizes the right of revolution, it cannot permit other states to intervene to prevent it."[3] When a state is in the throes of incipient revolution it is often difficult to determine which of several competing groups is "the government" and whether "the government" made any request for assistance. Professor Harris suggests that such difficulties demonstrate "one of the weaknesses of allowing intervention at the request of the constitutional government. . . ."[4]

(b) Intervention in Particular Circumstances

Above it was suggested that forceful intervention by one state against another might not violate article 2(4) if the intervention was not directed against the "territorial integrity or political independence" of another state and was not "inconsistent with the Purposes of the United Nations." Below are some examples that might fit these suggestions but remember, this whole line of argument is controversial, and some maintain that all uses of armed force by one state against another violate article 2(4).

---

3. Quincy Wright, *Subversive Intervention*, 54 Am. J. Int'l L. 521, 529 (1960).
4. D.J. Harris, *Cases and Materials on International Law* 744 (7th ed. 2010).

(i) *Intervening to Protect Nationals Abroad*

When a citizen travels abroad, the state to which he or she travels has an obligation to ensure that the alien is protected at least to the minimum international standard and to ensure that the alien's human rights are not violated (see Chapters 8 and 9). Not all states fulfill these obligations of care, so that aliens may find themselves in immediate danger without the time or means to leave the country. The aliens in question may have lived in the foreign country for some time and acquired considerable property, which may also be threatened. This type of situation raises the question of whether the alien's state may intervene to protect its nationals and/or their property. Such intervention always necessitates some use of force.

Several recent incursions by states into foreign territory have been justified, at least partly, on the basis of the claimed right to protect nationals or their property abroad; the 1956 invasion of Suez by a joint Anglo-French force in part to protect nationals and their property; the Israeli raid on Entebbe, Uganda, to rescue hijacked Israeli citizens in 1976; the United States 1980 attempt to rescue U.S. hostages held in Iran; the 1983 invasion of Grenada by U.S. military and troops from the Organization of Eastern Caribbean States, partly to rescue U.S. nationals stranded during a power struggle between various political factions; and the 1989 invasion of Panama by U.S. military forces, in part to protect U.S. nationals.

All of the above incidents have generated much controversy. There are often arguments about the facts: whether the nationals or their properties were really in any danger. There is also the fundamental question of whether such uses of force violate article 2(4) of the Charter. They certainly entail a "use of force" but it is disputed whether the force is directed "against the territorial integrity or political independent of any state, or [is used] in . . . [a] manner inconsistent with the Purposes of the United Nations."

These incursions do not fit easily into article 51's self-defence exception in that no "armed attack" has occurred in the territory of the invading state. Some scholars believe that because anticipatory self-defence was permitted under pre-Charter law and because article 51 speaks of "the inherent" right to self-defence, the right to resort to force in anticipation of an armed attack is permitted by article 51. For these scholars armed reprisals, which is what this type of intervention amounts to, is permissible provided it meets the requirements of necessity and proportionality.

(ii) *Humanitarian Intervention*

Over the years a number of states and various international scholars have maintained that there is a right to military intervention in the affairs of other states where the intervener is seeking to preserve or promote certain concepts that they regard as central to the framework of international law.

Most prevalent among the occasions stated to justify intervention are when the intervener is seeking to preserve or promote human rights or democracy or peace and security. None of these "rights to intervene" has received broad acceptance by the international community and thus cannot be regarded as established in customary international law. Nevertheless, every time a state does exercise force to intervene in another state to preserve or promote one of the favored interests and is not rebuked by the international community, the state's actions contribute to the development of an accepted state practice. Below are some examples where state military intervention has been justified on one or more of the above grounds.

The 1989 U.S. invasion of Panama occurred shortly after General Noriega had annulled the results of an election thought to have been won by his rival. President Bush wrote a letter to the Speaker of the U.S. House of Representatives in which he outlined a number of justifications for the invasion including "defend[ing] democracy in Panama. . . ." A draft resolution of the Security Council calling for U.S. withdrawal was vetoed by the U.S., the U.K., and France, although the General Assembly did pass a resolution calling the invasion "a flagrant violation of international law."

In 1971, a civil war broke out in Pakistan after East Pakistan had declared itself to be the independent State of Bangladesh. During the ensuing crisis more than one million refugees crossed from East Pakistan into India. India was sympathetic with the Bengalis and gave military assistance to the Bangladesh guerrillas. War broke out between India and Pakistan but two weeks later Pakistan surrendered. Writers have justified India's military assistance and her invasion on several grounds, including protecting Bangladesh's right to self-determination. The U.N. General Assembly had called on India to withdraw her force.

In 1979, Tanzania invaded Uganda in order to topple the brutal regime of Uganda's notorious dictator, Idi Amin. Although Tanzania justified her invasion on the basis of self-defence, others have condoned the military intervention on the basis of protecting human rights.

In 1999, the North Atlantic Treaty Organization (NATO) carried out a seventy-eight day bombing campaign against Yugoslavia in response to perceived widespread human rights abuses carried out by the Serb dominated government of Yugoslavia against the minority ethnic population of Kosovo Albanians. The legality of this invasion was the subject of much debate. Professor Louis Henkin concluded that "[i]n my view, the law is, and ought to be, that unilateral intervention by military force by a state or group of states is unlawful unless authorized by the Security Council." Nonetheless, Professor Henkin added that "many — governments and scholars — thought that something had to be done to end the horrors of Kosovo [and] that NATO was the appropriate body to do it . . ." Professor Ruth Wedgwood thought that "[t]he war over Kosovo . . . may . . . mark the emergence of a limited and conditional right of humanitarian intervention, permitting the use of force to protect the lives of a threatened population when the decision is taken by . . . a responsible multilateral organization and the Security Council does not oppose the action." On the other hand, the late Professor Jonathan Charney was clear in his view that "the NATO intervention through its bombing campaign violated the United Nations Charter and international law."

Yugoslavia filed multiple cases against individual NATO members in the International Court of Justice arguing that the bombing violated international legal norms. The Security Council was asked to condemn NATO's military action but the resolution failed with three votes in favor and twelve against. The Security Council has since endorsed an international civilian and military administration of the Kosovo region. Kosovo declared its independence in 2008 and has now been recognized as an independent state by roughly seventy other states. See also, *Accordance with International Law of the Unilateral Declaration of Independence in Respect of Kosovo*, Advisory Opinion, 2010 I.C.J. _____ (July 22).

(iii) *The Responsibility to Protect*

Recently, there has been a great deal of debate and some endorsement of a concept that has come to be known as "The Responsibility to Protect." This concept arises out of the knowledge that the international machinery to authorize the collective use of force, as originally envisioned in the Charter, has not materialized, and authorization by the Security Council for states to form coalitions and use force for acceptable emergency purposes is seldom granted. Yet because atrocities continue, the argument is made that states with the capacity to act to prevent catastrophes, or to react rapidly after they occur, have a responsibility to offer such assistance, including reconstruction after conflict. Such action is characterized as humanitarian intervention that, although recognizing the Security Council's primary responsibility to act, nonetheless places responsibility to act on states and "the international community" when the Security Council fails to authorize such protective action. Such proposals are controversial, favoring, as they must, richer and more powerful states. The concept of "The Responsibility to Protect" has been endorsed at the highest U.N. levels[5] but cannot be characterized as customary international law at this time.

(c) The Security Council's Power to Intervene

Article 24 of the U.N. Charter gives the Security Council "primary responsibility for the maintenance of international peace and security. . . ."

---

5. See, e.g., Report of the U.N. Secretary-General, In Larger Freedom: Towards Development, Security and Human Rights for All, U.N. Doc. A/59/2005 (2005).

United Nations members also "agree to accept and carry out the decisions of the Security Council in accordance with the present Charter." Art. 25.

Article 2(7) states a general limitation upon all organs of the United Nations with one exception:

> Nothing contained in the present Charter shall authorize the United Nations to intervene in matters which are essentially within the domestic jurisdiction of any State or shall require the Members to submit such matters to settlement under the present Charter; but this principle shall not prejudice the application of enforcement measures under Chapter VII.

Chapter VI of the U.N. Charter is entitled "Pacific Settlement of Disputes." Under this chapter the Security Council is given power to investigate disputes between states and to recommend appropriate settlement procedures.

Chapter VII of the Charter first grants the Security Council the power to "determine the existence of any threat to the peace, breach of the peace, or act of aggression and . . . [to] make recommendations, or decide what measures shall be taken in accordance with articles 41 and 42, to maintain or restore international peace and security." Art. 39. Article 40 gives the Security Council the power to "call upon the parties concerned [where there has been a threat to the peace, a breach of the peace, or an act of aggression] to comply with such provisional measures as it deems necessary or desirable. . . ."

(i) *Article 41 Measures*

Under article 41, the Security Council "may decide what measures not involving the use of armed force are to be employed to give effect to its decisions, and it may call upon the Members of the United Nations to apply such measures. . . ." The article then gives examples of the types of non-armed-force measures that may be employed and mentions "interruption of economic relations and of rail, sea, air, postal, telegraphic, radio and other means of communication, and the severance of diplomatic relations."

The Security Council has used its article 41 powers on numerous occasions, and there has been much debate on the effectiveness of such measures. For example, the Security Council ordered increasingly severe economic sanctions against Southern Rhodesia from 1965 through 1968 after the white government of Ian Smith had unilaterally declared independence from Britain. These sanctions were not lifted until 1979, when Rhodesia became the independent State of Zimbabwe. Economic sanctions were also applied to South Africa in an attempt to dismantle the government's apartheid policies. In 1963 the Council called for a voluntary arms embargo. When it became clear that the voluntary embargo was not effective, the Council imposed a mandatory arms embargo. More recently the Council has imposed a series of far-reaching economic sanctions on Iraq in the wake of its invasion of Kuwait. In 1992, the Security Council ordered Libya to hand over either to Britain or to the U.S. two named suspects in the Pan Am 103 bombing in Lockerbie, Scotland. When Libya did not comply, an arms and air embargo was imposed. These sanctions were lifted in 1999 when the accused men were handed over to be tried by a Scottish court located in the Netherlands. An arms embargo has been in place since 2004 on Sudan with respect to activity in the Darfur region. Iran has also been subject to sanctions for its suspected nuclear activity.

(ii) Article 42 Measures

If the Security Council determines that article 41 measures are inadequate "it may take such action by air, sea, or land forces as may be necessary to maintain or restore international peace and security. Such actions may include demonstrations, blockade, and other operations by air, sea, or land forces of Members of the United Nations." Art. 42. When the U.N. Charter was drafted it was assumed that member states would enter into agreements with the Security Council undertaking to provide standing forces to be used by the Council whenever deemed necessary. Article 43 outlines the mechanism for such agreements. In fact, no state has entered into such an agreement with the Security Council so that there are no permanent U.N. forces. Whenever the Security Council determines that armed force is necessary to maintain or restore international peace and security, it asks for states to supply forces on a volunteer basis, and agreements are reached between the Security Council and the states supplying forces with respect to the particular action contemplated.

In 1950, North Korea crossed the 38th parallel into South Korea and hostilities broke out. The Security Council called upon United Nations Members to "furnish such assistance to the Republic of Korea [South Korea] as may be necessary to repel the armed attack and to restore international peace and security in the area." Sixteen states offered assistance, and the Security Council recommended that Members providing assistance "make such forces and other assistance available to a unified command under the United States . . . [who was requested to] designate the commander of such forces . . . [and] at its discretion to use the United Nations flag in the course of operations against North Korean forces. . . ." The nations supplying forces to assist South Korea made agreements with the United States rather than the United Nations. The use of force had been authorized by the United Nations but it was the United States that led and commanded the expedition from the outset.

The legality of the Korean action has long been debated. Some authors maintain that absent U.N. forces mustered under article 43, the Security

Council has no power to authorize a U.N. force. Some have argued that the absence of the U.S.S.R. in the Security Council made the resolutions improper. Article 39 of the Charter gives the Security Council broad powers to decide upon the measures to be taken under article 41 or 42, which can include actions by the forces of member states. Such actions would not strictly be the actions of U.N. forces as such. Almost all of the states involved in the Korean action, however, regarded it as a U.N. action, admittedly led by the United States. The action could also be regarded as the exercise of the right of collective self-defence on behalf of South Korea, although the request and reporting requirements outlined in the *Nicaragua* case were probably not complied with.

After Iraq invaded Kuwait in 1990, the Security Council first imposed economic sanction and later authorized member states "to use all necessary means to uphold and implement Security Council resolution 660 (1990) [demanding Iraqi withdrawal] . . . and to restore international peace and security in the area . . ." This resolution was presumably within the scope of article 39, and there has been no suggestion that the Gulf operation was a U.N. action as such. A coalition of member state forces led by the United States and Britain removed the Iraqi forces from Kuwait five days after the offensive began on February 24, 1991.

(d) United Nations Peacekeeping Forces

Although there is nothing in the U.N. Charter that specifically authorizes the use of peacekeeping forces (in contrast to forces used to restore peace and security), such forces have been increasingly used in recent years. Technically, a force is only dispatched if the host country consents to its presence but if the governmental framework has collapsed this "consent" often occurs in highly confused circumstances. By the end of 1996, sixteen peacekeeping missions were operating under U.N. authorization. Twenty-nine peacekeeping operations were created between 1988 and 1996. Currently (2010) there are fifteen peacekeeping missions around the world and a good number of other peace operations directed by the U.N. Over time, these missions have become increasingly complex and often operate in dangerous situations. The expectation is that the demand for such missions will increase.

The legality of assessing expenses for peacekeeping forces was challenged by a number of states who refused to make any financial contributions assessed by the General Assembly under article 17 for peacekeeping forces in the Congo (ONUC) and the Middle East (UNEF). The General Assembly requested an advisory opinion from the International Court of Justice on the legality of the assessed expenses. In the *Certain Expenses of the United Nations* case, the Court ruled that the expenses were legitimate because they were assessed to fulfill the overall purposes of the United Nations, namely "to

promote and to maintain . . . peaceful settlement of [disputes]. . . ."
Advisory Opinion, 1962 I.C.J. 151, 171-172.

---

§10.5 THE *JUS IN BELLO*

The law described up to this point in the chapter is called *jus ad bellum*. It is the
law concerned with the right to use inter-state force. With few limited
exceptions the use of inter-state force is now prohibited by international
law but history teaches us that we do not always obey the law either at the
municipal level or the international level. Since at least the middle of the
nineteenth century, the modern laws of warfare have sought to create legal
norms applicable while armed conflict is in progress regardless of whether
the resort to force was permissible or not. Much of this law relates to inter-
state armed conflict (IAC) but increasingly the rules are also being applied to
internal armed conflict or non-international armed conflict (NIAC). Gradually a core code of conduct has developed that seeks to regulate the conduct
of war and protect victims of armed conflict both military and civilian. This
area of law is called *international humanitarian law*. The law that seeks to regulate
the types of force used is also found in the various conventions and some
customary law that seeks to prohibit and restrict the use of certain weapons.
Humanitarian law is closely related to human rights law since much of it
seeks to protect military and civilian victims of conflict. Humanitarian law is
the principal body of law applying in armed conflict but human rights law
continues to apply in conflict unless humanitarian law has a specific rule that
would oust the human rights rule. See *Legal Consequences of the Construction of a
Wall in the Occupied Palestinian Territory*, Advisory Opinion, 2004 I.C.J. 136
(July 9) at paras. 102-106. See also §3.11, The Effect of War on Treaties.

§10.5.1 The Regulation of the Conduct of Hostilities

(a) Modern Era History: The Hague and Geneva Conventions

U.S. President Abraham Lincoln is credited with promulgating the first
modern comprehensive code regulating the conduct of hostilities during
the United States Civil War. The *Lieber Code*, named after its chief author
Professor Francis Lieber, was an attempt to codify the laws of war and to
prepare them in a booklet that would serve as instructions to commanders in
the field. The first Hague Peace Conference convened in 1899 adopted the
Convention Concerning the Laws and Customs of War on Land. The Second Hague Peace
Conference of 1907 revised this Convention and adopted the *Convention
concerning the Laws and Customs of War on Land together with appended Hague Regulations.*

The Regulations were intended to form the basis of army manuals for the states parties to the Convention. These conventions and regulations were generally regarded as expressing the customary law of warfare as it existed at that time. They express the underlying principle behind the laws of warfare namely that force may only be used to achieve military advantage, that unnecessary suffering must be avoided and that if suffering is disproportionate to the military advantage gained its infliction is prohibited. From the middle of the nineteenth century, nations began to adopt conventions prohibiting the use of particular types of weapons. (See §10.5.3 infra.)

Thirteen conventions were adopted at the 1907 Hague Conference of which twelve were ratified. These conventions define belligerent status, forbid the use of force against undefended towns, regulate belligerent occupation of territory, set out the rights and responsibilities of neutral states, and prohibit the use of arms calculated to inflict unnecessary suffering. The four 1949 Geneva Conventions together with the two 1977 Protocols[6] now represent the current codification of the laws of war. All of these treaties, and many more, can be downloaded from the ICRC's web site at: http://www.icrc.org/ihl.nsf/INTRO?OpenView.

The four Geneva or "Red Cross" Conventions deal with the treatment of army and navy personnel wounded during combat, the treatment of prisoners of war, and the protection of civilians. A number of warlike practices are forbidden, such as torture, taking hostages, extra judicial executions, deportation, and wanton destruction of property. There are detailed rules on the protection of medical personnel, hospitals, and hospital ships and specific protections for noncombatants. The definition of a combatant came under increasing attack as rebel groups and guerrillas began to appear in many hostilities particularly after World War II. Protocol I tried to readjust the definition of combatant in light of the tactics of modern warfare but has remained controversial. The distinction between the civilian population and military personnel remains the bedrock for the provisions providing protection for civilians. Civilians are not to be the object of a military attack. The Hague Convention for the Protection of Cultural Property in the Event of Armed Conflict, 249 U.N.T.S. 215, protects cultural objects and buildings and those objects necessary to civilian survival, such as food, livestock, and drinking water supplies.

The main criticism leveled against the Geneva Conventions and Protocols is that they are based on the concept of "limited war," where war meant military forces fighting each other, the distinction between combatants and noncombatants was clear, and resources under military control — as opposed to civilian control — could be distinguished. In a world where "total war" is possible and where an entire nation's effort can be turned

---

6. 75 U.N.T.S. 31; 75 U.N.T.S. 85; 75 U.N.T.S. 135; 75 U.N.T.S. 287; 1125 U.N.T.S. 3; 1129 U.N.T.S. 609.

toward the war enterprise it is argued that the traditional laws of war no longer make sense. Before you are ready to throw out the conventional and customary laws of war, however, it is salutary to remember that all wars since World War II have in fact been limited wars fought with non-nuclear weapons. In many of these conflicts, the distinctions worked out in the conventions largely apply. A second major criticism leveled at the conventions is that many, if not most, current conflicts are the result of civil wars and that the conventions and protocols primarily address inter-state conflicts thus leaving internal conflicts largely unregulated by international law. The rise of international, non-governmental, paramilitary groups who launch attacks in a variety of locations throughout the world has also challenged the traditional application of the laws of war. The 1949 Conventions are indeed primarily concerned with international hostilities. However, each of the four 1949 Conventions has what is known as *Common Article 3*, which provides:

> *Article* 3. In the case of armed conflict not of an international character occurring in the territory of one of the High Contracting Parties, each Party to the conflict shall be bound to apply, as a minimum, the following provisions:
>
> (1) Persons taking no active part in the hostilities, including members of armed forces who have laid down their arms and those placed *hors de combat* by sickness, wounds, detention, or any other cause, shall in all circumstances be treated humanely, without any adverse distinction founded on race, colour, religion or faith, sex, birth or wealth, or any other similar criteria.
>
> To this end, the following acts are and shall remain prohibited at any time and in any place whatsoever with respect to the above-mentioned persons:
>
> (a) violence to life and person, in particular murder of all kinds, mutilation, cruel treatment and torture;
>
> (b) taking of hostages;
>
> (c) outrages upon personal dignity, in particular, humiliating and degrading treatment;
>
> (d) the passing of sentences and the carrying out of executions without previous judgment pronounced by a regularly constituted court affording all the judicial guarantees which are recognized as indispensable by civilized peoples.
>
> (2) The wounded and sick shall be collected and cared for.
>
> An impartial humanitarian body, such as the International Committee of the Red Cross, may offer its services to the Parties to the conflict.
>
> The Parties to the conflict should further endeavor to bring into force, by means of special agreements, all or part of the other provisions of the present Convention.
>
> The application of the preceding provisions shall not affect the legal status of the parties to the conflict.

This article provides a standard of treatment for noncombatants, the wounded, and prisoners in non-international armed conflicts. Protocol II develops these standards further and is specifically applicable to "all armed conflicts [not covered by article 1 to Protocol II] . . . which take place in the territory of a High Contracting Party between its armed forces and dissident armed forces or other organized armed groups which, under responsible command, exercise such control over a part of its territory as to enable them to carry out sustained and concerted military operations and to implement this Protocol." Protocol II, art. 1(1). The Protocol does not apply to "internal disturbances and tensions, such as riots, isolated and sporadic acts of violence and other acts of a similar nature, as not being armed conflict." Id. at art. 1(2). Trying to decide when the threshold level of violence has been reached sufficient to trigger the Protocol is obviously difficult.

The Protocol guarantees fundamental protection for noncombatants, the wounded, and prisoners. Certain activities are absolutely prohibited, such as torture, collective punishments, rape, enforced prostitution, and pillage. Special protection is given to children. Prisoners must be treated humanely, and no form of penalty may be carried out against prisoners unless pronounced by a court providing the fundamentals of fairness and impartiality.

The law applicable to internal hostilities is clearly in need of further development. Sassoli and Bouvier, the authors of a well-known textbook on international humanitarian law, state that they begin to see the distinct areas of international and internal armed conflict law moving together:

> In recent years, the IHL [international humanitarian law] of non-international armed conflicts is however drawing closer to the IHL of international conflicts: through the jurisprudence of the International Criminal Tribunals for the former Yugoslavia and Rwanda based upon their assessment of customary international law; in the crimes defined in the Statute of the International Criminal Court; by States having accepted that both categories of conflicts are covered by recent treaties on weapons and on the protection of cultural objects; under the growing influence of International Human Rights Law and according to the outcome of the ICRC [International Committee of the Red Cross] Study on customary international humanitarian law. (Footnotes omitted). I Marco Sassoli & Antoine A. Bouvier, *How Does Law Protect in War?* 250 (2d ed. 2006).

It remains to be seen whether the nations of the world are prepared to develop or merge these areas of law or to comply with the law once agreed upon.

Since their establishment in the 1990s, the International Criminal Tribunal for the former Yugoslavia and the International Criminal Tribunal for Rwanda have issued a number of judgments on a large variety of international humanitarian law issues. The International Criminal Court was established in 2002. It has now indicted several people and a few cases are now underway. (See Chapter 11 on International Criminal Law, where all three tribunals are discussed in more detail.)

§10.5.2 Specific Rules of International Humanitarian Law (IHL)

(a) Introduction

As noted above, the specific laws relating to armed conflict are found in the Hague Conventions, the four Geneva Conventions, the two Additional Protocols to the Geneva Conventions, and customary law. The laws are often very detailed covering a great range of subjects, such as the treatment of prisoners of war and rules regulating armies of occupation. Dealing with the complexity of all of these rules and their application is beyond the scope of this book. What follows are some materials on a few of the central rules of armed conflict.

(b) The Principle of Distinction and the Definition of Combatants/Military Objects and Civilians/Civilian Objects

The parties to the conflict must distinguish between civilians and combatants. Combatants and military objects can be attacked, and killing a combatant or destroying a military object is not a crime. (This is known as the combatant's privilege.) Civilians and civilian objects may not be attacked. All weapons must be able to distinguish between civilians and civilian objects, on the one hand, and military personnel and military objects, on the other. Indiscriminate attacks are forbidden. Although civilians or civilian objects may be killed, injured, or destroyed, such casualties are only permitted when the civilian destruction is incidental to attack on a legitimate military target **and** only when the civilian casualties are not "excessive in relation to the concrete and direct military advantage anticipated." Additional Protocol I, at art. 51(5)(b).

The principle of distinction is obviously dependent upon a careful definition of who or what is counted as a combatant or military object, and who or what is counted as a civilian or civilian object. Combatants in IAC are members of the armed forces of a party to the conflict (except for religious and medical personnel) and certain other persons who take a direct part in the hostilities. We find more detailed language in the definition of a prisoner of war in the Third Geneva Convention, article 4(A), which sets out requirements for lawful combatancy. If the requirements below are met, then the combatant is entitled to prisoner of war (POW) status if captured by the enemy. During the conflict the prisoner must be treated humanely and at the end of hostilities must be repatriated.

> Prisoners of war . . . are persons belonging to one of the following categories, who have fallen into the power of the enemy:
>
> (1) Members of the armed forces of a Party to the conflict, as well as members of militias or volunteer corps forming part of such armed forces.
>
> (2) Members of other militias and members of other volunteer corps, including those of organized resistance movements, belonging to a Party to the conflict and operating in or outside their own territory, even if this territory is occupied, provided that such militias or volunteer corps, including such organized resistance movements, fulfil the following conditions:
>
> (a) that of being commanded by a person responsible for his subordinates;
>
> (b) that of having a fixed distinctive sign recognizable at a distance;
>
> (c) that of carrying arms openly;
>
> (d) that of conducting their operations in accordance with the laws and customs of war. Geneva Convention III, art. 4(A).

These latter four requirements are cumulative and must all be fulfilled. There are a few other less important categories of persons who also fit the definition of POW, such as accredited "war correspondents" (art. 4(A)(4)) and civilians who spontaneously take up arms in a nonoccupied territory to resist an invading force (art. 4(A)(6)).

Example 10-6

When the U.S. attacked Afghanistan in the fall of 2001 after planes had crashed into the World Trade Center in New York and the Pentagon in Washington, D.C., the U.S. forces joined up with Afghanistan's Northern Alliance forces who were fighting the Taliban. You should assume that this war then became an international conflict although some scholars dispute this characterization. The Taliban forces had ousted the previous government and controlled about ninety percent of the country. The Northern Alliance forces seldom had distinguishable uniforms and many of the attached militias wore their tribal clothes. The U.S. forces generally wore U.S. uniforms, although there were reports of some wearing tribal clothing even when in combat.

If a member of the Northern Alliance forces wearing tribal clothing and no other distinguishing insignia were captured by the Taliban forces during combat, should that person be classified as a combatant and entitled to POW status? If a member of the U.S. forces only wearing the Afghan tribal clothes similar to those worn by the Northern Alliance were captured by the Taliban in combat, should that person be classified as a combatant and entitled to POW status?

Explanation

This question raises a number of issues: The first is whether a member of the Northern Alliance forces is a member of the armed forces of a party to the conflict. Assuming that is the case, then the issue is whether members of the armed forces have to meet the four cumulative requirements listed in Geneva III, article 4(A)(2) (see above), including the requirement for a fixed distinctive sign recognizable at a distance, or whether these requirements only apply to "other militias." Note that there is a period after clause (1), before mention of "other militias" in article 4(A)(2) of Geneva III cited above. The few courts that have examined the issue have determined that it was always assumed that regular armies would meet these requirements. If they did not, then they could be denied combatant/POW status. Assuming then that both the member of the Northern Alliance and the member of the U.S. forces must meet the requirement of wearing a fixed, distinctive, recognizable sign, the question then becomes whether tribal clothes meet that criteria. Professor Yoram Dinstein concludes that "irregular armed forces need not have any uniform, and suffice it for them to possess a less complex fixed distinctive emblem: part of the clothing (like a special shirt or a particular headgear) or certain insignia." The Conduct of Hostilities under the Law of International Armed Conflict 37 (2004). Provided the tribal clothes were distinctive enough and generally known to be what Northern Alliance warriors wore, the member of the Northern Alliance and the member of the U.S. forces might well be entitled to combatant/POW status. The tribal clothes would count as a fixed distinctive sign recognizable at a distance. (Without a doubt, the member of the U.S. forces would have violated U.S. forces internal rules that require the wearing of U.S. uniforms during combat, and might be reprimanded, but the violation of that internal rule would not mean that the international rule was violated.)

If the only permissible targets during conflict are enemy soldiers or military objects, in addition to defining combatants, we also need a definition of military objects. Additional Protocol I, article 52(2) provides the definition:

Military objects or objectives are:

> those objects which by their nature, location, purpose or use make an effective contribution to military action and whose total or partial destruction, capture or neutralization, in the circumstances ruling at the time, offers a definite military advantage.

This definition is perhaps intentionally broad and generic given the myriad objects that could make an effective contribution to military action and whose removal would offer military advantage; nonetheless, it is often criticized as too vague.

On the other side of the equation, civilians are those people who take no direct part in hostilities and are not members of the armed forces. Civilian objects are defined as any object that is not a military object. Additional Protocol I, art. 52(1). Civilians and civilian objects may not be attacked, but if civilians take an active or direct part in hostilities, they lose their civilian status and the protections that go with it. Additional Protocol I, art. 51(3). The question of what counts as direct participation in hostilities is difficult to answer.

Example 10-7

Below are the descriptions of civilian citizens of a country engaged in IAC:

(a) A driver of a truck delivering ammunition to troops.

(b) A driver of a truck delivering food to an army camp.

(c) A member of the civilian intelligence service who monitors data received from spy satellites and passes on data that may be useful to his or her nation's military efforts against the enemy.

(d) A person who supplies tires to his or her nation's army.

(e) A person who hacks into the enemy's military computer system causing it to crash and totally impairing the enemy's ability to wage war.

Which of the above civilians would you say is engaged in direct or active participation in hostilities?

Explanation

There are probably no definitive answers to these examples. However, the food deliverer seems the furthest away from direct or active participation in hostilities and the deliverer of ammunition and the computer hacker seem the closest to direct or active participation in hostilities. The intelligence gatherer and the tire supplier seem to fall in the middle of the spectrum. As the nature of warfare changes, it may be that the computer hacker could play the most direct or active part in hostilities. Certainly, an ability to make the enemy's military computer system crash could have a decisive effect on the outcome of hostilities. The hacker is not present on the battlefield firing weapons but the effect of shutting down the enemy's military computer system could be to immobilize the enemy just as surely as if the hacker had dropped a devastating weapon on enemy forces.

(c) Treatment of Those Captured in Armed Conflict

During a war, when members of the armed forces capture members of the opposing enemy forces, at whose hands they may well have risked life and limb, there may well be an urge to inflict immediate punishment on those captured. Over the centuries, clear laws have evolved requiring the humane treatment of those captured in warfare. If you wonder why any nation would sign up to such restraint, remember that when your own forces are captured, the law will also require restraint of the enemy thus protecting your own armed forces.

If the captured enemy is a lawful combatant in IAC then the Third Geneva Convention Relative to the Treatment of Prisoners of War, 75 U.N.T.S. 135, contains detailed provisions on treatment covering a multitude of requirements ranging from housing, food, and clothing to medical treatment and religious activities. Article 13 provides: "Prisoners of war must at all times be humanely treated." Although a POW can be tried by military courts for violations of the laws of war or violations of the laws and regulations of the detaining power, such courts must have certain essential guarantees of independence and impartiality. POWs cannot be tried for killing the enemy.

When it comes to interrogation, article 17, paragraph 1 requires POWs to give "only his surname, first name and rank, date of birth, and army, regimental, personal or serial number. . . ." This provision does not prevent the detaining power from asking more questions, and questioning may last for a period of time. However, if the POW declines to answer anything other than what is required by article 17, paragraph 1, then paragraph 4 of article 17 states:

> No physical or mental torture, nor any other form of coercion, may be inflicted on prisoners of war to secure from them information of any kind whatsoever. Prisoners of war who refuse to answer may not be threatened, insulted, or exposed to unpleasant or disadvantageous treatment of any kind. Geneva III, art. 17, para. 4.

In NIAC, as noted above, Common article 3 to each of the four Geneva Conventions requires that those:

> Who have laid down their arms and those placed *hors de combat* by sickness, wounds, detention, or any other cause, shall in all circumstances be treated humanely. . . .

The following acts are always prohibited:

> (a) violence to life and person, in particular murder of all kinds, mutilation, cruel treatment and torture;
> (b) taking of hostages;
> (c) outrages upon personal dignity, in particular, humiliating and degrading treatment;

(d) the passing of sentences and the carrying out of executions without previous judgment pronounced by a regularly constituted court affording all the judicial guarantees which are recognized as indispensable by civilized peoples. These provisions are expanded upon in Additional Protocol I, article 75.

It should also be added that the Convention Against Torture, 1465 U.N.T.S. 85, to which more than 140 countries are currently party, defines torture and prohibits it in any territory under a state party's jurisdiction. It also provides:

No exceptional circumstances whatsoever, whether a state of war or a threat of war, internal political instability or any other public emergency, may be invoked as a justification of torture. *Id.* at art. 2, para. 2.

What about treatment of persons engaged in armed conflict who are not lawful combatants? How must they be treated? Although some governments have maintained that international law does not address the issue of their treatment and that they can be treated in whatever manner the detaining power determines, this view has been firmly rejected by the vast majority of jurists and scholars. The fundamental guarantee of humane treatment is required with specific prohibition on torture, murder, corporal punishment, and mutilation. See Additional Protocol I, art. 75, the Convention Against Torture, art. 2, and Common Article 3.

Example 10-8

In an IAC an enemy general is captured. He is thought to know the enemy's specific bombardment plans for the next week. If the detaining power can learn of these plans, thousands of lives could be saved. The general supplies his full name, rank, date of birth, and serial number to his interrogators. He refuses to answer any further questions.

What may the detaining power do to persuade the general to divulge the enemy's battle plans?

Explanation

Presumably the general is a POW. He has supplied all the information required by the Geneva Conventions. The detaining power may continue to question him but he must at all times be treated humanely. He cannot be tortured, coerced, threatened or insulted, or exposed to unpleasant or disadvantageous treatment. If you think that these laws are too favorable to the POW, always remember that when your forces are captured, they cannot be made to expose your battle plans. It is also worth reflecting that although the detaining power may suspect that the general knows about future battle plans, he may not in fact have any such knowledge. Most experienced interrogators also agree that little reliable information is gained by the harsh treatment of detainees.

§10.5.3 Weapons Control

The great principle of the laws of warfare is that force is only permissible to achieve military advantage, and all unnecessary suffering is prohibited. The law distinguishes between combatants and civilians and lays down specific protections for civilians. States are not permitted to attack civilians or civilian buildings and may not use weapons that cannot distinguish between military and civilian targets. When it became apparent that certain weapons did not simply kill the enemy but inflicted great suffering in the process, conventions began to outlaw certain types of weapons.

(a) Historical Progression

For citations to weapons conventions, see http://www.icrc.org/.

The 1868 Declaration of St. Petersburg prohibited the use of certain explosive projectiles. The 1899 Hague Conference adopted a Convention forbidding certain weapons, and several Declarations regulated the use of expanding (dum-dum) bullets, projectiles and explosives launched from balloons, and projectiles diffusing asphyxiating or deleterious gases. A later Hague Conference of 1907 adopted Conventions regulating the laying of automatic submarine contact mines and bombardment by naval forces in time of war. The Protocol of 1925 prohibited the use of asphyxiating, poisonous, and other gases during time of war and forbade the use of bacteriological methods of warfare.

In 1972, the Convention on the Prohibition of the Development, Production and Stockpiling of Bacteriological (Biological) and Toxin Weapons and on their Destruction was signed. This Convention entered into force in 1975. In 1993 the principles and objectives of the 1925 Protocol and the 1972 Convention were reaffirmed and updated by a new Convention on the Prohibition of the Development, Production, Stockpiling and Use of Chemical Weapons and on their Destruction. The Convention, which entered into force in 1997, absolutely prohibits the use of chemical weapons "under any circumstance" and requires the destruction of all such weapons and any chemical weapons production facilities.

In 1980, the Convention on Prohibitions or Restrictions on the Use of Certain Conventional Weapons Which May Be Deemed to Be Excessively Injurious or to Have Indiscriminate Effects was adopted. Three Protocols were appended to the Convention: The Protocol on Non-Detectable Fragments (Protocol I), the Protocol on Prohibitions or Restrictions on the Use of Mines, Booby-Traps and Other Devices (Protocol II); and the Protocol on Prohibitions or Restrictions on the Use of Incendiary Weapons (Protocol III). A fourth Protocol on Blinding Laser Weapons was adopted in 1995 and entered into force in 1998. A fifth Protocol on Explosive Remnants of War was adopted in 2003 and entered into force in 2006.

In 1996, the international community amended the Protocol on Prohibitions and Restrictions on the Use of Mines, Booby-Traps and Other Devices. More recently, in September, 1997, the international community endorsed a treaty banning the use of land mines. The Convention was officially opened for signature in December 1997 and rapidly entered force. There are now over 156 states that have ratified the treaty, which entered into force in 1999. Most recently, the Convention on Cluster Munitions was adopted in May 2008 and entered into force in 2010.

(b) Nuclear Weapons

The creation of nuclear weapons heralded the possibility of mass destruction on a vast scale. The use of nuclear weapons during World War II by the United States against Japan proved that the devastation of such weapons was indeed unprecedented, not only with respect to the numbers of people killed and buildings razed, but also with respect to the number of subsequent initiatives to regulate nuclear weapons. These initiatives fall into four main categories: conventions or declarations that limit the spread or use of nuclear weapons; conventions that call for the reduction of nuclear weapons; conventions that declare certain areas of the world nuclear free; and conventions that prohibit the testing of nuclear weapons. Below is a list of some of the more important conventions in this area. The Advisory Opinion of the International Court of Justice on the *Legality of the Threat or Use of Nuclear Weapons*, 1996 I.C.J. 226, discussed below, contains a much more comprehensive list of conventions, resolutions, and declarations.

(i) *Conventions and Declarations that Limit the Spread or Use of Nuclear Weapons*

Treaty on the Non-Proliferation of Nuclear Weapons. Under this treaty the parties with nuclear weapons agree not to transfer nuclear weapons or nuclear explosive devices to non-nuclear states and not to assist such states in the manufacture or acquisition of such weapons. The non-nuclear parties agree not to receive such weapons or to manufacture or acquire them. All parties are permitted to develop nuclear energy for peaceful purposes.

The treaty was extended indefinitely in 1995, and the five declared nuclear weapon states gave various security assurances to the non-nuclear state parties. The 2000 Review Conference examined implementation procedures. The 2005 Conference brought into focus wide disagreements between those who wanted serious progress toward total nuclear disarmament and those who wanted to pursue enforcement actions against noncooperating member states, such as Iran. The 2010 Review Conference has faced similar concerns.

Declaration on the Prohibition of the Use of Nuclear and Thermo-Nuclear Weapons. This General Assembly resolution declares that the use of nuclear weapons violates the United Nations Charter.

(ii) *Conventions that Call for the Reduction of Nuclear Weapons*

Over many years, the U.S. and U.S.S.R., now Russia, have entered into a number of bilateral treaties on the reduction of nuclear weapons, most of which have now expired. In 2010, U.S. President Obama and Russian President Medvedev signed a new Strategic Arms Reduction Treaty (START), pledging to reduce their country's nuclear arsenals. The treaty was ratified by the U.S. in December 2010 and now remains to be ratified by Russia to become operative.

(iii) *Conventions that Declare Certain Areas of the World Nuclear Weapons Free*

Treaties prohibiting nuclear weapons in certain areas now cover the Antarctic, Outer Space, Latin America and the Caribbean, the South Pacific, parts of Africa, parts of Southeast Asia, and parts of Central Asia.

(iv) *Conventions that Prohibit the Testing of Nuclear Weapons*

A treaty now prohibits the testing of nuclear weapons in the atmosphere, outer space, and underwater for treaty parties. Some would argue that this prohibition has become customary law binding all states but others would disagree.

One hundred and fifty-three states have already ratified the Comprehensive Nuclear Test Ban Treaty (available at: http://www.ctbto.org/) but it will not go into force until forty-four designated states have ratified it. Thirty-five of the required forty-four states have currently ratified the treaty. Under this convention each state party "undertakes not to carry out any nuclear weapon test explosion or any other nuclear explosion and to prohibit and prevent any such nuclear explosion at any place under its jurisdiction or control." Art. I.

(v) *The I.C.J.'s Advisory Opinion on Nuclear Weapons*

The General Assembly of the United Nations submitted the following question to the International Court of Justice requesting an advisory opinion: "Is the threat or use of nuclear weapons in any circumstances permitted under international law?" The Court delivered its opinion in the summer of 1996. 1996 I.C.J. 226.

In order to answer this question the Court undertook a comprehensive review of a number of areas of law. For example, it reviewed international environmental law to see whether any of the principles of that law would outlaw nuclear weapons in all circumstances (see §13.7 below). The Court first examined treaty law and customary law but did not find any "comprehensive and universal prohibition of the threat or use of nuclear weapons as such" in either body of law. It next turned to international humanitarian law applicable in armed conflict. Some states argued that IHL was not applicable to nuclear weapons but the Court rejected that approach: "In the view of the vast majority of States as well as writers there can be no doubt as to the applicability of humanitarian law to nuclear weapons. The Court shares that view." *Nuclear Weapons* Advisory Opinion, *supra* at paras. 85-86. The Court then outlined the main principles of IHL:

> The cardinal principles contained in the texts constituting the fabric of humanitarian law are the following. The first is aimed at the protection of the civilian population and civilian objects and establishes the distinction between combatants and non-combatants; States must never make civilians the object of attack and must consequently never use weapons that are incapable of distinguishing between civilian and military targets. According to the second principle, it is prohibited to cause unnecessary suffering to combatants: it is accordingly prohibited to use weapons causing them such harm or uselessly aggravating their suffering. In application of that second principle, States do not have unlimited freedom of choice of means in the weapons they use. *Id.* at para. 78.

To these "cardinal principles" should be added the rule on collateral civilian damage known as the principle of proportionality. Judge Higgins in her dissenting opinion in the *Nuclear Weapons* Advisory Opinion restated the rule:

> The principle of proportionality . . . is reflected in many provisions of Additional Protocol I to the Geneva Conventions of 1949. Thus even a legitimate target may not be attacked if the collateral civilian casualties would be disproportionate to the specific military gain from the attack. *Nuclear Weapons*, Advisory Opinion, 1996 I.C.J. 226, at 587.

The rule in Protocol I prohibits an attack on a legitimate military target where the

> incidental loss of civilian life, injury to civilians, damage to civilian objects, or a combination thereof, . . . would be excessive in relation to the concrete and direct military advantage anticipated. Protocol I, 1125 U.N.T.S. 3, at art. 51(5)(b).

Example 10-9

You have no doubt read about the effect of nuclear weapons dropped in Japan toward the end of World War II, and you now know about many of the treaties that ban specific weapons because they violate the main principles of international humanitarian law (IHL).

Do you think that nuclear weapons can comply with the central principles of IHL as stated by the Court above?

Explanation

The three central principle of IHL as stated by the Court are: (1) weapons must be able to distinguish between civilian and military targets — civilians and civilian objects may not be targeted; (2) although civilians may end up getting killed or injured as "collateral damage" — where a military commander knows or should know that civilians may be harmed collateral to an attack on military personnel or military objects — the target must be abandoned where the civilian casualties are expected to be excessive in relation to the military advantage; and (3) no weapon may cause unnecessary suffering, even to those legitimately targeted.

In the two examples of the dropping of nuclear weapons at the end of World War II by U.S. forces on the cities of Hiroshima and Nagasaki, there were massive numbers of civilians killed and injured and widespread damage to civilian infrastructure. Because of the size of the bombs dropped, it is hard to conceive that those weapons could distinguish between military and civilian targets in urban environments. There has been a long debate over whether the use of the nuclear bombs aided in ending the war more quickly in the Far East and thus whether, ultimately, lives were saved. The calculation about collateral civilian damage (which was not made concrete until 1977), however, requires the calculation to be made for the particular attack, not for the overall war, and thus it does not seem possible that the scope of the civilian deaths and the destruction of civilian structures could be justified under the present collateral damage calculation.

Nuclear weapons also cause long-term suffering for those who are not killed immediately. There are many studies measuring the devastating long-term health effects on people who were at various distances from the center of the detonation. The health consequences are still being felt today more than sixty years later.

Some people have argued that newer generations of nuclear weapons, known as low-yield nuclear weapons, could be targeted entirely at a military target, such as an army marching in the desert or a naval warship in the middle of the ocean. If such uses of nuclear weapons were possible, it is argued, all of the military personnel could be killed instantaneously, and there would be no collateral civilian damage and no unnecessary suffering.

Such weapons used in such circumstances, it is argued, would comply with the rule of distinction, the civilian collateral damage rule, and the rule prohibiting unnecessary suffering. We do not, as yet, have a specific treaty forbidding nuclear weapons. In fact, the Non-Proliferation Treaty contemplates the possession of nuclear weapons by five named states.

§10.6 CONCLUSION

Those who are generally skeptical about the legitimacy or efficacy of international law tend to be even more skeptical about the laws of armed conflict. They remain convinced that armed force is either entirely, or largely, regulated by power and that militarily powerful states can (and/ or should be allowed to) do whatever they wish. Although all law experiences levels of noncompliance and varying levels of ineffective enforcement, we do not usually point to those factors as a reason to abolish the law in question or to abandon the attempt to subject the particular activity to a legal regime. All nations prohibit murder but murder occurs in all countries, sometimes it is quite prevalent for a variety of reasons. The percentage of murderers brought to justice also varies widely from country to country. Nonetheless, no one call for legalizing murder or for abandoning the attempt to regulate murder by law. In the modern era, every government that has waged war has argued strongly (even if sometimes incorrectly) that they were complying with international law. Sub-state groups tend to espouse ideological agendas. Their arguments are either that international law permits (or supports) their cause, or sometimes that they are not regulated by international law, or indeed any law. Most would disagree with such a view. Before you reject law as a useful tool in curbing resort to war and ameliorating its consequences, reflect on the alternatives. All law seeks to subject everyone to rules made applicable to all regardless of status or power. Law fundamentally rejects the notion that "might makes right." Without law operating in the arena of armed conflict, we are doomed to the terrible exigencies experienced by humanity before the dawn of legal systems. Without the *jus ad bellum* and the *jus in bello*, power will indeed determine what is permissible in the initiation and conduct of armed conflict.

International Criminal Law

11

§11.1 Introduction

§11.2 Definition of Crimes

    §11.2.1   Genocide

    §11.2.2   War Crimes

    §11.2.3   Crimes Against Humanity

    §11.2.4   The Crime of Aggression

§11.3 Individual Responsibility

§11.4 Defenses

    §11.4.1   Specific Defenses

§11.5 State Responsibility

§11.6 International and Hybrid (National/International) Criminal Tribunals

    §11.6.1   International Criminal Tribunals: Introduction

    §11.6.2   The Nuremberg Trials

    §11.6.3   The Tokyo Trials

    §11.6.4   The International Criminal Tribunal for the Former Yugoslavia

    §11.6.5   The International Criminal Tribunal for Rwanda

    §11.6.6   The International Criminal Court

    §11.6.7   Hybrid (National/International) Criminal Tribunals: Introduction

    §11.6.8   The Special Court for Sierra Leone

    §11.6.9   The East Timor Tribunal

§11.6.10 The Extraordinary Chambers in the Courts
          of Cambodia
§11.6.11 The Special Tribunal for Lebanon

§11.1 INTRODUCTION

All states have criminal codes that prohibit certain activity either when carried out within the state's territory or when committed by a national within or outside the state, or when the activity meets one of the other jurisdictional connections (see Chapter 6) and the state decides to prohibit and prosecute such activities. If the activity in question reaches beyond the state's borders, or is considered to be of universal concern, such as money laundering or terrorism, various methods of transnational criminal enforcement mechanisms have developed over time, such as sharing of information and extradition treaties (see §6.7).

This chapter deals with a related but distinct aspect of criminal law. There are certain crimes, such as genocide, war crimes, crimes against humanity, and the crime of aggression, which the international community has decided stand out as particularly heinous. As a result, either by treaty or custom, the community of states has determined that such activity should be prosecuted. The result is that such crimes can be tried either in national courts (provided the particular state adds the crime to its criminal code) or in an international or hybrid (national/international) criminal tribunal, provided a tribunal has been created with jurisdiction over the particular crime. The idea here is that the individual bears criminal responsibility for these crimes and that either national courts will try the individual or the international community will prosecute the individual using an international criminal court.

§11.2 DEFINITION OF CRIMES

Ever since the Nuremberg and Tokyo Trials, which occurred after World War II (see §§11.6.2 and 11.6.3), the definition of the crimes classified as international crimes has been undergoing intense examination and refinement. Each new international or hybrid tribunal will have a statute drawn up regulating its operations. The nature of the crimes that the tribunal can prosecute will be defined in detail. The definitions found in each new court's statute tend to differ somewhat although there are certain core concepts that have emerged.

§11.2.1 Genocide

In 1948, in the wake of the atrocities committed against Jews and other definable groups during World War II, the General Assembly adopted the Convention on the Prevention and Punishment of the Crime of Genocide, 78 U.N.T.S. 277. The Convention entered into force in 1951 and 141 states are now party to this treaty. The treaty makes genocide a crime "whether committed in time of peace or in time of war" (art. I) and the parties "undertake to prevent and to punish" this crime. *Id.*

Article II of the Convention defines the crime:

> In the present Convention, genocide means any of the following acts committed with intent to destroy, in whole or in part, a national, ethnical, racial or religious group, as such:
> (a) Killing members of the group;
> (b) Causing serious bodily or mental harm to the group;
> (c) Deliberately inflicting on the group conditions of life calculated to bring about its physical destruction in whole or in part;
> (d) Imposing measures intended to prevent births within the group;
> (e) Forcibly transferring children of the group to another group.

Historically, there had been very few prosecutions for genocide in national courts. More recently, German and Bosnian courts have convicted defendants of genocide. The newly established international and hybrid courts have also convicted several people of the crime of genocide. For example, Jean Kambanda, a former Prime Minister of Rwanda, pled guilty to genocide before the Rwanda Tribunal and was convicted in 1998. The same year, Jean Paul Akayesu, the former mayor of a town, was also convicted of genocide by the ICTR. More recently, in 2010, Yussuf Munyakazi, a businessman, was convicted of genocide and sentenced to twenty-five years in prison by that Tribunal. In 2010, the Yugoslav Tribunal also convicted two Bosnian Serb army officers for genocide for their part in the Srebrenica massacre of 1995 and another officer was convicted of aiding and abetting genocide.

All of these cases have discussed the various elements of the crime of genocide and have explained exactly what has to be proved by the prosecution to meet the requirements of the crime. A discussion of the precise elements of the various international crimes is beyond the scope of this book but materials focusing in depth on international criminal law will necessarily pay much attention to such matters including the necessary mental attitude (*mens rea*) required for conviction.

Example 11-1

In Cambodia, from 1975-1979 — when the Khmer Rouge government was in power — between one million and three million people died. In 2010, the Extraordinary Chambers in the Courts of Cambodia convicted Kaing Guek Eav of crimes against humanity and war crimes for his role in the death of at least 12,000 individuals in a prison camp where he was Deputy Chairman and later Chairman. See §11.6.10 below.

Why do you think Kaing was not charged with genocide?

Explanation

Although the general public tends to think of genocide as mass killing, the definition is much more precise (see definition above). The prosecutor has to be able to show that the alleged perpetrator had the "intent to destroy, in whole or in part, a national, ethnical, racial or religious group as such," and then demonstrate one or more of the acts listed in the definition directed toward the target group. Although a very small number of deaths would probably not count as genocide because it would be very difficult to prove that a particular group was being targeted, you should note that the definition does not include any number count. Perhaps the main problem in Kaing's case was the fact that virtually all of those killed were of the same national, ethnical, racial, and/or religious group as the perpetrator. He wasn't picking them out because of their distinguishing characteristics. To quote from the web site of the Holocaust Museum in Houston, Texas:

> Many genocide scholars believe these events [the Cambodian killings] do not qualify as genocide under the United Nations Convention, but instead call it an "auto-genocide" because it occurred across all of society instead of targeting one group. http://www.hmh.org/ed_Genocide_Cambodia.shtml.

§11.2.2 War Crimes

Chapter 10 examined the division of international humanitarian law into the jus ad bellum, the law with respect to the initiation of armed force, as well as the jus in bello, the law that applies to those involved in armed conflict. War crimes occur when individuals who are engaged in armed conflict, either international or internal, violate the treaty or customary law that applies in armed conflict. War crimes can also be committed by civilians when their illegal actions are facilitated by, or closely related to, the armed conflict. Prosecution, which may take place in national, military or regular, or in international or hybrid courts, usually concerns the more serious violations of the jus in bello. For example, in §10.5.2(b) above, the principle of distinction was examined under which parties to a conflict must always distinguish between civilians/civilian objects (which may not be attacked) and combatants/military objects (which may be attacked). Civilians may be attacked only, and only for so long as, they are taking a direct part in hostilities, or incidentally, as collateral damage to a legitimate attack on a military target where the civilian casualties are not "excessive in relation to the concrete and direct military advantage anticipated." API, at art. 51(5)(b). Once combatants or civilians are taken prisoner, they may not be attacked and must be treated humanely.

Example 11-2

The State of Artilla has been engaged in a bloody war with its neighbor, the State of Zuba, for three years. Civilians in Zuba are very supportive of their troops and, despite government regulations forbidding any civilian participation in the hostilities, the civilian population often takes potshots at enemy soldiers as they enter villages and towns. Captain Creeley was a platoon commander for the Artilla army. As he and his platoon approached a Zuma village, several shots were fired at them. Creeley had received information from Artilla intelligence services that there were no Zuma armed forces in the area. None of Creeley's men were killed by the gunfire but three were wounded, although not seriously. Creeley ordered his men to return fire, which they did. They saw five villagers fall to the ground. Creeley and his platoon waited fifteen minutes before advancing on the village. No gunfire was directed at them at this time. The sixty remaining villagers consisted of twenty children, ten very old men, twenty women, and ten teenagers. They were all huddled together weeping over the bodies of the five men who had been killed by Creeley's platoon. The only weapons in evidence were hunting rifles. One hunting rifle lay beside each of the five dead villagers.

Captain Creeley ordered the villagers to be lined up and shot. He personally shot all of them.

Can Captain Creeley be accused of war crimes (a) for ordering his men to return fire after the platoon had been fired on, which resulted in the death of five villagers; and (b) for shooting the sixty remaining villagers?

Explanation

Creeley cannot be accused of war crimes for ordering his men to return fire after the platoon had been fired on. As long as the villagers were directly participating in hostilities, they were legitimate targets. The fact that each dead man had a weapon lying beside him is evidence that each of those villagers were directly participating in hostilities. (Moreover, the platoon's response does not appear disproportionate.)

Creeley certainly can be accused of war crimes for shooting the remaining sixty villagers. Even if some of them had been involved in shooting at Creeley's platoon, by the time they were shot, they were all disarmed villagers who had been taken prisoner or interned as civilians. The villagers were either civilians, who cannot be targeted, or they were prisoners/internees who cannot be shot and must be treated humanely. Barring any surprise defense, not evident from the facts above, Creeley should be convicted. Cf. *U.S. v. Calley*, 22 U.S.C.M.A. 534 (1973); 48 C.M.R. 19 (1973); sub nom. *Calley v. Callaway*, 382 F. Supp. 650 (M.D. Ga. 1974); rev'd 519 F.2d 184 (5th Cir. 1975); cert. denied sub nom. *Calley v. Hoffman*, 425 U.S. 911 (1976).

There are numerous acts during warfare that can be classified as war crimes (which are beyond the scope of this book) but in general they will involve the targeting or abuse of civilians or those no longer participating in hostilities, or the abuse of those captured, or violating the various restrictions on the means and methods of warfare. If you would like to read a comprehensive list of war crimes, read article 8 of the ICC Statute, available at http://www.icc-cpi.int/.

In international armed conflict, war crimes include such acts as: acts directed against persons protected by the four Geneva Conventions of 1949 (e.g., civilians, prisoners, the wounded), such as willful killing, torture or inhumane treatment, wilfully causing great suffering, extensive destruction and appropriation of property, unlawful detention, and taking of hostages; or other serious violations, such as intentionally targeting civilians, attacking undefended towns and villages, killing or wounding a combatant who has laid down arms, attacking religious or educational buildings, refusing to take prisoners (i.e., killing anyone even if they have laid down their arms), using poison or poisoned weapons, committing rape, sexual slavery, enforced prostitution, or enforced pregnancy. In internal armed conflict (civil war), some of the acts that count as war crimes are directed against those taking no direct part in hostilities, such as murder; mutilation; cruel treatment; torture; taking hostages; passing out sentences not handed down by a regular court; attacking civilians; attacking medical personnel or medical buildings; attacking buildings dedicated to religion, education, art, science, or charitable purposes; committing rape; sexual slavery; enforced prostitution or enforced pregnancy; conscripting children under the age of fifteen into the armed forces; or refusing to take prisoners.

Just as in regular national criminal law, to prove the commission of an international crime various elements must be satisfied. Intent to commit the prohibited act maybe shown by evidence demonstrating the actual mindset of the alleged perpetrator or, depending on the crime, by showing that the perpetrator took unreasonable risks that a similarly situated person would know were likely to lead to the prohibited harm. The details of the elements of international crimes are explored in materials focusing in depth on international criminal law.

§11.2.3 Crimes Against Humanity

Crimes against humanity were listed as one of the crimes that could be prosecuted at Nuremberg and Tokyo after World War II. (See §§11.6.2 and 11.6.3.) This produced considerable controversy as the definition of the crime was far from settled. The definition in the London Charter of 1945 governing the Nuremberg Trials is found in article 6(c):

> Crimes Against Humanity: namely, murder, extermination, enslavement, deportation, and other inhumane acts committed against any civilian population, before or during the war; or persecutions on political, racial or religious grounds in execution of or in connection with any crime within the jurisdiction of the Tribunal whether or not in violation of the domestic law of the country where perpetrated.

Many scholars believed that an accepted definition of crimes against humanity was not part of customary law at that time. The principle that a person cannot be tried for a crime that was not prohibited at the time it was committed (*nullum crimen sine lege*) had long been part of criminal law, and yet several German and Japanese leaders were convicted of crimes against humanity when such acts had been committed in connection with other crimes within the Tribunal's jurisdiction.

The definition of crimes against humanity has undergone a number of changes. Originally, it was only thought of as a crime when carried out during, or in connection with, armed conflict. Indeed, the statute for the International Criminal Tribunal for the former Yugoslavia (ICTY, see §11.6.4) requires this connection. There we find the following definition:

Article 5
Crimes Against Humanity
The International Tribunal shall have the power to prosecute persons responsible for the following crimes when committed in armed conflict, whether international or internal in character, and directed against any civilian population:

    (a) murder;
    (b) extermination;
    (c) enslavement;
    (d) deportation;
    (e) imprisonment;

    (f) torture;

    (g) rape;

    (h) persecutions on political, racial, and religious grounds;

    (i) other inhumane acts.

However, by the time the statute was written for the International Criminal Tribunal for Rwanda (ICTR, see §11.6.5), the connection with armed conflict had been dropped. Article 3 of the ICTR's statute provides:

Article 3
Crimes Against Humanity

The International Tribunal for Rwanda shall have the power to prosecute persons responsible for the following crimes when committed as part of a widespread or systematic attack against any civilian population on national, political, ethnic, racial or religious grounds:

    (a) Murder;

    (b) Extermination;

    (c) Enslavement;

    (d) Deportation;

    (e) Imprisonment;

    (f) Torture;

    (g) Rape;

    (h) Persecutions on political, racial, and religious grounds;

    (i) Other inhumane acts.

The definition in the Rome Statute governing the International Criminal Court (ICC, see §11.6.6) similarly does not require a connection with armed conflict. It also uses the language "widespread or systematic attack [directed] against any civilian population" found in the ICTR's statute but goes on to elaborate the definitions of the various listed acts in great detail. It also adds other acts, such as "sexual slavery, enforced prostitution, forced pregnancy, enforced sterilization" as well as "enforced disappearance of persons" and the "crime of apartheid." As prosecutions for violations of international criminal law become more numerous, no doubt definitions of particular crimes will continue to be altered and developed.

§11.2.4 The Crime of Aggression

The London Charter governing the Nuremberg Trials of German leaders after World War II included the following crime:

> **Crimes Against Peace:** namely, planning, preparation, initiation or waging of a war of aggression, or a war in violation of international treaties, agreements or assurances, or participation in a common plan or conspiracy for the accomplishment of any of the foregoing. . . . Art. 6(a).

The Charter governing the Tokyo Trials of Japanese leaders also contained *crimes against peace* as being within the Tribunal's jurisdiction. Art. 5(a). The definition of the crime was substantially similar to the London Charter. Although there had been various attempts at prohibiting war throughout the ages, including the 1928 Treaty Providing for the Renunciation of War as an Instrument of National Policy, 94 L.N.T.S. 37, to which Germany and Japan were parties, it was not until the United Nations Charter came into effect in 1945 that there was any general agreement prohibiting the use of armed force. Article 2, paragraph 4 of the U.N. Charter prohibits:

> the threat or use of force against the territorial integrity or political independence of any state, or in any other manner inconsistent with the Purposes of the United Nations.

Armed force is only permitted for self-defence "if an armed attack occurs against a member of the United Nations . . ." (art. 51), or if force is authorized by the Security Council (art. 42). (See Chapter 10, §10.4.) Prosecution of German and Japanese leaders for waging wars of aggression was, therefore, highly controversial. Nonetheless, both German and Japanese leaders were convicted of crimes against peace.

The definition of the crime of aggression has continued to raise controversy. In 1974, the General Assembly adopted a detailed Resolution on the Definition of Aggression (G.A. Res. 3314), but it has been criticized as both too narrow and too broad. More recently, the Rome Statute governing the International Criminal Court lists "The crime of aggression" as a crime within the jurisdiction of the Court (art. 5). However, paragraph 2 of article 5 explains that the Court will not have jurisdiction over the crime of aggression until a definition of the crime has been adopted by the states parties to the Statute.

The Rome Statute was adopted in 1998 and entered into force in 2002 but it was not until the summer of 2010 that the definition of the crime of aggression was agreed upon at the Rome Statute Review Conference held in Kampala, Uganda. The definition adopted provides:

Article 8 *bis*
Crime of aggression

1. For the purpose of this Statute, "crime of aggression" means the planning, preparation, initiation or execution, by a person in a position effectively to exercise control over or to direct the political or military action of a State, of an

act of aggression which, by its character, gravity and scale, constitutes a manifest violation of the Charter of the United Nations.

2. For the purpose of paragraph 1, "act of aggression" means the use of armed force by a State against the sovereignty, territorial integrity or political independence of another State, or in any other manner inconsistent with the Charter of the United Nations . . .

There then follows a list of activities that qualify as acts of aggression ranging from the "invasion or attack by the armed forces of a State of the territory of another State . . ." to the "sending by or on behalf of a State of armed bands, groups, irregulars or mercenaries, which carry out acts of armed force against another State of such gravity as to amount to the acts listed above, or its substantial involvement therein." The language of this list substantially follows General Assembly Resolution 3314, and the latter provision was quoted by the ICJ in the *Nicaragua* case, 1986 I.C.J. 14 at para. 195 (Merits), as reflecting customary international law. Even though this definition of the crime of aggression is now part of the Rome State, the Review Conference also agreed that the ICC would not exercise jurisdiction over this crime until 2017 after a decision has been made by the states parties to activate this aspect of the Court's jurisdiction.

The use of armed force always arises in a highly politicized context. Those initiating the use of force are quick to explain their actions as being in conformity with international law. The recognition that force is subject to law is quite a concession, but a determination about the legitimacy of the use of force requires the careful sifting of much evidence. States will, however, often claim that evidence cannot be revealed because of security concerns or that its revelation would compromise the integrity of the state's sovereignty. As yet, the international community has shown considerable reluctance to submit the initiation of the use of armed force to legal standards triable through a judicial process, although it has clearly prohibited the use of force except in very limited circumstances. Nonetheless, during the post–World War II era some progress has been achieved.

Example 11-3

Saddam Hussein, the President of Iraq, ordered Iraqi forces to invade its neighbor the State of Kuwait in August 1990. Hussein cited several factors that he believed justified the invasion, including that the territory of Kuwait actually belonged to Iraq and that Kuwait was illegally siphoning oil from Iraqi wells. Iraq overran Kuwait and occupied the country for seven months.

The Security Council immediately condemned the attack and called upon Iraq to withdraw its forces from Kuwait and negotiate with Kuwait over its disputes. Later, the Security Council authorized member states of the U.N. to form a coalition and use force to drive the Iraqi troops out of Kuwait. The coalition attacked Iraqi forces in Kuwait in January 1991 and by February 25, 1991, Iraq had been driven out of Kuwait.

If, at the time, the ICC had been in existence and able to exercise its jurisdiction under the Rome Statute article 8 *bis*, would you conclude that Saddam Hussein could be indicted for the crime of aggression?

Explanation

There are two key issues here. The language of the Rome Statute article 8 *bis* (2) defines an act of aggression as "the use of armed force by a State against the sovereignty, territorial integrity or political independence of another State. . . ." This language mirrors U.N. Charter article 2(4). The question then becomes whether any of the reasons given for the invasion by Hussein would make the use of force fall outside the ambit of U.N. Charter, article 2(4). Most people would conclude that even if the allegation of illegal siphoning of oil turned out to be true, an economic dispute with another country is not an exception to article 2(4) and cannot be made to fit within the notion of self-defence under article 51. The territorial claim is more difficult. If, in fact, Kuwait was legitimately part of Iraq, then any use of force against Kuwait would arguably not be a use of force against another State. The difficulty with this argument is that at least since 1922, Kuwait's borders have been recognized by the international community. Until 1961, Kuwait was an independent principality under British protection. In 1961 Kuwait became a fully independent state. Waiting seventy years to pursue the claim may simply be too late. Pursuing the claim by armed force is also impermissible where alternative peaceful means such as arbitration or bringing a suit in the ICJ had not even been attempted and where the Security Council had required Iraq to enter into negotiations with Kuwait for the resolution of any disputes.

The second issue that colors the answer to this question is the fact that the Security Council condemned Iraq's attack and called for the withdrawal of Iraqi troops from Kuwait in binding resolutions. Once the Security Council issues binding resolutions, states must obey (U.N. Charter, art. 25). Later, the Security Council authorized the use of force to drive Iraq out of Kuwait. Iraq thus had no room to argue that its invasion was permissible. Although technically the Security Council's condemnation is not necessarily the same as a declaration that the invasion violated the Charter and thus was an act of aggression, it is very persuasive evidence that Saddam Hussein was considered to have violated the Charter. (Saddam Hussein was ultimately tried by a special court in Iraq for crimes against humanity. He was convicted and sentenced to death and was hanged on December 30, 2006.)

Example 11-4

During March and April 2003, a coalition of forces led by the U.S. invaded Iraq. President George W. Bush ordered U.S. troops to undertake the invasion. The main justification for the invasion was based on self-defence, because it was alleged that Iraq was producing weapons of mass destruction (nuclear, chemical, and biological) that were intended to be used on Western states. After twenty-one days of combat, Saddam Hussein was ousted from power but the battle continued for many months. No weapons of mass destruction have even been discovered in Iraq. Coalition forces currently (2010) remain in Iraq but have now begun a phased withdrawal. (A second justification for the invasion was that the action was already permitted by several Security Council resolutions passed in connection with the Iraq-Kuwait war. Since a very close reading of several Security Council resolutions would be necessary to resolve this argument, this Example will not explore this, or several other, justifications).

If, at the time, the ICC had been in existence and able to exercise its jurisdiction under article 8 *bis*, would you conclude that President Bush could be indicted for the crime of aggression?

Explanation

The answer to this question will depend upon whether the invasion is "inconsistent with the Charter of the United Nations. . . ." ICC Statute, art. 8 *bis* (2). That in turn will depend upon whether a feared threat of force at sometime in the future is sufficient to permit self-defence. The language of article 51 permits the use of force in self-defence "if an armed attack occurs against a member of the United Nations." Certainly, Iraq had not attacked the U.S. or any other nation in 2003. Some scholars read article 51 literally. In other words, without an actual armed attack, self-defence is not permitted. Is the fear of a possible attack sufficient to permit self-defence? Article 51 also speaks of the "inherent" right of self-defence, and some scholars maintain that this permits self-defence in the face of an imminent attack. There is not much evidence that anyone thought that Iraq had the capacity to launch an imminent attack. The Bush administration also announced the *Preemption Doctrine* under which it stated it believed it had the right to attack any state that might pose a possible threat to the U.S. or its allies at any time in the future. Very few international law scholars accept this interpretation of article 51. (See §10.4.)

§11.3 INDIVIDUAL RESPONSIBILITY

Before the middle of the twentieth century, international law was defined as encompassing the legal relationships between sovereign states. The only actors in the arena of international law were states. Rights and responsibilities under international law ran between and among states. Individuals, with one exception (see next paragraph), were viewed either as having no international legal rights or, at best, they might be viewed as deriving rights through their own state. The way that a state treated its own citizens was not considered as subject to international law. The state might torture or exterminate its citizens, or it might grant them generous pensions: Such activity was of no concern to international law.

There was one area where individuals did have some international rights, known as *responsibility for injury to aliens*, which was well established by the early twentieth century. The idea here was that although no state was obliged to permit noncitizens (aliens) to enter its territory, if it did so, it was automatically required to adhere to certain minimum standards of due care toward those aliens. So, for example, if a state admitted aliens as tourists and then suddenly arrested all of them and threw them in jail without charges or trials, that was considered to violate the minimum international standard. The state was free to treat its own citizens that way if it wished, but a minimum standard applied to the treatment of aliens. The alien's state could sue at the international level (provided there was an available forum) and seek compensation for the violation of the standard.

Gradually, starting with the U.N. Charter (1945) and the Universal Declaration of Human Rights (1948), the whole regime of human rights with its many enforcement mechanisms has developed. (See Chapters 8 and 9.) The human rights movement has largely focused on rights that individuals have under international legal standards against their own government but more recently, the idea that individuals have obligations under international law has gained traction.

Although the Nuremberg and Tokyo Trials after World War II (see §§11.6.2 and 11.6.3) were based on the idea that there were international criminal law standards applicable to individuals, those trials were, in many respects, an aberration, and no further international criminal trials took place until the International Criminal Tribunal for the former Yugoslavia was established by the Security Council in 1993. Although those who commit atrocities could, theoretically, always be prosecuted in national courts, that almost never happened because either the perpetrators held power or national law had created all sorts of immunities for high governmental officials (see §6.8). Often, after civil wars, the losing side would negotiate an amnesty agreement in return for laying down its arms. All of these mechanisms for avoiding accountability left the victims of international crime without a remedy. The idea behind international criminal law is that individuals can be held responsible for certain very serious offenses. Article 27 of the Rome Statute governing the International Criminal Court (ICC) makes it quite clear that high governmental rank will not immunize an individual from prosecution:

Article 27
Irrelevance of official capacity

1. This Statute shall apply equally to all persons without any distinction based on official capacity. In particular, official capacity as a Head of State or Government, a member of a Government or parliament, an elected representative or a government official shall in no case exempt a person from criminal responsibility under this Statute, nor shall it, in and of itself, constitute a ground for reduction of sentence.
2. Immunities or special procedural rules which may attach to the official capacity of a person, whether under national or international law, shall not bar the Court from exercising its jurisdiction over such a person.

Military commanders can also be held responsible not only for their own international crimes but also for any international crimes committed by troops under their command if they knew, or should have known, that troops were committing or were about to commit international crimes, and the commander failed to take measures to prevent the commission of such crimes or to ensure that such crimes were submitted for investigation and prosecution. (See article 28 of the Rome Statute for the ICC.)

Example 11-5

In the waning days of World War II, Japanese troops occupied the Philippines. The Japanese troops ran wild, committing widespread atrocities on military and civilian personnel throughout the country. The overall commander of the Japanese troops was General Tomoyuki Yamashita, who claimed that he did not know that his troops had ran amok and were committing war crimes.

1) Generally, can a commander of military troops be held responsible for the international criminal actions of subordinate forces under his command?

2) In what circumstances, if any, would you allow a commander to be exonerated if s/he was ignorant about the international criminal activity committed by subordinate troops? (See also §11.4.)

Explanations

1) Yes, a commander of military forces can be held responsible for the international crimes of subordinate troops if he or she knew, or should have known, that such activity was taking place and did not prevent such criminal activity or instigate investigation and prosecution.

2) In general, military commanders must set up a system of communication that allows them to be informed about the activities of subordinate troops. Failure to set up such a system of communication, which might well result in the commander's ignorance about the troops' criminal activity, would be no defense to the commander's culpability. However, if the enemy had systematically broken the commander's line of communication with subordinate troops and, if as a result, the commander could not have known of his troops' criminal activity, such ignorance might be accepted as a defense. This was one of a number of controversial issues in the military trial of General Yamashita and in various appeals from his conviction. The majority opinion in the U.S. Supreme Court refused to accept the defense of ignorance despite evidence that U.S. forces had severed Yamashita's lines of communication with his troops. This decision provoked vigorous dissents by some judges. See *In re Yamashita*, 327 U.S. 1 (1946).

The rapid creation of new international and hybrid criminal courts (see §11.6) since 1993 has firmly established the norm of individual responsibility under international criminal law standards. The daily increase in the number of individuals indicted and convicted for the commission of international crimes is affirmation of this standard.

§11.4 DEFENSES

As with criminal law in national courts, defenses to internationally prohibited activities have evolved over time but certain defenses now appear in most of the statutes governing modern international and hybrid criminal courts.

§11.4.1 Specific Defenses

A brief, truncated summary of defenses found in the ICC's Statute are: mental disease or defect; intoxication unless voluntary; defense of one's self or another; duress resulting from a threat of imminent death or serious bodily harm to one's self or another; a mistake of fact, or a mistake of law where such negates the mental element required by the crime; being ordered by a military or civilian superior to commit an unlawful act but only where the person did not know the order was unlawful and the order was not manifestly unlawful. This latter defense cannot be used with respect to orders to commit genocide or crimes against humanity that the Statute declares to be "manifestly unlawful." ICC Statute, art. 33(2). All of the above defenses are hedged about with conditions and provisos. The defense of duress did not appear in the ICTY's Statute.

Example 11-6

During the Balkan War in the 1990s, a young Serb soldier was taken to a farm by his superior officers. Several hundred Muslim men and boys were brought to the farm as prisoners. The young Serb soldier was ordered by his commander to fire at the prisoners as part of a firing squad that killed hundreds of the prisoners. The young Serb soldier alleged that, at first, he protested the order as illegal, but that his commander told him he could either participate in the firing squad or he could go and stand with the Muslims and be shot himself. The young Serb soldier then took part in the firing squad killing many prisoners. The soldier was later prosecuted for war crimes.

Would you allow the soldier's defense of duress?

Explanation

First, the mere fact that the soldier was ordered to kill the prisoners will not serve as a defense because the order would be deemed manifestly illegal. Even the lowest ranking soldier knows that he or she cannot kill unarmed prisoners, and it was clear that this soldier knew the order was illegal because he protested to his commander. Some statutes governing criminal tribunals would permit this defense of superior orders to be taken into consideration but only in mitigation of punishment. See ICTY Statute, art. 7(4). The more difficult issue is whether the alleged duress should count as a defense. Of course, the soldier will have to present evidence on the issue of duress, and it is certain that the commander will deny that he threatened the soldier with death if he would not participate in the firing squad. Commanders also almost always deny that they issued the illegal order but, in this case, the evidence of hundreds of dead prisoners and the testimony of the other firing squad members would tend to disprove such a denial. If other firing squad members testified that they heard the threat, that would lend credibility to the soldier's claim. If the case were tried under the ICC Statute, the defense of duress would be permitted because the duress did result from a threat of imminent death. If the case were tried by the ICTY, as it was, duress is not listed as a specific defense. A five-member appeals panel ultimately considered the case. Three members were not prepared to entertain the defense of duress, but two members would have allowed such a defense in this case, where the Muslims were going to be shot anyway and the soldier was threatened with immediate death. See *Prosecutor v. Erdemović*, 1997 I.C.T.Y. No. IT-96-22-A (Judgment of the Appeal Chamber).

§11.5 STATE RESPONSIBILITY

Under national law, many high governmental officials, such as heads of state, prime ministers, foreign ministers, and ambassadors enjoy immunity from prosecution in *foreign* states. See §6.8. Indeed, the I.C.J. implied that such immunity was required by customary international law. The *Arrest Warrant of 11 April 2000* (D.R. Congo v. Belgium), 2002 I.C.J. 3. Sovereign states also enjoy broad measures of immunity in *foreign* national courts for governmental activities but not for commercial activities. See §6.8.5. High governmental officials can, however, be prosecuted in their own *national* courts, provided that legislation or judicial decisions permit this. Similarly, a state may choose to allow its own citizens to sue their government in the state's own courts, provided this is permitted.

It was noted above, see §11.3, that high governmental officials can, however, be prosecuted in *international* and *hybrid* criminal courts provided the statute governing the particular court makes it clear that such persons are not immune from prosecution.

The question remains whether a *state* can be held responsible for international crimes for its acts or omissions. The materials in §4.4 should be reviewed at this time.

Bosnia and Herzegovina brought suit in the I.C.J. against the former Yugoslavia, later to become Serbia and Montenegro and from 2006 simply the Republic of Serbia, alleging violations of the Genocide Convention by Serbia during the Balkan War of the 1990s. Both states were party to the Convention. One of the major issues tackled by the Court was whether a state could be held responsible for violations of the Genocide Convention where no individual had been held responsible for the acts of genocide alleged in the suit. The Court examined article I of the Convention where parties "undertake to prevent and to punish" genocide. From this language the Court concluded: "the obligation to prevent genocide necessarily implies the prohibition of genocide." *Id.* at para. 166. The Court also noted article IX of the Convention, which states that:

> Disputes between the Contracting Parties relating to the interpretation, application or fulfillment of the present Convention including those relating to the responsibility of a State for genocide or for any of the other acts enumerated in

Article III, shall be submitted to the International Court of Justice at the request of any of the parties to the dispute.

From this, the Court concluded that the Convention permitted the Court "to find a State responsible if genocide or other acts enumerated in Article III [conspiracy to commit genocide; direct and public incitement to commit genocide; attempt to commit genocide; complicity in genocide] are committed by its organs, or persons or groups whose acts are attributable to it." *Application of the Convention on the Prevention and Punishment of The Crime of Genocide* (Bosnia and Herzegovina v. Serbia and Montenegro), 2007 I.C.J. 191 at para. 181 (hereafter *Bosnian Genocide* case).

Other parts of the *Bosnian Genocide* case examined the question of the attribution of genocide to Serbia on the basis of the conduct of various actors. *Id.* at paras. 385-395. Although the Court found that the massacre of roughly 7,000 Muslim men and boys in Srebrenica in 1995 was genocide (*id.* at para. 297), it decided that there was no evidence before the Court that persons or entities having the status of organs of Serbia perpetrated the acts of genocide committed at Srebrenica. *Id.* at para. 386. The Court determined that the genocide was "committed by members of the VRS [army of Republica Srpska] in and around Srebrenica from about 13 July 1995." *Id.* at para. 297. The officers in charge of the genocide were operating under orders from an entity known as the Republica Srpska and not on orders from The Federal Republic of Yugoslavia, later to become Serbia. Republica Srpska was a self-proclaimed state within Bosnia and Herzegovina with its own armed forces. Despite the fact that Serbia provided substantial financial support to Republica Srpska, that did not make the officers organs of Serbia. *Id.* at para. 388.

Nonetheless, the Court did find Serbia responsible for its failure to prevent genocide, which was equally an obligation under the Convention. Where the dangers of possible genocide were known to state leaders, where they had the means to influence the likely perpetrators and yet "manifestly refrained from using" such means, then the Court was prepared to find that Serbia violated its obligation under the Convention to prevent genocide. *Id.* at para. 438.

There are a number of other conventions that call upon states parties to prevent certain conduct, for example, the Convention Against Torture, 1465 U.N.T.S. 85, art. 2. Using the same logic as the *Bosnian Genocide* case, *supra*, it is reasonable to conclude that the state is also prohibited from committing torture. The definition of torture also requires that the act be carried out by "a public official or other person acting in an official capacity." Torture Convention, art. 1. Such officials may well constitute organs of the state. Thus their actions would be attributable to the state.

Most of the international law criminal cases have focused on individual responsibility, usually because the international criminal tribunals are given jurisdiction over *persons* who may be responsible "for the most serious crimes of international concern. . . ." ICC Statute, art. 1, rather than jurisdiction over *states*. The *Bosnian Genocide* case, *supra*, however, makes it clear that states can also be held responsible for commission of international crimes.

§11.6 INTERNATIONAL AND HYBRID (NATIONAL/ INTERNATIONAL) CRIMINAL TRIBUNALS

§11.6.1 International Criminal Tribunals: Introduction

In the post–World War II era, the attempt to develop international criminal law begins with the Nuremberg and Tokyo Trials, although these were not, strictly speaking, international criminal trials. The tribunals were established by the victorious allied forces after World War II to try leaders in Germany and Japan.

§11.6.2 The Nuremberg Trials

The International Military Tribunal was established by the London Charter in 1945, and the trials took place in Nuremberg, Germany. Twenty-four leaders of Germany's military, political, and economic spheres were accused of planning or committing crimes against peace, wars of aggression, war crimes, or crimes against humanity. Nineteen were convicted, three were acquitted, one was declared medically unfit for trial, and one committed suicide before trial. Another set of trials, the Trials of War Criminals before the Nuremberg Military Tribunals, was conducted at Nuremberg by the United States from 1946 to 1949. Of the 185 defendants, 142 were found guilty of one of more of the charges against them; 35 were acquitted; 4 committed suicide; and 4 could not be tried due to illness.

§11.6.3 The Tokyo Trials

The International Military Tribunal for the Far East was established in 1946 and prosecutions took place in Tokyo from 1946 to 1948. Twenty-seven Japanese leaders were charged with the most serious crimes of initiating or waging war, and 5,700 were accused of less serious war crimes. The Emperor of Japan and the entire imperial family were not indicted. The United States was a main participant in organizing and prosecuting those accused, although the judges and prosecutors came from a wide variety of countries. Seven of the twenty-seven accused were sentenced to death; sixteen were sentenced to life imprisonment; two others were sentenced to a term of years; and two died during trial. Of the 5,700 others accused, over 1,000 were either acquitted or were never tried, and the rest were convicted and condemned to death or sent to prison.

Many aspects of both the Nuremberg and Tokyo Trials have been criticized. Some describe the trials as nothing more than victors' retaliation. Although the Tribunals purported to apply established international law, many have argued that a number of the crimes, such as waging aggressive war, had never been declared illegal before the trials. The exoneration of the Japanese royal family was also extremely controversial.

§11.6.4 The International Criminal Tribunal for the Former Yugoslavia

In the wake of the Balkan War of the 1990s, the international community was concerned to reinforce the idea of individual responsibility for acts contrary to international humanitarian law. After a great deal of debate, the Security Council created an International Criminal Tribunal for the former Yugoslavia (http://www.icty.org/). Security Council Resolution 827 established the International Criminal Tribunal and stated its purpose as "prosecuting persons responsible for serious violations of international humanitarian law committed in the territory of the former Yugoslavia. . . ."

The Security Council asserted that it was acting under the powers conferred upon it by chapter VII of the United Nations Charter (arts. 39-51). Under article 39, the Security Council is empowered "to determine the existence of any threat to the peace, breach of the peace, or act of aggression and [to] . . . makes recommendations, or decide what measures shall be taken in accordance with Articles 41 and 42, to maintain or restore international peace and security." Article 41 permits the Security Council to "decide what measures not involving the use of force are to be employed to give effect to its decisions. . . ." Although the Security Council had never before used its powers to create an international tribunal, it is arguable that it is within the scope of its chapter VII powers.

The Secretary-General had been asked to draw up a report on the creation of a court to prosecute international crimes in the former Yugoslavia; the Security Council adopted the Statute of the International Tribunal, which was annexed to the Secretary-General's report. The Tribunal's Statute provides that it shall have the power to prosecute "persons responsible for serious violations of international humanitarian law . . ." (art. 1); "persons committing or ordering to be committed grave breaches of the Geneva Conventions of 12 August 1949 . . ." (art. 2); "persons violating the laws or customs of war" (art. 3); "persons committing genocide . . ." (art. 4); and "persons responsible for . . . [crimes against humanity] when committed in armed conflict, whether international or internal in character, and directed against any civilian population . . ." (art. 5). The Tribunal has also adopted rules of procedure and rules of evidence as authorized by article 15 of the Tribunal's Statute.

The Tribunal was established in 1993 and sits in The Hague in the Netherlands. It consists of three trial chambers each with three permanent judges and a maximum of six *ad litem* judges, and an appeals chamber of seven judges. This appeals chamber also serves as the appeals chamber of the Internal Tribunal for Rwanda (see below). The judges are elected by the General Assembly from a list submitted by the Security Council. They "shall be persons of high moral character, impartiality and integrity who possess the qualifications required in their respective countries for appointment to the highest judicial office. . . . [D]ue account shall be taken of the experience of the judges in criminal law, international law, including international humanitarian law and human rights." (Statute of the ICTY, art. 13.)

The Statute for the Tribunal also required the appointment of a prosecutor and created a Registry to carry out the administrative work of the Court. The Tribunal has indicted 161 people and has completed proceedings against 116 people. There are ongoing proceedings against twenty-six people. Only two indictees have not yet been arrested, Ratko Mladić and Goran Hadžic. The Tribunal hopes to complete all trials by 2012 and all appeals by 2013.

The first person to be tried by the Tribunal was Dusko Tadić, a low-ranking member of the Serbian military who was accused of a variety of crimes under the Statute. His trial proved to be a fertile ground for testing a number of the controversial aspects of the law of the Tribunal. The most radical attack mounted by Tadić's lawyers was the argument that the Security Council had no authority to create the Tribunal and that therefore the whole proceeding was without legal foundation. Although the trial chamber had determined that it lacked the power to consider the legality of its own creation, the Appeals Chamber was willing to tackle the issue. The Appeals Chamber undertook a thorough investigation of the Security Council's powers under chapter VII of the United Nations Charter and concluded that "the International Tribunal has been established in accordance with the appropriate procedures under the United Nations Charter. . . ."[1] The particular interpretation that the Appeals Chamber gave to particular articles of the Charter are of less importance than the fact that the Appeals Chamber considered itself empowered to address such questions. Whether the assertion of what is usually called "judicial supremacy" (the power of a court to pronounce upon the scope of the powers of the various branches of the U.N. system)

---

1. *Prosecutor v. Dusko Tadić*, Decision on the Defence Motion for Interlocutory Appeal on Jurisdiction, 1995 I.C.T.Y. No. IT-94-1-AR, at para. 47.

will stand the test of time remains to be seen. There is no doubt that the Tribunal's careful decisions on the scope of the crimes and numerous criminal procedural and evidentiary issues has contributed enormously to international criminal jurisprudence.

§11.6.5 The International Criminal Tribunal for Rwanda

A tribunal has also been established by the Security Council to prosecute the atrocities that occurred in Rwanda and neighboring states between January 1, 1994 and December 31, 1994. S.C. Res. 955 (1994). The International Criminal Tribunal for Rwanda (http://www.unictr.org/) sits in Arusha, Tanzania. Its structure and composition are very similar to the Yugoslav Tribunal. It originally functioned with the same prosecutor's office as the Yugoslav Tribunal but now has its own prosecutorial staff. The Rwandan Tribunal got off to a rocky start with allegations of bureaucratic mismanagement. Those problems appear to have been solved. Thirty-six cases have been completed. Eight detainees have been acquitted. Twenty-two cases are ongoing, and eight cases are currently on appeal. Two of the indicted are awaiting trial, and ten fugitives remain at large. The Tribunal had hoped to complete its work by the end of 2011 but it is likely to take longer.

§11.6.6 The International Criminal Court

Although war criminals were prosecuted after World War II in the trials at Nuremberg and Tokyo, those courts have often been described as victors' courts. They were established by the victorious allies after the Nazis and Japanese surrendered. The Yugoslav and Rwandan Tribunals were established by the Security Council but only have jurisdiction over crimes relating to conflict in particular geographic areas. For more than fifty years there have been those who have advocated the establishment of a permanent International Criminal Court.

In 1996, the General Assembly convened a Prepatory Committee to draft a treaty to establish a permanent international criminal court. The International Law Commission and the International Institute of Higher Studies in Criminal Sciences in Siracusa, Italy, had both produced drafts of texts for the establishment of the Court that were considered by the Prepatory Committee. In 1998, the U.N. General Assembly convened a diplomatic conference in Rome, Italy, to establish an International Criminal Court (http://www.icc-cpi.int/). The draft statute for the Court, known as the Rome Statute, was finalized at the Rome Conference and the treaty went into force on July 1, 2002, 2187 U.N.T.S 3. To date, 111 states have deposited their ratifications to the treaty.

The Court has been established at The Hague, the Netherlands. The Prosecutor's Office is investigating three situations referred by states, one situation referred by the Security Council, and one situation referred to the Prosecutor by a Pre-Trial Chamber. Four arrest warrants have been issued with respect to activities in Uganda. Three cases concern proceedings on activities in the Democratic Republic of the Congo. President Omar Hassan Ahmad Al Bashir of Sudan has been indicted for activities related to the Darfur region. Three other cases also concern Darfur. Pre-trial proceedings are continuing with respect to the Central African Republic. The Prosecutor has also been authorized to investigate the situation in Kenya.

The establishment of any major international organization is always difficult and time consuming. As the International Criminal Court settles down to a regular prosecutorial load, with carefully written judicial decisions on the details of the crimes listed in the Rome Statute, together with all the usual evidentiary and procedural issues that come before criminal courts, there is no doubt that this Court will shape the scope and nature of international criminal law for the future.

§11.6.7 Hybrid (National/International) Criminal Tribunals: Introduction

A recent development in international law has been the creation of hybrid (national/international) criminal tribunals. These tribunals are often established in the wake of armed conflict or other extremely serious crimes. They are usually characterized by an agreement between the United Nations and the country where the atrocities occurred and generally have a mix of nationally appointed judges and internationally appointed judges. The statutes that govern the operations of these tribunals often, although not always, apply a mix of national and international law. It is hoped that the combined national and international character of these courts adds to their credibility and legitimacy as they try to administer some measure of justice to victims. Below are brief descriptions of some of these hybrid tribunals.

§11.6.8 The Special Court for Sierra Leone

From 1991 to 2002, an extremely brutal war raged in Sierra Leone. Various factions, sometimes controlled by outside interests, fought over political power and influence over lucrative diamond mines. It is estimated that more that 75,000 people were killed in the war and many others had limbs hacked off by their attackers. Eventually, after peace was restored, the government of Sierra Leone requested assistance from the United

Nations in establishing a hybrid (national/international) criminal court. The Security Council authorized the U.N. Secretary-General to negotiate with Sierra Leone on the establishment of the Special Court, which came into existence in 2002. The Statute creates a Special Court (http://www .sc-sl.org/) that sits in Freetown, Sierra Leone, and has a mix of national judges appointed by Sierra Leone and international judges appointed by the U.N. The Special Court applies both national and international law under its statute and is authorized to prosecute "persons who bear the greatest responsibility for serious violations of international humanitarian law and Sierra Leonean Law" committed in the territory of Sierra Leone since November 30, 1996. The Court's statute permits prosecution for crimes against humanity; crimes applicable in non-international armed conflict; other serious violations of international humanitarian law; and certain sexual offenses under national law. This is the first court to try individuals for recruitment of child soldiers as a violation of international humanitarian law, and forced marriage as a crime against humanity.

Thirteen indictments have been handed down but two have been withdrawn owing to the death of the accused, one of which was Foday Sankoh, leader of the Revolutionary United Front. The trials and appeals of eight people have been concluded. The trial by the Special Court of Charles Taylor, the former President of Liberia, was moved to The Hague, the Netherlands, because of security concerns.

§11.6.9 The East Timor Tribunal

This hybrid (national/international) tribunal was created in 2000 by the United Nations transitional administration in East Timor. It was authorized to try serious criminal offenses including murder, rape, and torture that took place during the conflict between East Timor and Indonesia in 1999 as East Timor asserted its independence from Indonesia. A series of special panels took place from 2000 to 2006. Both national and international judges sat on the panels. Fifty-five trials were held of eight-eight people. Eighty-four people were convicted and four were acquitted. A number of Indonesians were indicted but the government of Indonesia refused to hand them over to the Tribunal. A large number of investigations were still ongoing when funding for the Tribunal came to an end.

§11.6.10 The Extraordinary Chambers in the Courts of Cambodia

This hybrid court (http://www.eccc.gov.kh/english/default.aspx) was established in 2003 after prolonged negotiations between the U.N. and the Cambodian government. The Court has authority to try members of the former Khmer Rouge regime leadership responsible for crimes occurring between 1975 and 1979, when between one and three million people died in Cambodia. Because of the considerable delay between the crimes and prosecution, many of the leaders are now very old or have died. One trial, against Kaing Guek Eav (Duch), a former prison chief, has been completed. He was convicted of war crimes and crimes against humanity on July 26, 2010. He was sentenced to thirty-five years, shortened to nineteen years because of time served or earlier illegal detention. Another trial against four senior Khmer Rouge leaders is scheduled to start in 2011.

§11.6.11 The Special Tribunal for Lebanon

In 2005, the government of Lebanon requested assistance from the U.N. for the establishment of a hybrid court to try those responsible for the attack on Lebanon occurring on February 14, 2005 (and possibly certain other attacks), which killed the former Prime Minister of Lebanon, Rafiq Hariri, as well as twenty-two other people. After Security Council authorization, the agreement to establish the Special Tribunal for Lebanon (http://www.stl-tsl.org/) entered into force in 2007. The judges, from Lebanon and from other countries, and the international prosecutor have been appointed. Lebanese law will be applied by the Tribunal, with the exception of the death penalty and the sentence of forced labor. The Tribunal is located in Leidschendam, the Netherlands, and began functioning on March 1, 2009.

CHAPTER 12

The Law of the Sea

§12.1 Introduction
§12.2 Internal Waters
 §12.2.1 Bays
 §12.2.2 Historic Bays
§12.3 The Territorial Sea
 §12.3.1 Measuring the Territorial Sea
 §12.3.2 Powers of the Coastal State in the Territorial Sea
  and Foreign Ships' Right of Innocent Passage
  (a) The Meaning of Innocent Passage
  (b) Coastal States' Right of Action Against
   Non-Innocent Passage
§12.4 Archipelagos
§12.5 International Straits
 §12.5.1 Definition of an International Strait
  (a) Customary Law
  (b) Treaty Law
 §12.5.2 Transit Passage Through Some International Straits
  (a) Transit Passage Contrasted with Innocent
   Passage
§12.6 The Contiguous Zone
§12.7 The Exclusive Economic Zone

§12.7.1   Coastal States' Rights in the Exclusive
          Economic Zone
§12.7.2   Foreign States' Rights in the Exclusive
          Economic Zone
§12.8   The Continental Shelf
§12.8.1   Delimitation of the Continental Shelf Between
          States with Opposite or Adjacent Coasts
§12.9   The High Seas
§12.10 The Deep Sea Bed
§12.10.1 The Deep Sea Bed Regime Under
          the 1982 Convention
§12.10.2 The Deep Sea Bed Regime Under
          the 1994 Agreement
§12.11 Settlement of Maritime Disputes
§12.12 Marine Pollution
§12.13 Jurisdiction Over Vessels
§12.13.1 The Genuine Link Requirement
§12.13.2 Remedy Where There Is No Genuine Link
§12.14 Prohibited Activities on the High Seas
§12.15 Jurisdiction Over Foreign Vessels
§12.15.1 Jurisdiction in Internal Waters and Ports
§12.15.2 Jurisdiction in the Territorial Sea
§12.15.3 The Right of Hot Pursuit
§12.16 Fishing on the High Seas

§12.1 INTRODUCTION

The law of the sea is one of the areas of international law where there was a good deal of settled customary law even before the twentieth century. It is also one of the great success stories of multilateral treaty making. In the 1950s important conventions were drafted by the International Law Commission. The first United Nations Conference on the Law of the Sea took place in 1958 and adopted four of the Commission's conventions: the Convention on the Territorial Sea and the Contiguous Zone, 516 U.N.T.S. 205; the Convention on the High Seas, 450 U.N.T.S. 82; the Convention on the Continental Shelf, 449 U.N.T.S. 311; and the Convention on Fishing and Conservation of the Living Resources of the High Seas, 559 U.N.T.S. 285. All of these conventions received a fair number of ratifications and all have entered into force. Parts of the Conventions represented existing customary law and parts have contributed to the development of customary law. Some pressing issues were, however, left unresolved by the Conventions, such as the breadth of the territorial seas and who, if anyone, had rights to the resources of the deep sea bed. To a large extent these conventions have been superseded by a Convention adopted after a series of United Nations conferences on the law of the sea that took place between 1974 and 1982. The United Nations Convention on the Law of the Sea (UNCLOS), 1833 U.N.T.S. 3, was opened for signature in Jamaica in 1982 and 155 states signed the Convention. The United States, which had been a major participant in all the preliminary conferences, refused to sign, largely because of its objections to the regime created for deep sea bed mining (Part XI of the Convention). Even though UNCLOS had received the required number of ratifications to enter into force by November 16, 1994, most of the industrialized states had initially refused to ratify the Convention. In order to accommodate the objections of the industrialized states, the United Nations Secretary-General initiated consultations that resulted in a 1994 Agreement Relating to the Implementation of Part XI of the United Nations Convention on the Law of the Sea of 10 December 1982, U.N. Doc. A/RES/48/263 (1994). This new Agreement went into force in 1996 and has received over 138 ratifications. The United States has signed but not yet ratified the Agreement. The Agreement modifies UNCLOS to the extent that the two documents are inconsistent. There is a complex series of provisions for states that have yet to ratify UNCLOS and states that have already ratified UNCLOS to become parties to the 1994 Agreement. One hundred and sixty states have now ratified UNCLOS.

The legal regime that emerges from UNCLOS and the 1994 Agreement can best be studied by looking at various segments of the waters of the world: internal waters, bays, the territorial sea, archipelagos, straits, the contiguous zone, the exclusive economic zone, the continental shelf, the high seas, and the deep sea bed. We shall "swim" through all of these waters and conclude with a section on jurisdiction over vessels.

§12.2 INTERNAL WATERS

Internal waters are those waters that lie within a state, such as lakes or rivers. The state exercises exclusive jurisdiction over these waters and can, if it wishes to do so, exclude other nations from entering these waters. The water that lies on the landward side of the baseline from which the territorial sea is measured (generally the low-water line along the coast), bays, and ports are also controlled by the coastal state and form part of the state's internal waters (see map below).

Lakes, bays that meet the Convention's definition, and rivers are all internal waters controlled by the coastal state.

Map of Internal Waters

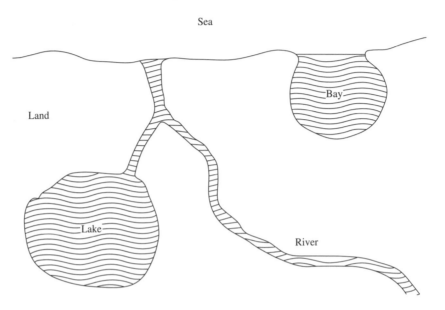

§12.2.1 Bays

It was agreed that the waters within a bay are internal waters but the basic problem confronting the drafters of the Convention was the definition of a bay. Coastal states are generally eager to define as much water as possible as within their jurisdiction, so the tendency was to try to define even large, shallow curvatures of the coastline as bays and thus claim them as internal waters. Under this theory, France and Spain could claim the whole of the Bay of Biscay between them, and Mexico and the United States could claim the Gulf of Mexico. Obviously such inclusive claims would not be acceptable. Article 10 of UNCLOS defines a bay narrowly as:

> a well-marked indentation whose penetration is in such proportion to the width of its mouth as to contain land-locked waters and constitute more than a mere curvature of the coast. An indentation shall not, however, be regarded as a bay unless its area is as large as, or larger than, that of the semi-circle whose diameter is a line drawn across the mouth of that indentation. Art. 10(2).

To constitute a bay, therefore, a body of water first has to satisfy the semicircular area test. This ensures that small coastal indentations are not counted as bays. The next problem was to decide from what point a bay's mouth would be measured and how wide the mouth could be. Article 10(3) states that "[f]or the purpose of measurement, the area of an indentation is that lying between the low-water mark around the shore of the indentation and a line joining the low-water mark of its natural entrance points." Article 10(4) provides: "If the distance between the low-water marks of the natural entrance points of a bay does not exceed 24 nautical miles, a closing line may be drawn between these two low-water marks, and the waters enclosed thereby shall be considered as internal waters." Thus an indentation having the configuration as shown in the map below would constitute a bay, and a straight line could be drawn across the entrance points so that all water on the landward side of the line would be internal waters.

Map of Bay Constituting Internal Waters

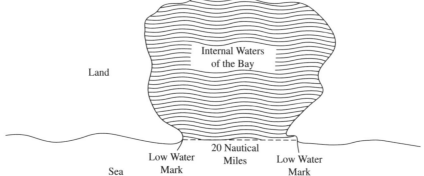

But what about deep indentations whose mouths are greater than twenty-four nautical miles across? Article 10(5) provides: "Where the distance between the low-water mark of the natural entrance points of the bay exceeds 24 nautical miles, a straight base-line of 24 nautical miles shall be drawn within the bay in such a manner as to enclose the maximum area of water that is possible with a line of that length." Thus the straight line would be drawn some way up the indentation to determine which area constitutes internal waters, as set out in the map below.

Map of Bay Where Only Part of the Waters Are Internal Waters

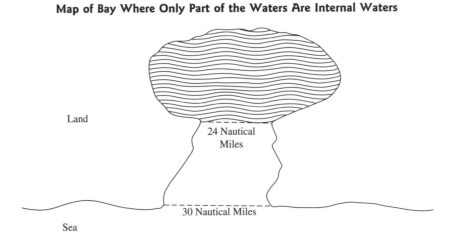

Example 12-1

Examine the map above.

Which part of the bay can be counted as internal waters by the coastal state?

Explanation

The natural entrance to the bay is greater than twenty-four nautical miles across, thus not all of the bay can count as internal waters. Proceed into the bay until the width is twenty-four nautical miles across. Next, determine if the remaining part of the bay meets the semicircular test (art. 10(2)). If it does, then all of the waters on the landward side of the twenty-four nautical mile-wide line are internal waters. If the waters so enclosed do not meet the semicircular test, proceed further into the bay to a part where both the maximum closing line and the semicircular test can be met. At that point, all of the waters on the landward side of the line will be internal waters.

§12.2.2 Historic Bays

Article 10 did not settle all issues related to bays, and article 10(6) specifically states that the "foregoing provisions do not apply to so-called 'historic' bays. . . ." A number of states have claimed large bodies of waters, some with entrance points hundreds of miles apart, as historic bays and entirely within the coastal state's internal waters. UNCLOS does not contain a definition of an historic bay, and the determination of whether a body of water constitutes an historic bay probably turns upon the length of time that the state has claimed the water as a bay and exercised jurisdiction over it and the extent to which other nations have been willing to accept that characterization. Canada claims as internal waters the whole of the Hudson Bay, which has entrance points fifty miles apart, though the United States disputes this claim. Libya claims the Gulf of Sidra (or Sirte) as an historic bay with a closing line of 300 miles. This is disputed by a number of states, including the United States.

§12.3 THE TERRITORIAL SEA

Prior to UNCLOS, there had been general agreement that a coastal state was entitled to claim a belt of waters around its coast as "territorial sea." It was agreed that the coastal state could exercise its jurisdiction over this belt of water even to the extent of excluding all fishing by foreigners in those waters. What was not agreed upon, however, was (a) the width of the territorial sea and (b) the extent to which the coastal state could prohibit foreign vessels from entering the territorial seas. The 1982 Convention resolved both issues. Article 2 of UNCLOS states:

> 1. The sovereignty of a coastal State extends, beyond its land territory and internal waters . . . to an adjacent belt of sea, described as the territorial sea.
> 2. This sovereignty extends to the air space over the territorial sea as well as to its bed and subsoil.
> 3. The sovereignty over the territorial sea is exercised subject to this Convention and to other rules of international law.

Article 3 defines the breadth of the territorial sea as "not exceeding 12 nautical miles, measured from baselines determined in accordance with this Convention." Normally the baseline "for measuring the breadth of the territorial sea is the low-water line along the coast. . . ." Art. 5.

For centuries states had disagreed about the breadth of the territorial sea. The Western industrialized states had generally claimed three nautical miles, the Scandinavian countries had claimed four nautical miles, and certain South American countries had claimed up to 200 nautical miles. Before the 1982 Convention, which for the first time permitted coastal states to claim up to 200 nautical miles as an exclusive economic zone (EEZ) (art. 57), the territorial sea was seen primarily in security terms or in terms of providing an exclusive fishing zone for the coastal state. (Can you think why the more powerful states should generally have favored a narrower territorial sea whereas the less powerful states generally wanted a broader territorial sea?) Once it was clear that the 1982 Convention was going to have a provision for a much expanded exclusive fishing (and other resources) zone it was easier to reach the compromise of twelve nautical miles as the breadth of the territorial sea.

§12.3.1 Measuring the Territorial Sea

The normal point from which to measure the territorial sea was agreed upon as the low-water mark along the coast (art. 5) but the International Court of Justice had permitted the drawing of straight baselines (that is, joining up certain low-water marks by straight lines rather than following every coastal indentation) in certain geographic circumstances. *Fisheries* case (U.K. v. Norway), 1951 I.C.J. 116. The 1982 Convention adopts the Court's ruling and provides for straight baselines "where the coastline is deeply indented and cut into, or if there is a fringe of islands along the coast . . ." (art. 7(1)). The same article also states that the "drawing of straight baselines must not depart to any appreciable extent from the general direction of the coast . . ." (art. 7(3)) and that "account may be taken, in determining particular baselines, of economic interests peculiar to the region concerned . . ." (art. 7(5)). A good number of states now employ the straight baseline method along portions of their coasts including the United Kingdom and the United States.

§12.3.2 Powers of the Coastal State in the Territorial Sea and Foreign Ships' Right of Innocent Passage

Although article 2 of UNCLOS made it clear that the coastal state's sovereignty extends to the territorial sea, it also stated that the state's sovereignty had to be exercised "subject to this Convention . . ." (art. 2(3)). A great debate had raged over whether foreign ships, and in particular foreign warships, had to ask permission from the coastal state before entering the territorial sea. Western nations tended to assert that all ships had the right to enter a coastal state's territorial sea provided the ship was exercising the right of "innocent passage." Eastern bloc countries tended to dispute this and argued either that all foreign vessels had to seek permission to enter the territorial sea or that foreign warships (as opposed to mercantile ships) could only enter the territorial sea after being granted permission by the coastal state. There was no general agreement on this issue but article 17 of UNCLOS resolves this long-fought battle by stating that "ships of all states, whether coastal or land-locked, enjoy the right of innocent passage through the territorial sea." Notice that article 17 makes no distinction between warships and mercantile ships but simply refers to "ships of all states. . . ." Note that there is no similar right of innocent passage for aircraft to fly over the territorial sea. Foreign aircraft must receive permission to fly over a state's territory or its territorial sea.

(a) The Meaning of Innocent Passage

The next battle was over the meaning of "innocent passage." Passage is defined in article 18, and article 19(1) states that "[p]assage is innocent so long as it is not prejudicial to the peace, good order or security of the coastal State." Article 19(2) contains a long list of activities that are automatically considered prejudicial to the peace of the coastal state, i.e., non-innocent. The activities listed include: the threat or use of force against the coastal state; practice with weapons; collecting information prejudicial to the security of the coastal state; launching or landing of aircraft or any military device; activities contrary to the customs, fiscal, immigration, or sanitary laws; serious pollution; fishing; research, or survey activities; interfering with communications or installations; and a final catch-all section, "any other activity not having a direct bearing on passage" (art. 19(2)(1)). What might such activities include? cruise ship dances on deck? captain's table lavish dinners? planning a pirate attack on another ship? The section is almost infinitely broad.

Article 20 requires submarines and other underwater vehicles "to navigate on the surface and to show their flag" when passing through the territorial sea. Article 23 requires "[f]oreign nuclear-powered ships and ships carrying nuclear or other inherently dangerous or noxious substances" to "carry documents and observe special precautionary measures established for such ships by international agreements."

Although the coastal state may not "hamper the innocent passage of foreign ships through the territorial sea . . ." (art. 24), the coastal state can regulate passage in a number of ways. It can adopt laws and regulations to protect navigation, cables and pipelines, living resources of the sea, the environment, and marine research; and can prevent violations of its customs, fiscal, immigration, and sanitary laws. Art. 21. It can also set up sea lanes and traffic separation schemes, particularly for inherently dangerous cargoes and nuclear vessels. Art. 22. The coastal state may take steps to prevent non-innocent passage (art. 25(1)) or even suspend innocent passage rights temporarily if such suspension "is essential for the protections of its security, including weapons exercises." Art. 25(3).

The coastal state may only exercise its criminal and civil jurisdiction over foreign vessels exercising the right of innocent passage in very limited circumstances. Arts. 27 & 28.

(b) Coastal States' Right of Action Against Non-Innocent Passage

One remaining difficulty is the question of what a state may do if it believes a foreign vessel is engaging in non-innocent activities in the territorial sea. Article 21(1) permits the coastal state to "take the necessary steps in its territorial sea to prevent passage which is not innocent." Article 30 states that "[i]f any warship does not comply with the laws and regulations of the coastal State concerning passage through the territorial sea and disregards any request for compliance therewith which is made to it, the coastal State may require it to leave the territorial sea immediately." Article 31 states that the flag state of a foreign warship shall bear the responsibility for any damage to the coastal state resulting from noncompliance of the warship with the coastal state's laws or regulations when passing through the territorial sea.

Although it is not entirely clear, it looks as if the 1982 Convention intends that the coastal state shall first request a foreign warship to stop violating the requirements of innocent passage and that if the foreign warship refuses to comply, the coastal state can order it to leave the territorial sea. Article 25(1) does not distinguish between warships and commercial vessels and simply permits "necessary steps" to prevent non-innocent passage. Three questions present themselves. First, what is permitted under "necessary steps" to prevent non-innocent passage in the territorial sea? Second, must a foreign warship be asked to comply with regulations before being asked to leave the territorial sea? Third, may the coastal state do anything to a ship engaging in non-innocent passage in the territorial sea beyond asking the foreign ship to leave and escorting it from the area?

Example 2-2

State A and State B have been on unfriendly terms for many years. State A's coastline is full of fjords and sounds that State A has always claimed as internal waters. State B has never protested this classification. State A has just detected a submarine from State B beneath the surface of the waters in the area of the mouth of one of its fjords. The mouth of this fjord is twenty nautical miles wide and the fjord runs inland for thirty miles, with a width ranging from twenty to five miles, after which it becomes a river.

What is State A permitted to do?

Explanation

First, you need to determine whether the fjord is properly classified as internal waters or territorial waters. Given that the fjord appears to meet the definition of a bay, it can be classified as internal waters. If State A has claimed it as an historic bay for many years and if other states have recognized it as such, it would also count as internal waters. Next, you need to ask exactly where the submarine was detected. If it is located seaward of a straight line drawn across the mouth of the fjord, it would be located in State A's territorial sea. If, on the other hand, it is located on the landward side of such a line it would be located in State A's internal waters.

If the submarine has entered the internal waters of the fjord, then State B's submarine has no right to be there without State A's permission. State A can arrest the vessel and the crew and subject the submarine and the crew members to its regular legal process. If, on the other hand, the submarine is only in the territorial waters of State A, then it has a right of innocent passage. To exercise innocent passage the submarine must navigate on the surface. The fact that it is not navigating on the surface means that it is arguably not exercising innocent passage. State A may well suspect that the submarine is spying or trying to collect evidence about State A's defense system. If there are reasonable grounds for believing that State B's submarine is engaged in non-innocent activity, then State A can request that the submarine should cease its non-innocent activity. If the submarine does not cease its non-innocent activity, then State A can escort it out of the territorial sea. What if State A considers that the submarine threatens its security? Some have argued that in such cases reasonable force can be used against the submarine. Others have argued that escorting the ship out of the territorial waters is all that is permitted. Some states have gone so far as to seize the intruding vessel, strip it down, arrest the crew, and only release them once they are convinced that no further threat is posed.

Example 12-3

Two small civilian planes registered in State C flew into the airspace of State D without permission. The pilots in the plane dropped leaflets over State D calling on the inhabitants "to rise up and overthrow your illegal, authoritarian dictators." State D complained to State C about this activity by these small planes and warned that State D would regard further infringements of its airspace as a threat to its security and would take "decisive action." State C issued a general warning to civilian aircraft reminding them that aircraft registered in State C did not have permission to fly over State D's territorial sea or the airspace above State D's territory. Some months later, the two small planes took off again intending to drop further leaflets over State D calling for revolution. The two planes were shot down by State D's air force and crashed ten nautical miles off the coast of State D. The bodies of the two pilots washed up on the shores of State D two days later.

Has State D violated international law?

Explanation

If the civilian planes were outside the territorial sea of State D and were not posing a threat of armed force against State D, then State D had no right to take any action against the planes. If the planes had violated State D's airspace without permission and did pose some sort of a security threat to State D, then, under the laws relating to the use of force, State D would be permitted to take necessary and proportional countermeasures. Most scholars would maintain that shooting down two unarmed civilian planes that were only suspected of having dropped political leaflets once previously and that may have been going to engage in the same conduct again, could not be counted as necessary or proportionate. Although the civilian planes may have violated the law by illegally entering State D's airspace, State D's response was grossly disproportionate and would require reparations. This answer might change if, as a result of the earlier leaflets dropped by the planes, there had been an uprising that had led to several days of rioting and hundreds of deaths. State D then might reasonably regard the activity of the planes as a severe threat to its security. Lurking throughout this question is the issue of whether international law recognizes the right of revolution against dictatorships and whether there is a right to some form of representative government. (See Chapters 4 and 8.) There would also need to be a factual examination of the system of government in State D. There is also the problem that presumably the pilots of the planes are not citizens of State D, which raises the issue of the extent to which private noncitizens may assist foreign uprisings. See Chapter 10, §10.4.3.

§12.4 ARCHIPELAGOS

After the International Court of Justice had permitted the drawing of straight baselines in certain geographic circumstances in the *Fisheries* case (U.K. v. Norway), 1951 I.C.J. 116, some archipelagic states began to wonder whether straight baselines could be drawn around the outside of their outermost islands, thus enclosing all the waters between the islands as internal waters. In 1955, The Philippines made such a pronouncement, and in 1957 Indonesia followed suit. Such developments did not please the international community because, at that time, it meant that foreign vessels had no right of passage through the enclosed waters. The 1982

Convention tackled the subject by creating a new regime for midocean archipelagic states (arts. 46-54).

Article 46(a) defines an archipelagic state as "constituted wholly by one or more archipelagos [which] may include other islands." An archipelago is defined as "a group of islands, including parts of islands, interconnecting waters and other natural features which are so closely interrelated that [they] form an intrinsic geographical, economic and political entity, or which historically have been regarded as such." Art. 46(b). States that form part of a mainland but have archipelagos lying off parts of their coasts are covered by article 7. The regime created for midocean archipelagic states permits the drawing of straight baselines "joining the outermost points of the outermost islands and drying reefs" (art. 47(1)) provided the baselines include the main islands, have a certain ratio of water to land, and generally (with certain exceptions) do not exceed 100 nautical miles. Art. 47.

The archipelagic waters enclosed by straight baselines are said to be within the sovereignty of the archipelagic state including the airspace (art. 49) but "ships of all States enjoy the right of innocent passage through archipelagic waters" (art. 52(1)), which passage may only be suspended if essential for security purposes. Art. 52(2). The archipelagic state "may designate sea lanes and air routes . . . through or over its archipelagic waters. . . ." Art. 53(1). This right of sea lane or air route passage to traverse archipelagic waters is "solely for the purpose of continuous, expeditious and unobstructed transit between one part of the high seas or an exclusive economic zone and another part of the high seas or an exclusive economic zone." Art. 53(3). This right of passage seems similar to the right of transit passage through international straits, see §12.5.2 infra. There does not appear to be any right to suspend sea lane passage through archipelagic waters.

The regime thus created for midocean archipelagos allows the drawing of straight baselines around the islands of the archipelago but gives both the right of innocent passage for ships through these waters and the right of sea lane passage for ships and aircraft through designated sea lanes or air routes through or over the enclosed waters.

§12.5 INTERNATIONAL STRAITS

Before the 1982 Convention permitted a territorial sea of twelve nautical miles, many states only claimed three nautical miles for their territorial sea. At that time most states regarded everything beyond the territorial sea as high seas and open to the vessels of all nations. This meant that many of the world's straits had a high seas passage through them because they were wider than six nautical miles. A high seas route meant that ships and aircraft did not have to ask permission of the coastal states to pass through the strait, nor did the ships or aircraft have to confine themselves to "innocent" activities. When it was agreed that the territorial sea would be widened to twelve nautical miles, it was immediately realized that many straits that previously had a high seas route through them would now be completely swallowed up by territorial sea. While the territorial sea regime allowed innocent passage for all ships, the limitations imposed by innocent passage were a far cry from the virtually unfettered passage permitted through the previously existing high seas route. Aircraft were given no right of innocent passage over the territorial sea, whereas they had been free to fly over a high seas route. A compromise was reached by the introduction of the concept of "transit" passage. First, however, a strait had to be defined, and here the drafters of the new Convention had a fair amount of customary law upon which to draw.

§12.5.1 Definition of an International Strait

(a) Customary Law

In 1949, the International Court of Justice had addressed the definition of a strait and determined that "the decisive criterion is . . . its geographic situation as connecting two parts of the high seas and the fact of its being used for international navigation." *Corfu Channel* case (U.K. v. Albania), 1949 I.C.J. 4, at 28. Remember, that at that time everything beyond the territorial sea was considered high seas. The Court also held that coastal states may not prohibit passage through international states "in time of peace." *Id.* at 29. All foreign vessels, including warships, had a right of innocent passage through such straits and did not have to seek permission of the coastal state to pass through the strait. *Id.* at 28.

(b) Treaty Law

The *Corfu Channel* case did not settle the question of the rights of passage through straits that connect one part of the high seas to a territorial sea. Article 16(4) of the 1958 Convention on the Territorial Sea and the Contiguous Zone provided a right of innocent passage through such straits but relatively few states had ratified this Convention.

§12.5.2 Transit Passage Through Some International Straits

The new transit passage regime created in the 1982 Convention applies only to "straits which are used for international navigation between one part of the high seas or an exclusive economic zone and another part of the high seas or an exclusive economic zone." Art. 37. (For the rules relating to the exclusive economic zone (EEZ), see §12.7 *infra*.) Article 55 defines the EEZ as "an area beyond and adjacent to the territorial sea . . ." not extending "beyond two hundred nautical miles from the baselines . . ." (art. 57).

Other types of straits are governed by different articles in the 1982 Convention. If, in a strait, there exists "a route through the high seas or through an exclusive economic zone of similar convenience with respect to navigational and hydrographical characteristics . . ." (art. 36) then there is no right of transit passage. Ships and aircraft must take the high seas or EEZ route and abide by the rules of those regimes, or if ships choose to traverse the territorial sea in such a strait they must abide by the rules of innocent passage. Article 38(1) provides that "if the strait is formed by an island of a State bordering the strait and its mainland, transit passage shall not apply if there exists seaward of the island a route through the high seas or through an exclusive economic zone of similar convenience with respect to navigational and hydrographical characteristics." The *Corfu Channel* case presented an "island" situation like the one described in article 38(1). The island of Corfu is owned by Greece which is "an island of a State bordering the strait and its mainland . . ." although the claim was against Albania, another state bordering the strait. Since transit passage does not apply in the island situation described in article 38(1), the right of innocent passage applies except that such a right of innocent passage through such a straight cannot be suspended (art. 45(2)) as it can in the territorial sea when "such suspension is essential for the protection of [the coastal state's] security . . ." (art. 25(3)). Where a strait connects the high seas or an EEZ and the territorial sea of another state (art. 45(1)(b)) the regime of innocent passage applies, which cannot be suspended (art. 45(2)).

Article 38 provides a right of transit passage for all ships and aircraft for international straits that connect one part of the high seas or EEZ and another part of the high seas or EEZ. This right of transit passage means "the freedom of navigation and overflight solely for the purpose of continuous and expeditious transit of the strait. . . ." Art. 38(2). Such passage does not exclude "entering, leaving or returning from a State bordering the strait, subject to the conditions of entry to that state." Art. 28(2). This right of transit passage "shall not be impeded. . . ." Art. 38(1). While exercising the right of transit passage, ships and aircraft must "refrain from any activities other than those incident to their normal modes of continuous and expeditious transit unless rendered necessary by *force majeure* or by distress. . . ." Art. 39(1)(c).

(a) Transit Passage Contrasted with Innocent Passage

How is the right of transit passage different from the right of innocent passage? Aircraft are given a right of transit passage through article 37 straits, whereas no such right of overflight is given to aircraft under innocent passage. This right of transit passage applies to military aircraft as well as civilian planes (art. 38(1) refers to "all . . . aircraft . . ."). Submarines must surface and show their flags when exercising the right of innocent passage (art. 20) but no such requirement is stated for transit passage, so presumably submarines may exercise the right of transit passage underwater. Article 19 has a long list of prohibited activities for ships exercising innocent passage. Articles 39-41 list less stringent restrictions on ships and aircraft exercising transit passage. The regulatory powers of the coastal states in transit passage (arts. 41 & 42) are more limited than those permitted in innocent passage (arts. 21-26).

Example 2-4

Study the map below.

Straits of Tiran

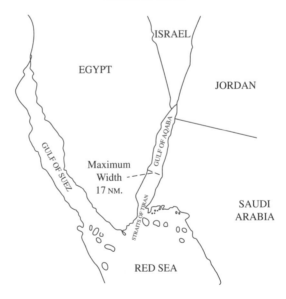

The maximum width of the Gulf of Aqaba is seventeen nautical miles. The only navigable channel into the Gulf is through the Straits of Tiran, which are three miles wide. All states bordering the Gulf claim the maximum territorial sea permissible under UNCLOS.

What rights do (1) a foreign ship and (2) a foreign aircraft have to pass through the Straits of Tiran? Can the coastal states suspend those rights and, if so, in what circumstances?

Explanation

The first thing to note is that the Straits of Tiran are not straits that connect "one part of the high seas or an exclusive economic zone and another part of the high seas or an exclusive economic zone." Art. 37. The Straits of Tiran connect one part of the high seas with the territorial seas of several states bordering the Gulf of Aqaba. The new transit passage regime thus does not apply to the Straits of Tiran. Article 45(1)(b) applies to straits that connect the high seas or an EEZ and the territorial sea in another state. The regime of innocent passage applies to such straits. Article 45(2) states that this right of innocent passage through such a strait cannot be suspended. As a result, a foreign ship has a right of innocent passage through the Straits of Tiran but a foreign aircraft has no such right. The foreign aircraft cannot fly over the Straits of Tiran without the permission of the coastal state over whose territorial sea the aircraft will be traversing. (Note, however, that in 1979, a peace treaty was signed between Egypt and Israel declaring the Straits of Tiran and the Gulf of Aqaba to be "international waterways open to all nations for unimpeded and non-suspendable freedom of navigation and overflight." 1138 U.N.T.S. 59. Although such a treaty only has two states parties, such treaties can create rights for third-party states if the treaty so intends, and third-party states either assent or can be assumed to have assented. See VCLT, art. 36).

§12.6 THE CONTIGUOUS ZONE

For centuries coastal states have asserted the right to exercise jurisdiction in the waters off their coasts in order to ensure their security or to protect other interests they deemed vital. In 1804, the United States Supreme Court stated "[A state's] power to secure itself from injury may certainly be exercised beyond the limits of its territory. . . . If this right be extended too far, the exercise of it will be resisted." *Church v. Hubbart*, 6 U.S. (2 Cranch) 187, at 234-235 (1804). The difficulty was in defining the limit of this authority. The Supreme Court noted: "[The exercise of this right] has occasioned long and frequent contests, which have sometimes ended in open war. The English, it will be recollected, complained of the right claimed by Spain to search their vessels on the high seas, which was carried so far, that the *guarda costas* of that nation seized vessels not in the neighborhood of their coasts. This practice was the subject of long and fruitless negotiations, and at length, of open war." *Church v. Hubbart, supra,* at 235.

The 1958 Convention on the Territorial Sea included a provision permitting coastal states to exercise control necessary to prevent violations of its customs, fiscal, immigration, or sanitary regulations in an area contiguous to its territorial sea but not to extend beyond twelve miles from the baselines. Art. 24. No agreement was reached on a security zone, which, given the capacity of modern weapons, would probably need a global limit. The Commentary by the International Law Commission on its Draft Articles for the 1958 Convention noted: "In so far as measures of self-defence against an imminent and direct threat to the security of the State are concerned, the Commission refers to general principles of international law and the Charter of the United Nations." 1956, II Y.B. Int'l L. Comm'n, at 294-295.

The 1982 Convention uses the same approach to the contiguous zone as the 1958 Convention and provides in article 33(1): "[I]n a zone contiguous to its territorial sea" the state may exercise the control necessary to:

> (a) prevent infringement of its customs, fiscal, immigration or sanitary laws and regulations within its territory or territorial sea;
> (b) punish infringement of the above laws and regulations committed within its territory or territorial sea.

> 2. The contiguous zone may not extend beyond 24 nautical miles from the baselines from which the breadth of the territorial sea is measured.

The contiguous zone gives a coastal state a grant of authority up to twenty-four nautical miles off its coast but for very specific and limited reasons. If a state claims a territorial sea of twelve nautical miles, it will be able to claim another twelve nautical miles for its contiguous zone. What exactly can a coastal state do to foreign vessels in its contiguous zone? How much power does the term "control" grant to the coastal state? Note that the contiguous zone under article 33 does not grant the coastal state the right to apply its substantive laws relating to customs, fiscal, immigration, or sanitary matters beyond its territorial sea. Professor Shearer states:

> Since laws on the substantive subjects of customs, fiscal, immigration and sanitary matters cannot be applied to the contiguous zone, it follows that an offence cannot be committed until the boundary of territorial waters is crossed by inward-bound ships. "Control" therefore must be limited to such measures as inspections and warnings, and cannot include arrest or forcible taking into port. It is arguable, however, and probably sustainable on the history of the British Hovering Acts and similar legislation elsewhere, that a coastal State might lawfully legislate to make it an offence to hover or to transship dutiable

cargoes in the contiguous zone and to carry out an arrest there because these activities are within the connotations of "prevention." I.A. Shearer, *Problems of Jurisdiction and Law Enforcement Against Delinquent Vessels*, 35 Int'l & Comp. L.Q. 320, at 330 (1986).

§12.7 THE EXCLUSIVE ECONOMIC ZONE

Many states had enforced an exclusive fisheries zone in their territorial sea for decades. These coastal states simply prohibited all foreign vessels from fishing in their territorial seas. Before the middle of the twentieth century most fishermen were employed on small boats that only had the capacity to fish fairly close to the shore. The building of much larger boats and the availability of refrigeration changed the traditional fishing patterns. Large "fish factory" ships put to sea for several months and caught and processed fish all over the world. Fish stocks began to dwindle, and nations with traditional fishing fleets were anxious to provide their fleets some protection. States began to make unilateral declarations extending their exclusive fishing zones beyond their territorial sea. Iceland claimed a twelve-mile zone in 1958. A number of Latin American states claimed 200-mile zones, which were the subject of numerous protests.

The 1958 Conventions could reach no agreement on a fishing zone but, by the time the 1982 Convention was ready to be signed, more than fifty states claimed various types of exclusive zones beyond their territorial seas. The 1982 Convention created a new EEZ:

> The exclusive economic zone is an area beyond and adjacent to the territorial sea, subject to the specific legal regime established in this Part, under which the rights and jurisdiction of the coastal State and the rights and freedoms of other States are governed by the relevant provisions of this Convention. Art. 55.

This zone "shall not extend beyond 200 nautical miles from the baselines. . . ." Art. 57. For the first time in history, international law recognized a zone, 200 nautical miles wide, in which the coastal state had the exclusive right to all of the natural resources, subject to certain limitations explained in other articles.

§12.7.1 Coastal States' Rights in the Exclusive Economic Zone

The coastal state is given "sovereign rights" in the EEZ but only for certain purposes: "exploring and exploiting, conserving and managing the natural

353

resources, whether living or non-living, of the waters . . . and of the sea-bed and its subsoil. . . ." Art. 56(1)(a). It is also given jurisdiction for the establishment of "installations and structures" and over "marine scientific research . . . [and] the protection and preservation of the marine environment." Art. 56(1)(b).

The coastal state is given the responsibility for determining "the allowable catch of living resources in its exclusive economic zone." Art. 61(1). It must also undertake conservation and management measures to prevent overexploitation of the zone (art. 61(2)) and promote "optimum utilization of the living resources. . . ." Art. 62(1). If the coastal state does not harvest the entire allowable catch it must give other states (including landlocked states) access to the resources by making agreements with other states. Art. 62(2), 69 & 70.

In order to enforce its rights in the EEZ, a coastal state may "take such measures, including boarding, inspection, arrest and judicial proceedings, as may be necessary to ensure compliance. . . ." Art. 73(1). Arrested vessels and crews must be released upon the posting of a bond but penalties for violations of the EEZ regulations may not include imprisonment or corporal punishment and the flag state must be "promptly notified." Art. 73.

The delimitation of the EEZ between states with opposite and adjacent coasts is to be worked out by agreement "to achieve an equitable solution." Art. 74(1).

§12.7.2 Foreign States' Rights in the Exclusive Economic Zone

All states are guaranteed the rights of "navigation and overflight" in the EEZ and the "laying of submarine cables and pipelines . . . compatible with . . . this Convention." Art. 58(1).

Example 12-5

State A has recently declared a 200-nautical-mile EEZ off its coastline. State B's fishermen have fished in the waters off State A for centuries, always remaining outside State A's territorial sea. State A used to claim three nautical miles as its territorial sea but it has recently extended that claim to twelve nautical miles. Neither State A, nor State B is a party to UNCLOS. State B's president announces at a press conference that "[w]hile we recognize State A's right to a twelve-mile territorial sea, our fishermen have an historic right to fish anywhere beyond State A's territorial sea."

Is the president of State B correct?

Explanation

No, the president of State B is not correct. UNCLOS permits states to claim up to 200 nautical miles as an EEZ. Even if State B and State A are not parties to UNCLOS, the regime of the EEZ is now accepted as customary international law. There are now 160 states parties to UNCLOS, and a number of non-parties have also claimed zones that are in conformity with UNCLOS. Although no state is obligated to claim an EEZ, every state is required to respect such claims by other states up to 200 nautical miles.

Example 12-6

For many decades, ships registered in the State of Lucas have traveled to the coastal waters of a neighboring state, Grassland, to take part in a month-long water festival. This festival involves sailing races and singing, eating, and drinking. Some of the Lucas-registered boats have operated as floating restaurants during the festivities and traditionally serve five-course meals washed down with much wine produced in the Lucasian vineyards. Both Lucas and Grassland are parties to UNCLOS. Recently, Grassland declared a 200-nautical-mile EEZ off its coast. The Grassland government also issued regulations stating: "Only ships registered in Grassland may engage in any form of economic activity within Grassland's EEZ. This regulation shall be interpreted to prohibit the buying and selling of food and any form of beverages by any non-Grassland registered vessel in Grassland's EEZ." The State of Lucas immediately protests this regulation and declares that it violates UNCLOS.

Does Grassland's new regulation prohibiting non-Grassland registered vessels from selling food and beverages in Grassland's EEZ violate UNCLOS?

Explanation

In all probability such a regulation would be deemed to violate UNCLOS. Although UNCLOS gives the coastal state the exclusive right to the economic resources **in** its EEZ, it does not prohibit other vessels from engaging in economic activity **on** another state's EEZ. The Law of the Sea Tribunal ruled that the buying and selling of fuel oil by a foreign vessel in another state's EEZ did not violate UNCLOS, and such activity could not be subject to a coastal state's customs zone. See *The Saiga* case (St. Vincent and the Grenadines v. Guinea), 1999 I.T.L.O.S. No. 2.

§12.8 THE CONTINENTAL SHELF

In 1945, U.S. President Harry S. Truman was the first to claim national rights in a continental shelf. 10 Fed. Reg. 12,303 (1945). The reason that this proclamation took place in the mid-1940s was that oil and mineral resources had been discovered in the continental shelf, and it had become technologically possible to harvest those resources.

The term "continental shelf" is used to describe the sloping ledge covered by water that projects from the coastline of many states. The breadth of the continental shelf varies very considerably, sometimes only projecting a few miles, sometimes extending hundreds of miles. The Truman proclamation encouraged other states to make similar claims, which they did, in rapid succession. The 1982 Convention defines the continental shelf as comprising:

> the sea-bed and subsoil of the submarine areas that extend beyond [the coastal State's] territorial sea throughout the natural prolongation of its land territory to the outer edge of the continental margin, or to a distance of 200 nautical miles from the baselines from which the breadth of the territorial sea is measured where the outer edge of the continental margin does not extend to that distance. Art. 76(1).

There are provisions for measuring the continental shelf when it projects beyond 200 miles (art. 76(4) & (7)) and wealth-sharing provisions for resources harvested by the coastal state from its continental shelf between 200 nautical miles and 350 nautical miles from the baselines (art. 82). The continental shelf may not be claimed by any state beyond 350 nautical miles (art. 76(6)).

The 1982 Convention makes it clear that the coastal state's rights in the continental shelf do not affect the status of the waters above it (art. 78). The coastal state's rights in the continental shelf are described as "sovereign" but only "for the purpose of exploring it and exploiting its natural resources." Art. 7(1). The coastal state is given exclusive rights to harvest the "mineral and other non-living resources of the sea-bed and subsoil together with living organisms belonging to sedentary species . . ." (art. 77(4)) and the right to "authorize and regulate drilling on the continental shelf. . . ." Art. 81. Other states are however given the right "to lay submarine cables and pipelines on the continental shelf . . ." (art. 79(1)) subject to the coastal state's right to "control . . . pollution from pipelines . . ." (art. 79(2)).

If the coastal state decides to exploit the non-living resources of its continental shelf beyond 200 nautical miles from the baselines then a system of payments to the International Seabed Authority is to be distributed "on the basis of equitable sharing criteria, taking into account the interests and needs of developing States, particularly the least developed and the land-locked among them." Art. 82(4).

§12.8.1 Delimitation of the Continental Shelf Between States with Opposite or Adjacent Coasts

One of the most intractable problems surrounding the issue of continental shelves has been the question of delimitation of the shelf when it is claimed by more than one state. The issue has generated a number of cases before the International Court of Justice. The 1982 Convention states that delimitation "shall be effected by agreement on the basis of international law . . . in order to achieve an equitable solution." Art. 83(1). "If no agreement can be reached within a reasonable period of time, the States concerned shall resort to the procedure provided for in Part XV." Art. 83(2). Part XV permits parties to the Convention to choose one of a variety of dispute settlement mechanisms, including the International Court of Justice and the International Tribunal for the Law of the Sea (art. 287), which is established under the Convention (see Annex VI), or binding conciliation (art. 284). A Commission on the Limits of the Continental Shelf is also established under article 76(8) and Annex II, and parties can request recommendations from the Commission, which are binding.

There are three different types of decisions that have contributed to this growing area of continental shelf delimitation law: (1) agreements between states delimiting their continental shelves (see *International Maritime Boundaries* (Jonathan Charney & Lewis Alexander eds. 1998)); (2) decisions of the International Court of Justice (e.g., *Continental Shelf* (Tunisia v. Libya), 1982 I.C.J. 18; *Delimitation of the Maritime Boundary in the Gulf of Maine Area* (Canada v. U.S.), 1984 I.C.J. 246; *Maritime Delimitation in Area between Greenland and Jan Mayen* (Denmark v. Norway), 1993 I.C.J. 38); and (3) decisions of ad hoc arbitral tribunals (e.g., *Delimitation of the Maritime Areas between Canada and France* (St. Pierre and Miquelon), 31 I.L.M. 1145 (1992)). Jonathan Charney, who was a leading authority on the law of the sea, summed up the juris-prudence of this area of law as follows:

> A primary criticism of the current state of this law is its indeterminacy. International law does not require that maritime boundaries be delimited in accordance with any particular method; rather, it requires that they be delim-ited in accordance with equitable principles, taking into account all of the relevant circumstances of the case so as to produce an equitable result. The equitable principles are indeterminate and the relevant circumstances are theoretically unlimited. Jonathan Charney, *Progress in International Maritime Delimitation Law*, 88 Am. J. Int'l L. 227, 230 (1994).

Charney hoped that "the continuing series of judgments and awards . . . [would] progressively refine the legal rules and their objectives." *Id.* at 233.

§12.9 THE HIGH SEAS

Under the 1958 Convention, the high seas were defined as any part of the sea that was not either territorial sea or internal waters. Since the 1982 Convention added new areas of the sea that were subject to certain rights conferred upon coastal states, the definition had to be changed. Article 86 of the 1982 Convention now defines the high seas as "all parts of the sea that are not included in the exclusive economic zone, in the territorial sea or the internal waters of a State, or in the archipelagic waters of an archipelagic State. . . ."

By the early seventeenth century the idea that the high seas should be open to all nations had been clearly articulated by the great Dutch jurist Hugo Grotius in his seminal work *Mare Liberum* (1609). This ancient principle has been preserved in the 1982 Convention, which states that "[n]o State may validly purport to subject any part of the high seas to its sovereignty." Art. 89. Article 87 reaffirms that "[t]he high seas are open to all States, whether coastal or landlocked. . . ." This article also confirms "freedom of navigation," "freedom of overflight," "freedom to lay any submarine cables and pipelines," "freedom to construct artificial islands and other installations permitted by international law," "freedom of fishing," and "freedom of scientific research." These freedoms must "be exercised . . . with due regard for the interests of other States . . . and also with due regard for the rights under this Convention with respect to activities in the Area." (The Area covers the deep sea bed, ocean floor, and subsoil, see §12.10 *infra*).

Article 88 of the 1982 Convention clearly states that "[t]he high seas shall be reserved for peaceful purposes." Many states engage in military maneuvers and the testing of conventional weapons on the high seas. The issue of testing nuclear weapons on the sea, land, or underground has generated much controversy. The Comprehensive Test Ban Treaty, which prohibits all nuclear weapons tests and nuclear explosions, was opened for signature in 1996 and has been signed by 182 states. U.N. Doc. A/50/1027(1996), reprinted at 35 I.L.M. 1439 (1996). One hundred and fifty-three states have already deposited their ratifications of the treaty, but it is not yet in force, as forty-four specific states must ratify the treaty before it goes into force. Currently, thirty-five of the forty-four states have deposited ratifications. (See also §12.14 *infra* and Chapter 10, §10.5.3 *supra*.)

§12.10 THE DEEP SEA BED

None of the 1958 Conventions had dealt with the deep sea bed largely because the possibility of economic activity on the sea bed was considered extremely remote. Rapid technological advances have made deep sea bed mining feasible. The discovery of manganese nodules and other minerals on the sea bed began to enhance the economic prospects for sea-bed mining. In the early 1980s, this mining was thought to be imminent but a decade long depressed market for certain minerals reduced the immediate prospects for mining.

The regime created for the deep sea bed in the 1982 Convention appears at Part XI with annexes (arts. 133-191). It is highly complex and only the briefest outline will be given here. The 1994 Agreement, which seeks to modify key provisions of Part XI, will also be sketched briefly.

The core dispute relating to the deep sea bed focuses on the issue of who owns the deep sea bed and who should control the assets resulting from any economic development of that area. Many developing countries felt that the deep sea bed was "the common heritage of mankind" (art. 136) and that any activities carried out in such an area should be "carried out for the benefit of mankind as a whole . . . taking into particular consideration the interests and needs of developing States. . . ." Art. 104. The industrialized states with the technological capacity to engage in deep sea bed mining tended to favor a free enterprise system with the spoils going to whoever managed to exploit an area first, similar to the freedom to fish on the high seas. A type of compromise was worked out between these two positions in the 1982 Convention but the developed nations initially refused to ratify the Convention principally because of dissatisfaction with the deep sea bed regime.

§12.10.1 The Deep Sea Bed Regime Under the 1982 Convention

The 1982 Convention defines as the "Area" "the sea-bed and ocean floor and subsoil thereof, beyond the limits of national jurisdiction. . . ." Art. 1(1). All activities in the "Area" are controlled by the International Seabed Authority (arts. 1(2), 153, 156-158). The principal organs of the Authority are the Assembly, the Council, the Secretariat, and the Enterprise. A system of "parallel access" is set up, whereby either the Enterprise or a public or private entity can undertake economic development of the Area but all such entities must enter into agreements with the Authority in order to carry out any activities in the Area.

A public or private entity applying to develop a site in the Area is required to submit applications to work at two equally viable sites. The Enterprise will award one site to the applicant and reserve the other site for itself or qualified applicants from developing states. This system essentially requires applicants to undertake site development work for their possible competitors. The applicant is also obliged to transfer any specialized technology used in the operation to the Enterprise and qualified developing states at reasonable rates.

The transfer of technology requirement is mandatory and again requires the applicant to reveal valuable information to its competitors. The idea behind these two requirements, parallel access and technology transfer, was to provide access to the resources of the deep sea bed to developing nations, but the Convention specifies that these requirements only last for ten years once the Enterprise has begun development of the deep sea bed.

There are also provisions for a heavy application fee of $500,000, an annual fixed fee of not less that $1 million, and other complex details relating to the financial terms of the contracts to be made by the Enterprise with applicants.

A number of industrialized states objected to many of the deep sea bed mining provisions. One category of objections related to the organizational structure of the various institutions created by the deep sea bed regime. The fear was that because key industrial states were not guaranteed seats on some of the constituent organs, those organs would be dominated by developing countries. The economic objections related to what was seen as discriminatory competitive advantage being given to the Enterprise at the cost of the applicants and the burden of heavy financial payments, limitations on production, and revenues being distributed to developing countries. It was hoped that the industrialized states would find enough advantage in the rest of the Convention to persuade them to accept the deep sea provisions, but his was not to be.

§12.10.2 The Deep Sea Bed Regime Under the 1994 Agreement

Under the auspices of the U.N. Secretary-General, consultations took place to try to resolve the various objections. By the summer of 1994 an agreement had been reached to modify the deep sea bed provisions of the Convention. This agreement went into force in 1996 and has been ratified by 140 states, 1836 U.N.T.S. 3. It modifies the 1982 Convention to the extent that the documents are inconsistent. The new agreement alters various parts of the decision-making process in certain sea bed institutions, limits the sea bed regime to the time when it becomes economically viable and then bases the regime on free-market principles. It also alters the fees and revenue structure of the Convention. Interesting legal issues were raised concerning the question of whether states that had already ratified the 1982 Convention could be bound by the changes in the 1994 Agreement since the 1982 Convention's articles of amendment made no provisions for the modification procedure envisioned by the 1994 Agreement. The 1994 Agreement attempts to deal with this dilemma at articles 395-400.

§12.11 SETTLEMENT OF MARITIME DISPUTES

The Convention also contains a mandatory dispute settlement mechanism for any disputes that arise out of the application or interpretation of the Convention. Parties to a dispute have a variety of fora in which to settle their differences. They may choose to go before the International Court of Justice or a newly created court, the International Tribunal for the Law of the Sea, including a Sea-Bed Disputes Chamber, or an arbitral tribunal, or a specialized arbitral tribunal. The International Tribunal for the Law of the Sea (http://www.itlos.org/) sits in Hamburg, Germany, and is now hearing cases and issuing judgments.

§12.12 MARINE POLLUTION

Environmental law, like many other areas of law, has often made progress in the wake of crisis. The law relating to marine pollution is no exception to this rule. A series of treaties have come into existence to deal with particular problems. Three areas have been of special concern, oil spills, the dumping of various types of refuse, and the release of nuclear waste. Each of these areas has generated multilateral and bilateral treaties and the brief descriptions below highlight some of the more important treaties.

The Convention for the Prevention of the Pollution of the Sea by Oil (OILPOL), 327 U.N.T.S. 3, prohibited the discharge of oil at sea and gave the flag state jurisdiction to prosecute violators. These prohibitions have been extended to cover other noxious substances by the International Convention for the Prevention of Marine Pollution from Ships, 1973, as modified by the Protocol of 1978 (MARPOL 73/78), which entered into force in 1983, 1340 U.N.T.S. 264.

When oil tankers ran aground and discharged large quantities of oil near a coastline, the coastal state was unsure what actions it was permitted to undertake to protect itself. In 1967, the *Torrey Canyon*, a Liberian-registered tanker, ran aground off the south coast of England, leaking massive amounts of oil into the sea. The British authorities bombed the tanker to minimize further damage. This incident gave rise to the International Convention Relating to Intervention on the High Seas in Cases of Oil Pollution Casualties, 970 U.N.T.S. 282, which permits parties to the Convention to "take such measures on the high seas as may be necessary to prevent, mitigate or eliminate grave and imminent danger to their coastline or related interests from pollution or threat of pollution of the sea by oil, following upon a maritime casualty or acts related to such a casualty, which may reasonably be expected to result in major harmful consequences." Id. art. 1(1).

The issue of compensation for damages caused by oil spills was addressed by the Convention on Civil Liability for Oil Pollution Damage, which imposes strict liability, 973 U.N.T.S. 3, with certain exceptions, on the vessel owners and requires compensation. An international fund was established by another Convention to provide for compensation where the polluting owner's assets proved insufficient, 110 U.N.T.S. 47.

The Geneva Convention on the High Seas, 450 U.N.T.S. 82, requires states to take measures to prevent the dumping of radioactive waste in the sea. Id. art. 25. There are also a number of conventions relating to dumping of different sorts of waste from ships and aircraft.

In 1978, another Liberian-registered tanker, the Amoco Cadiz, foundered off the coast of Brittany, France. It released most of its cargo of 230,000 tons of crude oil. This accident proved influential in the drafting of the 1982 Convention. Part XII of the 1982 Convention contains detailed provisions on the "Protection and Preservation of the Marine Environment" (arts. 192-237). The obligation to protect and preserve the marine environment (art. 194(1)) is imposed on all parties, and states must take measures "necessary to prevent, reduce and control pollution of the marine environment from any source . . ." (art. 194(1)). These measures include the control of pollution from vessels (art. 211). Enforcement of regulations can be carried out by the flag state (art. 217), port states (art. 218), or coastal states (art. 220(2)).

The Convention imposes obligations of "Global and Regional Co-operation," "Technical Assistance," and "Monitoring and Environmental Assistance." It also requires the regulation of pollution from land-based sources, from sea-bed activities, from activities in the Area, from dumping, from vessels, and from or through the atmosphere (arts. 197-212). Altogether the 1982 Convention provides an extremely comprehensive regime for the control of marine pollution.

§12.13 JURISDICTION OVER VESSELS

One of the pervasive problems connected with the law of the sea concerns the proper registration and control over vessels. For centuries, ships that have sought to evade the law have either shunned all registration (becoming a stateless vessel, see *infra* art. 92(2)) or have found a "registration of convenience," that is they have registered in states that have the fewest regulations surrounding registration and exercise virtually no control over ships once they are registered. You may have wondered why almost every oil tanker involved in an accident is registered in Liberia, Panama, or Honduras. The answer is that registration in these countries is relatively inexpensive, and these states exercise much less control over their registered ships than many other states. The minimum wages for crews are far lower than minimum wages in many countries. The ship owners can, therefore, operate their ships much less expensively than if they were registered in a state with more rigorous regulations.

The 1982 Convention guarantees that "[e]very State, whether coastal or land-locked, has the right to sail ships flying its flag on the high seas." Art. 90. Article 91 describes the nationality of ships:

> 1. Every State shall fix the conditions for the grant of its nationality to ships, for the registration of ships in its territory, and for the right to fly its flag. Ships have the nationality of the State whose flag they are entitled to fly. There must exist a genuine link between the State and the ship; . . .
>
> 2. Every State shall issue to ships to which it has granted the right to fly its flag documents to that effect.

Article 92 describes the status of ships:

> 1. Ships shall sail under the State of one flag only and, save in exceptional cases expressly provided for in international treaties or in this Convention, shall be subject to its exclusive jurisdiction on the high seas. A ship may not change its flag during a voyage or while in a port of call, save only in the case of a real transfer of ownership or change of registry.
>
> 2. A ship which sails under the flags of two or more States, using them according to convenience, may not claim any of the nationalities in question with respect to any other State, and may be assimilated to a ship without nationality.

Article 95, however provides warships with immunity from jurisdiction:

> Warships on the high seas have complete immunity from the jurisdiction of any State other than the flag state.

The articles above raise two related issues: (a) What exactly is a genuine link and (b) what may a State do if it knows or suspects that a ship has no genuine link with the state of registration?

§12.13.1 The Genuine Link Requirement

The 1982 Convention imposes a number of duties upon the flag state, which are spelled out in article 94. In general the state of registration is required to exercise "jurisdiction and control in administrative, technical and social matters over ships flying its flag." Art. 94(1). The state must "maintain a register of ships" and take jurisdiction over "the master, officers and crew" with respect to "administrative, technical and social matters concerning the ship." Art. 94(2). States must "ensure safety at sea" of their ships (art. 94(3)), and a detailed list of the measures to be taken to ensure safety are spelled out. Art. 94(3)-(5) & (7). Clearly if all states complied with the requirements of article 94, the enforcement of the requirements would in themselves go some way to providing a genuine link between the vessel and the state of registration.

Other factors have also been looked at to determine a genuine link. The Restatement of the Law Third, Foreign Relations Law of the United States §501, cmt. b states:

> "*Genuine link.*" In general, a state has a "genuine link" entitling it to register a ship and to authorize the ship to use its flag if the ship is owned by nationals of the state, whether natural or juridical persons, and the state exercises effective control over the ship. In most cases a ship is owned by a corporation created by the state of registry. However, in determining whether a "genuine link" with the state of registry exists, the following additional factors are to be taken into account: whether the officers and crew of the ship are nationals of the state, how often the ship stops in the ports of the state; and how extensive and effective is the control that the state exercises over the ship.

§12.13.2 Remedy Where There Is No Genuine Link

Article 94(6) of the 1982 Convention provides:

> A State which has clear grounds to believe that proper jurisdiction and control with respect to a ship have not been exercised may report the facts to the flag state. Upon receiving such a report, the flag State shall investigate the matter and, if appropriate, take any action to remedy the situation.

The Restatement Third §501, cmt. b states:

> Although international law requires a genuine link between the ship and the registering state, the lack of a genuine link does not justify another state in refusing to recognize the flag or in interfering with the ship. A state may, however, reject diplomatic protection by the flag state when the flag state has no genuine link with the ship. If another state doubts the existence of a genuine link, for instance, because there is evidence that the flag state has not

been exercising its duties to control and regulate the ship (see §502), it may request that the flag state "investigate the matter and, if appropriate, take any action necessary to remedy the situation." LOS Convention, Art. 94(6); . . .

The Restatement clearly thought that if a state did not in fact have a genuine link with a ship bearing its registration, then if the flag state tried to represent the ship before an international tribunal, the state against which the claim was filed could successfully move for dismissal of the suit on the ground that the flag state had no right to represent the ship because of the lack of a genuine link between the ship and the state of registration. This, however, was not the view taken by the first case raising this issue before the International Tribunal on the Law of the Sea. See *The Saiga* case, 1999 ITLOS No. 2 in Explanation 12-7 *infra*.

Example 12-7

In 1987, during the Iran-Iraq War, Kuwait found that a number of its oil tankers were coming under fire as they crossed the Persian Gulf. The Kuwait government requested military protection from the United States (and the United Kingdom). Since a proportion of the oil shipped from Kuwait was destined for the U.S. market, the U.S. government agreed to provide protection for eleven ships but only if the Kuwaiti vessels were reflagged as U.S.-registered ships. The ships were Kuwaiti owned, built in Japan, with Arab and Filipino crews.

The reflagging was accomplished by creating a corporation, Chesapeake Shipping, Inc., in Delaware. Its sole assets were the eleven tankers, and its sole activity was to charter the tankers back to the original owner, the Kuwait Oil Tanker Company, a Kuwaiti corporation. A number of waivers were granted on "national security grounds" from U.S. safety and inspection requirements. Initially only the captain was going to be a U.S. citizen, but after an outcry from the American maritime unions, the top five officers were required to be Americans.

Was there a genuine link between the reflagged oil tankers and the United States? If not, what were other states permitted to do about the lack of a genuine link?

Explanation

The link between the oil tankers and the United States was extremely thin. Clearly the United States (or the United Kingdom) is permitted to give whatever protection it deems fit to the vessels of other nations who may be vulnerable to attack. The decision to offer such protection is a matter of policy. The registration of vessels, however, seems to call for a much closer connection between the ship and its state of registration than merely setting up a paper corporation in the state of registration and requiring a few of the officers to be nationals of the home state. It is not clear what, if any, regulation or supervision the U.S. exercised over the oil tankers. Rigorous enforcement of U.S. safety and labor standards could have increased the link between the ships and the U.S. but the U.S. appears to have exempted the oil tankers from such regulations.

As for what other nations may do in light of such a weak link, it has been suggested that other nations could refuse to recognize the legitimacy of the registration thus rendering the ship stateless and subject to the jurisdiction of all states, but the Restatement rejects that view where the ship is properly registered. Some states might argue that the United States had no right to represent the tankers at the international level because of the lack of a genuine link. If an international court agreed, then a case brought on behalf of the tankers by the U.S. in an international tribunal might be dismissed on the grounds that because of the lack of a genuine link, the U.S. forfeited its right to represent the tankers.

The above suggestion of the legal consequences of the lack of a genuine link between a ship and its state of registration has, however, been rejected by the Law of the Sea Tribunal in *The Saiga* case (St. Vincent and the Grenadines v. Guinea), 1999 ITLOS No. 2. In that case the Tribunal ruled that when another state has grounds "to believe that proper jurisdiction and control with respect to a ship have not been exercised" (art. 94(6)), [t]hat State is entitled to report the facts to the flag State, which is then obliged to "investigate the matter and, if appropriate, take any action necessary to remedy the situation." *Id.* at para. 82. The Tribunal added that "the purpose of the provisions of the Convention on the need for a genuine link between a ship and its flag State is to assure more effective implementation of the duties of the flag State, and not to establish criteria by reference to which the validity of the registration of ships in a flag State may be challenged by other states." *Id.* at para. 83. The Tribunal also concluded that "there is no legal basis for . . . refus[ing] to recognize the right" of the ship to fly the flag of registration "on the ground that there was no genuine link between the ship" and the state of registration. *Id.* at para. 86. This ruling of the Tribunal has been heavily criticized. The reflagging of the Kuwaiti tankers caused a huge amount of criticism both from American and foreign maritime interests. After the cease-fire in the Iran-Iraq war, the reflagging was quietly dropped, and the tankers reverted to their Kuwaiti registration.

Later, in another case, the Tribunal ruled that Belize could not represent a ship before the Tribunal where the ship was not in possession of a current certificate of registration, even though the ship had previously been provisionally registered in Belize, but the provisional registration had expired and the ship had been "de-registered." In that case, France had arrested the ship for illegally fishing in the EEZ and Belize had sought the prompt release of the ship. France asked the Tribunal to dismiss Belize's claim for lack of proper registration. The Tribunal agreed with the French argument and dismissed the suit. *The "Grand Prince" case* (Belize v. France), 2001 ITLOS No. 8 (Prompt release).

§12.14 PROHIBITED ACTIVITIES ON THE HIGH SEAS

Certain activities are prohibited on the high seas. Article 99 of the 1982 Convention prohibits the transportation of slaves and declares that any slave taking refuge on board a ship "shall *ipso facto* be free." Article 100 imposes the obligation on all states to "cooperate to the fullest extent in the repression of piracy on the high seas. . . ." Piracy is given a highly technical definition in article 110.[1] States must also "cooperate in the suppression of illicit traffic in narcotic drugs and psychotropic substances . . ." (art. 108) and "cooperate in the suppression of unauthorized broadcasting from the high seas." Art. 109(1). Ships must also be registered and fly under the flag of the state of registration. Arts. 91 & 92.

What may a ship do if it comes across a vessel engaged in one of the prohibited activities?

When we were examining the bases for the assertion of jurisdiction by a state, we examined the Universality Principle. Chapter 6 §6.6. There it was stated that there are certain activities, including slavery, piracy, and operating a stateless vessel, that are considered sufficiently heinous to confer universal jurisdiction on all states. In other words, any state that finds the perpetrator is authorized to apprehend, try, and punish him or her, provided that the domestic laws of the particular state apprehending the suspect permit such a trial. Some scholars would add drug trafficking and hostage taking to the list. Although the 1982 Convention does not recognize this principle directly it does make certain provisions with respect to certain prohibited activities.

Article 105 provides that "[o]n the high seas . . . every State may seize a pirate ship or aircraft . . . [and] [t]he courts of the State which carried out

---

1. 1982 Convention, art. 101 defines piracy as follows:

Piracy consists of any of the following acts:

(a) any illegal acts of violence or detention, or any act of depredation, committed for private ends by the crew or the passengers of a private ship or a private aircraft, and directed:

(i) on the high seas, against another ship or aircraft, or against persons or property on board such ship or aircraft;
(ii) against a ship, aircraft, persons or property in a place outside the jurisdiction of any State;

(b) any act of voluntary participation in the operation of a ship or of an aircraft with knowledge of facts making it a pirate ship or aircraft;
(c) any act of inciting or of intentionally facilitating an act described in subparagraph (a) or (b).

the seizure may decide upon the penalties to be imposed. . . ." Such seizures can only be carried out by "warships or military aircraft. . . ." Art. 107.

Article 109 permits a number of different states the right to arrest and try those engaged in unauthorized broadcasting on the high seas: "(a) the flag state . . ."; "(b) the State of registry of the installation," if the broadcast is from an installation; "(c) the State of which the . . . [broadcaster] is a national"; "(d) any State where the transmission can be received"; or "(e) any State where authorized radio communication is suffering interference."

With respect to narcotic trafficking, article 108 only provides that the flag state of the suspected vessel "may request the co-operation of other States to suppress such traffic."

Article 110 provides for a "right of visit" in certain circumstances:

1. Except where acts of interference derive from powers conferred by treaty, a warship which encounters on the high seas a foreign ship, other than a ship entitled to complete immunity in accordance with articles 95 and 96, is not justified in boarding it unless there is reasonable ground for suspecting that:
(a) the ship is engaged in piracy:
(b) the ship is engaged in the slave trade;
(c) the ship is engaged in unauthorized broadcasting and the flag State of the warship has jurisdiction under article 109;
(d) the ship is without nationality; or
(e) though flying a foreign flag or refusing to show its flag, the ship is, in reality, of the same nationality as the warship.

2. In the cases provided for in paragraph 1, the warship may proceed to verify the ship's right to fly its flag. To this end, it may send a boat under the command of an officer to the suspected ship. If suspicion remains after the documents have been checked, it may proceed to a further examination on board the ship, which must be carried out with all possible consideration.

3. If the suspicions prove to be unfounded, and provided that the ship boarded has not committed any act justifying them, it shall be compensated for any loss or damage that may have been sustained.

4. These provisions apply *mutatis mutandis* to military aircraft.

5. These provisions also apply to any other duly authorized ships or aircraft clearly marked and identifiable as being on government service.

The above article obviously provides for a right of inspection in the circumstances outlined but it is not clear what powers the inspecting vessel has if its suspicions prove founded. May the inspecting ship arrest the crew and take them and the ship back to home port? May the crew be tried? If so, for what?

In general, it would be expected that a ship arrested, for example, for piracy would be tried for piracy in the courts of the arresting state, or a ship arrested for unauthorized broadcasting would be tried for that offense in the arresting state. (Note: The arresting state will need to have legislation permitting such an arrest and laws proscribing such activity.)

Example 12-8

A ship called "The Saucy Sam" was sailing on the high seas in the Pacific Ocean. It did not appear to be flying a flag. The coast guard from the State of Unity approached the ship, boarded her, found no documents of registration but did find a huge cargo of guns and missile launchers. When questioned, the captain and crew refused to discuss where the guns had been purchased or to where they were to be delivered. The coast guard arrested the ship and took it back to Unity. Assume that Unity has laws permitting such an arrest. After investigation it was discovered that the guns had been illegally purchased in State L and were destined for State M. There is no evidence that the guns were ever intended to arrive in the State of Unity.

For what crimes may the captain of "The Saucy Sam" be tried?

Explanation

Presumably the captain (and probably the owners of the ship) can be tried for sailing a stateless vessel. Whether they can also be tried for illegal ownership of guns or the intent to distribute guns illegally is more problematic. Some states take the view that there is no necessity for any nexus between the illegal activity and the forum state, and they have interpreted their laws (some would argue have stretched the interpretation) to permit such prosecution. *U.S. v. Marino-Garcia/U.S. v. Cassalins-Guzman*, 679 F.2d 1373 (11th Cir. 1982); *U.S. v. Garcia*, 182 Fed. App. 873 (11th Cir. 2006), cert. denied, 549 U.S. 1110 (2007). Such prosecutions may not provoke much sympathy for gunrunners or drug dealers but what if the cargo consists of items that are prohibited in some states but not in others, such as liquor or marijuana? Should teetotal states be allowed to prosecute vessels for carrying liquor simply because the ship is not registered? In theory, prosecution where there is the lack of any nexus to the forum state appears unjust and was probably not intended by the 1982 Convention, but in practice, the overwhelming majority of stateless vessels tend to be engaged in activities that are universally condemned, and they avoid registration or fly a false flag in an attempt to avoid any jurisdiction over their illegal activities.

§12.15 JURISDICTION OVER FOREIGN VESSELS

§12.15.1 Jurisdiction in Internal Waters and Ports

States may assert jurisdiction over foreign vessels in their internal waters on the basis of the Territorial Principle. The Restatement Third §512, cmt. c states:

> The coastal state may exercise jurisdiction with respect to a ship in port and over activities on board such ship, but in practice coastal states usually have little interest in exercising jurisdiction over such activities, except when the peace of the port is disturbed.

With respect to foreign vessels in port, the coastal state would generally rather have the master of the ship or the flag state exercise jurisdiction over foreign vessels, but there are exceptions to this disinclination to exercise jurisdiction. The general rule has grown up through a large number of bilateral treaties that forgo jurisdiction except when activity on board disturbs "the peace of the port," that murder and manslaughter disturb the "peace of the port" but that nothing else does, even multiple stabbings and chaotic fights on board. *Wildenhus' Case*, 120 U.S. 1 (1887).

§12.15.2 Jurisdiction in the Territorial Sea

The 1982 Convention makes it clear that the coastal state's sovereignty extends to the territorial sea (art. 2(1) & (2)) but that the sovereignty has to be exercised pursuant to the Convention and other rules of international law (art. 2(3)). Foreign ships are given a right of innocent passage through the territorial sea (art. 17), and we have already discussed what a state may do when it suspects a foreign ship is violating its right of innocent passage. §12.3.2(b)

The coastal state is free to extend its laws to the territorial sea, and to the extent that it does so, ships that violate those laws are subject to arrest but with rather large exceptions carved out by the 1982 Convention. Article 27 provides:

Criminal jurisdiction on board a foreign ship
1. The criminal jurisdiction of the coastal State should not be exercised on board a foreign ship passing through the territorial sea to arrest any person or to conduct any investigation in connection with any crime

committed on board the ship during its passage, save only in the following cases:

(a) if the consequences of the crime extend to the coastal State;

(b) if the crime is of a kind to disturb the peace of the country or the good order of the territorial sea;

(c) if the assistance of the local authorities has been requested by the master of the ship or by a diplomatic agent or consular officer of the flag State; or

(d) if such measures are necessary for the suppression of illicit traffic in narcotic drugs or psychotropic substances.

2. The above provisions do not affect the right of the coastal State to take any steps authorized by its laws for the purpose of an arrest or investigation on board a foreign ship passing through the territorial sea after leaving internal waters. . . .

5. Except as provided in Part XII or with respect to violations of laws and regulations adopted in accordance with Part V, the coastal State may not take any steps on board a foreign ship passing through the territorial sea to arrest any person or to conduct any investigation in connection with any crime committed before the ship entered the territorial sea, if the ship, proceeding from a foreign port, is only passing through the territorial sea without entering internal waters.

In general, then, the coastal state may not assert its criminal jurisdiction over foreign vessels passing through its territorial sea, with the few exceptions noted above.

With respect to the exercise of civil jurisdiction over foreign ships passing through the territorial sea, article 28 of the 1982 Convention also has a list of prohibitions with the result that the coastal state has very limited powers.

§12.15.3 The Right of Hot Pursuit

If a coastal state proclaims an EEZ of 200 nautical miles and prohibits all fishing by foreign vessels in the zone, and the coast guard finds a foreign vessel fishing within the zone, what may the coastal state authorities do? The coast guard can arrest the ship while the fishing vessel is in the EEZ but what if the fishermen head out to the high seas? Can the suspected ship be arrested on the high seas?

Article 111 provides for the right of hot pursuit from the various zones created by the 1982 Convention.

Right of hot pursuit

1. The hot pursuit of a foreign ship may be undertaken when the competent authorities of the coastal State have good reason to believe that

the ship has violated the laws and regulations of the State. Such pursuit must be commenced when foreign ship or one of its boats is within the internal waters, the archipelagic waters, the territorial sea or the contiguous zone of the pursuing State, and may only be continued outside the territorial sea or the contiguous zone if the pursuit has not been interrupted. It is not necessary that, at the time when the foreign ship within the territorial sea or the contiguous zone receives the order to stop, the ship giving the order should likewise be within the territorial sea or the contiguous zone. If the foreign ship is within a contiguous zone, as defined in article 33, the pursuit may only be undertaken if there has been a violation of the rights for the protection of which the zone was established.

2. The right of hot pursuit shall apply *mutatis mutandis* to violations in the exclusive economic zone or on the continental shelf, including safety zones around continental shelf installations, of the laws and regulations of the coastal State applicable in accordance with this Convention to the exclusive economic zone or the continental shelf, including such safety zones.

3. The right of hot pursuit ceases as soon as the ship pursued enters the territorial sea of its own State or of a third State.

4. Hot pursuit is not deemed to have begun unless the pursuing ship has satisfied itself by such practicable means as may be available that the ship pursued or one of its boats or other craft working as a team and using the ship pursued as a mother ship is within the limits of the territorial sea, or, as the case may be, within the contiguous zone or the exclusive economic zone or above the continental shelf. The pursuit may only be commenced after a visual or auditory signal to stop has been given at a distance which enables it to be seen or heard by the foreign ship.

5. The right of hot pursuit may be exercised only by warships or military aircraft, or other ships or aircraft clearly marked and identifiable as being on government service and authorized to that effect.

Example 12-9

The coast guard ship from the State of Eta notices that every time they catch sight of a ship called "Peace and Harmony" flying the Eta flag and duly registered in Eta, the "Peace and Harmony" always turns tail and heads in the other direction. The coast guard thinks this is suspicious. The "Peace and Harmony" is sighted in Eta's EEZ, and the coast guard decides to chase her. The Eta coast guard eventually catches up with the "Peace and Harmony" 300 miles off the coast of Eta and arrests the ship.

Did the Eta coast guard have the right to arrest the "Peace and Harmony" on the high seas?

Explanation

First, the coast guard had no "good reason to believe that the ship ha[d] violated the laws and regulations" of Eta except for the fact that the "Peace and Harmony" headed in the other direction whenever the coast guard came in sight, thus there would be no right of hot pursuit and the arrest on the high seas would be illegal.

But that answer is wrong because "hot pursuit" only applies to foreign ships. The coast guard ships do not need any special Convention right to chase ships that are registered in their own state (other than general national legislation giving such rights).

In general, where it is determined that there was no violation of the coastal states' laws in the zone in which the foreign ship was located when the chase started, then the pursuit will not be upheld. Similarly, if the laws in the various zones go beyond what is permitted by the Convention, the pursuit and conviction will not be upheld. *The Saiga* case (St. Vincent and the Grenadines v. Guinea), 1999 ITLOS No. 2.

Example 12-10

Suppose now that the Eta coast guard spotted a ship flying the flag of one of its neighbors, the State of Delta. The Delta ship appears to be fishing 120 nautical miles off Eta's coast. As the Eta coast guard approaches the fishing ship, they signal the fishing ship to heave to, but the fishermen turn the boat around and head out to sea. The Eta coast guard chases the Delta ship out to sea for another 100 nautical miles. Eventually the Delta ship changes course and heads for the coast. The Eta coast guard finally arrests the Delta ship when it is ten nautical miles from the coast of the State of Beta.

1) Was the pursuit of the Delta ship by the Eta coast guard illegal?

2) Was the arrest of Delta the fishing vessel by the Eta coast guard illegal?

Explanations

1) Initially the pursuit of the Delta fishing ship appears legal as the coast guard had "good reason to believe that the ship ha[d] violated the laws and regulations of" Eta (art. 111(1)). Prohibiting fishing by foreign ships in the EEZ is perfectly permissible (arts. 56 & 57). The ship was 120 nautical miles off the coast of Eta, well within the 200-nautical-mile maximum. The ship was signaled to heave to while it was within the EEZ, and there is no evidence that the chase was interrupted. Until the coast guard entered the territorial sea of Beta, the chase was legal.

2) Article 111(3) states that the right of hot pursuit ceases "as soon as the ship pursued enters the territorial sea of its own State or of a third State." Assuming that Beta has declared a territorial sea of twelve nautical miles

(art. 3), the Eta coast guard would have no right to enter the territorial sea for the purposes of arresting a foreign ship. The only right to enter Beta's territorial sea that the Eta coast guard has is to exercise "innocent passage" (art. 17). Arresting a foreign ship is not an activity "having a direct bearing on passage" (art. 19), and this would not be "innocent passage"; article 111(3) clearly states that the right of hot pursuit ceases when the Delta ship enters Beta's territorial sea. It is possible that the Eta coast guard could have radioed to the State of Beta and sought permission to enter Beta's territorial sea for the purposes of arresting the Delta ship. Provided Beta had given its permission for the arrest in its territorial sea, the arrest would be legal. Without such permission, the arrest would be illegal.

§12.16 FISHING ON THE HIGH SEAS

Before the twentieth century, activities on the high seas operated on the basis of freedom and commonage. The high seas were open to all states, as they still are (art. 87(1)), and activities were largely unrestricted. Fishing was the main activity on the high seas and, in general, the level of fishing engaged in permitted fish and marine mammal stocks to replenish themselves, though there were notably exceptions, such as certain species of whale. With the vastly increased fishing capacity now available, the balance has tipped very much against maintaining any sort of equilibrium of fish stock unless aggressive conservation and management is practiced. Many species have been fished either to extinction or almost to extinction, and some nations have prohibited the fishing of certain species in their EEZs, even for their own fishing fleets.

The 1982 Convention recognizes the necessity for the "conservation and management of the living resources of the high seas." Articles 116-120 deal with states' obligations to practice conservation and management of the high seas' resources.

The 1982 Convention, together with the 1994 Agreement, is a remarkable example of multilateral treaty making. It set out to provide a comprehensive code for the entire area of the globe covered by water. No legislative effort can ever be completely successful and will always need amendment and modification as circumstances change but the 1982 Convention stands as one of the most influential pieces of international law making of the twentieth century.

CHAPTER 13

International Environmental Law

§13.1   Introduction

§13.2   State Responsibility for Environmental Harm

§13.3   Establishing the Standard for State Responsibility
for Environmental Harm

      §13.3.1 Customary Law Standards

      §13.3.2 Declarations and Treaty Law Standards

§13.4   Hazardous Waste

§13.5   Atmosphere, Ozone, and Climate

§13.6   Nature, Flora, Fauna, and Other Resources

§13.7   Nuclear Fallout

§13.8   Other Regimes

§13.9   Guiding Environmental Principles

      §13.9.1 The Precautionary Principle

      §13.9.2 The Principle of Intergenerational Equity

      §13.9.3 The Principle of Sustainable Development

      §13.9.4 The Polluter Pays Principle

      §13.9.5 The Environmental Impact Assessment Principle

      §13.9.6 The Recognition of Differentiated Responsibilities
for Developed and Developing States

§13.10 Conclusion

§13.1 INTRODUCTION

International environmental law has been an area of dynamic growth, particularly in the last forty years. During the preindustrial era, states did not have much capacity to damage the globe but with the rise of the industrial state that changed. The mining of fossil fuels and the production of manufactured goods increased the capacity for environmental damage dramatically. Some decades passed before it was suspected that man's activities were the direct cause of changes in the environment, and further decades went by before the scientific proof was forthcoming that these changes were harmful and the direct cause of damage. Even with solid scientific evidence, it is taking some time for the international community to develop standards for state responsibility, agree on prohibited activities, and articulate remedies for violations of norms.

The area of international environmental law is closely connected to human rights law. The Universal Declaration on Human Rights was adopted by the United Nations General Assembly in 1948 and became the framework for the human rights system. It states that "[e]veryone has the right to work . . ." (art. 23(1)); "the right to a standard living adequate for the health and well-being of himself and of his family, including food, clothing, housing and medical care . . ." (art. 25). The International Covenant on Economic, Social and Cultural Rights, 993 U.N.T.S. 3, was adopted in 1966, entered into force in 1976, and now has 160 parties. It provides: "All peoples may, for their own needs, freely dispose of their natural wealth and resources . . ." (art. 1(2)). The Covenant recognizes "the right to work" (art. 6); "A decent living standard" (art. 7(a)(ii)); "Safe and healthy working conditions" (art. 7(b)); "the right of everyone to an adequate standard of living . . . adequate food, clothing and housing and . . . the continuous improvement of living conditions" (art. 11(1)); "the right of everyone to be free from hunger" (art. 11(2)); the State's obligation "to improve methods of production, conservation and distribution of food . . . by developing or reforming agrarian systems . . . to achieve the most efficient development and utilization of natural resources" (art. 11(2)(a)); "the right of everyone to the enjoyment of the highest attainable standard of physical and mental health" (art. 12(1)); "the right of everyone: (a) to take part in cultural life; (b) to enjoy the benefits of scientific progress and its applications" (art. 15(a) & (b)). Clearly those human rights cannot be fully achieved in a polluted and degraded environment. Thus the protection of the environment is often a crucial element in the achievement of human rights, particularly social, economic, and cultural rights. However, certain rights, such as the right to work or the right to food may, sometimes, be seen as clashing with environmental protection. People question why the habitat of the spotted owl must be protected at the expense of hundreds of jobs in logging.

The conservationists would reply that only by preserving the whole of our known ecosystem can we flourish. This debate remains controversial. How we balance the value that we give to protecting flora or fauna against the value that we accord to human needs has varied over time and the circumstances in which people perceive themselves.

§13.2 STATE RESPONSIBILITY FOR ENVIRONMENTAL HARM

Each state has a body of law describing what types of activities property owners are (a) required to engage in and (b) prohibited from undertaking. Early property law developed the notion of "nuisance" so that, for example, one property owner could sue his neighboring property owner for allowing thistles to grow in his fields, blow over into the adjoining fields, and ruin the existing crop. The property owner argued that he was entitled to relief for the damage caused by the invasive and destructive weeds. The courts began to describe such thistle growing activity as negligent, that is not in conformity with the accepted standard of care. The courts awarded damages for the resulting harm and also issued orders prohibiting such activity or requiring the thistle grower to chop down the thistles before they went to seed. There was no such similar body of law at the international level until the twentieth century when states began to realize that the activity of a particular state could cause substantial damage not only to itself but also to other states.

The original notion was that if a state wished to allow massive air or water pollution within its own borders that was no concern of the international community, but that if pollution made its way into another state, that gave rise to a legitimate claim on the part of the harmed state. Of course, it soon became apparent that pollution, in whatever form, is no respecter of national boundaries and that effective relief for the international community could only be found in a comprehensive regime that regulated the activities of a state within its own borders.

§13.3 ESTABLISHING THE STANDARD FOR STATE RESPONSIBILITY FOR ENVIRONMENTAL HARM

§13.3.1 Customary Law Standards

The first international environmental case did not occur until the 1930s in a dispute that had several phases and was finally resolved by an arbitral tribunal in 1941, the *Trail Smelter* case (U.S. v. Canada), 3 U.N. Rep. Int'l Arb. Awards 1905 (1941). In this case a Canadian company was engaged in smelting zinc and lead in the town of Trail, British Columbia, on the banks of the Columbia River about eleven miles upstream from the U.S. border. Over the years the smelting production increased, and by the 1930s more than 300 tons of sulfur were being released into the air daily. These fumes were alleged to be blowing into the United States and causing damage to property in the State of Washington. The United States and Canada referred the case to the International Joint Commission, and entity established to resolve such problems by a U.S.-Canadian Treaty. In 1931, the Commission awarded $350,000 to the United States in damages, which Canada agreed to pay. The Trail Smelter continued its operations, and a Special Arbitral Tribunal reached a decision in 1941 that compensation was due for the pollution caused between 1932 and 1937 and that in future the Trail Smelter was required to refrain from causing any damage to the State of Washington by smelting fumes. The tribunal was required to apply the "law and practice followed in dealing with cognate questions in the United States of America as well as international law and practice. . . ." *Id.* at 1912. The tribunal found that U.S. law on inter-state air pollution was the same as international law on such matters and thus it discussed what the international standard was.

The tribunal searched for a grand general principle to apply in the case and quoted with approval from an academic textbook: "A State owes at all times a duty to protect other States against injurious acts by individuals from within its jurisdiction." Clyde Eagleton, *The Responsibility of States in International Law* 80 (1928). *Id.* at 1963. Although this principle had not previously been applied to international environmental matters, it was broad enough to encompass air pollution provided the tribunal could agree on what constituted "an injurious act." The tribunal admitted that:

> No case of air pollution dealt with by an international tribunal has been brought to the attention of the Tribunal nor does the Tribunal know of any such case. The nearest analogy is that of water pollution. But, here also, no decision of an international tribunal has been cited or has been found. *Id.* at 1963.

Ultimately the tribunal concluded:

> That, under the principles of international law . . . no State has the right to use or permit the use of its territory in such a manner as to cause injury by fumes in or to the territory of another or the properties or persons therein, when the case is of serious consequence and the injury is established by clear and convincing evidence. *Id.* at 1965.

Canada was held responsible for the injurious conduct of the Trail Smelter and was obligated to ensure that the Smelter complied with the international standard. The Trail Smelter was ordered to "refrain from causing any damage through fumes to the State of Washington. . . ." *Id.* at 1966, and compensation was awarded.

The same general principles of state responsible for harm was reiterated by the I.C.J. in the *Corfu Channel* case (U.K. v. Albania), 1949 I.C.J. 4 (Merits). In that case two British warships passed through the North Corfu Channel in waters off the Albanian coast that the Court had determined to constitute an international strait through which foreign ships had a right of passage. The Channel had previously been swept for mines but, nonetheless, the British ships H.M.S. Saumarez and H.M.S. Volage struck mines and were severely damaged. Forty-four sailors died and forty-two were injured. The U.K. believed that the Albanian government had either laid the mines itself or had colluded with Yugoslavia in placing the mines in the Channel, but the U.K. lacked the evidence to prove either theory. The Court concluded that "the authors of the minelaying remain unknown. . . ." *Id.* at 17.

The U.K. then argued that, given the circumstances, the Albanian government must have known about the minelaying. The Court struggled with what knowledge might reasonably be imputed to Albania, what methods of proof should be permitted, and what burden of proof should be placed on the U.K. as the excerpt below reveals:

> It is clear that knowledge of the minelaying cannot be imputed to the Albanian Government by reason merely of the fact that a minefield discovered in Albanian territorial waters caused the explosions of which the British warships were the victims. . . . [I]t cannot be concluded from the mere fact of the control exercised by a State over its territory and waters that that State necessarily knew, or ought to have known, of any unlawful act perpetrated therein, nor yet that it necessarily knew, or should have known, the authors. This fact, by itself and apart from other circumstances, neither involves *prima facie* responsibility nor shifts the burden of proof.
>
> On the other hand, the fact of this exclusive territorial control exercised by a State within its frontiers has a bearing upon the methods of proof available to establish the knowledge of that State as to such events. By reason of this exclusive control, the other State, the victim of a breach of international law, is often unable to furnish direct proof of facts giving rise to responsibility. Such a State should be allowed a more liberal recourse to inferences of fact and circumstantial evidence. This indirect evidence is admitted in all systems of law, and its use is recognized by international decisions. It must be regarded as of special weight when it is based on a series of facts linked together and leading logically to a single conclusion.
>
> The Court must examine therefore whether it has been established by means of indirect evidence that Albania has knowledge of minelaying in her territorial waters independently of any connivance on her part in this operation. The proof may be drawn from inferences of fact, provided that they leave *no room* for reasonable doubt. . . . *Id.* at 18.

379

Albania admitted to having look-out posts a various points along the Channel. Experts were used to examine the area and report to the Court. On the basis of the Experts' Report, the Court concluded that "the laying of the minefield which caused the explosions on October 22, 1946, could not have been accomplished without the knowledge of the Albanian Government." Id. at 22. The Court thus determined that Albania's failure to warn the British ships of the danger violated Albania's obligation "not to allow knowingly its territory to be used for acts contrary to the rights of other States." Id. at 22. Albania was held responsible for the damage to the ships and the loss of life and was ordered to pay compensation to the U.K.

These early cases came about at a time when the idea of States having the capacity to injure other States by activities that had always been thought of as entirely within the control of individual States was just beginning to take hold. The general standard of care owed by a state to the international community has often been described as "due diligence." More recently, the Court characterized the standard as the "principle of prevention" in *Pulp Mills on the River Uruguay* (Argentina v. Uruguay), 2010 I.C.J. ___, at para. 101. Here the Court stated:

> A State is . . . obliged to use all the means at its disposal in order to avoid activities . . . causing significant damage to the environment. This Court has established that this obligation "is now part of the corpus of international law relating to the environment." *Legality of the Threat or Use of Nuclear Weapons*, Advisory Opinion, 1996 I.C.J. 242, at para. 29.

Again, more recently there have been suggestions that a "strict liability" standard should be applied in the case of activities recognized as ultra-hazardous. Under a strict liability standard states are liable for damage caused by their activities regardless of whether they exercised due diligence when undertaking the activities. Some conventions now apply a strict liability standard for certain dangerous activities, such as damage caused by objects emanating from human activity in space.[1]

§13.3.2 Declarations and Treaty Law Standards

In the latter half of the twentieth century individual states began to enact legislation to curb environmental damage within their own borders but the success of these efforts was dependent upon the particular political climate of the individual state. It soon became apparent that however stringent a state was in curbing its own activities, internal legislation could not protect it

---

1. See, e.g., Convention on International Liability for Damage Caused by Space Objects, art. II, 961 U.N.T.S. 187, 24 U.S.T. 2389, T.I.A.S. No. 7762, signed March 29, 1972, entered into force September 1, 1972, reprinted at 10 I.L.M. 965 (1971).

against environmental damage emanating from less responsible states. Thus a massive international effort was begun to draft principles and conventions in the environmental area.

The United Nations Conference on the Human Environment met in 1972 in Stockholm, Sweden, and issued a Declaration.[2] This type of Declaration is often characterized by grand statements of purpose. For example, Principle 2 of the Declaration states:

> The natural resources of the earth, including the air, water, land, flora and fauna and especially representative samples of natural ecosystems, must be safeguarded for the benefit of present and future generations through careful planning or management as appropriate.

Such statements are known as "soft law," insofar as they are not meant to create immediately enforceable legal rights. (See also Chapter 2, §2.9.) Rather, they represent the direction in which the international community is seeking to move and may, in time, come to represent the underlying norms that give rise to specific binding obligations upon states.

After the Stockholm Conference, the United Nations Environment Programme (UNEP) was created. The UNEP web site provides much useful information: http://www.unep.org/. Although this is one of the smaller U.N. agencies, it has been very influential in drafting a whole array of environmental treaties some of which have received widespread ratification. For example, the Convention on International Trade in Endangered Species of Wild Fauna and Flora (CITES), 993 U.N.T.S. 243, has 175 parties. Many of these treaties create ongoing monitoring systems and have periodic reviews of problems, progress, and need for further action. The latest triennial review by the parties of the CITES Convention took place in Qatar, March 13-25, 2010.

The international community also met at the Rio Summit in Brazil in 1992 at the United Nations Conference on Environment and Development. More than 170 nations and a host of non-governmental organizations met to create a framework for the environment for the next several decades. A Declaration on Environment and Development[3] was issued, which affirmed that "[h]uman beings are at the centre of concerns for sustainable development. They are entitled to a healthy and productive life in harmony with nature" (Principle I). The conference also adopted Agenda 21, which provides a broad ranging framework for the protection of the global environment. The Convention on Biological Diversity, 1760 U.N.T.S. 79, which

---

2. Stockholm Declaration of the U.N. Conference on the Human Environment, June 16, 1972, U.N. Doc. A/CONF.48/14/Rev.1 at 3 (1972), U.N. Sales No. E. 73.II.A.14 (1973), reprinted at 11 I.L.M. 1416 (1972).
3. [Rio] Declaration on Environment and Development, signed June 14, 1992, U.N. GAOR, 47th Sess., U.N. Doc. A/CONF.151/5/Rev.1 (1992), reprinted at 31 I.L.M. 874 (1992).

entered into force in 1993, has received over 190 ratifications. It has three main objectives: to conserve biological diversity; require sustainable use of the components of biological diversity; and to ensure the equitable sharing of benefits arising from the use of genetic resources. Parties are called upon to develop national plans for the conservation and sustainable use of biological diversity. The United Nations Framework Convention on Climate Change, 1771 U.N.T.S. 107, which entered into force in 1994, currently has 192 parties.

Gradually the international community has come to articulate a number of areas of environmental concern, and each of these areas has spawned its own declarations and treaties. It should be noted that the non-governmental organizations have been incredibly active and persuasive in the environmental area. States often drag their feet in agreeing to norms and in enforcing them because large industrial interests argue that stricter regimes will be too costly. Non-governmental groups, such as the World Wide Fund for Nature and Greenpeace International have no such constraints. This rapidly expanding group of declarations and treaties have also articulated certain principles that provide overall guidance on the standards to be applied. Below are listed some of the areas that have given rise to new legal regimes together with reference to the main treaties in force and the principles that have emerged from these areas of concern.

§13.4 HAZARDOUS WASTE

The Basel Convention on the Control of Transboundary Movements of Hazardous Wastes and Their Disposal, 1673 U.N.T.S. 57, defines hazardous wastes and sets controls and limitations on the transfer of such wastes between treaty partners. There is a similar convention applying specially to Africa: the Bamako Convention on the Ban of the Import into Africa and the Control of Transboundary Movement and Management of Hazardous Wastes Within Africa, 2101 U.N.T.S. 242. More recently, the Rotterdam Convention on the Prior Informed Consent Procedure for Certain Hazardous Chemicals and Pesticides in International Trade, 2244 U.N.T.S. 337, went into force in 2004 and currently has 127 parties.

Example 13-1

The Basel Convention on the Control of Transboundary Movements of Hazardous Wastes and Their Disposal, 1673 U.N.T.S. 57, entered into force in 1992. It has received 172 ratifications and, not surprisingly, regulates the transboundary movement and disposal of hazardous waste. Hazardous wastes are described in detail in annexes to the treaty and include cathode ray tubes of televisions. Under this treaty, the parties agree not to export hazardous waste to developing countries and to prevent the importation of hazardous wastes where there is reason to believe that such waste will not be managed in an environmentally sound manner. These particular provisions were drafted primarily to prevent developed states from paying developing states to take hazardous wastes off their hands for far less money than it would cost for the developed states to dispose of the hazardous wastes in an environmentally friendly manner.

State A is a highly developed state that is not a party to the Basel Convention. Almost every household in State A owns one or more televisions. Technological innovators in State A keep coming up with new forms of television, so that the population in State A replaces its televisions, on average, every five years. Individuals in State A pay a tax to the local municipality to remove the old televisions, which are then gathered together by the federal authorities of State A for disposal. State A has the capacity to dispose of the cathode ray tubes in the televisions in an environmentally responsible manner, but such disposal is costly.

Recently, the government of State A has entered into a ten-year agreement with a private disposal corporation in State B called "We Take It." State A intends to ship hundreds of tons of the old used televisions to State B including the cathode ray tubes. The cost of this contract is considerably less than it would cost State A to dispose of the televisions in an environmentally sound manner. State B is a developing state, which alleges that it can reuse some of the old televisions and can dispose of the cathode ray tubes if they are not used. State B has a chronic unemployment level of about twenty-five percent and states that it can provide a sizable amount of new employment by rehabilitating the old televisions and managing the disposal of the nonusable parts. State B is not a party to the Basel Convention.

A nonprofit organization called "Citizens Against Hazardous Waste Dumping" has branches in fifty-two countries, including State A and State B. This group has mounted a campaign against the shipment of the televisions from State A to State B. They estimate that fifty percent of the cathode ray tubes from the old televisions will not be usable, and they allege that State B does not have the capacity or the resources to dispose of the nonusable cathode ray tubes in ways that will not harm the environment.

The national laws of State A and State B do not prohibit the export or import of old televisions but also there are no specific statutes permitting such activity. The courts of both states incorporate customary international law into national law and will apply it in the absence of contrary national law.

The branch of the nonprofit organization "Citizens Against Hazardous Waste Dumping" located in State B brings a suit against the corporation "We Take It" in the courts of State B. They ask the court to rule that "We Take It" should be enjoined from carrying out its contract with State A. The court grants "Citizens Against Hazardous Waste Dumping" standing and proceeds to consider the merits of the case. How will the court rule?

Explanation

Assuming that all of the factual issues are resolved in the manner stated by the nonprofit organization in the Example, the principal question before the court will be whether customary international law prohibits the type of transboundary movement of the goods in question, including the cathode ray tubes. Currently there are 192 member states of the United Nations. Kosovo, Vatican City, and Taiwan are not members. All other states are members. The Basel Convention has received 172 ratifications. A further three states have signed but not yet ratified the treaty. Under the Vienna Convention on the Law of Treaties, 1155 U.N.T.S. 331 (see Chapter 3) states that have signed but not yet ratified a treaty are obligated "to refrain from acts which would defeat the object and purpose of a treaty . . ." (art. 18). This article is widely considered to be customary law. As a result 175 states are either bound directly by the requirements of the Basel Convention or are bound not to do anything against its object and purpose. The prohibition on the transboundary movement of hazardous waste, including cathode ray tubes, particularly when the movement is from a developed to a developing country was a central tenet of the Basel Convention and is clearly prohibited. Because of the Convention's near-universal adherence, the argument that such a prohibition is required by customary law is very strong. No doubt the nonprofit organization would also point to numerous national laws prohibiting the export or import of hazardous waste as well as various resolutions and directives to the same effect by regional and international organizations.

As a practical matter, the court might suggest a compromise. If there is a feasible way to sort out which cathode ray tubes are reusable and which are not before they leave State A, the court would obviously prefer such an option. If that is not feasible, then the court might require State A to take back all of the unused cathode ray tubes at no cost to "We Take It." That option would obviously raise the cost of the contract considerably and might not be acceptable to State A. On the other hand, State A would have gotten rid of some of its otherwise hazardous waste.

(Another issue, not mentioned in the Example, is whether the Basel Convention is contrary to the General Agreement on Tariffs and Trade (GATT), 55 U.N.T.S. 187, as modified under the World Trade Organization (WTO) framework. This agreement prohibits developed countries from using nontariff barriers to prevent developing countries' access to commodities or services. If waste disposal is considered a service or some of the old televisions can be reused and the remaining cathode ray tubes properly disposed of or returned to State A for proper disposal, then restricting access to waste disposal by developing countries could be viewed as a violation of GATT. Cf. WTO Appellate Body Report in the *Shrimp-Turtle* Case, WT/D558/AB/RW (Oct. 22, 2001), reprinted at 41 I.L.M. 149 (2002)).

Example 13-2

Assume that State I was party to a regional treaty regulating the disposal of all waste called "The Waste Disposal Convention." This treaty states that:

> The essential objective of all provisions relating to waste management should be the protection of human health and the environment against harmful effects caused by the collection, transport, treatment, storage and tipping of waste.

The Convention goes on to urge parties to "promote clean technologies" and "recycling." Each member state is required to become "self-sufficient in waste management by June 30, 2009 and not to export waste in any form after that date." These provisions of the Convention were enacted into State I's national laws in May 2009. State I has promulgated a national waste disposal plan to conform to the Convention's requirements. The plan has worked well throughout the country except in one largely urban area, which has sought a series of delays in implementation for a variety of reasons. There was violent opposition from local inhabitants, which was only controlled after deployment of the armed forces. Waste disposal plant construction was delayed in part because of the protests, and widespread fraud is being investigated in the awarding of the public disposal contracts. It is thought that organized crime gangs that have operated for many years in the area have systematically thwarted the central government's plans on waste disposal in this area. As a result, landfills are overflowing, and storage facilities no longer have any capacity. Litter fills the streets, and the smell of rotting garbage permeates the cities of the entire area. Hospitals report increases in serious food poisoning and lung infections. Several attempts to get State I to meet its obligations in this area by local, national, and regional administrators have all failed.

The enforcement arm of the regional government (which encompasses State I), known as "The Commission," sues State I in the regional Court of Justice. State I argues that it has done everything in its power to comply with the Convention and that any failure to comply should be excused under the doctrine of *force majeure* (superior force). This doctrine is found in many legal systems and basically refuses to find liability where the activity complained of was unforeseen and caused by an event or circumstances beyond the control of the party accused, making it impossible to carry out the required obligations. Generally *force majeure* events will be things like war, riots, earthquakes, strikes, or out-of-the-ordinary crimes.

It is clear that State I has failed to live up to its obligations under the Convention. Will the court permit the defense of *force majeure* to excuse State I from meeting its waste disposal obligations?

Explanation

The court would focus on whether the circumstances cited as relieving State I from liability were indeed beyond the control of State I and unforeseen, thus making compliance impossible. One suspects that the court would be unsympathetic to State I especially if the failure to comply with waste disposal obligations has been an ongoing problem over many years, as appears to be the case here.

The court would probably find that local opposition is almost always a feature of new waste-disposal plans and cannot be viewed as unforeseen; in any case, the violent opposition was controlled by the armed forces. As for the criminal gangs, the court would probably note that since gang activity has been in place for many years, it was not unforeseen. In any event, the court would be very reluctant to let State I off the hook on the grounds of protests or criminal activity because of the fear that many states might be able to cite such activity as preventing compliance with treaty obligations. In this case there are very real immediate dangers to public health as well as long-term danger to the environment. Compliance with the required standards is likely to be viewed as an urgent matter. Moreover, as State I has complied with the Convention in all areas except the one in question, State I clearly understands what is required and has the capacity to comply.

No doubt the court would call upon the parties to set a schedule for compliance and, if it had the power to do so, would impose heavy fines on State I. Cf. Case C-297/08, Comm'n v. Italy, 2010 E.C.R. ___, available at: http://curia.europa.eu/jurisp/cgi-bin. (Italy was found in violation of various European Directives on waste disposal in the area around Naples. The description of the almost total breakdown in waste disposal in the area is grim.)

§13.5 ATMOSPHERE, OZONE, AND CLIMATE

The principle first announced in the *Trail Smelter* case, *supra*, has found much more concrete expression in the Convention on Long-Range Transboundary Air Pollution, 1302 U.N.T.S. 217, which calls on parties to limit, gradually reduce, and prevent long-range transboundary air pollution. The Vienna Convention for the Protection of the Ozone Layer, 1513 U.N.T.S. 293, provides a mechanism for exchange of information and scientific research on the ozone layer. The 1987 Montreal Protocol on Substances that Deplete the Ozone Layer, 1522 U.N.T.S. 3, together with various adjustments and amendments, set limits on the production of chlorofluorocarbons (CFCs) and halons. The Helsinki Declaration on the Protection of the Ozone Layer, signed May 2, 1989, reprinted at 28 I.L.M. 1335 (1989), called for the phasing out of CFCs.

The pressing issue of global warming has received attention in the United Nations Framework Convention on Climate Change, 1771 U.N.T.S. 107, and the Kyoto Protocol, 2303 U.N.T.S. 148, to that Convention. The Stockholm Convention on Persistent Organic Pollutants, 2256 U.N.T.S. 119, also entered into force in 2004 and currently has 172 parties. The 2009 Copenhagen Climate conference failed to produce a legally binding document despite heroic efforts in some quarters, although a number of countries pledged to meet pollution reduction targets by specified dates.

§13.6 NATURE, FLORA, FAUNA, AND OTHER RESOURCES

Mention has already been made of the Convention on Biological Diversity, 1760 U.N.T.S. 79, and the CITES Convention, 993 U.N.T.S. 243. A nonbinding statement on the world's forests addresses management, conservation, and sustainable development of these vital resources, reprinted at 31 I.L.M. 887 (1992). The 1972 Convention for the Protection of the World Cultural and Natural Heritage, 1037 U.N.T.S. 151, imposes upon members "the duty of ensuring identification, protection, conservation, presentation and transmission to future generations of . . . cultural and natural heritage. . . ." Art. 4. The U.N. Convention to Combat Desertification, 1954 U.N.T.S. 3, has received almost universal ratification and entered into force in 1996. It requires various actions to support sustainable development at the community level to overcome desertification.

In a recent case in the International Court of Justice, *Gabčíkovo-Nagymaros Project* (Hungary v. Slovakia), 1997 I.C.J. 7, which concerned treaty obligations relating to the construction and operation of dams on the Danube River, Hungary argued that she was entitled to terminate a treaty with Slovakia because of "new requirements of international law for the protection of the environment. . . ." The Court determined that "newly developed norms of environmental law [were] relevant for the implementation of the Treaty . . . [and that the Treaty] require[d] the parties . . . to ensure that the quality of water in the Danube is not impaired and that nature is protected, to take new environmental norms into consideration. . . ." *Id.* at para. 112. The Court also noted that the "awareness of vulnerability of the environment and the recognition that environmental risks have to be assessed on a continuous basis have become much stronger in [recent] years. . . ." *Id.*

Example 13-3

The meridian frog (*hyla meridionalis*) is the only endangered amphibian in State S according to the official Catalog of Endangered Flora and Fauna prepared by State S's Department of Agriculture. State S lies within the region of Medi-Europa. A regional treaty in Medi-Europa called the "Convention on the Conservation of Medi-Europa Wildlife and Natural Habitats" lists the meridian frog as one of the strictly protected species. State S became a party to this treaty in 1999, the same year that the treaty entered into force. The relevant articles of the Medi-Europa Convention provide:

> Article 3: Each Contracting Party shall take steps to promote national policies for the conservation of wild flora, wild fauna and natural habitats with particular attention to endangered and vulnerable species, and endangered habitats.
>
> Article 4: Each Contracting Party shall take appropriate and necessary legislative and administrative measures to ensure the conservation of the habitats of wild flora and fauna especially those specified as endangered in Appendix 1.
>
> Appendix 1: The following species are declared endangered:
> . . . the meridian frog . . .

State S has passed no legislation implementing the provisions of this treaty despite becoming a party in 1999. Twenty years before that in 1979, State S ratified the Vienna Convention on the Law of Treaties, 1155 U.N.T.S. 331. That treaty entered into force in 1980. (See Chapter 3.)

There are only two areas left in the whole of Medi-Europa where meridian frogs survive. Both of these areas are in State S. One area is a wetlands area that consists of a number of streams, fens, and bogs. The other area is located near a river and a dam.

The wetlands area was owned by an old farmer who occasionally grazed sheep on the land but three months ago, he sold the land to a development company called "Buildup." There are no local zoning ordinances in the area and "Buildup" publically announced its plans to fill in the wetlands and construct a shopping mall in the area, which a corporate spokesperson stated "will bring hundreds of new jobs to this depressed area." The area has very few employment opportunities, with the result that most young people move away once they complete high school.

A group of conservation activists publicize the plight of the meridian frog on local and national television. They start a campaign called "Save Our Fragile Frogs." Soon there are marches by groups of conservationists with banners calling for everything from "Bomb Buildup Now" to "Make Buildup Extinct." In the meantime, a group of unemployed laborers from the area have organized counterdemonstrations. Their banners read "Food Not Frogs" and "Against Amphibians."

A group of *pro bono* lawyers who call themselves "Litigators for Life" take up the cause and file a suit against "Buildup" in the court with jurisdiction over the wetlands. They ask for a permanent injunction on any construction in the wetlands area.

The court grants the lawyers standing and proceeds to consider the case on the merits. How will the court rule?

Explanation

There appears to be no specific national law governing the dispute. Perhaps the court would regard the official Catalog drawn up by the Department of Agriculture, which lists the frog as an endangered amphibian as indicating a requirement to protect the frog. It would investigate the regulations surrounding the drafting of the Catalog. The court might point out that State S is a party to the Medi-Europa Convention and that one of the clear purposes of that Convention is the protection of endangered species and their habitats. The court might also point out that the Vienna Convention on the Law of Treaties provides: "Every treaty in force is binding upon the parties to it and must be performed by them in good faith." Art. 26. The court might berate the national legislature for not carrying out its obligation to pass protective legislation as required by the Medi-Europa Convention. Unfortunately, such raillery will not create the legislation. The only other legal avenue would be to examine whether customary international law requires the protection of the frog. The Convention on Biological Diversity, 1760 U.N.T.S. 79, has been ratified by almost every state. That treaty states that parties "shall, in accordance with its particular conditions and capabilities: (a) Develop national strategies, plans or programmes for the conservation and sustainable use of biological diversity. . . ." Art. 6. These strategies are known as Biodiversity Action Plans (BAPs). Such plans have now been promulgated by some countries, mostly developed countries, although the efficacy of any particular plan is hard to judge. Some developing states criticize such plans for favoring wildlife over human life. When it comes to requiring the protection of a particular species, even if the species or its habitat is endangered, it is difficult to argue that the protection of that species or habitat must, as a matter of law, take precedence over development projects, unless there is positive national law requiring such protection. State S appears to have no BAP.

As a compromise, the court might try to persuade the parties to come to some agreement perhaps suggesting that the developer should pay to move the frogs to another hospitable habitat (if any is available). Again, the conservationists could try to come up with another possible site for the shopping mall in the general area but one that would not threaten the frogs' habitat. If the sale of the land had not yet taken place but the farmer needed the money from the sale, the conservationist group could launch a campaign to raise money to buy the wetlands. (These types of campaigns are often

389

successful.) The group might also offer to buy the land from "Buildup" if the sale has been completed. Cf. Consultative Opinion: EAS CC9/2000, International Court of Environmental Arbitration and Conciliation, *Protection of the Meridian Frog* (Spain, 2000) available at: http://iceac.sarenet.es/Ingles/cases/EAS%20CC%209%202000.htm.

§13.7 NUCLEAR FALLOUT

The possibility of radioactive fallout from nuclear devices has caused concern for some decades. In 1961 the General Assembly of the United Nations issued a Declaration on the Prohibition of the Use of Nuclear and Thermo-Nuclear Weapons, G.A. Res. 1653 (1961), which stated that the use of such weapons "is contrary to the spirit, letter and aims of the United Nations and, as such, a direct violation of the Charter of the United Nations." In 1963 the Treaty Banning Nuclear Weapon Tests in the Atmosphere, in Outer Space and Under Water, 480 U.N.T.S. 43, was signed and entered into force the same year. In 1991 the General Assembly overwhelmingly endorsed "the complete cessation of nuclear-weapon tests and a comprehensive test ban. . . ." G.A. Res. 46/29 (1991).

In 1973, France indicated that it would carry out atmospheric nuclear testing in the South Pacific in the near future. Australia and New Zealand then brought the *Nuclear Tests* cases ((Australia v. France), 1974 I.C.J. 253; (New Zealand v. France), 1974 I.C.J. 457) against France, asking the International Court of Justice to declare that international law prohibited atmospheric nuclear testing. The Court ultimately dismissed the cases after France had unilaterally announced that the 1974 tests would be the last. The Court declared that:

> 51. In announcing the 1974 series of atmospheric tests would be the last the French Government conveyed to the world at large . . . its intention effectively to terminate these tests. . . . It is from the actual substance of these statements, and from the circumstances attending their making, that the legal implications of the unilateral act must be deduced. The objects of these statements are clear and they were addressed to the international community as a whole, and the Court holds that they constitute an undertaking possessing legal effect. . . .
>
> 52. Thus the Court faces a situation in which the objective of the Applicant has in effect been accomplished, inasmuch as the Court finds that France has undertaken the obligation to hold no further nuclear tests in the atmosphere in the South Pacific. *Nuclear Tests* case (Australia v. France) *supra*, at paras. 51 & 52.

The legal theory that unilateral statements made by high governmental officials are internationally binding was (and remains) controversial, and the dismissal of the suit, without a judgment on the merits, was certainly not what Australia and New Zealand had hoped for. However, it is worth remembering that the scientific evidence demonstrating injury caused by nuclear testing was considerably less robust than it is today, and there was (and still is) no treaty in force requiring the cessation of all nuclear testing. It has been suggested that if the Court had reached the merits of the case in 1974, it would have had to rule that there was no international law prohibiting atmospheric nuclear testing at that time. Such a ruling would likely have been wrongly interpreted as a positive endorsement of such testing. Perhaps the dismissal of the cases was the lesser of two unpalatable options. The court did add, however, that "if the basis for this Judgment were to be affected, the Applicant could request an examination of the situation in accordance with the provisions of the [I.C.J.] Statute. . . ." Id. at para. 60.

In 1995, France carried out a series of underground nuclear tests in the South Pacific that provoked widespread protests throughout the world. New Zealand, relying on the language of the Court's 1974 judgment, filed a "Request for an Examination of the Situation," asking the Court to declare that "the proposed nuclear tests will constitute a violation of the rights under international law of New Zealand, as well as of other States; . . . [and] that it is unlawful for France to conduct such nuclear tests before it has undertaken an Environmental Impact Assessment according to accepted international standards. Unless such an assessment establishes that the tests will not give rise, directly or indirectly, to radioactive contamination of the marine environment the rights under international law of New Zealand, as well as the rights of other States, will be violated." (New Zealand v. France), 1995 I.C.J. 288, 291 (Order of Sept. 22).[4]

The Court dismissed New Zealand's request stating that "in analyzing its Judgment of 1974, the Court has reached the conclusion that the Judgment dealt exclusively with atmospheric nuclear tests; . . . consequently it is not possible for the Court now to take into consideration questions relating to underground nuclear tests. . . ." Id. at 306. As a result the Court has not as yet delivered an opinion on the legality of nuclear testing. The Comprehensive Nuclear-Test Ban Treaty was opened for signature on September 24, 1996. States parties to this treaty "undertake [ ] not to carry out any nuclear weapon test explosion . . . at any place under [their] jurisdiction or control." U.N. Doc. A/50/1027 (1996), art. I(1). One hundred and eighty-two states have signed this treaty and 151 states have ratified it. To enter into force, the treaty requires that forty-four designated states ratify the treaty (art. XIV). To date, forty-one of the forty-four states have signed the treaty

---

4. Shortly after the Court's dismissal of the original suit against France, France withdrew from the compulsory jurisdiction of the I.C.J. (see Chapter 5, §5.3.2), thus it was not possible for New Zealand or Australia to initiate a new case against France.

and thirty-five of those (including France, the Russian Federation, and the United Kingdom) have ratified it.[5]

In 1986, an explosion at the Chernobyl (at that time in the U.S.S.R.) atomic power plant caused large amounts of radioactive emissions. The U.S.S.R. was slow to admit that anything untoward had occurred, and only when other countries presented evidence of increased levels of radioactivity did the U.S.S.R. reluctantly agree that an accident had occurred. This incident led to the Convention on Early Notification of a Nuclear Accident, 1439 U.N.T.S. 275, which requires parties, in the event of a radioactive accident, to "notify, directly or through the International Atomic Energy Agency . . . those states which are or may be physically affected. . . ." Art. 2. The Convention on Assistance in Case of a Nuclear Accident or Radiological Emergency, 1457 U.N.T.S. 133, provides for cooperation between the parties in order "to minimize its [the accident's] consequences and to protect life, property and the environment from the effects of radioactive releases." Art. 1(1).

In 1994, the General Assembly of the United Nations submitted the following question to the Court for an advisory opinion (see Chapter 5, §5.3.2): "Is the threat or use of nuclear weapons in any circumstances permitted under international law?" In the course of the Court's opinion it examined the effect of nuclear weapons on the environment and discussed whether environmental treaties or customary law prohibited the threat or use of nuclear weapons. *Legality of the Threat or Use of Nuclear Weapons*, Advisory Opinion, 1996 I.C.J. 226 (July 8).

The Court found that "the most directly relevant applicable law governing the question of which it was seized, is that relating to the use of force enshrined in the United Nations Charter and the law applicable in armed conflict which regulates the conduct of hostilities, together with any specific treaties on nuclear weapons that the court might determine to be relevant." Id. at para. 34. Nonetheless, the Court found that the unique destructive capacity of nuclear weapons had to be taken into account in examining the relevant law. Because the Court addresses the way in which environmental concerns impact the question before the Court, the section of the Court's opinion focusing on environmental issues is reproduced below. In many senses the Court's discussion of the environmental norms applicable to the laws of armed conflict serves as a paradigm for the application of these norms to all other spheres of human activity.

Opinion of the Court

27. In both their written and oral statements, some States furthermore argued that any use of nuclear weapons would be unlawfully by

---

5. For much useful information on the Convention, see http://www.ctbto.org/.

reference to existing norms relating to the safeguarding and protection of the environment, in view of their essential importance.

Specific references were made to various existing international treaties and instruments. These included Additional Protocol I of 1977 to the Geneva Conventions of 1949, Article 35, paragraph 3 of which prohibits the employment of "methods or means of warfare which are intended, or may be expected, to cause widespread, long-term and severe damage to the natural environment"; and the Convention of 18 May 1977 on the Prohibition of Military or Any Other Hostile Use of Environmental Modification Techniques, which prohibits the use of weapons which have "widespread, long-lasting or severe effects" on the environment (Art. 1). Also cited were Principle 21 of the Stockholm Declaration of 1972 and Principle 2 of the Rio Declaration of 1992 which express the common conviction of the States concerned that they have a duty "to ensure that activities within their jurisdiction or control do not cause damage to the environment of other States or of areas beyond the limits of national jurisdiction." These instruments and other provisions relating to the protection and safeguarding of the environment were said to apply at all times, in war as well as in peace, and it was contended that they would be violated by the use of nuclear weapons whose consequences would be widespread and would have transboundary effects.

28. Other States questioned the binding legal quality of these precepts of environmental law; or, in the context of the Convention on the Prohibition of Military or Any Other Hostile Use of Environmental Modification Techniques, denied that it was concerned at all with the use of nuclear weapons in hostilities; or, in the case of Additional Protocol I, denied that they were generally bound by its terms, or recalled that they had reserved their position in respect of Article 35, paragraph 3, thereof.

It was also argued by some States that the principal purpose of environmental treaties and norms was the protection of the environment in time of peace. It was said that those treaties made no mention of nuclear weapons. It was also pointed out that warfare in general, and nuclear warfare in particular, were not mentioned in their texts and that it would be destabilizing to the rule of law and to confidence in international negotiations if those treaties were now interpreted in such a way as to prohibit the use of nuclear weapons.

29. The Court recognizes that the environment is under daily threat and that the use of nuclear weapons could constitute a catastrophe for the environment. The Court also recognizes that the

environment is not an abstraction but represents the living space, the quality of life and the very health of human beings, including generations unborn. The existence of the general obligation of States to ensure that activities within their jurisdiction and control respect the environment of other States or of areas beyond national control is now part of the corpus of international law relating to the environment.

30. However, the Court is of the view that the issue is not whether the treaties relating to the protection of the environment are or are not applicable during an armed conflict, but rather whether the obligations stemming from these treaties were intended to be obligations of total restraint during military conflict.

The Court does not consider that the treaties in question could have intended to deprive a State of the exercise of its right of self-defence under international law because of its obligations to protect the environment. Nonetheless, States must take environmental considerations into account when assessing what is necessary and proportionate in the pursuit of legitimate military objectives. Respect for the environment is one of the elements that go to assessing whether an action is in conformity with the principles of necessity and proportionality.

This approach is supported, indeed, by the terms of Principle 24 of the Rio Declaration, which provides that:

> Warfare is inherently destructive of sustainable development. States shall therefore respect international law providing protection for the environment in times of armed conflict and cooperate in its further development, as necessary.

31. The Court notes furthermore that Article 35, paragraph 3, and 55 of Additional Protocol I provide additional protection for the environment. Taken together, these provisions embody a general obligation to protect the natural environment against widespread, long-term and severe environmental damage; the prohibition of methods and means of warfare which are intended, or may be expected, to cause such damage; and the prohibition of attacks against the natural environment by way of reprisals.

These are powerful constraints for all the States having subscribed to these provisions.

32. General Assembly resolution 47/37 of 25 November 1992 on the Protection of the Environment in Times of Armed Conflict, is also of interest in this context. It affirms the general view according to which environmental considerations constitute one of the elements to be taken into account in the implementation of the principles of the law applicable in armed conflict; it states that

"destruction of the environment, not justified by military necessity and carried out wantonly, is clearly contrary to existing international law." Addressing the reality that certain instruments are not yet binding on all States, the General Assembly in this resolution "[a]ppeals to all States that have not yet done so to consider becoming parties to the relevant international conventions."

In its recent Order in the *Request for an Examination of the Situation in Accordance with Paragraph 63 of the Court's Judgment of 20 December 1974 in the Nuclear Tests* (New Zealand v. France) *Case*, the Court stated that its conclusion was "without prejudice to the obligations of States to respect and protect the natural environment" (*Order of 22 September 1995, I.C.J. Reports 1955*, p. 306, para. 64). Although that statement was made in the context of nuclear testing, it naturally also applies to the actual use of nuclear weapons in armed conflict.

33. The Court thus finds that while existing international law relating to the protection and safeguarding of the environment does not specifically prohibit the use of nuclear weapons, it indicates important environmental factors that are properly to be taken into account in the context of the implementation of the principles and rules of the law applicable in armed conflict.

35. In applying this law [relating to the use of force and the conduct of hostilities] to the present case, the Court cannot however fail to take into account certain unique characteristics of nuclear weapons.

The Court has noted the definition of nuclear weapons contained in various treaties and accords. It also notes that nuclear weapons are explosive devices whose energy results from the fusion or fission of the atom. By its very nature, that process, in nuclear weapons as they exist today, releases not only immense quantities of heat and energy, but also powerful and prolonged radiation.

According to the material before the Court, the first two causes of damage are vastly more powerful than the damage caused by other weapons, while the phenomenon of radiation is said to be peculiar to nuclear weapons. These characteristics render the nuclear weapon potentially catastrophic. The destructive power of nuclear weapons cannot be contained in either space or time. They have the potential to destroy all civilization and the entire ecosystem of the planet.

The radiation released by a nuclear explosion would affect health, agriculture, natural resources and demography over a very wide area. Further, the use of nuclear weapons would be a serious danger to future generations. Ionizing radiation has the potential to damage the future environment, food and marine ecosystem, and to cause genetic defects and illness in future generations.

36. In consequence, in order correctly to apply to the present case the Charter law on the use of force and the law applicable in armed conflict, in particular humanitarian law, it is imperative for the Court to take account of the unique characteristics of nuclear weapons, and in particular their destructive capacity, their capacity to cause untold human suffering, and their ability to cause damage to generations to come.

The dissenting opinions in this case of judges Koroma, Weeramantry, and Shahabuddeen all have catalogs of the human and environmental disaster, including the risk of annihilating the entire human race, that necessarily accompany the use of nuclear weapons. The fundamental issue confronting the Court was whether, in light of the knowledge of the certain environmental and human disaster bound to follow the use of nuclear weapons (and understanding the legal limitations placed on the use of all weapons even during armed conflict), although such activity would normally be prohibited, there is, nonetheless, an exception carved out from this prohibition when a state exercises legitimate self-defense in circumstances where its very survival is at stake, presumably from the threat or use of illegal armed force. In the end, the Court found itself unable to answer this question. Having determined that the threat or use of nuclear weapons "would generally be contrary to the rules of international law applicable in armed conflict . . ." (id. at 266), the Court by an evenly divided seven-seven vote, with the President casting an extra vote in favor, as permitted for tied votes under the Court's rules, concluded:

> However, in view of the current state of international law, and of the elements of fact at its disposal, the Court cannot conclude definitely whether the threat or use of nuclear weapons would be lawful or unlawful in an extreme circumstance of self-defence, in which the very survival of a State would be at stake. . . ." *Id.* at 266.

(For further discussion of the *Nuclear Weapons Advisory Opinion*, see Chapter 10, §10.5.3(b)(v)).

Example 13-4

A highly industrialized state has recently developed a new weapon with phenomenal targeting accuracy. It can be delivered from drone aircraft that can be remotely controlled from 10,000 miles away from the actual location of the drone. This new weapon is called the "Deadly Richochet Rocket" or DRR because of its ability to keep bouncing around and destroying more targets. The weapon is indeed deadly. It kills all within its path and scorches the earth in a twenty-mile area surrounding the target. It also releases noxious fumes that kill off all vegetation within the same area. Vegetation will not regrow for at least ten years after being exposed to such a weapon.

Assuming that such a weapon can be used in a manner such that it targets only military personnel and military property, does such a weapon violate international environmental law?

Explanation

Although it may be hoped that the world community would immediately launch an effort to conclude a treaty banning such weapons because of their serious, long-lasting detriment to the environment, without a specific prohibition found in a binding treaty (or possibly customary law) the *Nuclear Weapons Advisory Opinion, supra,* tends to indicate that the use of the weapon, when exercising legitimate self-defense, to preserve the survival of the state, would not violate international law. (It should be borne in mind that the international community is getting ever more adept at banning specific weapons by treaty, as was the case for land mines: Convention on the Prohibition of the Use, Stockpiling, Production and Transfer of Anti-Personnel Mines and on their Destruction, 2056 U.N.T.S. 211, entered into force March 1, 1999, reprinted at 36 I.L.M. 1507 (1997).

§13.8 OTHER REGIMES

The Outer Space Treaties,[6] the Antarctic Treaty,[7] and the Law of Sea Convention[8] have been mentioned in other chapters. There are also a number of treaties and declarations relating to water courses, most notably the Convention and Statute on the Regime of Navigable Waterways of International Concern;[9] the Helsinki Rules on the Uses of the Waters of International

---

6. See, e.g., Treaty on Principles Governing the Activities of States in the Exploration and Uses of Outer Space, Including the Moon and Other Celestial Bodies, 610 U.N.T.S. 205, 18 U.S.T. 2410, T.I.A.S. No. 6347, opened for signature January 27, 1967, entered into force October 10, 1967, reprinted at 6 I.L.M. 386 (1967). (See Chapter 7.)

7. 402 U.N.T.S. 71, 12 U.S.T. 794, T.I.A.S. No. 4780, signed December 1, 1959, entered into force June 23, 1961. (See Chapter 7.)

8. U.N. Convention on the Law of the Sea, 1833 U.N.T.S. 3, signed December 10, 1982, entered into force November 16, 1994, reprinted at 21 I.L.M. 1261 (1982). (See Chapter 12.)

9. 7 L.N.T.S. 35, signed April 20, 1921, entered into force October 31, 1922.

Rivers;[10] and the Convention on the Protection and Use of Transboundary Watercourses and International Lakes,[11] which states that it is "intended to strengthen national measures for the protection and ecologically sound management of transboundary surface waters and ground waters." As each new area of human or natural activity is shown to present threats to the overall health of the ecosystem, so the law seeks to tackle these areas guided by normative environmental principles and practical requirements leading to proven or predicted solutions.

§13.9 GUIDING ENVIRONMENTAL PRINCIPLES

In the area of international environmental law certain rules have emerged as a form of operational principles working throughout the implementation of solutions to environmental problems. A number of these principles express overlapping concerns. It is disputed whether these principles are yet binding customary law or are still at the stage of moving toward binding obligations. Many of these principles can be found in a variety of treaties and other persuasive documents. Of course, the principles found in treaties are binding on the treaty parties.

§13.9.1 The Precautionary Principle

The 1992 Rio Declaration on Environment and Development states:

> Principle 15: In order to protect the environment, the precautionary approach shall be widely applied by States according to their capabilities. Where there are threats of serious or irreversible damage, lack of full scientific certainty shall not be used as a reason for postponing cost-effective measures to prevent environmental degradation. U.N. GAOR, 47th Sess. U.N. Doc. A/CONF.151/5/Rev.1 (1992), reprinted at 31 I.L.M. 874 (1992).

This principle has been discussed by Judge Weeramantry in his dissenting opinion in the *Nuclear Tests* case (New Zealand v. France), 1995 I.C.J. 288, at 342-344 (Order of 22 Sept.), where he notes that several treaties have already adopted this principle. He describes the principle by quoting article 7 of the 1990 Bergen ECE Ministerial Declaration on Sustainable Development: "In order to achieve sustainable development, policies must be based on the precautionary principle. Environmental measures must

---

10. International Law Association, Report of the Fifty-Second Conference, Helsinki, 1966 at 484, 52 Int'l L. Ass'n 484 (1987).
11. 1936 U.N.T.S. 269, signed March 17, 1992, entered into force October 6, 1996, reprinted at 31 I.L.M. 1312 (1992).

anticipate, prevent and attack the causes of environmental degradation. Where there are threats of serious or irreversible damage, lack of full scientific certainty should not be used as a reason for postponing measures to prevent environmental degradation." Id. at 342. Various judges in the Law of the Sea Tribunal in the *Southern Bluefin Tuna* cases (New Zealand v. Japan; Australia v. Japan), 1999 I.T.L.O.S. Nos. 3 & 4 (Request for Provisional Measures), have also discussed the principle; for example, the separate opinion of Judge Laing, paras. 12-21; the separate opinion of Judge Treves, paras. 8-9; and the separate opinion of Judge ad hoc Shearer, paragraph entitled "The precautionary principle/approach."

Example 13-5

Recently, there have been various suggestions that the information on global warming may not rest on as sturdy scientific data as was previously asserted. For example, Nicholas Kralev wrote:

> World weather agencies agreed this week to enhance data-gathering significantly and allow independent scrutiny of raw figures used in assessing climate change amid charges by critics that global warming scientific data were skewed. Warming put to new 'grand challenge': Temperature data face independent scrutiny, Wash. Times Feb. 26, 2010 at 1.

It was also reported that researchers in Britain had suppressed certain data and that the faulty data had been included in a 2007 U.N. report on global warming. Apparently, Britain's MET Office stated that these revelations do "not undermine the existing independent data sets that all reflect a warming trend."

State X is a developed wealthy country that has already begun an aggressive program to reduce greenhouse gases. State Y is a developing country. Seventy percent of its population lives on less than a dollar a day. Hunger is widespread. It was about to start imposing a ban on burning certain types of waste, which was to be gradually introduced over ten years as part of its effort to reduce global warming.

Applying the precautionary principle as enunciated in the 1992 Rio Declaration, *supra*, to their efforts at reducing greenhouse gas emissions, how should State X and State Y proceed in light of the doubts expressed about the reliability of the scientific evidence on which the conclusion of global warming rests? Below are three possible courses of action for States X and Y. Should State X and/or State Y:

A) Carry on as before?

B) Suspend all greenhouse gas emission reduction programs and await the outcome of the enhanced scientific data?

C) Convene their own experts for advice and then proceed with whatever program is suggested?

Explanation

The purpose of this example is to add to your appreciation of how difficult it is to make any decision when the principle to be applied is somewhat vague and when it is to be applied by states "according to their capabilities." The problem is compounded by the differing scientific views, not to mention political and business axes to be ground. Nonetheless, I strongly suspect that the drafters of the precautionary principle would reject option B as retrogressive; reject option C as unnecessary and duplicative; and endorse option A as embracing the notion that where there are threats of serious and irreversible damage, lack of scientific certainty should not be allowed to postpone action to prevent environmental degradation. State Y appears to be granted more leeway in starting its programs given its limited capacities.

§13.9.2 The Principle of Intergenerational Equity

This principle was aptly explained by Edith Brown Weiss:

> The starting proposition is that each generation is both a custodian and a user of our common natural and cultural patrimony. As custodians of this planet, we have certain moral obligations to future generation which we can transform into legally enforceable norms. In *Fairness to Future Generations: International Law, Common Patrimony and Intergenerational Equity* 21 (1989).

The 1972 Stockholm Declaration on the Human Environment states in Principle 1 that we all have "a solemn responsibility to protect and improve the environment for present and future generations." Judge Weeramantry in his dissenting opinion in the *Nuclear Tests* case, *supra*, 1995 I.C.J. 288, at 341-342 also states:

> The case before the Court raises . . . the principle of intergenerational equity — an important and rapidly developing principle of contemporary environmental law. . . .
>
> New Zealand's complaint that its rights are affected [by France's underground nuclear tests in the South Pacific] does not relate only to the rights of people presently in existence. The rights of the people of New Zealand include the rights of unborn posterity. Those are rights which a nation is entitled, and indeed obliged, to protect. *Id.* at 341.

§13.9.3 The Principle of Sustainable Development

Environmental protection is often weighed against the need, or some would say the right, to development. Early formulations of this need/right tended to focus on the right to economic development in order to create improvements in the quality of life. A wide variety of declarations and resolutions has also trumpeted a state's sovereign right to exploit its own natural resources. These statements began against the backdrop of a colonial system that was perceived as depressing the standard of living for Indigenous Peoples and fostering the exploitation of peoples and resources by the colonial powers at the expense of subjugated peoples. Nonetheless, by the 1970s it was understood that this claim to development was to be balanced against meeting the "developmental and environmental needs of present and future generations." Rio Declaration, *supra*, Principle 3.

The idea of "sustainable development" has been mentioned by the I.C.J. in the *Gabčíkovo-Nagymaros Project* case, *supra*, 1997 I.C.J. 7: "This need to reconcile economic development with protection of the environment is aptly expressed in the concept of sustainable development." *Id.* at 78. In the *Use of Nuclear Weapons* (Advisory Opinion), *supra*, the Court quotes Principle 24 of the Rio Declaration, which provides: "Warfare is inherently destructive of sustainable development. States shall therefore respect international law providing protection for the environment in times of armed conflict and cooperate in its further development, as necessary." *Id.* as quoted at para. 30. Again, in *Pulp Mills on the River Uruguay* (Argentina v. Uruguay), 2010 I.C.J. ___, the Court discussed sustainable development in the context of an agreement between the parties but went on to say when interpreting the agreement that it required "the need to strike a balance between the use of the waters and the protection of the river consistent with the objective of sustainable development." *Id.* at para. 177.

This principle seeks to temper the developmental activities of any particular generation by asking whether such types and levels of activity are sustainable over the long run. In other words, short-term profits should not be exploited at the expense of long-term degradation of the environment.

§13.9.4 The Polluter Pays Principle

Article 16 of the Rio Declaration states:

> National authorities should endeavor to promote the internalization of environmental costs and the use of economic instruments, taking into account the approach that the polluter should, in principle, bear the cost of pollution, with

due regard to the public interest and without distorting international trade and investment.

The idea behind this principle is that the cost of pollution should be calculated as a cost attributable to the party that engages in pollution, and that the polluter should bear the cost of any damages. See §13.3.1, *Trail Smelter* case (U.S. v. Canada), 3 U.N. Rep. Int'l Arb. Awards 1905 (1941).

§13.9.5 The Environmental Impact Assessment Principle

In recent decades there has been a movement to require states and other agencies to undertake environmental impact assessments (EIAs) prior to entering upon any major project. Principle 17 of the 1992 Rio Declaration states:

> Environmental impact assessment, as a national instrument, shall be undertaken for proposed activities that are likely to have a significant adverse impact on the environment and are subject to a decision of a competent national authority.

The Convention on Environmental Impact Assessment in a Transboundary Context, 1989 U.N.T.S. 309, requires parties to establish "an environmental impact assessment procedure that permits public participation and preparation of . . . environmental impact assessment documentation. . . ." Art. 2. The World Bank now requires an EIA for all projects that use Bank funds and effect any natural resources. A good number of states have also enacted national laws requiring EIAs on all major projects likely to impact the environment. The I.C.J. discussed an example of an EIA requirement under a treaty between Argentina and Uruguay in *Pulp Mills on the River Uruguay* (Argentina v. Uruguay), 2010 I.C.J. ___, at paras. 116, 119, 120, 121, 202, 203. The Court stated:

> In this sense, the obligation to protect and preserve . . . [under the agreement] has to be interpreted in accordance with a practice, which in recent years has gained so much acceptance among States that it may now be considered a requirement under general international law to undertake an environmental impact assessment where there is a risk that the proposed industrial activity may have a significant adverse impact in a transboundary context, in particular, on a shared resource. Moreover, due diligence, and the duty of vigilance and prevention which it implies, would not be considered to have been exercised, if a party planning work liable to affect the regime of the river or the quality of its waters did not undertake an environmental impact assessment on the potential effects of such works. *Id.* at para. 204.

§13.9.6 The Recognition of Differentiated Responsibilities for Developed and Developing States

Developing nations have often complained that they have more pressing needs than environmental concerns and that they should be subject to more relaxed standards while they are trying to supply basic necessities to their peoples and exercising their right to development. There is also resentment at the application of a so-called double standard. For example, it is argued, Europe chopped down all her forests centuries ago to engage in agriculture; now, when developing countries wish to do the same thing, they are told that they must not do so because it is bad for the environment.

Principle 7 of the 1992 Rio Declaration provides:

States shall cooperate in a spirit of global partnership to conserve, protect and restore the health and integrity of the Earth's ecosystem. In view of the different contributions to global environmental degradation, States have common but differentiated responsibilities. The developed countries acknowledge the responsibility that they bear in the international pursuit to sustainable development in view of the pressures their societies place on the global environment and of the technologies and financial resources they command.

This principle recognizes both the developed states major responsibility for environmental degradation and their primary responsibility for restoring the ecosystem's health. Some treaties now recognize the special needs of developing nations and provide less stringent standards for such states. For example, the Montreal Protocol on Substances that Deplete the Ozone Layer provides:

Any party that is a developing country and whose annual calculated level of consumption of the controlled substances in Annex A [various CFCs and halons] is less than 0.3 kilograms per capita . . . shall, in order to meet its basic domestic needs, be entitled to delay for ten years its compliance with the control measures. . . . Art. 5, 1522 U.N.T.S. 3.

Such treaties also provide for constant review of all countries' polluting activities and of the scientific knowledge available as it is updated. Delays, but not outright exceptions, are granted to developing states.

As noted at the beginning of this section, there is still much debate about the legal status of these principles, nonetheless, these principles are likely to be highlighted in any discussion of major projects throughout the world when they impact natural resources.

§13.10 CONCLUSION

The growth of international environmental law in recent decades has been phenomenal. The world is still developing effective enforcement mechanisms and relies heavily on the good faith of states to carry out their obligations under the various treaties. Some treaties have created their own inspection and verification systems,[12] and some international agencies undertake monitoring and reporting activities.[13] The continuing success of this remarkable movement will ultimately depend upon the willingness of the world's population to put long-term protection of the environment ahead of short-term economic success.

---

12. See, e.g., Treaty on the Southeast Asia Nuclear Weapon-Free Zone, 1981 U.N.T.S. 129, signed December 15, 1995, entered into force March 27, 1997, reprinted at 35 I.L.M. 635 (1996); African Nuclear-Weapon-Free Zone Treaty, signed September 13, 1995, entered into force July 7, 2009, U.N. Doc. A/50/426, reprinted at 35 I.L.M. 698 (1996).

13. See, e.g., Use of the Atomic Energy Agency in the Convention on Early Notification of a Nuclear Accident, art. 2, 1439 U.N.T.S. 275, signed September 26, 1986, entered into force October 27, 1986, reprinted at 25 I.L.M. 1370 (1986).

Table of Cases

Aaland Islands case, League of Nations O.J., Spec. Supp. 3 (1920), 64, 65

Abdullahi v. Pfizer, Inc., 562 F.3d 163 (2d Cir. 2009), cert. denied, 130 S. Ct. 3541 (2010), 8, 9, 10, 24, 260, 263

Accordance with International Law of the Unilateral Declaration of Independence in Respect of Kosovo, Advisory Opinion, 2010 I.C.J. _____ (July 22), 63, 76, 77, 78, 79, 289

Air Services Agreement case (France v. U.S.), 18 R.I.A.A. 416 (1978), 268

Aluminum Co. of America (U.S. v.), 148 F.2d 416 (2d Cir. 1945), 130

Alvarez-Machain (U.S. v.), 504 U.S. 655 (1992), 139, 154, 260, 262, 263

Anglo-Norwegian Fisheries. See Fisheries

Application of the Convention on the Prevention and Punishment of the Crime of Genocide (Bosnia & Herzegovina v. Serbia & Montenegro), 2007 I.C.J. 1, 22

Application of the Convention on the Prevention and Punishment of the Crime of Genocide (Bosnia & Herzegovina v. Yugoslavia), 1996 I.C.J. 595 (Preliminary Objections), 60

Arbitral Award of the Swiss Federal Council of 1922 concerning the boundary Between Colombia and Venezuela, I U.N.R.I.A.A. 228, 23, 166

Armed Activities on the Territory of the Congo (D.R. Congo v. Uganda), 2005 I.C.J. 168, 142

Arrest Warrant of 11 April 2000 (D.R. Congo v. Belgium), 2002 I.C.J. 3, 13, 137, 138, 147-149, 325

Asylum case (Colombia v. Peru), 1950 I.C.J. 266, 10, 11, 15

Attorney General of the Government of Israel v. Eichmann, S. Ct. Isr. (May 29, 1962); 16 Piske Din 2033 (1962), 138, 139, 154

Avena and Other Mexican Nationals (Mexico v. U.S.), 2004 I.C.J. 12, 23, 39, 40, 41, 55, 57, 58, 86, 145

Bin Laden (U.S. v.), 92 F. Supp. 2d 189 (S.D.N.Y. 2000) aff'd, sub nom. U.S. v. Odeh, 548 F.3d 276 (2d Cir. 2008), 135

Birch (U.S. v.), 470 F.2d 808 (4th Cir. 1972), 135

Brannigan and McBride v. United Kingdom, 258 Eur. Ct. H.R. (ser. A) (1993), 199, 202

Brogan and Others v. United Kingdom, 145-B Eur. Ct. H.R. (ser. A) (1988), 199, 202

Calley (U.S. v.), 22 U.S. C.M.A. 534 (1973); 48 C.M.R. 19 (1973) sub nom. Calley v. Callaway, 382 F. Supp. 650 (M.D. Ga. 1974); rev'd 519 F.2d 184 (5th Cir. 1975); cert. denied sub nom. Calley v. Hoffman, 425 U.S. 911 (1976), 314

Case of Certain Norwegian Loans (France v. Norway), 1957 I.C.J. 9, 116, 117, 119

Case of Mary Dann and Carrie Dann v. U.S., Case No. 11.140, Inter-Am. C.H.R., Report No. 75/02 (Dec. 27, 2002), 255

Case of Mayagna (Sumo) Awas Tingni Community v. Nicaragua, Inter-Am. Ct. H.R. (ser. C) No. 79 (2001), 255

Centre for Minority Rights Development (Kenya) and Minority Rights Group International on behalf of Endorois Welfare Council v. Kenya, African C.H.R. (2010), 251, 255, 257

Certain Expenses of the United Nations, Advisory Opinion, 1962 I.C.J. 151 (July 20), 292, 293

Chorzów Factory. See Factory at Chorzów

Church v. Hubbart, 6 U.S. (2 Cranch) 187 (1804), 351, 352

Clipperton Island Arbitration (France v. Mexico), 26 Am. J. Int'l L. 390 (1932), 105, 160

Comm'n v. Italy, 2010 E.C.R. _____, 386

Compulsory Membership in an Association Prescribed by Law for the Practice of Journalism, Advisory Opinion OC-5/85, Inter-Am. Ct. H.R. (ser. A) No. 5 (Nov. 13, 1985), 248

Continental Shelf (Libya v. Malta), 1985 I.C.J. 13, 18

Continental Shelf (Tunisia v. Libya), 1982 I.C.J. 18, 357

Corfu Channel (U.K. v. Albania), 1949 I.C.J. 4 (Merits), 22, 283, 348, 349, 379

Delimitation of the Maritime Boundary in the Gulf of Maine Area (Canada v. U.S.), 1984 I.C.J. 246, 18, 108, 109, 357

Delimition of the Maritime Areas Between Canada and France (St. Pierre and Miquelon) 31 I.L.M. 1145 (1992), 357

Dispute Regarding Navigational and Related Rights (Costa Rica v. Nicaragua), 2009 I.C.J. _____, 12

Doe I v. Unocal Corp., 395 F.3d 932 (9th Cir. 2002), 260-261

Domingues v. U.S., Case No. 12.285, Inter-Am. C.H.R., Report No. 62/02 (2002), 15

Dralle v. Republic of Czechoslovakia, Supreme Court of Austria, (1950) Int'l L. Rep. 155 (H. Lauterpacht ed.), 151

East Timor (Portugal v. Australia), 1995 I.C.J. 102, 75

Eastern Greenland case (Denmark v. Norway), 1933 P.C.I.J. (ser. A/B) No. 3, 30, 31, 159, 162

Ephraim v. Pastory, 87 I.L.R. 106 (Tanz. High Ct. 1990), 180

Ex Parte Pinochet, [2000] 1 AC 61; 1 AC 147, 19

Factory at Chorzów (Germany v. Poland), 1927 P.C.I.J. (ser. A) No. 9 (July 26) (Jurisdiction), 21, 23, 55, 85-87

Fawaz Yunis, a/k/a Nazeeh (U.S. v.), 924 F.2d 1086 (D.C. Cir. 1991), 133

Filartiga v. Pena-Irala, 630 F.2d 876 (2d Cir. 1980), 10, 220, 221, 259

Fisheries (U.K. v. Norway), 1951 I.C.J. 116, 15, 342, 346

Fisheries Jurisdiction (U.K. v. Iceland), 1973 I.C.J. 3 (Jurisdiction), 49, 50

Flores v. Southern Peru Copper Corp., 414 F.3d 233 (2d Cir. 2003), 9, 260

Foley Bros. v. Filardo, 336 U.S. 281 (1949), 130

Frontier Dispute (Benin v. Niger), 2005 I.C.J. 90, 64, 158

Frontier Dispute (Burkina Faso v. Mali), 1986 I.C.J. 554, 73, 110, 165

Gabčíkovo-Nagymaros Project (Hungary v. Slovakia), 1997 I.C.J. 7, 49, 50, 88, 387

Garcia (U.S. v.), 182 Fed. App. 873 (11th Cir. 2006), cert. denied, 549 U.S. 1110 (2007), 369

Grand Prince case (Belize v. France), 2001 I.T.L.O.S. No. 8, 367

Handyside v. United Kingdom, 24 Eur. Ct. H.R. (ser. A) (1979), 183

Ireland v. United Kingdom, 25 Eur. Ct. H.R. (ser. A) (1978), 202

Island of Palmas (Miangas) case (Netherlands v. U.S.), 2 R.I.A.A. 829 (1928), 159, 171

Italy (Gentini) v. Venezuela, Mixed Claims Comm'n, 1903 (Ralston, Venezuelan Arbitration of 1903) (1904), 21

J.W. Hampton, Jr. & Co. v. U.S., 276 U.S. 394 (1928), 32

Juan Humberto Sanchez case, 2003 Inter-Am. Ct. H.R. (ser. C) No. 102 (Nov. 25, 2003), 182

Kadic v. Karadzic, 70 F.3d 232 (2d Cir. 1995), 260

Kasikili/Sedudu Island (Botswana v. Namibia), 1999 I.C.J. 1045, 37, 167

Khulumani v. Barclay Nat'l Bank Ltd., 504 F.3d 254 (2d Cir. 2007), 259

Kiobel v. Royal Dutch Petroleum Co., 621 F. 3d 111 (2d Cir. 2010), 260, 262-263

Knab v. Republic of Georgia, No. 97-CV-03118 (TFH) 1998 U.S. Dist. Lexis 8820 (D.D.C. May 29, 1998) (mem.), 141

LaGrand (Germany v. U.S.), 2001 I.C.J. 466, 39, 40, 55, 86, 121, 145

Land and Maritime Boundary Between Cameroon and Nigeria (Cameroon v. Nigeria; Equatorial Guinea intervening), 2002 I.C.J. 303, 20, 158

Land, Island and Maritime Frontier Dispute (El Salvador v. Honduras), 1992 I.C.J. 351, 165, 166

Lawless v. Ireland, 3 Eur. Ct. H.R. (ser. A) (1961), 202

Legal Consequences for States of the Continued Presence in South Africa in Namibia (South West Africa) Notwithstanding Security Council Resolution 276 (1970), Advisory Opinion, 1971 I.C.J. 16 (June 21), 45, 75

Legal Consequences of the Construction of a Wall in the Occupied Palestinian Territory, Advisory Opinion, 2004 I.C.J. 136 (July 9), 52, 75, 87, 162, 229, 293

Legal Status of Eastern Greenland (Denmark v. Norway), 1933 P.C.I.J. (ser. A/B) No. 53 (Apr. 5), 30, 31, 159, 162

Legality of the Threat or Use of Nuclear Weapons,
Advisory Opinion, 1996 I.C.J. 226 (July 8),
24, 53, 120, 273, 304, 380, 392
Lubicon Lake Band v. Canada, Communication
No. 167/1984, U.N. Doc. Supp. No. 40
(A/45/40) (1990), 256

Magaya v. Magaya, 3 L.R.C. 35 (Zimb. Sup. Ct.
1999), 180-181
Marino-Garcia (U.S. v.)/U.S. v. Cassalins-Guzman, 679
F.2d 1373 (11th Cir. 1982), 369
*Maritime Delimitation in Area Between Greenland and Jan
Mayen* (Denmark v. Norway), 1993 I.C.J. 38,
357
Medellin v. Dretke, 371 F.3d 270 (5th Cir. 2004),
cert. denied, 544 U.S. 660 (2005), 57
Medellin v. Texas, 552 U.S. 491 (2008), 20,
58, 59
*Military and Paramilitary Activities in and Against
Nicaragua* (Nicaragua v. U.S.), 1984 I.C.J.
392 (Jurisdiction and Admissibility),
22, 119
*Military and Paramilitary Activities in and Against
Nicaragua* (Nicaragua v. U.S.), 1986 I.C.J. 14
(Merits), 25, 83, 88, 107, 115, 163, 273,
276-278, 281-286, 292, 318
Miranda v. Arizona, 384 U.S. 436 (1966), 39, 57
Murray v. The Schooner Charming Betsy, 6 U.S.
(2 Cranch) 64 (1804), 135

Namibia (South West Africa) case, Advisory
Opinion, 1971 I.C.J. 16 (June 21), 45, 75
New Jersey v. New York, 523 U.S. 767 (1998),
167, 168
North Sea Continental Shelf (F.R. Germany v.
Denmark; F.R. Germany v. Netherlands),
1969 I.C.J. 3, 15-17, 21
Nottebohm (Liechtenstein v. Guatemala), 1955
I.C.J. 4, 89, 90, 154
Nuclear Tests case (Australia v. France), 1974
I.C.J. 253, 30, 390
Nuclear Tests case (New Zealand v. France), 1974
I.C.J. 457, 390
Nuremberg Judgment, 6 F.R.D. 69 (1946), 177

Oil Platforms (Iran v. U.S.), 2003 I.C.J. 161, 280

Paquete Habana, The, 175 U.S. 677 (1900), 6, 7,
19, 24
Pfizer, Inc. v. Abdullahi. See *Abdullahi v. Pfizer, Inc.*
Presbyterian Church of Sudan v. Talisman Energy, Inc.,
582 F.3d 244 (2d Cir. 2009), 260-261

Prosecutor v. Duško Tadić, Decision on the Defence
Motion for Interlocutory Appeal on
Jurisdiction, 1995 I.C.T.Y. No. IT-94-1-AR,
329
Prosecutor v. Erdemović, 1997 I.C.T.Y. No. IT-96-22-A
(Judgment of the Appeals Chamber), 325
Prosecutor v. Furundzija, Case No. 17-95-17/IT,
Judgment of the Trial Chamber (10 Dec.
1998), 12
Protection of the Meridian Frog, EAS CC9/2000 Int'l
Ct. Env. Arb. & Conciliation (Spain 2000),
390
Pulp Mills on the River Uruguay (Argentina v.
Uruguay), 2010 I.C.J. _____, 86, 87, 380,
401, 402

Questions of Mutual Assistance in Criminal Matters
(Djibouti v. France), 2008 I.C.J. 177, 120

Reference re Secession of Quebec, 161 DLR (4th) 385,
2 S.C.R. 217 (1998), 19, 74, 75, 253
*Regina v. Bartle and the Commissioner of Police for the
Metropolis and Others Ex Parte Pinochet,* House of
Lords, U.K. (24 March 1999), 119 I.L.R.
135 (1999), 146, 147
Regina v. Hartely, 77 I.L.R. 330 (1978) (New
Zealand), 139
*Regina v. Horseferry Road Magistrate's Court, ex parte
Bennett,* 95 I.L.R. 380 (1993) (U.K.), 139
Regina v. Jones, [2006] UKHL 16, 19
Reparation for Injuries Suffered in the Service of the U.N.,
Advisory Opinion, 1949 I.C.J. 174
(April 11), 92
*Request for an Examination of the Situation in Accordance
with Paragraph 63 of the Court's Judgment of
20 December 1974 in the Nuclear Tests*
(New Zealand v. France) Case, 1995 I.C.J.
306 (Order of Sept. 22), 395, 398, 400
*Request for Interpretation of the Judgment of 31 March
2004* (Mexico v. U.S.), 2009 I.C.J. _____,
20, 58
*Reservations to the Convention on the Prevention and
Punishment of the Crime of Genocide,* Advisory
Opinion, 1951 I.C.J. 15 (May 28), 33, 185
Right of Passage case (Portugal v. India), 1960
I.C.J. 6, 11
Roper v. Simmons, 543 U.S. 551 (2005), 14, 190

Sahin v. Turkey, 41 Eur. H.R. Rep. 8 (2005), 245
Saiga case (St. Vincent and the Grenadines v.
Guinea), 1999 I.T.L.O.S. No. 2, 355, 365,
366, 373

Table of Cases

Samantar v. Yousuf, 130 S. Ct. 2278 (2010), 262

Sandra Lovelace v. Canada, Communication No. R.6/24, U.N. Doc. Supp. No. 40 (A/36/40) (1981), 256

Schooner Exchange v. McFadden, The, 11 U.S. (7 Cranch) 116 (1812), 150

Scotia, The, 81 U.S. 170 (1871), 7

Selmouni v. France, 1999-V Eur. Ct. H.R. 149, 182, 184

Shrimp-Turtle case, reprinted at 41 I.L.M. 149 (2002), 385

Sihadej Chindawongse (U.S. v.), /U.S. v. Boripat Siripan, 771 F.2d 840 (4th Cir. 1985), 145

Sinaltrainal v. Coca-Cola Co., 578 F.3d 1252 (11th Cir. 2009), 260

Smith v. U.S., 507 U.S. 197 (1993), 130

Social and Economic Rights Action Center and the Center for Economic and Social Rights v. Nigeria, Comm. 155/96, Afr. Comm'n on Human and Peoples' Rights (2001), 249

Soering v. United Kingdom, 161 Eur. Ct. H.R. (ser. A) (1989), 182-184

Sosa v. Alvarez-Machain, 542 U.S. 692 (2004), 260, 262-263

Southern Bluefin Tuna cases (New Zealand v. Japan; Australia v. Japan), 1999 I.T.L.O.S. Nos. 3 & 4 (Request for Provisional Measures), 399

Sovereignty Over Pedra Branca/Pulau Batu Puteh, Middle Rocks and South Ledge (Malaysia v. Singapore), 2008 I.C.J. 12, 64, 158, 164, 173

Sovereignty Over Pulau Ligitan and Pulau Sipadan (Indonesia v. Malaysia), 2002 I.C.J. 625, 64, 158

Stuart (U.S. v.), 489 U.S. 353 (1989), 38

Techt v. Hughes, 229 N.Y. 222, 128 N.E. 185, cert. denied, 254 U.S. 643 (1920), 51

Temple of Preah Vihear (Cambodia v. Thailand), 1962 I.C.J. 6, 41

Territorial and Maritime Dispute Between Nicaragua and Honduras in the Caribbean Sea (Nicaragua v. Honduras), 2007 I.C.J. 659, 23, 165

Territorial Dispute (Libya v. Chad), 1994 I.C.J. 6, 37

Trail Smelter case (U.S. v. Canada), 3 U.N. Rep. Int'l Arb. Awards 1905 (1941), 378, 379, 386, 402

U.S. Diplomatic and Consular Staff in Tehran (U.S. v. Iran), 1980 I.C.J. 3, 22, 47, 87, 88, 112, 141, 142

U.S. ex rel Mergé v. Italian Republic, 14 U.N.R.I.A.A. 236 (1955), 92

U.S. v. Aluminum Co. of America, 148 F.2d 416 (2d Cir. 1945), 130

U.S. v. Alvarez-Machain, 504 U.S. 655 (1992), 139, 154, 260, 262, 263

U.S. v. Bin Laden, 92 F. Supp. 2d 189 (S.D.N.Y. 2000) aff'd, sub nom. U.S. v. Odeh, 548 F.3d 276 (2d Cir. 2008), 135

U.S. v. Birch, 470 F.2d 808 (4th Cir. 1972), 135

U.S. v. Calley, 22 U.S. C.M.A. 534 (1973); 48 C.M.R. 19 (1973) sub nom. Calley v. Callaway, 382 F. Supp. 650 (M.D. Ga. 1974); rev'd 519 F.2d 184 (5th Cir. 1975); cert. denied sub nom. Calley v. Hoffman, 425 U.S. 911 (1976), 314

U.S. v. Fawaz Yunis, a/k/a Nazeeh, 924 F.2d 1086 (D.C. Cir. 1991), 133

U.S. v. Garcia, 182 Fed. App. 873 (11th Cir. 2006), cert. denied 549, U.S. 1110 (2007), 369

U.S. v. Marino-Garcia/U.S. v. Cassalins-Guzman, 679 F.2d 1373 (11th Cir. 1982), 369

U.S. v. Sihadej Chindawongse/U.S. v. Boripat Siripan, 771 F.2d 840 (4th Cir. 1985), 145

U.S. v. Stuart, 489 U.S. 353 (1989), 38

Velasquez Rodriquez case, Inter-Am. Ct. H.R. (ser. C) No. 4 (July 29, 1988), 247

Victory Transport, Inc. v. Comisaria General de Abastecimiento y Transportes, 336 F.2d 354 (2d Cir. 1964), cert. denied, 381 U.S. 934 (1965), 152

Western Sahara, Advisory Opinion, 1975 I.C.J. 12 (Oct. 16), 75, 160

Wildenhus' Case, 120 U.S. 1 (1887), 370

Wiwa v. Shell, 392 F.3d 812 (5th Cir. 2004), 260

Treaties and
Other International
Documents Index

The date listed is the date of the adoption or signing of the treaty.

1842 Treaty of Nanking (U.K.-China), 173
1868 Declaration of St. Petersburg, 303
1899 Declaration Respecting Expanding Bullets, 303
1899 Hague Convention Concerning the Laws and Customs of War on Land, 293
1899 Hague Convention for the Pacific Settlement of International Disputes, 105
1907 Hague Conventions I-XII, 294
1907 Hague Convention (IV) Concerning the Laws and Customs of War on Land, With Annex of Regulations, 293, 294
1907 Hague Convention (VIII) Relative to the Laying of Automatic Submarine Contact Mines, 303
1907 Hague Convention (IX) Concerning Bombardment by Naval Forces in Time of War, 303
1919 Covenant of the League of Nations, 72, 94, 106, 269
1921 Convention and Statute on the Regime of Navigable Waterways of International Concern, 397
1921 International Convention for the Suppression of Traffic in Women and Children, 176
1925 Geneva Gas Protocol, 303
1926 Convention to Suppress the Slave Trade and Slavery, 126
1928 General Treaty for the Renunciation of War (Kellogg-Briand Pact), 269, 317
1933 Convention on the Rights and Duties of States, 63
1945 Agreement for the Prosecution and Punishment of Major War Criminals of the European Axis Powers and Charter of the International Military Tribunal (Nuremberg or London Charter), 315, 316, 327
1945 Pact of the League of Arab States, 124, 251
1945 United Nations Charter, 20, 25, 33, 42, 43, 51, 72, 80, 93-98, 104, 106-110, 112, 115, 117, 120, 121, 158, 162, 177, 191, 229-231, 271-282, 285-287, 289-292, 317, 319-321, 328, 329
1946 Convention on the Privileges and Immunities of the United Nations, 94, 149
1946 The Tokyo Charter, 317, 327
1947 Agreement between the United Nations and the United States Regarding the Headquarters of the United Nations, 94, 149
1947 General Agreement on Tariffs and Trade (GATT) (modified in 1994 and now operative under the World Trade Organization (WTO) framework), 122, 384, 385
1948 American Declaration on the Rights and Duties of Man, 245-249
1948 Charter of the Organization of American States, 123, 245-247
1948 Convention on the Prevention and Punishment of the Crime of Genocide, 33, 43, 110, 227, 311, 312, 325, 326
1948 Universal Declaration of Human Rights, 27, 191-193, 376

1949 Geneva Convention for the Amelioration of the Condition of the Wounded and Sick in Armed Forces in the Field (Geneva I), 52, 138, 282, 294, 295, 302, 393

1949 Geneva Convention for the Amelioration of Wounded, Sick and Shipwrecked Members of the Armed Forces at Sea (Geneva II), 52, 138, 282, 294, 295, 302, 392

1949 Geneva Convention Relative to the Treatment of Prisoners of War (Geneva III), 52, 138, 282, 294, 295, 298, 299, 301, 302, 393

1949 Geneva Convention Relative to the Protection of Civilian Persons in Time of War (Geneva IV), 52, 138, 282, 294, 295, 302, 393

1949 The North Atlantic Treaty (NATO), 275

1950 European Convention on Human Rights, 243-244

1954 Convention for the Prevention of the Pollution of the Sea by Oil (OILPOL), 361

1954 Hague Conventions for the Protection of Cultural Property in the Event of Armed Conflict, 294

1958 Convention on Fishing and Conservation of the Living Resources of the High Seas, 336, 359

1958 Convention on the Continental Shelf, 17, 336, 359

1958 Convention on the High Seas, 336, 358, 359, 362

1958 Convention on the Territorial Sea and the Contiguous Zone, 336, 348, 352, 359

1959 The Antarctic Treaty, 64, 169, 305, 397

1961 European Social Charter (revised in 1996), 244

1961 Optional Protocol Concerning the Compulsory Settlement of Disputes to the Vienna Convention on Diplomatic Relations, 111

1961 Vienna Convention on Diplomatic Relations, 17, 46, 47, 111, 112, 140, 141, 142, 143

1963 Charter of the Organization of African Unity, 124

1963 Convention on Offenses and Certain Other Acts Committed On Board Aircraft, 132

1963 Treaty Banning Nuclear Weapon Tests in the Atmosphere, in Outer Space and Under Water, 390

1963 Vienna Convention on Consular Relations, 38, 39, 40, 41, 56, 57, 86, 87, 142, 144, 145, 146

1965 Convention on the Settlement of Investment Disputes between States and Nationals of Other States, 106

1966 Convention on the Elimination of All Forms of Racial Discrimination, 185

1966 First Optional Protocol to the International Covenant on Civil and Political Rights, 206-207

1966 International Covenant on Civil and Political Rights, 9, 27, 53, 73, 193-209

1966 International Covenant on Economic, Social and Cultural Rights, 27, 73, 209-221

1967 Treaty for the Prohibition of Nuclear Weapons in Latin America and the Caribbean, 305

1967 Treaty on Principles Governing the Activities of States in the Exploration and Uses of Outer Space, Including the Moon and Other Celestial Bodies (Outer Space Treaty), 170, 305, 397

1968 Agreement on the Rescue of Astronauts, the Return of Astronauts and the Return of Objects Launched into Space, 170

1968 Treaty on the Non-Proliferation of Nuclear Weapons (NPT), 304

1969 American Convention on Human Rights, 245-248

1969 Convention on Civil Liability for Oil Pollution Damage, 362

1969 International Convention Relating to Intervention on the High Seas in Cases of Oil Pollution Casualties, 362

1969 Vienna Convention on the Law of Treaties, 12, 16, 17, 20, 30-32, 35, 36-38, 41-45, 48-51, 54, 60, 118, 119, 181-186, 384, 388

1970 Hague Convention on the Suppression of Unlawful Seizure of Aircraft, 136

1971 International Convention on the Establishment of an International Fund for Compensation for Oil Pollution Damage, 362

1972 Convention for the Protection of the World Cultural and Natural Heritage, 387

1972 Convention on the International Liability for Damage Caused by Space Objects, 170, 380
1972 Convention on the Prohibition of the Development, Production and Stockpiling of Bacteriological (Biological) and Toxin Weapons and on their Destruction, 303
1973 Convention on International Trade in Endangered Species of Wild Fauna and Flora (CITES), 381, 387
1973 International Convention for the Prevention of Marine Pollution from Ships (MARPOL), 361
1975 Convention for the Avoidance of Double Taxation and the Prevention of Fiscal Evasion with respect to Taxes on Income and Capital Gains (U.S.-U.K.), 131
1975 Declaration on the Protection of All Persons from Being Subjected to Torture and Other Cruel, Inhuman or Degrading Treatment or Punishment, 221
1977 Convention of 18 May 1977 on the Prohibition of Military or Any Other Hostile Use of Environmental Modification Techniques, 393
1977 Protocol Additional to the Geneva Conventions of 12 August 1949, and Relating to the Protection of Victims of International Armed Conflicts (Protocol I), 81, 294, 296, 297, 299, 300, 302, 306, 313, 393, 394
1977 Protocol Additional to the Geneva Conventions of 12 August 1949, and Relating to the Protection of Victims of Non-International Armed Conflicts (Protocol II), 294, 296
1978 Protocol to the International Convention for the Prevention of Marine Pollution from Ships, 361
1978 Vienna Convention on Succession of States in Respect of Treaties, 60
1979 Agreement Governing the Activities of States on the Moon and Other Celestial Bodies, 170
1979 Convention on the Elimination of All Forms of Discrimination Against Women, 239
1979 Convention on Long-Range Transboundary Air Pollution, 386
1979 International Convention Against the Taking of Hostages, 136
1980 Convention for the Conservation of Antarctic Marine Living Resources, 170
1980 Convention on Prohibitions or Restrictions on the Use of Certain Conventional Weapons Which May Be Deemed to Be Excessively Injurious or to Have Indiscriminate Effects, 303
1980 Protocol on Non-Detectable Fragments (Protocol I), 303
1980 Protocol on Prohibitions and Restrictions on the Use of Mines, Booby-Traps and Other Devices (Protocol II), 304
1980 Protocol on Prohibitions or Restrictions on the Use of Incendiary Weapons (Protocol III), 304
1981 African Charter on Human and Peoples' Rights (Banjul Charter), 124, 248-249
1981 Algiers Accords, 122
1982 United Nations Convention on the Law of the Sea, 16, 17, 18, 33, 36, 121, 122, 337-357, 359-374, 397
1984 Convention Against Torture and Other Cruel, Inhuman or Degrading Treatment or Punishment, 10, 12, 27, 35, 36, 44, 45, 52, 147, 148, 238, 302, 326
1984 Joint Declaration of the Government of the United Kingdom of Great Britain and Northern Ireland and the Government of the People's Republic of China on the Question of Hong Kong, 173
1985 South Pacific Nuclear Free Zone Treaty, 305
1985 Vienna Convention for the Protection of the Ozone Layer, 386
1986 Convention on Assistance in Case of a Nuclear Accident or Radiological Emergency, 392
1986 Convention on the Early Notification of a Nuclear Accident, 392
1986 Use of the Atomic Energy Agency in the Convention on Early Notification of a Nuclear Accident, 404
1987 European Convention for the Prevention of Torture and Inhuman or Degrading Treatment or Punishment, 238
1987 Montreal Protocol on Substances that Deplete the Ozone Layer, 386, 387, 403

1989 Basel Convention on the Control of Transboundary Movements of Hazardous Wastes and Their Disposal, 382, 384

1989 Convention on the Rights of the Child, 14, 239

1989 Second Optional Protocol to the International Covenant on Civil and Political Rights, 207

1991 Bamako Convention on the Ban of the Import into Africa and the Control of Transboundary Movement and Management of Hazardous Wastes Within Africa, 382

1991 Convention on Environmental Assessment in a Transboundary Context, 402

1991 Protocol on Environmental Protection to the Antarctic Treaty, 170

1992 Convention on Biological Diversity, 28, 381, 387, 389

1992 Convention on the Protection of Transboundary Watercourses and International Lakes, 398

1992 United Nations Framework Convention on Climate Change, 28, 382, 387

1993 Convention on the Prohibition of the Development, Production, Stockpiling and Use of Chemical Weapons and on Their Destruction, 303

1994 Agreement Establishing the World Trade Organization (WTO), 122, 123, 384, 385

1994 Agreement Relating to the Implementation of Part XI of the United Nations Convention on the Law of the Sea of 10 December, 1982, 337, 360

1994 Arab Charter on Human Rights, 125, 251

1994 United Nations Convention to Combat Desertification in those Countries Experiencing Serious Drought and/or Desertification, Particularly in Africa, 387

1995 Protocol on Blinding Laser Weapons (Protocol IV), 304

1995 Treaty on the Southeast Asia Nuclear Weapon-Free Zone, 305, 404

1996 African Nuclear-Weapon-Free Zone Treaty, 305, 404

1996 Amendment to Protocol on Prohibition and Restrictions on the Use of Mines, Booby-Traps and Other Devices (Protocol II), 304

1996 Comprehensive Test Ban Treaty (not yet in force), 305, 358, 391

1996 Shanghai Cooperation Organization, 125

1997 Convention on Human Rights and Biomedicine, 9

1997 Convention on the Prohibition of the Use, Stockpiling, Production and Transfer of Anti-Personnel Mines and Their Destruction, 304, 397

1997 Extradition Treaty Between the Government of the United States and the Government of the Republic of India, 131

1997 Kyoto Protocol to the United Nations Framework Convention on Climate Change, 387

1997 Proposed American Declaration on the Rights of Indigenous Peoples, 255

1998 Protocol to the African Charter on Human and Peoples' Rights, 124, 249

1998 Rome Statute of the International Criminal Court, 316-322, 324, 327, 330, 331

1998 Rotterdam Convention on the Prior Informed Consent Procedure for Certain Hazardous Chemicals and Pesticides in International Trade, 382

2000 African Union Constitutive Act, 124

2000 Eurasian Economic Community, 125

2000 Optional Protocol to the Convention on the Rights of the Child on the Involvement of Children in Armed Conflict, 239

2000 Optional Protocol to the Convention on the Rights of the Child on the Sale of Children, Child Prostitution and Child Pornography, 239

2000 United Nations Global Compact, 258

2001 Stockholm Convention on Persistent Organic Pollutants, 387

2001 Universal Declaration on Cultural Diversity, 179

2003 Protocol on Explosive Remnants of War, 304

2006 Central Asian Nuclear-Free-Zone Treaty, 305

2007 Declaration on the Rights of Indigenous Peoples, 253

2008 Convention on Cluster Munitions, 304

2008 Optional Protocol to the International Covenant on Economic, Social and Cultural Rights, 213

2010 Treaty Between the United States of America and the Russian Federation on Measures for the Further Reduction and Limitation of Strategic Offensive Arms (New START Treaty) (not yet in force), 305

General Index

Aaland Islands, 64, 65
Accretion, 167, 168
Acquisition of territory, 157-173
Advisory opinions
    African Court on Human and
        Peoples' Rights, 250
    Canadian Supreme Court, 74-75
    Inter-American Court of Human Rights,
        247, 248
    International Court of Justice, 24, 120.
        See also advisory opinion cases at: 24, 33,
        45, 52, 53, 63, 76, 77, 78, 87, 92,
        107, 120, 160, 162, 227, 228, 229,
        273, 289, 292-293, 304, 305-306,
        380, 392, 401
Afghanistan, 100, 125, 280, 298
Africa, 45, 66, 71, 73, 75, 98, 124, 165, 180,
    222, 223, 243, 248-251, 255, 290,
    305, 331, 382, 404
African Charter on Human and Peoples'
    Rights/Banjul Charter, 124, 180,
    248-251, 257
African Court on Human and Peoples' Rights,
    124, 180, 248-251
African Union, 98, 124, 248-251
Aggression, 25, 52, 96, 230, 274, 277, 290,
    310, 316-319, 320, 327, 328
Agreement. *See* Treaties
Aircraft, 132, 136, 142, 170, 268, 343, 345,
    347, 348, 349, 350, 351, 362, 367,
    368, 372, 396
Air pollution, 378, 386
Airspace, 347
    rights of overflight, 268, 349, 350, 351,
        354, 358
Aliens, 8, 25, 74, 75, 76, 91-92, 100, 146,
    176, 259, 287, 321
    nationality of claims, 89-92
    standard of treatment, 176, 321
American Convention on Human Rights,
    184, 221, 245-248
American Declaration on the Rights and Duties
    of Man, 245-249
Annexation, 163
Antarctica, 64, 168, 169-170, 305, 397
Apartheid, 45, 66, 290, 316

Arab Charter on Human Rights, 125, 251
Arab League, 124-125, 133, 251
Arbitration, 23, 54, 102, 104, 105-106, 122,
    159, 160, 165, 171, 230, 269, 319, 390
    Iran-U.S. Claims Tribunal, 122
    Permanent Court of Arbitration, 105-106
Archipelagic waters/states, 337, 346-347,
    358, 372
Arctic, the, 64, 168-169
Armed attack, 35, 43, 65, 100, 124, 133, 142,
    162, 172, 201, 202, 228, 232, 234,
    236, 266, 267, 270, 271, 272,
    274-279, 280-282, 285, 287, 291,
    294-295, 297-298, 300, 303,
    306-307, 313-314, 316, 317-320,
    331, 333, 343, 365, 394
Arms embargo, 234, 290-291. *See also* Sanctions
Asylum, 10, 89, 108
Avulsion, 167-168

Banjul Charter/African Charter on Human
    and Peoples' Rights, 124, 180,
    248-251, 257
Baselines, 341, 342, 346, 347, 349, 352,
    353, 356
Bays, 337, 338-341, 345
Belgium, 13, 137, 147-148, 325
Biafra, 65
Biological diversity, 28, 381, 382, 387, 389
Biomedicine, 9-10
Blockades. *See* Sanctions
Boundaries, 18, 23, 37, 48, 60, 63, 73, 109,
    109, 138, 158, 165, 166, 167-168, 352,
    357, 383, 384, 386, 393, 398, 402
Burkina Faso, 73, 110, 165

Canada, 18, 19, 71, 74, 108, 109, 129, 152,
    169, 256, 270, 341, 357, 378, 402
Capital punishment, 13-16, 56, 99, 183,
    189-190, 207, 319, 328
Cession of territory, 158, 163
Charter of the United Nations, 20, 25, 33, 43,
    51, 72, 80, 93-98, 104, 106-110, 112,
    115, 117, 120, 121, 158, 162, 177,
    191, 229-231, 271-282, 285-287,
    289-292, 317, 319-321, 328, 329

Chemical weapons, 274, 303, 320

Children/rights of the child, 14, 53, 96, 132, 176, 194, 210, 216, 225-226, 237-240, 244, 246, 251, 255-257, 262-263, 296, 311, 313-314, 332

Civil war, 65, 167, 225, 233, 239, 286, 288, 293, 295, 314, 321

Climate change, 28, 382, 386-387, 399

Codification of international law, 16, 17, 24, 80, 294

Coercion, 42-43, 284, 301

Collective self-defence, 272, 274, 276-278, 280, 281, 285, 292

Colonies/colonialism, 6, 25, 65, 72-75, 78-79, 97, 158-159, 163-166, 172, 178, 249, 253, 283, 401

Common heritage of mankind, 168, 170, 359

Conciliation, 54, 104, 357, 390

Congo (Democratic Republic of), 13, 14, 137, 142, 147-148, 292, 325, 331

Conquest, 159, 162-163, 173, 265-333

Conservation, 99, 169, 170, 336, 354, 374, 376-377, 382, 387, 388-389

Consular immunity/rights, 22, 38-41, 47, 51, 56, 57, 86-88, 141-142, 144-146, 147, 371

Contiguous zone, 336, 337, 348, 351-353, 372

Continental shelf, 15-18, 21, 108, 109, 336, 337, 356-358

Conventions. See Treaties

Corruption, 41-42, 258

Countermeasures, 84, 265, 268, 281, 285, 346

Court of Justice of the European Union, 123

Crimes against humanity, 9, 12, 136, 147-148, 222, 234, 310, 312, 315-316, 319, 324, 327, 329, 332, 333

Criminal offences

International Criminal Court, 13, 31, 82, 101, 103, 222, 296-297, 316, 317, 321, 330-331

Nuremberg, 9, 177, 263, 315, 316, 321, 327-328

Rwanda, 13, 101, 226, 236, 296, 311, 316, 329, 330

state responsibility for, 80-82, 100, 325-327

Tokyo, 177, 310, 315, 317, 321, 327-328, 330

Yugoslavia, 12, 13, 25, 83, 101, 235, 296, 311, 315, 321, 328-330

Cuba, 6, 67, 137

Customary international law, 6-16

codification, 16, 17, 24, 80

environmental law, 48-51, 361, 377-380, 382-385

human rights, 8, 9, 10, 12, 14, 15, 16, 36, 190-193, 218-220

law of the sea, 6, 336, 348, 355

use of force, 43, 88, 138, 163, 269-270, 272, 276, 277, 282, 283, 286, 293, 294, 296, 297, 305, 318

Death penalty, 13-16, 56, 99, 183, 189-190, 207, 319, 328

Declarations, United Nations, 27, 72, 74, 76, 158, 162, 163, 177, 179, 180, 181, 190, 191-194, 209, 217-218, 220-221, 224, 243, 253-255, 272, 282-283, 305, 321, 376, 381, 390, 393, 398, 400, 401, 402, 403

Deep sea bed, 17, 359-361

Definition of international law, 1-3

Delimitation of continental shelf, 18, 108, 109, 357-358

Democratic Republic of Congo, 13, 14, 137, 142, 147-148, 292, 325, 331

Denunciation of treaties, 44-45, 190

Development, right to, 72, 191, 212, 249, 253, 257, 289, 381, 401, 403

Diplomatic immunity, 12, 46-47, 111-112, 139-144, 325

Discovery, 159-161, 171-172

Discrimination, 12, 76, 176, 180-181, 185, 187, 192, 194, 196, 199, 210, 211, 219, 226, 238-240, 246, 254, 256

Dispute settlement, 63, 103-126, 357, 361

Dumping, 361, 362, 383, 384

East Timor, 71, 75, 101, 332

Economic and Social Council (ECOSOC), 96-97, 98-99, 223, 254

Eichmann, Adolf, 138, 139, 154

El Salvador, 165, 166, 276-278

Embargo. See Sanctions

Entry into force. See Treaties

Environment

air pollution, 378, 386

biodiversity, 28, 381, 382, 387, 389

chemical weapons, 274, 303, 320

climate change, 28, 382, 386-387, 399

conservation, 99, 169, 170, 336, 354, 374, 376-377, 382, 387, 388-389

customary law, 377-380, 383-384, 388-389

deforestation, 387, 403

hazardous wastes, 382-386

liability for damage, 170, 362, 380, 385-386

marine pollution, 170, 354, 361-362, 391, 395-396

nuclear weapons, 169, 305, 307-308, 361, 380, 390-397, 398, 400-401, 404

oil pollution, 56, 82-85, 92, 197-198, 260-262, 361-362

ozone layer, 386-387

polar regions, 169-170, 305

Rio Declaration, 381, 393, 394, 398, 399, 401, 402, 403

state responsibility, 376, 377-380

Stockholm Declaration, 27, 381, 393, 400

sustainable development, 381, 382, 387, 389, 394, 398, 401, 403

U.N. Environment Programme (UNEP), 381

Equity, 21-22, 400

Erga omnes obligations, 136

Eritrea, 65, 71

Eurasian Economic Community, 98, 125

European Social Charter, 244

European Union, 9, 70, 98, 123, 125

Exclusive economic zone, 17-18, 341, 347, 349, 351, 353-355, 371-374

Executive agreements, 19, 32

Extradition, 131, 133-139, 146-147, 154-155, 183-184, 310

Extraterritoriality, 7, 130

Falkland Islands/Islas Malvinas, 164

Fisheries, 15, 17-18, 49, 50, 342, 353-354, 371, 373-374

Fishing, 6-8, 11-12, 336, 341, 342, 353, 358, 366, 371, 373-374

Flags of convenience, 362-367, 368-370, 371-373

Force. *See* Use of force; War

Foreign ships, 342-344, 351, 368, 370, 371-374, 379

Fraud, 41, 177, 215, 385

Friendly Relations, Declaration on, 162, 163, 272

Gender/sex discrimination, 176, 180, 181, 187, 192, 238, 239, 246, 255-256

General Assembly of the United Nations, 10, 13, 17, 24-25, 27, 45, 72, 76, 80, 93, 94, 95, 96, 97, 107, 120, 149, 162-163, 172, 191, 192, 209, 213, 222, 223, 224, 227, 229, 253, 254, 272, 277, 282, 284, 288, 292, 305, 311, 317, 318, 329, 330, 376, 390, 392, 394, 395

General principles of international law, 6, 20-22, 58, 108, 212, 270, 352, 379

General Treaty for the Renunciation of War/Kellogg-Briand Pact, 269, 317

Geneva Conventions on the Laws of War, 52, 81, 137, 138, 162, 282, 294, 297, 298, 301, 302, 306, 314, 328, 393

Genocide, 12, 22, 25, 33-35, 43, 60, 110, 136, 185, 188, 219, 227, 236, 238, 310, 311-312, 324, 325-327, 329

German reunification, 59

Germany, 15-17, 19, 39, 71, 85, 86-87, 90, 121, 145, 317, 327, 361

Global warming, 387, 399

Good offices, 104

Government, 6, 10, 30, 31, 47, 57, 58, 62-63, 64-69, 74, 80-85, 149-155, 282-286, 325-327

Greenland, 30, 31, 159, 162, 357

Grenada, 287

Grotius, Hugo, 385

Groups. *See* Non-state groups

Gulf War, 96, 233

Hague Conventions, 105, 136, 293-294, 297, 303

Harbors, 370. *See also* Internal waters

Hazardous waste, 382-386

High Commission for Human Rights, 177, 222-223, 224, 259

High seas, 6, 358, 367-369, 371-374

Hijacking, 100, 133-135, 136, 280, 287

Honduras, 23, 165-166, 176, 363

Hostilities. *See* Use of force; War

Hot pursuit, 371-374

Humanitarian intervention, 229, 231, 232, 287, 289

Human rights, 175-263

Alien Tort Claims Act, 8, 9, 259

Alien Tort Statute, 8, 9, 259

children, 8-10, 14, 53, 96, 132, 176, 194, 210, 216, 219, 225-226, 239-240, 244, 246, 251, 255-257, 262-263, 296, 311, 314, 332

Human rights (continued)
 complaints, 195, 206-208, 212-213,
  224-226, 242-243
 corporate responsibility, 101-102, 259-263
 customary law, 8, 9, 10, 12, 14, 15, 16, 36,
  190-193, 218-220
 European Court of Human Rights, 123, 182,
  183, 184, 199, 202, 207, 222, 243
 genocide, 12, 22, 25, 33-35, 43, 60, 110,
  136, 185, 188, 219, 227, 236, 238,
  310, 311-312, 324, 325-327, 329
 group rights, 2, 73-74, 99, 158-159, 177,
  182, 210, 232-234, 251-258
 Human Rights Commissioner, 177,
  222-223, 224, 259
 Human Rights Committee, 195, 241, 251
 Human Rights Council, 222, 223, 226, 242,
  254, 259, 261
 Indigenous Peoples, 45, 99, 158, 160, 210,
  212, 225-226, 239, 252-256, 401
 Inter-American Court of Human Rights,
  123, 182, 222, 245-248
 International Court of Justice, 226-228
 International Covenant on Civil and
  Political Rights, 9, 10, 186-187, 189,
  190, 192, 194, 195-209, 228, 238,
  240, 241, 242, 243, 246, 250, 251,
  252-256, 258, 261, 263
 International Covenant on Economic, Social
  and Cultural Rights, 190, 192, 194,
  209-221, 222, 225, 226, 228, 240,
  250, 251, 252-254, 261
 international criminal courts
  International Criminal Court, 13,
   31, 82, 101, 222, 296-297, 316,
   317, 321, 330-331
  Nuremberg, 9, 177, 263, 315, 316, 321,
   327-328
  Rwanda, 13, 101, 226, 236, 296, 311,
   316, 329, 330
  Tokyo, 177, 310, 315, 317, 321,
   327-328, 330
  Yugoslavia, 12, 13, 83, 101, 235, 296,
   311, 315, 321, 328-330
 legal positivism, 178-179
 natural law, 178-179
 non-governmental organizations, 96, 99,
  203, 240-242
 racial discrimination, 12, 185, 199, 219,
  238, 239, 240, 254, 283
 Security Council, 229-236

 self-determination, 181, 194, 209,
  252-253, 256
 self-executing treaties, 188-190, 195, 211
 sex/gender discrimination, 176, 180, 181,
  187, 192, 238, 239, 246, 255-256
 slavery, 176, 192, 194, 197, 199, 219, 226,
  239, 240, 246, 261
 torture/cruel, inhuman, or
  degrading treatment, 183-184, 192,
  194, 197, 199, 202, 210, 219,
  220-221, 225, 226, 238-240,
  242, 244, 260, 262
 treaty interpretation and reservations,
  182-188
 Universal Declaration of Human Rights,
  191-193
 war crimes, 222, 234

Immunity
 consular, 22, 38-41, 47, 51, 56, 57, 86-88,
  141-142, 144-146, 147, 371
 diplomatic, 12, 46-47, 111-112,
  139-144, 325
 for head of state and other ministers, 146-149
 for international organizations, 149
 sovereign, 149-152, 262
Independence, 25, 59, 63, 64, 65, 66, 67, 68, 69,
  70, 71, 72, 73, 74-79, 123, 158-159,
  165-166, 176, 231-233, 236, 246, 271,
  274-275, 282, 283, 286, 289, 290,
  317-319, 332
Indigenous Peoples, 45, 99, 158, 160, 210,
  212, 225-226, 239, 252-256, 401
Individuals, 2, 38, 39-40, 89, 100-101, 124,
  154, 176-178, 181-182, 188, 195-198,
  202, 205, 206-208, 210, 212, 213,
  215, 220, 222, 224, 225, 235, 241,
  243, 245, 247, 249, 250, 256, 257,
  260, 312, 321, 323, 332, 378
Innocent passage, 283, 342-347, 348-351,
  370, 374
Inter-American Commission on Human Rights,
  15, 123, 246, 247, 254
Inter-governmental organizations, 92, 93-97
Interim measures/provisional measures,
  121, 142
Internal waters, 337-341
International agreements. See Treaties
International courts
 International Court of Justice, 10, 14, 16,
  18, 20, 21, 24, 33, 37, 39, 94, 97, 106

advisory opinions, 107, 120, 227. *See also*
   advisory opinion cases at: 24, 33, 45, 52, 53,
   63, 75, 76, 77, 78, 87, 92, 120, 121,
   160, 162, 185, 227, 228, 229, 273,
   289, 292-293, 304, 305-306, 380,
   392, 396, 397, 401
   composition, 107-108
   contentious cases, 108-120
   enforcement of judgments, 107
   interim measures/provisional measures,
      121, 142
   judges, 107
   jurisdiction, 108-120, 226-227
   optional clause, 112-118
   President, 396
   reciprocity, 112, 117-119
   sources of law, 5-28, 108, 227-229
   stare decisis, 20, 23
   Statute, 20, 21, 23, 97, 107, 108, 109,
      110, 112, 113, 114, 115, 116,
      117, 118, 121, 122
   Sweden, 113, 115
   United States, 114-115, 119
   voting, 107, 396
international criminal courts
   International Criminal Court, 13, 31, 82,
      101, 103, 222, 296-297, 316, 317,
      321, 330-331
   Nuremberg, 9, 177, 263, 315, 316, 321,
      327-328
   Rwanda, 13, 101, 226, 236, 296, 311,
      316, 329, 330
   Tokyo, 177, 310, 315, 317, 321,
      327-328, 330
   Yugoslavia, 12, 13, 25, 83, 101, 235,
      296, 311, 315, 321, 328-330
   International Tribunal for the Law of the Sea,
      121-122, 361. *See also cases at:* 355,
      365-367, 373, 399
   Permanent Court of International Justice, 21,
      106. *See also cases at:* 21, 23, 30-31,
      55, 85-86, 87, 159, 162
International Covenant on Civil and
      Political Rights, 9, 10, 186-187, 189,
      190, 192, 194, 195-209, 228, 238,
      240, 241, 242, 243, 246, 250, 251,
      252-256, 258, 261, 263
International Covenant on Economic, Social
      and Cultural Rights, 190, 192, 194,
      209-221, 222, 225, 226, 228, 240,
      250, 251, 252-254, 261

International law
   definition, 1-3
   sources, 5-28, 108, 227-229
International Law Commission, 17, 24, 37, 41,
      47, 48, 51, 54, 80, 104, 186, 336
International organizations, 92-99, 149
   African Union, 98, 124, 248-250
   Arab League, 98, 124-125, 133, 243, 251
   Eurasian Economic Community, 98, 125
   European Union, 9, 70, 98, 123, 125
   governmental, 93-98
   international personality, 2, 92, 93
   League of Nations, 21, 45, 64-65, 72, 94,
      106, 158, 269
   non-governmental, 98-99
   Organization of African Unity
      (African Union), 98, 124, 248-250
   Organization of American States, 98, 123,
      237, 245, 246, 247, 248, 254, 255
   Shanghai Cooperation Organization, 98, 125
   United Nations, 93-98
International Red Cross/Red Crescent, 99, 294,
      295, 296
International relations
   states' capacity to enter into, 62-63, 65-69
International Seabed Authority, 359
International tribunals. *See also* International courts
   International Tribunal for Rwanda, 13, 101,
      296, 311, 316, 329, 330
   International Tribunal for the
      former Yugoslavia, 12, 13, 83, 101,
      235, 296, 311, 315, 321, 328-330
   International Tribunal for the Law of the Sea,
      121-122, 361. *See also cases at:* 355,
      365-367, 373, 399
Iran-Iraq War, 365-366
Islands, 37, 47, 64, 66-68, 105, 159-162,
      164, 165-166, 167, 168, 171-173,
      270, 342, 346, 347, 349, 358
Islas Malvinas/Falkland Islands, 164
Israel, 52-53, 63, 65, 87, 137, 138-139, 162,
      279, 287, 350, 351
Italy, 21, 68, 151, 269, 386

Jurisdiction, 127-154
   bases for national jurisdiction
      nationality, 130-132
      passive personality, 132-135
      protective, 135-136
      territorial, 128-130
      universality, 136-138, 146-148

Jurisdiction (*continued*)
  consular immunity from, 144-146
  diplomatic immunity from, 47, 140-144
  extradition, 131, 133-139, 146-147,
    154-155, 183-184, 310
  extraterritoriality, 7, 130
  genocide, 12, 22, 25, 33-35, 43, 60, 110,
    136, 185, 188, 219, 227, 236, 238,
    310, 311-312, 324, 325-327, 329
  head of state and other ministers'
    immunity from, 146-149
  hijacking, 100, 133-135, 136, 280, 287
  International Court of Justice, 108-120
  international criminal courts
    International Criminal Court, 13, 31, 82,
     101, 222, 296-297, 316, 317, 321,
     330-331
    Rwanda, 13, 101, 296, 311, 316, 329, 330
    Yugoslavia, 12, 13, 83, 101, 235, 296,
     311, 315, 321, 328-330
  piracy, 12, 136, 367, 368-369
  sovereign immunity, 149-152
  territorial sea, 18, 341-346, 349, 350-353,
    370-374
  terrorism, 125, 132, 136, 310
  war crimes, 13, 136, 137, 138, 147, 148,
    222, 234, 310, 312, 327, 333
Jus *ad bellum*, 267, 271-282, 293, 308
Jus *cogens*, 8, 12-16, 20, 36, 43, 186, 219
Jus *in bello*, 267, 293-308

Kellogg-Briand Pact/General Treaty for the
  Renunciation of War, 269, 317
Korean War, 291-292
Kosovo, 63, 69, 70, 74, 76-79, 231, 236, 275,
  288, 289, 384
Kuwait, 25-26, 96, 232-233, 281, 291, 292,
  318-320, 365-366
Kyoto Protocol, 387

Lakes, 337-338, 398
Landlocked states, 354, 357, 358
Lauterpacht, Hersch, 14, 71, 116, 118, 151
Law of the Sea
  archipelagic waters/states, 346-347, 372
  baselines, 341, 342, 346, 347, 349, 352,
    353, 356
  bays, 337, 338-341, 345
  broadcasting, 367-369
  contiguous zone, 351-353, 372
  continental shelf, 356-358, 372
  customs zone, 343, 351-353, 355

  deep sea bed, 358, 359-361
  dumping, 361, 362, 383-385
  exclusive economic zone, 17, 18, 353-355
  fishing, 6-8, 11-12, 336, 341, 342, 353,
    358, 366, 371, 373-374
  flags of convenience, 362-367, 368-370,
    371-373
  genuine link, 362-366
  Grotius, Hugo, 385
  high seas, 6, 358, 367-369, 371-374
  hot pursuit, 371-374
  innocent passage, 283, 342-347, 348-351,
    370, 374
  internal waters, 337-341
  international straits, 347-351
  International Tribunal for the Law of the Sea,
    121-122, 361. *See also cases at:* 355,
    365-367, 373, 399
  nationality of ships, 362-363, 368
  piracy, 12, 136, 367, 368-369
  pollution, 361-362
  prompt release of crew and ship, 366, 367
  slave trade, 136, 367-368
  stateless ships, 136, 363, 366, 367, 369
  straits, 347-351
  submarines, 343, 344-345, 350
  territorial sea, 18, 337, 341-346
  Tribunal for, 121-122, 361. *See also cases at:*
    355, 365-367, 373, 399
  United Nations Convention on the Law of
    the Sea (UNCLOS), 337, 338, 341,
    342, 343, 350, 354, 355-374
  use of force to detain ship or crew, 345,
    354, 366, 367
League of Arab States, 98, 124-125, 133,
  243, 251
League of Nations, 21, 45, 64-65, 72, 94, 106,
  158, 269
Liberia, 332, 361, 362, 363
Libya, 18, 25, 37-38, 141, 208, 291, 341, 357
London Charter. *See* International courts,
  international criminal courts,
  Nuremberg

Mali, 73, 110, 165
Mediation, 54, 104, 230
Medical research, 9, 262-263
Mexico, 7, 20, 23, 39, 40, 55, 57-58, 86, 105,
  145, 159-160
Mineral resources, 169, 356, 359
Minority groups, 65-66, 138, 176, 194, 199,
  219, 232, 251, 252, 255, 257, 275, 288

Moon, 168, 170, 397
Multinational corporations, 2, 101-102, 198, 258-263
Municipal courts
  executive agreements, 19, 32
  international law in, 18-20

Namibia, 45, 75, 120, 167. *See also* South West Africa
Nationality
  acquisition, 89-91
  of ships, 362-367
  state's right to represent citizen, 89-91
National security, 135-136, 198, 200, 243, 365
NATO, 231, 235, 236, 275-276, 280, 288-289
Negotiation, 54, 63, 97, 104, 235, 319, 332
Neutrality, 294
Nicaragua, 12, 22, 23, 25, 83, 88, 107, 115, 119, 163, 165, 166, 255, 273, 276-278, 281-286, 292, 318
Nigeria, 8, 14, 20, 65, 158, 249, 263
Non-governmental organizations, 96, 98-99, 203, 240-242, 382
Non-state actors, 2, 100, 247
Non-state groups
  protected groups, 99
  non-state actors, 100, 280
Norway, 15, 30, 31, 70, 116-118, 159, 162, 169, 342, 346, 357
Nuclear testing, 30, 305, 390-391, 395, 398, 400
Nuclear weapons, 304-308
  environmental damage, 380, 390-397, 401
  legality of threat or use, 120, 273-274, 358, 392-397
  non-proliferation, 308
  outer space, 170
Nuremberg Trials, 315-317, 327

Obligations *erga omnes*, 136
Occupation, 74, 76, 79, 160-162, 164, 165, 166
Oil pollution, 56, 82-85, 92, 197-198, 260-262, 361-362
Opinio juris, 13-14
Organization of African Unity (African Union), 98, 124, 248-250
Organization of American States, 98, 123, 237, 245, 246, 247, 248, 254, 255

Organs of the United Nations. *See* Economic and Social Council (ECOSOC); General Assembly of the United Nations; International courts: International Court of Justice; Secretary-General of the United Nations; Security Council of the United Nations; and Trusteeship Council
Outer space, 170, 305, 390
  Moon Treaty, 170, 397
  nuclear weapons, 305, 390
  Rescue and Return Agreement, 170
  sovereignty over, 170
Ozone layer, 386-387, 403

Palestine, 52-54, 63, 75-76, 87, 133, 162-163
Peaceful settlement of disputes, 103-126
Peacekeeping, 95-96, 292-293
Permanent Court of Arbitration, 105-106
Permanent Court of International Justice, 25, 206. *See also cases at*: 21, 23, 30-31, 55, 85-86, 87, 159, 162
Piracy, 12, 136, 367, 368-369
Poland, 85, 87
Polar regions, 168-170, 305
  Antarctica, 64, 168, 169-170, 305, 397
  Arctic, the, 64, 168-169
Pollution. *See* Environment
Ports, 337-341
Precedent, 20, 23
Prescription, 163-164
Prisoners of war, 81, 294-298, 301, 313-314, 324-325
Privileges and immunities
  consular, 22, 38-41, 47, 51, 56, 57, 86-88, 141-142, 144-146, 147, 371
  diplomatic, 12, 46-47, 111-112, 139-144, 325
  for head of state and other ministers, 146-149
  sovereign, 149-152, 262
Prompt release, 366, 367
Prostitution, 46, 296, 314, 316
Provisional measures, 121. *See also* Interim measures/provisional measures

Racial discrimination, 12, 185, 199, 219, 238, 239, 240, 254, 283
Ratification of treaties, 31-36
Reciprocity, 112, 117-119
Recognition, 69-70
  de facto government, 69-70
  non-recognition, 65-66
  Rhodesia, 65-66, 290

Red Cross/Red Crescent, 99, 294, 295, 296
Refugees, 230, 233, 288
Regional organizations, 98, 236. *See also* African
    Union; Arab League; Eurasian
    Economic Community; European
    Union; Organization of African Unity
    (African Union); Organization of
    American States; Shanghai Cooperation
    Organization
Relationship of international law to domestic
    (national) law, 18-20
Reparations, 21, 23, 55, 57, 85-88, 113,
    247, 346
Reprisals, 268, 281-282, 287, 394
Reservations to treaties, 14, 32-36, 113,
    117-119, 185-188, 205-207,
    213-214, 218-221, 227, 239
Resolutions
  General Assembly, 24-25
  Security Council, 25-26, 229-230
Responsibility to protect, 232, 289
Retorsions, 268
Rhodesia, 65-66, 290
Rio Declaration/Summit, 381, 393, 394, 398,
    399, 401, 402, 403
Rivers, 11-12, 47, 48-49, 166-168, 337-338,
    387-388, 397-398, 402
Rwanda, 13, 101, 236, 296, 311, 316,
    329, 330

Sanctions, 25, 66, 96, 230, 232-234,
    268-269, 290-292
Sea. *See* Law of the Sea
Secession, 19, 69, 70-79, 252-253
Secretary-General of the United Nations,
    97-98, 233
Security Council of the United Nations, 25-26,
    229-230
Self-defence, 84, 269-271, 276-281, 285,
    292, 317, 319-320, 396
Self-determination, 70-79, 94, 165, 172, 194,
    209, 252-253, 256, 283, 288
Sex/gender discrimination, 176, 180, 181,
    187, 192, 238, 239, 246, 255-256
Shanghai Cooperation Organization, 98, 125
Ships
  arrest, 366, 367
  flags of convenience, 362-367, 368-370,
    371-373
  foreign, 342-346, 370-373, 379
  genuine link, 362-366

hot pursuit, 371-374
  nationality, 362-363, 368
Sierra Leone, 101, 331-332
Slavery, 176, 192, 194, 197, 199, 219, 226,
    239, 240, 246, 261
Soft law, 26-28
Sources of law, 5-28
  custom, 6-12
  equity, 21-22, 400
  General Assembly resolutions, 24-25
  general principles, 20-22
  judicial decisions, 23
  jus cogens, 12-16
  Security Council resolutions, 25-26
  treaties, 16-18
  writers, 24
South Africa, 45, 66, 290
South West Africa, 45, 120, 167. *See also*
    Namibia
Sovereign immunity, 149-152, 262
Sovereignty
  air space, 275, 341
  conquest, 162-163
  contiguous zone, 351-353, 372
  continental shelf, 356-358, 372
  deep sea bed, 358, 359-361
  discovery, 159-161, 171-172
  exclusive economic zone, 17, 18, 353-355
  occupation, 74, 76, 79, 159, 160-162
  outer space, 170, 305, 390
  polar regions, 64, 168, 169-170, 305, 397
  territorial sea, 18
  uti possidetis juris, 73, 164-167
Stare decisis, 20, 23
State responsibility
  aliens, 100-101, 176, 287, 321
  environmental protection, 377-380
  imputability, 80-85, 379
  individuals, 81, 87-88, 100, 142
  reparations, 85-88
  responsibility to protect, 232, 289
States
  archipelagic, 346-347, 372
  boundaries, 63-64
  colonies, 6, 25, 65, 72-75, 78-79, 97,
    158-159, 163-166, 172, 178, 249,
    253, 283, 401
  defined territory, 63-64
  definition, 62-69
  government, 64-65
  landlocked, 354, 357, 358

Namibia, 45, 120, 167. *See also* South
West Africa
occupation, 74, 76, 79, 159, 160-162
permanent population, 64
recognition, 69-70
secession, 70-79
self-determination, 70-79
South West Africa, 45, 120, 167. *See also*
Namibia
succession, 59-60
Straits, 347-351. *See also* Law of the Sea,
international straits
Succession, 59-60
Sudan, 14, 124, 291, 331
Suez, 287, 350
Sustainable development, 381, 382, 387, 389,
394, 398, 401, 403
Sweden, 70, 113-115, 169, 381

Terra *nullius*, 158-159
Territorial sea
archipelagic states, 346-347, 372
baselines, 341-342
fisheries, 341-342
foreign ships, 342-346
Geneva Convention, 336
innocent passage, 283, 342-347, 348-351,
370, 374
internal waters, 337-341
landlocked states, 354, 357, 358
measurement, 341-342
passage through straits, 348-351
straits, 347-351
Territory
accretion, 167, 168
acquisition, 157-173
airspace, 347
avulsion, 167-168
boundaries, 63-64
cession, 158, 163
conquest, 159, 162-163, 173, 265-333
contiguity, 162
discovery, 159-161, 171-172
occupation, 74, 76, 79, 159, 160-162
outer space, 170, 305, 390
polar regions, 64, 168, 169-170, 305, 397
prescription, 163-164
terra *nullius*, 158-159
title, 157-173
uninhabited, 160-166
uti *possidetis juris*, 73, 164-167

Terrorism, 35, 44, 125, 132, 136, 310
Title, 157-173
conquest, 159, 162-163, 173, 265-333
discovery, 159-161, 171-172
occupation, 74, 76, 79, 159, 160-162
prescription, 163-164
uti *possidetis juris*, 73, 164-167
Tokyo Trials, 317, 321, 327-328
Torture/cruel, inhuman, or degrading treatment,
10, 12, 27, 35-36, 44-45, 52, 67, 76, 81,
136, 147-149, 183-184, 190, 192, 194,
197, 199, 202, 210, 219-221, 225-226,
238-240, 242, 244, 260, 294, 295-296,
301-302, 314, 316, 321, 326, 332
Treaties, 29-60
accession, 32
adoption, 17
breach, 45-47
capacity, 30-31
codification, 16
coercion, 42-43
corruption, 41-42
definition, 30
derogation from, 36, 43, 53, 198-200, 212,
218-221
entry into force, 36
error, 41
fraud, 41-42
fundamental change of circumstances, *rebus*
sic stantibus, 48-50
human rights, 44, 45, 52-54, 175-263
effect of war, 51-54
interpretation, 37-38, 182-185
invalidity, 41-44
jus *cogens*, 43-44
ratification, 31-32
reservations, 32-36, 185-188
self-executing, 58-59, 188-190
state succession, 59-60
supervening impossibility, 47-48
termination, 54, 190
Vienna Convention, 12, 17, 20, 30, 40, 41,
45, 48, 52, 181-186
war, effect on, 51-54
Tribunals. *See* International courts
Truman proclamation, 356
Trusteeship Council, 97

United Kingdom, 31, 65, 67, 71, 77, 78, 96,
107, 131, 151, 164, 169, 183, 283,
342, 365, 392

United Nations Charter, 20, 25, 33, 43, 51,
72, 80, 93-98, 104, 106-110, 112,
115, 117, 120, 121, 158, 162, 177,
191, 229-231, 271-282, 285-287,
289-292, 317, 319-321, 328, 329
Economic and Social Council (ECOSOC),
96-97, 98-99, 222-223, 254
General Assembly, 10, 13, 17, 24-25, 27,
45, 72, 76, 80, 93, 94, 95, 96, 97,
107, 120, 149, 162, 163, 172, 191,
192, 209, 213, 222, 223, 224, 227,
229, 253, 254, 272, 277, 282, 284,
288, 292, 305, 311, 317, 318, 329,
330, 376, 390, 392, 394, 395
Human Rights Commissioner, 222-223
Human Rights Committee, 195, 241, 251
injury of agents, 92
International Court of Justice. *See*
International courts
legal personality, 93-94
privileges and immunities, 94
Secretary-General, 97-98
Security Council, 95-96
Special Representative of the Secretary-
General, 259
Trusteeship Council, 97
United Nations Environment
Programme (UNEP), 381
United States, 8, 9, 10, 18, 22, 31-32, 38,
39-58, 59, 87, 88, 96, 107, 109, 112,
114-115, 121, 122, 130, 133, 149,
151, 163, 188, 189, 194, 206, 239,
270, 276, 280, 291, 293, 304, 327,
337, 342, 365-366, 378
Universal Declaration of Human Rights, 27,
76, 177, 179, 180, 190, 191-193,
209, 217, 218, 220, 224, 243, 245,
254, 321, 376
Universal Declaration on Cultural Diversity,
179
Use of force, 265-308. *See also* War
acquisition of territory, 162-163
Afghan War, 100, 280, 298-299
aggression, 316-320
armed attack, 162, 269-271, 272, 276,
277-282, 285, 287, 291, 317, 320
armed reprisals, 268, 282, 287
blockades. *See* Sanctions
civil war, 65, 225, 233, 239, 286, 293,
295, 314, 321
duress, 323-325

Geneva Conventions on the Laws of War, 52,
81, 137-138, 162, 282, 293-294, 297,
298, 301-302, 306, 314, 328, 393
Gulf War, 96, 233
humanitarian intervention, 229, 231, 232,
287, 289
Iran-Iraq War, 365-366
Iraq War, 280-281
jus ad bellum, 267, 271-282, 293, 308
jus in bello, 267, 293-303
Korean War, 291-292
laws and customs of war, 293, 298
NATO, 231, 235, 236, 275-276, 280,
288-289
nuclear weapons, 273-274, 304-308, 380,
390-397, 401
peacekeeping forces, 95-96, 292-293
preemption, 280-281
protecting nationals abroad, 287
reprisals, 268, 281-282, 287, 394
retorsions, 268
self-defence, 84, 269-271, 274-275,
276-280
anticipatory, 271, 276, 279, 281, 287
collective, 272, 276-278, 280, 285,
289, 292
preemption, 280-281
superior orders, 323-324
threat of force, 273-274
Uti possidetis juris, 73, 164-167

Vienna Convention on Consular Relations, 38,
142, 144-146
Vienna Convention on Diplomatic Relations,
17, 46, 111-112, 140-144
Vienna Convention on the Law of Treaties, 12,
17, 20, 30, 40, 41, 45, 48, 52,
181-186

War, 265-308. *See also* Use of force
Afghan War, 100, 280, 298-299
civil war, 65, 225, 233, 239, 286, 293,
295, 314, 321
Geneva Conventions on the Laws of War,
52, 81, 137-138, 162, 282, 293-294,
297, 298, 301-302, 306, 314,
328, 393
Gulf War, 96, 233
humanitarian law, 52, 53-54, 83, 199, 201,
228-236, 273, 293-308
Iran-Iraq War, 365-366

Iraq War, 280-281
jus ad bellum, 267, 271-282, 293, 308
jus in bello, 267, 293-303
Korean War, 291-292
NATO, 231, 235, 236, 275-276, 280,
    288-289
prisoners of war, 81, 294-298, 301,
    313-314, 324-325
Red Cross/Red Crescent, 99, 294, 295, 296
War crimes, 9, 12, 13, 101, 136, 137-138,
    147-148, 222, 234, 312-315, 322,
    324, 327, 333
aggression, 25, 52, 96, 230, 274, 277, 290,
    310, 316-319, 320, 327, 328
crimes against humanity, 315-316
individual responsibility, 101, 320-323
International Criminal Court, 13, 31, 82,
    101, 222, 296-297, 316, 317, 321,
    330

International Criminal Tribunal for
    Rwanda, 13, 101, 296, 311, 316,
    329, 330
International Criminal Tribunal for the
    former Yugoslavia, 12, 13, 83,
    101, 235, 296, 311, 315, 321,
    328-330
Nuremberg Tribunal, 9, 177, 263, 310,
    315, 316, 321, 327-328, 330
Tokyo Tribunal, 177, 310, 315, 317, 321,
    327-328, 330
Writers, 24

Yugoslavia, 25, 59, 69, 70, 96, 165, 275-276,
    288, 289, 328-330, 379
International Criminal Tribunal for the
    former Yugoslavia, 12, 13, 83, 101,
    235, 296, 311, 315, 321, 328-330
NATO bombing, 275-276